SOCIOLOGY
AUSTRALIA

THIRD EDITION

Judith Bessant & Rob Watts

ALLEN&UNWIN

First published in 2007 by Allen & Unwin

Allen & Unwin
83 Alexander Street
Crows Nest NSW 2065
Australia
Phone: (61 2) 8425 0100
Fax: (61 2) 9906 2218
Email: info@allenandunwin.com
Web: www.allenandunwin.com

National Library of Australia
Cataloguing-in-Publication entry:

Bessant, Judith.
    Sociology Australia.

    3rd ed.
    Bibliography.
    Includes index.
    ISBN 978 1 74175 016 4.

    1. Sociology – Australia. 2. Social change – Australia. 3.
    Australia – Social conditions – 21st century. 4.
    Australia – Social policy. I. Watts, Rob. II. Title.

301.0994

Set in 10/14 pt ITC Galliard by Midland Typesetters, Australia
Text design by Lisa White
Photo credits: Pedro Almeida, Matthew John and Sharyn Finger
Printed and bound in Singapore by Phoenix Print Media Pte Ltd

10 9 8 7 6 5 4

CONTENTS

Acknowledgments

There are many people without whom this edition of the book could not have been written. First and always, there are our students—past and present. We express our gratitude to those students we have taught through the 1990s and into the 2000s. We have relied upon them throughout the years to test many of the ideas and formulations found in the earlier editions of this book. Most willingly expressed their views after being asked to read and to use the book. This advice has helped us to rethink and rewrite this edition.

We want to thank postgraduate students and colleagues like Nick Halfpenny, who initiated the basic research involved in updating the tables; Hariz Halilovic, who worked on the second edition; and Janet Jukes, who updated and added to that work for this latest edition. We would also like to thank Pete Varitimidis for the technical and practical support he provided, as well as his extremely positive attitude. Without their work, our task would have been very much more difficult.

Colleagues like Martin Mowbray, Amanda Watkinson, Kerry Montero, Lois Bryson, Helen Marshall and Desmond McDonnell have helped in all sorts of ways, large and small. We also thank friends and family within and outside our own universities. Their support may not have always been directly related to this project, but without it the book would not have come to be, so thanks to both Sandy Cook and Bob Bessant. Thanks also to Dorothy and Bill Watts, who supplied their son with many cups of tea as he typed away—again—at Ocean Grove over the years. Our families have put up with the absences, distractedness and sometimes bad tempers which writing and then rewriting a book entails. To be the child of an academic must often be difficult. Rebekah and Macgregor, your mother is appreciative.

While the contemporary university is no longer as able to support intellectual work as it once did, many of our colleagues have given us material to read, together with helpful feedback and the type of stimulation with which universities have traditionally been credited. Special thanks to teachers like Sharon Andrews, Julia Thornton, Gillian Cavanagh, Cathryn Kriewaldt and Lisa Harris, who are working out what good teaching and learning look like in the social sciences. The School of Global Studies, Social Science and Planning at RMIT also provided a small amount of research funding to help with revising the data.

Elizabeth Weiss from Allen & Unwin has been her usual encouraging, cheerful, persistent and perceptive self. We are also grateful to the production team at Allen & Unwin, and particularly to Lauren Finger and Susan Jarvis for their expertise in editing and publishing this book.

INTRODUCTION

the heedless recklessness or hopeless confusion or complacent repetition of 'truths' which have become trivial and empty—seems to me among the outstanding characteristics of our time. What I propose, therefore, is very simple: it is nothing more than to think what we are doing.

Hannah Arendt (1958: 5)

Many ordinary Australians today seem to be worried, anxious or upset about how they live. If public opinion polls are to be believed, we no longer see the world as a safe place, and we feel the need to defend ourselves from terrorists intent on destroying the Australian way of life or attacking 'the West'. Many Australians appear to accept that they are engaged in a war against terror waged by radical or fundamentalist Muslims that began with the 9/11 attacks on New York and Washington in 2001. Australia joined with the United States and Britain in a 'Coalition of the Willing', first in an invasion of Afghanistan in 2002 and then an attack on Iraq in March 2004—apparently to prevent Iraq using its arsenal of 'weapons of mass destruction' against the West. In August 2005, an AC Nielsen poll showed that 70 per cent of Australians expected a terrorist attack in Australia in the next few years. Foxtel TV news polls in August 2005 suggested that more than 90 per cent of Australians were prepared to relinquish most of their civil liberties to have stronger security laws. In January 2006, one news poll found 87 per cent of those surveyed were fearful about terrorism.

Australians also speak about how they are caught up in structural change shaped by privatisation, deregulation, new technologies and globalisation. As a result, traditional values are seen as being in decline and Australians are apparently becoming more materialistic, selfish and amoral. The old regard for community has been killed off by rampant individualism, selfishness and hedonism. This is encouraged by new technologies like iPoDS, mobile phones, the internet, email and plasma and LCD televisions screens. Traditional values are also allegedly under attack from feminists and homosexual activists, purportedly leading to increasing divorce and separation rates, growing numbers of sole-parent families, the use of IVF to produce babies and a push by gays and lesbians for the right to marry. There are many opinion leaders prepared to argue that we need to get back to traditional values. Prime Minister John Howard in 2005 called for more pride in 'Australian values', while other government ministers have said that those foreigners living in Australia who do not subscribe to these values should 'clear out'.

Perhaps it was beliefs and fears like this that sparked Sydney's Cronulla Beach race riots in December 2005, which saw thousands of white Australians attack people described in the media as being of 'middle-Eastern appearance'.

Large numbers of Australians also believe that there are still too many unemployed 'dole bludgers' and 'welfare cheats' living off the taxpayer. The Howard Coalition government has used this belief to promote a succession of welfare reforms strengthening the idea of 'mutual obligation'—the view that everybody who receives income support should undertake education or training, be involved in a work-for-the-dole scheme or do community work.

Finally, many Australians complain that the cost of living is too high. It is widely believed that many younger Australians are no longer able to afford to buy their own homes. The costs of fundamentals like petrol, electricity, telephone and health insurance seem to be constantly rising.

So which of these beliefs and anxieties have any kind of rational or objective basis? How do Australians learn about these things? How might we begin thinking about these kinds of issues better? Asking these kinds of questions is one of the reasons we have written this book. We are committed to the idea that all of us can—and should—think intelligently and carefully about our society. We think it is vital to the collective well-being of all Australians that we are able to distinguish between the blind prejudices and rational beliefs mixed up in the above list of issues and anxieties.

WHY WE HAVE WRITTEN THIS BOOK

There are now any number of big sociology books, many published in Britain and the United States. Well-known British sociologists like Anthony Giddens, and writers like Tony Bilton and Michael Haralambos and their colleagues, for example, offer very comprehensive introductions to contemporary sociology. There are also many good Australian books by sociologists like Ray Juredeini, Alan Kellehear, David Holmes and Alastair Grieg. So why write another?

First, we are more interested in modern Australia than we are in sociology. Second, we have written this book because we have some important things to say about Australia. We are passionate about the idea that coming to terms with our own society is a crucial task that books like this should play. Third, we want to encourage good habits of mind, such as critical thinking. The list of social issues and common beliefs we outlined above suggest that many Australians might benefit from asking and pursuing some basic questions like:

- Are any of these things true?
- How would we know if they were true?
- Even if these things are nonsense, what are the consequences of people believing them to be true?

We think that there are many practical ways of thinking well and critically about these kinds of issues and about our present circumstances.

For all these reasons, we are not offering a conventional introduction to sociology. We take a non-conformist—indeed, often critical—view of sociology itself. While we do some of the traditional things that all sociology texts do, we also develop a thoughtful approach to long-held, often deeply conventional ideas and prejudices that have helped to define sociology.

For example, one product of the eighteenth century Enlightenment was the now-conventional modern idea that the triumph of science and rationality meant religious belief was no longer either credible or relevant. Sociology itself is a product of this Enlightenment idea, as early sociologists promoted the idea of a science of society. As a consequence, many sociologists over the past few centuries have either ignored religion—thinking it has disappeared from societies where 'science' now provides a new world-view—or treated it as an expression of irrational human beings. We believe that this prejudice against religion is not helpful—which is why we have a chapter on religion in Australia today. Religious belief and practice continues to give shape to people's lives and to exercise a profound influence on both culture and politics.

This suggests we need to be guided by what is going on around us rather than by any viewpoint of how a discipline like sociology should look. In short, if we are going to be thoughtful about our society, we also need to consider the way we use a discipline like sociology to try to understand what is happening around us. One of our key objectives in this book is to provide a guide to thinking carefully and critically about what it means to live in Australia today.

THINKING CRITICALLY

What does careful, critical thinking look like? It is not something we all do naturally and continuously as part of our day-to-day routines. Instead, we use the idea of 'common sense' to define the way we see and understand things in our everyday lives. These everyday activities and our commonsense ways of understanding them are durable and strong because of their pervasiveness, and because many of us share an almost unquestioning confidence in their naturalness. This is one reason why there is often a large gap between the kinds of intellectual and theoretical insights and discussions promoted by academics in general, and sociologists in particular, and the experiences of so-called ordinary people.

One obvious reason for this is that ordinary people do not use the same words and ideas as academic social scientists. Yet it is these words and ideas which help sociologists notice things that ordinary people neither see nor possibly care about. For example, we have just referred to change and globalisation, which Anthony Giddens (1990: 16) says lead 'to the reflexive ordering and reordering of social relations in the light of the continual inputs of knowledge'. Translated into non-academic language, this means that new kinds of knowledge and research help to change the way people think about and do things.

This way of writing may not sit easily with someone who has experienced change by losing a job or their marriage, or being diagnosed with cancer. Connecting these personal experiences to the way sociologists do research on unemployment, divorce rates or the causes of cancer is not always easy. This is partly due to the strange language sociologists tend to use, or the way some sociologists think about some of these issues. For example, sociologists talk about 'modernity' and 'post-modernity'. We suggest that using words like 'modernity' involves making generalisations about aspects of our social lives that simply cannot be generalised.

As you read this book, we ask you to be mindful of the gap between highly personal experiences of social changes—like being made redundant, having a friend suicide or choosing not to have children—and the bigger picture that concerns sociologists.

We discuss the idea that we are living in a time of intense change and crisis in which we continuously confront various fascinating and often frightening new experiences. Yet at the same time, for most of us, life continues in an often quiet, even dreary and routine way. In many ways, accepting the world as it is can be comforting. Questioning established ways of seeing ourselves, others and the social world generally can be disturbing. It is worth thinking about the things we claim to know, because sometimes our common sense offers only a partial view, which can fail to provide an accurate perspective on what is actually happening.

But how can we think critically if most of the time we are captured by how we live in our own part of the world? How can we think critically if we rely on common sense to understand what we are doing? Indeed why think critically at all? And how might we do it?

Thinking critically does not mean always trying to find faults, or being negative and destructive—although this is what many people imagine being 'critical' means. Thinking critically is both a practical and an ethical exercise. This is more important than ever because many people studying to 'become' teachers, social workers, nurses or psychologists may be asking—quite legitimately—why they have to do 'irrelevant' subjects like sociology when all they want to do is to learn how to teach, practise psychology or nurse.

The recent history and present activities of policy-makers and human service workers provide many examples of abuse and human pain brought about by professionals who have failed to think about what they were doing. For example:

- How did the thousands of German nurses and doctors who killed hundreds of thousands of psychiatric patients or people with intellectual disabilities between 1939 and 1945 do this without protest, even believing they were doing humanitarian work?
- Why did the Australian welfare workers who took tens of thousands of 'half-caste children' from their parents between approximately 1900 and 1970 believe that they were acting in the children's best interests?

- Why did authorities within church- and state-based institutions that were designed to care for and educate children and young people systematically ignore and deliberately conceal revelations of widespread neglect and abuse that occurred at the hands of those responsible for their well-being and schooling?
- Why did the urban planners and architects of the 1950s believe it was a good idea to remove people from slum housing and put them in high-rise towers of public housing?

In each of these cases—and there are many more—we see a failure or inability on the part of apparently well-educated professionals to think through what they were doing. They were either persuaded by delusional beliefs about the problem they thought they were addressing, or they failed to ask very basic ethical or duty-of-care questions before they acted in the ways they did.

Thinking critically is an indispensable skill for any professional. It is partly an exercise in understanding who we are as people and workers, and why we do certain things. Critical thinking is also related to understanding other people's ideas, feelings and activities. If we do not think about what we are doing, we can easily become involved in activities that are harmful and wrong. Most readers of this book are studying sociology as part of their formal education to become a human services professional. Given our history and the ease with which well-intentioned professionals can find themselves doing things that cause considerable pain and injury to others, it is important to be sure that our actions are both effective and ethical.

If readers become more thoughtful, then we have realised a key motivation for writing this book. However, there is more at stake here than simply a set of technical issues.

Thinking about our own activities and those of other people, and thinking seriously about how we see the world and how that world works, is a reflective activity that allows us assume some responsibility for the world in which we live. This kind of thinking is a vital part of any ethically defensible action, and is central to both thinking critically and being an ethically competent practitioner and a responsible citizen. We do not claim that we can spell out precisely what this means for you. What we can say is that there are three big questions which we need to keep constantly in the foreground of any conversation.

THE THREE BIG QUESTIONS

These questions have a long pedigree. They were first raised around 2400 years ago in the Greek city-state of Athens by philosophers like Socrates, Plato and Aristotle.

The first question asks 'what is true?' We rephrase this question in terms of 'what can we know?' or 'what can we know reliably?' How do we know that we know anything as distinct from merely believing something or having an opinion? How important are our senses like sight or smell in knowing what is true? And what role—if any—should scientific methods play in helping to access truth? Moreover, how important are intuition and feelings in grasping what is happening?

The second question asks 'what is the good?' In other words, what is the good or right thing to do? Is it ethical to put one's own interests ahead of those of others? Is our happiness the best measure of determining what is good?

In the light of these two questions we ask a third question. That question is 'what counts as good practice and good relationships with others?' Socrates reframed this as a question of justice. This is a practical question that ought to be asked by all of us, as we live with others. In other words, what do we owe to each other?

Each of these questions is central to what we mean by thinking. We may well believe that we spend a lot of time thinking. However, we are frequently mistaken about this. We want to encourage the kind of thinking that Hannah Arendt (1958: 5) was promoting when she said: 'The hardest thing to do is to think what we are doing.'

Universities were established to encourage this kind of thinking. As Alasdair Macintyre (1990: 215) puts it:

> When it is demanded of a university community that it justify itself by specifying what its peculiar and essential function is, that function which if it were not to exist, no other institution could discharge, the response of that community ought to be that universities are places where conceptions of, and standards of rational justification are elaborated, put to work in the detailed practices of enquiry, and themselves rationally evaluated, so that only from a university can the wider society learn how to conduct its own debates, theoretical or practical in a rationally defensible way.

The type of thinking to which Arendt and Macintyre refer is never an easy thing to do. Indeed, it can be quite painful. This may seem like a strange thing to say because we think most of the time. But that kind of thinking is different to what we are talking about here—which is to think critically in ways that reflect our contemporary situation. As Macintyre (1990) has argued, we need to constantly reflect on the older traditions involved in thinking about and defining whatever we mean by 'rationality' and to change our ideas about rationality if there is a case to do so.

We have already suggested that many Australians believe they live in a time of major change. Does that include the way we might think about and do sociology? We are inclined to think so.

NEW SOCIETY, NEW SOCIOLOGY?

Saying this does not imply a single way of doing sociology that needs to be changed. Between the 1940s and 1960s, however, many sociologists shared what Anthony Giddens has called an 'orthodox consensus' about sociology.

This orthodox consensus refers to the idea that sociologists from the nineteenth century, like Herbert Spencer or Emile Durkheim, and into the twentieth century, like Talcott Parsons, believed that sociology was the scientific 'something' referred to as 'society'. Society was understood as a social system that was identical with nation-states. 'Society' was an ordered, structured totality in which people as free and rational individuals were said to be socialised, coordinated and regulated to perform the roles ascribed to them by society through a process called socialisation. From that perspective, society was said to be an active source of coordination and order. Society created stable social roles, social rules and moral rules for people, and used them to create and reproduce the social order. These individuals interacted in predictable and coordinated ways, which were largely predetermined by the system's value consensus. Within this social system, society's many institutions (e.g. government, business corporations, families, schools and churches) and its many structures (e.g. the class system or the sexual division of labour) were said to be 'functional' to social order and continuity. They worked together to ensure stability and social order.

As a social system, society was also said to be 'objective', and therefore to permit scientific study. In other words, 'society' existed as a part of the external world—or reality—just like a rock or a chair. This view made the job of doing sociology relatively straightforward. Using scientific methods, sociologists named the social reality in ways they believed were accurate and unambiguous, and which demonstrated a correspondence between the external reality as they saw it and sociological knowledge.

Today there are probably very few sociologists who would defend this particular approach to sociology, though many continue to talk about sociology as the 'study of society'. Instead, we believe sociologists need to study 'the social'.

THINKING ABOUT THE SOCIAL

The word 'social' is a key adjective, yet it is rarely discussed explicitly in sociology. We all use the word 'social' as though it means something, and assume we are all talking about the same thing, but what does it actually mean? If we say something is 'political', 'economic' or 'psychological', is that different from something that is 'social'? Or are these all encompassed by the idea of social?

For simplicity's sake, let's say the term 'social' refers to the idea of relationships and connections between people. Some forms of connection or relationship are intimate and small scale, like our relations with family, friends and work colleagues. Some relations are very distant—even abstract—like our relationships with the editor who produces a newspaper that we read each day, or the leader of a foreign government we've seen only on television. The relationships may be pleasant or they may involve anger and violence. They are, however, vital aspects of social action involving people.

Talking about the idea of social by referring to 'society' tells us very little. We prefer not to use the term 'society' because it implies certain meanings that are problematic, and because society as an entity does actually not do or think anything. However, while we can get by without the idea of society, we cannot do without the idea of 'social'. Central to thinking well about our social lives is cultivating a 'sociological imagination' (Mills 1970).

A MODERN TAKE ON THE 'SOCIOLOGICAL IMAGINATION'

C. Wright Mills (1970) was a famous and outspoken American sociologist in the mid-twentieth century. He coined the phrase 'the sociological imagination' in the late 1940s as a way of explaining how sociologists could help ordinary people think about what they were doing. Encouraging people to develop a 'sociological imagination' is still a good idea. Wright Mills was suggesting that we need to constantly put our ordinary daily lives into a larger social and historical setting.

Take the business of travelling on a bus. Applying the 'sociological imagination' to this ordinary activity means asking questions like 'how many people and what kinds of organisation make this activity possible? How many of these people and organisations do I see or have contact with? What other kinds of social arrangements have to be put in place for this activity to continue to work smoothly? How many people benefit from this system of transport and who is disadvantaged by it? How has this activity changed over the past decades? How might it change in the future?' Far from taking this activity for granted and not thinking about it at all, the sociological imagination takes thinking about ordinary activities very seriously.

If exercised effectively, the sociological imagination enables us to understand our larger social and historical contexts. A sociological imagination helps us to understand that ordinary daily activities have a complexity we did not previously see.

The sociological imagination means lifting ourselves out of our own immediate part of the world and the commonsense view of the world that we have come to rely on. It involves trying to think about the social relations and history we cannot immediately see, but which invisibly shape our world and the way we understand it. It also involves placing our own personal biography into a bigger collective picture, where history and the many relationships and process we call 'society' come together. However (as we show in Chapter 2, where we map some of the ways in which sociology has been understood), although most sociologists agree that developing a sociological imagination is a good idea, they disagree about *how* to do it.

Developing our sociological imagination means that we can develop the idea of the social by increasing our sensitivity to what human relationships entail in ways that stop a lot of overly confident generalisations about the way things are. The sociological imagination imparts a useful kind of humility in the face of considerable complexity. According to David Bohmann (1991), we need to accept the indeterminacy in our social world as well as the knowledge that social scientists develop about that world. Bohmann argues that indeterminacy is central to understanding the quality of 'the social'—a point he elaborates when talking about the idea of social relationships.

Indeterminacy refers to the disordered, vague, ambiguous and contradictory aspects of our social relationships, experiences, beliefs, aspirations and actions. Accepting indeterminacy means accepting that nothing is simple or clearcut. It means acknowledging that, even when we use our most developed language capacities, reality always escapes the net of our language.

'Thinking sociologically' helps us to become more comfortable with indeterminacy in social relationships. It helps avoid the need to impose neatness and orderly categories where there are none. For example, it can help us to appreciate the fact that every action or relationship between people is characterised by indeterminacy, and to be comfortable with this.

Consider the relationship of 'friendship'. Friendship is a primary form of social relationship which works by *including* those who are called friends and by *excluding* those who are not. Similarly, the emotions of friendship can be experienced in ways that are contradictory. Friendship can offer great warmth and affection, yet it can also involve feelings of anger, guilt and betrayal—emotions that are often absent from more casual relationships. These contradictions, inconsistencies and discrepancies partly comprise what we mean by indeterminacy. Indeterminacy is central to what Georg Simmel (1949: 255) identifies as the 'innumerable forms of social life, all the with-one-another, for-one-another, in-one-another, against-one-another and through-one-another . . . associations accompanied by a feeling for, by a satisfaction in, the very fact that one is associated with others'.

Many of us often think we are free to act as we wish, but find we are actually constrained to act in ways we do not always understand. And, despite our intentions, many of our actions have consequences we did not anticipate.

Identifying or accepting the indeterminacy of our social lives is not a recommendation that we stop trying to interpret or influence the world, however. Some of the worst atrocities of the twentieth century—like the Nazi Holocaust and the Soviet terror—were a consequence of people promoting change. And the social sciences have played an important role in many acts of cruelty and evil. Given this, the urgent need for responsible political and social change becomes starkly evident. The social sciences can play a useful role in creating change that is cautious, respectful and reflective. As teachers, we agree with Herbert Spencer (1965), when he says that the aim of good education is not just knowledge, but also action.

Rapid and significant social change has become a defining feature of our contemporary experience. This does not mean that the changes taking place are all heading in one uniform direction, however. As many historians have argued, social change is an uneven and often contradictory process. One factor that led us to write the book is the recognition that, in a context of social change, more consideration needs to be given to the ways sociology can be done.

Like most other disciplines, sociology has a long history of argument about how best to develop a sociological imagination. (In Chapter 2 we map out some of the important differences in understanding sociology and suggest why they exist.) Most sociologists do, however, agree that the sociological imagination is a good idea, and that it involves:

- asking interesting questions;
- gathering evidence;
- comparing situations;
- understanding history; and
- testing different theories.

While we refer to something called 'mainstream sociology' from time to time, we are not suggesting that it is the only way to view the discipline. Rather, as Stepan Mestrovic (1997: 4) observes, it is more sensible to speak of sociology in terms of 'many little streams . . . all going in different directions'. We do not offer a new integrated model of sociology here, but suggest that there are some interesting questions and themes worth pursuing.

SIX KEY QUESTIONS IN THIS BOOK

Throughout this book we raise six central questions and focus on six themes:

- What is sociology, and how can we give contemporary expression to the sociological imagination?
- Who are we and how do we come to be who we are? This relates to the theme of self or identity.
- What changes are taking place in Australia, where are those changes coming from, and where might they take us? These questions relate to ideas like globalisation.
- In the context of a society said to be globalising, do we each enjoy an equal opportunity to make our lives the way we want them to be? This points to the theme of inequality.
- What is power, who has it, and who makes the decisions that shape the society in which we live?
- How do we know the modern world in which we live? This raises the theme of knowledge and the role of the media.

Identity, power, knowledge, inequality and globalisation are interconnected themes. Exploring how they are interrelated is one way we can understand the idea of 'social'. We have structured the book around these questions and themes.

THE STRUCTURE OF THE BOOK

We start with a discussion of sociology, its links to the modernisation process and the practice of the sociological imagination. We consider the various kinds of sociologies that have been developed and map them. We note that some of the differences in these various sociologies relate to the fact that different sociologists ask different questions, and therefore get different answers. Equally, different sociologists operate with different assumptions about the nature of reality and have different views about the best kind of theory of knowledge to apply.

Identity

Most people are interested in questions about who we are. Traditionally understood as the problem of how 'society' creates the 'individual', we recast this debate in terms of identity. Identity has at least two dimensions: internal and external. From the inside, we may see ourselves in particular ways and be interested in asking questions like: 'what does it mean to be a father? Who am I? How should I react to this person?' From the outside, we may wonder what kinds of relationships we enter into and why we enter into them. What does it mean to be an Australian in a multicultural society? Why do many 'adults' treat young people in the ways they do, and how does that influence the self-identity of certain young people? Does the way we act say anything about who we are? What does being a Muslim or a Christian mean today? Considering the question of identity may also make us curious about who is responsible for our identity. It may cause us to wonder where our ideas of self come from, and what it means to have a 'self'.

Globalisation

Globalisation has become a catchphrase and, like other popular words, it is used without people being clear about what it really means. We have little patience with people who use this category as if it explains anything (Giddens 1997: 519–33). Here, we use the word 'globalisation' as a shorthand way of referring to very complex processes of change.

For most of the twentieth century (especially the last decades), many people experienced the world as shrinking. Paradoxically, globalisation reflects a feeling that the world is also becoming more complex and larger. While globalisation means integration, it also means disintegration.

Globalisation refers to the rise of a global TV culture, but it also means the rise of extreme nationalist and racist divisions which have resulted in the return of genocidal and civil wars.

We are also experiencing enormous changes in relation to how we work, what we know and what we buy. Jobs are now taken from Australia and given to workers in cities like Seoul (Korea) or Mumbai (India). The new family car is likely to be made from parts designed and/ or produced in a dozen different countries. TV viewers can follow the Olympics or World Cup soccer action as it happens in a city 25 000 kilometres away. Billions of dollars are invested and reinvested in microseconds as electronic fund transfers zigzag across the globe. All this is part of globalisation, a process in which Australia is deeply involved. Given its significance and the degree to which we are part of the process, it is important that we have some understanding of globalisation—what it is, how it works and its social impact.

Inequality

Power and knowledge are important in Australia, which is marked by various social inequalities. Inequality, especially that related to the distribution of income and our socioeconomic status, helps shape our lives. Some Australians live comfortable and secure lives. Those who are financially poor die sooner, and often live with sickness in substandard housing on substandard diets. Many women, people from low socioeconomic backgrounds, many younger people, many recently arrived ethnic groups as well as a large proportion of Indigenous people are seriously affected by social and economic inequality.

Power

The processes of globalisation and the effects of unemployment and growing levels of inequality involve power. Saying that power is found in all social relations does not resolve the many complex issues about power. Some people exercise a lot of power while others have little. What is power? Why are there differences in the kind and amount of power people have? Is power simply about the wealth or money a person has? How does it relate to being a man or woman? How does power relate to being well educated, young, old or Aboriginal?

Knowledge

In Australia, we are moving towards an information or network society, where information plays an increasingly vital role. The term 'post-industrial society' emphasises the role and economic value of knowledge, and of information technologies and industries. Knowledge and knowledge-making are becoming more significant economically as the information economy evolves.

Power is also closely connected to knowledge. How much can we now rely on our direct experiences of the world for our knowledge of what is happening? What is the role of the educational and intellectual institutions that have for so long provided authoritative accounts of reality? We examine our reliance on the media and expert knowledge, and ask about the implications of becoming so dependent on them for what we know. The way we come to know the world also reflects the kinds of power and the resources we have in shaping our lives at personal, community, national and international levels.

It is important to note that, while these themes can be identified and separated from each other, they do not usually divide into distinct categories in the real world. The categories and experiences we talk about continuously blend, merge into and change each other. For example, the question of identity may raise questions about being Aboriginal or a mother, yet a person's context affects how they experience these aspects of their identity.

● ● ● PART ONE

WHAT IS SOCIOLOGY?

The idea that Australians now live in a time characterised by endless change has become a cliché. Indeed, the permanence of change has been accepted among social theorists ever since Karl Marx and Friedrich Engels wrote *The Communist Manifesto* back in 1848 and pointed to the way the European middle classes were creating a modern capitalist economy that set loose a permanent condition of change so total that 'everything that is solid melts into air'. That combination of economic change and political reform driven by the middle classes kick-started a permanent process of revolution in modern societies. It has become conventional to talk about this process of change by using terms like 'the modernising process' or 'modernity'. This in turn has led to much talk about the way we have moved into a period described as 'post-modern'. More recently, the word 'globalisation' has been used to define or describe this latest manifestation of change.

There is no doubt that those of us who live in Australia now, as well as those who have been writing sociology for the past two centuries, have been part of complex processes of social, economic, political and intellectual change. Yet what does this idea of permanent change mean? And what does 'modernity' mean, let alone 'post-modernity' or 'globalisation'?

Given that the development of social sciences like sociology took place in societies that were going through often-dramatic processes of social change, the claim of sociologists to be able to explain change takes on an extra level of interest. How, for example, have sociologists talked about processes of change, and have they anything useful or important to say?

What was an important sociologist like Zygmunt Bauman (1991) thinking when he attempted to explain the effort by the Nazi state after 1941 to kill as many of Europe's Jews as it could? This is the event widely referred to as 'the Holocaust'—a process that led to the murder of over five million Jewish people. Bauman used the idea of 'modernity' to explain this awful crime against humanity. Bauman (1991: 15) argues that features of modernity such as bureaucracy, science, technology, a modern army and modern political advertising can be used to explain the Nazi Holocaust. Is this an example of using an idea like modernity to obscure things rather than to illuminate or explain them?

In the first part of this book, we pay attention to sociology as a social science. In Chapter 1 we discuss the emergence of sociology as a distinctive way of thinking about the world, indicating some of the ways this developing intellectual tradition connected with the process of modernisation that was set loose some centuries ago.

In Chapter 2 we ask a basic question that anyone coming to sociology might find useful: how should we read sociology? Far from assuming that reading is a simple, uncomplicated activity, we outline a disciplined approach to reading that emphasises the need to be active and analytical, and to take nothing for granted.

In Chapter 3 we consider some of the ways sociologists have 'done' sociology. As with every other social science discipline, there are many different ways people who call themselves sociologists approach sociology. While we pay attention to some of these differences, we also offer a broad overview of how what C. Wright Mills called the 'sociological imagination' works.

In Chapter 4 we sketch out some of the ways in which this 'sociological imagination' can work to inform good research practices. We consider how sociological research can inform and promote change that is careful and respectful of people as well as being both effective and reflective.

Finally, in Chapter 5 we look at some of the issues at stake in the relationship between ethical ideas and values and the practice of sociology. As we argued in the Introduction, the question of ethical values is as significant as any issue when it comes to the search for truth.

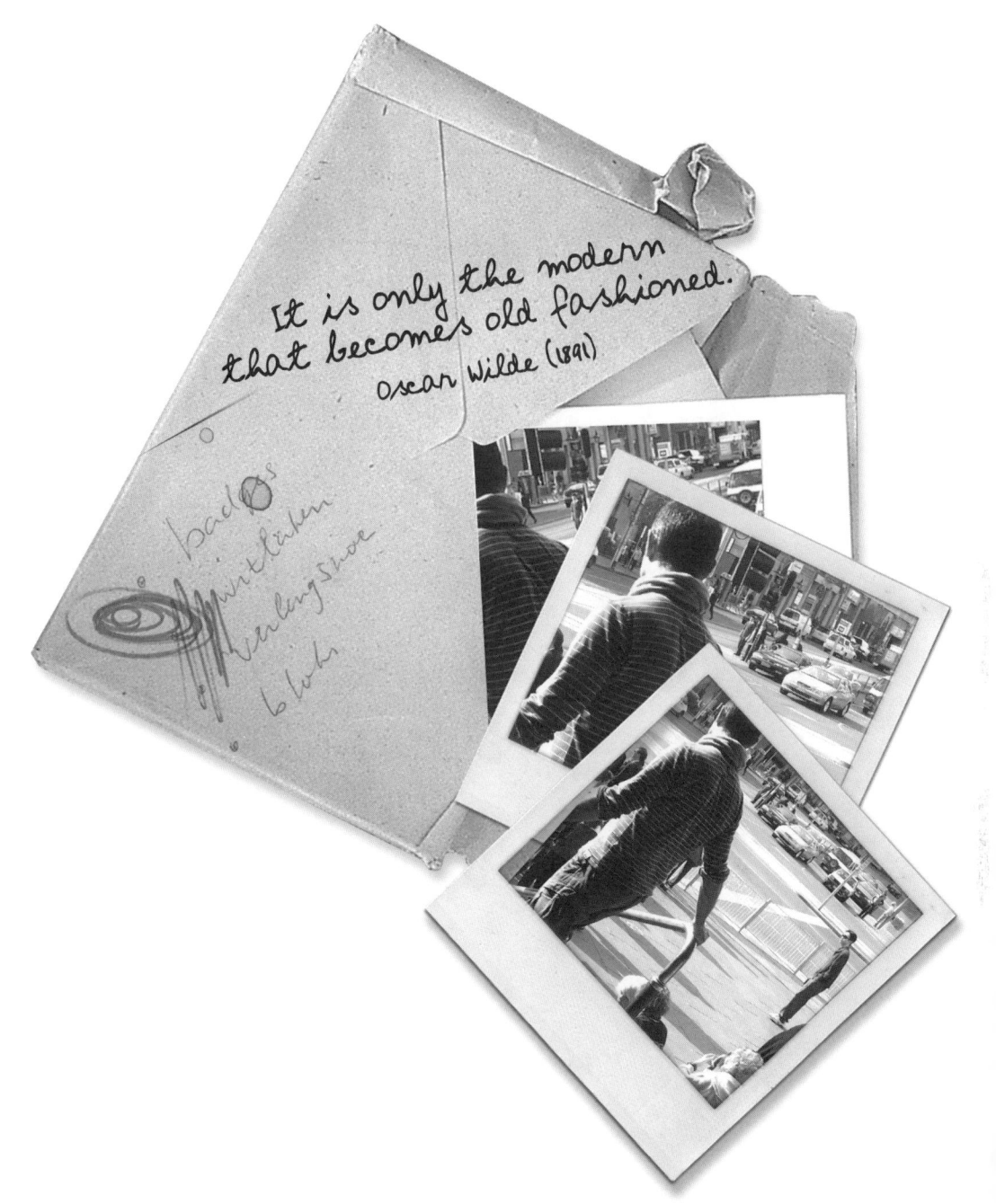

It is only the modern that becomes old fashioned.

Oscar Wilde (1891)

SOCIOLOGY IN AN AGE OF INSECURITY 1.

● ● SUMMARY

The idea that Australians now live in a period of accelerated change, leading to an experience Alvin Toffler (1974) called 'future shock', has become commonplace. In this context, there is also a lot of talk about how we are entering into new kinds of relationships with the rest of the world. To describe this process—which includes new technologies, the expansion of communication media and economic policies like free trade—many people have started using the word 'globalisation'. Whether 'globalisation' is a useful concept or a mischievous metaphor is one question to which we will return at the end of the book.

To place the discussion of globalisation into a larger context, we explore the idea that, in the seventeenth and eighteenth centuries, societies like Britain, Germany, France and later the United States began transforming themselves. They shifted from being societies and economies based on 'pre-modern' religion, peasant-farming economies, small-scale communities and traditional cultures to what is referred to variously as 'capitalist', 'industrialist' or simply 'modern' societies. We draw on Polanyi's (1973) model of the 'Great Transformation' to represent some of the key economic, political, demographic and intellectual changes that occurred.

It was in the context of the 'Great Transformation' that some people began speculating about why the process of change was happening and how it was happening. One result of that speculation was sociology.

● SOCIOLOGY IN AN AGE OF INSECURITY

After a long period of being relatively isolated from the rest of the world, Australia now has a much closer relationship with many countries. We can be in near-instantaneous contact with people around the world using a mobile phone or email, and we have access to non-stop global TV news services. Dramatic changes have taken place in the way we do business with the rest of the world—think of our reliance on Chinese imports for clothing, computers or foodstuffs. And, since the terrorist attacks in New York and Washington on 11 September 2001, there is a sense that we are no longer safe because terrorism has assumed a global dimension.

To describe these kinds of relationships, academics began to use the word 'globalisation'. They also used it when talking about economic policies like free trade or a deregulated financial system, which it is believed promote these closer links between Australia and the world. We also appear to believe that globalisation is a radically new feature of our daily lives. Sociologists like Bauman (1998), Giddens (1999), Beck (2000) and Pakulski (2004) have all used the concept and helped to give it considerable currency.

Some sociologists tend to adopt a generally favourable view of globalisation, like Giddens (1999), who argues that globalisation is just the latest phase of a larger process that sociologists call 'modernity'. Others tend to be more sceptical about such claims—for instance, Jan Pakulski

(2004), who argues that globalisation increases tendencies towards social inequality as well as promoting trends associated with modernity like 'universalistic orientations, rationalism, individualism and egalitarian values, trends reinforced by a popular culture hostile to hierarchy' (2004: 14).

As our earlier reference to terrorism suggests, the word 'globalisation' has been connected to many aspects of modern life typically defined as problems. From global sex tourism, global drug trafficking and the rise of global criminal networks to the restructuring of economies and the consequences of economic change with respect to poverty and unemployment, globalisation has had many negative features attributed to it. A decade ago, commentators like David Leser (1996: 4) were arguing:

> To be Australian today is, for many people, to be deeply insecure about the future. You . . . see this trauma in . . . the faces of those in the dole queues, in companies being downsized, in workplaces of increasing stress and competition, in traffic snarls, in isolated country towns, behind the walls of disintegrating family homes. It's no secret that the changes in Australian society have been staggering. No aspect of life remains unaltered. The catchwords have been globalisation and restructuring. The results have been declining wages, growing job insecurity, changing labour markets, soaring technological advancements, altering work practices and a redefinition of leisure. The Australian psyche has taken a pummeling.

In the new millennium, commentators like Lois Bryson (2001) continued making the link between the restructuring process associated with globalisation and serious social inequalities. According to Bryson, 'the gap between men's and women's wages has widened as have differences between women in strongly and weakly organised sections of the workforce' (2001: 96).

So are contemporary Australians right to believe that, after decades of being isolated, we have now entered a closer relationship with the rest of the world, and that this is a really new feature of our experience? How should we think about globalisation? Does it explain the things it is often used to explain?

As we will demonstrate, many beliefs rely on assumptions that may not be useful or credible. An assumption is an initial belief without which we cannot even ask a question, let alone answer it. As George Lakoff (1999, 2005) has observed, all our knowledge claims rely on assumptions that are built from simple but powerful metaphors and moral values. On what assumptions do our beliefs about globalisation rest?

We should recall, for example, that in *The Tyranny of Distance*, Geoffrey Blainey (1966) argued that Australians had always suffered due to the distances they had to travel to get to anywhere 'important'. This thesis relied on an evaluation of where British settlers saw the 'important' places as being. It failed to acknowledge that the region in which Australia was located—Southeast Asia—was less than 100 kilometres away by sea and was home to the world's longest-lived civilisation. Those who use the globalisation concept may similarly be relying unconsciously on an array of moral values and metaphors.

At the least, the current vogue for talking about 'globalisation' requires us to think about how sociologists have understood the past few centuries, which undoubtedly had involved major and persistent experiences of change in many societies. So, rather than engaging with the various debates about globalisation, we believe it is more useful to consider the 'big picture' of change over the past two or three centuries. We return to think critically about our various accounts about 'globalisation' in Chapter 16.

The idea that ours is a period of important change belongs to a larger story of change, which sociologists have referred to as the modernising process. That there is a close relationship between the emergence of sociology as certain ways of thinking and researching the social world and the experience of far-reaching changes in the way people have organised their economic, social and political and cultural activities is a core assumption which informs this book. Indeed, in several important ways the origins of sociology are to be found in the attempt to understand or explain the nature of large-scale change.

● FROM PRE-MODERN TO MODERN SOCIETY: THE BIG PICTURE

The kinds of societies we now live in are the results of a dramatic process of total change that has been taking place over the past 300 years. In the eighteenth century, members of the Scottish Enlightenment, including Adam Ferguson and Dougald Steuart, talked about the emergence of 'civil society', while Adam Smith talked about the growth of 'commercial society'. In the nineteenth century, Karl Marx wrote about the transition from the feudal mode of production to the capitalist mode of production. In the 1880s, Ferdinand Toennies referred to this process of change as the shift from *gemeinschaft* (or 'community') to *gesellschaft* (or 'society'). Around the same time, Arnold Toynbee wrote about the growth of 'industrialisation' while Werner Sombart described the evolution of 'capitalism'. In our own time, Anthony Giddens (1997) has written about the rise of 'modernity'.

Any attempt to generalise about processes of change in societies as different as China, Great Britain, Greece, the United States or Australia across a number of centuries must balance the need to simplify with a respect for complexity and difference—a balance not all sociologists have achieved. What the various models and stories of change all attempt to capture and describe is how societies in which people once lived a 'traditional' or 'pre-modern' way of life became 'modern'.

Traditional lifestyles

If we travelled in a time machine back to the Australian continent at the start of the eighteenth century, we would find Aboriginal and Torres Strait Islander people living a settled and traditional hunting and gathering lifestyle. They would have been doing this for at least 40 000 years. They harvested the land, waterways and seas to feed, clothe and shelter themselves. Their lifestyles were rich and diverse, complete with complex and sophisticated religious and spiritual belief systems. Moreover, Aborigines and Torres Strait Islanders lived in ways that were respectful of the constraints and fragility of the natural order. They were the first Australians to experience the dramatic shift into modernity, which—as for so many Indigenous peoples— involved a painful, even brutal, encounter with European peoples, culture and power.

Pre-modern societies

If we travelled in another time machine back to the England or Western Europe of the 1690s, we would find a society where most of the population lived and worked on the land. In Europe, China and India, people lived in what have been called pre-modern societies. This meant, according to Bilton et al. (1996) and Giddens (1997), that most people lived in small villages and engaged in agricultural production. They were born, lived, had their children, worked and died in these villages, often without moving more than a few kilometres. People rose with the sun and went to bed soon after nightfall. In these small worlds, people knew each other personally, and were often related through kinship networks of extended families, even clans. There are still large numbers of people living this way in countries like China, South America, Africa and even some parts of Europe. For historical accounts of pre-modern life, see Thompson (1968), Laslett (1979) and Braudel (1984).

People in such contexts experienced constant face-to-face interaction. In pre-modern societies, 'space' and 'place' coincided because most people lived in close proximity to one another and in small-scale, localised communities. People enjoyed (and often suffered) from the small-scale and intimate relationships that characterised these communities. Those interactions also provided them with most of the knowledge of the world they needed.

In traditional or pre-modern ways of life, the household was the primary economic and social unit. Most people in the household (including children) were required to work to make a living. Success and survival depended on hard work and earning a living from the soil, hoping that droughts, floods, epidemic diseases, war and other disasters would not occur too often.

By today's standards, most people and their households in these societies were materially poor. The difference between being well off and healthy and facing starvation and death was slight. Population levels were usually stable until something like the Black Death, which ravaged Europe in the fifteenth century, came along. The majority of the population were poor, ate what to most of us would seem monotonous diets, and would often go hungry.

Life was generally short. The average life expectancy was around 40 years of age. Infant and maternal mortality was high and sicknesses were common. For many women, pregnancy was a continuous condition. As Shorter (1988) has shown, midwifery practices in pre-modern Europe were usually barbaric—a far cry from the romantic images currently portrayed of the 'good old days' before white-coated doctors appropriated the women's business of having babies. Women gave birth to large numbers of children, their husbands moving on to new partners after their wife had died in childbirth.

In these societies, people developed elaborate belief systems or 'folk knowledge'—what we now call 'religion' and 'culture'. This was done by:

- other people telling them what was happening in the wider world;
- people seeing what was happening themselves; and
- a local wise person or priest telling them what they should believe.

Few people could read—and there was little for them to read anyway before the spread of book-printing after 1500 (Martin 1993). Folk knowledge included recipes and practices for curing illness, preventing disasters, contraception, assisting birth and keeping crops plentiful. Folk knowledge also included religious belief systems and what some people refer to as magic, which was intended to make the apparent chaos of the world meaningful and more manageable. People worshipped a variety of local gods, spirits and/or the Christian God. If anything unfavourable happened, an evil god or witchcraft was the usual explanation.

The fastest speed of travel was a fast walking pace or by horse. People were prey to diseases and infections they could not control. Violence, war and famine were never too far from intellectual and political life, especially as this related to religion, monarchical power and most importantly the local power elite—usually associated with great landowners.

Power was localised and personal. It was usually in the hands of the monarchy, wealthy landholders, the military, noble and religious families, and groups who 'looked after' locals in exchange for their obedience, loyalty, respect and taxes. The nobility, who comprised fewer than 5 per cent of the population, were extremely wealthy and powerful, and exercised extensive control over economic, religious, intellectual, political and legal matters in their community.

Community: The 'good old days'

In the late nineteenth century, sociologists like the German Ferdinand Toennies (1963) used the word 'community' to describe this way of life. Toennies personally experienced the shift from rural to urban life. Although it was probably not Toennies' intention, he helped romanticise the pre-modern community in ways that did not always accurately describe the harshness, pain or narrow-mindedness of that life. For Toennies, 'community' could be characterised as a close-knit grouping of farmers, based on what he called 'blood' ties. Community was also spoken of in terms of an intimacy among people and between people and their land. According to Toennies, this affinity with the land and communal conditions disintegrated as society modernised, trade and production expanded and people moved to larger cities. For German writers like Toennies and Max Weber, the modernising process was about the spread of rationality and science. The breakdown of community was associated with an alleged increase in selfishness as the basis of a new form of social organisation called 'society'—a concept used to define the individualised lives of people in cities.

Since the writings of Toennies (1963), the notion of 'community' has been associated with nostalgia for a lost way of life. As New Yorker Richard Sennett (1988) argues, the scale of the changes and its accompanying anxiety (especially in the nineteenth century) was so great that people looked backwards for reassurance:

> the destruction of the order 'feudalism' did not mean it was forgotten. Quite the opposite. It was idealized, tarted up, made the subject for regret. The idiocy and harshness of rural life were put out of mind, and the countryside became the place of pastoral ease in which deep and open human relationships seemed to have once existed. Everywhere in the nineteenth century the fragments of the old life which capitalism was shattering were being picked up and treasured as objects all the more precious because they were so vulnerable, too delicate and sensitive to survive the onslaught of material progress. Just as the village was idealised as a community, the stable family, with the younger generations taking their places in the order custom dictated was idealized as the seat of virtue . . . The citizen was offered a pastiche as a landscape of authority. Images of a broken world were pasted upon a canvas, tinted, and then presented as what trust, security protection, safety ought to be. Forming a community; belonging to one another—this social need was met with 'It once existed; we used to'. To retain a sense of reality, the citizen had to penetrate the haze of regret, to decompose that landscape, like a painter dissatisfied with collage who removes step by step what has been pasted together. (1988: 50–51)

Today, 'community' still implies a state of social order, moral consensus and stability in which traditional values, secure family life and harmony allegedly prevail (Eckersley 1992). Whether the pre-modern world was ever really like this is another question. Boswell's (1988) study of systematic child abandonment in Europe between 1000 and 1800 is one of the many historical works that suggest it was not.

● THE MODERNISING PROJECT

In Europe, Britain and America in the seventeenth, eighteenth and nineteenth centuries, traditional small-scale rural communities gave way to new ways of living characterised by two things: first, cities began increasing in size as populations shifted out of the country and into both old and new cities; and second, businessmen, engineers and entrepreneurs devised new ways of designing and organising economic production involving more intensive agriculture, the use of factories and new kinds of energy like steam and electricity to get things made and transported. The results were dramatic increases in wealth, the size and movement of populations, and major changes in health, longevity and family size.

For the last two centuries, writers have explained this revolutionary shift using different terms and emphasising everything from the role of ideas, state policy, demography and new technology to class struggle.

- Adam Smith in 1775 claimed that the rise of 'commercial society' occurred because of the growing use of the division of labour to generate economic wealth and increase the volume of trade.
- August Comte invented the word 'sociology' in the 1830s to name his 'science of society'. He saw historical change as being driven by successive changes in human knowledge as magic gave way to religion, which in turn gave way to scientific rationality.
- In 1848 Karl Marx developed a class-based theory of historical change, arguing that a mixture of economic, cultural and technological factors explained how a feudal order turned into a capitalist order dominated by a rising bourgeoisie which used the labour of the working class to generate and accumulate wealth.
- Lord Acton in the 1890s emphasised the role of ideas in his account of how the absolutist monarchies between 1400 and 1800 changed into a 'liberal democracy'. Also in the 1890s, another Englishman, Arnold Toynbee, wrote about how 'industrial society' emerged out of agrarian societies.
- In France in the same period, Emile Durkheim observed the shift towards modernity in terms of a transformation from a 'primitive society' (characterised by 'mechanical solidarity') into a complex modern society (characterised by 'organic solidarity').
- Between 1900 and 1920, the German Max Weber emphasised the interplay between science and rationalisation, the role of religious and moral values of the emerging capitalists, the economic power of capitalists and the rise of bureaucratic institutions in his story of 'modernity' as the triumph of 'instrumental rationality' or forms of scientific rationality that avoided any reference to ethical values.

Each of these accounts seems to capture some aspects of the modernising process without catching it in all its complexity. Because we think Karl Polanyi (1973) offers a useful synthesis of these various explanations, we draw on his account here.

● THE GREAT TRANSFORMATION

Karl Polanyi (1973) drew most of these factors together in his account of what he called the 'Great Transformation'. His account of social change addresses the process of modernisation that started in the seventeenth and eighteenth centuries and identifies six main factors:

- There was vigorous and rapid growth in new economic activity, characterised by the rise of capitalist financial, industrial and labour markets.
- Economic productivity rose dramatically. This originated with the development of manufacturing on a large scale of new farming, industrial and consumer products.
- People came to understand the world in terms of science and reason rather than the church, magic, witchcraft and faith.
- Populations grew in conjunction with movements of people migrating from the country to cities or from one country to another across the globe.
- New types of government emerged based on the nation-state. In many cases, these new systems of administration used democratic forms of representation to elect leaders or governments. The nation-states extended their control over the population to assist them in waging wars of conquest while also engaging in global trading expansion.
- This process saw the expansion of Western European economic and cultural activities across the world, which was characteristic of the nineteenth century and part of an 'era of colonialism'. It was a time when most European countries established colonies in parts of the world previously occupied by those who came to be identified as 'savages', 'natives' and 'heathens'.

Each of these key processes meant radical changes in the way people lived, worked, related to each other and understood the world. It was also an uneven process, leaving some people untouched even in countries like Great Britain—which arguably went through this process earliest. We discuss each of the elements outlined by Polanyi below.

Capitalism and the economic revolution

By the eighteenth century, the kind of economy now referred to as 'capitalism' was clearly emerging. As Braudel (1984) points out in his discussion of capitalism as a concept and a historical process, the word 'capitalism' only began to be used in the 1890s. Braudel nonetheless insists on the global nature of capitalist trading processes as far back as the fifteenth and sixteenth centuries. Capitalist economies included new methods of organising markets, trade and finance, as seen in Britain in the second half of the eighteenth century. (The development of this kind of economy was well underway when Britain colonised Australia in 1788, using convict labour to establish settlement in Sydney Cove.)

Capitalism

Capitalism is a social and economic system of production based on a radical distinction between a minority of people who own most of the productive wealth (or capital) and the majority of people who have to sell their labour if they are to survive. Buying and selling labour for wages is a defining feature of a capitalist economy. Historically, capitalism took off when labour became a commodity.

In Britain and Europe, the growth of capitalism depended on and reinforced the push to drive most farming people off the land they had lived on for centuries. All capitalist economies develop from and depend on fundamental social and economic inequalities like the unequal distribution of wealth. In Britain, in a process called enclosure which began in the sixteenth century, peasant farmers were forced off their land and had to look for work as free labourers in an urban labour market, where people either sold their labour or starved. In the European colonies like the Americas and Australia, the land had first to be cleared of the 'natives'; once that had been achieved, it was the colonial settlers' for the taking.

The development of modern capitalist economies through the eighteenth century was closely related to four other key changes:

- new forms of knowledge based on technological and natural sciences linked to new styles of applied technology such as steam engines and scientific farming techniques;
- new institutional arrangements for organising credit, investment and banking. This included the introduction of banks, the invention and widespread use of paper currency, the spread of shares bought and sold on stock exchanges, and the spread of rational techniques of accountancy;
- new styles of organising work, including the creation of factories and the extension and intensification of old techniques, like the division of labour, which saw jobs divided into increasingly smaller individual tasks, which were then distributed to different workers. Another essential requirement for industrialisation was the acceptance and spread of the 'work ethic' throughout the population. This meant accepting the belief that to be a 'good' person you had to be a 'hard worker' (see Braverman 1974); and

- the evolution of industrial capitalist economies in England and other European countries, characterised by changes in the quality and role of family formations and the sexual division of labour. As capitalist production techniques thrived, some of the basic economic and productive activities were removed from households. Thus the extended household and its economic role collapsed as economic activity gravitated towards the factory, pottery and mine. It was in this context that the smaller 'nuclear family' became prominent.

The nuclear family meant that women and men assumed new specific gender roles and relations. Most women remained subordinate, confined to supplying unpaid domestic labour in the household while most men engaged in paid employment outside the home. This meant that domestic labour was no longer recognised as 'real work'. It was unpaid labour which sustained the capitalist economy by providing a material base that allowed male breadwinners to sell their labour.

Economic revolution: The new productivity

The Great Transformation resulted in dramatic growth in the quantity of manufactured products. This seems to have occurred in waves, beginning with increases in agricultural productivity. The British economy was the first to experience this process, which began with a dramatic increase in farm production. This was followed by an even larger increase in the production of heavy industrial goods (e.g. steam engines, farm equipment and railway lines). For most of the Industrial Revolution, ordinary workers did not experience any dramatic improvement in their standard of living.

This only became apparent in the mid-twentieth century, when societies like Britain and the United States entered what is now described as the era of Fordism. In 1909 in the United States, Henry Ford designed and marketed the first low-cost mass-produced car (the Model T Ford). He decided to pay his workers more than the market rate so they could afford to buy the cars they produced on his assembly lines. Fordism involves mass production, mass advertising and mass consumption, fuelled by increasing wages.

For the first 70 years or so of the twentieth century, workers' incomes and working conditions became increasingly more secure, and they were encouraged to buy the abundant consumer goods they were producing. Mass consumption was promoted by the advertising industry as leading to certain lifestyles, based on the consumption of large quantities of goods. Mass media and advertising relayed the message that if you bought a certain car, toothpaste or cigarette, you would have high status and become sexy, attractive and happy.

Most of the economies which have gone through the modernising process in the past few decades, like Japan, Korea and China, have experienced similar processes to those just outlined, although the specific role of private business, government and international markets varies between countries.

The revolution in knowledge

The Great Transformation was not only about the rise of a capitalist global economy and a growth in wealth and production; it also involved the development and spread of new ways of thinking. It is not easy to say whether new economic and political activities came before changes in people's thinking about their worlds, or vice versa. Whatever the relationship, the Great Transformation occurred in tandem with new kinds of science, new ways of looking at the universe, and a steady decline in the authority of religious and magical ideas, practices and thinking.

Central to the Great Transformation was what has been called the 'scientific revolution'. As Stephen Shapin (1997) points out, the scientific revolution began with an assault led by Copernicus and Galileo on the traditional belief that the earth was at the centre of the universe. This was followed by Isaac Newton's 'discovery' of the laws of the cosmos. Newton's physics and his invention of calculus transformed people's understanding of the universe in the 1690s. Newton believed in God-the-watchmaker, who established the mechanisms of the universe and then left the laws of physics to keep its mechanisms ticking over. After Newton, the universe could be seen as an entirely godless place, where laws of motion and mathematics ruled.

The second major assault on traditional religious ideas came from Charles Darwin. In 1859, Darwin challenged the Biblical idea that God had created 'man' and other forms of life. According to Darwin, life was very old and had resulted from a process of continual development—or evolution—which depended on accidents of nature.

Darwinian evolution posed serious challenges to traditional forms of knowledge, which until then had rested securely and primarily on Christian faith and natural law. Darwin's theory saw science textbooks displace the Bible as the primary source of truth. The second half of the nineteenth century saw church-based learning, including church schools, increasingly replaced by secular education. Belief in God and the claims of religion were actively attacked throughout the nineteenth century, with the advocates of 'science' and 'reason' claiming that they alone could explain the world.

A key part of this scientific revolution in the nineteenth century was the rise of social sciences like psychology, economics and sociology, whose promoters set themselves the task of constructing a science that was able to discover the 'laws of society' or of the economy.

In the history of sociology, the idea that 'society' was a system just like the solar system became important to sociologists like Auguste Comte and Herbert Spencer from the 1840s on. Considerable attention was given from the 1870s onwards to developing an approach to describing and explaining social activities which used statistics. The rise of social statistics relied on the invention of such techniques as correlation coefficients by Francis Galton, Darwin's cousin. Increasingly, governments encouraged social scientists and professionals to remedy the many social and other problems that were being 'discovered'. Such assistance, it was argued, would allow governments to monitor the population for its health and well-being, as well as enabling them to manage society 'in the national interest'.

This 'scientific revolution' had other, more subtle, effects, including a new concept of time and the consolidation of beliefs about human nature, leading to important new ideas about individuals. In traditional society, time was seen and experienced in terms of the cycles associated with night and day, and through the longer rhythms of the seasons. In modern society, time required careful management—after all, 'time was money'. Time increasingly came to regulate our lives. The development of work sites like factories, mines and potteries required the strict management of time according to specific patterns of organised work (Thompson 1967).

In Britain and Western Europe from the seventeenth century on, we also see a distinctive approach to understanding the person as an individual. This idea—associated with John Locke's political philosophy of 'liberalism'—emphasised the rational, pleasure-seeking nature of people. Individuals were described as having inborn capacities like intelligence and rationality, as well as offensive and indecent 'animal' passions. According to this account (Seigel 2005: 35–49), individuals pursued their own interests by applying 'reason' to their life tasks. By the end of the nineteenth century economists were writing about 'rational economic man'.

The revolution in population

As dramatic as these changes in ways of thinking were, the demographic revolution was just as dramatic. The Great Transformation was the result of, and contributed to, our continuing population explosion. For example, the population in Europe grew from around 120 million in 1750 to 468 million by 1913 (Kumar 1978). There also began a tremendous migratory movement of people, which continues to this day. This demographic revolution took three forms: population growth, immigration and urbanisation.

Population growth

This resulted from a rise in birth rates and increased average life expectancy. This was due both to a major growth in productivity, especially of basic foods, and to improvements in the quality and quantity of housing and public health services. Everywhere, governments set about providing clean water and sanitation, which quickly did away with such chronic epidemic diseases as typhoid fever, dysentery, tuberculosis and cholera.

Immigration

The movement of populations (which continues today) escalated both between and within countries. Some of this movement related to the slavery that prospered between the seventh and nineteenth centuries, when 24 million Africans were enslaved. Ireland lost half its population after the Great Famine of the 1840s, as many fled their homeland to emigrate to the United States, Canada and Australia.

Urbanisation

As people were displaced and moved from the land, they moved to the big cities of Britain, the United States and Europe. In Britain in 1810, 20 per cent of the population lived in towns and cities. By 1910, this had grown to 80 per cent. As a result, these cities grew in size, creating new social relations and lifestyles.

Australia, despite images painted by the Heidelberg School of rural landscape artists and the stories of Henry Lawson about 'mates' in 'the bush', was already heavily urbanised by 1890. By this time, the majority of Australians lived in cities and towns along the coast. This pattern of urbanisation was not consistent—for example, the United States still had more people living in rural areas well into the 1940s.

In our own time, this process continues. At the start of the twenty-first century, China—which only recently began the process of modernising—has many cities like Beijing with enormous populations of between 15 and 20 million that are continuously expanding as millions of peasants leave the land and flock to the cities. Countries like China and India are experiencing rates of economic growth in which the gross domestic product (GDP) increases by between 5 and 8 per cent annually.

The political revolution

With all these economic, intellectual and demographic changes taking place, the political structures of Europe inevitably changed. Europe had a long history of monarchical states established by dynastic families. By the eighteenth century, many countries had governments with features we now identify as modern. These governments had extensive bureaucracies, which intervened to regulate economic activity, stimulate investment, raise taxes and control trade.

At the end of the eighteenth century and through the nineteenth century, the idea that ultimate power should rest within a government run by a royal family was challenged. The American War of Independence (1776–83) and the French Revolution (which began in 1789) introduced new ways of mobilising large numbers of people around ideas like 'democracy' and 'nationalism'.

There was increasing acceptance of the democratic idea that governments should respect the will of 'the people'. In 1864, American President Lincoln defined democracy as 'government by the people, for the people, of the people'. Sixty years later, women were given the vote in Britain and the United States, twenty years after Australian women.

Equally powerful was the idea that governments should represent a 'nation'—that is, a single ethnic community like 'the German people' or 'the American people'. This idea worked well only when a state had a single ethnic community within its borders. Many states, like the Austro-Hungarian Empire, had numerous ethnic communities. Nationalist ideologies which argued that the boundaries of a nation should represent a homogeneous and ethnically coherent national community became an important source of political and international tensions (Anderson 1989). By 1914, this idea would plunge Europe into a major war. The breakup of Yugolsavia after 1987 and the wars of the 1990s between Bosnians, Serbs, Kosovars and Croats had its origins in the ideology of nationalism. Together, democratic ideas and nationalist emotions generated significant political movements and change in most continents through the twentieth century.

Governments played a significant role in promoting modernisation. Through the nineteenth and twentieth centuries, governments became bigger as they expanded their control over many aspects of social, economic and cultural life. The promotion of the military and political power of a country was believed to depend on the capacity of governments to improve the quality of life of its populace, through the establishment of schools, hospitals, welfare systems and prisons to educate, punish, cure and manage citizens of the nation-state. To support the task of administering the population, governments drew on the knowledge produced by academics and professionals, and their claims to have expert skills. In the nineteenth century we also saw the growth of 'new' kinds of knowledge, especially in the social sciences.

Colonialism

The Great Transformation involved the massive expansion of European economic, cultural and political power over the globe in a process of 'imperialism' or colonisation. Europeans 'discovered' America in 1492. Over the next four centuries, many European countries—including Portugal, Spain, Holland, France, Germany and Great Britain—pursued a program of colonial expansion, exploring and acquiring 'unmapped' and 'primitive' territories around the world and sending out settlers to live in their colonies. This colonial expansion included the invasion of the Americas, Africa, India, China and Southeast Asia and the islands of Oceania and Polynesia, usually with destructive effects on the local people. The colonial expansion provided an ample supply of new resources, including slaves, foods, timbers and textiles, and drugs like coffee, tea, tobacco and opium, all of which were transported back to Britain and Europe.

By the nineteenth century, European countries had staked claims to various territories around the world. The economic benefits to the colonisers were immense. So too was the damage caused to colonisers and the colonised due to the spread of disease, war and racism: by the early twentieth century, some Australian states had only a small number of Indigenous people still alive. The 'winner' in the race for Empire was Great Britain. By the end of the nineteenth century, England had established so many colonies that it was said 'the sun never set on the British Empire'.

● SOCIOLOGY AND THE GREAT TRANSFORMATION

It might be thought that, if Polanyi's account of the Great Transformation is accurate, it must have been a shattering experience given the extensive damage done to traditional social relationships, institutions and beliefs. Yet we need to be cautious about how we understand such a long and complex process or what those going through the changes experienced and understood.

It is not clear that processes of change identified as dramatic by historians and sociologists were actually experienced as such by the people to whom they were happening. Not everyone in a given community or society will necessarily experience the same things as others in that community.

Second, it is not even very clear how much people in the seventeenth, eighteenth or nineteenth centuries knew about or understood about what was happening. Even today, where there are endless newspaper articles and nightly media analyses of processes like the spread of the web or the latest economic or political crisis, how many people fully understand the processes of change underway at the start of the twenty-first century? Finally, people experience and manage change in different ways.

In many ways, we continue to live in the shadow of the Great Transformation. This is so even as Australians move through a period of equivalent dramatic change. At least we can explore some of the ways intellectuals and writers dealt with it because they left us with records of their response.

The development of sociology was part of a modernising process that various writers tried to understand and explain. Sociologists understood and interpreted the Great Transformation in the terms provided by both conservative and progressive frames. That is, there were sociologists who resisted the dynamics of change they saw around them, while others enthusiastically promoted the processes of change. Both conservative and progressive interpretations affected the relevant societies in what Giddens (1984) has called the 'double hermeneutic'—that is, those interpretations (the various sociological stories) became part of the changing social reality, affecting the perceptions, beliefs and actions of those being studied. This took place as people used the sociological ideas to understand the changes and to promote their own interests. Sociological categories like 'society', 'deviance', 'anti-social' and 'socialisation' entered ordinary language and affected our commonsense view of the world. Finally, governments and other elite groups used sociologists, along with other social scientists, to shape, plan or change political, economic or social processes.

Sociology was used to investigate, regulate, plan for and police people within modern nation-states. The 'poor', 'delinquent', children, criminals, reformers, sexual and other deviants, the unemployed, factory workers, women and rural workers have all at various times been researched and written about, especially in the twentieth and twenty-first centuries. This involved governments, schools, armies and advertising agencies endeavouring to discover who and what was 'normal', and what could be done for those who were not 'normal'. The development of statistics and the use of large social surveys made this ambition appear an increasingly realistic project.

● INTELLECTUALS, SOCIOLOGISTS AND THE GREAT TRANSFORMATION

Intellectuals played a critical role in making sense of the Great Transformation. The development of social sciences like sociology, economics, criminology and anthropology was just one part of the 'modernisation' process. What makes sociology interesting, as well as complex, is the tremendous range of different values and approaches 'sociologists' have used to interpret the modernising experience.

Sociology effectively began in Europe and Britain in the eighteenth and nineteenth centuries, with more or less systematic attempts to describe or explain the various changes taking place in the way social relations and human conduct were changing. The work of a small group of intellectuals in Scotland after 1740, including David Hume, Adam Smith, Adam Ferguson and James Stuart, was especially important (Porter 2000). These members of the 'Scottish Enlightenment' reflected on the rise of what they called 'civil society'. They explored the rise of a commercial society and the paradox of individualism, considering how such a context produced social order. The Scottish Enlightenment left the legacy of a strong interest in the idea of progress and historical development. In France, another group of intellectuals usually referred to as the *philosophes*—men like Voltaire, Diderot Rousseau and Montesquieu—began reflecting on the nature of society. Montesquieu compared and contrasted countries like China with Europe and famously explained differences in national culture by reference to the kinds of weather places like Britain or Spain experienced. Rousseau put the question of social inequality at the forefront of leading social issues. Everywhere it seems Europeans came to feel increasingly confident that, just as sciences like physics and chemistry could explain the natural world, so a scientific approach might unlock the secrets of social and historical development—possibly even revealing laws of social change.

These inquiries influenced other writers in the nineteenth century, including Comte, Saint-Simon, Marx, Spencer, Toennies, Durkheim, Georg Simmel and Max Weber, who took up and extended the questions and answers their predecessors had proposed. By the twentieth century, sociology had emerged as a clear discipline in its own right, graced by writers like Robert Merton, Karl Mannheim, Talcott Parsons, Michel Foucault, Peter Berger, Alaine Touraine, Jurgen Habermas, Anthony Giddens, Pierre Bourdieu, Zygmunt Bauman and Ulrich Beck, who have continued to explore the meaning of modernity.

A history of sociology indicates that sociologists have always been divided about the value of the modernising process. Some worked within a progressive frame while others used a conservative one. Among sociologists, debates about 'modernity' were always intense. This meant theories or stories about the Great Transformation could be told using what George Lakoff (1999) calls either a 'conservative' frame or a 'progressive' frame.

● THINKING ABOUT FRAMES

There are major issues in establishing what we can know about anything with any degree of certainty. There are always a number of different ways of thinking about, or 'framing', the social issues of the day.

Our use of the word 'framing' signals that we are drawing on the work of George Lakoff (1999, 2005). Lakoff is an American cognitive scientist who has developed an original approach to understanding how people think, how we know our world and how we live in it. He does this by drawing on what he calls 'frames'. A 'frame' is a story partly made up of facts and partly of beliefs that also relies on values and feelings about things. It always consists of rich systems of metaphors.

Frames are not something odd or difficult to find. They are intrinsic to the way humans think and engage in both their ordinary daily activities and in important intellectual activities like physics, mathematics—and sociology. As Lakoff (1999) argues, any real insight into the nature of human beliefs and knowledge requires an appreciation of the role played both by metaphor and by moral values in the shaping of knowledge.

If we go back to the discussion of some of the important issues and anxieties that began this chapter, we will find that each of these beliefs and issues has been framed as particular stories. Take the idea that we are caught up in structural change shaped by 'privatisation' or 'globalisation', and that one result is that 'traditional values' are in decline and Australians are becoming more materialistic, selfish and amoral. This is a story framed by values, including the idea that change is not a good thing and that traditional values are inherently good or better than modern values. It is also a story infused with nostalgia for a time when traditional values were adhered to and supported.

Establishing that this is a story framed by certain values means we can also ask about how we know whether any of the key elements in the story are 'true' or 'factual' statements. Looking at all of the various stories at the start of this chapter, how do we check the 'truth' or otherwise of any of them? It will become clear that this issue prompts quite fundamental discussions and debates about the nature of truth and the role of the social sciences in producing knowledge.

For example, people who live in a particular society tend to hold certain ideas and beliefs about that place. For a long time, intellectuals and academic social scientists have referred to these ideas as 'common sense', 'ideologies' or 'folk wisdom', with a view to introducing the idea that their own 'theories' or 'scientific research' provided a better more solid basis for evaluating the beliefs that non-academics have. However, it is not so easy to draw a clear and simple distinction between what 'ordinary folk' believe and what academic scientists or intellectuals claim.

Any discussion about global warming, poverty, inequality or the falling fertility rate draws very heavily on the work of academics, experts or intellectuals. Yet there is very little general agreement among the experts about these and any other important social issues or policy debates. This is where Lakoff's work on frames is helpful.

A 'frame' is an unconscious, but very powerful, narrative that draws on authoritative metaphors and feelings to help us understand the world and to encourage us to construct certain moral and political attitudes and activities. Lakoff observes that: 'The frames we use come to us before any sets of data, facts or evidence are presented or relied on. Indeed the frames we use help us select in the evidence that will support the larger frame' (Lakoff 2005: 31).

At present, there is a tendency for us to divide into those who adopt a 'conservative' framework and those who adopt a 'progressive' framework. Lakoff accepts that this is a vast generalisation and overly simplistic; nonetheless, it is useful for helping to analyse and explain what is happening. But—and without suggesting for a minute that any one real person will fall into one or the other groups—we think he is right to suggest that there are two large clusters of frames on offer in Australia today. We are not suggesting that there are two clearly demarcated categories (progressive and conservative) that people fall into, but rather that we have particular orientations which lead us to see, think and feel in particular ways about social issues. Indeed, one person can have both conservative and progressive orientations on different issues at the same time.

According to Lakoff (1999: 117–29), a conservative moral world-view includes:

- the promotion of a 'strict father morality', which promotes self-discipline, self-reliance and responsibility, and upholds the morality of rewards and punishment. This involves endeavouring to prevent interference with the pursuit of self-interest by self-disciplined and self-reliant people. It also entails the promotion of punishment as a means of upholding authority, and for a lack of self-discipline;
- protecting moral people from external evils;
- upholding a traditional moral order;
- having conservative values and acting on them; and
- acting to support the moral order.

Lakoff explains that people who come close to having all these features are mythological 'model citizens'—wealthy, successful and law-abiding. They are supportive of a strong military system and a strict criminal justice system, oppose government regulation and are against affirmative action (1999: 163, 169–70).

Those with a progressive or liberal moral world-view, on the other hand, advocate:

- empathetic behaviour and the promotion of fairness;
- helping people who cannot help themselves;
- protecting those who cannot protect themselves;
- promoting fulfilment in life; and
- nurturing and strengthening oneself in order to achieve the above (1999: 165).

Lakoff argues that a person's general tendency influences the position they take on certain social issues. For example, those tending towards a conservative framework will be inclined to take the following position on certain social issues:

- The 'war on terror' does matter deeply because our national security is placed at risk by 'radical Islamists' and we need strong, determined leadership from our governments, including the suspension of civil liberties.
- Traditional values and standards are under attack or in decline because religion is not attracting as many believers as necessary.
- Family life is in a state of decline because there are too many selfish women who choose to work in the labour market rather than being a 'proper wife and mother'. The family is also under attack because there are too many degenerate and selfish gay and lesbian people.
- Big government is encouraging lazy welfare-dependent low-income Australians.
- Excessive taxation and overly generous welfare benefits are destroying incentive and self-reliance, and blunting the competitive edge of the national economy.
- The school system and bad parents are encouraging lazy, disobedient, drug- and alcohol-dependent children.
- Respect for authority is dead or dying.

Those who live and think within a more progressive framework tend to believe the following:

- The 'war on terror' is primarily a beat-up that is used by certain governments to conceal other motives, like the desire to protect their oil supply or to win elections.
- The big issues confronting us internationally are global poverty, the AIDS crisis in Asia and Africa, excessive military spending and global restructuring.
- Moral values need to be less rigid, and we need less authoritarian and more nurturing values that support the potential of human beings to develop.
- Governments need to raise taxes and do more to support people to get good education, find good jobs, have access to high-quality health care and support families in times of crisis.

- Governments need to provide more leadership by creating additional sustainable environmentally friendly business practices and community lifestyles, and more sustainable energy use like wind-power.
- If crime, 'broken families' and drug use are increasing, it is because there are unacceptable increases in poverty levels.

We use Lakoff's approach to framing social issues in several ways throughout this book. As we show, there is always more than one way of representing issues like:

- the changing roles and identities of women and men;
- changing attitudes towards and experiences of sexuality;
- family life and attitudes to marriage and child care;
- religious belief and action;
- crime and punishment;
- education;
- work and unemployment; and
- culture and Australian identity.

We use Lakoff's analytic approach to think about how we come to understand aspects of the world. This approach is helpful because it encourages a more critical or reflective attitude. The discovery that there are major issues and challenges involved in establishing the 'facts' of a case, and Lakoff's point that our values and feelings do make a difference in constructing our ideas about the world, help to remind us that we are still trying to answer three quite fundamental questions.

Using a conservative frame presents accounts of the Great Transformation as stories of loss. The losses may be about a decline in authority, social order, traditional community, hierarchy, traditional values, religious beliefs or the death of certain kinds of social relations, such as the father-dominated family.

Alternatively, a progressive frame will tell the story of the Great Transformation as an account of improvement, reform and growth—a story of progress. The growth may be in terms of more democracy, more wealth, better health, more schooling or improved quality of life.

Intellectuals have been as divided on this issue as everyone else. This is partly because they were part of the process they were trying to understand. Equally, these stories of loss and disorder or progress and reform have never just been intellectual and abstracted responses. Both sets of stories have always fed directly into the political and social processes of the day, and so contributed to the process of change itself.

Conservative frames

For many people who understand the world or their community within a conservative frame, the modernising process has long been seen as an erosion—even an attack—on authority and social order. The values and metaphors that go with this 'conservative' view are, of course, not stable: they change with the social and historical context. The poet Robert Southey saw the new-fangled steam train in the early 1820s as signalling a loss of respect for the older values of community and the stable, 'natural' order of green fields and forests, which industrialism and commercialism were destroying.

Working within a conservative frame, Emile Durkheim (1865–1917) painted a dark portrait of society and human beings. He did more than any other sociologist to shape and consolidate the idea of sociology as the scientific study of society as a system able to regulate its members. His was a sociology of social control. For Durkheim, society coordinated the actions of countless numbers of egoistic individuals, thereby creating and maintaining social order. Durkheim opposed the Marxist and socialist traditions, arguing that modernity was the inescapable result of a division of labour associated with industrialism. Weber (1868–1920) was another ambivalent pessimist, who saw modernity as a consequence of the expansion of rational techniques and bureaucratic institutions.

In our own times, arguments about 'the death of the family', the erosion of authority or the 'loss of community' reflect the long-standing feelings of bereavement and loss that have accompanied the modernising experience.

Progressive frames

Other intellectuals embraced the modernising process, however. For many nineteenth century British, American and European middle-class liberals and professionals, the modernising project was a necessary and inevitable developmental step in an idea of history as constant progress. For them, the Great Transformation was an inevitable yet welcome part of a longer historical struggle to improve peoples' lives, and to banish ignorance, poverty and distress. The Frenchman August Comte coined the term 'sociology' in the 1840s. As an optimist, he approved what he thought was the inevitable ascendancy of scientific reason and the displacement of the prejudices of religion. Socialists like Marx (1818–83) were angry optimists, who tied their social analysis to a belief in the inevitability of the collapse of capitalism. According to Marx, bourgeois society was a transitional phase heading towards a communist order of justice and freedom. Marx offers a sociology of liberation.

For writers like Spencer, Mill, Acton and the Australian Charles Pearson, what they saw of the change process across the nineteenth century promised greater democracy, freedom, wealth and the expansion of human capability and advancement. Some even saw certain laws of historical and social development operating. The implication was that there was little anyone could do to stop something so inevitable and necessary; equally, it would be foolish to step in to try to prevent the changes from unfolding.

The idea of inevitable progress was harnessed in campaigns for social reform. This faith in the idea of progress was also evident in the work of many who spoke on behalf of those injured by the process of modernisation. Socialists talked about the pain and alienation of the working class, and called on workers to struggle for a society without class divisions or exploitation. The radical and socialist working-class movements of the nineteenth century claimed that modernity had value only if workers could win material benefits from the process. The first women's movement, which fought for the right of women to vote, similarly told its story in terms of the inevitable spread of democracy and equality. Others campaigned against slavery: in America, the Civil War (1861–65) was fought over the issues of slavery and race.

Into our own time the work of the twentieth century American sociologist Talcott Parsons restated and 'popularised' the Durkheimian idea of society as a total social system without accepting its conservative, even pessimistic, overtones. For Parsons, society was an external objective: it had a life of its own and pursued its interests, if necessary, against those of its members. Modernity, for Parsons, was principally about patterns of universalising ideas and social values which guaranteed that modern social systems were rational, ordered and harmonious. Modern writers like Giddens, Bauman and Beck largely work with a similiar view of modernity.

But how much value is there to a concept like 'modernity'? The idea that ours is a period of modernity depends on agreeing that modernity is defined by techniques of administration involving bureaucracies, 'science' and technology. Modernity is the idea that societies are, first, reliant on the widespread dissemination of rational beliefs and scientific knowledge and/or, second, that they rely on the use of instrumental rational forms of social action produced by large-scale bureaucracies. Each of these propositions depends on the unstated assumption that the writer can authoritatively determine which beliefs are rational. Yet it is clear, as Mestrovic (1997) has pointed out, that in most so-called modern societies there are many influential belief systems like religion and nationalism, as well as pre-modern beliefs in magic or astrology. Many modern societies also rely on a belief in the inherent superiority of one ethnic community over another. None of these belief systems appears to be particularly rational. Rather than insisting on what may only be semantic distinctions, we need to pay much more attention to the curious and complex intermingling of 'scientific' and 'rational' ideas, and 'modern' techniques of social administration, with older and clearly quite durable ideas about 'community' and the 'state', a commingling evident in all 'modern societies' throughout the twentieth century and at the start of the twenty-first.

• CONCLUSION

From our viewpoint at the start of the twenty-first century, the changes that began over 300 years ago which we have called the Great Transformation involved a truly revolutionary change in the ways human beings lived. It generated great wealth and poverty, provoking vast social, political and military upheavals, and caused an enormous loss of human life. It has also produced tremendous improvements in the health, longevity, and cultural and material well-being of many people. Whether many people who actually lived through this period saw it in these terms is an entirely different question. As we argue in Chapter 9, the contemporary changes people refer to as 'globalisation' may represent another stage in the ongoing history of the Great Transformation.

Sociologists have been around throughout this entire process, telling stories—usually called theories. These theories rely on an idea of change that is told either in conservative terms as a story of loss of authority, tradition and order, or as a story of progress enlightenment, emancipation and progress.

Sociologists have been as divided on this basis as everyone else. But sociologists have always been an important part of the process they were trying to understand. In Chapter 2 we outline a useful approach to reading sociology or social theory before turning in Chapter 3 to survey some of the major traditions in the history of sociology.

Discussion questions

1.1 What is the 'Great Transformation'?

1.2 Would you describe the Great Transformation as a progressive or regressive process?

1.3 Which of the six factors Polanyi identifies in his account of the Great Transformation do you think was most important, and why?

1.4 Do concepts like 'globalisation' or 'modernity' mean anything, or have any value in helping you to understand our contemporary circumstances?

If social science
is the answer,
what is the
question?
Harold Garfinkel
(1988: vii)

. . . words still manifestly force the
understanding, throw everything into confusion
and lead mankind into vain and innumerable
controversies and fallacies.

Francis Bacon (1978 [1607]: 110)

2. READING SOCIOLOGY

- Summary

- Arguments

- Questions

- Claims

- Evidence

- Assumptions

- Metaphors

- Conclusion

- Discussion questions

● ● SUMMARY

Reading any kind of book or article requires a strong sense of purpose and method. In this chapter we outline a particular approach to reading which requires the reader to identify some key features of any kind of social science writing; namely: the questions addressed by the writer, the key claims, the main kinds of evidence being used and the key assumptions relied on by the writer. Along the way we also emphasise the key role played by metaphors. Is the idea that a person is a member of society a metaphor or a noun? Reading well entails being analytic and active. It also requires that the reader pay attention to the way ideas are framed and metaphors used to convey particular 'facts' and 'values'.

To understand what sociology *is*, it is necessary to be able to read and to think about the work sociologists *do*. And reading sociology well involves thinking about and interpreting what is written thoughtfully—or, as we say, critically.

Sociologists carry out research to make claims that a certain state of affairs in a community or society obtains. What they say is presented in the form of arguments. When we use the word 'argument', we could just as well have used words like 'stories' or 'frames'—as we began to do in the previous chapter. We have already used the term 'frame' in the way Lakoff (2005) uses that term. As we argued in the previous chapter, a frame is a story with facts *and* values *and* feelings in it, that uses both facts and metaphors to persuade the reader or listener of the truth of the story. A frame is an argument that comes out of a particular tradition or perspective, like Marxism, feminism, liberalism, queer theory or psychoanalysis.

Paying attention to frames is also helpful in dealing with the 'strangeness' which many people new to a discipline like sociology experience. Sometimes it seems that sociology is like a foreign language, replete with words ordinary people never use. This is a real problem. Sociologists either use ordinary words in really odd ways, or even invent new words or phrases like 'liquid modernity' or 'mechanical solidarity' that can be very frustrating even to knowledgeable readers. One way to deal with this is to systematically note words like this and use a sociological dictionary to get good definitions and keep a file of their meanings. Another useful strategy is to treat these words as clues to the frames being used. Queer theorists talk a lot about 'hetero-normativity', while people who admire the work of Michel Foucault talk about 'discourses', 'dividing practices' and 'government' a lot. As with learning a new language, there is no real answer except persistence.

We use the term 'argument' because most of us are familiar with this concept. We also use the term because we want to show how all arguments have a common structure which we can analyse—that is, show the component parts of an argument as a prelude to developing a thoughtful response to it. Finally, we use the term 'argument' because it describes how knowledge (or 'theory', 'research' or 'science') is produced and then communicated through books, reports and research articles to persuade the reader that what is being said is true or credible. It is important to be aware that, simply because someone—even an important or famous sociologist—says or writes something, this is never by itself a reason to believe them.

We have written this chapter for two reasons. One is to encourage a level of critical capacity on the part of readers to assess the worth of the arguments advanced by sociologists. We offer a very simple approach to reading actively and critically by directing attention to some of the key elements found in any argument offered by an academic writer. This involves pointing out some of the fundamental elements that constitute knowledge. Understanding the elements that make up knowledge also provides further insight into how we know anything at all.

Second, we want to develop the good habit of asking questions about things we usually take for granted. This involves paying greater attention to the ways in which we are invited or encouraged to see social problems or issues, and our tendencies to accept those particular framings.

In writing this chapter, we acknowledge the later work of Ludwig Wittgenstein (1953) and one of his proteges, Stephen Toulmin (1957). Toulmin provided an incisive account about how everyday knowledge is constituted and/or turned into the forms it takes in social sciences like sociology, economics or anthropology. As Wittgenstein said, the meaning of a word or sentence is found in the way it is used—it depends on the context. Toulmin pointed out that, in any argument, we can detect a structure—or a 'grammar'—of elements that makes up knowledge and is designed to convey a belief or claim about the ways things are. An argument does this in ways which persuade other people that the propositions are true.

In what follows, we offer an analytic framework for thinking carefully and critically about the *arguments* of sociologists. An analytic approach identifies the key parts of an argument.

People who are new to a discipline like sociology can get a good grasp of what is happening by paying attention to certain key elements in their reading. Thinking critically about sociology can also be assisted by asking how well each of the elements works in relation to the others.

Because we are interested in the ways sociologists construct arguments designed to persuade, we also need to discuss the techniques that are part of any exercise in persuasion. This is rhetoric: the study of techniques of persuasion. All knowledge, whether it depends on mathematics, empirical description or literary analysis, is an exercise in persuasion.

To discuss the techniques that are part of the art of persuasion, we need to ask how language is used in the rhetoric of sociology. Of particular importance is an understanding of how metaphors are used. Metaphors are fundamental to the ways we think about the world—indeed, as Lakoff and Johnson (1980) observe, without metaphors we literally cannot think. The problem is that our use of metaphors—like so much of the way we think—happens unconsciously. Paying attention to these aspects of thinking about and knowing the world significantly increases our capacity for good thinking.

● ARGUMENTS

Although it may seem like an oversimplification, there are only four central elements in any argument:

- the *question*, which provides the motivation for thinking about the world or for researching an issue;
- the main *claim*, which answers that question;
- some relevant *evidence* (or reasons) to sustain or support the main claim/s; and,
- finally and most crucially, certain *assumptions* which underpin each of these elements.

Together, these elements constitute an argument. For instance, in the following dialogue in a bar, notice how one person—Joan—constructs an argument:

> **Jim:** Who is going to win the final game? (The *question*)
>
> **Joan:** Oh, the Raiders are a sure thing. (The *claim*)
>
> **Jim:** Why do you say that?
>
> **Joan:** Well, they haven't lost a match now in thirteen games, their coach is the best coach in the competition and they're playing on their home ground. (The *evidence*)

In this case, the most crucial elements of the argument—namely, the 'assumptions'—remain implicit. It is assumed by Joan that the evidence she has used is a relevant and credible basis for a prediction. A little thought about this simple argument suggests (assuming Jim agrees the evidence Joan offers is accurate) that what holds the argument together is the assumption that it is possible to make accurate predictions about future events. This assumption underpins the question that was asked, and it underpins both the claim made by Joan and the evidence she offers.

The elements of this simple argument—question, claim, evidence and assumptions—provide the analytic structure of the more complex arguments sociologists develop by asking *questions* and making particular *claims* using certain kinds of *evidence* while relying on *assumptions* to do these things.

We now make some suggestions about how we can analyse the arguments that constitute sociological knowledge. And to make the value of that analysis apparent, we suggest that active reading begins by using this kind of framework with every piece of work the reader encounters.

● QUESTIONS

Academic research is always driven by explicit 'research questions'. When reading the work of academic writers, it is important that the reader both identify and understand the question the writer is addressing. This is important because often different writers disagree because different questions elicit different answers. It is also useful to be clear about what the question is in order to assess whether or how well it has been answered.

In most academic writing, the research question is spelled out in the introduction to the article or book. Such questions tend to combine words like 'what', 'why', 'how' and 'where', while some more sophisticated pieces of research and writing may ask 'how can we compare?'

Different disciplines tend to ask different questions. Among the key questions sociologists ask are:

- What is crime?
- How do we explain crime, or what causes it?
- How do we know crime, or how do we measure it?
- Who commits crime and who are its victims?
- What can we do to deal with crime, what can we do to deal with those who commit it, and how do we help those who suffer from it?

In terms of thinking carefully and critically, we can observe that not all questions are equal. There are good and bad questions. An example of a bad question is: 'Why is the moon made of green cheese?' Asking this question involves a logical fallacy called 'begging the question', which involves relying on a wrong assumption when framing the question. Even so, it is not possible to avoid making assumptions when framing the question.

As lawyers in a courtroom understand, no question is ever innocent. All questions rely on prior assumptions. That is, asking a question presupposes certain prior knowledge or beliefs. Every question relies on a raft of assumptions, including assumptions that the question is answerable and that the writer's own theoretical premises are sound. (We say more about this when we talk about assumptions.) Because assumptions are fundamental to all knowledge, we need to pay close attention to their role.

● CLAIMS

In most scholarly writing, the author makes it clear—usually in the introduction and conclusion—what their main claim or answer to the question is. This is also referred to as the writer's 'thesis'. The idea of 'claim' here refers to the main idea or point that the writer wants the reader to believe. In any large-scale and complex piece of writing or research, the main claim can be a very large and complicated structure of ideas and propositions.

Being thoughtful about an argument involves evaluating the claims that are made. It includes asking:

- how well an author answered the research question;
- whether it addresses a practical or ethical issue;
- how much it illuminates a previously not-clearly-understood part of the human or natural world; or
- whether it stands previous ideas on their head.

Like questions, claims depend on an array of unstated assumptions. For instance, in any piece of research based on evidence that was collected in an experimental laboratory, the credibility of the claim depends on the assumption that the research results can be reliably extrapolated or applied to other social settings. There are many examples of research carried out in psychology laboratories on the effects of televised film and cartoon violence on young children's disposition to emulate the violence they have seen. How good is the assumption that the evidence collected in a laboratory setting is applicable to what happens in a family's living room or a child's bedroom?

● EVIDENCE

All of the modern social sciences appeal to evidence. Like their colleagues in the other social science disciplines, sociologists collect, discover or use certain kinds of evidence to support their arguments. For this reason, disciplines like economics, sociology, psychology and sociology are treated as *empirical* enterprises. (By contrast, other disciplines like mathematics or some kinds of philosophy use deductive reasoning.) Leaving aside temporarily some important conceptual issues about what is meant by 'empirical', the credibility and value of the social sciences rest on the belief that they inform us of things that are 'real' or are discoverable in 'reality' because of the evidence they have assembled.

The credibility of a social sciences argument depends on an author's use of what they regard as evidence. In social sciences like sociology, the failure to supply evidence is a fatal weakness. Equally, a lot of critical attention is paid to the relevance and quantity of the evidence, as well as to the ways in which it was collected. As we will see, different kinds of sociologists collect different kinds of evidence. For some sociologists, crime statistics are important, while for others it may be evidence collected as participant observers, or in psychology laboratories.

For some sociologists, it is also important that the evidence can be gathered in the same way time and time again—in other words, that it is *replicable*. Without completely discounting the importance of good and relevant evidence, sometimes this concern results in the author overlooking the nature and validity of the assumptions that are relied on at each step of the argument.

There are a number of important things to note about what counts as evidence. First, different social science disciplines look for or accept different things as evidence. For example:

- Some psychologists rely on information gleaned from carefully designed and managed experiments run in specially designed laboratories or from the use of 'instruments' like aggression or impulsivity scales.
- In some kinds of sociology, a great deal of emphasis is placed on large-scale surveys which use questionnaires administered to large numbers of people which are then processed statistically using various tests of significance.
- In other forms of sociology, attention is given to obtaining insiders' accounts of events, their experiences and the meanings given to them.

It is because sociologists belong to a diverse discipline that they draw on a range of different kinds of evidence. Some sociologists believe ethnographic or participant observation research is far better than large-scale sample surveys, while others draw on photographs, cinema, advertising images or literary texts.

Finally, we live in a world where a vast, even overwhelming, mass of potential information exists. We need to select the evidence which is most relevant.

With regard to each of these three points, assumptions play a major role not only in shaping the questions we ask, but also in the claims we make and the kinds of evidence we discover, invent and use.

• ASSUMPTIONS

Assumptions are the most crucial part of any argument. An assumption is what we take for granted before we can proceed to ask a question or select evidence. Assumptions help us to define our questions, shape our claims and select our evidence.

Most of us believe that what we know depends on 'facts'. Such 'facts' come to us from the world through our various senses. If there is a dog sitting in the corner of the room, we know this because we can see it or sometimes hear and smell it. It is a 'fact' that the dog is there and our empirical senses tell us that this is so. This commonsense view is fine for discussing things like dogs and rocks; however, it makes no sense when it comes to many more complex issues.

This commonsense idea that there are facts waiting to be seen, smelt or counted is also not helpful for finding out about social things like the extent of unemployment, crime, gendered violence or poverty. To know about these we need to make—indeed, we cannot avoid making—assumptions.

The point we are making is that all our knowledge does not sit on rock-solid 'facts'. Instead, it relies on conceptual and cognitive abilities.

This idea of thinking about the world owes much to the work of Immanuel Kant (1724–1804). Kant argued that, while we 'know' things about the word based on our empirical senses (like sight, sound or smell), we can only organise these 'facts' by relying on what he called *a priori transcendentals*. These are concepts like 'time', 'space' or 'causality' that we require if we are to organise our sense impressions. They are made up of ideas that we have invented rather than those which come in as 'sense impressions'. For instance, the concept 'dog' refers to a furry, four-legged barking creature that we can see, smell and touch.

In the twentieth century, Gerald Holton (1988) showed how all 'hard sciences' like physics rely on *themata*, which are beliefs that we cannot verify by appealing to the facts, but simply assume to be true. He shows, for example, how Newton's rigorous account of the laws of the universe in *Principia Mathematica* (1687) relied on a themata called 'God'. Holton also reminds us of the origins of a themata like 'uncertainty' that reshaped twentieth century physics via the quantum revolution produced by physicists like Mach, Bohr and Heisenberg. What Holton called 'themata', Gadamer (1989) describes simply as rock-solid prejudices without which we cannot think.

Lakoff (1999) shows how metaphors supply many of these prejudices, and how metaphors appear to come from certain basic cognitive capacities that are 'wired' genetically into the human brain, or which reflect basic and vital social relationships.

The problem with assumptions (or themata, prejudices and/or metaphors) is that they are not always open to any further evidence or validation. A defining feature of any assumption is that it is rarely, if ever, spelt out. As Lakoff observes, most of our thinking processes—including our use of metaphors—are unconscious.

Metaphors are relatively easy to recognise, and they operate in every sentence you read or hear. The trick in identifying them is to ask whether something is a metaphor or literally a name or noun.

Establishing what assumptions are operating in a given piece of scholarship is not always easy. Assumptions are often elusive—they are found in the spaces between the words and in what is *not* said as much as in what is said. So how do we identify the assumptions operating in a particular argument? One way is to look at the elements in a piece of research or writing, and to ask what was implied by the author when they asked the question or selected the evidence.

We can generally identify the assumptions that are made by asking a few simple questions about the kind of question being asked and/or the kind of answer being sought. For example, is the question:

- descriptive;
- predictive;
- taxonomic;
- analytic;

- interpretive;
- explanatory; or
- evaluative?

What assumptions are made by the author in determining the kind of evidence that is needed? What assumptions does the author make about the central aspects and concepts being discussed? How has the material that will be useful as evidence been chosen? What assumptions link the evidence to the claims being made? Asking these questions will help to identify the assumptions holding an argument together. Once the assumptions have been identified, it is possible to think about and assess the value or credibility of the argument. If an argument relies on credible assumptions, it is likely to be a better argument than one which does not.

In analysing arguments, it also helps to identify particular *code words*. This is because we tend to use certain words to sum up our beliefs about the world. Certain key words allow us to spot particular belief systems and provide clues to the fundamental assumptions being made. Christians, for example, talk about 'grace' and 'sin'. Many feminists emphasise the role of 'patriarchy' and 'sex role socialisation', while economic liberals talk about 'market' and 'market forces'. Research also relies on belief systems. For example, researchers reliant on empiricist and/or positivist assumptions talk about 'co-variance', 'variables', 'representative samples' or the 'operationalisation' of concepts, while 'social constructionists' refer to 'symbolic systems' or 'discursive practices'. Experienced readers become adept at detecting the linguistic markers associated with particular belief systems.

What we mean by 'assumptions' refers to a polyglot assembly of beliefs sometimes bought together into what are referred to as theories. These may also be described in terms of 'paradigms', 'ideologies' or 'belief systems'.

Although we do not have the space to fully argue the case here, we assume that no one can do sociology simply looking at the facts of the world. People rely on their assumptions to live and work—and to do research—and do not usually like being required to examine what are often fundamental beliefs. These beliefs form part of their basic identity. In this way, sociologists—like all of us—come with already formed theories and beliefs that inform the kind of sociology they produce. This explains why controversies between different kinds of sociology can never be adjudicated by reference to evidence.

Broadly speaking, there are three kinds of assumptions (or themata) that inform the arguments we construct:

- We all have beliefs about the nature of reality that can then become assumptions inside a particular argument. These 'ontological' assumptions are our beliefs about the nature of reality. There are for example plenty of people who retain the Christian idea that all aspects of reality are manifestations of God, and therefore reality is orderly and spiritual. Alternatively, some people hold to an existentialist belief that no one made the universe, which just happened in one single 'Big Bang'.

- Second, we hold beliefs about the nature of good and evil, and whether humans can or should live good lives and how they should do this. These are political and ethical theories which address value questions about how to achieve justice or the good life. Values include different kinds of moral feelings along with more abstract ideas and principles: we may either feel an injustice very acutely or want to debate the principles that inform the idea of justice. Either way, our values are important and influence all our knowing and doing.

- Finally, we also hold on to epistemological or methodological beliefs about how we know anything about the world. Some of us appeal to faith, others to reason or rationality, while others prefer sticking to the facts. Over the past few centuries, the 'hard sciences' have given considerable weight to the idea that there is a thing called the 'scientific method', which we can use to establish credible knowledge. Holton (1984) reminds us of how Isaac Newton grounded his outline of scientific methods in his belief that there was a God—the Supreme Mathematician—who designed the universe so Newton could discover its laws. In the social sciences, these beliefs provide the basis for endless controversy.

Rhetoric and metaphors

Since Perelman and Olbrecchts-Tyteca's (1969) breakthrough text, there has been a modest revival of interest in the study of rhetoric in both the social sciences and the natural sciences.

By 'rhetoric' we mean all the techniques that we use to persuade other people of the authority and credibility of our knowledge. The study of rhetoric includes understanding how we try to be reasonable and persuasive by weighing and considering all the reasons, and not only the claims made by certain epistemologies, methodologies or logics, to secure access to the 'truth' (McCloskey 1999: 185).

We engage in rhetoric every time we attempt to persuade others of something. As McCloskey (1999) argues, we rely on a number of rhetorical techniques to secure all of our knowledge claims. Those techniques include the use of evidence or 'facts', various forms of logic and testing of validity, the construction and use of narratives, and the use of metaphors. The skilful use of each of these four elements constitutes a 'framework of authority' which writers use when endeavouring to convince an audience. Focusing on the techniques of persuasion in a study of rhetoric involves, among other things, refusing to accept positivist claims that statistical tests provide the only secure grounds for true knowledge. It also means rejecting those interpretivist claims that secure knowledge is gained only by mastery of hermeneutic and symbolic techniques.

The reason we need to be interested in rhetoric is summed up by Nelson et al. (1987: 3): 'Scholarship uses argument, and argument uses rhetoric. The rhetoric is not mere ornament or manipulation or trickery. It is rhetoric in the ancient sense of persuasive discourse.'

● METAPHORS

A central element of this turn to rhetoric has been a recognition of the way metaphors function.

What is a metaphor?

A metaphor involves understanding and experiencing one kind of thing by reference to another. It requires a translation of meaning from one place or thing to another. Metaphor involves the transfer or carrying over meaning by seeing or making an association between two apparently unrelated areas or objects that the metaphor somehow connects.

As George Lakoff and Mark Johnson (1980, 2003) demonstrate, we could not think or act without metaphors. Human thought processes are largely metaphorical. As Lakoff and Johnson note:

> Metaphor is pervasive in everyday life, not just in language but in thought and action. Our ordinary conceptual system in terms of which we both think and act is fundamentally metaphorical in nature . . . Our concepts structure what we perceive, how we get around in the world and how we relate to other people. (2003: 3)

As one illustration of this, they point to the way we think about arguments as war in terms of a series of ordinary phrases:

> Your claims are *indefensible.*
> He *attacked every weak point* in my argument.
> His criticisms were *right on target.*
> I've never *won* an argument with him.
> He *shot down* all my arguments.

As they go on to say:

> We can actually win or lose arguments. We see the person we are arguing with as an opponent. We attack his positions and defend our own. We gain and lose ground . . . Many of the things we do in arguing are partially structured by the concept of war. (2003: 4)

Think, for example, how a metaphor works when sociologists talk about the causal link between delinquency and the 'broken family' (Wells & Rankin 1991). The metaphor ('broken') invites us to think about people as something figurative ('a mechanism' that is 'broken'). It may also imply that there are experts who can intervene to fix the 'broken family'.

Metaphor is critical to our understanding of the world and the objects of sociological research like 'criminals' or 'broken families'.

How metaphors work

Metaphors have a variety of intellectual, emotional, creative and illustrative functions. They allow us to understand and imagine things in ways a 'literal' description cannot. For example, sociologists might refer to an 'epidemic of crime'. Using a medical metaphor like 'epidemic' constructs and shapes people's understanding in terms of something that is 'infectious' or highly 'contagious'. Understood as an 'epidemic', delinquent or criminal people are clearly dangerous—a threat to 'community health' and in urgent need of treatment if the infection isn't to become widespread. Like medical epidemics, the use of the term also implies that there are experts who can treat the problem with appropriate technical solutions. As Nikolas Rose (1990: 123) observes, talking in this way has a lot to do with the way certain acts 'come to symbolise a range of social anxieties, the decline of morality and social discipline, and the need to take steps in order to prevent a downward spiral into disorder'. There are different kinds of metaphors—or, to put this differently, there are different uses to which metaphors can be put.

Constitutive metaphors

Constitutive metaphors operate at a basic conceptual level. They make thought itself possible by helping to set up conceptual systems which we then use to define, explain and know the world.

Constitutive metaphors can involve big and basic concepts such as 'society' or 'culture'. For example, from the perspective of functionalist sociology, deviance or delinquency is explained by reference to a particular constitutive metaphor of society as an organistic living system. The use of figurative terms borrowed from the natural sciences characterises social relations in terms of something called 'society' as an organic assemblage rather like a biological or botanical system. The biological metaphor of society has framed the way some sociologists have thought, and in this way it has helped establish the basic discursive practices of sociology and sociology. From this basic metaphor, other subsidiary metaphors emerge referring to notions of 'social order'. This means that analogies can be made between the proper functions of parts of the body deemed necessary for a healthy life and the proper roles of people and institutions required for social well-being. Those individuals who do not 'internalise' their appropriate social role are identified as maladjusted and seen to jeopardise the social order (Klamer & Leonard 1994). This is a very powerful and seductive metaphor because it makes what is difficult to understand intelligible. Once such a metaphor is in place, it is extremely difficult to change.

Pedagogical metaphors

Pedagogical metaphors are often used in teaching or for describing and clarifying strange or unfamiliar phenomena. In this way, metaphors work to build a bridge between what people already know and what they don't.

Phrases such as 'feral adolescents' or 'lost generation' are examples of pedagogical metaphors. The idea of 'feral' suggests a wild, unsocialised and dangerous being. It conjures up an image of dishevelled, long-haired young people living in makeshift tepees deep in some rainforest who are committed to radical ecological politics. A metaphor like 'lost generation' has been used to talk about youth unemployment. It delivers a powerful message about young people as both victims and a threat.

Heuristic metaphors

Heuristic metaphors evoke comparisons and point to resemblances between things, helping to show us how we can think and talk about an observed phenomenon in terms that are already familiar to as. As Klamer and Leonard (1994: 112) observe, our use of heuristic metaphors proceeds 'by taking a fertile metaphor and relentlessly articulating the nature of its subsidiary domains, probing the properties of that terrain, and testing the connections'. Ideas like 'life cycle', 'culture' and 'subculture' are good examples of the fertility of heuristic metaphors in fields like youth studies and sociology.

An heuristic metaphor helps to begin an inquiry. Classic examples in sociological research and deviance theory include 'life-cycle' or 'life-stage' models. The metaphor of the life cycle, for example, allows us not only to explain, but to extend our inquiry and to develop models in order to describe in greater detail what is happening. (Such models, it might be added, also operate as useful pedagogical metaphors.) Classic notions of adolescence as a precarious, troubled phase (cf. Stanley-Hall 1904; Coleman 1974) in the life cycle invites us to treat those in that category as passing through a distinct and unique stage. Life-cycle metaphors borrow from the natural and biological sciences, enabling us to treat adolescence as a temporary status with specific cognitive, emotional and intellectual features. They include the idea of adolescence as a transitionary and typically troubled phase of 'storm and stress'. The heuristic power of such metaphors enables us to organise our thinking about particular aspects of young people and our relationships with them.

The term 'subculture' is an heuristic metaphor because it establishes a relationship between the collective activities of particular young people and the wider 'mainstream' culture. Subcultures are described by some (e.g. Hall & Jefferson 1976) as 'resistant' to the 'dominant hegemonic culture'. Members of the Birmingham Centre for Contemporary Cultural Studies (CCCS) in the 1970s and 1980s operated with a neo-Marxist understanding of subculture that demarcated young people in ceremonial fights against social order and assumed a clash between class and generation.

Heuristic metaphors can be expanded by relentlessly articulating the nature of their subsidiary domains. Adolescence as a period of 'storm and stress' constructs the adolescent as turbulent, unpredictable, susceptible to fits of rage and full of anxiety. Such a metaphor suggests a danger and threat. It invites us to imagine the adolescent as being in need of careful monitoring and governance as they tread the uncertain and rickety 'path' to responsible adulthood.

There is real value in paying careful attention to the use of metaphor in sociological theory and research. Each of the traditions that we have identified at work in sociology relies on and uses different kinds of metaphors in ways that matter deeply. When structural functionalists use words like 'structure' or 'social forces' they are using metaphors, because these words are not literally descriptive. Likewise, when symbolic interactionists use terms like 'social actor', 'moral panic' or 'social script' they are relying on metaphors. Understanding the cognitive role and function of metaphors and showing how specific metaphors constitute the object of research and theory provide a very important source of deep insight.

Sociological research and theory as we know it would not be possible without the use of metaphor. All researchers use particular metaphors in their daily work. This silently but powerfully informs the thinking of researchers and theorists—usually without there being an awareness of the metaphor or its capabilities.

● CONCLUSION

In this chapter, we presented a simple approach to reading and thinking about the work of sociologists. We did this because we appreciate that it helps to have some kind of method in mind when approaching central activities like reading and thinking.

We offered a very simple and practical approach to reading actively by directing attention to some of the key elements found in academic writing. By reading actively and looking for these elements, readers can develop sharper insights into what is being said while also forming a view about its credibility. We then briefly outlined the key role that metaphors play in shaping the way sociologists see and think about the world.

Discussion questions

2.1 What are the key elements of arguments?

2.2 What role do assumptions play in sociological arguments and research?

2.3 What is a metaphor?

2.4 Why do metaphors matter in sociology?

'... makes a good story', I said.
'Stories are all the human race has got, Dave. You just got to find the one you like and stay with it', he replied.
James Lee Burke, (2000), Purple Cane Road: 136

3. MAKING SENSE
OF SOCIOLOGY

- Summary

- The 'sociological imagination'

- Theory in sociology

- Clarification: Different kinds of theory

- Different ideas about reality and knowledge

- A potted history of sociology

- Seven sociologies

- The big picture

- Structural functionalism

- Marxism

- Feminism

- Weberian sociology

- Symbolic interactionism

- Critical theory

- Post-foundationalism

- Conclusion

- Discussion questions

● ● SUMMARY

It is not uncommon for people new to sociology to be completely baffled both by the language used and by the ways sociologists put their ideas together. In this chapter we outline some of the many approaches to the study of societies and social activities that constitute 'sociology'. While the idea of the 'sociological imagination' is a useful introduction to what sociologists do, it can gloss over the significant differences in the ways sociologists practise 'sociology'. This is evident even in the diversity of meanings attached to the word 'theory' when people talk about social theory. We offer a simple analytic approach to making sense of sociologists and point especially to the large differences in assumptions about the nature of reality and knowledge, and how this helps us to come to terms with the diversity of sociology. We then outline some of the defining characteristics of the seven kinds of 'sociology' we identify.

Many students—especially those new to sociology—end up being baffled by the language used by sociologists and/or by the way sociologists think. We spell out how it is possible to get a grasp of what sociologists say and think by providing a simple road map to the discipline.

As we show, being clearer means paying attention to the questions being asked by sociologists, which can include:

- Is social inequality becoming worse or better?
- Has a sense of community been aided or eroded by the spread of new technologies like the web or the mobile phone?
- Is anorexia a social phenomenon?
- How valid is Giddens' account of the 'double hermeneutic'?

Equally, we may need to ask and think about larger, more reflective questions like:

- What is sociology?
- What is a theory?
- What does it mean when we use the word 'social', and how does this differ from words like 'psychological', 'political' or 'economic'?
- How do social theory and sociology go together?

There are many different ways of answering these questions, which can be frustrating—especially for people who like simple, clearcut answers.

We have already suggested that sociology is neither simple nor ordered. There is no one definite or clear set of ideas, or body of research to which the words 'sociology' or 'social theory' can be unambiguously attached. Later we consider the various kinds of sociologies or 'traditions' to show that there are helpful ways of understanding what sociology is.

One way of understanding sociology more generally is to appreciate that it involves using and developing what C. Wright Mills (1970) called the 'sociological imagination'. Yet even if you could get all sociologists to agree that the idea of a sociological imagination was an attractive one, you would rarely get agreement on the best way to engage the 'sociological imagination'.

● THE 'SOCIOLOGICAL IMAGINATION'

When C. Wright Mills coined the phrase the 'sociological imagination', he was suggesting a way of thinking about and researching people's lives to show how they are connected to larger patterns of history and social processes. This was Mills' reaction to structural functionalism, which at that time was enjoying a period of intellectual dominance. Mills advocated Karl Marx's approach, which emphasised conflict, action and change, said to be driven by class conflict.

Four key ideas are central to Mills' account of the sociological imagination. The first is his distinction between the 'individual' and the 'social'. As Mills (1970) explains, in a city of one million people, the fact that a hundred people are unemployed is an *individual tragedy* for each of those people, but if forty thousand people are unemployed in a city of one million, a *social tragedy* exists. This distinction refers to the ways in which social networks produce their effects and how they are different from purely individual problems.

According to Mills, we are often unable to make this distinction because we rely too much on common sense. Mills also argues that we can only understand *what* is happening and *why* it is happening by revealing the effects on us of history and society. According to Mills, there is a larger history shaping our lives which is largely invisible—yet very real and powerful social factors shape what we think, feel and do. Finally, Mills was clear in his belief that we are free to choose and to act, but that we do not choose in a situation we ourselves have made. In this way, our capacity to choose and to act freely is constrained by our history and by our larger social context.

Giddens (1997: 19) provides a simple example of this account of the sociological imagination by talking about our morning coffee. Having our coffee is in one sense a very ordinary everyday activity: we reach for the jar, unscrew the lid, put a spoonful of coffee in a cup, pour in the water, add milk and drink. Applying the sociological imagination to this everyday activity means asking questions and seeking answers. It requires partial disengagement from the small part of the world in which we live and from the commonsense knowledge on which we rely. If we can make this break, we may be able to think about all of the social connections and the historical processes that shape our world and the way we live in and understand it. Drinking a cup of coffee takes on a surprising complexity when we ask questions like:

- Where did the coffee come from?
- Who made it?
- Why do I make it this way?
- Why do I drink it?
- What role does advertising play in my decision to drink it?
- Why do other people in other times or places start the morning with water, milk, rum or cow's blood?

Developing a sociological imagination means asking what, why and how questions—for example, what is unemployment, why does it happen and how does it affect people's lives? To answer these questions, we need to find out what is actually happening in the world. Sociologists agree that good sociology rests on evidence about the way things are. Yet finding out what is actually happening is not easy. As we argued in the previous chapter, we might want to hold on to the commonsense idea that the world consists of 'facts' that we can discover by using our senses. However, this will not get us too far with abstract concepts like poverty, inequality, unemployment or crime.

To say that we need to engage in social research involves starting a long discussion about how empirical research ought to be done. As we show below, there are many different views about what counts as evidence and how that evidence ought to be connected to sociological theory. As we have already argued, all of our questions, claims and the things we present as evidence rest on certain prior assumptions.

In short, if most sociologists say that developing a sociological imagination is a good idea, there is still no agreement about how best to do it or what it is that they will focus on. The trouble begins because different sociologists bring different assumptions and theories with them, and these ideas shape their work—including the kinds of questions they ask, the vocabulary they use and the kinds of things they will select as evidence.

Like most other disciplines, sociology has a long and rich history of argument, controversy and difference of opinion on how best to 'understand' or 'explain' social relations and society. It is impossible to offer a short, simple definition of sociology. Rather, we must accept that sociology is a complex and sometimes confusing mess of different ideas, theories, political or ethical values, research methods, controversy and debate.

● THEORY IN SOCIOLOGY

The word 'theory' is used a great deal by sociologists, frequently as if it is always entirely clear what is meant by the term—even though this is rarely the case. Academic sociologists generally attach a lot of value to theory; however, many also use the concept in ways that are not always clear to their students—and possibly not even to themselves. For this reason, before we look more closely at the history of sociological theory and the theoretical frameworks, we need to clarify what is meant by 'theory'.

● CLARIFICATION: DIFFERENT KINDS OF THEORY

The word 'theory' comes from the ancient Greek *theoria*, a word that has its origins in the idea of religious sacrifice, rituals and ceremonies.

> The *theoria* was initially the work of the *theoros*—used to describe anyone who was part of a delegation which attended religious festivals in a spectator role. To be a *theoros* involved becoming part of the religious reality via a process of contemplation.
>
> *Theoria* was the idea of being present to what is truly real. As Gadamer (1989: 124) points out, the ability to act theoretically is still defined by the fact that, in attending (i.e. listening) to something, one is still able to forget one's own purposes and to become absorbed into the stuff of reality. *Theoria* was true participation, not something active but passive (*pathos*)—namely, being totally involved in and being carried away by what one sees. This was possible only through becoming a true spectator—that is, someone who gazed intensely at something until they saw its truth.

These days, when the concept is being used clearly, 'theory' refers to a number of quite different kinds of intellectual activities. We need to be able to identify and respect these differences.

Bryan Turner (1996: 7–8) makes a useful distinction between two big uses of the 'theory' word. In our time, 'theory' tends to be understood either as a special statement possessing scientific and predictive/explanatory value, or as an interpretive statement in which the theorist explores issues of meaning and symbolic value.

The first sense of theory draws on the practices and assumptions of natural sciences like physics or chemistry. Here 'theory' refers to tightly defined deductive generalisations (or 'covering laws') that are said to have an explanatory and predictive capacity to explain or make sense of a mass of empirical data. A 'covering law' is a deductive generalisation which contains at least one universal law. An example may be: 'when events a and b occur, then by virtue of covering law x, y must follow'. Writers like Gottfredson and Hirschi (1990) rely on this interpretation when they use the word 'theory'. The aim of proponents of this view of 'theory' in social science is to generate statements which contain covering laws seen to be capable of explaining and predicting certain combinations of data. This approach is often seen as a key feature of the 'positivist' approach to scientific knowledge.

In its second meaning, 'theory' refers to any interpretation of social reality or human conduct. Advocates of this approach assume that the natural science view of explanations and predictions works well with chemicals or rocks, but does not work so well with human beings. They point to our capacity to act in relation to our feelings, moral, religious or political beliefs, human desires and intentions. According to this view, we can understand others by interpreting their feelings, beliefs, motivations or views of the world. For instance, writers like Max Weber and Peter Winch stressed the value of asking people to give accounts of their motives, reasons or beliefs when they did something. This approach belongs to a tradition of interpretive or hermeneutic social science.

Behind these two definitions of theory lie some large assumptions about the nature and objectives of human knowledge and the nature of reality itself. Around these quite different approaches to 'theory', very large arguments continue about how to do social science or criminology. (There are also large disagreements between people working inside these two large traditions.) The history of sociology can partly be written as a history of how these two competing frameworks influence sociologists to produce different kinds of sociology.

Apart from the distinction between theory as a scientific law and theory as an interpretive exercise, there is a third understanding of the word 'theory', although a better term might be 'paradigm' or 'framework'. In this sense, 'theory' refers to meta-narratives and interpretive traditions which offer large-scale understandings and explanations of human behaviour or social development—for example, talking about Marxism or feminism as a theory. Here the idea of theory refers to an interpretive scheme involving categories like 'class' or 'gender', which are then used to name actors and explain actions—often on the assumption that structure determines action. The point of this kind of theory is to produce a new way of seeing the world.

Fourth, theory can refer to recipes for action or practice in the same way that a recipe literally informs the practice of cooking a dish. That is, the theory is a reflection of a practice, represented as a set of components and way of ordering those components so as to produce good practice. An example is Egan's *The Skilled Helper* (1986), a book that looks at counselling practice abstracts and orders them, then uses them to inform communications practice classes.

Finally, 'theory' can be used pejoratively. This happens when one person says dismissively to another: 'You are just a theorist'. Here 'theory' refers to a process of speculation which engages a variety of deductive arguments, beliefs, prejudices or foundationalist claims about 'god', 'reality' 'truth', 'reason', 'society', and so on. In this sense, the word 'theory' refers to an exercise free from any confusion or ambiguity—and indeed, any regard for evidence.

In short, the word 'theory' refers to different kinds of intellectual activities. Sociology, like many other social sciences, relies on ideas and ways of understanding the world which have been around for several centuries. We need to be able to identify and respect these differences, and in particular to be able to identify and be thoughtful about the assumptions of particular writers and conscious of the larger traditions to which they belong.

● DIFFERENT IDEAS ABOUT REALITY AND KNOWLEDGE

Throughout history, people have developed a variety of ways to understand their world. These beliefs relate basic issues about:

- the nature of reality;
- ways to know reality; and
- the nature of human good and evil and how to live a good life.

Each of us inherits, acquires and selects from the large stories told about these issues. As we argued in the previous chapter, they help to shape what we believe in—what we feel comfortable with. We use these assumptions—or what Holton (1988) calls 'themata'—to develop particular kinds of knowledge about the world. As Holton (1988: 13–14) observes, themata are 'fundamental preconceptions that are stable and widely diffused beliefs that are not resolvable into or derivable from observation and analytic ratiocination'. Themata can be concepts like teleological drives, absolute time and space, causality, or ideas like 'beauty', gods or Creation. They are ideas that cannot be seen, measured or even derived from logical analysis: they just are, yet without them we cannot proceed to think and discover things or make science. When a physicist like Dirac (cited in Holton 1988: 15) says that 'A theory that has some mathematical beauty is more likely to be correct than an ugly one', beauty is a themata. Gadamer (1989) calls these foundational assumptions 'foundational prejudices' because, as Holton (1988) implies, there is no way of adjudicating between them by appealing to observation or logical analysis.

Some stories and their themata which are regarded as important include the following:

- According to Jews, Christians and Muslims, God created the world. It was an ordered and noble place until the first human beings disobeyed God and fell into evil. The world is a dark, often chaotic place, where evil in the form of change, disorder and materialism constantly threatens to break out. Heaven exists as another world, as an ideal of timelessness and perfection. God is known through faith or reason, and by obedience to a church or priest or through reading the Bible.
- For positivists, the world was created out of matter operating according to the physical laws of nature, which continue to shape human nature. Sociologists who are positivists believe human nature is a combination of anti-social impulses and biologically determined potential, and is best restrained by human-made rules and moral codes. (Another version sees humans as rational and good, well able to cooperate to establish the good life without too much interference by church or state; history has been a story of constant progress.) According to this view, the world

is basically orderly and predictable. We can be confident in our knowledge of the world only when humans use scientific methods of study.

- For existentialists, there is no intrinsic order or meaning in the universe—moral, physical or biological—except that which human beings in various social groups choose to confer on the universe, which is a godless and moral void. The universe may be meaningless, but culture and the expressiveness found in language create wonderful shaping patterns of belief and action.

In each of these stories, we find the three basic architectural elements needed to build a picture of the world. These are our views about:

- the nature of reality (or what philosophers call *ontology*);
- the ways we come to know that reality (or what philosophers call *epistemology*);
- the nature of human good and evil and how to live a good life (or *ethics*).

Ontology refers to our view about the nature of reality and what it looks like. There are many different ontologies. If we are religious, we may believe that reality and the universe are things God created and that the world obeys God's laws (i.e. natural law). If we are positivists, we may see the universe as the result of random physical events that are governed by various laws of nature. We may think that reality is orderly, rule-oriented and governed by laws of causality. We may argue that the natural world is different from the social world because humans can think, plan, act and reflect—something a stone or chair cannot do. We may think that the cosmos is less orderly and more chaotic, or we may just see this as a characteristic of social reality.

A long-held view is that there are some parts of reality (phenomena) we can see that are relatively impermanent. These parts of reality are characterised by change, but behind that world of phenomena exists the real changeless world (*noumos*) which is governed by God, or the laws of physics consisting of processes and structures that only certain people can see. The philosophers Plato and Kant both spoke of this kind of distinction between a reality of appearances which constantly change and a 'real' reality that is perfect and timeless, which is like some people's view of heaven. Sociologists engage with these more general ideas. They also address core sociological issues like whether 'society' is real and can be studied in its own right; whether 'individuals' (because they constitute society) are more real; or whether social relationships—or what Elias (1970) called 'figurations'—are more real than either society or the individual. (These issues are addressed in more detail in Chapter Five.)

Epistemology refers to how we obtain knowledge and establish an accurate account of reality. Most epistemological projects seek to establish some secure foundations for knowledge claims. Religiously inclined people rely on faith and the revelation of God's word found in the Bible to establish these as the foundations for belief. Others argue that only by searching scientifically behind the world of appearance can we uncover the 'real' structures of reality, and thereby establish some 'scientific' foundations. This view has been encouraged by some scientists and sociologists, who distrust anything that is not the result of rigorous methods of scientific investigation.

Some say that our ability to know the world is already wired into our brains at birth: this is the kind of rationalism associated with Descartes in the seventeenth century and Noam Chomsky in the twentieth century. Others say we need lots of facts that are based on our experience of the world, and that this gives us direct knowledge of the world. All this plus a considerable amount of thinking and we can grasp the nature of reality: this is empiricism. Empiricists say truth is obtained when we get the closest possible correspondence between our knowledge and the external reality. This, they say, is best done by careful experimentation or observation of the external world, and this process secures the foundations for true knowledge.

Opposed to most of these foundationalist programs is anti-foundationalism. Writers as different as Nietzsche, William James, John Dewey and Ludwig Wittgenstein, and in our own time Ian Hacking, Michel Foucault and Richard Rorty, argue that there is no external reality that has not already been selected for attention by our culture. These writers are variously pragmatists, constructivists and post-modernists. They argue that reality is always shaped by the language and stories (or 'discourses') used to describe reality. In their view, the best way we can engage with reality is through various interpretive research activities that involve listening to what people say about reality.

Ethics addresses questions like how to make choices about the right thing to do in a particular context, or how to tell the difference between good and evil. Ethical issues are central to politics, and to the shaping of our disposition to be either optimistic or pessimistic. If we decide that humans are essentially evil, then we may also argue that most people require a tight leash held by elites of powerful people who know what is best. Not surprisingly, powerful elites have tended to take this view, possibly to justify their maintenance of political control and in reference to authoritative sources of moral sanction like the church or the state.

Others may say we all have the capacity to tell right from wrong and we should leave it up to the individual. Kant, for example, argued that if we make the effort to put ourselves in another person's shoes, we can soon tell whether a particular action is good or evil. A more modern version of this, known as utilitarianism, says that good is what makes us happy and evil is what causes us pain—and that all of us can make this distinction.

The place and role of ethics in sociology involves some very difficult questions. Since Max Weber wrote his essay 'Politics as a Vocation' in 1919, it has been conventional for many sociologists to claim to be value-free, and to say that they are not seeking to promote any particular system of social or political values. However, this is both unwise and virtually impossible. It is clear, for example, that those espousing a positivist research model were actually promoting a deeply conservative political position. Since the 1960s, a variety of radical and critical styles of sociology have taken to proclaiming their commitment to revolutionary class struggle, liberal reform, feminist campaigns or anti-colonial and anti-racist positions as part of their teaching or research. Dealing explicitly with these different ethical systems is not always easy.

In any discussion of the various kinds of sociology, mapping their basic elements helps us to identify the differences between them. It is important here to remember that we are all theorists. All of us have views about our world and we each rely on some of the various assumptions identified here.

● A POTTED HISTORY OF SOCIOLOGY

Following is a brief history of sociology. For further historical accounts, see Giddens (1997: 1–14); Bilton et al. (1996: 575–616), Abraham (1973); and Nisbet (1974).

Sociology as an academic discipline emerged in the eighteenth century. Various philosophers and writers like the Frenchman Montesquieu and the Scots Hume, Smith and Fergusson produced books that later writers would describe as early versions of sociology. Much of this early effort was directed towards trying to understand the historical evolution of a commercial or bourgeois society called 'civil society', in which trade and wealth were becoming increasingly prominent. These early efforts relate to the beginnings of the Great Transformation.

Through the nineteenth century, a range of economists, lawyers, journalists, philosophers and historians in Britain, France, Germany and America, such as Auguste Comte, J.S. Mill, Karl Marx, Herbert Spencer, Arnold Toynbee, Ferdinand Toennies, Max Weber, Georg Simmel and Emile Durkheim, developed different versions of what Comte in the 1840s called 'sociology'. They identified many ways in which they thought such a 'science of society' could be developed. Some saw 'society' as equivalent to the 'natural universe', so the same features and laws were found in all societies. Others argued that history and particular kinds of economic arrangements defined particular kinds of societies. Each of them wrote important books and articles, which are now identified as part of classical social theory. Each was concerned about the growth of cities, the spread of factories and industry, and the rise of 'the cult of individualism'. Some could not contain their delight at the prospect of more radical social and economic change leading to a new socialist utopia.

There were no university sociology courses, journals, textbooks or conferences until the end of the nineteenth century. Durkheim became the first Professor of Sociology in 1887 at the University of Bordeaux, even though it had no Department of Sociology. The world's first Department of Sociology was established in 1893 at the University of Chicago. Sociology developed much later in Australia than almost anywhere else. Morven Brown was appointed Australia's first Professor of Sociology, at the University of New South Wales in 1958. Now most though not all Australian universities teach sociology.

Through the twentieth century, sociology increasingly secured a foothold in universities.

In North America, sociology assumed many of the features of a profession with its base in universities. Many people began calling themselves 'sociologists', and there were conferences, journals, textbooks, university courses and departments devoted to the study and development of sociology. Professional careers in sociology were also established, a series of specialisations developed (e.g. the sociology of religion, youth, work, family). Meanwhile, sociologists engaged in debate and controversy about what sociology was and how it should be practised.

It is a simplification (but a useful one) to argue that, for a period—roughly between the 1940s and the late 1960s—an 'orthodox consensus' associated with the work of Americans Talcott Parsons and Robert Merton, called 'structural functionalism', held sway. By the 1960s, this had been pushed from centre stage by a number of competitors like Marxism, Weberian sociology, feminism, symbolic interactionism and, most recently, post-modernism (or post-structuralism). Many of these traditions had been around for a very long time—even before the rise of Parsons' style of sociology. It is also unclear how solid or widespread the 'orthodox consensus' actually was.

At the start of the twenty-first century, there are many more 'sociological' people, journals, university departments and books than ever before. Equally, it is possible that there is even less certainty about what sociology is than there ever has been. At the same time, the work of people like Ulrich Beck (1999) and Derek Layder (1994, 1997) indicates that there is still a lot of vitality and good thinking being done by sociologists.

This brief history indicates why it is neither possible nor wise to offer a short, simple definition of sociology. Rather, we must accept that sociology has a history of different ideas, theories, political and ethical values, research methods, controversy and debate.

● SEVEN SOCIOLOGIES

It is useful to identify seven distinctive kinds of sociologies. These paradigms, or traditions, are:

- structural functionalism;
- Marxism;
- feminism;
- Weberian sociology;
- symbolic interactionism;
- critical theory; and
- post-foundationalism.

This is not a complete list; nor would everyone teaching sociology agree with it. It is also important to be aware that these traditions are not always clearly differentiated from one another—because they often connect very closely. In some instances, they share important similarities. And within each tradition, there are also important differences and sub-groups.

In some traditions certain ideas cluster, especially around key ideas about society, order, change and the nature of knowledge. Some feminists rely on Marx while others depend on ideas that come from the functionalist or post-structuralist tradition. For a long time, critical theorists borrowed from and blended aspects of Weber, Marx and Freud. There is often considerable disagreement about whether a particular writer actually believed what some people say he did. For example, was Durkheim really a 'positivist' who accepted Comte's work as Giddens (1982: 65–73) says? Most post-modernists, for example, reject some parts of Marxism and structural functionalism, while using the work of symbolic interactionists.

Sometimes there is a lot of confusion about who belongs in what tradition—for instance, some post-modernists reject 'grand narratives' about society, but then immediately contradict themselves. Finally, very rarely do things divide into just two simple choices or options. We need only recall how people constantly 'hover' between different ways of thinking, taking parts of ideas from various traditions. In short, ideas and the ways real people use them are never as neat or coherent as our summary implies.

Nonetheless, so long as these qualifications are remembered, it is useful to simplify things. To make the discussion as clear as possible, we have constructed an overview matrix which maps the seven schools. At various points, it is possible to see representatives of one tradition relying on ideas found in other traditions. We follow this with a more detailed overview of the dominant themes and views in each of the seven sociologies. In our discussion of each tradition, we have focused on one writer who offers a useful example of that perspective. We do not try critically to assess the worth of the ideas—as our later chapters indicate, we 'hover' between Marxism, feminism, critical theory and post-modernist perspectives.

● THE BIG PICTURE

Table 3.1 is set out in terms of two of the three basic elements (or the foundational prejudices) and one new element. Our approach takes into account:

- *ontology*—that is, the views held about the nature of reality and what it consists of; and
- *epistemology*, which concerns our views about what knowledge and truth are and how they can be secured.

The issue of the level of analysis is complex and significant. It will become apparent that different sociologies focus on different levels of social reality. Those with a phenomenological interest, for example, tend to focus on the inner quality of 'individual' or personal experience. 'Symbolic interactionists' focus on small-scale or micro-level interactions between small numbers of people. 'Structural functionalists', many 'feminists' and most 'Marxists' claim that

Table 3.1 The seven sociologies

	Structural functionalists	Marxists	Feminists	Weberians	Symbolic interactionists	Critical theorists	Post-foundationalists
1. Ontology Sociologists say society/social action:							
• is orderly and changes slowly	●						
• evolves through successive phases or stages	●	●					
• is characterised by conflict and changes, often dramatically		●	●	●			●
• is objective and shaped into social facts	●	●					
• consists of society structures and individuals	●	●					
• is socially constructed out of symbolic materials like language/ideas					●		
• depends on social inequality	●	●	●			●	●
• depends on moral consensus and social control	●	●	●	●		●	●
• depends on power		●	●	●		●	●
• recognises the determining influences of economic power		●					
2. Epistemology Sociologists use:							
• naturalist methods of natural sciences and seek truth	●	●		●			
• symbolic hermeneutic techniques of the human sciences to establish truth				●	●	●	
• social practices that produce whatever a given group calls truth		●	●				●
• critically analyse all knowledge claims			●			●	●
• deconstruct knowledge claims							●
3. Level of analysis Sociologists should theorise and do research on:							
• the whole of society	●	●	●	●			
• macrostructures like class, gender, ethnicity	●	●	●	●		●	
• institutions		●	●	●			
• social movements		●	●	●			
• patterns of knowledge			●			●	●
• face-to-face interactions		●			●		

the only level of social reality that is worth taking seriously is the entire social system. In other words, notions of 'society', 'patriarchy' or 'capitalism' are used to draw conclusions about the nature and causes of the micro-interactions between people in the social system.

Thus, when Durkheim (1897/[1951]) argues that 'society' is the cause of the rate at which individuals suicide, he is using his macro-level of analysis to explain a micro-level effect. This is the core of an important modern debate called the *structure-agency debate*: how much is 'society' the cause of what people do, and how much freedom do people have to act or think (see Giddens 1979)? We can see how a sociologist who operates only at a macro-level is likely to produce a quite different kind of sociology from the sociologist who looks at interactions at the micro-level. The question is whether a single sociological theory can work across all levels to provide a good explanation of what happens at every level.

● STRUCTURAL FUNCTIONALISM

Structural functionalism is the oldest kind of sociology. It is usually associated with August Comte (1798–1857), who coined the word 'sociology'. This tradition is also associated with the work of Herbert Spencer (1820–1903), Emile Durkheim (1858–1917) and the American Talcott Parsons (1902–79). Modern writers like Giddens refer to structural functionalism as the 'orthodox consensus' about sociology.

Emile Durkheim (1858–1917)

Emile Durkheim was a French Jew who experienced the anti-Semitism that characterised France in the second half of the nineteenth century (Lukes 1979). He was a deeply conservative pessimist, who was dismayed and disturbed by many aspects of French social and political life like socialism and democracy. Durkheim can be regarded as an early advocate for a form of politics that was later developed by Mussolini—corporatism, or Fascism.

Durkheim was a sober, middle-class, hard-working man, who appears to have had few if any vices. He is one of the most interesting and complex sociologists in this tradition, providing a nuanced and subtle account of the way culture works and of the tensions within modern society. Durkheim rejected any simple model of history as progress. He waged a continual war against Marxists and socialists while also working to professionalise sociology.

Durkheim began his academic life studying the role of moral ideas in teacher training. The world's first Professor of Sociology, he used the journal *Annales Sociologique* to develop a school of disciples. Unlike later sociologists, he worked closely with anthropologists like Mauss. In the 1890s he published books like *Suicide* (1897), *The Rules of Sociological Method* (1898) and *The Elementary Forms of Religious Life* (1912). It is said that he died heartbroken after the death, in 1916, of his son in the trenches of World War I.

Themes

In a general way, structural functionalism relies heavily on analogies with the human body. Key figures like Comte or Parsons also studied biology. Structural functionalism's members have been keen to promote the idea that a science like physics is a good model for a 'science of society'. It is a tradition which emphasises the idea that society causes us to act in particular ways, and this requires the use of proper 'scientific' rules and methods to establish laws of social development.

Talking about 'structural functionalism' overstates the actual extent of agreement between the writers said to belong to the tradition. The key writers in the structural functionalist tradition often disagreed. From Durkheim we receive a bleak and pessimistic story about the tensions of civilisation, while Parsons offers a more cheerful account of how modernity is about the rationalisation of those allegedly universal functional aspects that any 'society' needs to have fulfilled if it is to survive. Although structural functionalism is currently out of fashion, its ideas have been promoted by modern 'neo-functionalist' theorists like Jeffrey Alexander (1990).

Ontology

Structural functionalists say sociology is the study of 'society', its processes and structures, and that these can be understood as objective (or external) realities. According to structural functionalists, all societies tend towards equilibrium or social order; moreover, social order is what most people want (Durkheim 1897; Parsons 1971).

In the structural functionalist perspective, any society is just like the human body. The key institutional structures of a society work like the body's organs to keep society healthy and well. Remove any elements, or change any functions, and the whole system will be threatened.

Social order requires that every member of society works for the order and stability of that society. For functionalists, social health means the same thing as social order, which is guaranteed when:

- everyone accepts the moral values of their society; and
- all members of the community accept their roles. (This is done through a process which later American sociologists called 'socialisation'.)

Social order depends on there being a moral consensus. This means there is a general agreement in the society about social values and ways of seeing the world. According to this theory, 'society' establishes standards of behaviour and thinking which are 'functional' to that society. A crude version of this story says that if 'morality' collapses, so too does society.

Social order is achieved through extended and complex processes of socialisation, education and sanctions (i.e. punishments and rewards) and reinforced by social control agencies like schools, families, social workers and churches, which ensure that most people internalise the rules for 'right' behaviour (or norms).

Durkheim did not see religion, education, suicide or crime as individual activities; rather, he claimed that 'society' caused people to behave in certain ways. It is therefore the study of social facts and their structural causes that sociologists need to focus on, according to this tradition.

Epistemology

Many, though not all, structural functionalists argue that the use of 'scientific method' based on a hypothetico-deductive model (like Hempel's (1970) covering law model) will make sociology a real science. There is a strong positivist prejudice operating in structural functionalism. According to structural functionalists, good sociology depends on scientific research methods and a rigorous application of the rules for hypothesis construction, observation and analysis.

Structural functionalists are keen on uncovering 'objective social facts'—like the 'crime rate' or the 'unemployment rate'—that represent repeated or habitual activities. The study of these social facts can, it is argued, sustain the development of laws of social development. An enormous amount of sociological research, time and energy has been spent collecting and analysing statistics on family life, crime, health, education and religion.

According to structural functionalists, the social sciences are rational and useful to social progress. They play a role in the broader diffusion of reason and science and the rise of professions that will make society more beneficial to all.

Levels of analysis

Structural functionalists are interested in the whole of society—its structures and mechanisms for securing order and consensus. Many construct a history of social progress in which different kinds of society rise and fall. According to structural functionalists, societies have evolved through various phases in which rationality has become increasingly obvious.

● MARXISM

Marxism is often seen as the major competitor to structural functionalist theories because of the Marxist preoccupation with social change and conflict. The core elements of Marxism began with Karl Marx (1818–83) and his colleague Friedrich Engels (Marx & Engels 1971). Marx's writings (not all of them published in his lifetime) seeded an international movement of communist, socialist and revolutionary parties in the twentieth century (Kolakowski 1982).

Karl Marx (1818–83)

Marx was a German philosopher, sometime journalist, original thinker, hopeless politician and revolutionary who lived in exile after 1841, mostly in England (see McLelland 1978). He lived as an impoverished student all his life, even after he had married a woman from an aristocratic family. He drank too much, refused to earn a living and cried poor even though he was supported for most of his life by his friend and colleague Friedrich Engels, a wealthy industrialist. Despite his apparent poverty, Marx enjoyed trips to expensive spas in Europe to cure his alcohol-damaged liver. He had a ferocious temper (his family nickname was 'The Moor' after Shakespeare's Othello). He pursued fierce vendettas against his critics, and struggled unsuccessfully to establish an international workers' movement.

Marx's theory was a combination of Hegelian philosophy, French socialism and British political economy. His greatest work, *On Capital*, is a critical analysis of orthodox economic ideas as well as the mechanisms of trade, markets and currency systems in the nineteenth century. (Most of this book, like most of his other work, was published after his death.) His ideas often changed, and he never defined his terms systematically. His work stimulated the rise of socialist and communist workers' movements throughout the twentieth century. He achieved temporary fame while he was still alive after 1871, when the English press characteristically confused his 'communism' with the French 'communard' uprising in Paris in 1870–71.

Key themes

Marxists claim to offer a 'scientific' account of why radical social change is inevitable. Many Marxists have argued that modernisation meant the fullest development of a capitalist economy into a socialist phase culminating in communism. Various political leaders (Lenin, Stalin, Mao Zedong) called themselves Marxists, while intellectuals as diverse as Antonio Gramsci, Jean-Paul Sartre, Louis Althusser, Stuart Hall and the Australian R.W. Connell (1977) have also called themselves Marxists, if only briefly.

Until 1989 about half the world, including Russia, Eastern Europe and China, was in the hands of governments claiming to be Marxist. Marxism became important academically between the 1960s and the 1980s. Since then it has tended to lead a fugitive existence in universities.

Ontology

Marxists say that social reality is a complex historical process arising out of the ways societies organise their means of material production. Social reality is both historical and constantly changing because of ceaseless conflict between classes (Ollman 1975).

Marx believed it was not so much ideas that brought about change, but people's social relationships and activities. According to Marx, it was people earning a living, feeding, clothing and sheltering themselves that shaped history. The things Marx focused on included:

- social relations of production (i.e. family life and the organisation of work between bosses and workers); and
- the intellectual, technological and productive processes that constituted the 'forces' or 'means of production' (Avineri 1970).

Marx did not deny the role of ideas, however, and he spent much of his life critically analysing other people's ideas.

Marxists maintain that all historical societies are unequal, and that most people are in weak or subordinate positions because they are subject to the authority of powerful people and groups. In a capitalist society, most people belong to the working classes. Marxists since Marx have generally agreed that class structures and relationships are the paramount 'structures' shaping the social world. They also argue that in any society the primary kind of power is economic power over resources (like land, wealth or industry). In modern societies, capitalists are those who own the various forms of wealth (like land, finance or industrial capital); the working class, on the other hand, owns nothing but its labour power and skill. Both classes operate in a capital-intensive economy. Marxists say you cannot understand human action unless you relate it to people's position in the class structure.

History is the history of class conflict: the constant struggle between the classes over a share of the economic cake. Most Marxists until the 1940s held that capitalism would inevitably transform into a new kind of society—a socialist society dominated by working-class people.

For Marxists, social order is fragile. In part, this is because it depends on violence, coercion or ideologies designed to make an unjust order bearable. Maintaining social order is more successful when people's ideas are controlled through socialisation, education and ideology.

Finally, Marx's theory was critical. Marxists assume that human beings are 'naturally' creative and freedom-loving, but that under the conditions of capitalist production are alienated from their own essence or being (Ollman 1975).

Epistemology

There is a highly sophisticated philosophical framework informing Marxist analysis, which comes from the work of G.F.W. Hegel (1770–1830) and which rejects both positivism and empiricism. As Pinker (2000) shows, Hegel operated with a complex view about how communities develop knowledge that suits certain social interests, involving relationships between 'masters' and 'slaves'.

Marx derived from Hegel a way of thinking about complex, historically evolving forms of knowledge, emphasising the way both these patterns of ideas and the social processes of which they are a part are changing in a cycle of becoming and passing over. This is partly related to Marxism's respect for the concept of 'dialectics'. Dialectical imagination refers to the idea that we can understand our social world only in historical terms (see Ollman 1975; Harvey 1996).

Marx emphasised the value of critical thinking (or critique). This involves exposing ideas to various tests that demonstrate how prejudiced or incomplete the knowledge claims are. For some Marxists, ideology refers to ideas and knowledge which are untrue and unscientific, and which protect or promote the interests of powerful elites. According to this account, ideology makes it seem as if a capitalist society works well or reflects some natural order. The task of critique is to show how these claims actually reflect the social interests of powerful groups. According to twentieth century Marxists like Gramsci, we are socialised to accept and internalise the dominant values, which reflect the values and interests of the elites in that society. Social sciences are said to be part of the apparatus of ignorance and oppression, and can be challenged by a commitment to freedom or a desire to end oppression and exploitation. This results in a struggle for radical or revolutionary change.

Other Marxists (often called Western Marxists) have stressed the role of critical knowledge, which exposes ideology and distorted communication to critical analysis. Western Marxists drew on the work of Freud to offer an account of the culture and media industries to show why Western European countries had not gone through a socialist revolution. For Western Marxists, especially those allied with the tradition of critical theory (see below), all knowledge is partial and ideological.

Levels of analysis

For Marx, human history can best be understood in terms of phases or stages that are defined by the dominant mode of production. Societies have evolved through various phases typically defined and identified in terms of the dominant economic power groups (or classes) and the distinctive and dominant mode of production (slavery, feudalism or capitalism). Marxists also claim there is a need to examine the class structures of any society. This is a form of structuralism which gives priority to the idea of a class logic shaping human action and aspirations.

A considerable amount of modern Marxist research has drawn on the globalising logic operating in capitalism as a world order.

● FEMINISM

Feminism (along with post-modernism) represents one of the two really difficult traditions for mainstream sociologists. Feminism is both an intellectual tradition and a social movement. Feminists have deliberately undermined the confidence of nearly two centuries of 'male-stream' sociologists. Feminists have forced men to accept that women have always been a part of the social world, and that there are distinctive aspects of women's experiences that were left out of traditional social science (for good overviews, see Eisenstein 1984; Putnam Tong 1998).

It is conventional to suggest that there have been two waves of feminism. 'First-wave feminism' refers to the political and intellectual activities of women in many countries from the 1880s to the 1920s. These women worked on winning the vote (or suffrage) for women—a struggle that was generally successful by the 1920s.

The origins of 'second-wave feminism' are usually located in the 1960s. It refers to the pioneering work of such women as Germaine Greer (1967), Betty Friedan (1963) and Kate Millett (1971), and the subsequent growth of a vast and interesting body of feminist research and activism (Putnam Tong 1998; Grieve & Burns 1994).

This account of two 'waves' separated by a vacuum begs the question of what happened to women between the 1920s and 1960, when feminists continued to fight to have their women's work and ideas valued and recognised. Second, it overlooks the powerful contribution of the French philosopher and novelist Simone de Beauvoir, whose book *The Second Sex* (1973) provides a solid intellectual base for second-wave feminism. Third, it overlooks the growth of a small but interesting body of men's work, represented by the Australian R.W. Connell (1995). Finally, it ignores the fact that today feminism is very diverse, including:

- liberal feminism;
- Marxist and socialist feminism;
- radical feminism; and
- post-feminist (or post-modernist) feminism.

Both 'second-wave' feminists and later feminists, such as Naomi Wolf, Julia Kristeva, Sheila Jefferies and bell hooks, begin with the idea of patriarchy. Most feminists—especially those with a more structuralist view—argue that all women in Western societies are in a subservient position. They say that gender identities which reinforce unequal arrangements are maintained through the attainment of forced consent or secured by coercive sex-role socialisation. This comes in the form of sophisticated practices of advertising that 'program' girls and women, forcing them to internalise particular patterns of behaviour that secure their subordination to men and direct them towards certain types of conduct.

Germaine Greer (b. 1940)

Germaine Greer was born in Sydney, and became internationally famous as the author of *The Female Eunuch* (1967), one of the most important original texts of 'second-wave' feminism. Convent school-educated Greer went on to study literature at the University of Sydney before heading off to Oxford University, where she completed a PhD.

Greer has been active in feminist scholarship, writing a history of women artists, studies of menopause and the older woman, a history and critique of the practice of contraception, and most recently a retrospective account of feminism.

Greer is an enthusiastic controversialist, who uses humour and irony as well as heavily researched arguments to make her points. She maintains a high public profile as she continues to anger and delight both feminists and non-feminists with her outspoken views on menopause, aging and fertility control.

Ontology

Feminists have generally seen social reality as a complex process of gendered relations, in which the sexual division of labour and the distribution of material resources (land, property, wealth and ideas) are crucial to economic production and biological reproduction in all societies. Early feminists argued that, in any society, one of the principal kinds of power is gender power, reliant on the sexual division of labour. Men everywhere have formed the dominant gender, in turn constituting a form of society called a patriarchy. Men as a group have traditionally owned most of the wealth (land, finance or industrial capital) and have dominated the state structures, as well as the intellectual and creative institutions and practices. Women have not been completely passive or invisible, but they have largely been written out of history. Historically, most women have owned nothing except their capacity to sell their sexuality and/or their domestic labour (Barratt 1980). Yet many feminists are critical of the claim advanced by Marxists and socialists that economics or class relations are the most important factors, arguing that what is really important is how men relate to women.

Most feminists reject the idea that biology determines their destiny, and instead argue (following de Beauvoir) that gender is a product of social and cultural ideas informed by the power of men in patriarchal society. Feminists say that you cannot understand human action unless you relate it to a person's position in the gender structure. They maintain that most women are in weak or subordinate positions because they are subject to the authority of powerful men, both as individuals and in groups. For radical and separatist feminists, marriage, family life and heterosexuality constitute an institutional and ideological mechanism for the oppression and subordination of lesbians and of all women.

In the various kinds of structural feminism, patriarchal society is an external source of social and economic oppression by men of women. Social order is maintained only by various forms of violence. This includes potential and actual violence, including rape, as means of keeping women in servitude, while other ideological and coercive means are used to ensure the subjugation of women. For many feminists, patriarchy can effectively be challenged and a more equal society produced only when enough women understand that they are oppressed and when they appreciate the reasons for their oppression. Patriarchy can be challenged only through a struggle for formal and substantive equality, and this involves persuading men to share their power and their resources more equally.

We can see similarities with some kinds of Marxism. The argument is that women experience a form of 'false consciousness' (or ideology) that enables them to be party to their own domination and persecution, in the same way that Marxists argue 'the working class' can be free only when they realise they are oppressed by the dominant class.

Before the rise of post-modernist feminism, feminists gave primacy to the gendered nature of social structures and relationships. Post-modernist feminists stress the way women and men participate in the gendering of ongoing practices of identity formation (Connell 1995). Walby (1992) and Nicholson (1997) also reject the idea of a natural or timeless female nature as problematic.

Feminists with post-modernist sympathies argue that we need to appreciate the diversity of human experience. They say that women's bodies—most of which menstruate, become pregnant and give birth—cannot be seen as separate from our culture. Our gender identity can be understood only by appreciating the cultural meanings attributed to the body and what we do with it. Beauty and other aesthetic practices oriented towards the body, such as fashion, are used to distinguish between the sexual and social roles of men and women.

Thus, according to post-modernist feminists, ideas about 'femininity' and 'masculinity' actually prescribe what women (and men) should devote themselves to (Irigaray 1987; Nicholson 1997). Where post-modern feminists differ from the earlier feminists is in their claim that attempts to realise those ideals are not a form of passive submission. They may or may not be conscious acts or involve intentional choices. For post-modernist feminists, gender identity is an active process; it is not simply a question of being receptive to certain forces being acted out on you. How women negotiate the imagery of femininity according to post-modernist feminists is not a straightforward and direct process; rather, it is full of tensions, ambiguity, inconsistency and ambivalence. It is important to remember here that post-modernists see the self not as a unified, coherent and harmonious whole, but as fragmented by other entities such as ethnicity, class, political preference and age (Nicholson 1997).

Epistemology

It is impossible to define a single feminist epistemology. Some feminists argue that rationality, positivism and 'scientific method' are male inventions, and call for a distinctively feminist kind of epistemology. Other feminists have accepted some or all of these epistemologies and used them to do feminist research. Still others advocate critical theoretical or post-modernist and deconstructionist epistemologies.

Most feminists adhere to some form of critical approach to 'mainstream' (or, as it is often called, 'male-stream') theories and knowledge. They see their task as critical analysis coupled with emancipatory practices. Many set out to expose distorted communications and oppressive beliefs and practices. Because feminists claim that gender oppression is most effective when it is rendered invisible by the cloak of normality, they see the role of research as revealing what has hitherto been made invisible.

Central to most feminist research has been the liberation of women. This is why a primary aim of feminists' research is to reveal the oppressive structures and processes affecting women. Sometimes this is achieved through showing the positive history of women's achievements and struggles in the past. Other research shows the different forms oppression takes and what action can be taken to abolish or remove inequality and/or domination.

Levels of analysis

Most feminists do research and make theory which covers the societal level (i.e. patriarchy) as well as the institutional and the micro-levels around families or interactions between small numbers of people. Feminist research and theory covers everything from studies of organisations, the state and the private sector to settings like 'the family' and the schooling system.

Some feminists use a form of structural logic to uncover examples of a double standard. That is, when a certain activity is done by men, it is often defined as 'normal', legal and widely praised; when it is done by women, it is often seen as bad or immoral, is made illegal and is identified as unacceptable. A range of 'moral crimes' like prostitution or certain types of sexual behaviour by women fall into this category. Likewise, feminists point out that for a long time domestic violence and rape in and outside marriage were not detected or defined as major criminal problems.

● WEBERIAN SOCIOLOGY

The work of Max Weber (1864–1920) provides us with another set of approaches to studying social processes and historical development. Weber stressed the role of ideas (e.g. reason), institutions (e.g. religious organisations) and bureaucracies. This form of social theory, because it was developed against Marxism, shares much with Marxism—for example, Weber's acceptance of the important part played by economic processes in capitalist societies and his interest in inequality. However, far from sharing the relatively optimistic temper of most Marxists, Weberians tend to be ironic and/or despairing about the prospect of social progress. Weberians also argue that social life cannot be reduced to the economic domain: we must recognise the role of ideas and desires as part of the symbolic and cultural nature of social action. But Weberians are uncomfortable with the idea that our desires can be 'irrational'. This theory emphasises the unintended consequences of our actions.

Weber's insights have been picked up and adapted by modern Marxists, feminists, symbolic interactionists, critical theorists and post-structuralists like the Australian sociologist Anna Yeatman (1990).

Max Weber (1864–1920)

Weber was a brilliant, ambitious, obsessive and sometimes violent and suspicious academic who dominated Germany's social sciences from the late 1890s until his death in 1920 (see Weber 1974; Diggins 1996). He suffered from psychotic and depressive disorders which developed after the death of his bullying father. He had an apparently adoring wife, who accepted the lack of sex in the marriage. He avoided university teaching whenever he could, though he was highly regarded as a charismatic public speaker. Weber could also be a bully, who sued and threatened duels with anyone who criticised him. He enthusiastically supported Germany's declaration of war in 1914. Most of his biographers point to a series of unresolved tensions and contradictions in his own emotional makeup which are reflected in his social theory and research: Weber's characteristic tone is ironic and he respects ambiguity and contradiction. An atheist and a secularist, he pointed to the continuing role of religious values and practices. Likewise, he admired the achievements of nineteenth century science and rationality but spoke passionately about how we now all live in an 'iron cage of rationality'.

Weber began his academic career as a legal and economic historian, writing about the great Oriental religions. He hated Marxism and started (but never completed) an enormous study of capitalist economic and social processes so as to develop an alternative account (*Economy and Society*, 1978). As part of his anti-Marxist project, he discussed the growth of rationality and bureaucracies, wrote an important short study on the impact of religious ideas and practices on the growth of capitalism, *The Protestant Ethic and the Spirit of Capitalism* (1974), and also wrote about the vocation of the social scientist (1949). He died in the Spanish influenza epidemic of 1920.

Ontology

At the heart of the Weberian ontology is the claim that 'social reality' is different from 'natural reality' because social reality is symbolic and socially constructed. Social reality is a complex web of meanings that human beings create. We are constrained by it and yet orient ourselves within these systems of meanings, value orientations and symbolic constructions.

Strangely, for someone who lived most of his life under the shadow of emotional distress, Weber offers a narrowly rational account of action. Action is said to be rational and goal-directed because we pursue what we want through our values and religious beliefs, and we use language to both constitute and interpret these interactions. It is said to be causal because we find out what is happening by asking social actors to tell us what they are trying to achieve. In this account Weber was heavily influenced by the dominant neo-Kantian philosophy of his time, a philosophy that emphasised the creative role of human consciousness.

Weber was also heavily influenced by the German tradition of historical economics which traced historical change in institutions like the legal, banking or industrial systems.

Weber, like Marx, was interested in the large-scale shape of societies and the flow of history, and the role played in these larger processes by patterns of ideas (i.e. reason) and institutions like religions and bureaucracies. To this extent, he rejects Marxism's preference for the determining influence of material interests and economic power.

Like many other German intellectuals, Weber was pessimistic about modern societies. He believed modernity entailed the tragic triumph of reason and science. Science may have abolished the old symbolic order of magic and religion, but it replaced it with no comforting or ultimately meaningful symbolic order. The rational modern world, according to Weber, was now cold and heartless (Berger & Kellner 1974).

Weber wrote about large organisations and institutions like the church or bureaucracies as sites of social action in which norms, rules and other symbolic forms shape the kinds of human action possible inside them. These modern institutions have become our home in modernity, but we have lost any idea of why they do what they do. As a process of demystification, the world is emptied of the symbolic and ethical significance that religion and magic once conferred. Social action now takes place inside repetitive and institutional social forms. Money-making, productive activity and the deployment of power are some of the basic human activities. According to Weber, power can be understood in terms of normal functions which depend on there being a sense of legitimacy in the authority of the person or group who holds the power, as well as on an implied threat of physical violence.

Weber emphasises how modern bureaucracies reflect the achievements of rationality, while fewer and fewer people—apart from the experts who run things—now actually understand how or why these institutions do what they do. Technical reason triumphs at the expense of substantive rationality.

Weber did not doubt that human beings are constrained by their economic activities. Nor did he deny the role played by power in all of its guises. We are symbolic creatures and yet we are constrained by these symbolic systems.

Epistemology

Although Weber's work is ambiguous and difficult to summarise, it is generally accepted that he placed considerable reliance not on positivist research methods, but on techniques of understanding people. That is, Weber believed interpretation offered the best way of doing social research. He focused on the need to use our ordinary capacity to speak, listen, read and write.

Weber's own research relied on the historian's interpretive techniques of finding, reading and interpreting documents to reveal the causal flow of rules, meanings and norms that informed action. Weber did not do fieldwork, nor did he use participant observation techniques which the symbolic interactionists later developed, but this is one logical extension of Weber's views.

Levels of analysis

Weber was happy to construct large-scale theoretical accounts of whole societies and entire epochs of human history. He was also eager to construct normative accounts of social action and how it took place, and of how proper social science as an interpretive science should develop. He was not so good at linking his account of social action to the larger macro-stories he wanted to tell.

● SYMBOLIC INTERACTIONISM

In America from the 1920s, and especially at the University of Chicago, a group of sociologists developed an alternative to structural functionalism. This group of sociologists, who we are calling 'symbolic interactionists', developed from the distinctively American intellectual culture led by such thinkers as the pragmatists C.S. Peirce, William James and John Dewey; the group was also connected to the social psychology of G.H. Mead (1863–1931) and the urban ethnography tradition of Robert Park.

One branch whose members called themselves 'symbolic interactionists' was led by Herbert Blumer (1900–87), who emphasised the symbolic nature of social interaction and the idea that social reality is constructed by human beings. Subsequently, a European immigration resulted in Alfred Schutz (1899–1959) bringing the ideas of Husserl and phenomenology to America and into a phenomenological sociology that was associated with the work of Peter Berger (b. 1929).

Harold Garfinkel developed a parallel 'school' he called 'ethnomethodology'. Although there are important differences between these various groups, for simplicity's sake they are discussed as one perspective.

Peter Berger (b. 1929)

Berger is one of the most prolific and interesting representatives of the tradition of American symbolic interactionism. He brings his own brand of 'phenomenology' (the study of the quality of experience and consciousness) from his teacher, and fellow Austrian refugee and mentor, Alfred Schutz. His work reveals a fascinating tension between his practice as a sociologist and his other career as a leading Lutheran theologian. Berger came to America as a child after the Nazi occupation of Austria in the late 1930s.

Berger is the author of standard texts like *The Social Construction of Reality* (1971, with Thomas Luckmann). He fought for a long time to reconcile his belief in the socially constructed nature of reality with his faith, as a practising Christian, in the transcendental reality of God. He did this in books like *The Sacred Canopy* (1967) and *A Rumour of Angels* (1970). His pessimism has become increasingly evident in his writing on the loss of meaning in *The Homeless Mind* (1974, with H.F. Kellner), and in a similar vein he has decried the loss of authority of 'traditional' family values in *The War Over the Family* (1983, with his wife, Brigitte). Unlike many of his American symbolic interactionist colleagues, he has been willing to write about larger social issues and politically sensitive problems. He has also written the very popular introductory text *Invitation to Sociology* (1966).

Ontology

Like the Weberians, symbolic interactionists argue that social reality is not an objective or external fact. This means they reject the structural functionalists' approach to 'society' and to 'social facts' as objective realities. Symbolic interactionists assume that social action and social reality result from people giving meaning to events and objects, and agreeing about the meaning of these things and actions.

According to symbolic interactionists, social reality is whatever people define it as being. Symbolic interactionists emphasise that the social reality we live in depends on how we understand the meaning of each other's activities, words and gestures. They say social reality is the consequence of people's interactions, agreements and interpretive rules, and this involves the use of symbolic techniques of communication that are grounded in language. Human action, according to cultural anthropologists like Clifford Geertz, is symbolic action. Language is identified as an important part of interaction between people, and language is symbolic action. A lot of attention is paid to non-linguistic communication like gestures and body posture.

All social encounters involve and require constant interpretation, which helps people figure out what is happening around them. For example, if someone walks into the living room and winks at you, is this:

- an invitation to share a joke;
- a friendly acknowledgment;
- a sexual invitation; or
- an experiment in establishing how social interactions work?

What is actually happening is not the critical issue, because there is no special position from which a person can say what is 'actually' happening. From the perspective of theorists like

W.I. Thomas, the critical thing is to realise that we are engaging in interpretive processes, and that those processes shape how we see the world. The job of sociologists is to trace the interpretive strategies people use to act together and to understand each other.

Symbolic interactionists also follow Mead (1934) in arguing that the self is socially constructed. A 'self' is what we develop through interaction, and it is the result of learning how to play roles. The self has a 'me' and an 'I'. (The 'me' is the way you define yourself in a specific social setting, while the 'I' is the total picture you carry of yourself and is constructed from the ways other people have defined you.) Social reality relates to small-scale interactions taking place between selves. According to symbolic interactionists, it is through the process of role-taking that the self takes shape. They say that it is when we put ourselves in another person's position that we begin to develop self-consciousness, which is required for the development of the self. Role-taking means trying to interpret other people's viewpoints and responding from that imagined perspective in ways we think appropriate.

Epistemology

For symbolic interactionists, all knowledge is hermeneutic or interpretive in nature. Good sociological knowledge involves detailed ethnographic description or participant observation. Symbolic interactionists prefer interpretive and descriptive accounts of people's life-worlds, focusing on the meanings they attribute to certain things. They like looking, for example, at interactions between nurses and hospital patients, to explore how the medical staff interpret the behaviours of those in their charge.

Participant observation is one of the symbolic interactionists' preferred ways of obtaining information about how people experience their lives. Making observations from inside the group means the researcher gains an understanding of the values, knowledge and belief systems in other people's lives. Observation and interaction with those being studied is usually preferred to controlled experiments (used by many psychologists) and large-scale sample surveys based on questionnaires.

Levels of analysis

Symbolic interactionists do most of their research on the small-scale interactions between people. They say they are not very interested in macrosocial issues, though writers like Berger do in fact comment on large-scale social issues such as the status of the American family. They care more about micro-situations, and the interpretive techniques people use to act and to understand each other.

• CRITICAL THEORY

The 'critical theory' movement became an increasingly important and admired tradition within sociology in the 1970s and 1980s. It was largely the work of a group of German writers, who have produced provocative theory and research of very high quality. This represents the convergence of intellectual traditions not always believed to be compatible, such as Marxism, Freudian psychoanalysis and cognitive psychology, along with a big splash of Weberian sociology and flavourings of media studies, linguistics and literary analysis.

In 1923, a small group of Marxist intellectuals interested in cultural studies formed the Institute for Social Research at the University of Frankfurt (Jay 1972). This first generation of critical theorists was trying to understand what was preventing the European working class in advanced capitalist societies from waging the revolutionary struggle Marxism had predicted. Of this first generation of critical theorists, writers like T.W. Adorno and Max Horkheimer (1972), Herbert Marcuse (1972), Erich Fromm and Walter Benjamin produced studies of Nazism, mass culture and mass media, jazz, film, the psychology of authoritarianism and major studies of the Enlightenment. After 1933 most had to flee Germany, and many finished up in the United States, where Adorno, Horkheimer and Marcuse did research on the effects of mass culture and how it allegedly created a 'one-dimensional society'. They argued that people had become compliant—bought off by a consumerist culture centred on consumer goods and promoted by television. Adorno's work is important partly because he anticipates some of the post-modernist deconstructions of rationality.

In a second wave of critical theory, younger German theorists in the 1960s, including Jurgen Habermas, Claus Offe, Albrecht Wellmer and more recently Ulrich Beck (1992), began producing a comprehensive program of research and theory about the nature of capitalism, the modern state, the nature of Enlightenment, reason and a general theory of communicative action. One difference between first- and second-generation critical theory is the optimistic and modernist tone of writers like Habermas, which sits strangely with the gloomy and pessimistic work of Adorno. Rather than trying to describe a complex body of work, we concentrate here on second-wave critical theory. For a good overview of both generations, see Held (1980); for a discussion of how critical theory aligns with post-modernism, see Best and Kellner (1991).

Jurgen Habermas (b. 1929)

Jurgen Habermas is one of the great intellectual figures of the last half century. He has produced an extensive range of original work across many disciplines, including philosophy, ethics, social theory, politics, literary criticism and history.

Habermas is said to be a shy and reserved man. As an intellectual, he has been publicly associated with the German Socialist Party (SPD). His earliest work was an ambitious history and theory of the rise and fall of the public sphere of coffee houses, newspapers and public intellectuals. Then came studies of epistemology, where he outlined his theory of the interest base of knowledge and the status of the social sciences. This work was followed by a study of the crisis of the welfare state (*Legitimation Crisis*, 1973) and later by a two-volume study, *A Theory of Communicative Action* (1984–86). Since then Habermas has expanded his research into studies of discourse ethics and the role of norms in law.

Ontology

Second-wave critical theorists brought some of the elements of traditional Marxism, minus its class analysis and economic determinism, together with a Weberian focus on rationality and state structures, informed by a general interest in communication practices.

Critical theorists accept that most societies are unequal. Most citizens are in weak or powerless positions because they are subject to the authority of more powerful people and groups. In a capitalist society, most people belong to the working classes. This fundamental inequality affects the type of social action and knowledge that is permissible. Critical theorists agree with the symbolic interactionists that social action and social reality are the product of people giving meaning to events and objects. At the same time the kinds of knowledge people produce and the uses to which they put that knowledge reflect the existing structures and power relations of society.

Perhaps what is most distinctive about their view of social reality is their insistence on the contradictory nature of societies and communities. Contemporary critical theorists developed an overall systems approach to modern capitalism while claiming that capitalism is intrinsically disorganised not least because of basic contradictions between different state activities. Both Offe and Habermas argued that modern capitalism is disordered, disorganised and in constant crisis. They argue that class consciousness is not as important as it once was, because of the success of the mass media industries in eroding radical working-class consciousness and the welfare state representing a successful class compromise (Offe 1983, 1996).

Habermas (1973) and Offe (1996) argue that the modern state attempts to do three contradictory things:

- ensure that the economy is profitable for the corporate sector;
- invest in the kind of human capital necessary to supply a well-educated and skilled workforce appropriate to an advanced society and economy; and
- ensure that the inevitable unequal effects of a successful economy (e.g. poverty, unemployment and homelessness) do not become a problem by funding significant and costly social security programs.

Critical theorists argue that balancing the needs of these three systems is impossible, and that modern states keep lurching into fiscal crises as they try to balance their budgets, but produce political crises as they discover they need to spend more money in order to keep political support for the social order intact.

Epistemology

The sophisticated work of first-generation critical theorists such as Adorno, Marcuse and Horkheimer reflected the impact of both Hegelian and Husserlian phenomenology on Marxist dialectics. The epistemological premises of second-generation critical theorists have been more 'conventionally' critical (Jay 1972)—although, as Best and Kellner (1991) point out, there are important convergences between, for example, Habermas (critical theory) and Foucault (post-modernism). Like the more general Marxist tradition, critical theorists assume that knowledge is impregnated by social values and political interests.

The task of the 'critical theorist' is to reveal these interests in shaping particular scientific or political claims—to play a role in liberating people by showing the effects of distorted communication.

Levels of analysis

Critical theorists engage in a kind of social systems analysis. Societies, economies and states are seen as complex systemic wholes that tend towards crisis and conflict. Societies are shaped by the interweaving of institutional logics, systems needs and patterns of knowledge with contradictory effects.

Critical theorists emphasise a logic of economic, administrative and political power found in a technostructure that works on behalf of capital. The main exponents of critical theory were not concerned with the social realities that exist in microsettings (e.g. particular schools or families), though there is no reason why this should continue to be the case. The interest of critical theorists has tended to be in the larger social structural effects of power and policy process (Offe 1996). Habermas has also worked at a high level of conceptual abstraction in his attempt to delineate social action as rule—and norm-oriented.

• POST-FOUNDATIONALISM

Post-foundationalism represents one of the most radical assaults on the kind of sociology that has taken an approving and optimistic approach to the modernising process. Many sociologists neither like nor approve of anti-foundationalism. It does not help that there is considerable disagreement among those identified with post-foundationalism.

An early version of post-foundationalism was developed in America through the work of the pragmatists, including C.S. Peirce, William James and John Dewey between the 1870s and the 1930s. The most distinguished modern exponent of this view is Richard Rorty. A different kind of anti-foundationalism began in the 1950s and 1960s among French intellectuals like Roland Barthes, Jean-Francois Lyotard, Jean Baudrillard and Michel Foucault. It spread across the world through the work of Anglo-American writers like Terry Eagleton and Frederic Jameson.

Anti-foundationalists reject the idea that a single scientific or truthful account of reality is possible. Its proponents are critical of Marxists, positivists and the orthodox style of sociology exemplified by Parsons—indeed, of most of the social sciences that grew out of the Enlightenment belief in reason (see Harvey 1989; Best & Kellner 1991; for a good, simple introduction, see Eagleton 1988).

Those anti-foundationalists who identify themselves as 'post-structuralists' (like Foucault) or as 'post-modernists' (like Lyotard) argue that modern societies have evolved through various phases or stages, passing from 'traditional' through the 'modern' into the 'post-modern'. They claim that we have moved into a new 'post-industrial' (Touraine 1971) or 'post-modern' era (Lyotard 1984).

Post-foundationalists emphasise the idea of multiple knowledges, ethical and moral rules, and the multiple forms that social and political movements can take. They reject claims that there is a truth that exists outside discourses and language practices. They also reject claims made by some Marxists and feminists that there is a single logic of power and oppression based on class or gender, arguing instead that a multiplicity of powers exists alongside a diversity of positions, each of which calls for political struggle.

There is a large question that is implicitly raised by Berman (1982) about whether post-foundationalism is really all that new, or whether it is simply taking the 'project of modernity' to its logical end-point. In one way, anti-foundationalism is simply one more version of the anti-Enlightenment belief that there is no objective basis either for believing in 'scientific reason' or for optimism about social progress.

There is justifiable concern about the jargon-ridden, cryptic and obscure way in which some post-modernists write. This cannot be said of writers like Rorty (1999) or Hacking (1999), whose work is characterised by great clarity. Similarly, there are reasons to be apprehensive about the ethical relativism that characterises the work of some post-modernists. However, the work of a post-modernist ethicist like Levinas (1996) points to great ethical authority which addresses that concern. But there can be no denying the often healthy impact of scholarship by Garland (1991) on criminology, Hunter (1993) on education or Rose (1990) on psychology which draws on Foucault's work.

Michel Foucault (1929–84)

Foucault is the most famous and important intellectual figure among twentieth century post-structuralists. He produced an extensive range of original work in the areas of philosophy, ethics, social theory, politics and history. This writing was combined with numerous public intellectual interventions concerning crime and punishment and the French government's treatment of Algerians and political prisoners. He was a public intellectual, and a homosexual devotee of sadomasochism.

After a troubled youth, which included several suicidal episodes, Foucault found himself at the centre of the French intellectual training system. From the 1950s, he travelled widely and taught in Sweden, France, Germany and the United States, while working from a Parisian academic base where he became a 'star' public intellectual from the 1960s. He produced original and, in his early phase, very 'difficult' books dealing with the history of epistemology and the evolution of distinctions between 'normal' and 'abnormal' people, including a history of madness (*Madness and Civilization*) and a history of the rise of modern prisons (*Discipline and Punishment*). He wrote original and challenging accounts of scientific practice, a radical *History of Sexuality* (in three volumes), and a history of the rise of state biopolitics. He died of AIDS in 1984.

Ontology

Post-foundationalists argue that we cannot directly access reality because we can comprehend it only through the terms given to us in the languages we speak and the discourses we use to name and to know reality. Some push this line hard: Baudrillard (1987) argues that, in a world saturated by the media, there are only media images: he went too far in describing the US military intervention in Iraq in 1991 as a simulation.

Most anti-foundationalists tend to argue that both social reality and knowledge are socially constituted. However, they also say all knowledge is inextricably bound up with power. In making this claim, post-modernists take the radical deconstruction of Western rationality found in the anti-philosophy of Friedrich Nietzsche (1844–1900), who argued that the will to know relies on the will to power. Power, according to most post-modernists and post-structuralists, relies on claims to know certain things. In particular power relies on a claim to be able to access truth. Most anti-foundationalists reject a belief in the possibility of an 'absolute truth'. They assume that people who claim to have the truth are actually using a variety of social or political techniques to force other people to accept this claim.

The social sciences (or the 'human sciences') have been of particular interest to writers like Foucault, who studied how sociologists went about the job of constructing truths about certain types of people. From a Foucauldian perspective, the main purpose of the human sciences was to define, categorise and regulate people by using criteria like 'rational' to define the irrational, and 'normal' to define the abnormal. For Foucault, micro-power serves to distinguish between those who are defined as 'normal' and those who are not.

Foucault argues that if we understand how language is organised into 'discourses' then we will gain insight into their power effects.

Epistemology

From the perspective of the anti-foundationalists, the social sciences are part of the apparatus of control and regulation; post-structuralists see their own task in being critical or deconstructive. Anti-foundationalists reject the value of what they see as 'grand narratives', or large, over-arching accounts about class or gender power which carry the idea that there is a single social system.

Some anti-foundationalists would even argue that 'society' and the 'individual' are discursive fictions, because all knowledge is discursive and there is nothing that can be called knowledge that can exist outside language or discourse. If there is also no truth, social science needs to deconstruct grand narratives and discourses. Moreover, 'building knowledge' is suspect because it is likely to carry a 'will to power'.

Levels of analysis

Most anti-foundationalists say they do not theorise about entire societies or classes or gender groups, though many actually adopt a high level of generality. The anti-foundationalist approach shares the Marxist and some feminist preoccupations with the way power is used to define certain people and behaviours as bad or irrational. Most anti-foundationalists like Foucault also reject mainstream Marxist and feminist claims that power is a single, unitary logic that flows across society in a uniform way. They say that power is dispersed and disparate—that is, it is everywhere and fragmentary. In this way most anti-foundationalists disagree both with the Marxist idea that power is organised economically in terms of class and with certain feminist claims that patriarchal power shapes everyone's lives.

Most post-structuralists see power not necessarily as hierarchical and moving from the top down: they see it as dispersed and localised. Although this is a simplification, most post-structuralists combine the radical's interest in power and the symbolic interactionist's interest in the way particular practices inside specific institutions like gaols, hospitals and schools are used to control people.

Finally, despite their rejection of grand narratives, writers like Foucault can fall into making the same kinds of generalisations that he and other post-modernists have criticised. Foucault, for instance, is happy to talk about what he calls 'epistemes', which are described as clusters of ideas that are very influential and remain effective for centuries.

● CONCLUSION

In this chapter, we have tried to map clearly the intricate and complex ways in which writers across a variety of sociological perspectives have tried to understand some of the big issues and changes that have characterised the modernising process. The point of this has been to indicate that there is no single way of doing sociology, or of putting the 'sociological imagination' into action. Throughout the book we will critically inquire into the various claims made from within a variety of sociological perspectives. In Chapter 4 we explore some of the practical ways we can start to do sociological research.

Discussion questions

3.1 Which tradition of doing sociology do you most identify with? Can you say why this is so?

3.2 Have you ever thought about the nature of 'reality'? Has the reading of this chapter altered anything about the way you think about this?

3.3 Can you establish any links between your own ethical views and the kinds of political beliefs you hold?

... what good is it to strive after a knowledge of reality, if the knowledge we acquire cannot serve us in our lives?

Emile Durkheim (1982: 85)

4. DOING SOCIOLOGY

- Summary

- Social research as a form of
  social action

- What is good social research?

- Doing social research

- Conclusion

- Discussion questions

● ● SUMMARY

In this chapter, we argue that everyone can find out what is going on around them, and that we can all do social research. Unfortunately, social research has often been mystified by sociologists concerned with boosting their credentials as serious scientists or important scholars by making their methodological apparatus more complex and sophisticated at the expense of clarity or usefulness. Here we attempt to take some of the mystery out of social research. We outline what makes good research, and we spell out how it might be done. We suggest some of the steps that anyone who is thoughtful and hard-working can take, and explain how to keep a social research project on track by paying attention to certain basic ethical ideas.

Doing social research is a good way of 'doing sociology'. It is also a useful and practical activity. As Bob Connell (1975: 1) argues: 'Useful research on many problems can be done with small resources and should be a regular part of the life of any thoughtful person involved in social action.' Doing social research is one way we can become smarter about what we do and why we do it. While it is true that quite a lot of social research is useless, poorly performed and read by only a few people, when we do good research it can play a major political and practical role in our collective lives.

Research can help to establish the existence or the sources of social problems. It can put pressure on governments or corporations to fix problems or to develop effective policy responses. It can even play a role in large-scale social change, as evidenced by Touraine's (1979) action research project which became part of the Polish Solidarity movement of the 1970s and 1980s which helped to dismantle the one-party rule of the Polish Communist Party. As Bourdieu's (1999) very large research project suggests, it can help us to appreciate the real complexity and suffering that occurs in the wake of economic restructuring by giving voice to the experiences of large numbers of people. More often it is social research produced by expert social researchers to help governments or community organisations solve a range of practical problems; researchers like Harding, Lloyd and Greenwell (2002) want to chart the growth of economic disadvantage.

In the context of the new types of work now emerging, social research skills are increasingly being emphasised by employers. Corporations and governments, as well as many agencies in the community sector, are eager to promote and use research. Yet, whatever its practical value, social research remains a mysterious and, for some, an intimidating activity in which few people engage.

There are many reasons why people do not do more research. Many feel that they do not have the time or skills to do it. Others experience a dramatic loss of confidence when they attempt to read a sophisticated research paper. Perhaps too many academics unconsciously or consciously give the impression that research is something lay people should best leave to the professionals. This is unfortunate, because much of the complexity surrounding research is illusory. Research can by done by most people as long as they follow a few simple rules and do some careful thinking. You can develop your own expertise as you go. Here we promote the idea that social research is an activity ordinary people can and should pursue.

By research, we mean any process of discovery that makes the effort to be both ethically informed and sensitive as well as seeking to persuade by the careful presentation of relevant evidence and which respects basic logical criteria. Trying to discover what is going on or why it is going on is the curiosity that energises research. Being curious to know what is happening and engaging in a systematic process of discovery should be a central part of contemporary professional activity.

We begin by making a sociological point about social research: it is a form of social action in which *anyone* can engage. However, to develop a practical version of the 'sociological imagination' by engaging in social research means leaving behind the commonsense world of social action.

● SOCIAL RESEARCH AS A FORM OF SOCIAL ACTION

Social research is a form of social action. There are, of course, many different types and logics of social action. And, as we show later, there are also many different types and logics of social research, which flow from the various perspectives and assumptions sociologists use to make sense of the world (see Chapter 3).

Sociologists like Giddens (1979) have consistently stressed our capacity for agency—for example, our ability to be self-aware, to know what we are doing, to choose what to do, and to give good accounts of that action. Giddens argues that we are self-interpreting, symbolic and expressive creatures who are rational because we seek to direct, interpret, monitor and change our activities. It is in this sense that we can talk about research as one form of social action.

Social action usually has the following features:

- Most social action involves interactions between two or more people. Sometimes, as in the case of reading a book, one of the persons (the author) is not actually present and it appears to be a solitary activity; however, we would suggest that this is still a rich and complex social interaction.
- It is conventional to say that social action has a purpose, and is therefore rational. Sometimes the reason for an action only becomes clear to us later. Then we may offer a post facto explanation of our motives. And occasionally we do things for which there is no entirely satisfactory account.
- Social action relies on a rich array of symbolic codes and rules, including spoken and non-verbal body language, and all the interpretive activity which speaking and listening involves. Most social settings also involve complex rules for interacting.

- Social action can involve basic creative and negotiation processes in which the very terms of the interaction are negotiable. This occurs in the complex relationship-building activities of a date, where the prospect of having sex with the other person enters the mind of one person. Very intricate questions about intimacy, touching and language are involved in negotiating this situation.
- Finally, social action is reflective. It enables us to provide accounts of our action. Indeed, social action can be open to a wide range of interpretations and rationalisations from both those doing it as well as those observing.

In the light of these criteria, good social research is one of the more 'rational' forms of social action:

- It is often goal-directed (it is 'rational'). A lot of research is shaped by what is called the research question, which drives many of the processes of research.
- It involves establishing working relations with other people (it is social).
- Social research relies on symbolic codes (especially language) in the form of research questions and research instruments like surveys or questionnaires, designed to reveal distinctive patterns of belief or action.
- Social research involves people being very clear about what they are doing and why they are doing it (i.e. it is reflective).

Finally, the various 'sociologies' we mapped out in the previous chapter produce very different kinds of research activities—the diverse beliefs and assumptions sociologists make about knowledge and social reality shape the research practices in which they engage. Each of the sociologies makes different assumptions about:

- the nature of the social reality it wants to investigate;
- the best way to know reality; and
- the best or most appropriate level of reality at which to work.

These assumptions help to determine how various sociologies 'know' the world. The different assumptions mean differences in:

- the kinds of questions sociologists ask;
- the kind of evidence sociologists regard as credible and relevant; and
- the logic of the explanations and interpretations they will develop. Some research depends on assumptions about causality, while other research accepts a high degree of indeterminacy.

It is impossible to address the complexity of issues relating to social research that arise from the different sociologies. Here, we have tried to simplify the various approaches to doing social research while leaving the more complex issues of assumptions about reality or knowledge to be addressed by students or researchers.

● WHAT IS GOOD SOCIAL RESEARCH?

Social research is about all the forms of social action, and is itself a form of social action which can interpret, monitor and change other social activities, relations or institutions.

Wadsworth (1997) identifies five criteria for good social research:

- There is an interesting or significant social problem or issue worth investigating.
- The researcher can transform the problem into a clear research question.
- There is a relatively systematic process of inquiry and the use of particular methods of investigation.
- The research produces useful information, which underpins credible claims or answers to the question/s.
- A good research process is systematic and rigorous. It is also trusted as being reliable by those to whom it is presented, or who are going to try to use it.

Let's examine these points in more detail.

Research is problem-driven

Good social research often starts with the idea that there is a social problem or an issue that needs to be investigated, or that something needs to be discovered. It may be a specific problem about social relationships (i.e. domestic violence), or it may relate to an organisational issue—for example, a union may want to know why workers are not joining. Research is often motivated by personal curiosity and the belief that there is social value in pursuing a problem.

Good research question

To produce good research, it is necessary for the project to be driven and disciplined by one or more simple, clear questions. The research question gives shape to and steers the process of investigation. As we showed in our discussion of reading sociology (Chapter 2), it is vital to identify the question or questions being asked. As a reader, this means you are engaging with the intentions of the person whose work you are reading. As a researcher, being clear about the questions being asked adds clarity and purpose to your research. If there are any doubts or anxieties about the direction of your reading, thinking or collection of information, you can simply return to your research questions, which provide a constant point of reference. Good research also *answers* the research question. This means that any activities in which you engage to perform the research need constantly to be connected to the question.

Good questions are, to an extent, open-ended. In other words, they presuppose a genuine discovery process. Your research questions should start with 'Why . . .?', 'What . . .?' and 'How . . .?' This may seem obvious, but it is surprising how often we see research that has little direction and simply doesn't answer a question or address a claim.

Systematic

Good research involves a relatively systematic process of inquiry and the use of particular methods of investigation appropriate to answering the question.

Good social research is shaped and informed at every stage by the research question. The researcher then develops or adopts a methodical and systematic approach to unearthing evidence, facts, ideas and connections. Researchers need to use appropriate techniques that are relevant to their questions.

This idea of systematic and methodical process can, however, be misunderstood to mean that you use only a certain kind of statistical set of techniques. This is not what we mean. By 'systematic' or 'methodical', we mean that researchers explore all the angles, trying to read as much as they can of what has already been written about their research topic. Researchers also try to spell out the possible connections, and try to get as much relevant information as possible to give the research credibility.

Useful

Good social research produces useful information which underpins credible claims and answers the basic questions. It also relies on relevant existing information and evidence. Evidence is the information that can be used to form general conclusions relevant to the research questions. You may have uncovered what you think are explanations for why the school retention rate is growing. These explanations or interpretations will have some credibility if you are able to collect data and put in place a chain of information which you think will convince a reasonable person about why the school retention rate is growing.

Credible

A good research process is trusted as being reliable by those to whom it is presented or to those who will try to use it.

Systematic and rigorous research ensures that most of the relevant material is discovered, read about, considered, thought about and connected. This relates to the question of credibility. Credibility ensures that the audience (of university teachers, politicians, funding bodies or the community) can have confidence in the findings and conclusions.

Criteria for credibility

- The research question should not rely on implausible assumptions or beliefs. Establishing the research question also means accepting that some people who do not share your assumptions may be upset about how you frame the question.

- The answer generated by the research process should be relevant to the research question: it should answer the question. This depends on choosing relevant evidence that enables you to answer the question.

- Good research acknowledges that others have already thought about and performed research on the issue you are looking at. (This is another reminder of the social nature of social research.) It is a good idea to read all the recent research relevant to your question.

- Credibility requires that you have provided enough relevant evidence to support all the major claims you make. Once more, there are important questions about what kinds of evidence count as relevant. Given the diversity of sociologies (which do not always have a common view on what is relevant evidence), there will always be some sociologists who do not like the evidence presented.

- In developing, writing up and presenting the research, it is useful to anticipate and respond to any possible criticisms or alternative viewpoints. There are, however, limits to the extent to which this is possible and/or desirable.

● DOING SOCIAL RESEARCH

There are a large number of possibilities for doing social research in terms of the questions that might be posed, the assumptions that may be relied on, or ways of finding out about the social world. This makes it difficult to be too prescriptive about how social research should be done. For good examples of a non-prescriptive approach, see Wadsworth (1997) and Giddens (1997: 537–57). One way of proceeding is to use a *process approach*, which leaves the more substantive issues and difficulties alone. The process approach to research is outlined below.

Stage 1: Establishing the research question

It is vital to begin by addressing a problem that is important via a question or set of research questions. With students, a teacher will probably establish a clear question, or allow them to define and refine their own question. Consultants and people working in an organisation may be aware that a problem exists, but might take longer to clarify the precise question.

To develop your research question, it is useful to:

- talk to people like teachers, other students, other researchers or colleagues. This helps you to clarify your thoughts, and it is helpful to get feedback and questions on your ideas; and
- spend time researching your topic. It is necessary to read around the topic in order to see what—if any—previous research or theoretical material exists that is relevant. Check relevant academic or research journals to see what has been done by other Australian and international researchers.

The point is to scan the existing material to see what has already been done and to provide yourself with some new ways of thinking about your topic. This process helps you to refine the question. You may need to do a more thorough and focused survey, but that can be left until later in the process. It is imperative that you take time out to think, reflect on and sketch out your thinking and ideas about the topic or problem. This also helps sort out your research question.

Try to think about the research as a genuine inquiry into the problem, rather than in terms of what you want to prove. Once you have a version of a question, it can be beneficial to test it out on friends, family or colleagues. Remember to keep the question as simple as possible—the answer can be as complex as you want it to be.

Stage 2: Identifying, reading and reviewing relevant research and theoretical literature

Assuming that you have a useful research question, you can begin doing more intensive work on the relevant research literature. In most cases, there will already be previous review material and theoretical reflection on the issues you are trying to tackle. Not all of it will be good, or agree with your way of thinking.

- Identify other relevant research literature.
- Find out where it is and whether you can access it.
- Begin to collect it. Make sure you organise your material in ways that make it easy to find again. This will involve constructing a bibliography to record the work you have referred to. (There are now several good computer programs that make this tedious work relatively painless.)
- Read the material and start to think about it. This may involve making notes.

Much of the research material will be found in books, reports, monographs and journal articles. These are very easily accessed using key words and search engines to explore electronic databases for relevant research. There are also other economic, psychological, anthropological, political, policy, criminological, organisational, social work and educational journals that may carry relevant work.

There are other sources of information, like the Australian Bureau of Statistics (ABS), which produces social statistics on population, economic and a wide range of social activities. The ABS takes a census every five years and publishes regular descriptive details about families, young people, women, migrants and Indigenous people. If you are interested in finding out about particular government programs and policies, it is worth talking to people in the respective federal, state or local government departments. Do not overlook government and university archives.

Research materials may be found in specialist organisational resource collections, or on special websites established by governments, organisations, companies, universities and individual researchers. University libraries often have collections of postgraduate theses. Most also have large current collections of international journals. There are specialist resource centres in most states, including the websites of major research centres (e.g. the Australian Institute of Criminology in Canberra or the Australian Institute of Family Studies in Melbourne), welfare and advocacy organisations (the Brotherhood of St Laurence and most major churches), foundations and peak organisations (e.g. the Australian Council of Social Services, the Business Council of Australia or the Australian Council of Trade Unions). It is important to be systematic in identifying, reading or copying this material. It is also imperative to keep the material in good condition or to store electronic versions in accessible files.

Stage 3: Choosing and developing a research method, design or technique of inquiry

If you have a clear question and have started to find out how other people have researched the issues you are looking at, it is timely to think about how you will collect the evidence you need to answer your research question. It is vital that whatever method you choose will help you to get credible answers. This is not always a simple matter. The kinds of assumptions or prejudices you are working with will lead you to favour certain theories. Your theoretical preference will then shape the research question, and you will be disposed to look for certain kinds of evidence or to rely on certain research techniques.

Good social research establishes a simple logical link between the 'how' and 'why' of the research. If you are clear about the question (the 'why' or the 'what'), the 'how' should be relatively obvious.

Do not assume that only certain techniques or methods of research can be used or are acceptable. Many people seem to think that social research has to use survey techniques and involves large amounts of data which are subjected to statistical treatment and presentation. The technique that is most acceptable and assists in giving your research credibility is the one which helps you answer the questions.

Potential research techniques include the following.

Social surveys and questionnaires

For some sociologists, doing social research means using a social survey. The survey is a quantitative form of research because it involves generating numerical data for statistical analysis. Social surveys are often regarded as more 'scientific' and/or 'objective' than other forms of social science research. However, while social surveys are a good way of collecting a large amount of simple information, they may not always reflect the complexity of social reality.

Elaborate methodologies have been established around questions concerning the size and composition of the sample (i.e. the group that the researcher establishes to represent the whole population). This is said to be necessary for generalisations to be made—to be able to apply the results to the entire population of interest.

A social survey uses some form of random selection process to select a sample of people which is then seen to represent the entire population. This is because it is not practical to survey the entire population of a country like Australia or even a city like Sydney for reasons of cost and complexity. A number of other assumptions are then made:

- People will not purposely lie about what they think or do.
- People will not be influenced by the questions or the researcher.
- People will be able reliably to report what they actually do.
- Simple and clear-cut questions are most likely to accurately capture the beliefs or activities of survey respondents.
- People's statements about what they think or do are not just spur-of-the-moment responses, and do reflect stable beliefs or patterns of activities.

The validity of many of these assumptions is questionable. In certain areas of life—people's sexual activity, their financial dealings, or even issues like who does the housework—we know that people will not, or cannot, reliably report what they do. It is also unclear whether a set of uncomplicated questions or choices can do justice to the complex nature of social existence.

The advantage of the survey questionnaire is that it can collect large amounts of information by sampling the views, beliefs and activities of large sections of the population. This allows the researcher to claim that patterns of beliefs or activities are current in a society or a community at a particular time.

Establishing a random sample involves selecting people by chance. It is assumed that the larger a random sample, the more confidence the researcher can have that the sample will be representative of the population. For other research questions, however, a representative sample is established to construct a microcosm of the population. Most research involves a narrow range of issues and/or focuses on a specific group of people, so a representative sample can be appropriate and is usually easier and cheaper to establish.

Most surveys involve distributing a questionnaire (known as the survey instrument) to the sample. This is a set of questions on paper which can be handed out or mailed to people and then returned, completed, to the researcher. Handing out a small questionnaire, which can be filled out quickly on the spot, usually achieves a better response rate than mailing out a survey. Mailouts of questionnaires usually have a lower rate of return and are more costly to administer.

When designing a questionnaire, the research question and population of interest should be kept in mind. It is also important to remember that surveys are good at collecting large amounts of relatively simple data. There are a number of factors to consider when designing a survey questionnaire:

- It needs to be carefully designed, and should always be road-tested to iron out problems.
- The questions need to be clear and unambiguous.
- You will need to choose between using open-ended questions and closed questions. Open-ended questions are aimed at capturing the diversity and complexity of what you are looking at, but are not always easy to feed into a computer program. Closed questions are designed to force people to choose between options to make coding and analysing the answers relatively easy.

Finally, you must decide on the kinds of statistics you will use and how extensive your use of various testing procedures will be. Again the point of reference should be the research question.

In general, if you plan to use a questionnaire, it is useful to get advice and support from people who have done it before. You should also consult some of the guidebooks to social research (e.g. Wadsworth 1997; de Vaus 1995 or Hoyle, Harris and Judd 2002).

Participation and observation techniques

A different approach to social research, often referred to as qualitative research or ethnographic research, comprises a range of participant and observation techniques that are designed to explore the complex and symbolic aspects of social life.

These qualitative approaches involve building a picture of social action in order to tap into the meanings and explanations of the people in whom you are interested. This is done through either close observation of or participation in the activities of the people you want to research (Stanley 1990). For symbolic interactionists, these approaches are seen as indispensable to 'good' sociology. This kind of approach can be effective, but it cannot be used to support large-scale claims about whole societies or communities. As with quantitative research, there is a tradeoff between the quality of the data and the scope revealed by ethnographic research.

There is a long tradition of ethnographic research in sociology, much of it connected to the symbolic interactionist tradition. The Chicago School of Urban Studies pioneered an interest in the 1920s in 'criminal' and 'delinquent' cultures. This exercise involved white, middle-class researchers going into working-class neighbourhoods and reporting on the ways of life, patterns of communication and the expressive activities of 'the poor', 'the criminal' and 'the deviant'. This was similar to the way European anthropologists reported on the 'primitive' peoples of Asia, Australia or Africa (Whyte 1955). Since then there have been many examples of this style of research, including Hunter S. Thompson's account of his years riding a Harley with the Hell's Angels (participant observation) and Laud Humphreys' account of male sex in public toilets (observational research).

Ethnographic research produces the most complex pictures of social realities. Ethnographers assume that it is only when you have become exposed to, or become part of, a complex social reality that all the elaborate rules, invisible meanings, motives, ambiguous actions and feelings that make up a social reality become clear enough to be seen and reported on.

Ethnographic research is also hard to do well. It can take a long time to find a group of people that will be prepared to accept the researcher's presence, or to 'discover' what is happening and how people understand what they do. There is always the danger that people will either mislead the researcher or play elaborate games with them.

Ethnographic research can also be dangerous. Some of the activities that are reported on can be illegal or involve violence or other physical and emotional dangers. This method also raises ethical issues about the social role and status of the researcher, who may or may not let on that he or she is a researcher.

Finally, there are questions about how to present the findings that will be respectful of the complexity of the social settings and integrity of the people being reported on, while preserving coherence and credibility. Much of the best ethnographic research has been done by people who have a rare capacity to write well and intelligently, like Sennett and Cobb (1989) or the examples of Australian community studies by Wild (1974) or Bryson and Thompson (1977).

Action research

Action research is close in spirit to ethnographic research because it often involves the social researcher being, or becoming part of, a larger social or organisational group. It is different from the more usual kinds of social research, which often stress the need for an emotional and ethical objectivity or detachment. As well, most research finishes when the writing up and dissemination are complete, and when the recommendations for action (if any) have been made. Action research is an approach to research that is directed towards informing and guiding various forms of social action. It can take on a more committed and political quality. For this reason, some feminists and Marxists like developing action research projects.

The defining characteristic of action research is a commitment to making the research process a key part of the change process. The social researcher shares a commitment to using research in an ongoing fashion to report on a situation that usually involves a group of people pursuing some kind of change. Action research involves feeding research findings into the context of the original source of the material, implementing the findings and then repeating the whole cycle of research again, feeding it back into the group and so on . . . It assumes that the research process needs to be linked to larger processes of change, and that the researcher has an ethical or political obligation to be part of the larger social process.

Action research is usually connected to notions of participation and democratic involvement by people in a change situation. It is promoted in the various social movements. In Australia, Kemmis (1981) has used action research as a way of democratising school communities (see also Stringer 1996).

Individual interviews

These involve the researcher asking questions on a one-to-one basis. A structured questionnaire—known as a schedule of questions—may be used, or it may be best to have an unstructured discussion. A combination of these techniques can also be used. Issues which must be addressed include choosing interviewees; obtaining parental consent for interviews with minors, or arranging translators where necessary; and how interviews will be recorded—for example, using audio or videotapes, or taking notes—and written up afterwards.

Group interviews and discussions

An alternative to one-to-one interviews is to set up one or more small groups of people who can help you with your research. Sometimes researchers use what is called a focus group, with between six and eight people exploring a number of themes in depth using a relatively open yet structured approach. A group can be particularly effective for working with people who might be nervous about individual interviews, and the group setting can generate some interesting exchanges.

Selecting the best method

Each method is good for getting a certain kind of answer, but each has limits. The method you select should always reflect your research question and what you want to find out. For example, if you want to know what a group of young people actually do in a shopping mall, it is next to useless to ask them to fill out a questionnaire—it is far better to observe them in action and then ask follow-up questions. Equally, if you want to know what a lot of people think about a political leader or party, it is better to use a large-scale and simple survey questionnaire. To illustrate this point we have constructed a short and simple thought exercise (see box).

Thought exercise: Linking questions and methods of getting information

We have asked five possible research questions below and identified five possible methods of getting information. Connect the question to the method most likely to generate some useful research.

Questions

1   What status do young graffiti artists have in the community?

2   What activities do fourteen- to seventeen-year-olds carry out in shopping centres?

3   What do young people think about the quality and relevance of youth services in the suburb of Plenty Valley?

4   What reasons and explanations do young graffiti artists give for engaging in this activity?

5   Are there any statistically significant connections between family size, income distribution and schooling in the regional town of Bellingen and the incidence and location of graffiti?

Methods

1   A simple analysis of statistical data already gathered by an organisation like ABS or AIFS on family size, schooling and income by local census districts, and evidence in the police station about the location and numbers of graffiti 'attacks'.

2   Participant observation of a group of young people in a shopping centre.

3   A detailed content analysis and examination of press or media reports about young people.

4   In-depth unstructured interviews with a small number of young people observed doing graffiti.

5   The design and mail-out of a postal questionnaire to 600 adolescents in the town of Bellingen.

Stage 4: Carrying out the method/s of inquiry and collecting information

While careful thinking about your questions is an important part of reliable social research, the actual collection of information can be either the most difficult or the most delightful part of the research process—or both. Often the frustrations and the joys of this phase of the process are inseparable. Each method presents its own problems. Some approaches are time consuming, difficult or even dangerous; others are boring and require lots of administrative time, effort and money to work well. There are several problems that seem to crop up time and time again.

Finding your sample or interviewees

There is one practical problem that raises itself in any discussion of research with people: if you want to talk to a certain group of people, they may not want to talk to you. Or, once found, interviewees may not want to talk unless special conditions of confidentiality or non-attribution are accepted. This is often the case with young people, who fear contact with authority, or with policy-makers and decision-makers.

Locating or accessing a range of research materials

Although we are said to live in an information age, research materials are not always easy to find. Indeed, the proliferation of research materials can mean that the researcher confronts both a vast and unreadable bulk of material as well as a sense that much of this material is not easily accessible. Some data already collected may be stored in cities far away, or may cost money to extract even if immediately available on the internet.

There are always going to be constraints of time, distance and money that affect your capacity to get specific kinds and amounts of information. You need to be flexible and practical in your approach to this issue. At a certain point, you may need to say to yourself: 'I do not have any more time to give to this project.'

Storing or recording the information

Another problem people face relates to storing and accessing the research materials as they accumulate. There are no easy answers, apart from disciplining yourself to keep the materials in a useful filing system with plenty of identification tags.

You may have problems if people do not want to be taped. Others may want to hear the tape before they give permission for you to use it. Transcription of tapes is costly and time consuming, and may involve the use of special equipment and trained personnel. You might have 300 hours of wonderful tape recordings, but you cannot sit down and replay every tape to find the bit you need every time you need it. There has to be a way of indexing, storing and accessing the information, and the need for this increases as the amount of research material grows. You might need to use special computer programs to store and index written material, or you might need elaborate filing systems.

You need to be able to access information easily and quickly, especially when it comes to incorporating it in any written report or other research output. It is vital that you identify all interviews with date, time, place and names of participants. You need to be able to safely store audio- or videotapes; likewise, all articles, books and reports should have their bibliographical details recorded. It is sensible to ensure that all computer disks are backed up, with at least one up-to-date copy stored in another place.

Stage 5: Thinking about and interpreting the information you have collected

Typically, much of the thinking, analysing and integrating processes go on when you are collecting information and when you are writing it up. This is a mysterious process: your brain is sorting, comparing, contrasting, looking for the big picture and small, discrepant counter-examples; it is hard to impose discipline. Sometimes significance, links and implications are self-evident, all seeming to flow easily from the material. But it is not usually so simple.

Again, it is vital that the research data and information you have collected be approached in the light of the research questions with which you began. Interpreting the findings of your research is a disciplined process, best approached by working from what you set out to investigate.

If you have loads of quantitative data, a range of standard tests of validity and significance can be applied to them. If you have a large amount of interview material, you may want to look for patterns or interesting connections. Equally, however, the discipline of using the questions to unpack the research material should call on your imagination and creativity, so that you begin to ask new questions or make lateral or interesting connections and leaps.

Stage 6: Writing up or organising research results for presentation

Research is carried out for all sorts of audiences: lecturers, thesis examiners, journal editors and readers, and specific organisations like governments, business companies or community agencies. Each of these audiences and consumers has expectations, rules and conventions which need to be taken into account.

If you want to link your research to some process of social change and social action, it is important to get the research to an audience of people who will do something with it. Three key questions help to ensure that the right links are made between a piece of research and a change process:

- What action do you want to follow from your research?
- Who will need to have the research in order to give effect to the action outcomes?
- What are the best ways of getting the research into those people's hands?

This calls for some strategic thinking, in which the researcher/s and their organisation try to establish who has a role to play in putting the action outcomes into effect (e.g. journalists and media organisations, key decision-makers and policy-makers at the appropriate level of government).

A written report is usually an effective way of presenting the information and analysis. It needs to:

- be kept as short as possible;
- be attractively presented and designed;
- have an attractive title and cover; and
- contain a short and useful summary.

Do not forget to involve the media. If there is anything of interest in your research, the media may want to pick it up. This can involve contacting local journalists, TV or radio producers and preparing a media release—possibly even staging a press conference.

● CONCLUSION

Research is a basic skill which should be developed by all university students and a growing number of professional workers so that it becomes a part of their daily practice. Yet too few people do the kinds of simple but thoughtful research that might help them to design better services and programs, evaluate their own activities and identify problems that need to be tackled in their work or in their community.

Research should be a normal and valued part of work practices, yet many workers see research as being beyond their scope of practice. We hope that we have indicated some good reasons why this attitude can and should change, as well as indicating some ways to begin conducting good research activities.

Discussion questions

4.1 Is there a single set of techniques for doing good social research?

4.2 What is social research, and what should it reflect?

4.3 What is the role of the research question?

4.4 Which techniques of research are most useful?

4.5 What ethical issues are most important in social research?

The modern social
sciences are
intellectually
vacuous and
ethically
nihilist

Alfred Schutz
(1986 [1940]: 29)

5. ETHICS AND SOCIOLOGY

● ● SUMMARY

This chapter explores the complex relationship between sociology and ethics. First, we discuss the narrow and technical issues raised by the idea that social research should be carried out with a regard for ethical practice. A checklist of questions is then provided, which will be useful when doing research. Second, we turn to some larger issues, like the silence of sociology in the face of evil. We argue via a case study that conventional sociology has failed to address some central problems raised by radical evil. Moreover, the preoccupation with structural explanations has the effect of rendering sociologists unable to explore processes of moral deliberation, which amounts to a refusal of the moral.

Talking and writing about ethics has become very popular in recent years. It is now common, for example, to hear moral language being used by politicians when they talk about 'mutual obligation' to explain why jobless people must now work for their social security payments. We hear *some* business and marketing companies talking about business ethics, and about their social responsibilities. There are even consultant ethicists who advise companies and governments on ethical issues and the drafting of codes of ethical behaviour. In the context of attempts to mobilise popular support for the so-called 'war on terror', neo-conservative politicians have begun talking up the idea that what Australians really need now is to defend the 'core Australian values'.

We all confront ethical issues or questions in our everyday lives. Should you buy something you really want from a company known to exploit its workers? Should you tell your friend that the boy she is head over heels in love with is seeing someone else? What should a teacher do when a student submits an essay that is obviously plagiarised? Sometimes the issues assume an extra weight—such as when a woman wonders whether she should have an abortion, or when a person who is HIV positive anguishes over whether or not they should tell the person they are about to have sex with.

All these are 'practical' questions that involve judgments. Indeed, the first part of any practice is judgment—which happens when we consider what we should do and why we should do it. The second part of practice is the actual doing. These ethical questions centre on the single most significant question we ever have to confront: how ought we to live? Every time we find ourselves asking 'what should we do?' in a situation where there are alternative choices and outcomes, we are engaging in ethical deliberation. Ethical practice involves answering the question 'why should I do x?'

We address the challenges posed by the idea of ethical values in two ways. First, we consider the question of what doing good social research requires with respect to ethical practices. What is good social research? What ethical considerations should researchers pay attention to? Second, we consider the fraught relationship of sociology to the very idea of ethical values. As we indicate via a case study, sociology has not been distinguished by a strong regard for ethical issues.

If the last century suggests anything, it is that the problem of evil is a very real one, signified by state-sponsored military terror and violence. Confronted with the problem of state genocide and other grotesque crimes against humanity, sociology has simply decided to close its eyes. Why and how has this been possible?

Let us begin with a simple clarification about why ethics is an issue of fundamental interest to us all.

● WHAT ARE ETHICS?

First, the terms 'ethics/ethical' and 'moral/morality' are often used in ways that assume their meanings are obvious to all and/or that there is some important distinction between them. Both sets of words point to a common interest in doing what Aristotle in the fourth century BCE set out to do, namely to clarify what the nature of the 'good' is. As Aristotle (1976: 63) points out, all human activity is ethically oriented:

> Every art and every investigation and similarly every action and pursuit is considered to aim at some good. Hence the Good has been rightly defined as that at which all things aim.

On the nature of the 'good', Aristotle says:

> What is the highest of all practical goods? 'It is happiness', say both ordinary and cultured people, and they identify happiness with living well or doing well. (1976: 66)

As one of the most influential living philosophers, Richard Rorty (1999), points out, ethical discussion and deliberation begin when we discover that one person's idea of the good does not coincide with another's. As Rorty (1999: 73) puts it:

> Morality and the law . . . begin when controversy arises. We invent both when we can no longer just do what comes naturally when routine is no longer good enough or when habit and custom no longer suffice These will no longer suffice when the individual's needs begin to clash with those of her family or her family's with those of her neighbours . . .

Think of the many cases of cannibalism committed by shipwrecked sailors at sea. There are twelve sailors in a lifeboat after their ship has sunk. In order for most of the survivors to live, one or two of their mates must be killed and eaten. What is the nature of the good here? In a very simple sense, the fact that we are social creatures living communally creates the conditions in which the discovery has to be made that our interests in any given situation may not coincide. As anthropologists and sociologists have long tried to explore and explain, the existence of authoritative moral or ethical rules and codes promoted by religions and political systems is one attempt to help resolve this difference of interests.

Ethics has at least two clear and distinct meanings. Barnes (in Aristotle 1976: 21) makes a useful initial distinction when he suggests that there are two kinds of ethical judgment. The first group comprises substantive moral judgments like:

- It is good to pay back debts.
- It is good to protect life at all costs.
- It is wrong to kill or do violent things to another person.
- Do unto others as you would have them do unto you.

Barnes calls these *ethical judgments*. They are specific statements about how we should act in a given situation.

Barnes calls the second kind of judgment *meta-ethical statements*. These are the kinds of things philosophers since Socrates, Plato and Aristotle have been generating and exploring. They relate to the logic of moral discourse, and address questions like:

- Are the words used in moral discourse factual or prescriptive?
- Are there valid or consistent ways of applying certain ethical principles?
- Should all statements containing the 'should' word be treated as universal prescriptions?

This second kind of statement is the preserve of moral philosophers. As Barnes (in Aristotle 1976: 19–20) observes:

> It is tempting to regard as the specifically philosophical aspects of moral philosophy precisely this self conscious study of the logic of moral discourse: if moral philosophers hope by their philosophising to make us better men, their proprietary path to that goal is meta-ethical—the articulation and elucidation of our thought about moral matters will, they trust, lead us to judge well and to act rightly.

In our own time, important philosophers like John Rawls (1999) and Jurgen Habermas (1998) have attempted to clarify the principles of justice and fairness by reference to the processes all of us engage in when we speak to each other, through what Habermas has called a 'theory of communicative competence'.

● THE ETHICS OF GOOD SOCIAL RESEARCH

Increasingly, undergraduate students in Australian universities are expected to engage in field research—as distinct from library or internet-based research. Research which involves working with other people inevitably raises a host of ethical issues. It also means that ethics clearances need to be sought and approved before that research starts.

People doing research and organisations like universities are now, more than ever before, subject to popular and official concerns about ethical conduct. Today all universities, most social research centres and research funding bodies require what is commonly referred to as an ethics clearance before any research involving contact with people or creatures like mice or monkeys can begin.

Much of the current interest in ethical issues is pragmatic, developing from fears of legal action and the rising costs of insurance premiums should specific kinds of research be proved to have produced serious harm to individuals or to whole communities. In this regard, insisting on close regulation of research becomes part of the management of risk. It now seems incomprehensible that, in a modern country like the United States, without any official ethical clearance or regulation, millions of young Americans were vaccinated in the 1950s and 1960s as part of an experiment to protect children from polio. Likewise, well-documented cases involving the drug thalidomide (shown to cause serious birth defects), intra-uterine contraceptive devices that led to death or disability, or breast implants which resulted in long-term illness for many women have made it clear that there are major legal and financial costs associated with research which fails to discover that some things are too dangerous to use.

If researchers carry out experiments or other types of research activity involving people in ways that cause them harm, the institutions in which they work are legally liable. The prospect of lawsuits has moved many senior administrators to insist that all research be subject to rigorous regulatory processes. This requirement has gone so far that, in places like universities where most of our social research is performed, not only do academic researchers require ethics clearances, but so do undergraduate and postgraduate students.

● RESEARCH IS POLITICAL

Awareness of the ethical dimensions of research also involves a recognition that any kind of social research is a deeply political activity which involves making claims about how we ought to see reality. From Bacon in the seventeenth century to Foucault in the twentieth, writers have accepted that knowledge is power. In the wake of what is referred to as the 'scientific revolution', social and natural scientists have acquired tremendous authority and credibility, based on their claims to expertise.

Research is a political activity in a number of ways. First, experts who create knowledge themselves draw on deeply political discourses in the production of that knowledge. Over the past two centuries, a considerable amount of social research has been racist, class-bound, misogynist—or at least blind to gender—and ageist.

From the 1890s to the 1940s, eugenically inclined social scientists carried out basic and widely admired research which constituted a whole range of problem groups by constructing elaborate 'scientific' enterprises that referred to 'maladjusted youth', 'juvenile delinquents' and 'anti-social youth cultures'. Much of the current 'youth at risk' research literature continues this tradition—see Bessant et al. (2005).

For most of the twentieth century, social scientific research resting on racist assumptions has legitimated research into the 'problem' of intelligence among Afro-American 'blacks'. Into the 1990s, Wilson and Herrnstein (1985) 'confirmed' that American blacks were biologically inclined to lower intelligence than white Americans.

Similarly, social scientific research using allegedly objective techniques, from Burt (1938) to Farrington (1994), consistently 'proved' that working-class children were less intelligent and more likely to become criminal than their middle- and upper-class counterpart. Because such research informed our knowledge of the world, it had quite practical effects in terms of shaping government policies in areas such as education, immigration and crime prevention.

Social research also has political consequences. This is what Giddens (1990) called the 'double hermeneutic' effect. 'The double hermeneutic' refers to an interactive process that begins with social scientists collecting data from the social world as part of their research work. The material is then analysed and theorised before the research results are fed back into the community. This feedback process has the capacity to change the social world, often in major ways. This means that those who are the objects of research can be changed quite directly by the material produced about them. In social sciences like sociology, criminology and psychology, and in allied vocational training programs like education, social work and counselling, academic research has been seriously implicated in changing social practices. For example, parents regularly become anxious about their child's IQ or cognitive skills, relying on expert constructions of these abilities.

In addition, research has political effects because governments rely on the activities of experts and researchers to provide detailed and sophisticated statistical knowledge about the whole population. It is through research processes that social problems and issues are defined. Large-scale statistical (epidemiological) research has been able to establish a link between smoking tobacco and a variety of major health risks, or between defective diets and the incidence of developmental defects like spina bifida. Governments can then step in to fix or regulate the problem—for example, by posting health warnings on cigarette packets.

This process does not always work smoothly or without paradox: good intentions can produce bad effects. For example, a researcher may decide to carry out a study on young people living in poverty because she is concerned with issues of social justice and wants to draw attention to the conditions in which these people live. Her research may produce journal articles, conference papers or a book, all of which feed into a popular understanding of 'the problem' of a 'juvenile underclass'. In direct contrast to what the researcher intended, her data may produce precisely the opposite outcomes. The media may, for example, pick up on the research and represent the subjects of the research as a threat to community safety. This may also feed into popular prejudices and mistaken information that 'the poor' are more likely than others to be criminal.

The following considerations suggest why social research has to be thought about carefully.

● ETHICS CLEARANCE

An ethics clearance process is now normal in most research organisations, and is something with which undergraduate students can also expect to have to comply. Most authorities who monitor and regulate social research only require an ethics clearance if the researcher actually comes in contact with people or animals that feel. However, consideration of the impact of your work also needs to be given when you are dealing with things that do not feel—like documents, papers and so on.

The ethics clearance process should filter out any obvious problems with a proposed research project. However, members of ethics committees may draw on the same discourses, or be part of the same culture, as the researcher. This makes recognising the problematic assumptions underpinning research projects very difficult. Likewise, preventing undesirable outcomes is not always easy. It is often very difficult to foresee with any accuracy how your research can be put to use by people with agendas that are quite different from your own.

In order to perform research that is ethical, it is important to think and reflect on what you are doing. The following questions provide some basic guidelines for ethical research.

Guidelines for ethical practice in social research

- *Are those you are researching likely in any way to be disadvantaged or harmed in any way as a result of your research?* This also goes to questions of trust and confidentiality. It is impossible to know how others might use or interpret your findings. It is, however, possible to safeguard participants against many of the more obvious possible negative responses by considering the agenda of those sponsoring the research and by the researcher reflecting on and being very clear about their own reasons for doing the research.

- *Is it appropriate to protect the identity of those you are researching, and can you ensure that their identity remains anonymous if appropriate?* If the answer is yes, then ensure that there are no identity markers, like identifying details around the information participants provide, that would enable others to recognise who they are. This also means making sure any data collected is kept in a safe and secure place.

- *Is there a power dynamic at work in the relationship between yourself as researcher and those you are researching?* As a researcher, you are usually in a power position in relation to your research participants. This calls for a recognition of the power difference in the relationship and a sensitivity to its implications. Recognising the power differential also means guaranteeing that participants in the project provide their informed consent (see below).

- *Will you need to obtain informed consent because the people you propose to research are young or in some other way vulnerable and dependent?* It is common practice now for social researchers to obtain informed consent. This involves the participant knowing clearly what the research is about and what it is to be used for. To achieve this, the researcher needs to communicate in language that the participant can easily understand.

  Obtaining the consent of a participant is part of ethical practice because it means the researcher must seek permission or authorisation from the participant or their guardian to use the material they provide. This not only helps to protect the participant, it is also an act of respect and acknowledges their power to say no and the value of the data to the researcher. Ethical social research also means not obtaining that authorisation through deceit, bribery or coercion.

  Questions about who has the legal and moral capacity to provide consent is another issue. For many young people, the consent of parents is required. If the research is being performed within an institution or agency like a school, the relevant authorities also need to provide their permission for the project to proceed. These requirements can make doing certain kinds of research extremely difficult, if not impossible.

- *Are there any legal issues involved in the research you propose to carry out?* Research can sometimes have legal implications. For example, the people you are researching may be involved in criminal or illegal acts, either as perpetrators or as the victims of a crime.

  This means your research could be subpoenaed in court and used against your participants. This might be a problem for those doing research on issues such as paedophilia, the use of illicit drugs or violence in the workplace. There are some basic steps to help prevent this from happening:

  - Think ahead and ask yourself whether the research is likely to reveal information about illegal activities. If it is important to report on a matter where there are serious moral or legal issues it may be best to report the matter to the police and exclude the persons involved from the research.

  - For other matters phrase questions so as to require only general answers that do not allow too much explicit detail to emerge.

- Design the consent forms so the person cannot be identified through the tapes and other research material.
- Double-code the material so that you are the only one who could possibly establish the participant's identity.

- *Is the proposed research likely to raise sensitive or emotionally stressful issues?* Research sometimes requires the participant to discuss issues that are painful or stressful. To deal with this ethically, the researcher first needs to be sensitive to the fact that their questions or interventions are causing pain or distress. This may sound obvious, but some people can be oblivious to the pain they are causing others.

  It may also be helpful to have some referral cards with you in case the research provokes a response that requires further help. It is not a good idea to counsel the participant yourself unless you know precisely what you are doing.

- *Are there any issues of power or inequality involved in being a member of a research team?* Are junior members of the research project team being exploited? Dealing with this ethically means being aware of the power relations in the group and making sure that:
  - one person is not being excluded from decision-making processes;
  - one person does not get all the hack work;
  - one person is not bullied or intimidated by the others; and
  - no one is exploited.

- *Is anyone likely to be deceived about the use to which the research will be put or the nature of the questions to be asked?* It is unethical to obtain material by deceit. Some researchers attempt to justify lying to those involved in the project by arguing that it is the only way they can access the data. For example, a researcher may go into a school to obtain information about students, but can only get official entry on the condition that they inform the school of their findings. This is fine as long as the student knows that the information they offer will be relayed to school officials (i.e. the principal). If the researcher gets the information from students but tells them that it is in complete confidence, this becomes a serious problem. Not only is it obtaining information by deceit, but it is denying the students' right to natural justice and can land the researcher in serious legal trouble. It is also very likely to damage those being researched. Gaining information by deceit also raises questions for certain methodologies such as participant observation. This is when a researcher goes into a group and pretends to be one of them. Participant observation is a well-practised approach, and has produced some fascinating information. However, full disclosure is essential.

● THE PROBLEM OF EVIL

In some important respects, sociology has failed conspicuously to deal with some of the most momentous instances of staggeringly bad behaviour in the past century. This is what we mean by the 'problem of evil' and the failure of sociology. The problem of evil was framed by Christian theologians on the basis that if God was all-good, all-knowing and all-powerful, how come He allowed humans to suffer from disease, war, poverty or hunger?

Given that some of us no longer think within a framework of believing in an all-good, all-knowing and all-powerful God, Arendt (1963) and Neiman (2002) remind us of the point of thinking about evil post-theologically. For the problem of evil remains. This time it implicates very powerful governments and the experts they rely on to inform them about what is happening in the world. Take cases like the genocide that erupted in Rwanda in 1994 and Bosnia in 1995, or the refusal/inability of American governments to either protect the victims of Hurricane Katrina in 2005 in New Orleans, or to deal with the aftermath in an effective, humane and timely way. In each case, the problem of evil implicates three elements of civic policy.

The first question is 'what is true?' We can rephrase this question in terms of 'what can we know?' or 'what can we know reliably?' The second question is: 'what is the good?' This concerns how we ought to act, especially in relation to each other, and what kind of good our actions serve to promote. And, in the light of our answers to these two questions, we must go on to ask a third question: 'how then ought we to live with each other?' This is the great practical question which Socrates memorably reframed as the question of justice. Our inability to address these three questions can result in human suffering on an appalling scale.

The modern problem of evil implicates the relation of knowledge and power no less than the older theological framework did. The modern framing of this old problem implicates the institutionalised forms that both scientific knowledge and political power now take.

Let's examine the two cases of Rwanda in 1994 (where 800 000 Tutsis were killed over 100 days in front of a UN peacekeeping army) and the murder of 8000 Bosnians (again in front of UN soldiers, this time in just four days, in July 1995). In both cases, neither the UN nor the most powerful state in the world, the United States, either protested or did anything to stop the killings. The defence mounted to justify this inactivity was that 'we did not know what was happening until it was too late'. The US Ambassador to the United Nations was Madeleine Albright. In her (2003) *Madam Secretary: A Memoir*, she stresses that the conspicuous failure on the part of the United States or the United Nations to act to prevent genocide is best explained by a lack of accurate information.

Yet, in one of her footnotes, Albright tells a small and pointed story of one of her visits to the killing fields in Bosnia some years after the event. The mass graves were close to a row of houses. As she (2003: 188) says: 'According to the residents no one had heard the screams of the people being executed. More likely they did hear, and they did nothing.' Albright's memoirs testify to the inadequacy of the international community's response to the two crises. They also point—albeit silently—to the problem of how knowing what is happening, good judgment and good conduct depend on each other.

The culpable failure of superpowers like the United States or of international agencies like the United Nations—agencies set up in the wake of the awful discovery of the Nazi 'Final Solution'—to prevent genocide is one thing; however, it is matched by the failure of social sciences like sociology or criminology to pay attention to the problem of state crimes against humanity. Radical evil, like the genocidal murder of millions of innocent people, is a problem that now implicates both power and knowledge.

Among the many factors that explain this, one is the way modern social sciences have failed to think through the relationship of the social and the ethical. This is a failure that is grounded in the constitutive schema that have shaped the disciplinary practices and self-understandings of sociologists.

The problem of evil and the silence of sociology

It is no exaggeration to say that the social sciences have managed to ignore the worst kinds of state violence in a way that is simply incredible. Key social science disciplines like criminology, sociology and social theory have lapsed into near-complete silence about the scale of the violence and abuse of human rights committed by governments across the twentieth century.

This is especially odd given that sociologists and criminologists have done truckloads of research and produced numerous volumes of theory on 'ordinary' violence and street crime, from street mugging, assault and theft to rape and homicide. Yet the highly organised and systematic criminal violence perpetrated by states against their own citizens and the citizens of other states is on a scale that exceeds the experience of ordinary crime by an order of magnitude that seems almost to defeat our imaginative capacity.

It is difficult and perhaps pointless trying to document the absence. Archer and Gartner (1978: 219) noted several decades ago that: 'Violence by the state is strangely absent from most discussions of the problem of violence.' Not much has changed since. David Friedrichs (1998) has published a benchmark two-volume collection of articles on the theme of criminology and 'state crime'. As Friedrichs (1998: i) observes, his book was published at the end of the twentieth century, yet: 'It is dismaying to confront the general neglect of the topic of state crime in the criminological literature. State crime as a major focus of criminological attention has yet to be realized.'

Crimes against humanity are no less striking an absence in sociology. Zygmunt Bauman (1991) observed that mainstream sociologists and criminologists had long ignored, and continue to ignore, the specific case of the Final Solution. This is even more true of the many other examples of state-sponsored violence marking the political landscape of the twentieth century.

In what was designed as an exhaustive and authoritative UNESCO survey of twentieth century sociology, Neil Smelser (1994) makes no reference to the Holocaust, or to any other forms of state crime. No less striking is the way major figures from Parsons, Merton and C. Wright Mills through to Foucault, Giddens and Bourdieu have simply ignored the problem. This silence is repeated in any number of standard sociological textbooks. If denial is typical, we can also acknowledge that there has been a distinguished—if short—roll-call of important sociologists like Collins (1975) and Chalk and Jonasson (1990), and social theorists from Bauman (1991) to Agamben (1997), Elias (1999), Keane (2001), Sofsky (1997, 2003) and most recently Mann (2005) who *have* paid attention.

Why is it that conventional sociologists, criminologists and social theorists have had a problem recognising state-sponsored crimes against humanity? David Friedrichs (1998: xvi) is surely right to suggest that:

> the conceptual, definitional and methodological issues in the realm of state crime are especially daunting . . . [though] any systematic treatment of state crime must grapple with these issues. State crime, political crime, human rights issues and 'legitimate' military, diplomatic and domestic initiatives are entangled in complex ways and must be disentangled.

Among the obvious 'conceptual' problems is that most sociologists and criminologists define crime in terms of whatever their governments define as criminal. Since governments rarely identify the bad things they do—especially when they descend into 'radical evil' as criminal activity—it is not surprising that state crime has proved difficult for criminologists and sociologists to recognise, let alone think about.

Yet the difficulty runs far deeper than this and has more to do with the role of what Bohme (1977) calls 'constructive schemes'. These constructive schemes provide what Fuller (2005: 27) calls the 'default beliefs', which most people—including particular kinds of social scientists—feel they need in order to be able to move through the world. It is simply, as Fuller notes, that most of us do not decide to think anything in particular and find it more convenient to move through a world already equipped with default beliefs—in this case, about what sociology 'is' or what a criminologist 'does'. Such constructive schemes help to constitute the characteristic problems, methods and theoretical explanations that conventional practitioners of the social sciences regard as credible or proper. One result has been to render state crime nearly invisible.

So what is it about the constructive schemes of sociology or criminology that has helped to blank out crimes against humanity?

It is certainly not because sociologists have not been interested in the fact of ethical ideas. Even sociologists, who have often been quite complicated about the role of moral values in sociology, have had to pay attention to ethical ideas and issues. Sociology is, after all, about people and their social relations. Sociologists from Talcott Parsons to Robert Bellah in America, or Emile Durkheim to Michel Foucault in France, have continuously been interested in ethical ideas and practices. Sociologists have variously insisted that 'society' and 'social order' are ultimately the accomplishment of a communal moral or ethical order. Others have pointed to the determinative role played by religious systems of belief and practice. Others have raised questions about how much social order is a product of power and morality embedded in what Foucault has called the practices of governance and truth. All have understood that there is a close and complex relationship between social life and our ethical ideas, values and practices.

Yet sociologists have not had a straightforward relationship with ethics. On the one hand, while happy to describe and explain the social origins and functions of moral ideas, the broad-church positivist tradition whose adherents wish sociology to be a 'proper science' has explicitly rejected any idea that sociologists should either bring their own ethical values into their research or that sociologists should offer moral advice to people or communities.

Indeed, Durkheim's contribution to sociology had the effect of decreeing that 'society' was the source of all the important moral ideas and this obliterated any idea of an autonomous source of moral values. In his famous essay 'Homo Duplex: the Dualism of Human Nature and its Social Conditions', Durkheim explored the human sense of being split into two elements. This, he said, has been variously understood as animal/human mind/body or body/spirit. Durkheim (1973: 159, 162) insisted that the real split was between 'nasty animalistic and egoistic individualism and the higher order of reason and moral life embodied in the society'. It is not too difficult to see here how, for Durkheim, 'society' had replaced 'God' as the source of moral and rational capacities. The consequence was an insistence on Durkheim's part that the collective life of any society provided a source of rational analysis and moral values superior to and more authoritative than anything individuals could come up with. Yet other sociologists have insisted that the discipline has a moral or political duty to act as advocates for disadvantaged groups like the working class, women, colored people or homosexuals.

Most recently, what we have called 'anti-foundationalism' has rejected much of the language and assumptions relied on previously. Writers influenced by Foucault say there is no objective social reality waiting to be 'discovered'. They say the advocacy of liberation relies on meta-narratives that are false and politically dangerous.

Finally, even discussing ethical issues has not been helped by certain widespread intellectual trends in Anglo-American societies. Through the nineteenth and twentieth centuries, institutions from governments through the mass media to universities have increasingly accepted and promoted the idea that ethical questions are merely 'subjective' matters lacking the kind of weight or authority which 'facts' possess. This is the tradition Alasdair MacIntyre (1981) calls 'emotivism', which he claims has swept over moral philosophy and much of Western society in the past two centuries.

Emotivism is the idea that all ethical principles or values are equally valid because ethical values are simply the expression of feelings. As such, 'values'—unlike 'facts'—have no real validity or authority. It is argued that values cannot be rationally assessed or compared. Each value is as good as any other. How, then, have sociologists dealt with the issues of moral choice or ethical deliberation? We suggest here that they have not done very well. We begin by illustrating this general point with a famous dispute that erupted in the field of 'Holocaust' studies in the 1990s about how to explain the actions of ordinary German men who were asked to kill Jews—and did.

The actions of ordinary men

In 1992, Christopher Browning published *Ordinary Men*, an account of the murderous work of the 101 Battalion of *Ordnungspolizei* (or 'Order Police'). Browning follows the story of how, in 1942, the 101 Battalion was ordered to take part in the systematic shooting of thousands of Jews in Poland as they followed the German army invading Russia. The Order Police were made up of a cross-section of 'ordinary' middle-aged German men, considered unsuitable for active front-line military service but deemed sufficiently useful for a range of basic tasks which included the mass killing of unarmed civilians.

The controversy between Browning and his critic, Daniel Goldhagen (1996), raises the problem of how well conventional sociological explanations are able to deal with the human drama of people struggling to act ethically.

Battalion 101 has a special status in the historiography of the Holocaust because of the circumstances of its first exercise in mass murder. Goldhagen, like Browning, focuses on the occasion of the first killing operation by Battalion 101 in the Polish village of Josefow when its commander, Major Wilhelm Trapp, outlined the nature of their duties to the entire battalion of nearly 500 men. Trapp was by all accounts extremely uncomfortable and upset about the orders he had received. He had been ordered to spare only those Jewish men able to work. The rest—the old, the sick, women and children—were all to be shot. Unusually Trapp gave the men in his battalion the opportunity to volunteer not to take part in the operation. On this first occasion only ten or twelve men took the opportunity to absent themselves from the action that was about to commence. The rest of the battalion began the killing of all the Jews, other than able-bodied men, they found in the village. The victims were trucked outside the village before being marched into the nearby forest and shot.

In his 'revision' of Browning, Daniel Goldhagen (1996: 181–3) wants to use Battalion 101 as evidence of his proposition that all or most Germans were 'eliminationist anti-Semites', and that what they did was done out of conviction.

Goldhagen agrees with Browning that the Order Police were not a specifically Nazi agency, nor were they screened for ideological soundness or military fitness. They were by all accounts poorly trained and had the lowest status of all of the various German military and police agencies. Goldhagen rightly emphasises (1996: 217–18) the human drama and the morally outrageous activities of these men on that long day. Many of the killers were soon covered in blood, bone and brain matter. Some of the men found the experience horrifying and a small number absented themselves from the killing operation over the course of the day. However, almost all of the men of Battalion 101 'chose to carry out their lethal tasks' (Goldhagen 1996: 222).

How should we understand this moment? Why did so few 'ordinary men' refuse to take part? Why did so many kill people who constituted no threat to them? And, given that many of the perpetrators were clearly distressed by what they did, why did they do it? (Implicit in any discussion of this event is the obvious question: what would we have done in that situation?)

Goldhagen draws a typically 'sociological' conclusion from this case that here is prime evidence of a nearly universal German commitment to 'eliminationist anti-Semitism'. These 'ordinary Germans' killed the Jews of Josefow because they wanted to, because they were committed to a 'virulent anti-Semitism' and 'wanted' to play their part in the Final Solution. Goldhagen (1996) takes a 'sociological' view of the problem by identifying an element of German culture with a commitment to eliminationist anti-Semitism as a way to explain the conduct of these 'ordinary men'.

As Zygmunt Bauman (1991: 210) argues, if one consequence of the 'sociological imagination' has been the conflation of the 'moral' with sociological categories like 'structure', 'social order' or even 'society' itself, then we should give up looking for 'individual' moral consciences or indeed any serious idea about ethical life.

Can a conventionally framed sociological account offer us any insight into the process of people engaging in a process of moral deliberation as they struggle to act ethically? In effect, Goldhagen's account renders irrelevant any issue of moral deliberation on the part of these 'ordinary men'—and indeed, he does not seek to elucidate the experience at all. Given his account, there is no need—he is only interested in asserting the righteousness of his own moral outrage within a conventional sociological account of why the men of Battalion 101 did what they did.

The resistance/collaboration distinction may well echo the fundamental distinction drawn between 'good' and 'evil', but it may also only serve to deflect or even distort the effort needed to follow people as they deliberate and make complex or difficult choices.

• SOCIOLOGY AND THE REFUSAL OF THE MORAL

Conventional sociology, or what Giddens has called 'mainstream sociology', seems not to have accepted the possibility of being a moral science in several ways that matter. From its inception in the last quarter of the nineteenth century, modern sociology has been intensely preoccupied with promoting itself as a science. Likewise, it has been almost obsessed with certain expressions of deviance, pathology and criminality represented in street crime, organised crime, urban gangs, football hooliganism, domestic violence and the 'underclass'.

Most of the great names in the sociological pantheon (including Durkheim, Parsons, Wirth, Merton, Becker, Douglas, Erikson and Lemert) gained their reputations with studies of deviance or 'social pathology'. Crime, violence and anti-social behaviours associated with criminals, 'pathological families', the unemployed, the 'colored races', 'the poor' or their current manifestation, 'the underclass', have generated both intense interest and continuing disapproval on the part of sociologists.

Amongst a host of possible interpretive responses, the bulk of sociologists who have worked within what is conventionally referred to as the 'structural functionalist' paradigm have affirmed the 'commonsense' view shared with professionals, the police, the journalists and the politicians of the day that juvenile delinquency, sexual violence or predatory crime are reprehensible. These phenomena were also explained as a consequence of inadequate or non-existent 'socialisation', a problem in turn linked variously to ecological conditions (e.g. 'slums') or to economic or cultural impoverishment. The neo-Marxist response associated with the 'new criminology' of the 1970s revised that approach, arguing that delinquency and working-class predatory crime were better located within an interpretive framework in which class structure and modes of resistance or adaptation were emphasised.

Most recently, and in spite of Colin Sumner's (1992) powerful obituary for the sociology of deviance, the social sciences have been busy rehabilitating the 'social pathology' models of the 1890s. This older discourse has been refashioned to take account of the alleged emergence of an 'underclass' of 'welfare dependents' who lack adequate 'social capital' and confront 'social exclusion' and whose lives can be assimilated to the management of risk. The 'underclass' has been (re)discovered in many Western societies complete with biological and cultural dispositions to criminality, unemployability, promiscuity, drug use and welfare dependency. That there is an elective affinity between this kind of social science and economic liberal governments eager to advance individual responsibility, tough law and order agendas and fiscal restraint should not go unremarked.

What Giddens has called 'mainstream sociology' continues to practise a more or less explicit refusal of the moral both in its representation of social conduct as structurally constrained and in its treatment of the 'normative' ordering of conduct.

Within sociological discourse, 'structure' has usually meant those 'unacknowledged structural constraints' that possess a degree of stability and 'causal efficacy'. Among the classical theorists (typically understood to include Comte, Marx, Spencer, Weber and Durkheim), there was early established a powerful link between the idea of 'society' and the idea of 'structure'. 'Society' became nothing more than an orderly system for producing moral constraints, and thereby shaping human conduct. On this basis, 'individual free will' was a myth.

As a consequence, a host of sociological, quantitative and cultural determinisms have long thronged the sociological courtyard, with serious negative consequences for any attempt to understand how people actually engage in moral deliberation or make choices about how to act. For, ultimately, moral deliberation is something people *do*. Richard Rorty's (1999: 88) recent call for a radical revision of philosophy willing to create new ways of being human rests on the basic insight that any decent ethics will insist on the primacy of the agent point of view.

In a general sense, the 'sociological imagination' and the Kantian inquiry into practical judgment have both been central to the Enlightenment project. Yet a central and immanent problem in the Enlightenment project has been the inability to reconcile, let alone establish, a dialogue between these two core aspects of that project.

The Kantian account of ethical judgment and practice presumes a distinctly un-sociological, autonomous, rationally calculative and ethically competent individual. However, what Pierre Manent (1998) calls the 'sociological viewpoint', or Wright Mills (1965) the 'sociological imagination', simply conflates the moral with whatever exists as a moral consensus in any given social setting. In effect, sociology has refused to constitute itself as a form of moral science. It does this because the ideas of 'structure' and 'structural determinism' are so crucial to the history of sociology. For those many sociologists—dead or alive—who have hankered after explanatory potency or disciplinary credibility, the idea that social structures can be used to 'explain' human action/social change/political change has exercised a deep and continuing appeal and authority. That this results in a paradox where the major theorists working within mainstream sociology recognise the central role of morality in securing social integration while simultaneously using the idea of structural determinism to refuse any inquiry into the processes of moral deliberation hardly requires comment.

● CONCLUSION

The central question is how we are to bring together into one frame an inquiry that is at once ethically sensitive, yet alert to the push and pull of the social. In the work of important-because-marginal sociologists or social theorists like C. Wright Mills, Peter Berger, Alvin Gouldner, Norbert Elias, Zygmunt Bauman, Phillip Rieff and Agnes Heller there is a vital and urgent concern with moral issues that works to preserve the integrity of that concern.

Discussion questions

5.1 Identify three or four key values that matter deeply to you, and try to say why they matter. Do you always do things in ways that respect these values?

5.2 Do you think Australians share a core set of common values? If so, what are they?

5.3 Does growing up in a community that is strongly committed to capital punishment mean that you would accept the ethical rightness of this kind of conduct, or that this makes it right?

5.4 Is deceit ever justified in doing social research with other people?

● ● ● PART TWO

IDENTITY: BEING YOURSELF, BEING AUSTRALIAN

We're friends together because we own Australia, everyone of us no matter who—white and black. We come together, join in . . . That will be all right. That will make it better from that big trouble. You know before, Captain Cook made a lot of cruel, you know. Now these days, these days we'll be friendly, we'll be love each other, we'll be mates.

—Hobbles Danayarri of the Yarralin people (1980), cited in Day (1996)

Most of us, at some time, ask ourselves questions about our self. Malfred, a character in the Janet Frame novel *A State of Siege* (1990: 144), does just this:

Who am I then? Where do I creep, crippled, or fly dancing? I could put my hand over my life, obliterating it, disposing of it as I would an insect: there's no reason why others should not do this also . . . All my life there has been someone within listening distance of me . . .

A question like 'Who am I then?' is not a trivial one, nor is it easily answered. For, as Frame observes, we invariably ask this question within 'listening distance' of others.

What we call our 'private' or inner life is always lived out in close proximity with other people. What does this mean for the experience of being a person? On the one hand, there is the question of what that proximity with family members, friends and acquaintances means for our inner sense of self. Getting clarity about our feelings and sense of purpose sometimes requires withdrawal from the company of others. Sometimes that proximity makes it hard to work out whose voice is providing the answers. On the other hand, the life that we live with others can provide us with a sense that we are more than whatever is locked up inside our skull. These relations bring us pleasure and pain, and it is our contact with others that can enrich a sense of self, challenging us to do new things or to think new thoughts.

The chapters in this section use a wide array of theory and research done by contemporary social scientists to explore what it means to be a person living in Australia today.

Only a few decades ago, sociologists would have discussed these issues in terms of the role played by society in constructing a variety of social roles (like 'mother', 'teenager', 'student', 'social worker' or 'Christian') via a process called 'socialisation', seen as integral to constructing an 'individual'. In the sociology of the 1950s and 1960s, successful socialisation was said to make for a well-adjusted or socially conforming person, while failed socialisation produced deviants like homosexuals, drug addicts or communists.

This older sociological narrative about society making the individual has been replaced with a more complex story about identity and the idea that having or being a certain kind of person involves a much messier process of making 'identities'. Our discussion is couched in terms of key identity markers, such as our gender and sexuality, the family we grow up in, our age, ethnicity and religion, and how these various identity markers come together to influence who you are as an Australian in the early twenty-first century.

How strange these people are.
How strange I am.
How strange we are.
Norbert Elias (1998: xi)

Few ideas are both as
weighty and as slippery as
the notion of the self.

Jerrold Seigel (2005: 3)

OURSELVES: 6.
MYSELF, YOURSELF

• • SUMMARY

In this chapter, we explore the concept of the 'self'. Many people talk about the 'self' by referring to the idea that we are all 'individuals'. Where does this idea come from? We look at both old and new stories about the self. How does the idea that we are all individuals relate to the sociological idea that we are whatever society makes us? We look at the way many sociologists have explained how the self comes into being using the idea of socialisation, and outline some problems with the traditional model of socialisation. We suggest that by turning this into a question of identity, we can better understand the idea that our 'self' has both an inner and an external quality.

Many of us spend a lot of time trying to understand ourselves—perhaps as much time as we spend trying to understand other people. It is never easy understanding either ourselves or others. Turgenev (1974), a nineteenth century Russian writer, wrote that 'the heart of another is like a dark forest'. Other people suggest that even self-knowledge often escapes us. Hannah Arendt (1968), a twentieth century philosopher, claimed there are certain things hidden from us always, and some things only others can know. Parker Palmer (1998: 13) talks of the 'mystery of self' when he writes that our self is:

> an evolving nexus where all the forces that constitute my life converge in the mystery of self: my genetic makeup, the nature of the man and woman who gave me life, the culture in which I was raised, people who have sustained me and people who have done me harm, the good and ill I have done to others, the experience of love and suffering—and much, much more.

Traditional sociology, like the structural functionalist kind or the Marxist variety, has not always been very interested in talking about the self—perhaps because its advocates saw this as an interest best left to other disciplines like psychology. Durkheim (cited in Seigel 2005: 489) set the benchmark with his declaration that, without social control exercised by 'society', rationality and moral order would collapse because 'our capacity for feeling is insatiable and a bottomless abyss' while human desire in all its awfulness 'becomes insatiable, even morbid'. The exception to this was the interest shown in face-to-face encounters by those working within the symbolic interactionist tradition, like Blumer (1969) or Goffman (1974)—even though, as Layder (1997: 25) insists, they did so by adopting an excessively rational view of the person—treating them almost as some kind of computing machine.

The avoidance of the self altogether and/or the insistence on banishing 'irrational' elements like feelings and values from their topics of research produced a long-term—and disastrous—distortion on the part of mainstream sociology. Alan Sica (1988: 1) makes this point when he asks why so many sociologists and social theorists:

of personality, organisations, social change, even of deviance [have] laid such emphasis upon, even rel[ied] on the notion of rationality in human action? And why has it therefore suppressed or judged irrelevant systematic tracking of 'irrationality' as a factor in social behavior, as moreover an essential invariant element of lived experience?

This neglect has only begun to be corrected quite recently (e.g. see Layder 1997; Barbalet 1998; Katz 2002).

How odd is it, then, that the reluctance on the part of most sociologists to address the self in its rich complexity occurs in a context in which we are increasingly encouraged to explore our self or to talk about ourselves in public? Whole professions of counsellors and therapists exist to help us to understand ourselves, or to fix our emotional problems. Modern TV talk shows like *Dr Phil* or *Oprah* encourage ordinary people to talk at great length about personal issues. We have armies of experts advising us on 'how to be a better person', or questionnaires waiting to be filled out in popular magazines to measure our emotional well-being. In the light of these developments, Phillip Rieff (1996) suggested that Anglo-American societies in the second half of the twentieth century were seduced by a culture of the therapeutic at some cost to what Rieff argues are important traditional values like a clear distinction between good and evil.

Like Derek Layder (1997: 24), we emphasise the point that people are complex and contradictory beings who have 'an emotional and cognitive depth' and are able to explore questions about the nature of social interaction and social processes within a discernibly sociological frame. That we can and must link up the psychological and the social is suggested by Thomas Nagel (1986), who says any credible idea of self has to accept that it must take into account both the inside story of self implied every time we use the word 'I' and the idea of a self suggested from the outside.

In this chapter we ask a few basic questions:

- What is the self, and how does it come into being?
- Where does the idea that we are 'individuals' come from?
- How useful is the traditional sociological perspective which says that 'society' makes us who we are?

● WHAT IS THE SELF?

A question like this provides a clue in its use of a word like 'self'. There are other words we might have used, like 'person', 'personality, 'individual', 'subject', 'agency', 'ego' or 'the I'. In each case, the word comes out of a tradition and a certain way of thinking which has already framed how we might think—even if it does so unconsciously. As Alasdair Macintyre (1988) insists, words cannot easily be removed from their tradition of use, nor are they fully understood until the point of that tradition is understood.

Take the idea of 'person'. The word 'person' comes from the Greek *prosopon*, meaning the mask worn by actors in the open-air theatres of Athens two and a half centuries ago. That word was taken into Latin as *persona*. It carries the same idea—namely a mask that is worn but is 'animated', or made to live by the sound or spirit of the actor. From *persona* we get the English 'person', 'personality' and 'personhood'.

This implies a number of things about the person and their personality. It suggests that we go into the public world hidden behind a mask: our public face is something worn when we are in public, and is not necessarily the same as the 'real' or private self behind the mask. It also suggests a lack of authenticity and a certain shallowness. Seigel (2005: 17) says 'personhood' or personality has a dignity conveyed by social recognition. This is what sociologists like Weber call 'status'—the honour or value that people give to the aspects of the person they can see.

Keeping this basic point in mind, it is clear that questions of 'self', 'person', 'identity' and 'subjectivity' have long been a major preoccupation not only of contemporary sociologists, but of ancient philosophers and theologians as well as contemporary psychologists, historians, bio-ethicists, journalists and other experts.

Contemporary experts are involved in doing research and developing theories about how selves develop and interact. Different occupations rely on very different models, or theories, of the self. These models are important because they inform the activities of these professions and activities. At the same time, these theories depend on ideas with a long history, and/or are found spread widely throughout our society. In other words, many 'ordinary' people believe or use versions of these stories.

As Seigel (2005) reminds us in an overview of the past three centuries of European thinking about the self, there are three broad traditions available—some of them with a very long pedigree:

- One treats it as a product of our capacity for rationality, thought and reflection. Its origins lie in the oldest of the stories we have available—the idea that 'soul', 'reason' or other divine attributes were planted in humans' bodies by the gods or a god. In the eighteenth century, philosophers like Kant designated Reason as the primary source of an autonomous free self.
- A second tradition locates the self firmly in the body. From the seventeenth and eighteenth centuries this kind of story was told by rationalists and the *philosophes* of the Enlightenment. Men like Condillac insisted that the self was whatever the physical structures of the body (conceived of as a system of levers) and the brain (as a kind of computing machine) made possible.
- A third, even more recent, tradition treats the self as the consequence of social interactions. The self is a social product.

The urge to 'theorise' or to explain things appears to be a very old and well-established human inclination. From the earliest stories and texts, we find human beings telling stories in order to understand themselves and their world. We still tell stories for these reasons.

We need to consider closely the accounts people give about being a person. How do Australians talk about the idea of 'self'? How do they deal with each other? Is the way Australians do this different from how people in other societies do these things? Perhaps the best place to start is with the claim that we are all 'individuals'.

● THE SELF AS INDIVIDUAL

In Australia today, many people answer the question 'Who am I?' with the response that they are 'a woman', 'a Muslim', 'a plumber', 'a computer operator', 'an Italian', 'old', 'a homosexual' or 'a mother'. (These answers, as we suggest later, are all identity markers.) Many of us will also answer by saying 'I am an individual'. But what does this mean? If asked what an 'individual' was, most Australians would say that being an individual involves believing things like:

- Each of us is unique.
- Each person has the ability to reason.
- Each person has their own beliefs.
- Each of us is free to choose different ethical values.
- Each of us should have a say in who governs us.
- Each of us has a right to own property.

The word 'individual' comes from the Latin word *individuum*, meaning 'indivisible'. It is close in meaning to the very old idea of the atom as the basic building block of all matter because it carries the sense that societies are made up or built out of individuals.

Yet, as Seigel (2005: 107–10) reminds us, the idea of the self-as-individual is an idea which understands:

- the individual as a property-owning subject;
- the concept that a person's body is one of the important things they own; and
- that the individual is responsible for him or herself to secure their livelihood and life chances by hard work.

These ideas about the individual are part of a tradition of ideas called liberalism, or what C.B. McPherson (1968) has called 'possessive individualism'. This set of meanings tells us that this idea of individualism has relatively recent origins in the seventeenth century—a time that marked the origins of market capitalism and the closely related political philosophy of liberalism associated with John Locke (1632–1704). Liberalism is a very large and diverse tradition of ideas. Its advocates variously emphasise the relative weight to be given to self-interest, the needs of the community as a whole and the kind of roles governments should play. As Isaiah Berlin (1969) points out, liberals have also promoted divergent ideas about 'liberty' or freedom. Some have promoted 'negative freedom'—that is, being free from oppression and interference by the state—while others have advocated for 'positive freedom'—the idea that each of us should be supported by governments in order to flourish.

In our time the revival of a narrow version of economic liberalism has led to extreme views, such as ex-British Prime Minister Margaret Thatcher's claim that: 'There is no such thing as society'. Clearly there is a real society—though the ways sociologists have used the idea have not always been helpful. Stephen Fuchs (2005: 34), in defending a traditional sociological idea, mirrors Thatcher when he says that 'society does not "consist" of persons'.

In any society, of course, there are real people. And real people are social beings caught up in real social relationships. They are neither perfectly free 'individuals', nor are they forced to believe or act by something called 'society'.

● STORIES ABOUT THE INDIVIDUAL

The idea that we are individuals draws on several sophisticated stories, some of which have a long history. The Christian–Jewish–Muslim story says that human beings were created by a god in his own image, and that he gave these creatures free will and rationality, then banished them from the Garden of Eden when they disobeyed him.

The theological story: We are the children of God

The oldest story, which still has currency today for Christians, Jews and Muslims, is the Creation story found in the Christian Bible (2500–1500 BC) and the Jewish Pentateuch. In the two stories found in the first book of the Bible, Genesis, God ('Yhwh') made human beings in the god's own image: one tells of a sexless god making 'man and woman'; the other tells of a male god making 'Adam' and then 'Eve' to be his 'helper'. These are the Dreaming stories of many people in the West.

Using these stories, the Jewish and Christian traditions built an elaborate account of human beings as the creatures or 'children' of their god. These stories tell how human beings are made partly from the sinful and 'natural' body (or clay), which dies, and partly from the godlike parts (or soul), which is immortal. The Judaeo-Christian tradition claims that human beings belong to their god and must obey him, although they can choose not to. (This is because god gave humans the capacity to be 'free moral agents', which includes the ability to disobey the god.)

To see how pervasive this idea is, think about modern debates on abortion or euthanasia. Traditional Christians say that only the god (now called God, to make the point that Christians believe there is only one god) gives us life and only 'He' may take it, because all life 'belongs' to God. Liberals, feminists and rationalists disagree, believing that each person 'owns' their life and may freely dispose of it as they wish (or, in the case of abortion, the pregnant woman may remove the foetus from her body). These debates rely on issues of ownership: either that god owns us, or we own ourselves.

Aboriginal stories, totems and the self

Another spiritual story, which links the self to a cosmic order, is found in the stories Australian Aboriginal groups tell about their origins. These may be far older than the Judaeo-Christian stories. One such story was told by the Wurunderjeri people in the area now called Melbourne (Broome 1984: 1). The Wurunderjeri believed an act of creation took place when Bunjil took some pieces of bark and breathed human life into them. Until then the world was both lifeless and formless—except for super-creatures like Bunjil. Bunjil shaped the land and made it fruitful; he gave the men spears and the women digging sticks, and showed them how to hunt and gather food. Bunjil then laid down a code of behaviour for the humans, or the Wurunderjeri.

'Dreaming' stories are designed to ensure that every person, living or dead, knows they have a place within a physically and spiritually united world. They tell of the time when the world was made, and when the animals, plants and rocks that became totems were established.

Totem was the foundation of identity, of self, for the Aboriginal people. A totem is usually a thing, an animal or a plant with which each person is identified as part of their being. Among the Urbanna people, for example, there were two classes of people known as the Mathurie and the Wirawawa. Within each of these two classes were six totems: for the Mathurie there were totems like the Inyarrie (wild duck), Wutnimmera (green cicada), Matla (dingo), Waragutie (emu), Kalaththura (wild turkey) and Guti (black swan); among the Wirawawa there were the Kurar (cloud), Wabma (carpet snake), Kapirie (lace lizard), Urantha (pelican), Kutnichilie (water hen) and Wakalia (crow). In this group, a Wirawawa woman could only marry a Mathurie man. Only certain totems could marry: a cicada man could marry only a crow woman, or a water hen woman could marry only a dingo man.

To have no totem was to have no existence. To be born into a tribe was to be born into a totem which gave you a sense of identity, because it linked you to all of the other people born into that totem. It established a particular place for the self in the country to which the group belonged and which it looked after.

Modern people tell their own version of a Dreaming story, which explains how we come to be who we are.

The Enlightenment story: We are all born as free, rational individuals

The important modern belief that each of us is an individual came together in what we can call the Enlightenment model, which drew heavily on core elements of the scientific world-view associated with Isaac Newton. This model of humankind came to achieve high status through the nineteenth century by integrating elements of the religious story. It still operates in a lot of modern social science. This pictured the self as an autonomous individual, well integrated and rational. It drew on four clusters of ideas.

The first of these was the British liberal tradition (Arblaster 1988). The development of liberal individualism has had a complex history in societies like Britain and America, which went through the Great Transformation. Liberalism emerged as a set of very subversive ideas, which the social and political elites of the seventeenth and eighteenth centuries rightly saw as dangerous to their dominance. This intellectual tradition was put together by English and Scottish writers like Thomas Hobbes (1588–1679), John Locke (1632–1704), Adam Smith (1723–90) and Jeremy Bentham (1748–1832).

In seventeenth century England, Hobbes wrote of a time when all humans lived in a 'state of nature', full of violence, war and uncertainty. In a story that looks very similar to an Aboriginal Dreaming story, writers like Hobbes and Locke say that certain people came together and, via a 'social contract', agreed to give up certain powers and freedoms in order to create government and the 'civil society'. The creation of 'civil society' meant the flowering of social order and the emergence of wealth—and poverty. Built into this story was the idea that government was the creation of people coming together and agreeing to form a state.

John Locke, in the late seventeenth century, thought only men of property should be involved in forming government. Locke argued that all individuals had certain basic inalienable rights. Among these was the right not to be the property of others. Locke added that everyone had a right to own property but in practice only a few could do so. Those few, he thought, should also have the right to form a government.

La Mettrie argued in the 1740s that humans are nothing but calculating machines who cannot help but be rational, operating according to some kind of in-built logical process. This idea has resurfaced with a vengeance in the cognitive sciences attached to the development of the computer since the 1970s.

Third, Jeremy Bentham in the late eighteenth century argued that all humans are selfish hedonists who seek to rationally maximise their happiness and minimise pain. This idea is foundational to most kinds of economic theory, and continues to dominate the teaching of ethical philosophy in most universities in the Anglo-American world. Peter Singer, the founder of 'animal liberation', is only the latest in a long line of utilitarians to use this fundamental idea creatively.

Finally, at the end of the eighteenth century, Immanuel Kant drew all of these ideas together into a powerful account of a single, solidary, autonomous individual as a well-integrated rational being. Kant's *Ich* (or ego) recognises the role of experience in shaping our development into a distinctively human being able to be rational and commanded by ideas about the good. The Kantian idea of the self says we are all ethically driven to do what is both rational and good.

These elements make up a kind of foundational Enlightenment story about 'the self' as an autonomous individual, an integrated ego (see box).

The autonomous individual

- According to the Enlightenment account, our life is an integrated whole lived as a smooth curve—a slow progression from childhood through to adult maturity, shaped by our experience as we are educated and make choices that advance our happiness.

- It involves a developmental curve that starts with the child as innocent, unformed and passive; the adult mature rational self is represented as a fixed structure, as a stable, known and entirely knowable centre of consciousness.

- The self is represented as rational/logical *and* empirical, calmly taking aboard experience then both using it and being used by it to form ideas and build up rational knowledge. This account depends on the idea that we use memory to fix things—in a similar way to a photograph—to capture and to keep experiences, images and ideas.

- Our self is understood in terms of a model of autonomous individuals. The self is represented as an undivided, integrated, coherent psychic entity. (The very idea of 'individual' means something that cannot be divided.)

- This model emphasises rationality, which we use to refashion and make sense of the ideas given to us by experience, pursuing rational goals and rationally promoting our happiness.

The French Revolution (1789–1814) drew on some of these ideas in ways that have not yet stopped being unsettling: revolutionaries argued that, simply by virtue of being a member of the nation (or a citizen), a person was entitled to certain rights, like the right to select a government. Socialist and working-class movements took up the argument and pushed relentlessly to open up what had been monarchical and aristocratic governments established on the basis of a birthright to rule. Through the nineteenth and twentieth centuries, the 'democratic revolution' saw more and more governments being voted into office by popular elections.

In the liberal tradition evident in the work of Locke, Bentham and John Stuart Mill, individuals are a strange combination of interests governed by 'reason' and threatened by unruly passions (or emotions) like envy, greed or lust. A rather darker view of the self was developed by Freud at the end of the nineteenth century. While Freud is conventionally seen as a psychologist, his ideas also entered into mainstream sociology minus the critical bite he gave to them.

The Freudian story

Even in the eighteenth century, some people did not accept the Enlightenment model. Proponents of the counter-Enlightenment or Romantic movement argued for the role played by feelings and nature. As Jean-Jacques Rousseau, the first great theorist of the romantic era, argued in the 1760s, human beings had once enjoyed a natural state. Entering into civil society we became unequal, our lives distorted by social hierarchies, authoritarian government and the requirements of custom and convention. To live in civil society was to be deformed morally. Only by returning to nature could we restore something of that natural grace.

By the end of the eighteenth century, poets like Goethe, Wordsworth and Coleridge were emphasising the value of getting in touch with the 'natural self' revealed by our dreams and by those elements of the self untouched by society.

By the start of the twentieth century, Sigmund Freud (1856–1939), a Viennese Jewish physician and psychologist, was taking these ideas further as he constructed a very unsettling view of how we become adults.

- Rather than seeing infants and children as innocent, unformed and passive, Freud maintained that the child is already alive with instincts, fantasies and desires.

- Freud reversed the foundationalist Enlightenment idea that the self is a passive photographic film on which experience is imprinted. He insisted that when we 'see' the world we do so by way of projection in just the way a film projector throws out an image onto the world as the passive screen.

- For Freud, the self is not a single, well-integrated individual entity, but a fractured affair in which psychically we are the sum of four warring parts: the *id* (our instinctual drives); the *super ego* (a kind of moral policeman); the *unconscious*, into which we plunge all the desires and fantasies which the super ego bans; and the *ego*, the public face we present to the world and to ourselves.

  Freud says we are mostly unaware of how this psychic architecture actually works because most of the mechanisms for holding it together are unconscious.

- For this reason, Freud rejected any simple idea of causality. To the extent that he retained any sense that our psychic life reveals causation, it is in the form of over-determination, in which complex and multiple layers of feeling, pain, experience, fantasy, desire and repression overlay each other as the ego strives to lead a life worth living.

- Freud subverts any notion that rationality could be what we think it is. In its place, rationality becomes a deeply ambiguous illusion where our ideas can become symbolic expressions of things we do not know about.

  All human thought is an accommodation between the ideas and memories that are consciously available (the preconscious) and the unconscious—all those ideas, feelings, desires, traumas and fantasies that have been repressed or forgotten.

- Hence Freud's idea that no one is 'normal'. The price of living with each other in the blessed state of civilisation is that we must repress all those desires and fantasies and instincts to kill or destroy or have sex with each other in ways which would rapidly prove intolerable and destructive of our social relationships. Civilisation in Freud's hands becomes a fragile achievement constantly threatened by the potentiality for violence or self-destruction.

- Finally, nothing after Freud can ever be seen as simply what we say it is. Freud reminds us that words, feelings, images, dreams, fantasies and desires are expressive and are carried symbolically—often in ways that transform them.

Freud subverts our commonsense belief that everyone is always telling the truth about their emotional life or their normal conduct. Indeed, says Freud, anything that is available to our consciousness is being sent into the world to deceive and mislead either ourself or someone else.

The sociological argument: Society makes us individuals

Through the nineteenth and early twentieth centuries, sociologists struggled to come to terms with the idea of the modern rational individual through debating what was known as the 'social question' (Collini 1979.) The social question refers to a set of interrelated issues arising out of the French Revolution, including persistent social movements promoting democratic ideas, the spread of poverty and of socialist ideas leading to chronic social anxiety about the poor and the working class. In France, key nineteenth century French sociologists such as August Comte (1798–1857), Alexis de Tocqueville (1805–59) and Emile Durkheim (1858–1917) were obsessed with the question: 'how is social order possible?' They were dismayed by what they saw as the destructive consequences of hyper-individualism and democracy. This anxiety about democracy was partly based on the French experience of revolutions (in 1789, 1830, 1848 and 1870), which created considerable social and political change. Comte was far more optimistic about this question than Durkheim, who tended to privilege the needs of society over the individual, seeing in the democratic ethos a source of social and moral disorder. Tocqeville, who travelled across America in the 1830s, returned convinced that democratic governments which pursued equality ended up destroying liberty—an idea which would return with a vengeance in the 1980s at the hands of economic liberals like von Hayek.

Writers in two countries which narrowly avoided revolutionary upheaval, Germany and Britain, produced more optimistic accounts. In Germany, Max Weber emphasised the shaping role of ideas (like science and rationality) and institutions (like bureaucracies) in promoting modernity. He travelled to America in 1904 and returned convinced that the highly individualist theology of Protestant churches supported both a vibrant political democracy and a highly conformist and conventional social order. In Britain, early sociologists like L.T. Hobhouse (1864–1930), Herbert Spencer (1820–1903) and in the United States like Lester Ward, Albion Small and W.G. Sumner developed a more distinctively liberal model of sociology (Bannister 1987). In this model, the relationship of the individual to society was identified as a key problem which was resolved by the structures of society. Finally, this idea of structure drew on the work of French and British anthropologists interested in the interconnected character of social structure: any change in one institution produced changes everywhere else.

By the mid-twentieth century, the American sociologist Talcott Parsons (1902–79) and protegés like Robert Merton had developed what Giddens called the 'sociological orthodoxy'; it was held in great respect at least until the 1970s. Variously referred to as 'structural functionalism' or 'American sociology' (Benton 1984), it drew together the French preoccupation with social order, the Freudian idea of developmental stages and the repression of instinctual drives, the anthropological interest in structures and institutions, the Weberian interest in ruling ideas and the classical liberal interest in individuals.

Parsons produced the modern sociological myth of the socialised individual. In effect, this theoretical model argued that modern societies were able to produce 'individuals' who wanted to support the dominant moral consensus and so maintain social order. If this model is unpacked, we find five core claims:

- Society is a system where every part (from individuals and their moral beliefs to their institutions, like family or religion) is interconnected. Change one part and all other parts are affected. As a system, each society works towards promoting its own internal social order or equilibrium while protecting itself from disorder.
- Any society is a total and consensus-based system of moral values and beliefs, which guide and determine each individual's activities and roles.
- Individual identity is derived from social structure. That is, society creates the types of individuals that meet its needs. Each society ensures that its individual members acquire their identity through the socialisation process.
- Successful socialisation ensures that people fill their social roles and realise the functional needs essential to social order and the survival of society as a system.
- Some people fail to be socialised properly and become deviants—or criminals. These deviants have to be 'dealt with' in order to protect social order.

The classical sociological story drew in part on the religious story about 'human nature' as greedy, irrational and violent. Without God's intervention, human beings would naturally indulge themselves in 'animal-like' behaviours.

Emile Durkheim (1858–1917) developed a sociological version of this idea. He argued that humans had two sides. One was full of individualistic animal instincts and drives. The only way this kind of individualism could be dealt with was by immersion in a society that was prepared to exercise moral authority and bend the individual to the will of society, enhancing the human capacity to obey moral rules and to acquire self-control.

In North America, Talcott Parsons wrote about how the 'internalisation of social norms' ensured that social order was maintained. This required two things: the establishment of society-wide moral and social codes for living together successfully; and a process of educating and disciplining human beings to enable them to live collectively in peace. This is a story of 'society' as an objective structure or system of rules and processes that forces members to work for the health and integration or what is called the 'functioning' of the social order or system. This became the cornerstone of what is sometimes called 'classical sociology' or 'structural functionalism'.

The classical sociological story assumes that all behaviour is learned and that all behaviour is routine and predictable. In effect, it implies that all we know, think or feel is 'planted' in us by society. Socialisation induces a spontaneous desire to be cooperative by mobilising emotions like shame, guilt, punishments and rewards.

It needs to be emphasised that the classical tradition allowed for some people to be different (or deviant). The classical sociological theorists claimed that people could be different in three ways: they could be slightly different (or deviant); they could be naughty or delinquent; or they could be criminal. If people stepped out of line too far, society would step in to treat the deviant, the delinquent or the criminal. As long as it did not get too large, the population of the deviant, delinquent or criminal was even said to have a positive function or value in maintaining social order, by showing people what they could expect if they ever contemplated such behaviour.

• SOCIALISATION AND THE SELF

Classical sociologists like Durkheim and Parsons emphasised the constraining nature of society as an objective fact. According to this account, society forces us to behave in ways it wants. The tradition of structural functionalist sociologists, from Durkheim (in the 1890s) to Parsons (in the 1950s), relied on something like an image of 'society' as a factory assembly line.

● SOCIALISATION

'Socialisation' is a word given to the process of becoming a member of a particular society. It involves a lifelong process of learning to think, feel and behave in regular, predictable ways deemed appropriate to the demands and interests of society.

In writing about learning to be a member of society, Durkheim emphasised the external constraints that constitute society:

> When I fulfil my obligations as brother, husband or citizen, I perform duties which are defined, externally to myself and my acts, in law and custom. Even if they conform to my own sentiments, and I feel their reality subjectively, such reality is still objective, for I did not create them: I merely inherited them through my education . . . (Durkheim 1938: 1–2)

Until the 1970s, most sociologists after Durkheim and Parsons were content to develop an orthodox body of theory and research which showed how socialisation processes worked to promote social order. Committed to developing sociology as a profession, these sociologists devoted a lot of research time to primary and secondary socialisation. According to this orthodox consensus, primary socialisation was the process of imprinting society on the infant and child—usually within the family.

Primary socialisation

Orthodox sociologists say that the primary socialisation process involves:

- developing language;
- learning cognitive skills (reading, writing, perception, thinking and counting);
- internalising appropriate moral standards, attitudes, aspirations and identities as 'wife', 'teacher' or 'teenager';
- being socialised in terms of social roles, like 'child', 'club member', 'patient', or 'girl';
- learning how to control feelings and desires by 'internalising' self-control mechanisms like shame and guilt; and
- learning how to behave in role-specific ways.

Secondary socialisation

This is a lifelong process of learning how to adjust and conform to the expectations, roles, values and behaviours of 'society'. It relies on such activities as going to school, attending church, watching television, working for other people, reading the newspaper or going to a psychiatrist.

THE PROBLEMS WITH SOCIALISATION THEORY

Durkheim consistently emphasised the way 'society' educated individual feelings and commitments, promoted morality and inculcated emotions like guilt and shame through such key institutions as the family and the school. However, leaping from this fact to the proposition that we can act, think or feel only in accordance with the way that an entire 'society' wants us to may be stretching the bounds of credulity.

As Fatteh (1997: 35) has suggested, contemporary societies like Australia are characterised more by moral and social diversity than by a single moral or cultural order. The sociology of Durkheim and Parsons, which attempted to make sense of 'modern society', drew on descriptions and models of small-scale, harmonious and homogeneous pre-modern societies in places like nineteenth century Australia, the Pacific islands and Africa.

This observation suggests we need to ask some questions about the orthodox sociological story of society socialising us:

- Has there ever been a large and complex society with just one way of thinking, acting or feeling?
- Does society socialise us, or do quite particular people and groups provide us with examples of certain types of behaviour and ways of thinking?
- Does learning simply mean passively imitating and absorbing what is put before us? Or does it involve making choices, selecting what we agree with or find acceptable?
- Are we so tightly constrained by 'society' that we cannot modify the language we use or the rules of social interaction? On their own account, how could changes ever take place in society? Most structural functionalists have dealt with this problem by using the idea of deviance to explain change.

In raising these questions, we do not doubt that Australians speak, think and act in ways they have learned from other people. Learning itself is a curious and complex process involving elements of imitation, selection and modification. So how useful is the claim that individuals learn the culture of their society through socialisation (Haralambos et al. 1997: 6)?

SOCIAL ORDER AND MORAL CONSENSUS

The orthodox account of society suggests that large, complex 'societies' exist in which there is general agreement, or consensus, about how people feel, behave and decide what is right or wrong. In Australia, the legal system supplies one such set of rules about what is right or wrong. Yet we also know that not all of the rules are either obeyed or believed to be right. We do not believe that such a society with such social/moral consensus has ever existed. If that is so the classical account of 'society' socialising 'the self' collapses.

Classical sociology tells a story of a programmed human behaviour that is predictable, orderly and constrained. The classical sociological account is very close to the psychological account given by behaviourists like Pavlov, Skinner and neoclassical learning theorists—that all human behaviour is a set of learned responses to stimuli. But it is clear that, while the classical socialisation theory suggests otherwise, we are not unthinking programmed machines that respond involuntarily by doing X every time we encounter Y. The orthodox sociological story is limited because it fails to explain how we act creatively and how we respond to novel stimuli by making new links. Nor can this account explain the diversity of beliefs and practices that exists in complex societies. The classical socialisation story also denies our ability to be agents, acting according to our knowledge, beliefs and feelings. Finally, though this raises different issues, the classical tradition is not able to explain how social change takes place. Indeed, when sociologists from this tradition try to explain things like war and revolutions, they say that these kinds of social change take place because 'society' was ready for change, or they argue that people who promote change in any area of life are 'deviants'.

If there are major problems with the socialisation account offered by classical sociology, what can we put in its place? Two ideas—social agency and identity—are relevant when we speak about the self as a social being. Most traditional sociologists addressed the question of identity by default, as they pursued issues related to the large-scale change of whole societies (i.e. the problem of social order, the role of class or industrial society). Such orientations and preoccupations were not necessarily wrong, but tended to leave 'real' people out of the story. In answering the question 'who are we?' we argue that our self is a complex of identities, which are shaped in and by different social relationships and activities found in particular quite real networks—or what Elias (1998: 101–3) has called 'figurations'. In this way, we get closer to a richer understanding of what the idea of 'social' actually refers to.

● BEING SOCIAL AND IDENTITY

Sociologists like Anthony Giddens (1979) argue that we are self-interpreting, symbolic and expressive creatures who are rational because we seek to direct, interpret, monitor and change our activities. He has consistently stressed our capacity for agency, by which he means our ability to be self-aware, to know what we are doing, to choose what to do, and to give good accounts of why we did what we have done.

It is true that we are creatures of habit, who like to do the same thing day after day. Equally, however, we can and often do choose what we do. We can reflect on our activities, and we can to some extent change these activities and the ways we think. This is just another way of talking about the role and relevance of the sociological imagination in our everyday life. Even when we are alone and engaging in an apparently solitary activity like writing a letter, we are still using deeply social capacities like language to constitute our ideas.

The idea of social agency captures the point that we mostly act together with other people with whom we have some kind of relationship and that we use social media like language to do these things. Social agency involves people negotiating and planning with each other to do certain things and then acting and interacting around those plans.

Most of us do not make difficult choices every hour of the day. We do, however, exercise agency. Agency also means drawing on a range of ethical values when confronting choices about what to do or how to act. As Giddens (1984: 3, 22) writes:

> To be a human being is to be a purposive agent who has reasons for his or her activities and is able, if asked, to elaborate discursively upon these reasons . . . As social actors all human beings are highly 'learned' in respect of knowledge which they possess, and apply, in the production and reproduction of day-to-day social encounters.

Because we as human beings have agency does not mean we have complete freedom about what we will do, partly because we are constantly interacting with other people. It is therefore likely that we will never have full agency or total freedom to determine what we personally like or want. As Karl Marx argued in the mid-nineteenth century, we make our own history, but not under circumstances of our own choosing.

The idea of agency is useful because we too frequently assume that society will not let us do certain things. Here we confront the problems created by the way sociologists have talked about society as if it were a 'structure' external to people. Norbert Elias (1998: 101) puts this point very well:

> One can see more clearly . . . the illusionary character of any conception of society which makes it appear that norms or rules have a power of their own, as if they were something outside and apart from the groups of people . . . I have some reservations with regard to the standard expressions such as that which we use when we say that a society or group *has* a structure. One can easily interpret this manner of speaking as if the group were something apart from the people who form it.

The idea that we are social beings means that we live in a series of long- and short-term relationships, or figurations. We live in relatively small figurations of mutual relationships of dependence and independence. Those figurations set up rules and expectations on which we act. Frequently we negotiate minor or major changes. We can try to change people's attitudes and if we don't succeed we can leave one figuration and try another. We can be creative with the rules or with language, even as they shape us. We can change the rules of an organisation. We can even, as many Europeans found themselves doing in the late 1980s, change an entire economic or political system.

More problematic is the assumption that agency implies we are rational creatures. The account of agency found in Giddens is an overly rationalist one which ignores, for example, the role of emotion in our lives (Mestrovic 1997: 77–111). Giddens also overstates the extent to which humans are able to understand fully the nature of their own emotional life or motives, let alone those of other people. Yet the idea of agency remains useful if it reminds us that most of us can provide a reason for what we have done or for what we propose to do.

The major obstacle to our agency is often other people: whether it is our family, our workplace, school, a community group or the law, there will always be people who do not agree with us. Sometimes we comply with what they want, sometimes we do not; at other times, we accommodate their expectations and compromise.

Emphasising the nature of our social agency means understanding that:

- we are people who have ethical ideas, feelings and desires who can plan for a future and are capable of great creativity, and that we live and work with other people;
- our lives are informed by these values, ideas, emotions and intentions, which we use each day to make choices and shape our lives in interaction with other people;
- we have the ability to reflect on our own beliefs and actions and to communicate these self-understandings to other people; and
- we are aware that there are limits put on our actions by our social relationships with people we can both see and touch, as well as with unknown people like law-makers.

We are neither the creature or puppet of society, nor are we entirely free or autonomous individuals. There is no clear distinction between the self and an external social world. Real people are linked through what Norbert Elias (1978) called 'figurations': real relationships of mutual dependence and independence that change continually.

● FIGURATIONS AND IDENTITY

Figurations are not structures, like 'class' or 'gender', but are actual, empirically discoverable chains of mutual relationships found everywhere from families to supermarkets, churches, rave parties, offices and neighbourhoods. We are not separable from these figurations: they are larger wholes, though not as large as a whole society. A figuration refers to all the people we can identify with whom we have face-to-face relationships. Some of these relationships are very persistent and powerful, like those we have with our families and friends. Some can be less intense but persistent, like those with work colleagues or fellow members of a sporting team. It will include people who can exercise a powerful influence on our lives because they are teachers, priests or bosses. These figurations are shaped by factors like whether we are living in a large city or a small rural town and by the kind of access we have to transport, sporting and leisure activities and the mass media.

We should not forget that we can also have quite important relationships with people we have never actually met. These might include leaders of various organisations of which we are members, people whose views or lifestyle we admire who we encounter in the media, or people we 'meet' via emails and on the internet. It is within these figurations that we encounter the fact that all of us develop and carry identity markers.

Our identity is usually indicated by names like 'girl', 'doctor', 'student', 'white', 'woman', 'unemployed' or 'heterosexual'. These names carry different messages about our social existence and how we (and others) see and feel about ourselves. Some of the names we use refer to our physical appearance; others refer to our family or collective histories—for example, 'I am divorced' or 'I was a junkie'. Some of these names or markers may also refer to being part of a group—'I am a nun' or 'I am an Iraqi'.

We each have numerous identities, which are concerned with social relationships. This is because markers like those just mentioned refer to the existence of other people, each bearing a complex of identity markers. These markers are used in constructing a sense of self and help to shape the ways people act, think or feel in a given situation. The self is social, because to have a social identity means being part of a set of social relations.

Each of these identity markers indicates or requires the existence of someone who is the same or who is different, and it is that similarity or difference that is used to help say who we are. For instance, a person cannot be a 'mother' without having a 'child'. This typically involves an actual relationship between a mother and her child (a relation of difference), while it presupposes a relationship of difference at the linguistic level (i.e. 'mothers' have 'children') and a set of actual relations of similarity with other mothers. In the same way, being a 'teacher' involves manifold actual and logical relations of similarity (with other 'teachers') and of difference (with 'students').

We use a medley of identity markers to say who we are, who we want to be and who other people are. We emphasise different markers according to time and place. The key markers include age, family, parental status, friends, sex, gender, occupation, class, status, leisure activities, religion, ethnicity, race and education. We also use many other markers, like clothing and taste in music.

Erving Goffman (1969) described the ways we shape our 'self' in the presence of others. Many people are skilled at presenting themselves to others so that they show themselves off to best advantage. They show some facets of their self while deliberately hiding others.

If we are to understand the 'self' as social and as involving identity markers, we need to work with certain considerations.

The self is historical

The self is historical because the ways in which people understand themselves, define themselves and prescribe how they and others should live constantly change.

In Athens in the fifth century BCE, it was quite acceptable for adult men who were 'citizens' to have sexual relations with adolescent boys. These days, such behaviour is defined as criminal and morally abhorrent. In nineteenth century England, a woman was not defined in law as a 'person' because to be defined in that way it was necessary to own property. As women could not lawfully own property—or bequeath it—they could not identify themselves as persons. Further, the meaning of a word can alter over time, because the meaning given to a particular identity marker changes according to the social context. For example, defining yourself as a Christian in Rome around 200 CE was not the same as defining yourself as a Christian in Adelaide today.

Identities are double-sided

The category of identity accepts that there is an internal–external dimension to the self—identity is neither internal nor external, but both.

Identity refers to our internal, private experiences—the way we think, our feelings and how we perceive the world. The way we experience and feel about ourselves also shapes how we perceive and respond to others. This is not to say that the way other people identify us does not influence how we experience life and how we see our self, however. The ways we experience and feel about ourselves help shape our relations with others.

Inner and outer aspects of identity

Identity refers to the way we relate to and understand ourselves, and to how other people understand us and relate to us. How others perceive you helps them figure out how they will deal with you. This aspect of identity often relates to how our skin colour, gender, body shape and abilities, accent, sexuality, age and dress are perceived. (It also relates to the stories they may have already heard about who others think you are.)

Features of our self, such as our physical demeanour and skin colour, carry particular meanings. They signal particular stories about who we are supposed to be on the inside and help shape the ways the outside world responds to us. There are, however, often enormous discrepancies between how we feel and identify ourselves and how certain other people see and behave towards us.

Identity is often fragmented or divided

Consider our gender identity. Freud said that the first thing you notice about a person you have met for the first time is whether they are male or female. Men and women share some experiences. But some writers believe they also interact, think and feel in ways that are different from each other. However, although gender is important in shaping a person's understanding of identity, it is only one element of one's self.

As R.W. Connell (1995) argues, what it means to be a man or a woman not only varies in different places and times, but can be very different for people in the same place and time. He maintains that these differences depend on who a person is, who they are with and what they are doing. As Connell notes, our identity as a 'man' or a 'woman' is often dependent on our social context, and this can be uncertain. Most Koori men are different from most Lebanese men in a number of ways. Most Nyungar women are different from most Greek women. Middle-class professional heterosexual Anglo-Celtic men tend to experience things differently from most young Italian lesbian women.

We cannot assume that all of those identified as belonging to a particular social category, like 'women' or 'the elderly', have a common existence. This type of thinking is called essentialism.

Essentialism

Essentialism is the assumption or claim that all people over a certain age, or who have a certain skin colour, or who are either male or female, or who do the same job or have the same religion will therefore all have the same kinds of beliefs, needs and desires, and behave in the same way. Essentialism is a consequence of our will to generalise. When we generalise, we assume that a group like 'the elderly' or 'women' can actually be defined or described by reference to a particular set of supposedly shared characteristics. Hence all elderly people enjoy playing lawn bowls and are forgetful, dependent or fragile. Or all women are emotional, caring, soft and not very physical. This, of course, is not only inaccurate, but can be offensive, even harmful. A 70-year-old man may have more in common with a twelve-year-old girl than he does with another man of his own generation. The same applies to all the other social categories used to identify people according to gender or ethnicity.

In short, we often experience tensions—even contradictions—between certain aspects of our identity. Most of us have parts of our identity that are counter to other aspects of our identity. For example, we may be in a permanent heterosexual relationship and also have homosexual desires. We may identify ourselves as a practising and committed Catholic, but be divorced. There are constant tensions in our identities which can cause great problems if they are not managed well or resolved.

Identity is fluid and changeable

Our identities are fluid because we are involved in social practices that are constantly shifting and changing. Many of the stories we tell about ourselves and the accounts others give about us alter continuously.

Our identity is rarely resolved. To be a person who is a waged 'worker', a 'wife', a 'mother' and a 'Catholic' is to enter a variety of relationships and social practices that can be fulfilling and happy yet at the same time extremely difficult, tension-ridden and contradictory. Similarly, a young woman may get married and experience herself in the first months as a blissfully happy 'wife'. This role may, after some years of growing stress and abuse from her partner, turn into an identity that she experiences as painful and sad. Our 'identity' can change as our social relations change. Further, other people may sometimes want to define your identity in ways you find unpleasant, discriminatory or oppressive.

Identity is fluid

Identity can be ambivalent, powerful and variable, but it can also be resistant to change. The different aspects of identities may help us feel we are 'together' as a person, or they may lead to us feeling divided. Our identities may also be in a state of flux, and we may value certain aspects of our identities in ways that are different from the ways other people regard them.

Identity and language

The fact that we use words like 'story' to talk about identity indicates that language is important in constituting our identity; using language is, after all, a basic social practice in which we all engage. It is through language that we know the world; and it is through language that we name our self and others.

As Giddens (1987a) argues, language is good for demonstrating the double-edged nature of social life. Language exists before we do. It is already there as a set of rules for speaking and writing effectively or 'properly'.

We can use the speech rules (of grammar and syntax) to create new words and meanings, even as we learn the existing meanings of words to name a world that already exists. We can also use language to bring new aspects of the world to consciousness or to bring about change. Equally, language constrains us because it limits us. To a large degree, language has already defined much of what we can think, say and feel.

● CONCLUSION

The identity markers we use to construct and delineate an understanding of self indicate a set of intricate and persistent social relationships in which we work towards being our self. They also indicate a range of specific relationships that we enter throughout our life.

Rather than saying something as abstract as 'human beings create society and are at the same time created by it' (Bilton et al. 1996: 15), we maintain that:

- We experience our self within those social relations which we encounter on a personal, face-to-face basis as well as on a more extended and 'abstracted' basis, such as through the media.
- Similarly, though—even when we are not totally aware of it—we help to reshape the already existing relationships and practices we encounter.

The complex relations between the 'inner' and the 'outer' elements of self are fully on display when we consider the way all of us think about and deal with particular groups of people on the basis of the way they look or behave. We have argued that identity depends in part on the way identity markers to do with physical appearance or social status are used to construct understandings and expectations about whole groups of people. Sometimes this can be a relatively benign or minor matter, with few serious consequences. Sometimes, however, it can have deeply troubling consequences for large numbers of people. This can be the case when we turn to the way we use the markers of age in relation to children and young people. In this context, families provide a key figuration. In Chapter 7 we look at families in Australia.

Discussion questions

6.1 Which identity markers do you think are most important for knowing and talking about your self? Are these different from the markers you might use to discuss other people?

6.2 How valid are arguments that society, through the socialisation process, creates or shapes the individual?

6.3 Do you think people who lived in Rome 2000 years ago were very different from people who now live in Australia?

6.4 How much agency do you think you currently possess? Who or what constrains your agency?

The life I share with my partner of 10 years, and our two children is so joyous —what with all the love and support— that sometimes I forget that I am actively discriminated against by our Government. So it's most helpful that Philip Ruddock's [Attorney-General's] department has instigated the change to wedding ceremonies that now makes sure I will be reminded that 'marriage is the union of a man and woman' (The Age (7/1/2006) and not for people like us. Thanks Phil.

—Letter to The Age 9 January 2006—

OURSELVES IN FAMILIES 7.

● ● SUMMARY

How Australians make families in a context of far-reaching change has become a hot issue. Because how we think about things makes a difference, we explore some of the ways we can think about families. Is there only one kind of family? How do people form families? How crucial is the family? We examine critically some of the answers to these questions as well as make suggestions of our own. We then turn to the widespread belief, in a time characterised by ideas like 'globalisation' and 'restructuring', that the family is in trouble—maybe even dead. Is the family dead or dying? To address this question, we ask whether there was ever a time when the traditional family was alive and well.

In Australia, families have always mattered. The significance of families has both a rich personal dimension and a very intense public quality.

Families matter to us personally because each one of us has connections to some kind of family. We all have a biological father and mother. Many—though not all of us—grew up in close proximity to our mother and/or father. This is so even though the rate of divorce since 1975 has meant the creation of many 'step-families' and 'blended families'. Although there has been a long-term historical trend over the last 200 years for families to be smaller, many of us have brothers and sisters, aunts and uncles, grandparents and occasionally great-grandparents. With the growth in step- and blended families, many of us also have half-brothers and half-sisters, step-parents, step-siblings and double sets of grandparents.

Many people enjoy being in families, and we spend large amounts of time in them. Australians live much of their private lives in families—eating, sleeping, talking, gardening, watching TV and relaxing at home (Hartley & McDonald 1994: 6; Bryson et al. 1997). Inside families, we experience some of our strongest emotions. These feelings range from love and tenderness through jealousy to murderous rage. Families are supposed to protect and nourish us emotionally, physically and spiritually when we are young and vulnerable. However, many people—especially children and women—are abused sexually, physically or emotionally, and the majority of murders occur inside familes. As McDonald (1994: 4) writes: 'Nothing in our society brings greater joy than being part of a happy, supportive family; nothing in our society brings greater devastation than being part of a family that is destructive of the individual personalities of its members.'

Equally, nothing expresses the public mood of contemporary anxiety as much as the controversies that swirl about modern families. Ideas about 'family values' matter deeply in the arguments that make up what some commentators call the 'culture wars' waged between conservatives and progressives. The fact that there is an ever-expanding industry of experts on the family, including social workers, psychologists, lawyers, counsellors, doctors and teachers, has helped to keep the debate about the modern family alive.

It is not surprising, then, that families are one of the most controversial of all social institutions (Gilding 1997). The political significance of families has become a prominent feature of modern Australian politics. Since July 2005, Senator Steve Fielding has represented a Christian party in the Senate calling itself Family First. There is also intense public discussion about the consequences of putting infants into long-term child care.

Some of this debate has followed the move to locate homosexual and lesbian sexuality in the mainstream. Since the 1990s, gay activist members of the Rainbow Sash movement have publicly protested against the Catholic Church ban on gays taking Holy Communion. Having successfully advocated to decriminalise homosexual activity—Tasmania was the last state to do so in 2000—a variety of gay and lesbian groups have created a great deal of momentum and public discussion as they pursue the right to same-sex civil unions—or marriage.

As well as heat, a degree of paradox shadows the debates that rage about modern family life. In the 1970s, feminist and Gay Lib activists developed pungent critiques of patriarchal marriage and family forms. Equally, Christian groups like Women Who Want to be Women or the Australian Family Values Association defended marriage and family life. Today, gay and lesbian activists defend their right to form families, and children and even get married. There is also evidence that gay and lesbian couples are using IVF technologies to have biological children of their own. The same Christian groups that once defended family values and marriage have now become much more discriminating, suggesting that only heterosexual couples have a right to marry or to establish families. The same 'pro-family' groups have been campaigning for a restoration of 'traditional family values' and the right of children to be cared for at home by their mothers.

Governments and policy-makers are being forced to address new kinds of issues, partly arising out of this pressure to change public opinion and partly because of what new technologies like in-vitro fertilisation (IVF) techniques have made possible. One recent case that unfolded in 2002 catches the novelty of the times.

In 2002 a lesbian police officer (Haley) wanted to have a baby with her partner (Joy). The problem was that the *Infertility Treatment Act* did not permit single women or lesbians the right to access the IVF program. So Haley and her male friend (Mark), who was also gay and a policeman, presented to an IVF program as a married couple and were subsequently successful in Haley getting pregnant. They had a son. They were subsequently brought to court charged with providing false information to the IVF program, but the magistrate in the Melbourne Magistrates Court dismissed the charges.

Human rights groups and feminists supported the arguments of this young lesbian couple about their right to access the IVF program. They attacked the inequity of the IVF legislation, pointing out—rightly—that it contravened the *Equal Opportunity Act*, which prohibits any discrimination in the provision of services like health care, banking services or education on the grounds of marital status or sexual orientation. There were also arguments mounted that gay or lesbian couples were just as able to parent effectively as 'straight' parents. Conversely, Catholic conservatives like Bill Muehlenberg, a spokesperson for the Australian Family Association, argued that the risk of child sexual abuse doubled in families lacking the biological father, and that a child needed both biological parents to achieve emotional health and independence.

The historical ironies in these arguments are striking. In the 1970s, lesbian feminists were busily attacking marriage and the family as patriarchal instruments of oppression. Now they are busily defending the right of lesbians to marry and form families by having children and raising them. In effect, they have become passionate defenders of the principles of marriage and families. Equally, the conservatives who were busily defending marriage and children in the 1970s are now only half-hearted defenders of marriage. They now say that only certain people (heterosexuals) should have the right to have families, and that not everyone has a right to marry or to have children.

Subsequently the right of gay and lesbian couples to access IVF treatment has been confirmed. The same IVF treatment has led to no less complex policy debates about the right of children who are the product of sperm donors to know who the biological father is, and to have access to them at a later stage in their life.

In short, the family is controversial today. The debates about the modern family are one aspect of the economic, social and political changes that have become increasingly apparent over the past 25 years, and which we use the word 'globalisation' to name. So how should we think about all of this controversy?

● THINKING ANALYTICALLY ABOUT THE CONTROVERSY

It is clear that much of the debate about modern family life reflects the effort made by conservatives, who have energised the discussion by claiming the 'traditional family' is dead or dying. Let us take this idea seriously and apply the kind of analytic approach we outlined in Chapter 2 to thinking about sociological arguments. We can do this best by posing one research question and then systematically looking at the assumptions and the role played by values in shaping such a claim, as well as looking to the kinds of evidence that we might need to examine.

The question we can purse is simply framed: is the 'traditional family' dead or dying? Framing such a question depends on a number of assumptions, the most obvious being that there once was a time when the 'traditional family' model dominated. As we will see, there is a presumption made by many who are caught up in the 'war over the family' that there once was such a traditional family form called the 'nuclear family'—a family made up of a heterosexual couple called mum and dad and their children.

Coming to terms with this research question means asking other questions like:

- Is there or was there ever a 'traditional family' form or model?
- How universal or popular was the 'nuclear family' of mum, dad and the kids?
- Do families have social 'functions' to fulfil and how useful is it to talk in these terms?
- Do patterns of growing childlessness, increasing numbers of unmarried couples and childless couples or rising divorce rates spell the end of 'the traditional family'?

● THE FAMILY: NUCLEAR AND UNIVERSAL?

When people talk about the 'modern family', they usually do so in terms of something called the 'nuclear family'. The word 'nuclear' suggests that the family is an atom or a basic building block of society (see box).

The nuclear family

The 'nuclear family' is usually defined as a family where:

- there are no more than two generations living under the one roof (i.e. parents and children);
- the mother and father are married;
- the adults have a sexual relationship based on affection;
- the children are the biological products of the two parents. This means there is a genetic connection between parents and children, and between the children as siblings;
- the children are dependent, passing through infancy, childhood and adolescence until they leave the home to establish another nuclear family of their own; and
- the family stays together, at least until the children reach maturity and independence.

One of the major reasons why the 'nuclear family' model has achieved some kind of popularity has to do with the work of a famous social scientist called George P. Murdock. Over half a century ago, Murdock (1949) did a study of some 250 societies around the world. In that study, Murdock (1949: 2) claimed that: 'The nuclear family is a universal human social grouping . . . and exists as a distinct and strongly functional group in every known society.' Central to Murdock's account of the nuclear family is the idea that 'the family' has certain functions to fulfil. Murdock's use of the concept 'function' points to his place in the structural functionalist tradition. Murdock writes about the nuclear family as 'a strongly functional group in every known society' (1949: 2). Much of the modern anxiety about families begins with this belief that families have a vital function in society, associated with the reproduction of society and the socialisation of children.

● FUNCTIONS OF THE FAMILY

The idea of function is a key concept in the structural functionalist sociological tradition. It implies that people and institutions exist only because society needs them for its survival and health. It derives from the work of nineteenth century sociologists like Comte, Spencer and Durkheim, who relied on metaphors taken directly from biology and physiology (Canguilhem 1990).

Murdock was a functionalist in this tradition. He claimed that the family existed because it fulfilled four functions for 'society' (see box). (Note that this makes the family the creation of society and not of people.) Whenever we confront large generalisations or stereotypes like these, we need to ask whether there is evidence to support them. Do all families, across the globe, live out these ideas and do these things? And what sense, if any, is there to the idea of functionality?

Functions of the nuclear family

- **Sexual function.** The family organises and channels sexual activity in ways that promote an ordered, well-behaved society. This was said to be functionally good because, if people were able to have sex whenever they wanted, chaos and anarchy would follow.

- **Reproductive function.** A society needs to ensure there are enough children to carry on the society, so the family assists society to reproduce itself and so survive over time.

- **Educational function.** The family is the institution where infants and children are socialised, or taught what to think and how to behave in socially approved ways.

- **Economic function.** The family is socially useful because it promotes the sexual division of labour. The woman (as wife and mother) does unpaid domestic labour, including child-rearing, while the man (as husband and father) goes out of the household to hunt for food or work for wages. Economic cooperation works best between people who habitually live together. It also guarantees the economic functioning of an entire society.

● PROBLEMS WITH MURDOCK

There are any number of problems with Murdock's argument, particularly his core claim that the 'nuclear family' was or is universal. First, he ignored evidence of the many times and places where families did not conform to his model. In Australia, Aboriginal communities exhibit very different patterns of family formation, with an obvious preference for quite extended family patterns and far larger average household sizes than is common among non-Aboriginal families. Adams (1960) points out that many families in Central and South American societies do not include a regularly resident male father figure—a feature also of many modern Afro-American families. In many communities in Micronesia, men live apart from the women and children in large communal huts. In Muslim societies, some men—providing they can afford it—lawfully have numerous wives and children by them all. Murdock's insistence on the universality of the nuclear family disguises the actual diversity of family forms. As Fox (1967) explains, the alleged universality of the nuclear family can be sustained only if you are prepared to ignore the many exceptions which exist.

Second, there are numerous examples of families simply failing to exhibit the functions Murdock ascribes to the nuclear family. In Gough's (1967) study of the historic pattern of family life in Kerala in southern India, men did not economically support their wives—nor did they acknowledge or support their offspring. Moreover, men and women routinely had numerous sexual relationships. Among the Nayar, it was important only that a man (any man) would claim to be a child's father.

Third, Murdock's portrait of the family overstates the positive aspects of the nuclear family. As David Morgan (1975: 21) points out wryly: 'Murdock's nuclear family is a remarkably harmonious institution. Husband and wife have an integrated division of labour and have a good time in bed.' Morgan is suggesting that Murdock's picture bears little relationship to the lived reality of many people. We would be hard pressed to find a time in the last thousand years of European history when family life actually conformed to the idealised narrative about nuclear or traditional families. As John Boswell (1990) points out, one of the standard ways European families limited their family size between 1000 CE and the late eighteenth century was to abandon unwanted babies at special places where other people could adopt these children. Even more interesting is Boswell's (1994) discovery of incontrovertible evidence that both the Catholic and Orthodox churches had liturgical means of recognising same-sex unions, and that same-sex couples took advantage of this up until about the twelfth century when these churches outlawed same-sex unions.

On the larger question of how marriage has been constructed, we know that the idea of couples marrying 'for love' is a relatively recent innovation. Amongst Europe's elite families across the last 1000 years, and until quite recently, marriages were arranged affairs designed to secure the transmission of property or to build political alliances. If members of these families wanted love or sex, they took mistresses or lovers—rather in the way Prince Charles handled his marriage to Princess Diana. Among the 'lower orders', many unions never received the blessing of church or civil law. Thomas Hardy's novel *Tess of the D'Urbervilles* reminds us of how, in the early nineteenth century, men in rural England would take a wife they no longer wanted to the local market and sell her! Third, the very high death rates associated with childbirth meant that many husbands routinely married many times, and that 'blended families' were common. Factors like these suggest the 'good old days' were not as 'traditional' as some conservatives would like us to believe.

Murdock's work is a good example of how some people generalise about (or essentialise) the family. They assume that there is just one set of relationships and activities that identifies or defines the family. Margrit Eichler (1983: 1) has called this the 'monolithic family' myth. She has this to say:

> If we free ourselves from the monolithic notion that families have a particular structure and instead operate on the assumption that the structure of families is (and always has been) fluid, there is no reason to concern ourselves with the thought of the 'death of the family'. At the same time there is also no need to downplay the importance of the changes that have already taken place and that continue to take place. (1983: 26)

The claim that there is only one pattern of attributes that define the Australian family is a considerable stumbling block to thinking about issues like marriage, divorce, sex, children and caring for people. More generally, 'essentialism' inhibits good careful thinking.

● MODERN AUSTRALIAN FAMILIES

Many Australians probably subscribe to Eichler's monolithic family myth. This means they will believe some, or all, of the following propositions:

- If a man and woman marry, they do so because they fall in love and will eventually have children.
- If children are present in the family, they are/ought to be the biological—or legally adopted—children of the couple.
- Both parents are/ought to be involved in raising and socialising the children, with the woman playing the key child-care role.
- The two adults have sex only with each other (not with other partners, and certainly not with their children), and the children do not have sex with each other.
- All the members of the family live together in the one residence, and there is one household economy.
- Family relations are characterised by mutually supportive, warm and close emotional relations.

Those who advocate this monolithic family model seem to forget that Australian families do not look a lot like this.

The idea of family has numerous meanings and resonances that are embedded in our cultural, religious and linguistic history. When we speak of the family, we refer to relationships that are 'familiar' (as in 'close' and 'well known'). The word *familia* in Latin literally meant 'household', and included everybody who lived under a very large roof. The word *familius* actually referred to a 'servant'. It is useful to remember that in 1545, when the English word 'family' began to get a lot of use, it meant 'the group consisting of parents and their children, other relatives, servants, etc.'

If we turn to the modern context in Australia and use the evidence gathered by the Australian Bureau of Statistics (ABS), we will see that modern families include a wide array of living arrangements and relationships, including:

- married 'heterosexual' couples and their child or children;
- married and unmarried couples with adult children—between 1986 and 2005, the proportion of 20–24-year-olds living at home increased from 42 per cent to 49 per cent (ABS 2005b: 39);
- blended families;
- sole-parent families;
- childless couples, or those whose children have left home;
- single persons;
- lesbian and gay couples (married and not married and with and without children).

It is this diversity that has led to sociologists like Aspin (1987: 16) opting for a wide-ranging definition of the family as a group of:

- at least two members, comprising either two adults or one adult and one child, or one adult living apart from the family group, but regarding the group as his or her family;
- members related to each other through marriage, blood ties, adoption or interaction; and
- members with certain positions and undertaking the roles expected of them.

Likewise, the National Council for the International Year of the Family (Cass et al. 1994: 7) made the same point in its definition of the family, which included:

two parents with dependent and older children, sole parent families, step-families, blended families, siblings caring for each other, spouse/partners caring for each other, networks of relatives extending well beyond the household, families caring for elderly members and those with a disability, families whose structures and relationships may differ according to race, ethnicity, religious faith and cultural background.

Using the most recent (2001) Census data available, we find that, at the start of the twenty-first century:

- There has been a modest increase in the number of couple families from 1982, when they made up 28.7 per cent of families to 2001, when they made up 35.6 per cent of all families (de Vaus 2005: 1). Of these couples, 43.25 per cent had no children living with them—up from 1982, when 37 per cent had no children living with them. (This is largely a result of the ageing process, as many of the couples are older people whose children have left home.)

- The tendency to avoid marriage has become a relatively strong trend, though the marriage rate goes up and down from year to year. In 2001, some 72 per cent of people lived with their partner prior to some more formal marriage arrangement.

- Couple families with children are a minority of Australian households, families and couple families. They represent a declining percentage of families, amounting to a 20 per cent decline between 1976 and 2001 (de Vaus 2005: 1). Equally, of couple families with children, 90 per cent are in a family with both parents, while 5.5 per cent are in step-families and 4.4 per cent are in blended families.

- Sole-parent families are increasing. There was a big growth in this kind of family from 1966, when they made up 7.1 per cent of families, to 2001, when they made up 22.6 per cent of families (de Vaus 2005: 2). The vast majority of these families— around 89 per cent—are headed by women.

- While it is difficult to get a tight grip on the divorce rate, de Vaus (2005: 2) estimates that between 32 and 46 per cent of marriages in existence in 2001 will end in divorce. Of divorces in 2001, some 51 per cent involved a child or children under eighteen— down from 1971 when 67.5 per cent of divorces affected a child or children under eighteen.

- There has also been a big increase in the number of people living by themselves. In 2001, 25 per cent of households comprised people living alone (de Vaus 2005: 2).

- For all of the anxiety about same-sex couples in 2001, they only represented a small minority—around 0.55 per cent of household couples.

- Likewise, for all of the discussion and anxiety about the ethical consequences of IVF technology, fewer than 2 per cent of all births in 2001 were a consequence of IVF technology (de Vaus 2005: 2).

While this is a highly selective snapshot of families and households in 2001, it points to considerable diversity in the way Australians now live.

● DEATH OF THE FAMILY?

There is considerable contemporary anxiety about the death or breakdown of the family. This anxiety usually involves several claims:

- Claim 1: Factors like increasing divorce, sole-parent households or childlessness are dangerous anti-family trends.
- Claim 2: Family life is under threat, in particular because women are 'selfish' and are neglecting their 'traditional' roles and 'natural' responsibility to care for their husband and children.
- The assumption underpinning these claims is that 'the family' was historically a static entity and that it was part of the 'good old days' when everyone knew their place and had a place. There was no divorce or illegitimacy, and everyone lived 'happily ever after'. According to this story, in the mid-1970s the good old days ended and the 'nuclear family' went into crisis.

There are a number of assumptions that need to be carefully checked before we can accept or reject this story of the decline—or death—of the family. One has to do with the historical assumption that 'once upon a time' the traditional or nuclear family was the dominant norm. For the 'death of the family' story to be convincing, we would need to find a time in Australia's white history when the 'nuclear family' and 'traditional family values' were alive and well.

● THE NUCLEAR FAMILY IN AUSTRALIAN HISTORY

There are some peculiar patterns in Australia's history that mean we should not expect to find a stable 'traditional' or 'nuclear' family pattern. The only time the modern 'nuclear family' was dominant was in the period from the late 1940s to the 1970s. However, this may suggest why Australians who remember this time believe that a far longer chapter of history has come crashing to an end.

First, we need to remember that the pre-white invasion period was dominated by complex, highly intricate Aboriginal family forms. These family forms exhibited complex totemic and linguistic systems for defining and managing sexual and relational identities. As Alison Palmer (2000) shows, Aboriginal families bore the brunt of colonial dispossession in colonies like Queensland as the white invaders gained a foothold over the land and systematically evicted the Indigenous people from their land. This process followed a demographic catastrophe typical of many European colonising processes, as Indigenous peoples were wiped out by European diseases and the survivors of that mopped up by policing and military operations.

Second, it is hard to find a period in Australia's white history (i.e. between 1788 and the start of the twenty-first century) when family life conformed to an idealised image of the nuclear family. Rather, we see persistent evidence of significant historical disruptions and changing patterns in family formation.

Australia, like many other societies settled by European immigration and exhibiting the features of a colonial economy, had more men than women for a long time. Robert Hughes

(1986) gleefully points out the implications of this for thinking about homosexuality in Australia's colonial history! In contrast, in 2006, women make up slightly more than 50 per cent of the total population (ABS 2006b: 6). In the convict period (roughly from 1788–1858), convict men were housed in dormitories or on household farms as servants, while free men lived in boarding houses and hotels. This pattern also produced very large households, averaging around ten persons—roughly twice the size of British households at this time. The later history of the Australian colonies was punctuated by disruptive economic depressions, wars and gold-rushes, all of which had major effects on family formation.

With the gold-rushes (1851–65 and the 1890s) came an influx of men into Australia, and a considerable amount of internal migration as men chased the latest gold discoveries. This meant the separation of many families as fathers/husbands went off to the goldfields. The consequences of these kinds of events on the way people formed relationships and established families were striking, as Peter McDonald (1988) found.

Families in Victoria in the 1880s

McDonald's (1988) research on late nineteenth century families in Victoria discovered that households were larger than they are now, and that nuclear families (i.e. mother, father and children) comprised just over half of all households. He also found that there was considerable complexity in the family arrangements (see box). It was not unusual to have one or more aunts, grandparents and cousins living in the same household as the parents and children.

Victorian families in the late nineteenth century

- There were 224 000 occupied dwellings with a total of 1 130 000 people, or 5.04 persons per household.
- Of this total, over 503 000 persons formed a nuclear family setting.
- There were five primary kinds of family unit:
    - Type 1: 160 000 families of two adults plus 343 000 children (aged one to fifteen);
    - Type 2: 20 000 widowed women plus 30 000 children (aged one to fifteen);
    - Type 3: 12 000 widowed men with 17 000 children (aged one to fifteen);
    - Type 4: 14 000 childless couples;
    - Type 5: 18 000 single-person households.

There were also:

- 3000 orphans;
- 151 000 never-married males aged fifteen to 30;
- 120 000 never-married women aged fifteen to 30;

- 50 000 men aged 30+;

- 20 000 females aged 30+; and

- 22 000 widowed men and women.

All of these were scattered among the first four basic types of household. We know 18 000 individuals formed a single-person household and the remainder (346 000) were distributed among the other household types. These were presumably older children, aunts, uncles, cousins, nieces and nephews linked to one of the four basic types. The 'nuclear family' was an important style of family, but it was not the only family form in late nineteenth century Australia.

In the twentieth century, major destructive events like wars and economic crises have continued to disrupt families. Two world wars meant many men departed for military service, leaving women at home or at work in the paid labour market. Many men never returned, or if they survived the killing fields they came back with their health shattered: Australia lost 60 000 men in 1914–18 alone. More recently, smaller wars like Korea and Vietnam saw husbands and sons go overseas for years at a time to be killed, wounded or imprisoned. Two great economic depressions (1890s–1910 and the 1930s Great Depression) saw the birth rate plummet and families break up as men went away for extended periods in search of work.

Only in the years from 1945 to 1975 do we see a flowering of the modern, stable nuclear family. As John Murphy (2000: 20–30) shows, the marriage rate increased after 1945 (when it was 160 per 1000 eligible population) to peak at 240 per 1000 population in 1970. This affirmation of family life took place in a context of considerable postwar political and international insecurity, and dramatic economic change.

The social experience of marriage in these years after 1945 became ubiquitous, and formed the demographic foundation for widespread representations of domesticity in popular magazines and in political rhetoric. This marriage boom meant men and women made substantial investments—both emotional and material—in the idea of domesticity and family life. However, the flood of divorces which began with the passage of the no-fault clause in the new *Family Law Act* 1975 suggested that, for a significant number of Australians, that investment had not paid off.

So far, we have explored the worth of the assumption that the traditional or nuclear family has actually been the dominant long-term form taken by Australian families. This was true for only a relatively short period of time. If we turn to our own time, what does the evidence about things like the rates at which people get married or divorce or have children suggest? How do we best make sense of the contemporary evidence about our living arrangements?

● CONTEMPORARY TRENDS

We have seen that at the start of the twenty-first century the most common form of family is still the two-parent-plus-dependent-child-or-children family—though it must be noted that this now only accounts for less than a third of all families. This is followed by couples without children, who make up almost another third of families. Then there is a small but increasingly significant number of sole-parent families. There has been a big increase in the number of people living alone.

How should we understand this pattern?

First, we need to understand that the statistics reflect a lot of inevitable—even natural—changes in the way people live. Hartley and McDonald (1994) argue for a 'families in transition' model, reminding us that all families have their own histories. They suggest (1994: 6–19) these are not totally distinct families, but are snapshots of people and families at different stages of their lives.

That is, each of us has a history, and each family has its own specific history of change. Some changes have to do with the fact that people grow up, leave home or get older. Other changes relate to the choices people make. Many sole-parent families were once two-parent families. Many couples without children have either had children or will have them in the future. Families take on new shapes as they become smaller or bigger.

Second, it is clear that there are also some fundamental changes going on—like the reduction in the average number of children each woman now has and the propensity to marry or to divorce.

● DECLINING FERTILITY RATES

There has been a long-term decline in the numbers of children born to women—or what is called the 'fertility rate'. This is the number of live births per 1000 women in any one year. The average size of households and families has been shrinking for over 200 years. Between the gold-rush period (1851–65) and World War I, the average household size was about five persons; by the 1980s, this had declined to around three persons. This, as Snooks (1994) points out, is 'part of the first major change in average household size in Western society in 1000 years', the importance of which 'cannot be overestimated' (1994: 66).

On average women are having fewer children. In the 1860s the rate was over six live births per woman. Accompanying the sharp rise in marriage numbers after 1945 was a sharp rise in the fertility rate (3.6 births per woman); however, this rise did not last, and there was a subsequent sharp downward trend in the birth rate. In 1988 the fertility rate i.e. children per woman was 1.84 and by 1999 it was 1.76 (ABS 2006b: 29). This shift began in the 1960s with the development and use of the birth control pill, which coincided with a shift towards smaller families and married women getting jobs.

By 2001, the fertility rate per woman was 1.75—not enough to replace the population. The only thing that is currently stopping the Australian population actually shrinking is immigration. Caldwell and Ruzicka (1978: 95) noted some time ago that fertility rates were declining. That decline is shown in Table 7.1.

Table 7.1 Fertility rates 1861–1996

Year	Fertility rate
1861	6
1881	5
1901	4
1925	3
1960	3.5
1975	2
1996	1.8

The fertility rate is the number of live births per 1000 women in the year nominated; thus, in 1861 there were six live births per 1000 of population.
These figures only cover the non-Aboriginal population. As is well known, Aboriginal Australians now have a very high fertility rate.
Source: ABS (1997d).

Women are also having their children later in life. In 1971, 66 per cent of married women gave birth to their first child before age 25. In 1994, only 22 per cent of women under 25 had a child. In the 1990s, about 33 per cent of women had their first child after their thirtieth birthday, while over 40 per cent of all women giving birth were now over 30.

• THE DECISION TO MARRY AND DIVORCE

It is also the case that, at the start of the twenty-first century, many more Australians than ever before are likely to experience major changes in their family relationships. Since the 1970s, more Australians have either delayed getting married or avoided it altogether. Many people move through cycles of marriage, divorce and remarriage.

While marriage remains popular, there are many more people in de facto relationships. Many younger people are living together, and seem to be approaching marriage with more caution. In 1975, only 15 per cent of people lived together before marriage. At the beginning of the 1990s, Callan and Noller (1991) argued that younger Australians were uncertain—even suspicious—about marriage. In 1991, about 8.2 per cent of all couples were in de facto relationships. By the 1990s, over 60 per cent of couples who married had lived together first, and by 2005 that rate had risen to 76 per cent. In the decade between 1984 and 1994, the percentage of births outside marriage rose from 14.8 per cent of all births to 25.6 per cent (ABS 1996b: 30). More people are marrying later than at any time since the 1940s.

In the 1930s, around 30 per cent of women in their twenties had married. In the years just after World War II, people married younger than at any previous time. Now, at the beginning of the twenty-first century, marriage is being delayed significantly. In 2005, the largest number of people getting married were in the 25–29 years age group, and the median age for men and women marrying for the first time has steadily risen to 29.2 for men and 27.2 for women in 2005 (ABS 2005b: 29).

What of the divorce rate—the key kind of evidence for the 'death of the family' pointed to by conservatives? Here the evidence is ambiguous. The divorce rate has retreated from its high point in the years immediately after the introduction of the *Family Law Act* 1975. But the divorce rate remains higher than at any point before the 1970s. Indeed, Australia recorded its highest number of divorces ever in 2001, when some 55 300 divorces were recorded.

As Table 7.2 shows, the *Family Law Act* had its most dramatic impact between 1975 and 1980 (when upwards of 60 000 divorces were being granted annually). Since then, divorce rates have stabilised.

Table 7.2 Australian divorce rates (per 1000 currently married)

Year	Men	Women
1976	18.9	18.8
1984	11.9	11.9
1989	10.8	10.7
1994	12.0	12.0
1999	12.7	12.7
2001	13.1	13.1
2005	13.2	13.1

Source: ABS (2005d: 3).

To summarise the statistics:

- Some 5 per cent of marriages end in divorce within five years.
- Around 17 per cent of marriages end in divorce within ten years.
- Approximately 28 per cent of marriages end in divorce within twenty years.
- Some 37 per cent of marriages end in divorce within 30 years.

In the first decade of the twenty-first century, many couples with children will experience parental separation or divorce. Just over a half (52 per cent) of marriages will last more than 30 years. In other words, about 48 per cent of married couples will divorce. The high divorce rate means a big increase in blended families and sole-parent families.

Blended families and step-families are becoming more common. In 2005, around 8 per cent of couple-plus-children families had step-children from a previous family. In other words, some 450 000 children and young people live in step- or blended families.

Sole-parent families

There is also a significant increase in the number of sole-parent families. However—and contrary to what many talkback radio hosts believe—most sole parents are not teenagers who got pregnant. (Only 3 per cent of sole parents are teenagers who have never been married.) Most sole parents are between 25 and 49 years old, and most became sole parents following a separation, death or divorce. There are many more sole parents who are single because their partner has died (11 per cent) than there are teenage mums.

In recent years, sole parents—especially single mothers—have received a lot of bad press. It is suggested that some women deliberately get pregnant so they can receive government income security, while critics argue that households without a male upset the natural order and place the children at risk of anti-social activities such as delinquency. While it is true that levels of poverty are high amongst sole-parent households, many of the stereotypes generated about sole parents are misleading and harmful. Such stereotyping can lead to damaging and dangerous practices, as Jane, a 39-year-old single mother of two, tells (see box).

Jane's story

When I went for my last job interview, halfway through it the bloke said: 'I see you're not married.' I knew he wasn't supposed to make those kind of comments, but what could I say? I felt so angry with him, and I knew exactly what he was getting at. He pretended to be on my side, saying that he knew what it was like having young children because he and his wife had to run around after theirs. I thought to myself, 'You bastard, I bet I work twice as hard as you and your wife.' He then asked what would happen on the school holidays or when one of the kids got sick. So I said they'd go to their grandmother's, which was a complete lie because the grandmothers on both sides live interstate. All he was worried about was whether I might have to take time off work to look after the kids—all that for $10 an hour.

The other thing I noticed when I separated from Greg was that I stopped being invited to people's places for dinner. When I was married we were always going to people's homes. I also noticed that when John [a single father] was on his own he seemed to get asked for dinner so often. I think people feel sorry for men on their own and want to help out, look after the kids, provide meals or invite them around for dinner. If you're a single mum it's a completely different story. People seem to think there's something wrong with you. There's this idea that you're bad or immoral in some way. And there is this incredible fear that you're going to run off with the husbands. I can't remember the last time I was asked out to someone's place for dinner.

• EXPLAINING CHANGES IN 'THE FAMILY'

There are at least two key factors that have helped to reshape modern families:

- changes in women's identity, producing changes in the sexual division of labour, most notably leading to increased numbers of married women entering the paid workforce; and
- more reliable forms of birth control, enabling women to control their own fertility.

Changes in women's identity

One important reason for new family arrangements is the change that has occurred in the way women have redefined their identity as women, daughters, wives/partners and mothers. Fuelled by any number of factors, including the feminist movement from the 1960s on, the redefinition of women's identity has produced some major changes in the sexual division of labour.

Sexual division of labour

The sexual division of labour refers to the idea that there is—or ought to be—a difference between men's and women's work based on the characteristics said to define 'masculinity' and 'femininity'.

A long-standing sociological theory—relying on structural functionalist assumptions—suggests that society lays down a template or a matrix of what it means to be feminine or masculine, to which members of each gender are expected to conform. Sociologists traditionally have called this the sex-role model. Whatever the validity of this structuralist view of sex roles, there can be little doubt that something very important has happened in women's relationship to the labour market.

It must be noted that the key change is *not* about more women entering paid employment. Australian women have been involved in the labour market through the twentieth century. In 1966, about 50 per cent of all women were in the paid workforce. By 2005, the female participation rate was 53.9 per cent (ABS 2006b: 108). However, the fact that women have long enjoyed significant access to paid work does *not* mean they have been treated fairly as workers: women have never been paid as much as men; they have always been more vulnerable to unemployment; and they have mostly done part-time and casual jobs.

What has changed is the number of *married* women in the workforce (Probert 1997). Since the 1970s, growing numbers of married women have entered the labour market. In 1947, only 6.5 per cent of married women were in the labour force. By 1966, approximately 29 per cent of married women were working full- or part-time. By 2000, this rate had nearly doubled with around 56 per cent of married women in the labour force. Married women aged 20–24 had the highest labour force participation rate. In 2005, over two-thirds of women in couples who were also mothers were in the labour force, compared with some 30 per cent of women who were sole parents.

The household division of labour

The fact that there are now more married women (with dependent children) in the paid workforce seems to have produced little, if any, change in the division of labour inside the family unit. While many women (and some men) say they support more equality in the home, there is little evidence of any significant change in the number of men actually doing more housework or child care (Bittman & Pixley 1997). Many men still think it is enough to 'help out' around the house rather than assume fundamental responsibility for the housework or for child care. Similarly, many women still believe it is their responsibility to organise the house, cook, clean and look after the children—as well as doing paid work.

Good evidence about who does what in terms of child care and housework comes out of time-budget surveys of domestic work. These surveys show that, in single (male) income-earning families, the average time spent by fathers on child care is six minutes a day. Men do the same amount of child care and domestic work in dual income-earning families. Table 7.3 offers one summary of research on the division of labour.

Women do approximately 90 per cent of child-care tasks and 70 per cent of all family work. Bittman (1991) found that Australian women did 70 per cent of the unpaid domestic work and spent 36 hours a week on domestic work while men put in about 14.5 hours of unpaid work.

Where both partners work for an income, research shows that women make more adjustments in juggling both paid and unpaid work than their male partners. For example, women work less overtime and spend more time looking after children when they are sick. Women are also less likely than men to be in positions where they are required to shift interstate or overseas with their jobs and expect the family to follow.

Given that there are many households where one or both parents engage in full-time paid work, how does the time and energy given to work outside the home affect family relations? As recent research (Gilding 1997; Bittman & Pixley 1997) suggests, there appear to be more tensions in households as parents try to keep down a job and still have time to pick the children up from school (or after-school care), help them with homework and get them to netball and basketball training, as well as just spend time with them.

Table 7.3 Division of labour in a range of household tasks by workforce status (married couples only)

Housework type	Wife not in paid work	Wife in part-time work	Wife in full-time work	All couples (%)
1. Laundry				
Husband more	1	2	7	3
Equal	5	5	16	9
Wife more	94	93	77	88
2. Cleaning bathroom				
Husband more	3	3	9	5
Equal	7	7	11	5
Wife more	90	90	80	86
3. Cooking evening meal				
Husband more	3	4	10	6
Equal	8	12	19	13
Wife more	89	84	71	81
4. Doing dishes				
Husband more	6	8	12	19
Equal	23	30	32	28
Wife more	71	62	56	63
5. Taking out garbage				
Husband more	51	54	60	55
Equal	24	28	24	25
Wife more	25	18	16	20
6. Taking children to appointments				
Husband more	5	4	7	5
Equal	30	31	47	35
Wife more	65	65	46	60

Source: Glezer (1991: 10).

More women are seeking greater equality in terms of access to economic resources and decision-making in their lives. Spender (1980) points to one important consequence of changes to women's identities: women now outnumber men in initiating divorce proceedings. These changes in women's capacity to define their own lives have been complemented by dramatic changes in their capacity to control their fertility.

Increasing control by women over their fertility

Historically, women had little control about when they became pregnant. Average rates of between thirteen and sixteen pregnancies per woman until the nineteenth century reflected the relatively poor contraception technology then available. Unreliable birth control techniques were overlaid with powerful ideas about God's will and 'the rights' of men, while the fact that other women also had large families provided added pressure to conceive as often as possible. Only in the early 1960s did relatively effective means of controlling fertility become widely available to women in the form of the birth control pill.

Since then, more freely available contraception—including the widespread advertising of condoms, which was illegal until the 1970s—plus the growing availability of legal abortion have given women more control over pregnancies than ever. They now have the ability to choose when or whether to have children, and to limit the number of pregnancies. Declining birth rates and a big increase in the number of married women in paid employment indicate the choice many women now want to make.

● CONCLUSION

Sometimes popular ideas or expectations about families become confused with the way things actually are. As Robinson and Watson (1995: 5) put it: 'As a society, we expect the family to nurture, to protect, guide and provide refuge for all its members; we believe that a happy family is the basis of a good life and a strong nation.' Many cultural pessimists talk about the 'death' or 'breakdown' of the family (Eckersley 1993: 10–11). They also point to the rise of 'dysfunctional' families—by which they mean sole parents, divorced parents, alcoholic parents, homosexuals, mentally ill parents, delinquent children, and so on (Ochiltree 1990). Ironically, 'traditional' nuclear families with an authoritarian father-husband who does paid work while the wife-mother stays at home may no longer be very 'functional'; instead, non-traditional families with a working wife-mother may be highly functional.

Contemporary concerns that the 'nuclear family' is dying depend to a large extent on the assumption that a strong and healthy family—sometimes referred to as a 'functional' family—has long been the basis of social order, morality and even civilisation itself. Much of today's conservative framing of a story of decline depends on a cultural pessimism that in turn relies on the mistaken belief that we once had 'real' families living 'real' (i.e. 'traditional') family values. This assumption ignores the complex history of how human beings have established their living arrangements.

Perhaps the modern anxiety about families reflects Australians' recent experience of political and economic change. Unemployment and rapid economic change have also affected many Australians, and contributed to a widespread sense that the change process is out of control.

Modern Australian families are diverse. We will continue to see a variety of ways of people working inside their families to make their lives as happy, secure and coherent as they can—but not always under circumstances of their own making.

Discussion questions

7.1 Is it realistic to assume that there is a single entity called 'the family'?

7.2 How universal is the nuclear family?

7.3 Do families have social functions?

7.4 How useful is it to talk about the functions of the family?

7.5 Do patterns like increasing childlessness (child-free families) or rising divorce rates mean the death of the family?

7.6 How pessimistic should we be about current trends in divorce rates?

'Wait until you have children of your own', she says
to him in one of her bitter moods. 'Then you'll know'.
What will he know? It is a formula she uses, a
formula that sounds as if it comes from the old days.
Perhaps it is what each generation says to the next,
as a warning, as a threat. But he does not want to
hear it. 'Wait until you have children'. What nonsense,
what a contradiction! How can a child have children?

J.M Coetzee, Boyhood (1998: 162)

8. BEING YOUNG: AGE AND IDENTITY

- Summary

- Being young

- The status of children and young people

- Social science as prejudice

- The idea of childhood

- The idea of adolescence

- Adolescence as agony and adjustment

- Sociologists on adolescence

- Youth culture

- Social constructivism and post-modernism

- Moral panics and young people as problems

- Generalising about adolescence and youth culture

- Young people and globalisation

- Youth at risk

- Problems with risk talk

- Conclusion

- Discussion questions

● ● SUMMARY

In this chapter, we begin by outlining some of the serious disadvantages and injustices that are normally experienced by many children and young people. We trace this situation back to the ways young people are talked about by adults and experts as 'troubled' and/or as 'trouble-makers'. This preoccupation owes a great deal to two key concepts: 'childhood' and 'adolescence'. We discuss some of the ways adults—especially professionals and experts—have constructed influential ideas about the phases of childhood and adolescence in what is called the life cycle. We explore the ways adults and experts construct and reproduce highly prejudicial accounts of young people, and consider the implications of this practice. We then turn to the idea of youth culture, and show how the modern media and some key social sciences represent young people as a threat to social order. In a short case study designed to reveal the need for care in constructing causal arguments, we critically analyse claims that youth unemployment 'causes' high rates of youth crime, and indicate why this assertion needs to be treated cautiously.

● BEING YOUNG

In our society, age—particularly being a child or a young person—is a crucial identity marker. This has a major impact on how young people are seen and treated, and on the experience of being young. Being young is an experience common to all of us, though we all will have experienced it differently. Unlike some other identity markers, which tend to be permanent—like being 'male' or female or having a particular skin colour—being young is not a permanent source of identity.

Most of us take pride in the idea that we are part of a humane, civilised and democratic society in which all people, regardless of their circumstances, have basic human needs and rights. We tend to be shocked when we discover that these principles are being denied. The discovery that women and coloured people have frequently been treated in demeaning, abusive and exploitative ways has driven major social movements designed to ensure that their human rights were respected. That discovery has yet to be made about children and young people.

We have certainly seen substantial progress in the way young people are treated. The following statement by the United Nations, in a report on the status of young people, makes the general point that we have come a long way. Prior to the 20th century, children were for the most part regarded as inferior and subordinate to adults, and childhood was a period of life that was often brief and regarded as a stage of passage to adulthood. (UN 2005; see also Canadian Council on Social Development 2002)

At first glance, the confidence expressed in the UN report seems well placed. After all, there is a lot of talk about the importance of giving people a fair go, to say nothing of the fact that young people are now encouraged to participate in the social and political life of our community or, as John Ralston Saul (1997) puts it, that we now behave toward them as if their personhood is recognised. In the West, we no longer have children working long hours down coal mines, up chimneys or in factories, suggesting a kind of progress that goes beyond material ideals and embraces democratic citizenship. In New Zealand, Australia, the United States and the United Kingdom, for example, most young people receive a basic education, there is ample health care and laws exist to protect young people from various forms of abuse. Currently we also hear much official talk about the democratic virtues of youth participation and the need to hear young people's voices.

However, sitting oddly alongside such evidence of progress is a lot of other evidence that contradicts any claims that we now treat young people as if we recognise their personhood and citizenship. That is why we are sceptical. We are not convinced by the claim that children and young people are now fully participating members of society, or by the use of indicators of narrowly defined notions of 'progress' which point to literacy levels, education retention rates and other similar measures of well-being in the bid to demonstrate how enlightened and progressive the social treatment of our children and young people has become.

In this chapter, we ask some simple questions:

- What is the ethical status of children and young people?
- Why does our community sanction this representation of children and young people, and the subsequent treatment of these two groups?
- What role has been played by core concepts like 'childhood' and 'adolescence' in producing the social practices and attitudes that result in the kinds of civil disabilities so many children and young people experience?

We suggest that the popular collective image of ourselves as an inclusive democratic society is at odds with our general treatment of young people. We will suggest that this is a consequence of popular attitudes and expert discourses, as well as of government policy-making which continues to define and treat young people in ways that exclude them from all sorts of normal social activity and enable them to be treated with discourtesy and a lack of regard for their basic human rights (Bessant 2004; Carson et al. 2000; Lansdown 2001; Matthews et al. 2000).

● THE STATUS OF CHILDREN AND YOUNG PEOPLE

Most young people in Australia continue to be subjected to discriminatory practices that would not be tolerated if applied to any other section of the population. Australia's children and young people continue to inhabit a space that lies outside the normal rule of law. Status is a key sociological idea here.

Status refers to the way we attribute value to other people. Children and young people enjoy at best an ambiguous, moral and civic status. Too often they live outside the full protection of the law, and outside the kind of moral and civic spaces others take for granted (see box). Indeed, in some ways young people have the status of an outsider.

Infringement of young people's rights

- Young people are denied basic rights, including frequent denial of access to public spaces. In Australia, local governments, public institutions and commercial enterprises like shopping malls pass youth curfew regulations and 'no young people on the property' policies to keep young people off the streets during certain hours or out of certain spaces. This emulates the long-standing denial of the right of free access to public transport, hotels or even certain areas of cities by blacks in Australia and the United States under the aegis of discriminatory regulations. For example, in October 2004 the Consumer Affairs Department in Victoria banned 'under-age' events in licensed venues in Melbourne's central business district. This decision came weeks after an assault on a security guard at an under-age venue.

- In the late 1980s and early 1990s, the Northern Territory and Western Australian governments enacted mandatory sentencing legislation in response to populist law and order campaigns to address 'rising crime rates'. This legislation was deeply inimical to the rights of young Indigenous people.

- The rights of young people to freedom of movement, speech and assembly are frequently curtailed. Many politicians, parents and teachers refuse students permission to participate in political activities like protest marches when those activities occur during school hours. In many cases, this involves appealing to truancy laws.

- Police can lawfully apprehend and relocate a young person without that young person having committed an offence other than being out at night or carrying paraphernalia that can be used to chrome (e.g. plastic bag, spray can).

- The 1997 report by the Australian Law Reform Commission (ALRC) and Human Rights and Equal Opportunity Commission (HREOC), *Seen and Heard: Priority for Children in Legal Processes*, found that children and young people are systematically excluded from legal processes.

- Young people continue to be routinely subjected to various kinds of social and economic injustice. The 'youth wage' ensures that some young people do not receive equal pay for equal work.

- Children can apparently be beaten and punished with impunity, especially by their parents. We see occasional attempts to force law reform on this issue to make the physical assaults on young people that many parents call 'discipline' a crime. Some young people continue to be beaten and punished with impunity. Yet such proposals are still liable to provoke community outrage.

Despite talk of progress and self-congratulatory statements about how enlightened 'the modern world' is, we still have a long way to go in treating young people as citizens and people with the capability to exercise human agency, and the power of logical argument and moral reasoning. In most countries, young people do not enjoy citizenship status in terms of a legal entitlement to participate in democratic practices and other key social activities. Yet young people provide most of the fighting personnel for national and local militia. In some countries, children as young as seven and eight are regularly recruited or kidnapped to serve as soldiers (Human Rights Watch, http://hrw.org/children). In the genocide that has been taking place in Darfur since 2004, children as young as ten are being used to carry out a horrifying exercise in mass murder. In South American countries like Brazil, 'cleaning the streets' involves campaigns perpetrated by death squads, who torture and systematically shoot to kill homeless children and young people like vermin (Human Rights Watch, http:// hrw.org/children; United Nations 1995). In most 'developed' and 'developing' countries, too many young people live in extreme poverty. Australia, for example, has the highest rate of child poverty after Russia, the United States and Italy (Bradbury & Jantti 2001; Neville 2002: 8).

Young people, by virtue of their relative inexperience, vulnerability and absence of certain legal rights, are also readily subject to sexual, physical and emotional abuse. Without legal entitlements and social rights to shield themselves, young people are less able to defend themselves in ways that most others can. Furthermore, the continuance of policies that allow many young people to live in poverty, to be subject to systemic mistreatment and exploitation, raises ethical questions about youth policy and the values or interests which inform such policy. Our idea of social progress aligns with the work of T.H. Marshall (1950), Henderson (1996) and John Ralston Saul (1997), whose work suggests it can be measured to some degree by the quality of our democratic culture.

Young people are assumed to lack the attributes that entitle them to the kind of just and fair treatment that adults enjoy. In other words, to be a child or a young person in Australia is to experience high levels of social disadvantage, unequal treatment and a lack of respect, both legally and socially, that is as shocking as the casual way this circumstance is routinely denied or covered up.

You can usually tell who is seen to be not fully human or a non-person by whether they are treated in the following ways:

- Typically, they are talked about in their presence as if they are not there. Children and young people continue to be treated in this way.
- They are regularly subjected to prejudicial treatment which is seen as normal and natural, and which is often legal.
- They are regularly denied a range of human rights—something which is also generally considered right and unproblematic.

Most young people are treated in these ways. Young people are believed to:

- lack the intellectual capacity for logical thought and explicable principles that produce appropriate values and beliefs;
- lack the capacity for moral judgment or even plain common sense;
- be closer in nature and status to animals—which makes it right, proper and normal to act in ways that deny their full human civilised human status; and
- be unable to adequately speak for themselves, despite constantly being talked *about*.

The Australian philosopher Raimond Gaita (2000) has argued that such denials of what he calls our 'common humanity' carry a cost: they are usually followed by other negations that those deemed to be 'un-people' must endure.

Why and how has the inferior status of children and young people come about? As we will show, the immediate answer is to be found in the representation of children and young people by modern social sciences like sociology and psychology. Behind this can be found larger and quite persistent ideas that constitute a history of the concepts of childhood and adolescence.

● SOCIAL SCIENCE AS PREJUDICE

One immediate reason for the prevalence of discriminatory attitudes towards young people is a long and complex history of scientific research that has been highly influential in shaping popular and expert understandings of young people, including underwriting the idea that they are 'naturally' meant to be subordinate and dependent. As Rom Harre (1986) has argued, social sciences like psychology and sociology have constructed a compelling, and now conventional, story about human development understood as a series of inevitable and necessary evolutionary stages:

> developing *human beings change not only in respect to what they know they can do, but also and most importantly with respect to what their society permits them to do, that is what they may do.* Certain classes of persons have certain rights and obligations to the display of competences, while others, regardless of their state of knowledge are forbidden to make public use of them. (1986: 294, our emphasis)

As we show a little later, what was called the 'child studies' movement in the nineteenth century evolved during the twentieth century to occupy critical space in most of the social sciences. The result has been a tradition of 'human developmental theory' or 'life-cycle theory'. This tradition was the work of a long line of psychologists, sociologists and criminologists from Cyril Burt, Jean Piaget, Erik Erickson, Kohlberg and Talcott Parsons through to contemporary figures like Michael Rutter, John Farrington and Gary Catalano. The tradition of developmental studies has had a significant influence on how most of us now understand the intellectual, social and emotional development of young people. More recently, this tradition has been criticised (Harre 1986; Danziger 1994; Fernandez-Armestos 1997; Rose 1991). Yet, despite these important critical insights, the mainstream ideas remain deeply embedded in our collective understandings of 'youth'.

In its various forms, 'human developmental theory' has helped to consolidate a dominant view of young people that became a primary obstacle to their capacity to engage in challenging experiences and opportunities to extend themselves.

The contemporary common sense that childhood or adolescence constitutes a natural stage in human development owes a lot to the work of figures in psychology like the great twentieth century Swiss psychologist Jean Piaget. Piaget declared that children were simply incapable of doing any of the cognitive tasks associated with normal adults (Fernandez-Armestos 1997: 18). Piaget believed children were capable only of what he called 'pre-logical, primitive thought', while adults 'naturally' practised higher forms of rationality which occupied the top rungs of the cognitive ladder. No less influential has been the work of the moral philosopher Kohlberg, who built on Piaget's 'scientific model' of cognitive development, producing his own influential model of the moral stages of development. These ideas have proved incredibly influential—so much so that they are still taught in most university undergraduate psychology, early childhood and teaching courses. As Rom Harre (1986) notes, the 'stages' of human development were:

> studied by attempting to map their pre-given order onto some other pre-given order, namely that of Piagetian cognitive development. In other words, success or failure in the research was measured by the extent to which the mapping was achieved. *Neither of the pre-given orders were themselves subject to critical scrutiny.* (1986: 295, our emphasis)

Implicit in these accounts was the simple idea that the child or adolescent was a pre-social 'animal' in contrast to the fully human civilised status of adult human beings. The consequences of this are on display in the *Oxford English Dictionary* (*OED*) definition of 'youth', which defines it as a quality or condition of the young: 'freshness, vigour, wantonness, rashness'. ('Wantonness' is defined by the *OED* as 'undisciplined', 'ungoverned', 'unmanageable', 'rebellious', 'lascivious', 'unchaste', 'lewd', 'frisky', 'frolicsome', 'impelled by caprice or fancy', 'unrestrained', 'spoiled', 'petulant'!)

Decades of developmental psychology have established the 'scientific fact' that children and young people are emotionally, ethically and intellectually less able than adults. As we suggest later, this is not to say that the emotional and intellectual lives of young people are necessarily the same as those of adults. Rather, the point is that the differences have been interpreted through a hierarchical adult-centric view of the world in which children and teenagers have been understood as deficient and/or inferior to adults.

Young people represent a group about which experts, the media and policy-makers love to generalise. However irrational and prejudiced these beliefs are, they have undoubtedly influenced politicians and government policy across the past century. Images of young people as agents of social disorder have long been staple elements of journalism. Journalistic generalisations about 'Generation Z' or 'the Net-generation' are rife. Worse still is the way the media regularly report on and exaggerate official, popular and academic concerns about problems believed to be uniquely experienced by young people, like homelessness, alcohol and drug use, criminal activity and delinquency, pregnancy and sexual promiscuity, suicide or high levels of unemployment. Australian newspapers 'discovered' a new 'underclass' of juvenile offenders, drug-users and anti-social vandals a decade after an equivalent 'discovery' in America. Notwithstanding the possibility that the 'discovery' testifies more to the wish fulfilment of certain well-meaning academic researchers than to any real discovery, the 'youth underclass' has been explained in terms of economic recession, globalisation, youth unemployment, the death of the family and the breakdown of the welfare state (see White 1993, 1994). Prejudices like this have meant that, over the last decade, developmental theory has been resuscitated to buttress the idea that there are large numbers of 'anti-social' young people (e.g. Rutter et al. 1998). This in turn has sponsored the development of the idea that it is possible to measure risk factors and identify those who are at risk of becoming 'anti-social'. A lot of money is being spent on this kind of research and on so-called preventive programs. (For a detailed critique of this, see Bessant et al. 2003.)

In this chapter we assess the validity of some of the popular prejudices entertained by adults and experts about young people. Are young people aged between thirteen and 25 all that different from the rest of us? How much is adolescence a biological process? Are young people in more trouble, and do they cause more problems, than other age groups?

We begin by trying to establish where the deeply prejudicial ideas about young people come from. We do this by establishing what some of the key words, like 'childhood' or 'adolescence', mean. The ways in which we define childhood and adolescence shape the way in which we respond to children and teenagers. They also influence how young people and children see and define themselves, even when these stories bear little or no relation to the lived experience of many young people.

As we show, the core idea of adolescence as a time of turbulence and transition to adulthood depends on the prior idea of 'childhood'.

• THE IDEA OF CHILDHOOD

In societies like Australia, it is now generally expected that all children will have a childhood. What does this mean? The French historian Phillipe Aries (1973) was the first historian to observe that, until the seventeenth and eighteenth centuries, European children were defined and treated like 'small adults'. They routinely worked and dressed as fully grown people, and engaged in most adult activities as soon as they were physically able to. Children as young as twelve married; many children worked for wages or in the household economy until the late nineteenth century; and some very young kings and princes led armies to battle in medieval times.

The modern story of 'childhood' began in the seventeenth and eighteenth centuries, when middle-class people and philosophers like John Locke and Jean Jacques Rousseau argued that children should be treated as 'dependent', sexually innocent and vulnerable. Through the nineteenth century, an emerging ideology of 'childhood' found its most robust expression among the Anglo-American and European middle classes. Novelists like Charles Dickens elaborated a powerful story about innocent children needing protection from adult values and behaviours. Young people began to be dressed in children's clothing. At the behest of activists like the Earl of Shaftsbury, who called themselves 'child savers', young people were increasingly excluded from the labour market and prevented from earning an income. The child savers became great advocates for moral education, sponsoring the Sunday School movement and then, from the 1870s, supporting the passage of legislation in most Western countries to make it compulsory for children to attend schools for long periods. Schools as institutions guaranteed children's dependence and helped to keep them out of the labour market. The fact that children were working for wages was enough to define them as delinquents. Adults began worrying about children who missed out on having a 'childhood'.

Intellectuals and activists like Froebel and G. Stanley Hall contributed to the development of the 'child study' movement from the 1870s onwards, promoting ideas about teaching children and managing their psychological and physical health in places like kindergartens (or 'child gardens'). Taking its cue from the work of Charles Darwin, a great deal of scientific work began on identifying the stages of 'normal' development in activities like reading, writing and moral judgment. (Implicit in this work was the idea that the development of children into adults mirrors the development of different species or 'races' of people from 'savagery' to 'civilisation'.) This research, now called life-cycle theory, continues to this day, buttressed by techniques like the measurement of intelligence.

Today the fact you are a child means (among other things) that you are defined as innocent, vulnerable and weak; that you are in need of protection from certain aspects of the adult world, such as sex, gambling, working for a living and all the other markers of independence; and that you need to be 'saved' or sheltered from those things in order to have a childhood.

The creation of childhood has meant treating children not as independent beings, but as 'dependants'. This project of defining and managing childhood provided the backdrop for the subsequent development of a similar project around adolescence.

● THE IDEA OF ADOLESCENCE

In 1904, G. Stanley-Hall published a book called *Adolescence*. It has helped to define many of the key social science prejudices about young people ever since. It has been conventional since then to think that being an 'adolescent' or a 'youth' is best explained as a biological state and that the problems which allegedly define adolescence are the result of a clash between biological drives and social constraints. These are essentialist arguments dependent on stereotypes that imply all adolescents do the same things, or feel and think in the same ways.

The biological story

No one can deny that complex genetic and biological processes characterise the lengthy process involved in a baby's growth through childhood into adolescence and adulthood. Human babies are born weak, small, vulnerable, speechless living creatures who need to be cared for intensively for a far longer period than any other animal.

Equally, there are biological factors operating in the period called puberty. However, becoming an adolescent is not just about biology (Sercombe 1997). A range of social relationships and often complex cultural and economic factors also shape our developing identity as children or young people—remembering that 'identity' refers both to our own experiences and to the ways others treat us. These factors include:

- the meanings and value other people attribute to being a child or an adolescent in our community; and
- the social expectations set up by other people about appropriate behaviour.

These social and cultural factors vary significantly from one social context and from one historical period to the next. Being a child, for example, is quite a recent Western phenomenon.

Adolescence as a recognised phase in the life cycle was 'discovered' in the early twentieth century. The idea of adolescence saw the dependence of childhood extend into what later came to be known as the 'teen' years.

● ADOLESCENCE AS AGONY AND ADJUSTMENT

This idea of adolescence was developed by a number of people, of whom G. Stanley-Hall is recognised as the most influential. Stanley-Hall was an American 'child studies' expert, psychologist and an advocate for racial hygiene at the beginning of the twentieth century. He argued that adolescence was a precarious section of the path from childhood to adulthood. This passage involved an insecure and unstable period of transition and adjustment in preparation for adult life.

The turbulence allegedly resulted from the hormonal, physical and emotional changes conflicting with society's rules. Adolescents, although physically developed, were prohibited from giving expression to activities (especially sex) that were reserved for adults. (Hall himself had an obsession bordering on mania about the evil effects of masturbation.) Sexual expression for teenagers was taboo because they were said to be socially or emotionally irresponsible, and not mature enough to accept adult responsibilities and the identity related to adult sexuality.

From this biological base, Hall told a story about how the need to control the outbreak of sexuality for a decade or more inevitably created stresses and trouble both for the adolescent and for those around them. Through the twentieth century, the idea that 'the adolescent' is naturally irresponsible, emotionally unstable, rebellious, difficult and almost certainly deviant has been retold endlessly by generations of social scientists, and is now widely held to be a basic truth by most adults.

• SOCIOLOGISTS ON ADOLESCENCE

Since Hall's work, the idea of 'adolescence' has become part of a larger sociological story told about 'society'. One important sociological approach to adolescence draws on structural functionalism. Sociologists like Talcott Parsons and Robert Merton played a major role in embellishing the story about adolescence as a difficult life-cycle stage.

To be an adolescent in the terms set up by this sociological story was to already be a 'deviant'. In the 1990s, some people (including youth workers) started to talk about 'feral adolescents'. Metaphors like 'feral' point to the idea of 'wild' and unrestrained children carrying on like animals. Likewise, in the development of social science risk-based research, we see old prejudices at work. Farrington (1994) has defined 'anti-social' behaviours in terms of being 'troublesome and dishonest' in primary school, being 'aggressive and frequent liars' between the ages of twelve and fourteen, being a 'bully' at fourteen, and engaging in 'heavy drinking', 'heavy smoking', 'using prohibited drugs', 'heavy gambling' and frequent, early, unprotected and promiscuous sex by eighteen. It is salutary to remember that West and Farrington (1977) had earlier included having an 'anti-establishment attitude' in their definition of 'anti-social'.

It is no secret that, in Australia—as numerous health and social surveys conducted in the late 1990s have indicated—many young people at eighteen have engaged in 'heavy drinking', have 'used prohibited drugs' and have engaged in frequent, often unprotected sexual activities. A substantial minority of young people are also engaged in 'heavy gambling' and 'heavy smoking'. The proposition that these activities signify 'anti-social behaviour' in a society where these attributes and activities are also widely practised and used as hallmarks of sophisticated behaviour by many adults is an interesting idea. Does Farrington really want us to believe that the behaviours to which he refers are actually capable of 'interfering with the smooth running of Western society'?

The very ubiquity of behaviours such as bullying, cheating and lying might suggest that they have hardly impacted on 'the smooth running of Western society'. Yet it is important to think about this framework, even if it is wrong. This is because, if most adults believe such stories, these beliefs will lead to quite real and practical consequences. As we have already seen, Australian governments have passed laws imposing night curfews, requiring young people to attend school, and preventing young people from having sex, buying alcohol or tobacco, engaging in paid work and gambling before a certain age.

One of the most influential ideas about young people is the long-standing notion that all young people are different from adults, and from what sociologists ever since the 1930s and 1940s have called a 'youth culture'.

• YOUTH CULTURE

The idea of a 'youth culture' developed from the already existing category of 'the adolescent' as well as the classical sociological account of society. The term 'youth culture' defines young people as rebellious, difficult and even deviant.

In Germany, Karl Mannheim developed the first social-psychological account of youth culture in the late 1920s. In the United States, Talcott Parsons developed a sociological theory of youth culture in the 1940s.

Parsons' story about youth culture identified certain differences between all young people and the adult population, claiming that these differences were organised generationally as well as culturally around common values, aspirations and behaviours. He defined youth culture as 'more or less specifically irresponsible' (Parsons 1963: 32), and claimed that young people formed a definite culture that was 'antagonistic' to adults, teachers and institutions. We need to remember that, when Parsons identified youth culture as irresponsible, World War II was raging as 'responsible' adults called out millions of young men to kill each other—as well as tens of millions of ordinary civilians—with a deadly intent never seen before or since.

During the 1950s and 1960s, many Anglo-American sociologists agreed that adolescents had grouped together in cohesive opposition to responsible adults. James Coleman (1961: 4), for example, claimed adolescents belonged to 'a relatively autonomous culture, controlled internally by a system of norms and sanctions and largely antithetical or indifferent to that offered by parents, teachers and clergymen'. Like Parsons, Coleman saw youth culture as deviant, the result of a social process of age segregation in which 'the adolescent is dumped into a society of his peers' (Coleman 1961: 4). Bennett Berger (1963: 331) agreed, claiming that the youth culture was dangerous: 'from the perspective of the major institutions of social order, youthfulness is excess; it is implicit or incipient disorder; for society it is a "problem" that requires handling, control, co-option or channeling in socially approved directions.'

Yet this tradition—though it continues to influence a lot of contemporary research done on 'youth'—has not gone without challenge. Beginning in the late 1960s, Marxists, neo-Marxists, and feminists initiated a more critical tradition of scholarly research of youth cultures, challenging many of the original formulations of the American tradition of functionalist sociology.

Neo-Marxist and feminist accounts of youth culture

In Britain, neo-Marxist writers associated with the Birmingham Centre for Cultural Studies (CCCS) (Clarke et al. 1976; Brake 1985) argued that youth culture was not a generalised reaction by all young people, but was better understood primarily as a 'working-class' phenomenon, as rebellious working-class teenagers opted not to promote revolutionary struggle against capitalism and an exploitative labour market, but rather chose to express their frustrations and rebelliousness through football riots, street fights or loud music.

In Australia, writers like Rob White (1990), who was heavily influenced by neo-Marxist theories, argued that local 'youth cultures' involved young people in a struggle for space in cities and streets increasingly controlled by private property and police.

Feminists influenced by this tradition pushed the critique even further as they observed the tendency to actually talk about the experience only of boys when it seemed they were talking about both young men and women. As feminists like Angela McRobbie (1980) and Kerry Carrington (1993) note, the youth culture literature is preoccupied with what boys do, and ignores young women's experiences and interests. Carrington has done much to illuminate the darker side of sexism at work among young working-class men and women in Australia.

Running in parallel with the neo-Marxist and feminist critiques, an entirely novel kind of critical challenge has been mounted by social constructionist, post-structuralist and post-modernist writers.

• SOCIAL CONSTRUCTIVISM AND POST-MODERNISM

As we showed in Chapter 3, modern sociology has been affected by various critical challenges to long-standing sociological orthodoxies. The oldest of these critical traditions came from a loose coalition of symbolic interactionists and social constructivists. In the 1960s, writers like Blumer et al. (1969) and Cicourel (1976) rejected the structuralist approach favoured both by the structural functionalists and by those kinds of feminism and Marxism that also emphasised structural explanations using categories like 'class' and 'patriarchy'. The symbolic interactionists argued that what we call social reality is actually socially constructed by institutions that invent social categories and use social institutions like schools and police or techniques like social statistics to create social order.

A different but parallel challenge came from writers like Michel Foucault (1977, 1979), Jean François Lyotard (1984), Nikolas Rose (1990) and Ian Hacking (1999, 2002), who raised fundamental questions about the status of the claims to scientific status by the social and medical sciences.

An even broader challenge mounted by people working under the rubric of 'post-modernism' and 'cultural studies' has focused attention on the way images generated in the media, or discourses produced by experts and scientists, can take over the representation of social problems and of groups of people. The many excesses of post-modernism—like the too-easy dismissal of the idea that there is anything real about social reality—have been rightly identified. As Hacking (1999) puts it, you can believe that paying rent is just a social construction but try not paying your rent and the idiocy of the position will become very clear. Nonetheless, one of the benefits of this approach has been to challenge the tendency to construct stereotypical generalisations about groups like women and young people. Another has been to challenge the simplistic use of structuralist arguments that use abstractions like 'society', 'class' or 'patriarchy' to explain social processes.

In a nutshell, a variety of social constructivist, post-modernist and post-structuralist writers have promoted a more critical attitude to talking about and using categories like 'youth' or 'working class'. (In saying this we are not implying that there was much agreement between these traditions—only that together they have sponsored a more critical approach.)

In Australia, writers like Tait (1992, 1995) and Kelly (1998) have disputed claims that social scientific knowledge is or can be objective. This is evident in their suggestions that the categories we operate with do not refer to things that are simply material or natural (Kelly 1998). In other words, categories like 'youth' (Mizen 2004) and sub-categories like 'youth homelessness' or 'youth cultures' (Tucker 2004: 81–9) cannot be regarded as objective 'things' because they are produced by researchers (Tait 1992, 1995: 123–34). They emphasise the way that knowledge is developed and maintained through social processes. This means that how we see, understand and know the world is not simply extracted from nature, but is made or negotiated by people (Hopkin 1996: 12–17; Aitken 2001).

The most important legacy of this constellation of social constructivist, post-modernist and post-structuralist writers has been to focus on the ways various understandings of the world are linked to certain types of social action. For example, the kinds of theory and research done on illicit drug use by young people produced by law enforcement agencies and by traditional sociologists of deviance and mainstream criminology have emphasised the deviant status and law-breaking aspects of young drug offenders. Conversely, as biomedical and psychological experts intervene in the field of drug use, they have represented the problem as a health issue.

Finally, and because of this variety of social constructivist, post-modernist and post-structuralist writers, there is now a much greater stress on the ways that knowledge and how we live are culturally and historically specific. This means that ways of talking about specific groups or kinds of people—like 'the delinquent' or 'child'—are seen as specific to a particular culture and its institutions, and as such are socially constructed (Carrington 1993). More recently, writers working from these traditions have drawn our attention to the role of cyberspace and electronic communications, and the ways in which new identities and new forms of collective action have evolved (Melucci 1996; Hopkin 2002; Aapola et al. 2005). Here consideration is given to ways in which 'youth culture' is deeply political, and to how the idea of cultural citizenship provides a useful way of understanding style, music and sub-cultures (Harris 2001; Giroux 1997). New music forms, new styles of dress and identities and new music are deeply political activities because these actions challenge conventional relations, institutions and power relations. These kinds of socio-political pursuits are evident in new forms of political space now available through cyberspace, in which young people have opportunities to narrate themselves, to speak from the actual places where their experiences and daily lives are mediated in ways that are largely denied to them in the traditional public sphere (Bessant 2000; Meekosha 2002: 67–88).

Arguably one of the most fruitful products of this move away from a simplified neo-Marxist and structuralist framework is found in the work of Stanley Cohen (1972). Cohen has blended together elements of neo-Marxism and social constructivism to develop an interesting account of the way the modern media have used and generated stereotypes of young people who were turned into 'folk devils' to whip up what he called 'moral panics'.

● MORAL PANICS AND YOUNG PEOPLE AS PROBLEMS

Cohen's work began with the recognition made by some other writers, like Pearson (1983), that young people as a group have repeatedly been discovered to be 'problems' needing to be controlled and regulated. 'White' Australia (like other comparable societies) has a history of public anxiety about young people which goes back to the first decades of settlement at Sydney Cove in the 1790s (Avril 1992: 319–24). In the 1870s, the media 'discovered' larrikins, and the activities of street gangs (or 'pushes') in Melbourne and Sydney provide one early precursor to the contemporary 'discovery' of youth at risk (Murray 1974).

Throughout the nineteenth and twentieth centuries, persistent moral outrage was expressed in newspapers about the actions of 'gangs' of 'anti-social' and 'delinquent' young people. Cohen (1972) called these processes of media outrage and public response 'moral panics'. The generation of moral panics about young people became especially prevalent in the second half of the twentieth century (Bavin-Mizzi 1995).

A 'moral panic' refers to the way sections of the media exaggerate and 'over report' a situation, which then provides the basis for a backlash driven by the concern and fear set loose by the media about the behaviour of young 'folk devils'. Cohen argues that the ways in which a situation is initially 'reported' by the media can be critical to the later progress of a moral panic, as that is how most people form their initial impressions of both deviance and disasters (Cohen 1972: 23). According to Cohen (1972: 22–3), a moral panic evolves in four stages:

- A condition, episode, person or groups of persons emerges to become defined as a threat to the values and interests of 'society' (Cohen calls these groups 'folk devils').
- The threat is presented in a stylised and stereotypical way by the mass media.
- The moral barricades are 'manned' by editors, bishops, politicians and other right-thinking people.
- Socially accredited 'experts'—typically academics—pronounce their diagnoses and solutions, and governments are urged to 'do something'—usually involving tougher police or preventative strategies.

The condition then disappears or submerges—only to be 'rediscovered' again, and again . . .

In the 1950s, the first modern Australian moral panic about young people erupted over the wickedness of young bodgies (men) and widgies (women). Bodgies initially dressed in expensive 'zoot suits' (with jackets that reached down to the knees) and later in blue denim jeans and t-shirts, while widgies wore tight tops and flowing dresses. They gathered in 'dens of depravity' called milk bars, where they publicly engaged in dancing—and kissing! In the 1950s, this behaviour was extremely upsetting to many 'respectable citizens', and from the perspective of the Australian press it was very threatening. The degree of overstatement in the media is indicated in this report (cited in Braithwaite & Barker 1977):

> Sydney, Saturday: A mob of more than forty screaming, snarling, gouging Bodgies last night turned Lidcombe Park into a battlefield, rioting over widgies and booze. Brawling Bodgies used jagged bottles, billets of wood, fists and rocks to batter each other.

Moral panics over juvenile crime, adolescent gangs, pop music and teenage immorality have continued to erupt at regular intervals. There were clearly elements of this process set loose in December 2005 when thousands of young people clashed repeatedly on the beaches of Cronulla in what the media quickly dubbed 'race riots'. Historians like Pearson (1983) remind us that this kind of representation of young people has a remarkably long history, going back at least to the late eighteenth century. We should not see contemporary representations of youthful disorder, lawlessness and misrule as genuinely 'new'.

So are young people really so different from their parents? Can we generalise about young people as if they are a single group with a single set of tastes or behaviours, as experts and sections of the media like to do? How useful is the idea of youth culture?

● GENERALISING ABOUT ADOLESCENCE AND YOUTH CULTURE

Should we talk about young people as if their age is the only identity marker that matters? Are all young people identical to each other just because they are aged between thirteen and 25 years? Here we encounter the problem of essentialising again. Perhaps the only safe generalisation to be made is this: most generalising statements about young people are at best half-truths—and some are just plain wrong. While experimentation, experiencing crisis or being troublesome may characterise the lives of some young people some of the time, such experiences equally well describe the lives of other people. Young people are not an homogeneous group: they are as diverse as the rest of the community.

Generalising about 'young people' or 'adolescents' ignores the fact that most young people often have more in common with their own parents and relatives than with their immediate networks—or figurations—of friends. Consider young people's leisure tastes. Many adults pick on teenagers' music. Yet the Australian Broadcasting Authority (ABA 1996) found that young people had a wide range of musical tastes spanning the entire range of music styles, from dance and techno to heavy metal and rock.

Even more disturbing from the point of view of those experts and media pundits who want to talk up the troublesome nature of young people is the fact that most young people are just like their parents and live ordinary—even boring lives—shaped by the moral standards, codes of behaviour and expectations of their family and community. This conclusion is supported by the work of Daniel and Judith Offer (1968, 1969, 1970, 1988), who have spent their careers researching what they called 'normal youth'. Over a lengthy career, Daniel and Judith Offer argued against the notion that young people were more traumatised or more trouble-making than other sectors of the population. The point Daniel and Judith Offer make is supported by others, including Roberts (1983).

The same kinds of reservations need to be developed about the idea of 'youth culture'. On the one hand, it is plain that for some young people identification with a larger group of other young people or with a style of music, clothing or behaviour matters a good deal. Since the 1950s, all kinds of youth cultures—like the bodgies and widgies, punks, skins and Goths; styles of music like metal, rap or techno; or particular scenes like the surf scene of the 1970s or the rave scene of the 1990s—have provided the basis for young people to get together and develop a range of expressive activities (Braithwaite & Barker 1977; Stratton 1992; Willis 1990; Savage 1992).

This, however, does not mean that the kinds of ways in which youth culture has been deployed to date have added much deep insight into the lives of ordinary young people. There have been a number of critiques of the core concept of youth culture, whether put to work by the mainstream kind of sociology or by neo-Marxists (Tait 1992: 13–17; Sercombe 1992: 51–4). This critique makes the simple but telling point that too often the more conventional accounts of youth culture are crass exercises in unrestrained prejudice. Tait (1992) argues that writers like Cohen, Hall and Brake offer an overly determinist and economistic account of youth culture. Clarke (1982) and Walker (1988) claim that this model romanticises the 'resistance' of young working-class men. Nor does this rule out the need to ask important questions about how much the activities and aspirations of young people intersect with, and may even be driven by, commercial interests in the recording, media, clothing and cosmetic industries, and how much they represent young people's own values and interests.

In the final part of this chapter we turn to some issues about the experience of being young at a time of considerable social and economic change.

● YOUNG PEOPLE AND GLOBALISATION

Young Australians, along with Australians of all ages, have been caught in a number of major changes over the last 25 years. Australia, for example, has long ceased to have the kind of industrial economy and workforce that characterised the first three-quarters of the twentieth century. From the early 1990s into the early years of the twenty-first century, Australians have embraced an information-based and service economy symbolised by the development of digital technologies like the internet and the mobile phone (Pakulski 2004). The internet provides for hitherto undreamt of ways of working and doing business (including internet banking and shopping), getting an education or enabling people to relate to each other. These are producing dramatic shifts in the nature of young people's experience.

One of the important changes relates to the ways 'the transition' from 'youth' to 'adult' status is now occurring. Through the nineteenth century and until the early 1970s, most young people engaged in full-time work as soon as they were able to do so, either by working for wages or contributing to the household or farm economy. After the introduction of mass compulsory schooling in the 1870s, the great majority of young people got work immediately on leaving school, and most young Australians had left school by age fifteen or sixteen. In the years after 1945, Australians enjoyed their first lengthy period of full employment. Paid work offered independence and some level of responsibility, including the chance to contribute financially to the household economy, to live apart from parents, to save for a car and house, and to get married and have children. Into the late 1970s, most young people did not complete secondary schooling to the equivalent of Year 12, and university or post-secondary education remained a minority option.

At the start of the twenty-first century, all of this has changed. Take, for example, the role of universities. What once were small-scale institutions offering an education to a minority of the population—mostly elite and middle-class males—have become mass tertiary education institutions offering an unprecedented variety and diversity of undergraduate and postgraduate education. In 1946, there were just over 17 000 university students representing 2.3 per cent of the seventeen to 22 years age group. By 1966, the number of universities had doubled and the student population had increased by 500 per cent to 91 000, representing 7.8 per cent of the seventeen to 22 years cohort (Little 1970: 3). The next three decades saw even more significant increases. Between 1975 and 1996, the number of Australians in higher education rose from 273 137 (1975) to 631 025 (1996) (Marginson 1997: 186–7). By 2005 there were over 900 000 students studying at universities and another 1.1 million in TAFE colleges. This increase meant that, in terms of the participation rate in post-secondary education, Australia—which in 1975 was in the lowest quarter of OECD states—had by 2005 moved into the top 20 per cent of OECD member-states. Even allowing for the increased proportion of overseas students—which became a staple part of Australian university enrolments in the late 1990s as universities moved to increase their income from this source—this shift to a mass tertiary education system is undoubtedly an increasingly significant part of the experience of young people.

If the old industrial economic order involved a relatively simple transition from school to the full-time workforce around the age of sixteen for most young people, the new service economy sees increasingly complex relations between education and paid work—a connection that begins in the late secondary years and continues on through the years of post-secondary education. In effect, increasing numbers of young people are now combining dual careers as students and workers.

Between 1983 and 2005, the labour force participation rate for all people (aged over fifteen) increased slightly from 60 per cent to 63 per cent while the rate for fifteen to 24 year-olds stayed remarkably stable, hovering between 68 and 69 per cent. Yet this stability masked significant shifts in the experience of full-time and part-time employment on the part of 15–24-year-olds (ABS 2005c).

For much of the 1980s, these shifts had a lot to do with persistently high rates of youth unemployment coexisting with a sizeable full-time labour market for young people. Through the 1980s, fifteen- to nineteen-year-olds had unemployment rates (as defined and measured by the ABS) of over 20 per cent. Unemployment remained a problem into the mid-1990s.

Although there are problems with estimating the youth unemployment rate, the ABS rate stayed consistently high through the 1980s and 1990s (ABS 1997b). It was 19.9 per cent in 1986, 15.7 per cent in 1989, 23.8 per cent in 1992 and 20.7 per cent in 1996. However, it is important to note that by the middle of the first decade of the twenty-first century, the youth unemployment rate had dropped to around 15 per cent.

Even more significant was the radical disintegration of the full-time youth labour market and the construction of a large part-time youth labour market. Since the mid-1970s, the full-time labour market for young people has disintegrated, while the part-time labour market has grown enormously. From the early 1980s, increasing numbers of young Australians had trouble finding full-time work as its availability shrank dramatically (see Table 8.1).

Table 8.1 Youth labour force, 1975 and 2005 (%)

	1975		2005	
Labour force status	15–19	20–24	15–19	20–24
Full-time	45	86.4	31.3	66.9
Part-time	13.4	7.6	68.2	33.6
Unemployed	12.9	5.9	15.5	8.7
Labour force participation	58.3	82.3	56.3	79

Source: ABS (2006a).

The disintegration of the full-time youth labour market has been extraordinary. Back in 1983, some 72 per cent of fifteen- to 19-year-olds were in full-time work. By 2005, this had been cut by more than half. For all young people aged between fifteen and 24, the full-time labour market accounted for 83 per cent of that group. In 2005, fewer than 32 per cent of fifteen- to ninteen-year-olds had full-time work, while only 52 per cent of fifteen- to 24-year-olds were in full-time work.

No less dramatic has been the marked increase in the part-time youth labour force. In 1983, around 22.8 per cent of fifteen- to 19-year-olds were in part-time work; by 2005, this had climbed to 68 per cent. In 1983, only 18 per cent of fifteen- to 24-year-olds were in part-time work; by 2005, this had risen to 48 per cent.

The changes in the pattern of full-time and part-time work carried out by young people is closely related to their increased involvement in secondary and post-secondary education. The most common pattern is for full-time students to work on a part-time basis. The smaller numbers in full-time work tend not to combine this with study, while part-time students do not tend to work part-time. In 2005, 65 per cent of the fifteen- to ninteen-year-olds and 82 per cent of full-time twenty- to 24-year-old workers were not studying.

It is not surprising to discover (using ABS data) that nearly two-thirds of those young people in part-time employment work in just two industries: the retail sector and food and alcohol outlets. In 2005, 52 per cent of fifteen- to ninteen-year-olds worked in retail, and another

11 per cent were working in 'accommodation, cafes and restaurants'. The ABS chooses to suggest that 'lower levels of educational attainment and work experience' explain why young people are generally employed in the less skilled and less well-paid jobs that are found in these industries. Our later discussion of McDonaldisation examines why part-time employment—especially in the fast food and rationalised service industries—is now the dominant option for many young workers.

There is a good case for thinking about the links between globalisation and new patterns of social inequality (Pakulski 2004). Equally, there are problems with an undiscriminating use of a generic idea like globalisation when it is applied to a group like young people, who have already been subjected to excessive generalisation—even stereotyping.

From the mid-1970s, when evidence about the effects of youth unemployment first began to gather, young people began to be represented as 'victims' of unemployment and restructuring; by the mid-1990s, it had become fashionable to blame globalisation. This victim status heightened popular concern about 'rising' rates of juvenile crime, suicide, homelessness and substance abuse. As well as young people being 'casualties of change' (Eckersley 1988, 1993), researchers and commentators promoted the idea that young unemployed people were graffiti artists, delinquents, gang members or young offenders, and as such a menace to social order. The result has been the recycling of expressions of concern and alarm about troublesome young people, most recently captured in the now-fashionable discourse about youth at risk.

● YOUTH AT RISK

Stories about young people as victims or threats to social order have become a standard part of public discussion. As 'victims', they are engaging in self-destructive behaviours (including anorexia, drug abuse and suicide). Some writers insist that this is because our 'culture' or 'society' has lost the traditional moral code that helped young people feel confident about themselves and their place in the world (Eckersley 1993, 2004; McDonald 1995). It is not difficult to see the 'classical' sociological account operating here.

Young people also continue to regularly be represented as major causes of crime, anti-social behaviour, drug abuse and social disorder. 'Bad kids', whether they be graffitists, train-surfers, drug-takers or rave party-goers, remain a staple feature of media reports and commentary (Bessant & Hil 1997; Rutter et al. 1998; National Crime Prevention 1999). In either case, the source of the trouble can quickly be located in global economic integration, changes to the youth labour market and unemployment and the breakdown of the 'welfare state'.

After decades of talking about 'delinquency' and 'anti-social youth', the currently favoured framework uses the language of risk to make sense of young people as either victims and/or threats. This model argues that risks are now so widespread that almost everyone is at risk, which has led governments to develop preventative programs and policies:

- In 1998, the Howard Liberal-National Coalition government introduced changes to Australia's income support for young people in a unified and means-tested system known as the Common Youth Allowance. The justification for this 'reform' was to better meet the needs of 'at-risk' young people.
- In 2004, a multi-million dollar research program was established under Professor Fiona Stanley to identify risk factors in the first five years of a child's life as a prelude to interventions designed to prevent them becoming a teenage delinquent.
- In 2006, Victoria's Parliamentary Drugs and Crime Committee released a paper adopting the risk model in its recommendations for an alcohol prevention strategy.

The 'at risk' category works in a time of major social transformation as an index of deficiency, usually located in the person or group deemed to be 'at risk'. For commentators like Eckersley, 'youth at risk' are the 'miner's canaries' of our society in crisis. The at risk category signifies the 'crisis' and apparently novel hazards and problems that characterise our era as dangerous, difficult and crisis-ridden. According to Eckersley, these include:

> pressures of increasing urbanisation, industrialisation, centralisation, mechanisation, individualisation, of growing populations, increasing global economic competition and accelerating change, of a strengthening material and economic domination of our lives and a weakening spiritual and moral influence. (Eckersley 1992: 18)

As Kelly (1998: 22) points out, these features mirror Giddens' (1990) 'risk profile of modernity'. The restructuring of the labour market and economy coincided with the collapse of the full-time youth labour market that began to occur in the 1980s (Wooden 1998: 35; Dryfoos 1990; Langmore & Quiggin 1994; Quiggin 1997; Bell 1997). The restructuring process has given rise to a range of specific anxieties about youth homelessness, youth suicide, juvenile delinquency, and drug use and addiction.

The restructuring process has meant that youth encounter 'new morbidities' that present major obstacles to becoming adults. Batten and Russell's (1995: 1) position is typical:

> The term 'at risk' is used to describe or identify young people who, beset by particular difficulties and disadvantages, are thought likely to fail to achieve the development in their adolescent years that would provide a sound basis for a satisfying and fulfilling adult life.

The result is a lot of research and policy advocacy that rolls out the same old prejudiced and over-generalised stereotypes that have shadowed young people over the last century. The at-risk literature depends on popular and social scientific discourses about adolescence as a period in the life cycle that is inherently troublesome. Given this basic assumption, it is not surprising to find that the empirical and social scientific work on risk factors appears to set loose the potential for an almost limitless field of discovery of risk factors. As Batten and Russell (1995: 1) indicate, 'modern scientific understandings' of the adolescent stage in the life cycle mean that the psychological, biological, economic and socio-cultural factors are such that 'all youths are in some sense at risk'. The factors that allegedly constitute 'at risk youth' extend from indicators of specific disadvantage (like gender, aboriginality or physical disability) to indicators that appear to be common to all fourteen- to 25-year-olds.

The 'risk factors' identified by the authors of the 'Pathways to Prevention' study (National Crime Prevention 1999: 11) are derived from numerous longitudinal studies and include 'genetic and biological characteristics of the child, family characteristics of the child, family characteristics, stressful life events and community or cultural factors'. They are also heavily— yet silently—dependent on long-standing views about the essential nature of adolescence.

Casting a net far enough to include all young people makes a corrective response not only a 'necessity', but also a responsible solution: it sanctions any intervention as long as that response is justified in terms of 'reducing' the risk factors.

● PROBLEMS WITH RISK TALK

There are three key problems with risk talk. The first is that the persistent search for the predictive factors that 'cause' crime, unemployment, youth suicide or homelessness is essentially fruitless. The criminologist Jack Katz (1988: 5) summarises this point in a discussion about the search for the 'causes' of crime:

> Whatever the validity of the hereditary, psychological, and social-ecological conditions of crime, many of those in the identified causal categories do not commit crime. Many people who do commit crime do not fit the causal categories. Many who do fit the background categories and later committed crime, go for long periods without committing or attempting to commit the crime to which the theory directs them.

Moreover, the cataloguing of risk factors depends on a vast literature produced since the 1940s on troubled and troublemaking young people, much of which is committed to identifying the emotional, psychological, cultural and social deficits both of the offenders and their families. There appears to be a high degree of insensitivity to issues of class, gender, age and ethnicity in the selection of populations for research, evidenced by the refusal of mainstream social scientists to systematically research the families and the lives of elite or middle-class white people—a framework which all too accurately mirrors the policing and regulatory activities directed against populations which are socially disadvantaged.

The fact that the researcher's political and moral values are reinserted into the categories being measured, and that they are central to the research discourse, is also ignored. As Caspi et al. (1995) point out, categories like 'inadequate parental supervision', 'impulsivity', 'sluggishness', or the all-consuming 'at risk' category, tend to reveal more about the ethnocentric and class-centric views and prejudices of the researchers than they do about the world to which they are applied.

Finally, the reductionism that underwrites most empiricist research has the effect of blanking out the actual social world in which the research is being done—a world which includes both the researcher and the research population. Positivist researchers like to reduce their analyses to single or 'cluster' explanations of complex social phenomena. Thus, in locating the onset of delinquency in the 'family dynamics' of poor or working-class families, the researchers abstract such behaviour from its wider social and economic contexts, simultaneously ignoring their own cultural norms while silently using them to locate deficiencies in the lives of the (subordinated) research populations. The frequent emphasis given to the 'internal dynamics' of 'the family' or the 'community'—as in the case of the Pathways Report (National Crime Prevention 1999)—means that any of these larger social contexts are located in the vague hinterlands of the 'environment'. Thus 'factors' (even if related to structural conditions) become abstracted artefacts appropriate only for purposes of measurement rather than for any sort of reflexive or theoretical exercise.

This is not to deny that there are issues which are worthy of research and policy-making. For most of the period of economic crisis since 1975, an 'incomplete education' has been defined as the key factor that places the young person at risk of unemployment (Ainley et al. 1984; Dryfoos 1990; Bradley & Stock 1993; Dwyer 1997). For Meredith Edwards (1998: 25), the enormity of the problem of 'youth at risk' created by their opting out of education is obvious. An unfinished education is said to also place the young person at risk of other social ills like psychological depression, juvenile crime, suicide, homelessness and drug abuse. Those at risk of unemployment are students who either leave the education system too early, or who show signs of leaving in the foreseeable future. The idea that young people ought to remain within the education system has become so normative that the primary objectives of most institutions' learning outcomes appear to be directed towards the demands of the labour market (Marginson 1997).

Historically, paid employment was seen as 'functional' in terms of providing the basis for social integration and a secure transition along the road from adolescence to adulthood. Young people without work were seen as problematic because they lacked an occupation to organise lives.

What are the consequences for young people of the shifts which have occurred in the youth labour market? We do not know much about how young people have actually experienced these changes, since they have no point of comparison in their own experience. However, while it is clear the full-time youth labour market has disintegrated, this has not meant the wholesale creation of an aimless, socially disconnected generation of young people.

In the first decade of the twenty-first century, most fifteen- to nineteen-year-olds are in either full-time work or in a mixture of full-time study and part-time paid employment. One effect of the increasing exclusion of young people from the full-time labour market has been a further extension of life spent in the institutions that used to characterise dependence. Many young people are now staying on longer at school and university. However, there is evidence of growing dissatisfaction with this option: almost 15 per cent of teenagers, or some 187 000 young people, are now neither in full-time study nor in full-time work (Dusseldorp Skills Forum 1998).

Growing numbers of young people are staying on longer in the parental home, with over 40 per cent of 26-year-olds doing so in 1996. This is the 'never-empty nest' syndrome (Hartley 1989).

A second effect is stress as students try to deal with a combination of economic stress and the strains of being both a full-time student and a part-time worker. There is also mounting evidence of high levels of economic distress among sections of the modern student population. This problem has not been helped by the evolution of an increasingly punitive social policy framework at the national level. Governments are encouraging families to take more responsibility for their children by imposing ever-tighter eligibility tests and other requirements that remove the opportunity for independent social security payments to young people. Since 1998–99, young unemployed people have been compelled under the Howard government's doctrine of mutual obligation to either study or work for the dole: people who work for the dole are specifically excluded from the normal protections afforded by industrial laws and awards.

• CONCLUSION

The way some adults talk *about* rather than *with* young people points to a long-standing tendency towards social ventriloquism—the tendency to speak on behalf of others. Rarely do we directly hear the voices of young people in discussions about youth. Many people might find our claim that children and young people are denied basic human rights and citizenship rights surprising. After all, young people have some of the fundamental formal rights of any citizen. Citizenship, however, has been closely connected to individual freedoms—including freedom of the person, the right to own property, freedom of speech and the right to justice. These are all rights that most young Australians do not have.

Young people have a special status in contemporary Australian communities derived from their position as financially, socially and emotionally dependent on older people (usually their parents). Their dependent status is connected to the idea that young people are in need of care and protection. These perceptions generally owe much to a history in which youth, adolescence and childhood have been defined as innocent, naive, vulnerable, inherently troublesome and transitional.

Changing this situation, however, depends on overcoming a few obstacles. In the eyes of many people 'the problem' we refer to is not a problem at all. This is because it is generally seen as truth that children and young people lack rationality and competence for good moral judgment. For any kind of social change to take place, there first needs to be a general recognition of the prejudices that exist, and this includes an awareness of how science and scientific methods often recycle prejudices about young people by reinforcing beliefs that it is natural for children and youth to have subordinate and dependent status.

There is a need to talk more with young people, with a view to establishing how *they* experience their lives. Identity is very much about the differences between the way we experience ourselves and the way others treat us. Our identity and behaviour are often interpreted in ways that have little if any relationship to the ways in which the person being discussed understands and experiences him or her self. This proposition is even more strikingly confirmed when we turn to the issue of gender in the next chapter.

Discussion questions

8.1 Are all fourteen-, sixteen- or nineteen-year-olds basically the same?

8.2 How useful is it to talk about 'youth cultures' when people are interested in talking about the activities and beliefs of young people?

8.3 Why do young people attract so much critical attention? Is it because they are so different from adults?

8.4 What is a 'moral panic'? Is there evidence of one happening in the current week's newspapers and/or current affairs TV shows?

Bull, a very large and heavy set young man, awoke one morning to find that while he had slept he had acquired another primary sexual characteristic ... a vagina ... I'm sick thought Bull to himself. I'm really sick.

Will Self, Cock & Bull (1993: 103–5)

SEX IN AUSTRALIA 9.

- Summary

- Why questions about sex matter

- Sex and gender

- Essentialism and the sex/gender issue

- Problems with biological determinism

- Problems with sociological determinism

- Gender inequality

- Patriarchy and the sexual division of labour

- Sexual division of labour

- Men's work

- Women's work

- Changes?

- Unequal consequences

- Changing sexualities?

- Heterosexism

- Actual sexuality?

- Sexuality and fluid identity

- Conclusion

- Discussion questions

• • SUMMARY

In this chapter, we suggest ways of thinking about sex as a key marker of identity. Today, there are more questions than there are settled answers about what it means to be a man or a woman. What is gender, and is it different from sex? How much are sex and gender natural phenomena and to what extent are they social or cultural? What is sexism? Are women and men becoming more equal, and how important is it that men and women be different? Have gender identities and relations changed in recent years, and if so in what ways?

Our identity as 'male' or 'female' is one of the most basic aspects of our being. As Sigmund Freud observed a century ago, when you meet a person for the first time, the very first thing you notice about them is whether they are a man or a woman. Yet what words do we use to capture this central fact? Is it the 'sex' or 'gender'? Zilla Eisenstein (1988), a famous feminist sociologist, summed up a conventional understanding when she said: 'Sex is the realm of biological raw material and gender reflects human social intervention' (1988: 81). As we will see, it may not be quite so simple.

Our gender and our sex are central identity markers. While accepting that being a person means being more than a man or a woman, our sexual identity is implicated in many of the feelings and thoughts we have about our self, as well as the kinds of relationships we have with each other.

Love and sex are also a matter of profound interest and preoccupation. Men, it is suggested, have a sexual thought every ten minutes. Many men and women are preoccupied with relationship issues. Music, films, television, the media and books are saturated with ideas, discussions and portrayals of sex and love. Advertising routinely uses sexual images to make toothpaste or chocolate seem more desirable. So when we say sex is vital to our identity, we refer to a wide spectrum embracing everything from quite personal and private issues through to broad public issues about gender and the roles men and women are expected to play.

In this chapter, we ask a few basic questions:

- What is sex and/or gender?
- How does sex relate to our sense of self, to our identity?
- Are there any significant changes taking place in the ways sexual and gender identity are lived out?
- Have traditional male and female roles changed in any significant way over the last quarter-century? Does greater public visibility and increased acceptance of gay and lesbian relations signify the 'homosexualisation' of our culture?

● WHY QUESTIONS ABOUT SEX MATTER

It is widely believed—especially by conservatives—that 'traditional' values and institutions like the family are under attack, or even dead. Much of this concern centres on the claim that traditional sexual roles, values and practices are under assault by feminists, lesbians and homosexuals. Human sexuality is both fascinating and deeply puzzling, as shown by a story told by one of the most famous economists of our time, Professor D. McCloskey, author of some nine books (see box).

Professor McCloskey writes (1999: 7–8)

I was, and am, a professor of economics and of history at the University of Iowa. From age eleven, I had been a secret cross dresser a few times a week. Otherwise I was normal, just a guy. My wife had known about the cross-dressing since the first year of our marriage when we were twenty-two. No big deal, we decided. Lots of men have this or that sexual preference. Relax we said. By 1994 aged fifty-two, I had been married these three decades, had two grown children, and thought I might cross dress a little more . . .

McCloskey's marvellous book *Crossing: A Memoir* (1999) is a profound, sensitive and moving essay about identity, sexuality and one person's journey into self. He tells the extraordinary story of how Donald McCloskey became Deidre McCloskey. We follow him in and out of a series of painful operations, with significant financial and social costs as Donald transforms himself into Deidre. He endures much physical and emotional pain, and financial hardship, and his wife and children disown him. As he observes:

My crossing—change, migration, growing up, self-discovery—took place from 1994 to 1997 beginning in my home in Iowa . . . I visited womanhood and stayed . . . I did not change gender because I liked colourful clothing [Donald did not] or womanly grace [Donald viewed it as sentimental]. The decision was not utilitarian; my gender crossing was motivated by identity not by a balance sheet of utility. I say in response to your question Why? 'Can't I just be?' You, dear reader, *are*. No one gets indignant if you have no answer to why you are an optimist or why you like peach ice-cream. And incidentally, why do you think you are the gender you were officially assigned to at birth? Prove it!

How should we understand McCloskey's story? In particular, what does it suggest about the role played by nature and nurture? Was he born a trans-sexual or was he just a cross-dresser who decided to make a permanent change? These questions are well discussed by Garber (1993) and by Greig et al. (2003: 138–52).

Trans-sexuals are people who realise early that they are trapped in the wrong body. (Psychiatrists, call this 'sexual dysmorphia'.) Sociologically, these people have been reared by their parents to reflect the body—and the genitalia—they were born with. Biologically, they also have all the normal sex chromosomes that correspond with being either a boy or girl. This may be so, yet they feel they either want to dress like the other sex or become them. How is this to be explained? This case indicates that neither biological nor sociological explanations seem to be all that useful.

That we need to think about this is suggested by an episode of the ABC TV series *Australian Story* screened in 2004. It followed the landmark case heard by the High Court in 2003 that 'found' that it was possible for a man, who had once been a woman and who then had gone though gender reassignment surgery to become a man, could lawfully marry her (female) partner. The Australian government and its then Attorney-General (Darryl Williams) decided to appeal the case. They argued that the court's judgment was offensive to traditional values and subverted the traditional idea of what marriage is supposed to be all about. Adding extra bite to this story was the fact that the lawyer representing the woman had herself once been a leading male lawyer who had gone through gender reassignment to become a leading female lawyer. The Commonwealth's appeal was subsequently dismissed and the person was finally able to marry her (female) partner.

• SEX AND GENDER

Conventionally, the term 'sex' has referred to the essential biological characteristics and processes at work in human bodies, while 'gender' has referred to the social and cultural expectations that are grafted on to our bodies by socialisation. But is the distinction really so clearcut?

Sex

The term 'sex' has been used to refer to what were seen as clear biological distinctions between female and male bodies.

Speaking genetically, most men and women have different sex chromosomes (XY in men and XX in women), and also have different hormones. These genetic traits mean that most women have a vagina, ovaries and breasts, tend to have less body hair, and are typically shorter than men. Most women also have the ability to give birth to babies. Most men have a penis and two testicles, typically have more facial and chest hair than women, and are usually both taller and more muscular than women.

We now know that it is not always so simple. One of the consequences of the international Human Genome Project, which set out to map the human genome in the 1980s and 1990s, was the discovery that the fragment of genetic material in human DNA that transforms the foetus—which always starts out as female—into a male *if* there is an XY chromosome present is fragile and subject to mutation. Consequently, there are a significant number of people who are genetically indeterminate—that is, they may have additional sex chromosomes. This means that, while to all intents and purposes they look to be either male or female, there is a more complex picture under the surface. The sporting world was rocked in the late 1980s when a number of very large and muscular women who had been competing at Olympic Games in track and field and swimming events were found after genetic examination to have male chromosomes—which, it was claimed, gave them an unfair advantage.

The normal foetal development process starts with a foetus that is female. If the XY chromosome is present about seven weeks after conception, that chromosome should cause a flooding of the foetus with testosterone, leading to the development of a penis and testes. In some small, isolated communities, this process can be delayed until puberty, when girls suddenly transform into boys. One of the authors of this book has visited an island where this process has been happening for several generations. That it has caused some consternation in the community is an understatement.

Gender

The word 'gender' is often used to refer to the social, cultural and psychological qualities of being 'male' or 'female'. Many sociologists believe that what it meant to be masculine or feminine is carried in our heads because society puts the notions there, and these in turn inform and shape our social actions, our bodies and our relationships.

In our society, masculinity has traditionally meant being:

- strong and protective;
- assertive;
- a breadwinner;
- intellectually rational (good at electronics and 'hard' disciplines like mathematics, engineering, etc.); and
- not good at expressing emotions.

On the other hand, femininity means being:

- soft and understanding;
- caring, nurturing and supportive;
- passive, forgiving and patient;
- intellectually limited, but emotionally expressive and talkative; and
- useless at mechanical or electronic work.

How accurate is this? As Greig et al. (2003: 134–5) point out, there are any number of possible ways of connecting the biological and the social, including the following:

- It is all sex and there is no gender.
- It is all gender and there is no sex.
- Sex determines gender.
- It starts with sex and then gender gets added.
- Gender takes over and determines sex.

For a start, we think the conventional distinction between sex as biological and gender as social is too simple. The biological and the sociological accounts of sex and gender both suffer from the usual problems that determinism sets loose when people start to construct stereotypes or engage in what we have referred to as essentialism.

● ESSENTIALISM AND THE SEX/GENDER ISSUE

On the one hand we have biological determinists who claim that sex and gender are natural. They believe biology shapes human behaviour and identity in universal ways. For example, the fact that men have testicles and penises, or are muscular, is used to argue that all men are strong, competitive, tough, hunter-gatherers, aggressive, intellectually rational and emotionally inadequate. Similarly, because women have uteruses, breasts and give birth, it is argued that they are soft, caring, passive, nurturing, love children and are intellectually restricted and emotionally sensitive.

On the other hand, there are sociological determinists who insist that sex and gender are all about social construction. Sex-role socialisation theorists claim that 'society' determines which roles and characteristics are functional. Furthermore, primary and secondary socialisation ensure that every new member of society is educated and fitted into his or her appropriate sex role.

As American sociologist Harold Garfinkel (1967: 122–8) observed several decades ago, many people who firmly believe in a 'natural' account of sex are committed to arguing that:

- There are only two sexes—female and male.
- Every person is either a male or female.
- Sexual identity is unvarying—that is, you are either male or female, and you remain that way forever.
- Genitals are the identifiers of sex—males have penises and females have vaginas.
- The division between male and female is an objective, natural and timeless fact.

Both biological and sociological determinists rely on gender essentialism. This is the claim that a single set of rudimentary gender characteristics defines the identity and experiences of a person. Gender essentialists claim that all women or all men share certain characteristics with all other women or men. This requires overlooking other aspects of the person's identity, like their age, religion, ethnicity and social class.

Both biological and sociological determinists also seem to cling to the idea that any explanation must be given in terms of one factor or the other: it is either biological or it is sociological. This intellectual disposition seems to be deeply rooted in Western dualist metaphysics. We prefer the kind of fuzzy logic that has been gaining ground in various new kinds of mathematics and information technology.

There are many problems with the logic of both biological and sociological determinism. Let us look at biological determinism first.

● PROBLEMS WITH BIOLOGICAL DETERMINISM

As writers like Lacquer (1980) remind us, from the time of Plato through to the Enlightenment of the eighteenth century and later, Europeans believed in a 'one-sex model'. That is, while 'man' and 'woman' were acknowledged to exist, human bodies were believed to derive from a single ideal or archetypal body. There are no prizes for guessing that the ideal body was a male body, from which the subordinate female body had been split off.

Into the eighteenth century, anatomists were able to scientifically 'prove' this story by showing how a woman's vagina, when suitably drawn and described, looked just like the male penis. They also maintained that, just as men ejaculated semen at orgasm, so women also produced a kind of 'semen' when they 'came'. It is this Platonic story that also gives us the charming idea that 'love' is what happens when a man and woman recognise each other as having been originally part of one body.

Lacquer reminds us that sex, like all other 'natural' things, is surrounded and reshaped by the cultural and symbolic discourses and stories that have gathered over time in a given society. The implication of this is that we never encounter the natural as it 'really' is, but only as it is given to us in a cultural framework of belief and practice. Bourdieu (1994) calls this cultural framework of practice a 'habitus', or 'second nature', emphasising how many things frequently feel and look to be the natural way of doing things.

Sociologists and anthropologists have also pointed out for some time now that definitions of what it means to be masculine or feminine vary dramatically across different times and places. Margaret Mead's study of gender (1963 [1935]) in three different communities demonstrated that, while in some communities men were strong, tough breadwinners, in others they were not; equally, not all women were soft, caring, passive and nurturing. Since Mead, many researchers have provided evidence to demonstrate that being masculine and feminine can be a different experience historically and geographically.

Third, many homosexual men and women demonstrate that it is possible to be both stereotypically masculine or feminine, and yet not to want to have sexual relationships or emotional attachments in the way 'real' women and 'real' men are supposed to. For example, very feminine lesbian women may feel a strong emotional attachment and sexual desire towards other women who present as stereotypically feminine. Equally, many 'straight' women and men do not fit the traditional gender stereotypes.

In short, biological determinism starts to collapse before the evidence of actual diversity. The same kinds of problems confront sociological determinists.

● PROBLEMS WITH SOCIOLOGICAL DETERMINISM

Sociological determinism is the idea that 'society' or 'structures' determine behaviour and identity. Many sociologists, including feminists in the 1970s and 1980s, argued that sex and gender were products of what a particular society said a woman and man ought to be. Sex-role socialisation theorists claimed that society determined what roles and characteristics were functional. Furthermore, primary and secondary socialisation ensures that every new member of society is educated and fitted into his or her appropriate sex role.

Feminists in the 1970s and 1980s gave these sociological ideas about gender and sex-role socialisation a distinctive twist (Hughes 1997). According to feminists at this time, structure determined identity. The feminist story maintained that all females who were successfully socialised as women were the victims of the social system. Exponents of feminism in the 1970s and 1980s replaced the idea of society with the concept of patriarchy—that is, a society dominated by men, which was identified as a universal and timeless system of gender-based oppression.

A lot of effort is undoubtedly put into teaching children to behave in gender-specific ways. We do learn many of the things related to being male or female. Research into sex-role socialisation suggests that young children learn early what their sex is. Peterson (1997), for example, claims that from eight months of age children are sensitive to sex differences in adult physical appearance. Even so, they may still have trouble distinguishing themselves, or other children, correctly as 'boy' or 'girl' for some time after they have learned to speak. Even children aged between four and seven may use the language of sex 'incorrectly'.

Further, 'gender constancy'—or the idea that we are permanently one sex or the other—can take some time to develop. Young children, for example, believe that having a different haircut can change your gender (Peterson 1997: 260). It is also common for young children to dress, and take on the name and persona, of the opposite sex.

Equally, it is clear that in most societies there are dominant views—or sex norms—about what is appropriate behaviour for boys and girls. Many parents, for example, have clear ideas about the 'right' colours in which to dress their babies, and how they should relate to little boys and girls. Fagot et al.'s (1985) work indicates that many parents expect boys to be physically rough and able to take a 'tumble', while their daughters are encouraged to be less physically active and more talkative. By the age of two, these expectations are identified as predictors of how well girls and boys are adjusting to their respective sex roles. At the same time—and especially in adolescence—young people are inclined to imitate certain sex-role models from their own gender group. Parents are said to be particularly strong role models (Russell 1989).

Privileging sex-role socialisation as the explanation for why people behave as men or as women cannot account for the actual diversity of sexual and gendered behaviour, however. Nor does it allow for the possibility that both our sexuality and our gender identity are a complex overlay of biological factors and social processes in which both determinism and choice play a part.

Gender essentialists ignore all the evidence suggesting that there are no universal or timeless characteristics exhibited by all women and all men at all times. They also rely on a view of determinism that seems to deny us any kind of choice.

There are influential ideas at work defining and valuing social practices which continue to regulate the behaviour of many Australians in terms of prescribed masculine and feminine behaviours. Yet 'manliness' and 'womanliness' are no more essentially a single set of characteristics than being 'Australian' or 'young' or 'Catholic'. Brown and Jordanova (1982: 390) make the point that:

> there is no such thing as woman or man outside of a social setting; men and women, and femininity and masculinity, are constituted in specific social settings with factors like our age, class, marital status and so on impacting quite heavily on how we shape our gender identities.

Sociological determinists ignore the fact that gender is not an orderly or tightly definable category within any large or complex society. Even if there are dominant societal or patriarchal norms about how a proper man or woman is supposed to behave, this does not mean that everyone actually conforms to these norms. Increasing numbers of Australian men—referred to as 'metro-sexuals'—spend a lot of their time in gyms pursuing a buffed body, and wear colognes, moisturisers and jewellery. Many women now pursue paid jobs, and some engage in body-building exercises that have traditionally been exclusive to the male domain.

When people use a notion like masculinity or femininity to 'explain' why someone has done something (e.g. Polk 1994), such accounts rely on essentialist definitions of masculinity or femininity that select one or more characteristics and use those to define the substance of femininity or masculinity. A major limitation of the attempt to encapsulate femininity or masculinity by reference to behaviours like risk-taking, possessiveness, the need to compete and aggression is the arbitrary choice of what is identified as the essence of femininity or masculinity. This selection often tells us more about the writer than anything else.

Second, sociological determinists assume that babies and children are passive vessels that are filled and shaped through the sex-role socialisation process with whatever society prescribes as the appropriate sex-role characteristics. The problem with this account is that people are always making choices about how to act and feel. Children are very capable of asserting themselves in terms of the kinds of clothing, toys or hairstyles they want, and often do this against the wishes of their parents.

Gender cannot be defined as if it were some kind of object—like a chair or a rock. Such an approach to understanding gender leads to 'essentialist' accounts based on an appeal either to 'nature' or to 'society', both of which are problematic. Gender is not open to essentialist descriptions. There is no evidence to support the claim that all women or all men, by virtue of their nature or their socialisation, can be defined according to a single set of characteristics.

Gender is a matter of identity involving both the things that are given to us biologically *and* culturally to work with. Identity is also a process of working out how to live as we negotiate between the flow of consciousness, ideas and feelings that come from within us *and* the ideas and expectations of others that mark out the domain of the social.

In important ways, this means that there is a basic historical quality to our identities. This means first that each of us has a personal history of evolving into a particular kind of man or woman. Equally, and in the larger sense of the idea of a collective history, the gendered identities of men and women are not timeless, but relate to their historical context.

Gender identity is fluid and changeable

Even within the same society, women and men have diverse experiences of age, ethnicity, religion and class, and these experiences intersect with being masculine or feminine. Being a young Australian-Italian Catholic male is a very different experience from being a young Australian-Arabic Muslim male. Some men body-build, while others never do strenuous exercise. Some women have babies, while others do not. Our identities as women and men are developed in complex sets of interactions in specific social and material contexts. These identities can be both unchanging and fluid.

Australian feminists Carol Johnson (1993) and Kerry Carrington (1993) emphasise the diversity of women's and girls' experiences and women's capacity for agency, and warn against essentialising gender categories. They are critical of older feminist arguments which claim that all women have in common certain experiences related to being subject to masculine/patriarchal oppression. Some women from different ethnic minority backgrounds have argued that such assertions fail to appreciate the issues of cultural difference, and that many of the oppressive practices 'Western women' refer to are in fact not experienced by them as oppressive. Further, the assumptions made by some Western feminists that they (certain ethnic minority groups) are oppressed are in fact themselves oppressive and even disempowering. The idea that to be a woman (regardless of one's socio-cultural, political or personal history) only means 'oppression under patriarchal domination' has successfully been challenged.

There is now much broader acceptance by feminists that two or more women can be positioned in such ways that mean they may have more in common with a man than they do with each other (Yeatman 1990: 154). Tsolidis (1993: 56), for example, has noted how many 'black' women say they have more in common with men of their own indigenous community than they do with 'white feminist' women.

Many factors play a part in the shaping of ourselves as women and men, mothers and fathers, wives and husbands or as same-sex couples. In some circumstances, we may have opportunities to accept or reject certain expectations. As she explains in her account of growing up in a 'strict Greek family', Penny's immediate family provides her:

> main source of information about how a Greek female should prepare herself for her own family. Much of this came from conversations with my mother. For example, I might be peeling the potatoes in the sink and my mum might come out with a statement like: 'I hope you're watching how I am making the casserole, Penny because one day you'll be doing this for your family.' Oh those dreaded words—'one day' and 'family' don't go too good in the same sentence. Although I do plan to have a family—one day, I still believe that a woman of the house need not do all of the housework. (Bessant, 2004 Interview)

Gender essentialists overlook our capacity for choice—or what philosophers call 'agency'. For some people, however, their social circumstances are such that their agency can be very limited or even non-existent. This is why no discussion of gender identity can be complete until the problem of inequality is taken into account. As we will see, there is plenty of research evidence pointing to considerable inequality between women and men.

● GENDER INEQUALITY

A number of questions provide an indication of the problems women still face in Australia:

- Why are women's average weekly earnings in Australia in 2005 still only two-thirds of men's average weekly earnings?
- Why is it that Australia has not yet had a woman prime minister?
- Why has our High Court up to 2006 only had two women judges?
- Why do women make up fewer than 6 per cent of company directors in the top 100 businesses?

- Why do so few male partners of working women assume full-time child-care responsibilities or full-time work in the home?

PATRIARCHY AND THE SEXUAL DIVISION OF LABOUR

One answer to each of these questions is that Australia, in common with most other societies, is a 'patriarchy'. This is a social system in which men as a group dominate and oppress women as a group. In patriarchal systems, men have more wealth, status and power than women.

Feminists in the 1970s identified patriarchy as the 'master' system, and sex-role socialisation as the social process that produced gender roles and identity and consequently reproduced the system of inequality and oppression. Gender (like 'class' in the Marxist tradition) came to be the key to everything—often at the expense of other identity markers like class, ethnicity, religion, status and biography.

They could point with some force to the role played by a variety of belief systems, particularly 'sexism', which relies on the idea that there are a number of real or imagined differences between women and men. Those differences are usually said to be either natural and universal, and are used to explain why men are supposedly superior to or dominate women.

SEXUAL DIVISION OF LABOUR

Regardless of the value of a category like patriarchy, or how 'masculinity' and 'femininity' are defined, there is a clear sexual division of labour in Australia. This refers to the idea that specific activities are identified as men's work while others are defined as women's work. It should be noted that there is no universal pattern in the specific activities that are defined as men's or women's work: what men do in one society may be done by women in another.

Aboriginal Australians and white Australians have for a long time lived and worked in ways shaped by a sexual division of labour. When white colonists encountered Aboriginal societies, there was evidence of a clear sexual division of labour (Broome 1984: 14–19). In Victoria, for example, Aboriginal men went hunting or engaged in war-making while the women gathered the vegetable food, tended the camp and did the basic child care. There was also a very clear division in terms of symbolic and ritual activities, with 'women's business' and 'men's business' carefully segregated.

For the 200 years and more since the white occupation of Australia began, Australia has had an established sexual division of labour that also reflected the organisation of a capitalist economy. One of the key features of any capitalist economy is the existence of a large number of people who sell their labour for wages.

In white Australia, most men have been the major breadwinners and done what economists call 'productive work'. Women have also always been employed in the labour market. However, marriage marked the end of economic participation for many women—at least until the 1970s. Up to that time most married women ceased paid work when they got married or fell pregnant. They then took over most of the household work, involving cooking, cleaning and caring for children and other dependants.

It wasn't always this way historically, however. Before the emergence of modern capitalism, economies were household-based. This meant that family households produced farm foods, textiles and other goods, and they did this work based on an understanding and expectation that everyone in the household contributed. This was the dominant mode of production in countries like Britain until the eighteenth century, or in places like Italy, Greece or Turkey until quite recently. It remains a popular mode of production in many African and South American countries.

From the eighteenth century, the new capitalist economies saw men physically move from their households and go into factories, mines or offices, where they worked for wages.

• MEN'S WORK

For more than 200 years, most Australian men have sold their labour in the labour market. Some have been professionals who have sold their services; some have worked farms or run small businesses. A small number have owned large quantities of capital, from which they derived an income.

Men's privileged access to the labour market was part of the larger sexual division of labour. Married women took primary responsibility for work in the home, including domestic and child-care work. Conversely, wage work and productive work done outside the household was defined as men's business, and done largely by men. This traditional sexual division of labour was accompanied by important economic, cultural and psychological features.

Men assumed a psychological identity as breadwinners, as most of the (male) population sold their labour power on the labour market. To be a good breadwinner was for a long time a primary mark of a 'real' man. A set of cultural, psychological and social practices and expectations developed around access to work and its meanings, especially among men. The 'industrial society' relied on the expansion of a labour market and the development of a 'work ethic'—a set of moral rules, such as: 'It is good to work hard, to save hard, and to be independent and self-reliant'. This goes with a set of feelings like shame, anxiety or guilt.

Paid employment has always been important to male identity. It helps define who a man is. Paid work also helps structure our life worlds. The way time is organised, for example, often assumes that five days out of seven are devoted to work.

• WOMEN'S WORK

The sexual division of labour meant that, until the 1970s, most married women stayed at home and organised the household economy. But there have always been Australian women in the labour market, especially before marriage or having children, while many have stayed on in part-time work.

Women have always been an important part of the labour force. If we look at the proportion of all women (over fifteen and under 65 years) who are working in full-time jobs, there has been little growth for 60 years or more. According to Probert (1997: 2):

- In 1933, 25.5 per cent of women aged fifteen to 65 worked full-time.
- In 1986, 26.9 per cent of women aged fifteen to 65 worked full-time.
- In 1997, 28 per cent of women aged fifteen to 65 worked full-time.

The other kind of work women have done is unpaid household work. Over twenty years ago, economists like John Ironmonger (1989) set out to measure the economic value of the various kinds of work women did in the home by calculating a proper wage for it. In the 1980s, this produced estimates that women's household work was worth up to half the total value of GDP. The economic value of this domestic work in 2005, according to economists' estimates, is more than $410 billion a year.

• CHANGES?

There is evidence pointing to some significant changes in this 'traditional' pattern over the past quarter-century. The Australian labour market has become increasingly feminised since 1975 (Probert & McDonald 1996), and there have been changes in the labour force participation rates of men and women since 1985. The labour force participation rate is the proportion of the total population aged sixteen to 65 in the labour force. The labour force participation rate allows us to measure both the male and female participation rates. The evidence seems to show that more married women are entering the labour market and more men are leaving it (see Table 9.1).

As Belinda Probert (1997) has pointed out, there is a popular view that in the past few decades the participation of women in the labour force has risen, especially for 25–54-year-olds. However, as Probert has shown, the participation rate for young women did not rise significantly from 1966 to the mid-1990s. This was due to the collapse of the full-time youth labour market and the complementary dramatic rise in education participation (ABS 1996a: 72–3). The 25–34 age group experienced the largest growth in work participation, with comparatively smaller rises for older women (DEET 1995: 27). Probert (1997) argues that if we look at the volume of women's work, measured in terms of equivalent full-time units, we find only a small rise in the number of women working, from 31 per cent of working-age women in 1933 to 37 per cent of working-age women in 1993.

What this adds up to is that there are now more married women in waged work. There has been a significant increase in the proportion of married women (or women in couple relations) with paid jobs. And there are fewer men working full-time in Australia than ever before (as we see in Table 9.1). Such data have led commentators to speak of the 'feminisation of the workforce' (see box).

Table 9.1 Key trends in the Australian labour force, 1985–2005

	1993	**1995**	**1999**	**2005**
Total labour force ('000)	7.2	8.6	8.9	9.4
Participation rate	60.5	62.6	63.3	63.2
Male participation rate	75.9	73.9	73.8	72.8
Female participation rate	52.5	52.7	51.7	53.9

Source: ABS 2005c: 108.

The feminisation of the workforce

The feminisation of the workforce is due to a number of factors:

- More women want waged work and want to combine domestic and paid work.

- There are more supports (e.g. flexi-time and flexible child care), enabling more women to combine paid employment with child care. There has been a notable decline in the number of traditional men's jobs, especially in manufacturing and heavy industries.

- There has been a corresponding growth in service industries, which require new skills—especially in areas like social and community services—and are based on part-time employment. It is thus not surprising that the majority of employees in the largest industry sector in Australia, the social and community services sector, are women (about 66 per cent). The community services sector has 1.5 million workers, and includes occupations such as teaching, social work, medicine and nursing, which involve working with people.

- Many employers are now 'downsizing' by sacking male workers and replacing full-time positions with part-time jobs. This trend suits many women with dependent children.

One 1997 report indicated that in Australia between 1990 and 1997, only 2500 permanent full-time jobs had been created, compared with over 500 000 new part-time jobs. Most new jobs created in Australia since 1975 have been filled by women, because the majority of new jobs have been part-time. It should be noted however that the ABS analysis of women's workforce participation rates does not take into account the effect on women's employment of the shrinkage in full-time work and the growth in part-time work.

Yet some things do not change. Certain core aspects of the division of labour remain intact, despite some important changes. First, the female participation rate—especially for married women—depends on factors which reflect the different status of women, such as:

- the availability of affordable child care;
- access to part-time work, to accommodate school and kindergarten schedules;
- the birth rate, which has declined; and
- the child/family-friendliness of workplaces.

Despite the rise in female participation rates, especially of married women, women continue to leave the workforce at an earlier age than men (DEETYA 1997).

Second, the labour market has been, and remains, profoundly divided between women's and men's jobs, with only about 25 per cent commonality. (Sociologists call this occupational segregation.) By 2006, for example, some 24 per cent of men worked as electricians, plumbers and carpenters, compared with only 2 per cent of women (ABS 2006b: 121).

Women's income from wages still tends on average to be lower than men's. In 1994, women's pay (including overtime, over-award pay and measured result payment) averaged 85 per cent of men's average wages (ABS 1996b: 112). This means women tend to be more flexible in terms of how they enter and leave the labour market. Most women cannot say they have been in a full-time waged job for more than ten years. In 1995, only 591 000 women, compared with 1.2 million men, had been in their jobs for more than ten years (ABS 1995: 111).

Finally, even though there are increasing numbers of married women in the labour market, women who are in couple relationships continue to do most of the housework. And most women with children provide the daily (and nightly) care for those children. For most women, 'paid employment' still includes part-time waged work. This is usually combined with unpaid domestic and child-care work.

• UNEQUAL CONSEQUENCES

It is now widely accepted that the greatest social change over the past few decades has been the increase of the proportion of married women in the labour force. Yet the division of labour continues to have a major impact on women's lives, reinforcing the long-standing unequal status of women as a group. There is no shortage of good research to provide evidence about the extent of gendered inequality in Australia.

One consequence of this division of labour has been that men as a group tend to be more economically and politically powerful, and to have more prestige than women. Gender inequality characterises the social relations between women as a group and men as a group. Despite the 'feminisation of the labour market', a gendered division of labour remains a noticeable feature. Most women continue to work in a narrow band of female-dominated occupations, and most are excluded from senior positions and top income-earning jobs.

Australian women still earn less on average than men

Despite acceptance in 1969 of the legal principle that men and women doing the same job should get paid equally, men's and women's wages are still (on average) unequal. Table 9.2 shows that women in full-time work (in 1985–94) earned on average between three-quarters and four-fifths of the income men in full-time work were earning.

Table 9.2 Female/male ratio of average total full-time adult weekly earnings, 1985–94

Year	Female/male ratio
1985	0.79
1986	0.79
1987	0.79
1988	0.79
1989	0.79
1990	0.79
1991	0.80
1992	0.82
1993	0.80
1994	0.82

Source: ABS (1996b: 114).

Again, we need to be careful about the extent to which we generalise. As Katie Hughes (1997) points out, this does not mean that individual women cannot have more money, wealth, power or prestige than some or even most men. However, more women are poor, and women tent to be closer to poverty and economic insecurity than men. There is evidence to show that poverty, like the workforce, has been feminised. One of the strong findings of recent research is that to be a woman and a sole parent means almost certain poverty (Saunders 1994; Shaver 1998). As Shaver (1998: 277–89) shows, sole parents, older single women whose children are over sixteen and the wives of unemployed men are more likely to be poor.

As Gregory and Hunter's (1995) research suggests, although women's participation rate has risen, not all women enjoy equal access to paid employment. Like men, woman's ability to obtain employment is affected by her socioeconomic status. Hunter and Gregory used census data to examine the social and economic characteristics of each census district (each one consisting of roughly 700 households across Australia), and ranked these census districts by socioeconomic status. Between 1976 and 1991, the employment-to-population ratio fell generally. High-income, high-status neighbourhoods did much better than low-status, low-income neighbourhoods. This also has a gender aspect (cited in Probert 1997: 7):

- For men in the top 5 per cent of high-income, high-status socioeconomic status (SES) areas, the employment-to-population ratio fell by 9 per cent.
- For men in the lowest 5 per cent of SES neighbourhoods, the employment-to-population ratio fell by 37 per cent.
- For women in the top 50 per cent of SES areas, the employment-to-population ratio rose by 16 per cent; however, the ratio for women in the bottom 10 per cent of SES areas fell by 17.5 per cent.

These findings highlight the fact that not all women experience work in the same way. Being poor or working class, or living in particular neighbourhoods, can affect the way people cope with changes in employment.

To date we have focused on the large-scale shifts in the sexual division of labour. Do any of these changes affect more intimate aspects of our lives? Does the 'feminisation of the workforce' impact on the way men and women relate to each other? If gender relations are changing, is this having an impact on the ways Australians conduct their sexual lives and relations? Have the rise of feminism and the increasing number of married women in the workforce created a 'crisis of masculinity', as some writers like Biddulph (2004) claim? Can we use a process like the feminisation of the workforce to account for major shifts in the public acceptance of gay and lesbian sexuality?

● CHANGING SEXUALITIES?

Sexuality relates to the ways we experience our gender identities and our bodies, and how we use our bodies in terms of physical movement, decoration, adornment, display, sexual pleasure and reproduction. Many sociologists argue that, even in the most private aspects of our lives, social conventions, rules and symbolic systems shape our conduct, feelings and experiences. They say that sexuality is a set of practices shaped by social definitions and prescriptions.

In Western societies, Christian churches have traditionally expressed hostility to many expressions of sexuality. There is a long history of church attempts to regulate and control sexuality by using shame, fear, guilt and, when all else fails, the law. As Foucault (1986) shows, the early Christian Church drew on 'pagan' Greek and Roman codes of practice to regulate sex. Foucault demonstrates how the Greek practice of encouraging older men to enter into erotic relations with boys was severely regulated and driven by the fear that, for an older man, losing control or seeking to have anal intercourse would render that man effeminate and/or animal-like.

The subsequent development of Catholic natural law teachings took up these views, which rendered sex acceptable only when it was performed inside marriage—and then only when the husband and wife wanted to have children. This animus against unrestrained sexuality or sex for pleasure mimicked similar views found in Judaism. Masturbation was defined as a venial sin, birth control was wicked and immoral, abortion was evil, and homosexuality was regarded as offensive to the natural order. Today there are still many people who subscribe to these beliefs, and they continue to provide the official belief system of the Catholic Church.

One effect of this was to sanction a staggering degree of hypocrisy accompanying unremitting efforts to regulate people's sexual lives by a variety of legal and policing mechanisms. Modern governments continue to define the legal basis of sexuality by stating when young persons may legally have sexual intercourse, or when they can marry without parental permission. In Australia, we are forbidden to engage in certain sexual activity in public (e.g. masturbation and intercourse) because such activities are defined as immoral and a public nuisance. Marriage laws determine legal sexual relationships in marriage. Rich (1984) argues that if heterosexuality is experienced by many people as normal, this is because desire for the opposite sex is something that has been imposed, managed, organised, propagandised and maintained by force. For a long time, deviant sexuality has been legally prohibited, with punishments attached. (In some US states, husbands and wives may not legally engage in fellatio or anal intercourse.) In Tasmania, sex between consenting male adults in private was unlawful until 2000.

The results can sometimes take on a ludicrous quality. In America, the case of President Bill Clinton springs to mind (see box).

Regulating moral values: President Bill Clinton

The official American value system continues to be shaped by a conservative Christian view about the place of sex in marriage. Clinton, who was a self-proclaimed Christian and whose fondness for extra-marital sex was well known before his election to the presidency in 1992, was nearly impeached by the Republican Party in 1998–99 for his well-known affair with a young female staffer at the White House and his pathetic attempts to lie his way out of the mess. The impeachment process fell apart when the editor of a man's magazine called *Hustler* offered a million dollars for each provable case of senior Republicans engaging in sexual hanky panky. Within days of offering this reward, four of the most senior Republicans running the case for family values against Clinton had resigned.

Gagnon and Simon (1973) argue that sexuality involves complex social processes and rules. They argue that the situations and behaviours we see and experience as 'sexual' are socially defined in that way. The ways situations and behaviours are identified and experienced as sexual is the result of organised 'sexual scripts' which provide frameworks of meaning for the people in those situations. Gagnon and Simon illustrate the ways sexual scripts are constructed and learned by people in different settings and ages. In a later book, they argue (Gagnon & Simon 1987) that these sexual scripts work on three different levels:

- a general cultural level, where the scripts operate at the level of institutions (e.g. large-scale organisations and the law) to prescribe 'normal' sexual life;
- the interpersonal level, where people apply their understanding of what is appropriate to another person in what evolves into a 'sexual act'; and
- the intra-psychic level, which is concerned with how we construct our desires and fantasies.

This sociological approach to human sexuality is well illustrated when we look at some contemporary stories men in particular tell about themselves, in which they are constructed as the sexually aggressive creature pursuing the more passive female. This story is what some writers call 'heterosexism'.

● HETEROSEXISM

According to heterosexists, sex is what women have 'done' to them by men. Men, it is said, experience desire, have erections which they cannot really control, and initiate the sex. Women are either receptive or not. Further, 'proper' sex means 'penetrative sex with ejaculation'. Heterosexists also believe that all men want sex at every opportunity, that most men are promiscuous, and that their penises direct their lives. According to heterosexist accounts of sexuality, sexual desire is always heterosexual, and desire is for those of the opposite sex—that is, women find men sexually arousing and men find women sexually attractive (Walker 1988: 99–102).

Heterosexism also sees as 'fact' the idea that women have different sexual needs from men. The claim is made that most women, unless they are immoral, are sexually passive and generally uninterested in sex. Further, women's sexuality is said to be responsive to men's desires. According to heterosexist discourses, women like 'their' men to be strong, good providers and virile. Women also supposedly feel secure and comfortable as a support person, preferring to defer to the authority, knowledge and strength of the man.

R.W. Connell (1995) argues that this story validates the need for men to embody power, to fill out social, physical, intellectual, emotional space by occupying and dominating rooms, groups, disciplines and books. The embodiment of masculine power is also exhibited publicly, in demonstrations of sporting prowess and the need to be successful in sport, the workplace and the market. It follows, according to heterosexist discourses, that gay men are not 'real men' and are easily distinguishable by their 'feminine' manners and gestures. Similarly, by virtue of the reality that they do not find men sexually attractive, lesbians fail to be 'real women'.

Some feminists argue that heterosexism is an elaborate attempt to prescribe how women and men should be. So what does 'real' sexuality look like?

● ACTUAL SEXUALITY?

Like many aspects of human activity, our sexuality is complex. And it is not easy to make robust generalisations about what people actually do sexually. We get a clue about the central problem here when we consider the problem of getting men to give accurate self-measurements of their own erect penises. In the late 1990s, the condom manufacturer Ansells asked their male customers to send in self-measurements, supplying a tape measure with each pack of condoms. The results suggested Australian men had undergone a secret evolutionary process to become penile giants. Given the sensitivities about sexual activity, people are often unwilling to engage in full disclosure.

No such problem appears to have affected the single most famous and long-lived research project inquiring into human sexuality, which began in the United States in the late 1930s. Alfred Kinsey was an American zoologist who gave up studying wasps and turned to the study of human sexuality. Kinsey started a huge sexual research project at Indiana University that has now been going on for some 70 years. It was designed to collect thousands of sexual histories given to his researchers by ordinary American men and women across the entire age range. He wanted to know when people started having a sexual life, when they had their first orgasm, who and what they had sex with and how often they engaged in sexual activities.

In his first report on male sexuality, published over half a century ago and resting on some 50 000 interviews, Kinsey (1948) made some 'shocking' discoveries:

- Most men started masturbating at puberty and masturbation remained a lifelong practice even among married men.
- Marital sex hardly began to contain the enormous and prolific sexuality of most men.
- Most men had had their first sexual experience with a woman in the mid- to late teen years.
- A majority of men had had extra-marital sex with a prostitute or a non-professional sexual partner.
- A substantial minority of men had had sex to orgasm with animals.

- A third of the men interviewed had experienced at least one orgasm with another male.
- There were purely 'heterosexual' men and purely 'homosexual' men, but both groups were statistically 'small' and 'abnormal', while in the middle there was a continuum of desire and patterns of practice as men in particular sought out sexual opportunities as the need arose. This idea rested on evidence gained from close and detailed interviews suggesting that most men had erotic images and dreams featuring other men.
- Kinsey also showed the effects that class, religion and geographic region had on these patterns of sexual activity: crudely put, working-class boys and boys in rural settings started earlier, while middle-class men had more 'inventive' sexual lives.

Kinsey concluded that human sexuality cannot be put into the simple pigeonholes prescribed by the heterosexist story. As he put it, 'nature does not know about or construct pigeon holes'.

Kinsey's research suggests that, while there are ongoing attempts by all sorts of groups to regulate sexual life—including governments, churches and more recently experts who write 'how to have sex' advice books—this does not quite contain the anarchic qualities of actual human sexuality.

Despite considerable public discussion about sex in magazines and on TV, much of the controversy about it is riddled with anxiety. Many men continue to worry about their ability to have erections at will and whether they 'measure up' to being a 'real' man. Equally, many women are concerned about their body size and shape. Some feel anxious about their breast size, the amount of cellulite on their thighs and/or their ability to reach orgasm.

● SEXUALITY AND FLUID IDENTITY

The discussion about heterosexism suggests a strong connection between identity and sexuality. But what is that link? Again the inside/outside problem is relevant. The story told by Gary Wotherspoon (1986: 111–12) (see box) raises many interesting questions about sexual identity.

Gary's story

Gary is a Sydney academic who is now in his late fifties. Here he remembers his teenage years:

> With schoolmates, with neighbours, with relatives, or with strangers I began a highly active sex life that lasted with only minor breaks (with two notable exceptions) for almost 25 years. Ignoring the solitary pleasures of masturbation—so frowned

upon by the medical and religious professions in my day—I would probably have had sex with another person at least two or three times a week over this quarter-century . . . I had probably the fairly standard heterosexual experiences of my peer group.

In our social group one had 'girlfriends'; relationships could last from a month or so to several years. Sexual activity depended on how long you had been going out together, how committed the girl felt you were and how both sets of parents viewed the situation. 'Heavy petting' was deep tongue kissing, breast fondling, vaginal stimulation: all of these indulgences were fairly commonly practised among our group. Actual intercourse was rare . . . Many of our peer group assured us that, once engaged to marry, sexual activity increased. But it was fairly dull, unimaginative stuff. None of the girls in our group were known to like oral sex; cunnilingus and analingus might as well have been places in Ireland for all we knew of them. I was, however, lucky enough to have as a neighbour a girl who was as sexually experimental as I was and we certainly enjoyed fucking.

Gary now identifies himself as gay, and is a leading historian in the gay movement. His story opens up some important questions about the social nature of sex and gender. For example, is 'being homosexual' a fact confirmed by the sexual activities we engage in, or by the emotions and fantasies we carry with us? If older research by Kinsey (1948) is plausible, what sense do we make of the fact that, while only about 10 per cent of men identified themselves as 'homosexual', between a quarter and a third of the men in his study had had at least one sexual experience to orgasm with another man? Or how do we deal with the fact that some people engage in homosexual behaviour while they are in single-sex prisons or single-sex boarding schools? Similarly, some sex workers may have both male and female clients, but claim heterosexual identities (Moore & Rosenthal 1993: 106–7).

Some women and men 'know' early in their lives that they are 'homosexual', 'heterosexual' or 'bisexual', and do not deviate from that realisation. Others discover this through experiment, while some switch interest and desires according to mood or occasion. This indicates that it may not be wise to maintain a close and fixed connection between our sexuality, which can be fluid and diverse, and our identities (as masculine or feminine). If psychologists like Jung are right, all of us carry 'feminine' and 'masculine' features, and being psychologically 'healthy' means achieving a balance.

● CONCLUSION

It may well be that 'once upon a time' men and women staked their identity in terms of traditional gender and sex roles. However, it is apparent that, in the last 50 years or so, all sorts of traditional understandings about sex and what it means to be a man or a woman have begun to change:

- Identity politics took off in the 1960s with the feminist movement. Australian writers like Germaine Greer, Dale Spender and Eva Cox challenged the idea that women are 'naturally' suited to being mothers and housewives. The women's movement has promoted gender equality, and has been a major challenge to the nuclear family and to women's role in it.
- The gay movement, led in Australia by writers like Denis Altmann, challenged the idea that heterosexuality is a natural and necessarily desirable identity.
- Men's movements have emerged to encourage men to look at their roles in domestic violence and to promote a more equal relationship between men and women.
- Most governments in Australia have accepted that women have a right to be treated equally and should not be subject to sexual assault, harassment or gender-based discrimination in their paid employment.

These developments have been successful to varying degrees. Political parties have struggled with 'affirmative action' for women. At state level, two women—Carmen Lawrence (Western Australia) and Joan Kirner (Victoria)—have served as premiers. Australia has still not had a woman prime minister, nor does it have a parliament like that in Sweden, where half of the MPs are women. In the home, while many women deny they are feminists, there is a general trend towards women being more assertive about identifying their needs and acting to have those needs met; however, domestic violence still affects too many women.

We can be sure about only one thing: sex and gender will remain controversial talking points.

Discussion questions

9.1 Are men and women different? If so, in what ways? How should we talk about these differences?

9.2 In what ways can differences between men and women become a basis for inequality between them?

9.3 How can we distinguish between what is 'natural' and what is 'cultural' in relation to sex and gender?

9.4 How useful is the explanation of sex role socialisation (and/or patriarchy) in explaining patterns of inequality in men's and women's lives?

9.5 Do gay men attract more social disapproval than lesbian women? If so, why?

Man is certainly stark mad: he cannot make a flea and yet he will be making gods by dozens.

Montaigne, (1994) 'Apology for Raimonde de Sebonde' from his Essays (1580–1588)

RELIGION IN AUSTRALIA 10.

● ● SUMMARY

Mainstream sociologists and social theorists over the last century have endlessly promoted a portrait of modern societies as places where science and reason have triumphed. Yet religious belief continues to inform the lives of large numbers of people who live in modern societies—like Australia. Religion is another key source of identity. If anything religion is emerging—again—as a significant source of political and social activism. We see this especially in the regeneration of conservative political ideas that are helping to reshape contemporary Australian public life. In this chapter we explore the contemporary character of religion in Australia. We begin with some basic questions about religion and spirituality before turning to the sociological tradition and the arguments of two great sociologists, Durkheim and Weber. We conclude with a brief discussion of the social significance of the contemporary revival of religious faith.

Here are some of the things that many contemporary Australians see or do on a daily basis:

- On large city streets around lunchtime, lines of colourfully clothed, drum-banging, chanting and cymbal-crashing devotees of Krishna weave through crowds of often bemused shoppers.
- At sunrise each day in certain suburbs of Melbourne and Sydney, thousands of Muslim men gather to say the first prayers of the day in mosques.
- The authors of this book give lectures several times a week in a multi-million dollar 800-seat lecture theatre built by a small inner-city church in Melbourne. The church invested in this venue to house the several thousand Christians who take part in Sunday worship each week, accompanied by rock bands.
- In bookshops all over Australia, book buyers find walls of bookshelves on religion, spirituality, New Age cults and astrology.

Despite this evidence of religion in our society, most sociologists have long argued that the forces which produced modern societies were secularising processes that would kill off any religious impulse or practice. This assumption underpinned Hans Mol's (1971) classic study of religion in Australia.

This led, as Australia's leading sociologist of religion Gary Bouma (2003: 626) puts it, to making 'religion, and the sociology of it irrelevant'. Yet, against this confident expectation on the part of so many sociologists that religious belief and action would die out, it remains a persistent feature of all modern societies, including Australia (see Bouma & Hughes 2000). Indeed, it is impossible to understand societies as different as the United States, India, Saudi Arabia or Vietnam without paying attention to the religious beliefs and practices of their citizens.

Religion remains important for many reasons, two of which are that it continues to provide an important source of identity for most Australians, and it informs some of the most significant aspects of modern life.

● RELIGION AND IDENTITY

Consider some basic information drawn from ABS data collected since 1947 outlining a profile of religious identity in Australia (Table 10.1). The table first shows that in the 1940s we had no 'exotic' religions like Buddhism or Islam, and most Australians were content to declare themselves Anglicans. What this meant is not certain. In the 1950s, for example, it was commonplace for many Australians to claim that they were 'C of E' (Church of England). The joke version of this was the proposition that 'C of E' really meant they went to church 'at Christmas and Easter'.

Second, this table reveals that in 2001 most Australians still claimed some kind of religious affiliation. Religion clearly continues to be an important source of identity for many Australians. As Bouma (2003: 629) observes: 'A rich diversity of spiritualities has found its expression in the 2001 Census.' Yet it is also worth noting that, over the past half-century, there has been a shift towards rejecting a religious basis of identity. Until the 1970s, one in ten Australians may have had no religious commitment. In the last two Censuses of 1996 and 2001, that proportion increased markedly so that today it seems that one in four Australians either declares they have 'no religion' or else refuses to answer the question. While the ABS Census data offers a snapshot of religious affiliation, how important is religion as a source of identity?

Table 10.1 Selected religious affiliations of Australians by Census years, 1947–2001 (%)

Type	1947	1971	1996	2001
Anglicans	39	31	22	20.7
Catholics	20.7	27.0	27	26.7
Protestants	22.1	17.2	11.3	10.1
Jews	0.4	0.5	0.55	0.4
Buddhists	–	–	1.1	1.9
Muslims	–	0.2	1.1	1.5
No religion	0.3	6.7	16.5	15.5
Not stated	10.9	6.1	8.7	9.8

Source: Bouma (2003: 629).

The Australian Community Survey (1998) asked how important a variety of options were in the ways people might describe themselves. The list included:

- gender;
- age;
- education;
- the country you or your ancestors came from;
- occupation;
- family income;
- social class; and
- character and personality.

How are we to understand the 'finding' that only 10 per cent of respondents said their religion was the single most important category in describing who they are? Another 11 per cent said their religious identity was extremely important, but 43 per cent said it was not important at all. Compared with most other factors examined in this survey, religion did not rate highly among Australians in their self-descriptions. Being Australian, one's gender, the person's job or occupation, income, education and country of origin all had greater significance. At the same time, it is worth noting that two-thirds of people completing the Census in 2001 identified themselves as Christian and for some others, like many Jews and Muslims, religion clearly does continue to matter.

Yet while this research suggests that religion is not central to the lives of many Australians, other considerations need to be kept in mind when trying to understand religion in contemporary Australia. There are, for example, always questions about how one aspect of our identity (in this case, religion) relates to other markers such as gender or sexuality. Ethnic identity also makes a difference. Religion might also relate to the ways some people claim to know a particular culture and its values. One way in which a particular culture is said to be known (both by insiders and outsiders) is by reference to certain connections—real or imagined—between religion and politics.

To 'have' a religion is one way we continue to answer questions like 'who am I?' or 'who are you?' As we will see, while it may seem that religion is a less important aspect of a person's identity than gender or ethnicity, this may be misleading. If our sense of self—or our 'identity'—comprises many different political or ethical beliefs, as well as social relations and other markers, then religion is yet another core source of identity.

Like all identity markers, a person's religious feelings and beliefs point to how we experience ourselves or others. Like all identity markers, our religious beliefs or practices have distinctive inner, or 'subjective', states of mind. They also have distinctive external manifestations, like styles of dress (such as the Muslim *hijab* or the Orthodox Jew's *yamulka*) or forms of conduct—like fasting at Lent or Ramadan, or the celebratory use of food at Friday night Jewish Shabbat. In some cases, a religion will literally inscribe itself on the believer's body—for example, the Jewish and Muslim practice of male circumcision.

Finally, religions work to define the outsiders which some members of a given community may need in order to consolidate a sense of 'community'. In Australia, Catholics and Protestants vilified each other until the 1960s—much as they do in Northern Ireland even now. Jews famously have been objects of campaigns of hatred—even violence and mass murder—over the past thousand years as anti-Semites found in Catholic Orthodox and Protestant Christian churches and communities mobilise themselves against Jews. The contemporary vilification of Muslims in Australia is a more recent version of anti-Semitism.

Yet if major figures in sociology are to be believed, then none of these things should be happening or should be making a difference. Yet they are.

As we noted earlier in this book, sociology began as part of the Enlightenment project, committed to the idea that science and rationality actually characterised the modern world, banishing all irrational phenomena along the way. Clearly such predictions overlooked some important features of the modern world, such as the continuing appeal of religious commitment and identity. For various reasons, religion has not received a lot of attention from mainstream sociologists over the past few decades. One reason for this is that mainstream sociologists have tended to be uncomfortable when dealing with 'irrational' social phenomena.

In this chapter, we identity five questions that deserve an answer:

- What is a religious experience?
- Is there anything distinctively social about religious beliefs and practices about which sociologists can say something insightful?
- How have sociologists approached the question of religion?
- What and how should we think about religion sociologically?
- Why does religion make a difference in a community like Australia in our time?

● THE RELIGIOUS EXPERIENCE

Any answer to an important question like 'what is a religious experience?' depends on what is meant by the key idea, in this case 'religion'. This question was first posed by figures like the psychologist William James and the sociologist Emile Durkheim in the late nineteenth and early twentieth centuries. There are at least three dominant ways people in our time have answered it.

Religious observance

One answer comes from people who are themselves members of a religious community. They frame their answers on the basis of being members of a particular religious group or sect. For example, a Catholic will say it means, among other things, to have been baptised, to have learned the Catechism, to attend mass on Sunday and take confession, and more generally to have entered into a state of belief in God and identity as a fully confirmed believer in the Catholic faith. This approach to religion sees it as an entry into a communion with the divine order of the world—a world made by or inhabited by one god. This is the kind of answer that a person who is part of a community of believers—be they Christians, Buddhists or Muslims—is likely to give. They will use the language, forms of conduct and beliefs that identify them to themselves and to others as belonging to that community.

Religion as spirituality

A related but different answer might be offered by someone in a religious community of believers, but it will tend to focus on certain inner qualities of mind, belief or feeling. Such a response might describe the inner state of beliefs or feelings of a 'spiritual' kind.

In 2001, more than 400 000 church-going Australians completed questionnaires as part of the National Church Life Survey (NCLS) regarding the nature of faith and church life in Australia (Christian Research Association 2005). Survey respondents came from more than 7000 churches and nineteen denominations across the country. Catholics were included for the first time, although they had participated in the separate but parallel Catholic Church Life Survey in 1996, when the previous NCLS had been held. Given the Catholic teaching that all Catholics are obliged to attend Sunday mass, it is not surprising that marginally more Catholics seemed to go to church than Anglicans and other Protestants (87 per cent compared with 84 per cent of Anglicans and Protestants). Curiously, though, Catholics were a little less likely than people of other denominations to be regular worshippers at the parish where they completed the survey (78 per cent Catholics compared with 83 per cent of Anglicans and Protestants).

The survey suggests interesting things about 'spiritual' experiences. Three-quarters of respondents said that, during church services, they usually or always experienced 'a sense of God's presence', while among Catholics almost the same proportion reported a sense of fulfilling their obligation—a much higher proportion than for attendees of other denominations. On the other hand, non-Catholic attendees were more likely to experience what was described as 'growth in understanding of God', 'joy', 'inspiration' and 'spontaneity' in church services.

Understandably, those disposed to belief in a certain god, or gods, and a particular religious community will want to claim that the experience of such feelings is evidence that their religion is true and that their god is real and powerful. That is, the state of feeling referred to as 'spiritual' is typically explained and understood as emanating from the god or heaven.

Equally significant was the way these people reported on their sense of 'belonging' to a certain community of like-minded people. This was reported as the experience of belonging to one's parish or congregation, and was quite high—79 per cent of both Anglican and Protestant attendees said that this was either strong and growing or strong and stable. The figure was less for those attending Catholic parishes (68 per cent).

Spirituality and the religious experience come in many shapes. They might be experienced as a result of practices like prayer, meditation, starvation, extended sleeplessness or attendance at a revival meeting. Here the idea of spirituality or spiritual experience relates to reports of feeling strong or high emotions, or even experiencing ecstasy or out-of-body experiences.

The word 'spirituality' might be thought to encompass more than the kinds of feelings experienced by someone who is attached to an institutionalised practice of religious belief or worship. It may be open to people like Aldous Huxley who used drugs like mescalin and LSD to experience 'reality'. It may also be the kind of experience some people get when they go out on a starry night and gaze at the black star-studded night sky. It might refer to a sense of awe, wonderment and beauty experienced in a walk through a forest. These kinds of experiences are often described as spiritual. They can involve a sense of oneself as small and/or insignificant before the largeness of the cosmos. Or a spiritual or religious experience may relate to a sense that many aspects of life remain mysterious and significant.

Religion as a way of life

If you do not belong to a given community of belief, you may explain religious experience as the consequence of certain communal or social practices or a way of life. From this perspective, a religious experience is a social phenomenon, generated by a collective way of life. It is the consequence of people agreeing to do certain things together and over time developing rituals, specialised vocabularies and, on occasion, experiencing high feelings in a space established by the collective.

From this perspective, religion is a way of producing a certain kind of social order by organising social relations and practices. As classic sociologists from Durkheim through to Parsons have pointed out, for a long time, religious practice and belief have provided a basis for articulating codes of moral belief with a view to regulating human conduct. On a small scale, this relates to organising the lives of priests or clerics. Thus those who manage the religion establish rules for membership, run regular meetings and act together in ways that involve rites of entry and collective identity for nuns, monks or priests.

The effect of religion extends past the patterns of life established for and by priests or clerics, however. Religious personnel and their organisations also attempt to shape the life of a larger number of people in a given community—perhaps even in a large nation-state. Their capacity to do this rests on their ability to persuade the larger community that there are problems of existence or life that they alone can handle. For some people, the claims advanced by religious groups can be very attractive.

In all cultures, we see the success with which two kinds of reality are proposed, with the boundaries between policed by a priestly caste. The first reality is the mundane—and it is where most of us are said to live. The second is the divine or sacred reality which only a privileged few are said to be able to access. The way in which priestly power is secured is by establishing that only the ordained can access the divine, or can mediate and manage relations between the gods and the human world. For this reason, the priestly castes of all the world's religions have guarded their privileged status. It is typically they who can see or to talk with the gods. It is a claim buttressed by relying on esoteric clothing and rituals, theatre, music and the use of specialised languages like Latin.

As Walter Burkert (1987) has observed, at the heart of any idea about a divine or sacred reality is the practice of 'sacrifice'. This is retained in the Christian practice of communion, which involves the symbolic act of eating 'the host' or the body of the Christ and drinking his blood. This is said to give us the 'sacred' order—an order ruled by priests whose functions began as the managers of 'sacrificial' processes which involved the killing of people, animals or even the gods or their images. Should these techniques that sustain the mythos of the exclusive and privileged status of the priestly caste fail, there are always terror, violence and the law courts to fall back on to keep people in a state of obedience.

All of the great world religions, from Judaism, Hinduism and Christianity to Islam and Buddhism have articulated certain values and rules for living in the world and with each other. In the process of constructing myths about creation, the order of the world and the nature of human life, all these religions have helped to shape the larger culture of the communities in which they have flourished. They have proscribed rules about dress, listed the foods that can be eaten or not, established patterns of work and holidays that typically reflect old rituals of sacrifice, written the rules about who cannot and can and have sex with whom, when and how, and legislated on how family life or economic activities are best organised.

If you are a non-believer and a little sceptical about all of this, you might decide that religious beliefs are actually quite problematic and even dangerous. This way of thinking takes us some way towards a sociological approach to religion. It is an approach that suspends any readiness to take religion as a believer does—as giving us some access to the divine order—and instead asks about the kinds of social purposes religion fulfils.

This was Karl Marx's attitude when he made his famous quip about religion being 'the opiate of the masses'. Jurgen Habermas (1999: 175) was also making this point when he declared that religion serves only to legitimate political and economic arrangements that benefit certain elites: 'religious and metaphysical world-views . . . have the form of doctrines that can be worked up intellectually and that explain and justify an existing order in terms of the world order they explicate.'

Habermas's theories owe a lot to the traditions of Marxism and critical theory. This predisposes him to argue that religion is an 'ideology'—in other words, that it is a belief system which works to serve the social and political interests of elite groups and the particular economic and political arrangements that enable them to enjoy great wealth or power. In effect, rather than treating religious belief or practice as whatever religious believers say it is, Habermas treats religion as an intellectual veil that covers up social arrangements which benefit a small number of people at the expense of a large number of people.

Conservative sociologists from Durkheim to Parsons have tended to argue that religion need not be taken at face value, but that from a functional viewpoint it serves to preserve social order or bolster respect for traditional values and traditional institutions like marriage or a given political order. Other sociologists, influenced by critical traditions, adopt a more starkly sceptical stance of the kind adopted by Habermas. Yet this distinction between 'conservative' and 'critical' sociologists does not quite catch the complex ways sociologists of various dispositions have handled the issue of religion.

● HOW HAVE SOCIOLOGISTS APPROACHED THE QUESTION OF RELIGION?

Looking back over the history of sociology, we see several tendencies when sociologists address religious belief or practice. Generally speaking, sociologists have been uncomfortable with anything that smacks of irrationality, and there is general agreement that religious belief is 'irrational'. One consequence is that religion has tended to disappear from sociology. In the intellectual foundations of any discipline there are assumptions, or what writers like Holton (1988: 31–53) calls 'themata' and Gadamer (1989) defines as 'prejudices'. One of the foundational assumptions of sociology is a strong preference for 'rationality' over 'irrationality'.

There is a long tradition, beginning with the 'founding father' of sociology Auguste Comte, of active hostility directed against religion in all of its forms. Many sociologists—especially those who accepted the value of scientific method or the progressive movement of collectivist responses to social problems like poverty or unemployment—became ardent advocates for the progressive modernisation of social life, denying the role or value of religion. In this way, mainstream sociology became a stronghold of secular thought.

It is likely that many sociologists are agnostic or anti-religious, which may have encouraged many sociologists to ignore religion. This may be why Western and Najman (1999) simply pay no attention to the phenomenon of religion in Australia in their otherwise comprehensive textbook. A third tendency operating among sociologists, beginning with pioneers like Emile Durkheim, was to treat religion as a source of important social activities that performed vital 'functions' like securing social order.

To appreciate these various sociological responses to religion, we need to remember that sociology grew from the Enlightenment project—a project that was preoccupied with the idea of reason and with giving greater weight to scientific knowledge as a basis for social, political or economic progress.

In the seventeenth century, men like Galileo and Newton did not conclude that this affected their Christian belief in God, who they treated as a great mathematician. However, this confidence in the ability to hold simultaneously to a belief in God and in scientific method did not hold over the following centuries. By the eighteenth century, *philosophes* like Hume, Condorcet and Diderot began to subvert Christian belief by insisting that scientific method was more rational than any religious belief. The rationalist-scientistic version of the Enlightenment project was expressed by eighteenth century philosophers like David Hume (1882), who regarded religion as just one aspect of superstition. Hume did not spare his contempt for those in the grip of religious delusion:

> the mind of man is subject to certain unaccountable terrors and apprehensions proceeding either from the unhappy situation of private or public affairs, from ill-health, from a gloomy or melancholic disposition . . . Weakness, fear, melancholy together with ignorance are the true sources of superstition . . . superstition is favorable to priestly power . . . (1882: 144–5)

It was on this basis, as David Harvey (1989: 27) has argued, that the men who created the Enlightenment believed:

> That there was only one possible answer to any question. From this it followed that the world could be controlled and rationally if we could only picture and represent it rightly. But this presumed that there existed a single correct mode of representation which, if we could uncover it (and this was what the scientific and mathematical endeavors [of the Scientific Revolution] were all about), would provide the means to Enlightenment ends.

This Enlightenment project and the scientific rationalism of the past few centuries were not just about a philosophy of science, but also entailed a belief in a purposeful historical process which issued forth in social progress.

Given the origins of sociology in the Enlightenment, how would sociologists deal with the apparently irrational character of religion? While there is a substantial sociology of religion, mainstream sociologists have tended until recently to do what they have done to other apparently irrational factors like emotions or violence: ignore the problem altogether.

● DURKHEIM ON RELIGION AND ITS SOCIAL FUNCTIONS

Durkheim was preoccupied with the problem of social order. He understood this in terms that were then popular in the late nineteenth century. As a European and a Frenchman, he had abundant evidence to confirm his view that social order was precarious. In the previous century, France had gone through numerous revolutions (1789, 1830, 1848 and 1870), suffered catastrophic military defeats and experienced the birth pains of industrial development. Durkheim was also a deeply committed pessimist, much influenced by his encounter with the greatest philosopher of pessimism, Arthur Schopenhauer. Durkheim believed that 'individuals' needed to be disciplined or regulated by 'society'.

For Durkheim, society is a single, coherent moral order based on a single moral consensus. Anything that threatens that moral order needs to be dealt with severely, since any loss of moral coherence threatens social order. To describe that possible state of moral anarchy, Durkheim used the idea of 'anomie'.

Because Durkheim was a positivist, he did not accept religious explanations for religious belief. Equally, he saw religion as having a powerful role in maintaining social and moral order. Indeed, Durkheim came to believe that religion was the most powerful way society secured its hold over us and made its power both real and visible. This led the American philosopher Kenneth Burke (1944) to the shrewd insight that 'society' became a new 'god' concept, possessing many of the characteristics formerly attributed to God. Burke suggested that, as the new 'god' concept society took on the role and character once said to belong to God, 'it' became all-knowing, all-powerful and all-good, and must be obeyed.

This is the approach Durkheim adopted in his last work, *Elementary Forms of Religious Life* (1965). Durkheim (1965: 416) acknowledges that:

> . . . the men who lead the religious life and have a direct sensation of what it really is . . . feel that the real function of religion is not to make us think [or] to enrich our knowledge
>
> . . . but rather it is to make us act, to aid us to live. The believer who has communicated with his god is not merely a man who sees new truths of which the unbeliever is ignorant but he is a man who is stronger he feels within him more force either to endure the trials of existence or to rise above them it as though he were raised above the miseries of the world because he is raised above his condition as a mere man he believes that he is saved from evil.

Durkheim went on to argue that the beliefs of believers cannot be purely illusory and that 'these religious experiences rests upon a specific experience whose demonstrative value is in one sense not one bit inferior to that of scientific experiments though different from them'. This may seem like a curious thesis for someone like Durkheim, long identified as a positivist. However, Durkheim (1965: 419) saved the day for positivists by arguing that the underlying reality which sets loose this religious experience is not a god, but rather society itself, which 'develops the moral forces and awakens this sentiment of a shield, of a refuge and of a guardian support which attaches the believer to his cult'.

Whatever is meant by 'the sacred' or 'the divine' is simply an effect of society as a powerful collective entity. The fact that 'society' is the secret motive source of religious impulse does not mean that the effects are weak or insignificant. Durkheim (1965: 229) suggests this is how and why objects like statues, holy relics or symbols become sacred objects, able to inspire feelings.

For Durkheim (1965: 229), whatever is real about the experience of religion is a consequence of powerful emotions and dynamics set loose by groups of humans, not by the gods. His description of this is quite powerful:

> If collective life awakens religious thought on reaching a certain stage of intensity, it is because it brings about a state of effervescence which changes the conditions of psychic activity. Vital energies are overexcited, passions more active, sensations stronger; there are some only produced at this moment. A man does not recognize himself, he feels himself transformed . . .

As he (1965: 224) argues, when a society becomes aware of itself, it achieves a concentration of itself:

> Now this concentration brings about an exaltation in the mental life which takes form in a group of ideal conceptions where is portrayed the new life thus awakened the collective ideal which religion expresses is far from being due to a vague innate power of the individual, but it is rather at the school of collective life that the individual learns to idealize. It is assimilating the ideals elaborated by society that he has become more capable of conceiving the ideal.

Thus religion is powerful because it is a socially sanctioned and constructed source of ideal values for assigning meaning to the human condition.

So what happens if the religious impulse is abolished or reduced in scope as a result of the spread of the idea that religious belief itself is unreliable or irrational? In particular, what happens in a community when an alternative way of thinking about knowledge—such as the scientific world-view that took hold of Europe through the nineteenth century—comes to provide a dominant way of thinking about the world but seems unable to supply convincing answers to important ethical questions.

These are the questions about modernity that preoccupied Max Weber in the decades after 1890.

● WEBER ON MODERNITY AND RELIGION

The sociological story of how we came to live in 'modernity' is usually sourced to Max Weber (1866–1920). Weber devoted considerable time to articulating his proposition that the modern age is best characterised by the dominance of a certain style of rationality, especially the institutionalised form it took in the modern world as 'bureaucracy'.

The strength and relevance of Weber's work lie in the way he grounded his account in a fundamental inquiry into social life. His particular account of modernity rests on a larger inquiry into the very nature of all social action. He constructed this model or typology of human action as a series of what he called 'ideal types' or logical constructions. As Weber (1947: 117) acknowledges, real human action rarely—if ever—conforms to just one of these types of action.

Weber claimed we could understand all human action as oriented or designed in one of four ways:

- traditional conduct, which refers to the way we do things because it is the custom—the way it has always been done;
- action which is directed by feelings or emotions, which Weber took to be a prime example of irrational behaviour;
- *wertrational* action, or 'value rationality'. According to Weber (1947: 116), this kind of activity encompasses activities informed by 'a conscious belief in the absolute value of some ethical, aesthetic, or religious form of behavior entirely for its own sake and independently of any prospects of external success'; and
- *zweckrationalitat*, or 'instrumental rationality', the consequence of deliberate calculation by an actor of the most efficient means of achieving an end.

Weber suggests it is 'instrumental rationality' that precisely characterises the modern age and defines the modern economy: market-based activities are almost pure expressions of efficient, rationally calculated economic activities designed to maximise people's happiness. Here we get the famous Weberian equation: 'modern' equals 'rational'. This equation looks simple. It is, however, anything but. Rather it points to a series of problems that Weber struggled to deal with.

According to Weber, instrumental rationality is the defining feature of modernity. This entails that those societies that have taken the path to modernity have privileged instrumental rationality as the central, even defining, feature of modern life. On the one hand this has taken two forms. First, modern societies have installed a dominant regard for certain kinds of scientific knowledge. Second, modernity is characterised by the triumph of the bureaucratic organisation of social life. In each case, Weber argues, the effect is to outlaw value-driven activities.

Weber takes for granted the conventional empiricist or positivist account of 'proper' scientific knowledge based on scientific method. This involves understanding knowledge in terms that rest, for example, on Hume's 'is/ought' distinction. Hume had argued in the eighteenth century that values can never—or should never—play any role in authentically 'scientific' knowledge.

This is because, as Hume believed he had demonstrated in the 1740s, we cannot derive 'ought' statements—that is, statements of value—from descriptions of what is or what we loosely call 'facts'. Facts are 'empirical' or 'objective', while values are 'subjective' and lack any basis in 'fact'. (It is important to know that not all modern philosophers treat this view as credible. Hilary Putnam (2005), among others, has demonstrated why the 'is/ought' distinction is a primitive and non-defensible view of whatever people mean by 'facts' and of whatever people mean by 'values'.)

Equally, bureaucracy is understood to require the functional division of labour, impersonality and instrumental-rationality (*zweckrationalitat*), enabling the functionaries to act only as impartial or even objective rule-followers. This does not mean bureaucracies are informed by scientific knowledge, only that they appear to act without reference to any moral values.

Weber (1947, 1958) developed his 'ideal-typical' account of bureaucracy in the context of his larger interest in techniques of coercion, domination and the legitimisation of these dispositions. Weber emphasised the hierarchical rule-bound nature of bureaucracies reliant on the subdivision of technical tasks and on the 'routinization' of behaviours. We are now all familiar with and possibly even accept this conventional account of bureaucracies that suggests how the bureaucrat is merely part of the administrative machinery. Weber suggests, for example, that the bureaucrat bears no responsibility for his actions since he merely follows rules. He does not make them. This characterisation underpins the proposition which many later social theorists recycled: namely, that bureaucracies blind the functionaries to the ethical import of their decisions or actions (Merton 1967).

According to Weber, the problem was that, while the 'triumph of Reason' provided humans with a more rational grip on the world of things, scientists, bureaucrats and professionals were committed to excluding emotions and values from scientific knowledge or bureaucratic practice and thus were unable to address the fundamental questions of value or meaning.

Weber himself seems to have felt acutely the dilemmas this set of circumstances apparently posed. His own struggles to reconcile his powerful emotions with his rationality led to a long period of psychotic breakdown. Much of Weber's scholarly work addressed the role of religions. Weber's (1974) best known work, for example, explores the connections between Protestantism and the rise of capitalism in the early modern period.

No one could underestimate the role played by science and technology in constantly transforming our world and as the basis upon which people now live, work and play. No one could doubt that we continue to live in societies where bureaucracies, both state-run and private, continue to administer large parts of our social experience. Yet there are problems with Weber's account of the role played by reason in the modern condition. He failed to clarify the ways we can understand the idea of rationality itself, or on the basis on which we are to accept his case that ethical or religious ideas are intrinsically 'non-rational'.

There are four ways we have understood 'rationality'. If we think about each one of them, on what basis might we say that either ethical or religious ideas are not rational?

The oldest idea is of 'rationality' as counting or measuring. Rationality defines certain kinds of knowledge based on measurement or counting exercises and is designed to give us some kind of explanatory or descriptive account of the way things are or can be calculated to occur by using numbers. But is there any basis offered by this understanding of rationality to say why this kind of knowledge-making activity is superior to any other kind of knowledge?

As Weber reminds us, 'rationality' has also been understood as the criterion of efficiency that is applied to our choices between different activities—to be rational means achieving an economical fit of means to ends. This understanding simply relies on a prejudice of the value of efficiency or speed.

Third, rationality is understood as what Hegel meant when he said 'the rational is the real'. Rationality is contrasted with irrationality: irrational people, so it is said, substitute whatever they imagine or fantasise to be real for 'the real'. Thus rationality or reason involves the capacity to engage with reality effectively or accurately and in effect stands as a synonym for the 'truth'.

Finally, any idea of human action as rational could be understood as pointing to two aspects of our human-ness. It presupposes that we do what we do because the kinds of actions that we think of as human mean that we have an intention or idea that we give effect to by acting it out, and that our thoughts are 'father to the deed'. Additionally, the idea of rationality implies that for each such action a rational actor is able to provide a rationale for why they did what they did. This approach is what Weber, among others, has proposed as part of his *verstehende* approach, or method of doing sociology (*verstehen* is the German word for 'understanding'). Weber thought it possible to put ourselves into the shoes of another and grasp their understandings of things. Rationality on this score entails the ability of one actor to give another person an account of why they did what they did and to do so in ways that are comprehensible or intelligible to that other person. This is an important idea, but it is not able to solve certain problems.

If rationality is to be understood as the ability of a person to give another person an account of why they did what they did that is comprehensible or intelligible to that other person, then this is only going to be possible in certain circumstances. It requires among other things that for such an account to be plausible or 'understandable', the audience has to share the basic perceptions and beliefs of the other person. For instance, someone who is a Jehovah's Witness may be able to explain to another Jehovah's Witness why they refused to allow their sick child to receive a blood transfusion by pointing to a certain text in the Bible and this will be accepted as a good or rational reason. To a non-Jehovah's Witness it may seem completely non-rational.

If we think our way through the various ways of using the word 'rational', it seems that religious belief may be understood as 'irrational' or 'rational'. If we want to count things, then we cannot go out and measure or weigh 'God'. Equally, rationality as efficiency does not seem to work all that well for those who want to argue for a 'God concept'. However, if by rational we simply mean a capacity to give a credible or comprehensible account of our beliefs and action that are acceptable to others, then religious belief is comprehensible to others and so meets the test of rationality quite well. It is on the basis of this view that some modern writers now argue that the fact that all knowledge systems rest on prejudices, including the 'scientific method' model, then there is no final basis for authoritatively defining religious belief as irrational: it is just a different system of belief or practice like astrology, marathon-running or physics. Each has its adherents and devotees and each may fail to persuade some people of its credibility.

In contrast to the views of Weber, a lot of human activity continues to be shaped by moral or ethical objectives, many of them with their origins in religious belief and practice. Plainly, most humans continue to be informed by explicit or implicit values and ethical ideas.

Finally and most crucially for this discussion, religion is not missing from our world in the way Weber suggests it should be. Our world has not got rid of religious belief. Large numbers of Australians still read their horoscope each morning, have lucky numbers or wear lucky items of clothes, and believe that their dreams are prophecies of their own future. And religious affiliation and practice remain crucial aspects of many people's lives.

● WHY DOES RELIGION MATTER IN OUR TIME?

The signs are everywhere. In spite of Max Weber, modern societies and modernising societies alike continue to provide a home to a lot of religious belief. Religious belief and practice in all of their numerous forms and expressions continue to be important. For example, in the dramatically modernising economic powerhouse that is contemporary China, and in spite of decades of attempts by the Chinese Communist Party to eradicate religion, we see persistent attendance at Taoist temples and the maintenance of household shrines by hundreds of millions of Chinese. All this points to the continued appeal of traditional forms of Chinese religious belief.

In the United States, the most modernised and scientifically powerful society on the planet, upwards of 80 per cent of Americans profess to be practising Christians, while a clear majority accept the Biblical accounts of Creation. Every twentieth century president from McKinley to Bush has been an active and committed Christian.

Religion also continues to lie at the heart of the great conflicts of our time. The all-too-successful attempts by governments and social movements to mobilise sectarian sentiment remind us just how relevant religious identity remains. This is confirmed by the numerous conflicts and forms of violence that erupt globally—conflicts that rely on links between religious and ethnic identity and political mobilisation.

In the name of religion, groups of Muslims, Jews, Catholics, Protestants, Hindus, Sikhs and Orthodox Christians persistently advocate various forms of violence, including large-scale conflict, terror and torture in the ways they have done for decades, or in some cases even centuries (see box).

In the name of religion

Religious identity currently lies at the heart of some major global conflicts:

- In the state of Israel and the putative state of Palestine, Israeli Jews and Palestinian Muslims fight each other over land that has enormous religious significance for both communities. In August 2005, the Israeli state began moving Orthodox Jews off land they had seized illegally in the Gaza Strip in order to try to get the peace process back on track. Equally committed radical Palestinian Muslims continue to carry out suicide bombing attacks on civilians in Israeli cities, a practice emulated sporadically with bloody results in cities like New York, Barcelona and London.

- In the former Yugoslavia, Croatian Catholics and Serbian Orthodox Christians fought each other throughout the 1990s, producing tens of thousands of victims of rape, terror and mass murder. In 1995 UN troops stood by and watched helplessly as 9000 Bosnian Muslims were systematically executed in Srebrenica and only US military intervention prevented another mass killing of Bosnian Muslims in Kosovo in 1999.

- In the United States, President George W. Bush routinely invokes a distinctively American Christian fundamentalism to denounce Islamic fundamentalism. The kind of Christianity being invoked is suggested by the fact (reported in US opinion surveys) that a majority of Americans believe that each day they are surrounded by angels—wearing wings. Equally, there are daily denunciations of America's anti-Islamic stance and its 'degeneracy' and 'immorality' by Muslim clerics in countries like Saudi Arabia, Indonesia and Iran.

- In Northern Ireland, Protestants and Catholics still face an uncertain future after a century of terrorism and violence on both sides.

Religion also makes its mark in Australia on a wide range of domestic issues and discussions (see box).

Religious issues in Australia

- Fundamentalist Christians of various denominations—including Catholics, evangelical Anglicans and Pentecostalists, as well as various Muslim clerics—argue that abortion and homosexuality are 'sins', and that gays and lesbians should not be allowed to marry, to have or to rear children, or to work in religious schools.

- The Catholic Church, under the leadership of successive conservative leaders like Pope John Paul II or Cardinal George Pell, has consistently refused to ordain women as priests on the grounds that women lack the male identity ascribed to God. On the basis of this argument, the Catholic Church, as a large employer of teachers in its church schools, denies women equal opportunity—a right which is a legal requirement for all other organisations.

- This refusal to recognise the human rights of women is matched by the refusal by too many people in positions of responsibility to acknowledge that sexual abuse of children by adults takes place and is a crime. Cases of sexual abuse perpetrated by Catholic priests continue to be discovered where senior church figures have conspired to do nothing or to conceal the crimes.

- Various religious groups found in Christian and Islamic communities continue to rail against 'selfish women' who will 'refuse' to fulfil their 'traditional' and 'proper' roles as wives and mothers by going out to work and/or placing their children in child care.

- In some outer suburbs in our bigger cities, new evangelical churches offer a beguiling mix of almost theatrical religious worship conducted by charismatic preachers. In some cases, this is combined with incendiary and anti-Semitic denunciations of Muslims as enemies of Christ, and claims that all good Christians ought to embrace the idea propagated by US President George W. Bush after the 9/11 attacks that the United States had a duty to embark on a 'new Crusade against Islam' (see Bouma 2001).

- The idea that religion helps to define 'Australian culture' and 'Australian values' has become a popular one in Australia, especially among radio show hosts and neo-conservative politicians.

● CONCLUSION

As we have indicated, the last two ABS Censuses (of 1996 and 2001) paint a general picture of Australians' religious belief and conduct. Approximately 70 per cent of the Australian population claim to be 'Christian' while 17 per cent claim no religious faith. By 2001, some of the key smaller Christian groups, led by the Uniting Church Presbyterians and Salvation Army, were shrinking in numbers. The biggest single Christian faith group, the Catholic Church, declined slightly when set against the 5.7 per cent growth in overall population. Buddhism and Islam, on the other hand, have grown considerably since 1996. The numbers claiming to be Buddhist grew the most of any of the religious communities, with Buddhists making up 2 per cent of the entire population—or around 400 000 people—while Islam also grew by 40 per cent in the same period as a consequence of significant immigration and of conversions among local Australian-born young people. At the same time, the numbers claiming 'no religion' declined. According to the 2001 Census, around 70 000 Australians now claimed to be 'Jedi' worshippers, following a campaign to get Australians to declare themselves in this fashion as an argument in favour of removing all reference to religion from the next Census, which was carried out in August 2006.

The continued significance of religion calls into question some of the fundamental aspects of sociology's story of modernity. The work of twentieth century American sociologist Talcott Parsons restated and 'popularised' the Durkheimian idea of society as a total social system. For Parsons, society was an external objective; it had a life of its own and pursued its interests, if necessary, against those of its members. For Parsons, modernity was principally about patterns of universalising ideas and social values that guaranteed that modern social systems were rational, ordered and harmonious. Modern writers like Giddens, Bauman and Beck largely work with a similar view of modernity.

However, the continued significance of religion suggests that we need to question the value of a concept like 'modernity'—the idea that societies are both reliant on the widespread dissemination of rational beliefs and scientific knowledge, and on the use of instrumental rational forms of social action produced by large-scale bureaucracies. Each of these propositions depends on the unstated assumption that the writer can authoritatively determine which beliefs are rational—and those that are not. Yet, as Mestrovic (1997) points out, most modern societies maintain many influential belief systems like religion and nationalism, as well as pre-modern beliefs in magic or astrology.

Many modern societies also rely on a belief in the inherent superiority of one ethnic community over another. None of these belief systems appears to be particularly rational. Rather than insisting on what may only be semantic distinctions, we need to pay much more attention to the curious and complex intermingling of 'scientific' and 'rational' ideas and modern techniques of social administration with older quite durable ideas about 'community' and the 'state'—a commingling evident in all modern societies throughout the twentieth century and at the start of the twenty-first.

Discussion questions

10.1   Why does religion continue to be important for many Australians?

10.2   Is religion a source of positive values in the modern world?

10.3   Are all religious beliefs irrational or pre-modern and all scientific beliefs rational and modern?

Borders are scratched across the hearts of men
By strangers with a calm judicial pen,
And when the borders bleed we watch with dread
The lines of ink along the map turn red.

Marya Mannes (1959)
'Gaza Strip' from Subverse: Rhymes for Our Times

IDENTITY, MULTI-CULTURALISM, AND IMAGINED COMMUNITY 11.

• • SUMMARY

In this chapter, we consider the issue of Australia's national identity in a period of globalisation— a process allegedly eroding the identity and authority of the nation-state and the attractions of local ethnic identity. We first consider ideas like colonialism, race and racism, and look at some of the problems inherent in these ideas as we explore the colonial experience which produced both dispossession and a demographic catastrophe for the Aboriginal people. We then use the idea of ethnicity to examine the patterns of immigration and immigration policy in Australia—especially since 1945. Both the history of black and white relations and the entry of large numbers of non-British immigrants to Australia after 1950 raise large questions about Australia's identity and the problem of inequality.

Contemporary life presents us with many puzzles. If we believe what some of the leading sociologists of our time say, religious faith ought to be disappearing or to have died out completely. So too ought the willingness of people to say things like 'I am an Aussie' or 'I am Vietnamese'. Yet identity which is defined in part by our ethnicity continues to be a central part of many Australians' daily experience. This aspect of identity is also associated with deep feelings, and generates plenty of controversy.

Over the last 150 years, sociologists have argued that modern society was on a path of ever-increasing progress and rationality, which meant 'irrational' and 'pre-modern' belief systems like racism, religion and nationalism were doomed to disappear. In 1999, Anthony Giddens argued that 'globalising' tendencies were the latest expression of centuries-old processes that define the modernisation process—or what he calls 'the project of modernity'. For writers like Giddens, globalisation is the latest and most benevolent expression of all those rational, scientific and technological practices, values and beliefs that are said to have made the modern world. At the start of the twenty-first century, Giddens believes we are even further along the pathway towards the comprehensive 'rationalisation of the world'. While Max Weber emphasised the role of science, capitalist methods of production and bureaucracy, Giddens points to the spread of global TV and mobile phone coverage, the global advertising and marketing reach of transnational corporations like McDonald's, Nike and Sony, and of course the dramatic spread of the internet. The consequences include the construction of a global culture in which we all live in a small global village, making patriotism, racism and nationalist sentiment redundant. Strangely enough, though, this has not happened.

Over the last decade, questions of ethnic identity and national identity have provided a series of major flashpoints in Australian public life (see box).

Identity flashpoints

- Beginning in 1991, successive Australian governments decided to defy the usual international conventions established by United Nations refugee policies and treaties, and to detain asylum seekers arriving in Australia in high-security detention centres. ('Asylum seekers' is the name given by authorities to people who are seeking status as refugees.) Adopting this punitive regime led to the incarceration of children as well as adults in conditions which created 'sites of legal exceptionality' (Agamben 1997), where their rights to legal protection were dissolved. This was justified by the idea it would deter asylum seekers from coming to Australia. Public support was secured by representing them as 'illegals', 'queue jumpers' and even as 'terrorists' and 'criminals'. Subsequent campaigns to end this policy have seen church leaders, lawyers and human rights activists mounting protest marches and political pressure to end the policy.

- In September 1996, Pauline Hanson MHR, a newly elected Independent who had been ejected from the Queensland Liberal Party for her racist views, electrified Australian political debate when she made her 'maiden speech' in parliament on 10 September 1996, in which she claimed that Australia was being overwhelmed by Asians and that Aborigines were getting unjustified welfare support from 'soft' governments. Hanson went on to create the One Australia party before she lost her parliamentary seat and served a prison sentence for electoral offences (of which she has since been cleared) and has most recently become a TV celebrity.

- In the late 1990s, neo-Nazis and white supremacists firebombed a number of Asian restaurants in Perth, and desecrated public sites commemorating the role of Nyungar people.

- Following the terrorist attacks of 9 September 2001 in New York and Washington, Muslim women were assaulted in suburbs in Melbourne and Sydney and mosques attacked. In terms of the paradigm that Edward Said (1997) has called 'Orientalism', sections of the Australian media have treated the terrorist attacks as a contest between the 'West' and the 'Rest'. Drawing on books by Bernard Lewis (1994), Samuel Huntington (1996) and Judith Miller (1997), local journalists like Janet Friedrichsen have portrayed local Muslim communities as part of a challenge by a militant atavistic premodern culture driven by hatred of all Western political thought and values understood as secular, rational and tolerant. On the basis of this mobilisation of fear, anti-terrorist legislation has been introduced (Hocking 2004), suspending long-standing legal rights deemed necessary to 'defend the homeland'.

- In 2004, hundreds of thousands of people marched in cities across Australia to support the process of reconciliation between black and white Australians.

- In December 2005, a week of race rioting brought Aussie flag-waving young men into repeated violent conflict with other young Australians identifying as Lebanese on the beach at Cronulla. Some Sydney radio commentators used the word 'white' to describe the young Aussie flag wavers, while others argued that the riots demonstrated the racist underbelly of modern Australian society.

In stressing the contemporary role of ethnic identity and the political mobilisation of people supporting multicultural toleration as well as people promoting racism and cultural conflict, we do not mean to imply that this is a new phenomenon. Quite the reverse, in fact. The contemporary politics of ethnicity cannot be explained without understanding the history of modern Australia. In that history, the matter of ethnic identity has always been central both to relations between Indigenous peoples and British settlers who colonised the continent in 1788, and to the subsequent role played by immigration in a country geographers have conventionally referred to as 'a region of recent settlement'.

In fact, as historian David Day (1996) reminds us, our continent has one of the longest continuous histories of human settlement. What we call modern Australia began in 1788 with a process of colonisation by British military forces that initiated a process of 'dis-settlement'. The colonial period (1788–1901) saw a British socio-cultural, economic and political order imposed on a country long settled by people whom those settlers had initially called 'Indians' and later referred to as 'Aborigines'. That invasion unleashed a demographic catastrophe for the Aboriginals, and led to the dispossession of their land and widespread social disintegration.

At the start of the twenty-first century, the history of black and white relations is still being interpreted and revised—often in highly controversial terms, as the so-called 'history wars' indicate (Attwood 2005). Equally key issues like Aboriginal land rights remain to be properly resolved, as the continued failure to conclude a treaty with the Indigenous peoples suggests.

Colonisation also started a process of immigration which, across several centuries and a number of phases, has decisively shaped the character of contemporary Australian society. At a time when some politicians talk up the need to defend 'core Australian values', we need to remember that in 2005 almost one in four members of the Australian population was born overseas. And what had been a predominantly British culture until the 1970s—signified by the fact that the largest intake of migrants continued to come from Britain—has changed markedly. In 2005, British-born migrants made up only 24.5 per cent of all overseas-born. People born in China and Vietnam each made up 4 per cent of the population born overseas, while in the decade up to 2005, Sudanese migrants and refugees had the highest migration growth rate at nearly 26 per cent, followed by people born in Afghanistan (12 per cent) and Iraq (11 per cent), pointing to the significant role played by war and famine in producing population movements on a global scale (ABS 2005b).

As has so often occurred in our modern history, immigration continues to supply much of the dynamic behind recent population growth. Indeed, since the 1990s, were it not for immigration Australia's low fertility rate would be leading to population shrinkage. Into the twenty-first century, Australia continues to bring in over 100 000 migrants annually. In 2004, 117 600 migrants arrived, while 2005 saw 128 740 settlers come to Australia—the greatest number of migrants since the early 1980s (ABS 2005b). If foreign students who elect to stay on after study are included, this figure rises to about 175 000 new settlers up to June 2005.

Using immigration to add to the local population has been an ongoing part of our history. Governments in Britain and in colonial Australia encouraged immigration from Britain, and from the 1850s the gold-rushes and economic growth attracted a steady stream of British migrants. By the 1890s, the colonies were animated by a kind of Australian nationalism which supported the project of a federal government which came into effect in 1901. Australian nationalism also gave voice to the objective of building a 'white Australia'. In that 'white Australia', Asians and 'coloureds' were not welcome. The codification of the 'white Australia' policy after 1901 was supported by all political parties into the 1960s. Only after 1950 were substantial numbers of non-British immigrants encouraged to come to Australia. (Yet, even into the 1990s, British immigrants were the most numerous component of immigration.) In the early 1970s, 'white Australia' ended and Australia began experimenting with an official commitment to 'multiculturalism' (Lopez 2000). What 'multiculturalism' actually means remains deeply contested and the policy commitment to multiculturalism has become a major source of continuing public controversy. Even as Australia became an increasingly multi-ethnic society, with significant numbers of settlers from Asia, Africa and India, public intellectuals like Geoffrey Blainey (1984) rejected the new orthodoxy, arguing that Australia should remain proud of its British heritage. Because we are still caught in the web of history, the legacies of colonialism and racism have yet to be adequately understood, let alone resolved.

In a period said to be defined by globalising trends, Australians and their government policy elites and opinion-makers are still engaged in a painful and yet-to-be-completed process of determining how best to understand ourselves as a nation-state. Some of this debate has to do with our status as a 'former' British colony. Australia remains one of the few normal-sized countries in the world to have a national flag bearing the flag of another country. Most of the major ex-British colonies like India, Canada, Kenya and South Africa have their own flags.

Australia's head of state—the British Queen—continues constitutionally to be the head of state of another sovereign nation-state. In the 1970s and 1980s, there was a tussle over the national anthem which was finally resolved by making 'Advance Australia Fair' the legal anthem. In a major test of popular feeling, a Constitutional Referendum was held in 1999 to seek support for an Australian republic that would have meant replacing the British sovereign with an Australian head of state. The referendum proposal to do so was defeated narrowly, largely because the advocates for a republic were unable to agree on a single model for a new head of state. Anti-republican groups used this problem to great advantage.

Some of this debate has to do with the various views within the community of the cost and benefits of globalisation. One source of controversy addresses the special relationship successive Australian governments have constructed with the United States. This has both political and economic elements. The willingness of both Labor and Coalition governments to follow the United States into military invasions in Iraq (in 1991 and again since 2003) has been one source of contention. No less contentious has been debate about the role of the Australian–United States Free Trade Agreement (signed in 2005) in either securing or eroding our 'national interest' (Weiss et al. 2004).

Finally, relations between our Indigenous people—who make up around 1.5 per cent of the population—and the dominant 'white' society remains as unresolved as ever. As the forced dissolution of the Aboriginal and Torres Strait Islander Commission (ATSIC)—the first exercise in democratic Aboriginal self-determination—in 2004–05 suggests, these relationships will continue to be a source both of controversy and some shame—especially given the abundant evidence of Indigenous disadvantage.

In short, if ethnicity is central to identity, it is a deeply conflicted and puzzling aspect of contemporary Australia. It seems clear that, far from disappearing in the wake of modernisation or globalisation, our ethnicity continues to matter both for individuals and for discussions about national identity. This consideration suggests the value of addressing several questions:

- What does ethnicity mean and why does it matter?
- How is a discussion couched in terms of ethnicity different from older ideas like race?
- Why and how does history matter in the discussion of ethnic identity and national identity?
- Why is ethnicity a key source of controversy and conflict?

● ETHNICITY AND RACE: IMAGINED COMMUNITY

There is now a general view that the concept of race is a discredited and unscientific way of thinking about collective identity, especially if it promotes the view that humans do belong to different races and that there are fundamental differences in intellectual or ethical ability based on natural or biological factors. The preferred modern way of thinking and talking about collective identity—especially among social scientists—is the term 'ethnicity'. As Marek Kohn (1999: 7–13) argues, however, the complacency with which the idea that racial thinking is now defunct has been accepted may well be disguising the fact that racial thinking has never gone away—just changed some of its vocabulary.

The capacity of human beings to look for ways of identifying people who are *in* a given community and those who are 'foreign' to that community is an extremely long-standing one. Our word 'ethnicity' comes from the period of Classical Greek communities organised around city-states like Athens and Sparta: *ethnoi* was the word the Greeks used to name a 'foreigner'. Recalling this indicates that everyone can be a foreigner to someone else, so we are all in fact 'ethnic'.

We see here a fundamental logic for organising and regulating social relationships which, after Francois Dubet (1993), we call the 'logic of community'. 'Community' is one of the classic concepts in sociology; however, it is notoriously difficult to get agreement about what it means. With Dubet, we see 'community' as a way of thinking about collective identity based on the simultaneous practice of inclusion and exclusion. That is, a community is based on decisions taken to define who is part of that community. This is achieved by defining who is 'outside' of or 'foreign' to that community. This builds on Georg Simmel's (1950) early twentieth century attempt to construct a basic framework for thinking about social life or Carl Schmitt's (1996) no less basic attempt to construct a theory of politics. Both point to the basic distinction we all make between 'friends' and 'enemies'. In an abstracted sense, we can say that the logic of community builds on the logic of 'friend/enemy' to construct what we can call an 'imagined community'.

The idea of an 'imagined community' draws on the work of Benedict Anderson (1989). The potency of the idea of national identity is suggested by powerful emotions like patriotism and the willingness with which so many men in particular have been prepared to sacrifice their lives in military conflict fought for love of country. Anderson says this is testimony to the power of the idea of community constructed over the last few centuries. The construction and cultivation of the idea that 'we' are part of a national community, or a particular ethnic community, depends, according to Anderson, first on the emergence of print technology and the spread of literacy. More recently, it relies on the spread of new media technology like radio, film and TV. In both cases, the idea of 'country', 'nation' or a 'community' based on 'race' or 'ethnicity' is a tribute to the work of writers, academics, political elites, novelists and journalists. It is these groups of the intellectually trained who focus on the special—even unique—value of a language, a geography, a history, a culture and the ways of eating certain foods, wearing certain clothes and cultivating a certain life in common that makes the imagined community into a reality. Constructing the idea of community is done in a variety of ways: by writing histories of communities, telling stories about a given community, making speeches, writing poetry, building universities, creating museums, establishing national days (like Anzac Day) and erecting statues.

It is no accident that the growth of the idea of nation and nationality occured in the same time frame as the birth of what Hannah Arendt (1954) called 'race thinking'. While appeals to special national identity rest on many factors, the idea that 'we' are a special, unique and more valuable group than other groups seems to play a special role. The older idea of 'race', which points to the belief that 'blood ties' define a given community in natural or biological terms, has proved to be a persistent idea over the past few centuries.

● RACE AND RACISM

Race thinking became epidemic and virulent in the nineteenth century. However, it had long been in the air Europeans breathed—even if the 'race' word itself was not much used. It owes much to the writers and intellectuals who gave us the Enlightenment, ostensibly the source of science, rationality and the impulse to modernity that some sociologists persist in talking about.

The Nigerian writer Emmanuel Eze (1997: 3) reminds us that the greatest of the Enlightenment philosophers, Immanuel Kant—the man who wrote so compellingly about universal Reason and Freedom and the need to obey universal and inviolable ethical laws—was also a racist. Kant, who is still held up as the acme of Enlightenment Reason, spent more time giving lectures on race than he did on Reason and ethics. Kant held that:

> The tallest and most beautiful people . . . are on the parallel that runs through Germany . . . The inhabitant of the temperate parts of the world, above all the central part [i.e. Europe] has a more beautiful body, works harder, is more jocular, more controlled in his passions, more intelligent than any other race of people in the world . . .
>
> The Negroes of Africa have by nature no feeling that rises above the trifling . . . Hume challenges anyone to cite a single example in which a Negro has shown talents . . . still not a single one was ever found who presented anything great in art or science or any other praiseworthy quality . . . (Kant 1997 [1764])

While we may want to believe that this nonsense has stopped being taken seriously, unfortunately this is not the case, as the publication in 1994 by Herrnstein and Wilson of their book, *The Bell Curve*, indicates. This book demonstrated 'scientifically' that American Afro-Americans are 'naturally' less intelligent than white Americans as measured by IQ scores.

Racism begins with those tendencies to invent or construct community which are inherent in most human groups. Those tendencies include constructing belief systems based on generalisations about those who are part of the 'in' group and those who are outside—or 'other'—that is, the 'logic of community'. Racism also depends on generalisation. Generalising is always dangerous, but racism extends the logic of generalising and uses physical markers like skin/hair colour and 'scientific' truths about intelligence and behaviour to construct 'truths' about certain people, ignoring the actual diversity found in all groups of people.

Racism refers to practices justified by the premise that there are distinct groups of people known as 'races'. They are said to be distinctive because members of those races allegedly share certain 'natural' or 'biological' characteristics. Racists believe that these biological characteristics explain why some races are naturally superior to others. They include:

- levels of intelligence;
- levels of civilisation or culture;
- fitness to survive;
- being more natural or animal-like; and
- standards of morality.

Racist beliefs include the following claims:

- Blacks have lower IQs than whites and are 'sexually promiscuous', but they make superb athletes, boxers, dancers or singers.
- Aborigines are lazy, drunken and dirty people.
- Asians are sneaky, or inscrutable, intelligent, cruel, industrious—and hard-working.
- Jews are inscrutable, intelligent, mean, avaricious—and hard-working.
- British people are intelligent, tolerant, industrious—and hard-working.

Many Australians still erroneously believe that some races are naturally superior or inferior. Yet there is more genetic variation between individuals in a single community than there is between national communities. Approximately 85 per cent of genetic variation occurs between individuals within the same country, while a further 5–10 per cent comes from differences between people living in different countries on the same continent.

Geneticists have pointed out that if there are 50 000 genes in each human, only ten of them determine skin colour. Racists claim that there is a relationship between skin colour and other human capacities (e.g. intelligence or morality), which they claim are also genetically based. These claims are misleading and dangerous. There is no known genetic basis for saying that the genes which determine skin colour determine other genetic factors like intelligence—assuming that 'intelligence' is genetically based at all (Jones 1993).

The geneticists' conclusion is that genetic variation is something individuals carry, not races. The point here is that genetic variation, the operation of genetic mutation and the proportion of junk material in the human genome make it impossible to use a genetic marker to identify a group as a 'race'. This is a useful point, but it does not deal with the fact that racist beliefs and ideas—however irrational or lacking in evidence—do have practical effects. These beliefs have been used to justify everything from normal activities such as education, health, birth control and immigration policies through to slavery, torture, exploitation and the genocide of whole peoples (see box).

The dark side of racism

- The southern states of the United States refused to give Afro-Americans—who had historically been brought to America as slaves until the Civil War (1861–65) 'freed' them—any civil rights, including the right to vote or attend 'whites only' schools, until 1968.

- The Nazi government in Germany between 1941 and 1945 systematically killed at least 4.5 million Jews, along with millions more 'racially unfit' people in death camps like Auschwitz and Treblinka.

- Australian governments maintained a White Australia policy between 1901 and 1973 to keep 'coloured' people out, a policy which had the support of all the major political parties.

- The dominant Chinese people (the Han) have pursued racist policies against minorities like the Tibetans since the 1950s.

- Turks carried out the first modern genocide against Armenians in 1916–17.

- In Malaysia there has been racial tension between Malay and Chinese people.

- After Independence and Partition created India and Pakistan in 1947, Muslims and Hindus slaughtered each other in the millions.

- In Rwanda, the Hutu killed about a million Tutsis in 1994–95.

- The Balkans have seen Croats, Serbs and Muslims engage in horrific violence, with evidence of genocide—especially by Serbs directed at Bosnians and Muslims.

- In Indonesia, at least 500 000 ethnic Chinese were killed in 1966–67.

While racial thinking had authority conferred on it by a lot of scientific research, it fell rapidly into a twilight zone after 1945 and the discovery of what racial science had done in Nazi Germany. At the urging of international bodies like the United Nations, and of social scientists, 'ethnicity' has become the new and preferred way of talking about collective groups of people using things like common language or a shared history.

● ETHNICITY

Ethnicity is the idea that certain differences and similarities exist in the group that are symbolic or cultural in origin, and that those features provide a source of group and personal identity. Ethnicity stresses the role and importance in a community of shared factors like:

- territory or geography;
- language;

- belief systems—especially religious ones;
- styles of clothing, food, music and dance;
- ways of living or 'culture'; and
- history.

In this sense, ethnicity is usually very close to the anthropologist's idea of 'culture' as the totality of exclusive, shared ways of living, thinking and acting within a large group. Even so, as Goldberg (1993) points out, many people use the term 'ethnicity' when they are referring to 'race', or to the alleged inherent superiority (or inferiority) of one ethnic group over another. 'Ethnicity' is combined with the idea of 'race' by people who claim there are cultural differences at a group level. Thus Yinger (1981: 20) claims that: 'An ethnic group perceives itself and it is perceived to be different in some combination of . . . language, religion, race and ancestral homelands with its related culture.' The discussion about ethnicity stresses culture, socialisation and choice rather than nature or biology as the basis of ethnic difference. However, this does not mean it is a problem-free idea.

What's wrong with ethnicity?

Ethnicity is a very fluid concept, because the ethnic status you ascribe to a group is determined by the criteria people use to define ethnicity. This is another way of saying that it is very much a constructed identity, and depends on all the technologies and discourses that Anderson (1989) tells us have gone into an 'imagined community'.

Many so-called ethnic groups are themselves subdivided into smaller groups. For example, Yugoslavs have drawn lines that make distinctions between groups like Croats, Slovenians, Serbs and Bosnians. In turn, people within these groups use religion to mark further points of difference (like Muslim Bosnians or Catholic Croatians).

Territorial criteria give one definition of ethnicity; religion or language can give another. For example, when we talk about ethnicity in Melbourne, do we refer to markers based on country of origin when we speak of Lebanese, Turks, Palestinians or Israelis? Or do we refer to religion as a marker of ethnic difference, and speak of Muslims, Christians or Jews? Or do we use linguistic markers, and make reference to categories such as English, Arabic, Yiddish, Hebrew or Turkish speakers?

What boundaries exist in Australia between ethnic groups, and what makes one group 'ethnic' and another not? For instance, there is a small group of traditional rural Australians living on farms with a particular lifestyle. Why aren't rural Australians an ethnic group? We may ask similar questions about the idea of British ethnicity or Anglo-Celtic ethnicity. Many people who were born in England, for example, do not see themselves as 'ethnic', but those from Wales and Scotland increasingly do.

As Richard Sennett (1988) has reminded us, the very idea of community can be simultaneously both a positive thing, enhancing pride, social cohesion and a sense of belonging, and a bitter divisive and destructive idea—as those who have been excluded in order to construct someone else's sense of belonging to a community can testify.

● AUSTRALIAN RACE RELATIONS: ABORIGINES AND ABORIGINALITY

Most of us know that modern Australia was established at Sydney Cove in January 1788. It is sometimes forgotten that this was but a small moment in a much longer and larger process of European colonisation, which took off after Columbus 'discovered' the Americas in 1492.

Over the next 400 years, much of Africa, Asia, the Americas, Australasia and Oceania was invaded by European traders, missionaries and military forces. Many indigenous people were killed, but millions more died from European diseases after the first contact with the Europeans. Colonisation meant local populations lost their traditional lifestyles as their lands were taken by the Spaniards, the Dutch, the French, the Portuguese, the Belgians, the Russians, the Germans and the British, who either established direct colonial rule or set up regimes favourable to their interests.

Though racism has been conventionally treated as a distinctively nineteenth century belief system, Irene Silverblatt (2004) reminds us that racial thinking was integral to the sixteenth century invasion and conquest by the Spaniards of their South American empire. Critical to this process was the widespread belief that Europeans were inherently superior to and deserved to rule over 'their' colonies and the people they had acquired. Moreover, they thought they had God's support for their activities. These ideas led to the imposition of racial categories and new ways of regulating the various ethnic groups brought together in the Spanish empire, including the indigenous peoples, African slaves and European settlers. The construction of empire was everywhere imagined by the Europeans to involve bringing 'civilisation' to 'savage' peoples.

Manning Clark was a sensitive, progressive Australian historian. He started his much admired six-volume history of Australia thus: 'Civilisation did not begin in Australia until the last quarter of the eighteenth century' (Clark 1962: 3). This statement, for which he later apologised, indicates the extent to which white racist beliefs were shared even among many educated white Australians until recently.

Indigenous history in Australia

Indigenous Australians appear now to have been here for at least 60 000 years. This first process of settlement may have involved two waves of immigration (Day 1996: 8). Archaeological evidence has suggested that these first immigrants were a population of large, heavy Neanderthals. Some of these ancient skeletons are more than 1.8 metres tall, with massive bone structures. It is likely that their ancestors were part of a first wave of arrivals—perhaps 100 000 years ago. The second wave of immigrants was a smaller, more slender population group. It is likely that these people arrived around 50 000 years ago. Although we are not sure precisely how or when they travelled, it is likely they crossed a land bridge from southern India and then traversed uncharted waters in canoes or simply waded through low coastal waters to reach what became Australia.

Despite the perception of many Europeans that Indigenous peoples 'all looked the same', there was a rich and diverse pattern of 500–700 Aboriginal communities across the continent, with approximately 100–1500 people in each grouping and around 600 people on average in most communities (Elkin 1954: 11).

They lived in different environments, had different ways of living off the land, used different weapons and utensils, and practised different rituals and codes for living, marrying and dying. Some initiated young men into manhood by knocking their front teeth out; others practised circumcision or cut open the shaft of the penis. Girls were similarly initiated into 'women's business', which included giving the girls access to certain forms of special knowledge. Some groups of Aboriginal people lived nomadic lives, while others built permanent houses or stone huts, dug dams and developed elaborate water systems to trap fish. Far from living in splendid isolation, those groups living in what is now the Northern Territory had trading relations with Indonesians, who fished here centuries ago, and this in turn intersected with elaborate trading networks that crossed the continent of Australia (McBryde 1987: 253–73).

Across Australia, there were approximately 250 different language families. Wurm (1972) suggests there was a phonological and grammatical similarity between these languages, which created a rich diversity in the vocabularies: 'a situation unique in the world' (1972: 31).

There was no common 'Aboriginal' language, and most groups could not always communicate effectively with each other.

The history of white Australia began in January 1788, when a small invasion force of soldiers, and male and female convicts, took possession of 'New South Wales'—a small part of what was then called 'New Holland'. As Day writes (1996: 2), the 200 years since 1788 have not been good for Aboriginal Australians. The British invasion and the establishment of British colonies had two primary effects:

- A demographic catastrophe took place involving an initial and drastic reduction in the Aboriginal population. As Tim Rowse (2005: 312–13) notes, this catastrophe was followed in the twentieth century by a remarkable recovery.

- The practice of colonists moving the Indigenous peoples off their land—most often on to designated native reserves and settlements—led to a spiritual and cultural dispossession, signalled by the invention and use of the word 'Aboriginal' and ultimately of policies designed to 'assimilate' Indigenous peoples. One of the more recent techniques used to regulate Indigenous peoples involved the twentieth century use of 'welfare interventions', which stripped large numbers of young Aboriginal children from their families and relocated them in white families and institutions. In New South Wales alone, over 10 000 children of the 'stolen generation' were removed in the years to 1970 (Sidoti 1997: 8).

● THE DEMOGRAPHIC CATASTROPHE—AND RECOVERY?

We do not know how many people there were in Australia in 1788. Estimates of the numbers of Aboriginal people at that time have ranged from 300 000 to over a million (ABS 2006a: 21). John Mulvaney (2002) has recently suggested a mid-range estimate of approximately 750 000. This compares with the current ABS Census-based enumeration which gives an Indigenous population in 2005 of 492 700 (ABS 2005a). As Rowse (2005) makes clear, there is a complex history of changes in how Indigenous people were identified and counted which also needs to be taken into account when assessing the demographic impact of colonisation.

One of the first effects of European invasion was a dramatic drop in the Aboriginal population. N.G. Butlin (1983), using some complex demographic techniques—and some now debatable assumptions about the initial population size—was probably close enough when he suggested that by 1805 only 50 per cent of the 1788 population in New South Wales were still alive. In Victoria by 1830 (i.e. before settlement began there), it had dropped to 25–30 per cent.

Using the racial categories in popular use until the 1960s, the scale of the demographic losses was extreme. By 1921, there were some 52 738 'full-bloods' alive, and by 1954 this had declined to a low point of 39 415 'full-bloods' (Rowse 2005: 321). If we used the racist distinction between 'full-blood' and 'half-caste' we would see that, in Victoria, there were over 15 000 full-descent Aborigines in 1835, and by 1922 there were fewer than 88. By the 1870s, there were no 'pure-blood aboriginals' left alive in Tasmania; the last Aborigine, a woman called Truganini, was 'exhibited' in the Hobart Zoo. Indigenous numbers in places like Western Australia and the Northern Territory proved more robust.

How and why did this catastrophe occur? The so-called 'history wars' is primarily a debate between historians like Henry Reynolds and Keith Windschuttle about the use of words like 'genocide' and the extent to which there is good evidence of an intent to use violence to kill off the Indigenous peoples (see Attwood 2005). Our view is that there is some good evidence that some Aboriginal people were shot and poisoned, especially when they showed any signs of resistance. Alison Palmer (2000: 40) estimates that between 5000 and 15 000 Aboriginals were killed in Queensland between 1840 and 1897. Yet it now seems clear that most of the initial devastating population loss was due to the impact of new European diseases. Many Indigenous people died in advance of the actual appearance of whites, their deaths a result of the dramatic spread of European illnesses and diseases to which they had no immunity (e.g. colds, diphtheria, smallpox, tuberculosis and chickenpox).

The sexual exploitation of Aboriginal women and girls had a more ambiguous, albeit just as damaging, effect on the population. Many European men raped many Aboriginal women and/ or entered into long-term relationships with Aboriginal girls, though usually not involving legal marriage. Many of what used to be called 'half-caste' children were born due to this behaviour. Their descendants make up a significant proportion of the modern Aboriginal population.

Until the 1950s, the colonial and Commonwealth Censuses used the racial categories distinguishing between 'full-blood' and 'half-caste' Aboriginal people. These Censuses fail to take into account the large numbers of children born to Aboriginal and non-Aboriginal parents. On this basis Rowse (2005) suggests that, while we can accept the large story of a dramatic population decline, there has been a recovery of sorts. Through the first decades of the twentieth century, he points to a recovery of population numbers partly explicable by changes in identifying and counting 'Aborigines' and partly because of a big increase in the numbers of children born to Aboriginal people and non-Aboriginal people. Between 1921 and 1944, state Censuses suggest a static total number of 'full-bloods' and 'half-castes' of around 68 000, with a significant increase occurring.

Table 11.1 Indigenous population, 1966–2001

Census year	Numbers
1966	101 978
1971	115 953
1981	159 897
1986	227 645
1991	265 458
1996	352 970
2001	410 002

Source: Rowse (2005: 322).

• CULTURAL AND SPIRITUAL DISPOSSESSION

In parallel with this demographic decline, the Indigenous people were also dispossessed of their culture (including their languages and arts) and their land. During the nineteenth century, the

Gidja, Djawun, Miriwung, Aranta, Koori, Nyungar and many other Indigenous Australians lost their identity. Instead, they became what the Europeans called them—'Aborigines'. At the very moment the Indigenous people became 'Aborigines', their ability to tell their own stories about themselves and their world began to diminish. They thereby ceased to be a heterogeneous people with a rich and diverse history, and became 'savage', 'uncivilised' and 'prehistoric'.

Attwood (1989: 149) notes that:

> The concept 'Aborigines' has been generally used as though such a self-consciously identified group had existed at first contact with Europeans, but this is to prescribe retrospectively a definition to the Aboriginal peoples at a period when they had no such sense of themselves. Before 1788 or even much later, they did not conceive of themselves as 'Aboriginal' any more than the European invaders thought of themselves as 'Australians'.

Attwood (1989: 149) sums up the situation:

> Before the coming of Europeans, one cannot regard 'Aborigines' as a homogenous group. Theirs was a world of small groups and narrow divisions . . . they defined themselves in terms of their specific relationships with the land and other Aborigines. Across the continent they used different names for themselves which generally signified that they thought of themselves as a particular group and considered other Aborigines to be strangers and savage.

One fundamental result of the process of dispossession entailed by the invention of the 'Aborigine' was that until 1968 they had no formal civic rights or legal status as Australian citizens. This meant they could not, for example, own property, vote, or even be counted as part of the Australian population at Census time. (The 1942 *Citizenship Act* allowed only Aboriginal people with 'some white blood' to apply for status as citizens.) A constitutional referendum finally gave Aboriginal people citizenship status in 1967—about 60 years after Australian men had decided that even women were citizens and should be allowed to vote. This meant that Indigenous peoples could be counted as part of the Australian population and they could vote and stand for election.

Along with cultural dispossession came the eviction of Aborigines from any land the white settlers wanted. In 1787, a British newspaper informed its readers that the territory of New South Wales was 'formed of a virgin mould, untouched since the Creation' (cited in Day 1996: 49). Court rulings in the 1820s confirmed what any sensible English person had already 'known'—that Australia was *terra nullius*. According to British law, Australia was a land that had not been occupied or farmed by anyone, and therefore it belonged to no one until the

British occupation. This meant there was no illegality involved in British people occupying the land. There was no need to buy the land from Aborigines or for treaties.

This useful legal finding would justify decades of dispossession, and would be overturned partially only in June 1992. (The High Court's finding in the *Mabo* case was that, where Aboriginal people could show continued use of land not already leased or in possession of the Crown, they could claim 'native title' over that land.)

● ABORIGINAL PEOPLE TODAY

Contemporary Aboriginal communities experience many of the same social and economic problems as indigenous peoples in Canada, New Zealand and the United States. While there are encouraging signs of improvement in some social indicators, the overall circumstances of the Indigenous peoples suggest they are the most disadvantaged group in Australia.

There is a powerful connection linking low social and economic status and poor health. Indigenous people tend as a group to be less healthy, and to have shorter lives. It continues to be a problem that Aborigines have a lower life expectancy than white Australians: in 2005 for men, life expectancy is 59.6 years and for women it is 64.8 years (compared with 76 years for non-Aboriginal men and 82 years for women). Indigenous infant mortality rates, at thirteen infant deaths per 1000 live births, are much higher than for the white population (ABS 2005a). At the same time, the Indigenous fertility rate is much higher, and as a group Indigenous people show a much younger age profile than the larger society, with a median age of 21 years (compared with 36 years for non-Indigenous people).

One feature of the Indigenous population is that nearly 40 per cent are under fifteen years of age, compared with 22 per cent of the total population, while 68 per cent of Aborigines are under 30, compared with 43 per cent of all Australians. One implication of being both young and Aboriginal is that it increases Indigenous people's visibility to police and other law enforcement agents. Certainly it is hard to explain the incredible rates of imprisonment of Aborigines other than by some explanation concerning racist policing practices. In 2004–05 the Aboriginal imprisonment rate was 1663 per 100 000, compared with 139 per 100 000 of the white population (ABS 2005a).

Indigenous people are also less well educated, though that is changing with a steady growth in the numbers of Indigenous people in primary and secondary schooling as well as rises in the retention rates from 20 per cent in 1994 to 32 per cent in 2002. The 1996 Census (ABS 2000: 22) showed 57 per cent of Aboriginal people aged sixteen were students, compared with 83.5 per cent of all Australians. In 1996, 3 per cent of Indigenous people had never attended a school, compared with 0.7 per cent of all Australians. Only 2 per cent of Aborigines had a university degree, compared with 10.4 per cent of all Australians. That situation has now improved, with 10 per cent of Aboriginal people now possessing some post-secondary qualification. In remote

Australia, literacy in English continues to be a problem: 5 per cent of Aborigines spoke no English, while another 26 per cent said they did not speak English well (ABS 2006a: 22).

As with schooling, there have been improvements in Aboriginal employment and unemployment rates. The proportions in mainstream employment rose from 31 per cent in 1994 to 38 per cent in 2004. However, as a group Aborigines tend to be more likely to be unemployed than non-Indigenous people—though again their unemployment as a national average has fallen from 24 per cent in 1994 to 13 per cent in 2004. This is twice the unemployment rate for non-Indigenous people. Over half of the Aborigines who were unemployed had been unemployed for more than twelve months.

Most of the employment available to Aborigines in remote and rural Australia has been a result of the Community Development Employment Project (CDEP) scheme, in operation since 1977. CDEP is important in rural Australia because it supplies more than half of all jobs held by Aboriginal people.

The effects on income are accordingly stark. Australian Aborigines usually have far lower incomes than most non-Indigenous Australians. Aborigines receive a lower income on average than the total population, and there are fewer high income-earning Aborigines. Back in 1994, the real mean equalised gross household income for each Aboriginal household was $158 compared with $310 for each 'white' Australian household (ABS 2006a: 23). This had improved slightly by 2004–05, when the real mean equalised gross household income for Indigenous households was $394 a week—still only 60 per cent of the real mean equalised gross household income for non-Indigenous families. This reflects the fact that the Aboriginal population has a higher than average reliance on social security payments.

In terms of the level of government welfare and related support to the Indigenous population, the criticisms mounted by the likes of Pauline Hanson about 'disproportionate' or 'excessive' amounts of government support are simply untrue. Since the 1990s, welfare, health care and education support provided specifically for Aborigines has rarely exceeded more than 2 per cent of total budget outlays—a level proportionate to the 2 per cent of the total population that Aborigines represent. (Whether more resources ought to be devoted to Aboriginal welfare, rather than less as Hanson implies, is a matter for urgent debate.)

Finally, the housing options open to Indigenous people have their own consequences. Images of rotting timber and tin shanties, cardboard shacks, canvas tents and piles of rubbish are often associated with Aboriginal housing. However, this picture is not true for the large proportion of Aboriginal people. It is true that they are far less likely to own or to be purchasing their own houses. Even in the major cities and towns, only 34 per cent were home owners, while over half were renting their homes from private and government housing agencies. In rural areas, most of the rental housing (57 per cent of housing stock) is owned and supplied by Indigenous community groups. These are the homes needing most repairs, and about which people express most dissatisfaction.

There is one 'big fact' about Indigenous people that helps to explain many of the problems related to being Aboriginal in Australia today. Unlike most Australians, who live in the major capital cities, most of Australia's 492 000 Aboriginal people at the start of the twenty-first century live in rural and provincial Australia (see box).

Where Indigenous Australians live

- Only 30.3 per cent of Aboriginal people live in the major capital cities, compared with 62.7 per cent of all Australians.

- Over half of all Aborigines live in two states: New South Wales (29 per cent) and Queensland (27 per cent).

- Some 42 per cent of Aboriginal people live in provincial cities, compared with 23.2 per cent of all Australians.

- Around 27.3 per cent of Aboriginal people live in rural Australia, compared with 14 per cent of all Australians.

- Of the capital cities, Darwin has the highest proportion of Indigenous people (10.3 per cent); this is followed by Hobart (3.2 per cent).

- Indigenous people represent only 4 per cent or less of the total population in each state and territory—except in the Northern Territory, where the figure stands at 30 per cent (ABS 2005a).

For these reasons, many Indigenous people are invisible to the far more numerous Australians who live and work in the big cities. The big cities are where most of the paid jobs are. They are also where the best housing, health and education services are to be found.

It is in remote and rural Australia that the often graphic media images of Aboriginal people living in conditions of poverty characteristic of Third World countries take on a certain grim reality. One of the biggest problems in Australia is that, even after decades of efforts to redress these problems by white governments using conventional methods and approaches, little has been achieved. If this is a somewhat depressing portrait, there has been movement towards improving the political and economic status of Australia's Indigenous population, though it has been patchy at best.

● ABORIGINAL POLITICS

On 3 June 1992, the High Court of Australia issued the *Mabo* judgment. This overturned 170 years of legal practice, which stated that land could be taken by the British without dispossessing or depriving any Indigenous groups of their rights and entitlements. (The *Mabo* case is named after Eddie Mabo, a Torres Strait Islander who took a claim to the High Court that British annexation had not extinguished native title to land.)

The *Mabo* judgment maintained that Aboriginal title to the land still existed, so long as Aboriginal people could demonstrate an 'abiding connection with their land through laws, customs, beliefs and ceremonies'. In 1993, the Keating Labor government passed the *Native Title Act* 1993, which established a process through which Indigenous people could pursue land title claims. The *Native Title Act* does not permit the extinction of any prior land titles held by farmers or householders. Most Aboriginal claims to title will affect only Crown land. Despite this, many farmers, mining companies and conservatives claimed that non-Indigenous land-owners—including householders in the suburbs—would be dispossessed by this loss of rights to 'their' land. In a subsequent ruling (the *Wik* judgment), the High Court provoked the Coalition Howard government (1996–) to legislate to protect white interests at Aboriginal expense.

At the start of the twenty-first century, progress towards a process of national reconciliation between 'white' and Indigenous Australians remains a controversial subject. In spite of one Royal Commission (1991) into Aboriginal deaths in custody, young Aborigines continue to die in greater numbers now than before 1991, while the grossly disproportionate numbers of Aboriginal arrests and imprisonment rates in several states, particularly Western Australia and Queensland, points to the persistence of racist policing practices.

Political debate about Aboriginal policy remains prone to racist and misleading claims that Aborigines get an unfair share of 'white' resources. In the first decade of the twenty-first century, the Howard government—while it backs the reconciliation process—has steadily refused to issue a formal apology to the 'stolen generations'. A new low moment in black–white relations was reached in 2005 when the Howard government formally disbanded the ATSIC Commission—the first and only exercise in establishing a form of democratically elected Aboriginal 'government'. The excuse offered for this political coup rested on allegations of corrupt practice by the political representatives and bureaucratic officers employed by ATSIC. That there was evidence of some level of corruption in the disbursement of funds to support Aboriginal health welfare and education is undoubted; however, that this corruption was greater than that normally accompanying any process of distributing funds involving politicians of any kind was never discussed.

Debates about the history of black and white relations in the colonial era and the contested nature of contemporary relations between Aboriginal people and other Australians is one reminder that identity in a multicultural society is never going to be without conflict. The same can be said of the way immigration has shaped modern Australia.

• IMMIGRATION DEBATES

Immigration is central to modern Australian's individual and collective identity. Modern Australia is a society made up of people born overseas and their children, as well as the descendants of earlier generations of immigrants. The period since 1945 has had the most dramatic effects of any time in our modern history. Between 1945 and 1975, large-scale immigration from increasingly diverse countries and regions brought a far wider range of ethnic groups to Australia than had hitherto been the case, although the pattern of immigration confirmed the long-standing preference for British migrants. Since the 1980s, that preference has ceased to exert any influence on patterns of migration. In consequence, Australia has proportionately both a higher number of migrants in its population than any other country in the world (apart from Israel) and a more diverse pattern of ethnic communities.

There is general agreement that, comparatively speaking, Australia has been one of the most successful examples of a multicultural society, with a good record of intra-ethnic relations since the 1940s. Australia has not been scarred by the kinds of extreme intra-ethnic violence that has characterised countries like Britain, France, Germany or the United States. This claim needs to be tempered by the appalling record of black–white relations after 1788. It also needs to be acknowledged that Australia has not managed to completely avoid certain strains and tensions about its identity as a modern multicultural society defined by the quality both of the tolerance shown and the level of mutual respect. As always, the history of how we have come to be the kind of society we are needs to be understood if we are to deal well with our contemporary circumstances.

• COLONIAL IMMIGRATION

It is conventional to treat the period since the sixteenth century as an era marked by large-scale movements of people across the globe (Castles & Miller 1993). This ignores the fact that the entire million-year-plus history of our species has been marked by constant population movement or migration. The creation of a 'white Australia' after Federation in 1901 was one small part of that vast global process.

As has long been acknowledged, immigration is a kind of push-me, pull-me process. First, there have to be motivations—even pressures—which lead people to want to migrate. Sometimes people actually have little choice. Economic factors like unemployment, poverty, even famine and the disruptions following a civil or military disturbance provide one set of motivations. Equally, there have to be attractions and a willingness on the part of prospective host societies to make them sufficiently attractive to would-be migrants—particularly those who faced extreme hazards in getting to Australia in the nineteenth century. All of these factors have been a persistent part of modern Australia's experience of immigration.

In the first instance, poverty and the disturbances that accompanied Britain's pioneering leap into industrialisation provided one source of immigrants. These were the people who came to Australia involuntarily as convicted felons. By the 1780s, Britain's gaols were filled to overflowing and Britain faced a penal crisis as one long-standing depot for receiving the overflow—the American colonies—was closed down after Britain 'lost' its American empire in 1783. Though there is some debate about the precise mixture of motives that led to British settlement in New South Wales, the drive to empty its gaols was one factor. Between 1788 and 1852, approximately 170 000 convicts—the majority of whom were English, with a significant admixture of Irish—were sent from Britain to New South Wales, Tasmania and Queensland. Most were men. Australia began as, and remained for some considerable time, 'a man's country'. (In 1881 there were 1.2 million men to 1.03 million women. As late as 1971, men still dominated: there were 6.4 million men to 6.3 million women.)

Both the policy-makers in Britain and the colonial administrators early understood that free immigrants offered a more secure basis for the growth and development of the Australian colonies. By the mid-1830s, pressure mounted to end the flow of convicts into the Australian colonies and, although Australia was a long way from Britain and Europe, it proved attractive to prospective migrants. In the nineteenth century, given the long distances travelled in small and vulnerable sailing ships on a long sea voyage, it was also a hazardous experience. But there were serious pressures mounting in a number of countries that pushed people to migrate to Australia in the nineteenth century.

England during the 1840s suffered a severe economic depression, with unemployment, poverty and famine. There was also considerable anxiety in some quarters about the threat such large numbers of jobless, hungry and angry 'labourers' represented to social order. By the 1840s, more than 40 000 free settlers were arriving annually in Australia. In Ireland, the great potato famine of the 1840s produced mass poverty and hunger. Canada, the United States and Australia reaped the benefits of the exodus of Irish settlers. Yet there were also other non-European countries where circumstances were pushing people to migrate.

In Imperial China, the economic and political dislocation following the Western seizure of territory around Canton and Shanghai (in modern Kuangchuo province) impelled millions of Chinese out of China and into Southeast Asia and/or across the Pacific. The 'gold-rush' era after 1851 made places like California and Australia highly desirable destinations for Chinese migrants. A significant number of Chinese men came to Australia in the 1850s in search of gold, and stayed on either as farmers in rural areas or as merchants in cities like Sydney and Melbourne.

Finally, though this is less well remembered, the colonisation of Queensland after 1859 led to a short-term experiment in creating a slave economy. Queenslanders systematically raided a number of Pacific islands, kidnapping thousands of people in an operation called 'blackbirding'. The captives were brought back to work in the developing sugar cane industry. Together, these

'Kanakas' and the Chinese may well have turned Australia into a multicultural society. However, that opportunity was well and truly rejected as economic development and the political process led to a white racist response.

● AUSTRALIA: WHITE AND IMPERIAL

By the 1880s, 'Australia' was a series of thriving British colonies, each exporting mineral or agricultural products to Britain's export-oriented industrial economy. Australia was seen by both local and British-based elites as a whites-only extension of Britain and the British Empire. This came to be part of the 'common sense' of most Australians. All shades of political opinion in the Australian political community came to accept a conventional kind of white racism as a fundamental framework for thinking about the world and Australia's place in it. From the 1880s, many 'well-educated' Australians were convinced that population pressure from the 'masses of Asians' to the north of the country would force them to move south and 'swamp' the country.

In Britain and the colonies, it was accepted as a matter of fact that there was a 'natural', colour-coded hierarchy of races: white races were at the top, the swarthy races of Europe were next, the 'yellow' Asian races came further down the ladder and last were the black races, closest in intelligence and nature to monkeys. This thinking 'justified' keeping the races separate. Even advanced liberals like Alfred Deakin believed that the white races had a 'duty to civilise' the 'coloured races', who ought to be both happy and grateful for the effort that white imperialists made in 'civilising' them and promoting their evolution into a more advanced species.

One major policy implication of this racial sentiment was that immigration into Australia was to be encouraged only for white—and preferably British—settlers. From the late 1880s, various colonial governments passed racial exclusion legislation designed to repatriate ('send home') black Pacific islanders who had been brought to Australia as indentured labourers, as well as Chinese labourers brought to Australia in the 1840s and 1850s. Many Chinese left Australia in the 1880s as a result of mass protest campaigns to evict them, though small numbers stayed on.

In 1901, the first legislation passed by the new Commonwealth parliament was the *Immigration Restriction Act* 1901. This 'white Australia' legislation was based on a racist belief in white supremacy. As Australia's first prime minister, Edmund Barton (cited in Gibb 1973: 100–1), said: 'We know that coloured and white labour cannot exist side by side; we are well aware that China can swamp us with a single year's surplus of population . . .'. The Act gave the Commonwealth government the right to administer to any person wishing to enter Australia a test (in any language) to determine their fitness to enter Australia; it was not uncommon to find 'coloured' persons who arrived in Australia being given tests in Icelandic or in medieval French. (This technicality was used to avoid giving offence to the Japanese government by naming Chinese or Japanese people in the legislation.)

The 'white Australia' policy enjoyed strong community support through to the 1970s. It was not until after the election of the Whitlam government in 1972 that the policy was officially dropped. By 1973, Australia was on its way to becoming a 'multicultural society' (Lopez 2000), though the extent of popular support for this was unclear.

● POSTWAR IMMIGRATION, 1947 TO THE 1980s

The addition of four million settlers to Australia's population in the four decades after 1947, while nothing like the scale of the immigration which changed the United States between 1870 and 1914, was central to the redefinition of our society as multicultural. Castles (1992) has divided the history of Australian immigration since 1947 into three periods:

- assimilation (1947–65);
- integration (1965–72); and
- multiculturalism (1973–).

Castles' periodisation is based on the dominant understanding by governments as spelled out in official policy statements identifying how the social and cultural impact of the migrants would best be dealt with.

These phases, though they have a pleasing appearance of precision, are not all that clearcut. This periodisation serves best to remind us that for a long time governments have played a dominant role in determining the character of our society and culture. They also remind us that governments have tried to tell a story about social order through a process of legitimation based on policy statements that promote a certain view of the national community. To put this another way, this process of developing immigration policies has relied on a variety of understandings of Australia as a certain kind of 'imagined community'.

Assimilation, 1947–65

In 1945, the postwar Labor government under the leadership of 'Ben' Chifley established a new Department of Immigration to plan and run a large-scale immigration program. This novel experiment in a planned immigration policy was part of an ambitious process of post-war reconstruction designed to rebuild Australia by modernising and industrialising the economy and enhancing the country's security. The need for a policy of postwar reconstruction reaffirmed the role of immigration policy as a key part of the long-standing policy consensus Paul Kelly (1993) calls 'the Australian settlement'. As one of the pioneering sociologists of immigration, Jean Martin (1978), notes, successive Australian governments from 1947 made immigration into a policy device designed to address the economic development needs of Australia.

It also was believed that a program of mass immigration would protect Australia from Asia by filling a large and 'empty' continent with people. For many Australians, the threat of Japanese invasion in 1942 had been a frightening experience. Being a member of the British Empire had long encouraged Australians to refer to Japan and China in the 1930s as the 'Far East'. The onset of the Pacific War in 1941, the Japanese bombing of Darwin and the shelling of Sydney by Japanese mini-subs in 1942 revealed the fallacy of that geographic misapprehension.

In 1947, the Chifley government's immigration policy contracted initially to bring in large numbers of British migrants and a small number of refugees from north and central Europe. The official policy aimed at attracting ten British people to one non-British settler. Large numbers of British migrants were attracted by a generously subsidised immigration ticket (so-called 'ten pound Poms') and the guarantee of a job at the end of the voyage to Australia.

In 1947, Arthur Calwell, Australia's first Minister for Immigration, argued that British migrants would 'settle in' easily. Non-English migrants might be a greater problem, so northern Europeans with fair skin from countries like Holland, Germany, Poland and the Baltic countries—rather than the 'darker' Italians and Greeks—were the first choice in 1947. These were the first non-English speaking background (NESB) people to come to Australia as migrants in the postwar period. It was assumed that a process of assimilation would begin as soon as the immigrants arrived in Australia. NESB migrants would 'automatically' learn English when they entered the workforce, while their children would 'automatically' be absorbed into Australian culture by a 'natural' process.

By 1951–52, the supply of migrants from northern Europe began to diminish. In seeking more migrants, Australia turned to southern European countries like Italy, Greece and Yugoslavia. Many migrants from those countries entered into indentured labour arrangements, to work at the government's direction—usually for two years—in certain industries. This meant that, as soon as the new migrants disembarked from the ships, they were bussed to migrant hostels, where they were housed in Nissan Huts made from corrugated iron, which were conveniently located in major industrial areas. Many of these workers were at work within days of their arrival (Freeman & Jupp 1992).

Throughout the 1940s and 1950s, the formal elements of the 'white Australia' policy were retained. Equally influential figures like Calwell, who was himself a fluent Mandarin speaker, and his Liberal government successors were committed to opening the way to more open relations with Asia. The introduction of an educational policy under the Colombo Plan involved a carefully managed program that brought significant numbers of ethnic Chinese, Indonesian and Indian students into Australian universities.

Integration, 1965–72

By the 1960s, while Australia had attracted many migrants, governments and the few migration experts believed that the policy of 'assimilation' was not working. Social scientists like James Jupp and Jean Martin produced research showing that many non-English speaking people were living in what were described as 'ghetto suburbs'. Many were concentrated in working-class, industrialised areas with low wages, low skill levels and poor access to health and educational services. The children of some migrants were not 'automatically' learning English, nor were they doing well at school. Worse, there was even evidence of dissatisfied migrants returning home.

For a few years, the federal government entertained the idea of 'integration'. This saw the introduction of special grants, special education projects and other community initiatives to integrate migrants into 'the Australian way of life'.

Multiculturalism, 1973–

In 1973, the first Labor Party government in 23 years—the Whitlam government—dramatically reformulated the national immigration policy framework. After Whitlam had formally abandoned the 'white Australia' policy, his Minister for Immigration, a very colourful Italian migrant named Al Grassby, announced that Australia was now a 'multicultural society' (Lopez 2000).

'Multiculturalism' at that time meant that governments could speak of a 'family of the nation' while also recognising that NESB migrants had special welfare, health and educational needs. In the 1970s and early 1980s, much of the rhetoric of multiculturalism referred to maintaining a space for cultural diversity within a common 'Australian' framework. By 1989, the Hawke Labor government's 'National Agenda for a Multi-cultural Australia' recognised three dimensions of multiculturalism:

- the right of all Australians to express their specific cultural identity while sharing a common Australian culture;
- the right of all Australians to equality of treatment and opportunity; and
- the need to maintain and develop the skills of all Australians, regardless of their cultural background.

Subsequent immigration policy formulations under the Howard Coalition government have retained the rhetoric of multiculturalism while seeking to more or less subtly emphasise the 'fact' that Australia has a core national identity grounded in its Anglo-Irish origins. The politics of the post-9/11 period has also seen a not-so-subtle ramping-up of anti-Muslim sentiment by some high-profile ministers in the Howard government, like Brendan Nelson and Bronwyn Bishop—who called for the banning of Muslim girls wearing their hijabs to public schools in mid-2005.

These shifts in the understanding of what Australia's multicultural immigration policy framework means have been accompanied by different kinds of debates about the value of immigration, something which has shadowed a quite marked shift in our population profile.

On the one hand, and especially since the 1980s, Australian immigration policy has resculptured our population profile. This policy has generated often-heated debate about the optimal numbers of migrants. Governments and some business lobby groups have consistently argued that Australia depends on immigration for continued population—and economic—growth. Equally, some distinctly racist elements have aligned themselves with environmentalists to argue that Australia is already over-populated. In periods of high unemployment, it is not surprising that concerns are voiced about the impact of large immigration intakes.

Successive redefinitions of Australia's multicultural policy and reassessments of what the economy needs have seen some significant shifts in the annual immigration intakes. For most of the 1990s, Australia kept its intake under 90 000 people per year, as shown in Table 11.2.

Table 11.2 Annual settler intake 1993–99

Year	Number of immigrants
1993	76 330
1994	69 768
1995	87 428
1996	99 139
1997	85 752
1998	77 327
1999	84 143

Source: ABS 2005b.

However, as the twenty-first century began, policy-makers started to increase the annual migration intake. For example, in 2004 net migration added 117 600 people to our population, while it added 128 740 to our population in 2005—a record intake for the past two decades (ABS 2005b). Second, the source of migrants has continued to shift towards 'non-traditional' countries. Back in the early 1970s, approximately 47 per cent of all migrants to Australia came from Britain, and there was no intake from Vietnam or India. Since the 1980s, Australia has begun to take in a significant number of 'Asian' migrants. This trend is captured in Table 11.3, which shows the main country of birth of the population in 1971 and 2000.

Table 11.3 Main country of birth of the population, 1971 and 2000

Country	1971	2000
United Kingdom	1 081 300	1 164 200
New Zealand	74 100	374 300
Italy	288 300	241 600
Former Yugoslavia	128 600	210 700
Vietnam	700	174 500
China	17 100	168 900
Greece	159 800	141 200
Philippines	2 300	123 500
Germany	110 000	120 100
India	28 700	110 400
Malaysia	14 400	97 800
Netherlands	98 600	90 100
South Africa	12 200	80 600
Lebanon	23 900	79 300
Poland	59 500	68 400
Indonesia	7 700	67 400
United States	26 800	65 800
Hong Kong	5 400	56 900
Total	2 545 900	4 517 800

Source: ABS 2005b.

In the 30 years between 1971 and 2000, the proportion of migrants arriving from Britain dropped considerably, while countries like Hong Kong and Vietnam became more significant sources of immigration. In 2005, some 21 780 migrants came to Australia from the United Kingdom—less than 9 per cent of the total intake.

Under recent changes to immigration law, foreign students who have studied in Australia can stay on if they meet certain criteria. If these students are added, there is a major increase in the number of young Asians who arrive in Australia as long-term visitors for educational purposes and who elect to stay on. In the year to June 2005, this would make our actual immigration intake closer to 170 000 people.

This shift in the ethnic profile of immigration is captured in a series of annual snapshots captured in Table 11.4. It points to a pattern of changes that reflect the movement of political and economic factors operating globally like wars, recessions, famine and political change processes taking place over the last few decades in places like Lebanon, Hong Kong and South Africa.

Table 11.4 Country of birth of settler arrivals, 1970–2000

Country	1970		1980		1990		2000	
	No.	% of total	No.	% of total	No.	% of total	No.	% of total
China							36600	8
Former Yugoslavia							28300	6
Germany	18700	2						
Greece	56000	7						
Hong Kong					27500	4		
India							16400	3
Italy	62700	8						
Lebanon			16400	5				
Malaysia					26600	4		
New Zealand			39800	11	82500	13	80600	18
Philippines					36900	5		
South Africa			10200	3			21400	4
United Kingdom/ Ireland	369100	47	86200	25	107000	17	48600	11
United States	13700	1						
Vietnam			30600	8	38900	6		
Yugoslavia	63500	8						

Source: ABS 2006.

On the other hand, the dramatic rise and fall of Pauline Hanson's One Nation movement is a reminder that ethnicity and immigration policy are both controversial and volatile. One Nation proved to be a passing fad, unable to attract enough voters. Recent surveys done in 2005 suggest that most Australians are happy about the current ethnic profile of the population, which has seen a major increase in the numbers of African and Asian migrants. Likewise, there is no evidence to support the claim that high rates of immigration cause unemployment (Withers & Pope 1985: 560). On the contrary, the available evidence indicates that it is only recently arrived migrants, especially those with little or no English, who suffer from high rates of unemployment.

The role played by fear, prejudice and over-generalising has been evident in the most recent manifestation of controversy about ethnicity.

● ASYLUM SEEKERS OR 'QUEUE JUMPERS'?

Since the early 1990s, Australian Labor and Coalition governments have run a policy of detaining 'asylum seekers'—people seeking refugee status who have arrived in Australia without papers or approval. Australian governments now routinely incarcerate men, women and children in high-security detention centres while the government assesses their claims to be treated as asylum seekers—as required under international law. Given that this process may take years, this detention amounts to indefinite prison sentences, often exceeding those given to people convicted of very serious offences. In a shameful judgment late in 2004, the High Court found that there was no legal impediment to detaining asylum seekers for the term of their natural life as their processing in detention centres was simply an administrative process where the principles of natural justice and English common law did not apply. Many other countries which have received asylum seekers have welcomed them, looked after their often grievous psychiatric and physical health problems, given them support to find jobs and settled them in the community.

Many asylum seekers do not have passports and would not be given them by their governments even if they asked. They are held under conditions of extreme secrecy and hardship, involving the denial of basic human and legal rights. Given that many of these people are the victims of civil war, persecution, torture and illegal detention, the effects on them of their treatment in these centres can only be imagined.

Until late 2000, successive governments had the complete backing of the Australia media in their approach to asylum seekers. Only a series of attempts to cover up scandals and serious criminal activity inside the detention centres led to a reassessment by the media. The major political parties have continued to routinely justify these inhuman practices on the grounds that Australia needs to persuade these people not to come to Australia by making their treatment as punitive as possible.

The shameful implications of this policy in terms of our legal obligations under international law were on display in the so-called '*Tampa* affair' of October 2001 and the shocking involvement of the Australian government in the deaths of some 365 asylum seekers in the seas off Indonesia in a boat known only as *SIEV IX* (Marr & Wilkinson 2004). The Howard government has refused to name those killed on the grounds that to do so would compromise Australia's national security—a posture that has not addressed the grief of their many relatives in Australia.

The credibility of the Howard government's multicultural commitment has been compromised further especially since the 9/11 terrorist attacks in the United States due to Australia's membership of the Bush Administration's 'Coalition of the Willing' in a so-called 'war against terror'. This has led the Australian government to embark on an invasion of Iraq defined by the UN as an illegal action. It has also involved the systematic mobilisation of insecurity as part of a renewed politics of fear directed at the Islamic community, in which real Australians are called on to engage in a war by the West against the (Islamic) Rest (Scruton 2004). It is not hard to see in the polis of fear lingering traces of an anxiety about our place in the world that has always seemed to cultivate both racism and fears of the 'Asian masses'.

• CONCLUSION

Over 25 years ago, Andrew Jakubowicz (1981) argued that multiculturalism diverted attention from other more serious forms of inequality, such as economic inequality, and that this happened by focusing on relatively insignificant cultural issues (1981: 13):

> Multi-culturalism is regressive because in some of its guises it often trivialises more serious social issues of inequality, founded in socio-economic structures, gender relations, and racism . . . it does not question the need to define the nation and to draw boundaries of inclusion and exclusion. Human identity must become transnational.

The ethical value of rethinking identity in transnational terms may be a very good idea. Yet the Australian experience suggests that it faces some major obstacles. The emotional appeals of thinking in terms of 'imagined communities' and relying on patriotism or the imagined superiority of one's own community of blood ties, common language or religious affiliation show no signs of diminishing, even in an era of globalisation.

Meanwhile, real people continue to kill, torture, exclude and imprison each other across the world, relying on claims about the superiority of their ethnic and racial identity. In Australia, patriotism—which is usually seen as a high civic virtue—can on occasion be appropriated by scoundrels and villains. It is also the price we pay for being nostalgic about a past long gone. Discerning what is truly valuable about our past is a practical task. As J.M. Coetzee (1999) has one of his white protagonists say to another white man, both of whom are caught up in the attempt to make sense of South Africa's history of white racial oppression:

> So at last you have apologized . . . You are sorry . . . But I say to myself, we are all sorry when we are found out. The question is not are we sorry? The question is, what lesson have we learned? The question is, what are we going to do now that we are sorry?

Discussion questions

11.1 What have been some of the impacts of Australia's long history of racism on contemporary Australian society?

11.2 Why do racists believe what they do, and what is wrong with their arguments?

11.3 Do Aboriginal people really receive more welfare, education or health services than they deserve—as the One Nation movement insisted?

11.4 Why do some immigrants receive more criticism than others?

11.5 Can or should we ever generalise about whole groups of people on the basis of their race or ethnicity?

● ● ● PART THREE

GLOBALISATION, AUSTRALIA AND SOCIAL CHANGE

It's no secret that the changes in Australian society have been staggering. No aspect of life remains unaltered. The catchwords have been globalisation and restructuring.

—David Leser (1996)

The idea that we live in a time of unprecedented change has become one of the essential truisms or clichés of our time. For some Australians, this idea is linked to changes in the kinds of work they do. For others, it has to do with the seemingly endless release of new computers or software programs, new mobile phone features, new digital TV and digital cameras or any number of electronic gadgets. For yet others, it may have to do with the dramatic escalation in fear and anxiety associated with the apparent threat posed by Islamic terrorism—especially since the attacks on New York and Washington of 11 September 2001, Bali in 2003 and most recently in London in 2005. For some, it may have to do with the sense that there are basic problems looming in our environment to do with things like global warming or the depletion in oil supplies. Or it may be linked to a sense that traditional values and institutions from the family or to the role of government are changing in unhealthy ways.

'Globalisation' is the favoured buzzword most often used to describe or explain this sense that we live in a time of exciting change and/or of anxiety-provoking new problems. The possibility that 'globalisation' is so empty of precise meaning may explain why this very large and empty semantic bucket is applied to everything and anything.

Over the next five chapters, we want to examine some key aspects of the change process, as well as establishing whether traditional sociological ideas and approaches to explaining social change, or newer ideas like globalisation, have any value in making sense of these changes. Conventional sociology has long emphasised the progressive and benevolent character of what has been called the modernisation process. Modernisation (along with associated concepts like modernity) has generally been associated with things like the spread of science and technology, economic development and rising standards of living, the decline of traditional and 'irrational' beliefs like religion, and the spread of democracy. Some contemporary sociologists like Giddens (1991a) and Beck (1998) tend to see globalisation as simply another stage in the evolution of modernity, although some writers acknowledge that this process also brings about painful disruption and a range of social problems.

We focus here on some key themes. Those who talk about globalisation or stages in social development like modernity or post-modernity argue that the future of paid work as we have traditionally known it has become problematic as we move into post-industrialism, with serious consequences for the distribution of economic resources like wealth and income and the growth of poverty. Other writers point to dramatic changes in government policy over the past 30 years, and suggest that we are witnessing the death or disabling of the nation-state and the decline of the welfare state. It is also suggested that, courtesy of the spread of new forms of cybernetic and digital technologies, a new kind of 'post-modern' or 'information' society is evolving.

We begin in Chapter 12 by exploring the idea that major changes are taking place in the design and distribution of paid work that raise big questions about the future of work.

In Chapter 13, we turn to two major themes in modern sociology: class and inequality. Here we investigate a traditional sociological argument that societies like Australia reveal a persistent pattern—or structure—of extensive inequality organised around the distribution of economic activities and resources like income or capital. The idea of class is said to refer to ways a society both represents and organises the distribution of wealth—a factor common to all capitalist economies. Then, in Chapter 14, we ask what evidence there is that Australia is a society of equals, or whether there are trends towards increasing economic and social inequality. Is there any good evidence of an increase in the numbers of people living on low incomes? We ask how we can research inequality, and whether we can measure it or think about it using concepts like poverty—the concept often associated with it.

In Chapter 15, we turn to the question of power and the state and the regulation of social life. There has been an escalation in anti-government and 'small-government-is-good' rhetoric in the past few decades. There have also been major policy changes affecting the relations between government and society. The behaviour of multinational and transnational companies also raises questions about the power of modern governments.

If it is true that big businesses can move in and out of nations, or shift billions of dollars electronically in seconds, or threaten the loss of employment or a favourable credit rating, who actually holds power in the modern nation: the state or the transnational companies? Does this mean that governments have become irrelevant or powerless?

We suggest that governments are more important today than ever before, and have extended their influence over their populations more than in any other time. Governments continue to spend a large share of national resources on vital social, cultural and economic activities. The need for the rule of law and regulation of increasingly chaotic economies if anything has grown. Global ecological issues and the continuing crisis of unregulated international economic activities are also critical tasks for responsible government. In short, the reported 'death of the nation-state' may be exaggerated.

At the same time, as we show in a discussion of the idea of 'social order' and the traditional idea of 'deviance', there is a more general sense in which social regulation continues to be a major feature of societies like Australia.

It is often argued that globalisation is being promoted by the extension of information-based and media industries. So in Chapter 16 we examine the role of the modern media. If 'globalising' means the extension of new multinational media companies and new information technologies like satellite television, email and the internet—all of which intensify the flow of information—what effects is any of this having? In what ways, if any, is the role of the modern mass media changing?

Finally, we turn to the theme of sustainability and ask questions that need careful attention, like: What does sustainability mean? Why are more and more people recognising sustainability as a significant social issue? Why has the concept of 'sustainability' caught on in the way it has? Does the work of Ulrich Beck (1992) on 'risk society' illuminate or obscure our understanding? What does the fact that 'sustainability' has become a concept central to both the significant social conflict and political debate in our time tell us about our society?

In a short conclusion, we revisit the question of globalisation.

In Australia … the recent and significant reshaping of the industrial relations regime through the Workplace Relations Amendment (Work Choices) Act 2005 (Cth), in part a response to globalisation, threatens possibilities for balancing work and family responsibilities given an expected decrease in employment security implicit in the Act.

Charlesworth, S., Douglas, K., Fastenau, M and Cartwright, S., editorial, in 2006, in Charlesworth, S., Douglas, K., Fastenau, M and Cartwright, S. (eds), Women and Work 2005: RMIT Centre for Applied Social Research, Melbourne, p.1.

12. AUSTRALIANS AT WORK

- Summary

- The Australian Settlement, 1901–75

- The end of the Australian Settlement

- The future of work

- What is work?

- A history of work

- Work and capitalism

- Defining and measuring employment
  and unemployment

- The ABS and employment/unemployment
  statistics

- The problem with work

- Explanations

- Australia restructured?

- Conclusion

- Discussion questions

● ● SUMMARY

In this chapter we discuss one of the important features of the way Australia has experienced change in the way paid work is organised and distributed. We begin with what has been called 'the Australian Settlement'. Australian governments from 1901 attempted to protect Australians from aspects of the world they found threatening—economic competition, economic insecurity or invasion by 'coloured' people. The Australian Settlement was especially successful between 1945 and 1975 when Australians enjoyed a long economic boom and full employment. Since the 1970s, we have seen changes to the way work is done, the kinds of work available and who has access to the labour market. We then develop a framework for thinking about the way work as we have known it is being transformed. The distribution of paid work is becoming more unequal. Full-time employment is disappearing as an option for some people. Too much work is a problem for some, and too little or no work the problem for a large minority. We examine what unemployment is, and consider how it is defined and measured. We also ask what is wrong with the official measurements of unemployment. Finally, we critically analyse some of the explanations for why unemployment and under-employment have become major social problems in countries like Australia.

Back in 1961, Russian astronaut Yuri Gagarin saw planet Earth as a ball in space—a globe. The word 'globalisation' describes what Robertson (1992: 8) refers to as the 'compression of the world and the intensification of consciousness of the world as a whole'. The term 'globalisation' is now used to make sense of almost every aspect of our contemporary experience of social, political, economic, military and diplomatic matters (Robertson 1985, 1992; Bureau of Industry Economics 1989; Harris 1993; Lloyd 1995; see Waters 1997 for an overview of the literature). It is a term that can be over-used, and in ways that are unhelpful—especially when it is suggested that globalisation is both novel and is having unprecedented effects.

Waters (1997: 3) defines globalisation as 'a social process in which the constraints of geography on social and cultural arrangements recede and in which people become increasingly aware that they are receding'. Waters is pointing to the effects of new technology and media on 'shrinking' time and space, and giving people access to what is said to be a single global culture. Yet this is not such a new process. The single greatest shrinkage of time and space came in 1871 when Australians—living on the continent that is most distant from Europe—were connected to a global telegraph system in Britain, enabling the transmission of news in minutes. Even so, there can be little doubt that, since the late 1980s, global TV and the spread of the internet have connected more people to each other in ways that are both visual, immediate and cheap than has been possible with any other technology. This means that Australians are entering into new kinds of relationships and having experiences not possible in the past (see box).

Global communications and entertainment

- TV viewers can end the evening with programs like Dave Letterman's *Late Show* or NBC's *Today*, shown live from New York. Or they tune in via cable TV to 24-hour-a-day world news programs on CNN.

- Many young people are listening to music and words written in black suburbs of Los Angeles and now easily downloaded from the web on to iPods and other MP3 players.

- Families can eat at McDonald's in Sydney, Adelaide or Townsville—or in almost identical fast-food restaurants in China, Russia, France, Albania or America.

- Banks, finance companies and stock exchanges increasingly work a 24-hour day buying and selling currency, bonds or shares on stock exchanges around the world using information technology to move money or financial products on a global basis.

- In 2005, more that 60 per cent of Australians used the internet at least once a week. The internet enables people to work in 'virtual' ways with other people they have never met and are unlikely to meet. They may buy an airline ticket in Sydney that is 'logged in' by a worker in Bombay. Or they may establish a close relationship characterised by a degree of 'virtual intimacy' with a colleague through email or through direct dial-up telephone or video-conferencing links from their home computer.

- When natural disasters occur, like the tsunami of Christmas 2004, television images of the disaster quickly prompt a major aid response by voluntary organisations and governments. The downside of this is that no less awful disasters—like famine in Somalia or the Sudan—can numb the response of television audiences.

- People can drive a car that was designed in Munich, using an engine manufactured in Tokyo, a car body made in Korea and a sound system made in Sweden, and assembled in Adelaide.

- One of the authors of this book travelled from Australia to Disneyland in California and bought a packet of coloured pencils. The pencils were decorated with the Disney cartoon character Donald Duck. The pigments and slate powders used to make the lead for the pencils originated in Spain, while the wood used to surround the lead came from Australia. The pencils were manufactured in the Philippines and exported to the United States, where they were packaged and sold—in this instance, to Australians. The pencils were then transported to Australia via London and Bali and ended up in a child's pencil case in a Melbourne primary school classroom.

It is also plain that globalisation refers to all kinds of processes that are changing the relationship between governments, businesses, police and military activities, and environmental regulation.

Meetings of the World Economic Forum or the World Bank now routinely attract protestors who are intensely critical of globalisation. For both critics and advocates, globalisation is understood to mean major changes in the way goods and services are made, global moves to introduce free trade by knocking down tariff barriers, deregulating the currency and financial systems, reducing wages and weakening unions, and selling off public assets like state-owned banks, schools or telecommunications companies.

Its advocates argue that globalisation will mean cheaper commodities, an end to world hunger and poverty, greater diversity of goods, a higher standard of living for everybody and better customer service. However, critics of globalisation—like Pusey (2003)—claim that large numbers of Australians have paid a huge price because of changes in the way governments intervene, which Pusey attributes to a mixture of economic rationalism and globalisation. These critics point out that unemployment and under-employment have become nearly permanent features of contemporary life in many Western societies. Critics of globalisation argue that, because of it, governments have faced cuts to tax revenues, beginning in the 1980s, meaning that health, welfare and education services are suffering. These critics say that the rhetoric of 'freedom of choice' has been used to defend attempts to reduce working conditions, weaken unions, cut real wages and promote high levels of overwork and anxiety among those workers who are still employed. The critics say there is mounting evidence that more people are living in poverty or on social security benefits, while already affluent people become more and more wealthy.

In this chapter we ask some basic questions, then return to the larger question of 'globalisation' in Chapter 20.

- What has been happening in Australia since the early 1980s?
- Is there any evidence to suggest that Australians are doing better or worse economically?
- What were things like before the 1980s?
- Given the centrality of the paid work we do, what has happened to work?

In order to address these questions, we need to start by sketching a picture of employment in Australia through the twentieth century.

• THE AUSTRALIAN SETTLEMENT, 1901–75

In 1901, Australia was a British colony with a small population of just over three million English, Scottish and Irish descendants of immigrants (including convicts), mostly found in the big coastal capital cities like Sydney and Melbourne. Its political and administrative institutions and all aspects of its culture were essentially British.

At the start of the twentieth century, Australia was about to get a new federal government, in addition to the old colonial governments in each state. It was effectively a white racist society. 'Coloured' people were not welcome, while it was confidently expected that the few remaining Indigenous people would die out within the next few generations. It was also a country where working-class people had come to play a larger role than was usual anywhere else. From the 1850s on, workers had organised a large and powerful union movement that had pursued a range of policies and established institutions designed to secure a high average standard of wages for workers and their families. By 1901, the union movement had established a workers' party called the Australian Labor Party (ALP). In 1899, the Queensland ALP won an election and formed the first democratically elected workers' government in the world.

Economically, in 1901 Australia was very well off and probably had the highest average standard of living of any country on Earth. This owed a great deal to the fact that Australians had developed an economy based on the production and sale of primary products to Britain. In 1901, nearly 35 per cent of all workers were in primary production. In comparison, in 2005 fewer than 8 per cent of workers were in primary industry. Our standard of living was also due to the fact that governments had long played a major role in investing in everything from roads, water and sewerage systems, ports and railways to public health and education.

Given this backdrop it is perhaps not surprising that for the next 70 years or so after Federation in 1901, successive Australian governments evolved a framework of social and economic policies which Paul Kelly (1992: 2–5) has called the 'Australian Settlement'. Kelly says the Australian Settlement was designed to protect Australian's high living standards (then the highest in the world) and to protect the racial and cultural identity of a white colony. It had four key policy elements, the first three of which were in place by 1910, with the last added in the 1940s:

- maintenance of a 'white Australia';
- tariff protection to support Australian industries;
- a legal minimum, or 'basic', wage to support Australian families; and
- full employment and a 'welfare state'.

A 'white Australia'

The very first legislation passed by the new Commonwealth parliament in 1901 was the *Immigration Restriction Act* designed to control the numbers and types of people entering Australia. The 'white Australia' policy refused 'coloured' people entry to the country. Unions, political parties from both sides and business all supported 'white Australia' into the 1960s and 1970s.

Tariff protection

From 1901, the Commonwealth government adopted a high tariff policy. (A tariff is a tax paid on imported goods designed to raise their cost.) Support for this policy came from unions and industries, which thought that it would protect workers, employment and company profits from overseas competition. Although tariffs had an economic justification, they were also a statement about being 'safe from undesirable elements' in the wider world. Even as late as the 1960s, Australian furniture carried stamps saying the product was made by 'European-only labour'.

A basic wage based on family needs

In 1907, the Arbitration and Conciliation Court (now called the Australian Industrial Relations Commission) established a minimum wage level for all workers in a case brought to it by the Sunshine Harvester company seeking a tariff protection certificate. Justice H.B. Higgins, who was in charge of the court, agreed to the certificate if the company agreed to pay their workers a minimum or basic wage. Higgins calculated the amount needed to meet the needs of the average worker, his wife and three children. The *Harvester* judgment made it illegal for companies seeking tariff protection to pay workers below the basic wage. By the late 1920s, all workers were covered by a basic wage judgment made every few years by the Arbitration and Conciliation Court. This was an early practical exercise in social justice (Castles 1998; Bryson 1992).

Until the 1940s, white Australia, tariff protection and the basic wage system fitted together very neatly, although unemployment remained a persistent problem—especially in the Great Depression of the 1930s.

Full employment and a welfare state

In 1945, the Chifley Labor government issued a White Paper on Full Employment announcing that henceforward the first priority of the national government was the maintenance of employment for all workers. Between 1945 and 1975, Australian governments assumed responsibility for securing the economic conditions to ensure that all who wanted employment could have it. ('All' was understood to mean men and unmarried women only.) Using economic policies and ideas drawn from the work of the English economist J.M. Keynes, Australia developed a mixed economy and a welfare state. The mixed economy was achieved through a combination of government investment in infrastructure, universal income taxation and regulation of the banking system. The welfare state involved an extension of the original *Old Age Pensions Act* of 1910 by providing for low-cost, means-tested income benefits for people who were unemployed, sick, disabled or for divorced or separated women with children.

From 1945 to 1975, Australians enjoyed an unprecedented economic boom, with constant economic growth, low unemployment, high levels of investment and increased availability of consumer goods like cars and TVs. So high was the demand for labour that, from 1947, Australia encouraged very high rates of immigration, including from countries other than Britain. This would transform Australia into a multicultural society, though the ban on 'coloured' migrants was not lifted. Australian protectionist policies remained fully in force across a wide array of areas including censorship.

● THE END OF THE AUSTRALIAN SETTLEMENT

However, all the elements that made up the Australian Settlement have now been abolished or radically amended. The concept of 'globalisation' can be used to explain the changes that began taking place in the 1970s and which have continued on into our time. As Bob Catley (1996: 222–3) puts it, 'the globalising of Australian capitalism . . . has become unavoidable, necessary and desirable'. Michael Pusey (1991) argues that this occurred because elite bureaucrats in Canberra adopted an ideology called economic rationalism. For more complex explanations of this, see Beilharz (1994) or Bessant et al. (2006).

Since the 1970s, successive Labor and Coalition governments have slowly dismantled the Australian Settlement. This process became especially obvious after 1983, when leading unions, businesses and the Hawke Labor government used the Accord framework to promote deregulation and economic modernisation by opening Australia to the global economy. (The Accord refers to a series of agreements between the ALP government and the trade union movement to promote deregulation while protecting low-paid workers.)

The results were striking. Through the 1970s, the 'white Australia' policy was abolished. Since 1974–75, Australia has pursued a 'multicultural' policy, attracting hundreds of thousands of migrants from Asian and African countries.

Tariff protection was reduced first in 1974, when the Whitlam Labor government cut tariffs by 25 per cent. Since 1985, tariffs have progressively been lowered, with a target of very low to zero tariffs by 2008.

The 'basic wage' no longer exists, and the whole of Australia's industrial arbitration and award system has been deregulated. Since 1996, the Howard Coalition government's industrial relations reforms have weakened the role of unions, workers have been able to sign an individual employment contract, and there has been a steady reduction in minimum award conditions which all employers are required to take into account. In 2006 most employers were freed from having to take account of unfair dismissal protection for workers.

Official government support for full employment effectively ended between 1975 and 1979. One result has been record levels of unemployment (in 1982–84 and 1989–93), and the number and types of jobs available have been left increasingly to market forces. This has resulted in dramatic rises in long-term under-employment, represented by a very large proportion of casual, low-paid and part-time jobs.

We want to look at what has happened to paid employment for two reasons. First, the kinds of jobs that are available play a vital role in shaping the kinds of lives people lead, determining the resources to which they have access, like housing, education or health services, and the opportunities they have for leisure. The second reason has to do with the fact that, for several decades, writers like Barry Jones (1982), Robert Reich (1994), Stanley Aronowitz and Anthony Di Fazio (1994) and Jeremy Rifkin (1996) have all argued that there are long-term technological and social processes at work that are putting a large question mark over the very future of work. As Rifkin (1996: xvi) puts it:

> We are entering a new phase in world history—one in which fewer and fewer workers will be needed to produce the goods and services for the global population . . . For the whole of the modern era, people's worth has been measured by the market value of their labour . . . now new ways of defining human worth and social relationships will need to be explored.

● THE FUTURE OF WORK

It is possible that your age will play a role in how you feel about work, and whether you are anxious about its future. For example, if you are in your thirties, forties of fifties, you will be able to recall a period less than a decade ago when unemployment was a major problem. However, if you are eighteen you may be less likely to answer in this way because your recent experience is of a plentiful supply of work.

A quick snapshot using ABS statistics from the *Australian Year Book 2006* reveals a highly complex situation (Commonwealth Bureau of Statistics 2006). Several key features stand out about the contemporary patterns of work (see box).

Contemporary patterns of work

- The total labour force (including workers and the unemployed) has increased from 8.7 million in 1994 to just over ten million at the end of 2005 (ABS 2006a). This includes both full-time (7.1 million) and part-time (2.9 million) work.

- The number and proportion of people in paid employment has continued to increase over the last decade. The proportion of the total population in employment increased from 43.7 per cent in 1994 to 47.9 per cent in 2004–05. *Note*: This is still a minority of the total population.

- The unemployment rate as a proportion of the labour force has fallen from 6.6 per cent in 1999–2000 to 5.1 per cent at the end of 2005. In 2005–06, the unemployment rate hovered between 5.0 per cent and 5.5 per cent. (Through most of the 1990s, it hovered around the 8–11 per cent level.) However, this good news needs to be tempered with the recognition that this data reflects decisions taken by the ABS about who actually gets to be counted as unemployed.

- Important shifts have occurred in the respective rates at which men and women are in paid employment. The female participation rate has increased from 45.7 per cent in 1984–85 to 56.5 per cent in 2004–05, while the male participation rate has declined from 75.9 per cent in 1984–85 to 71.8 per cent in 2004–05.

- There has been a dramatic change in the ratio of people engaged in part-time work. In 1988, part-time work accounted for 19 per cent of workers, and in 1994 it accounted for 24 per cent. Since then, that rate has climbed even higher. In 2004–05, some 28.4 per cent of workers were working part-time. Australia has the highest proportion of part-time workers in the world.

- There have also been major changes in the kinds of industries which employ people. Back in 1969, nearly 29 per cent of the workforce was employed in secondary industry or manufacturing. By 1989–90, this had declined to 15 per cent, and by 2004–05 it was 11 per cent. Conversely, the services sector has kept on growing, and now accounts for 74 per cent of all workers.

On the face of it, such data may suggest that there is really nothing much to worry about in terms of issues like the future of work. Yet a close examination of the evidence suggests that there is an unequal distribution of paid employment. Some people have too much work while others have too little. In some industries, full-time employment opportunities have disappeared following the adoption of new styles of work organisation, the introduction of new technologies, the relocation of industries from one country to another, and the replacement of many full-time jobs with part-time work. Question marks also hang over the future of work due to what Ritzer (1993) has called the 'McDonaldization of work'.

● WHAT IS WORK?

Grint (1991) describes work in the following way: 'Work is more than employment but less than all forms of social activity; indeed employment is a form of work but not all work is employment' (1991: 32). Work is conventionally distinguished from leisure activities or a hobby, though how it is different is not always clear.

Most people would say that working relates to having, or doing, a paid job. For many people, an essential characteristic of work is getting paid. This might help to explain why some forms of work tend to be invisible, like women's housework.

How should we think about housework or volunteer work—both of which are significant but largely hidden kinds of work, done largely by women. This is codified in contemporary economic measures such as the gross domestic product (GDP), which calculates the value of paid labour but does not include the value of domestic and caring work done mainly by women (Waring 1987). As Ironmonger (1989) and others have shown, if the value of housework and other forms of unpaid women's work were added to GDP, it would blow the GDP out by between 50 and 75 per cent. In contemporary terms, it would be worth anywhere between $300 billion and $450 billion!

● A HISTORY OF WORK

For the longest and unrecorded part of human history, every human being had to work in order to survive. Killing wildlife, gathering edible nuts and roots and collecting water were fundamental to survival for all those hunter-gatherers who lived off the land. And the earliest fossil evidence suggests that our earliest human ancestors had developed a sexual division of labour, with work divided into 'men's work' and 'women's work'.

With the move into human settlements some time around 3000 BCE in places like modern India, Iraq, China and Turkey, we see new forms of work organised around farming—that is, the production of food crops of livestock or grains and the beginnings of urban communities. It is then that we start to get an even more complex division of labour. This is marked both by the specialisation of labour, as some people engage in tasks like metal work, clerical work or farming work, and more fundamental status distinctions which seem to deserve a word like 'class'. 'Class' here means the place people occupy as groups in the ownership and control of economic resources. (For a more extended discussion of this concept, see Chapter 13.)

By the time the Greeks—and later the Romans—had evolved their distinctive kinds of economies organised around great cities, sophisticated production techniques and trading, the social institution of slavery was established as a long-term basis for getting much of the social production of the means of life organised. In places like classical Athens, slaves made up a clear majority of the population.

Aristotle's theory of work

Aristotle, who lived in the sixth century BCE, offered an early theory of work. It was based on the premise that, while all animals laboured, only humans worked. His point was that, while a bee or a beaver built elaborate constructions like a hive or a dam, they did so because they were genetically programmed to do so. However, said Aristotle, humans worked first by imagining and designing what they would do. What distinguished the worst architect from the best bee was the architect's use of intelligence and imagination.

What Aristotle did not do—and indeed in some sense could not afford to do—was reflect on the social arrangements which made it possible for him to theorise. As a Greek gentleman, he relied on the work of the slaves who ran his estate, cooked and served his food and possibly even supplied their bodies for his sexual pleasure.

In the subsequent evolution of 'traditional' or pre-modern societies in Europe into what is sometimes called feudal society, small numbers of people took control of vast tracts of land—typically by military expropriation. The nobility, in conjunction with the Christian church, enjoyed the wealth and lived off the labour of their slaves (now called serfs) or tenants. In these traditional societies that survived the collapse of the Roman Empire around the fifth century AD, most people were either slaves/serfs who worked for their owners or else struggled as peasant farmers to make a living from the soil on which they lived. They did this by growing crops and through the use of their animals; they also clothed themselves and paid rent to a local lord or land-owner. Sometimes farmers sold their surplus (if they had any) at a local market in exchange for cash or other goods and services. By the fourteenth and fifteenth centuries, more complex economies had evolved in the great European cities, with a highly complex division of labour based on trades and crafts. In these cities, there was the beginning of a working class, who survived by selling their labour to employers.

Two and a half thousand years after Aristotle, in a Europe which had largely abolished the institution of slavery, other highly advantaged men would offer their own theories of work in the radically different context of a Europe that was developing an economic system we now call 'industrial capitalism'.

In 1861 in Britain, Samuel Smiles wrote a best-selling book (called *Self-Reliance*) about the virtues of hard work. At the same time, another advantaged German male called Karl Marx—who lived in genteel poverty off the proceeds of his friend Friedrich Engels' ownership of highly profitable factories in Manchester—was developing an influential account of the evils of the capitalist mode of production and the role played by the working class. Marx looked forward to a time when the need to work would be abolished as everyone lived in a communist utopia where labour-saving devices did what human labour had previously done. In 1904 another gentleman scholar, the great German sociologist Max Weber, argued that the 'Protestant ethic' set up a powerful moral incentive for people to work that made the development of modern capitalism possible.

While the word 'capitalism' tends not to be used so much any more, it still has analytic and empirical value.

● WORK AND CAPITALISM

The rise of industrial capitalist societies that began in and after the sixteenth century in Europe saw growing numbers of people living in cities. The growth of larger and larger cities is one index of the growth of distinctively capitalist ways of organising an economy. Capitalist economies have three defining features:

- the existence of a labour market;
- unequal power in economic decision-making and unequal access to key economic resources; and
- a sexual division of labour.

Each of these features is interdependent.

The labour market

For a labour market to exist, there needs to be a section of the population that is able to buy the labour of others who want to sell it. This is a highly simplified way of beginning to think about class in the ways used by both Marx and Weber. By 'class' both Marx and Weber meant the chief kinds of economic resources available in a given society and the different groups that own them. In our kind of society, there are people who own capital—including land, property or financial resources from which they derive further income. In Australia, there are also people who sell their labour—either to employers (wage earners), to clients (fee-for-service professionals) or to customers (owners of small businesses).

In 2004–05 about 80 per cent of the adult population worked for wages, 6.5 per cent owned incorporated businesses while about 13.6 per cent ran small businesses as shopkeepers, manufacturers or professionals (ABS 2006a). This pattern of employment rests on an underlying pattern of ownership of basic resources (see box). In Australia, this broadly divides into two kinds of resource: capital and labour. The different kinds of capital include finance capital (shares and other investments), property (land and rental properties), industrial capital (industrial plant and equipment) and informational capital (like the Google search engine); types of labour are physical and intellectual labour, and skills.

> ## Ownership of capital and labour resources in Australia
>
> - A small number of Australians (around 10–14 per cent of the adult population) own around 75–90 per cent of Australia's wealth or productive capital (for various estimates of the distribution of wealth, see Greig et al. 2003: 96–8). The Commonwealth Bureau of Statistics 2006, which uses the idea of 'net household worth', estimates that the top 20 per cent of households own 59 per cent of 'net household worth' (see Chapter 14 for more discussion).
> - Around 14 per cent of the adult population sell their services (as doctors, plumbers or lawyers) to the rest of us, or operate small businesses.
> - Some 75 per cent of adults have no capital assets with which to earn their living, so must rely on selling their capacity to work to an employer. If they cannot do this, they must rely on government social security benefits. Into the twenty-first century, governments play an important economic role as providers of income support schemes to the 34 per cent of Australians (both adults and children) who rely on social security for an income.

The fact that there is a labour market is therefore closely connected with the distribution of economic resources and this creates a situation marked by considerable inequality in economic power.

Unequal power

The second key feature of any capitalist economy is the fact that there are unequal power relations in the use and control of economic resources. There are many examples of this inequality:

- Subject to certain legal restrictions, owners and managers of businesses can hire and fire workers as they wish.
- Owners and managers can order or direct workers to do things they would not otherwise do in pursuit of the manager or owner's business objectives.
- Many workers experience a loss of control over the work they do. This can be the result of a deliberate process of 'deskilling' workers so managers can better control the flow of work. If workers are not very skilled, they are less likely to complain when managers tell them to 'speed up' or do things differently.
- Many employees have little if any control over the way businesses are run—they are excluded from policy-making.
- In terms of priorities, workers' interests often come after the interests of investors, banks, owners and shareholders.
- The loss of control may be so great that workers even have to wait for a set time or seek special permission to go to the lavatory (see the discussion of McDonaldisation below).

This inequality of power was one major historical reason for the creation of unions in the nineteenth century. If they belong to strong unions, workers can enhance their bargaining position, or at least protect themselves from the worst effects of the imbalance in power. However, union membership has fallen away quite strikingly in the last three decades: in 1976, 51 per cent of all employees were union members. Between 1988 and 1994, union membership fell from 46 per cent of all male workers to 38 per cent, and from 35 to 31 per cent of all female workers (ABS 1995: 106). By 2005, the unionisation rate for all workers had fallen to under 22.7 per cent (Commonwealth Bureau of Statistics 2006). That this reflects distinctively Australian circumstances is suggested by some international comparisons. In Sweden, 90 per cent of workers were in unions through the 1990s, while in the United States only 16 per cent of workers were unionists in the 1990s.

Finally, in terms that merit analysis, all capitalist economies continue to rely on the oldest and most entrenched social relations that define work: the sexual division of labour.

The sexual division of labour

Since the rise of capitalism, more men than women have been in full-time paid employment (as we saw in Chapters 6 and 8). Paid work has relied on the prior sexual division of labour, understood as a split between paid public full-time work (largely done by men) and unpaid household labour (largely done by women).

These three primary defining features of any capitalist economy are strongly connected to the way paid employment is distributed. Before we can discuss this, however, we need to return to a basic question: what do we know about patterns of employment and unemployment?

● DEFINING AND MEASURING EMPLOYMENT AND UNEMPLOYMENT

One of the problems with measuring employment and unemployment relates to the fact that how these things are counted depends on who is counting, why they are counting, and what criteria or evidence they use to count.

What is unemployment?

When people talk about unemployment, they may well assume that the official ABS unemployment rate is based on facts—like the numbers of people who are unemployed. Establishing what we mean by unemployment is at least as difficult as working out what we mean by work. Let's look at the data in Table 12.1.

Table 12.1 Unemployment in Australia, 1994–2005

	1994	1996	1998	2000	2002	2004	2005
No. unemployed	888 500	736 500	737 800	626 300	663 300	586 000	543 600
Unemployment rate (%)	10.2	8.1	8.0	6.6	6.7	5.8	5.1

Source: ABS (2005c; 2006a).

Defining unemployment as all those people without paid jobs would mean a huge population of the unemployed, including babies, children at school, young people in universities and TAFE colleges, people in gaols and hospitals, people doing domestic work, volunteer workers and the elderly. So if unemployment doesn't mean everyone who isn't working in a paid job, who *does* it include? Wickham and Hunt (1994) maintain that defining particular types of people (like 'the unemployed') depends on the needs and administrative practices of governments and experts. This point is very relevant to understanding the category of 'unemployed' and the way unemployment is counted.

Counting unemployment depends on those who do the counting deciding what a person has to do to be classified as unemployed. And that, as we will see, depends on a prior understanding of who is employed and who is in the labour force (see box).

Who counts the unemployed?

A number of agencies or departments in Australia produce unemployment statistics. Each uses different ways of determining who meets the requirements so they can be counted as unemployed. Further, each agency produces different estimates of the number of unemployed people in Australia. The two key agencies are the Australian Bureau of Statistics (ABS) and Centrelink.

Australian Bureau of Statistics

The ABS is the biggest producer of social and economic statistics in the country. Its data are used by governments, researchers and the media because the ABS is generally seen as the supplier of the most authoritative estimates of the unemployment rate. To establish the unemployment rate, the ABS uses representative sample surveys rather than surveying every single household in the country. (Once every five years, on Census night, the ABS takes a 'statistical snapshot' of every Australian household.)

Centrelink

To qualify for unemployment benefits, people must first apply to Centrelink. We get some idea of how many people are unemployed from the numbers of those registered with Centrelink as being in search of work. However, it is important to realise that many people who are unemployed do not register. In July 1994, 7 per cent of men and 17 per cent of women wanting full-time work were not registered, and a massive 64 per cent of unemployed women and 60 per cent of unemployed men wanting part-time work were not registered (ABS 1995: 103).

Each of these agencies uses a different definition of 'unemployed'. In both cases, someone has to meet a list of eligibility criteria before being defined as 'unemployed'. They use a number of tests, including whether you have worked, your income, the type of activities you have been engaged in, and assets tests. For example, if you voluntarily left your last job, you are not eligible to be counted as unemployed by the CES/Centrelink for three months.

● THE ABS AND EMPLOYMENT/UNEMPLOYMENT STATISTICS

The ABS uses the International Labor Organisation (ILO) definitions of 'employment' and 'unemployment' to establish the unemployment rate—partly to make international comparisons with other countries possible. According to the ILO and the ABS definition of 'unemployment' and the unemployment rate, in order to be unemployed you must first be in the labour force. Defining and counting the labour force gives us a labour force participation rate. To be counted in the 'labour force' you have to be aged between sixteen and 65 years, and to have worked for income for one or more hours per week in the survey period and/or have been actively looking for work in the survey period.

A person in the sample used by the ABS can only be defined as officially unemployed if they:

- are over fifteen years and under 65 years of age;
- have actively looked for work in the four weeks prior to the survey;
- are able to start work in the survey week; and
- have not worked for more than one hour during the survey week.

Having made these definitional decisions, the ABS can then 'count' the unemployed. Of course, the ABS does not actually count more than a large sample of people. It uses a representative sample of 30 000 households which is carefully designed to be representative of the whole population.

Problems with the ABS definitions and measures

The definition of the 'labour market' means that many people are not defined/counted as unemployed, and this acts to reduce the ABS unemployment rate. For example, those who are jobless and who have given up 'actively' looking for work are not counted as unemployed.

They are placed in another separate group: the 'discouraged worker' category. There are a large number of people who are not counted as unemployed, yet want paid employment.

We get some sense of the scale of this problem if we compare (in Table 12.2) the unemployment rate with the other two categories of people: those the ABS definition treats as 'marginally attached to the workforce'; and 'discouraged jobseekers', who don't have jobs but have given up looking for work. Ever since Stricker and Sheehan's (1982) pioneering work, labour market researchers have consistently drawn attention to the problem of what they call the 'hidden unemployed'—that is, people excluded by the way the ILO/ABS definition of 'labour force' and 'unemployment' constructs the unemployment rate.

Table 12.2 Unemployment, 'marginally attached to workforce' and 'discouraged jobseekers', 1994–2004

	1994	**2000**	**2004**
Unemployed (no.)	888500	626300	586000
Marginally attached to workforce	773300	823900	855300
Discouraged jobseekers	106500	106500	82000

Source: Commonwealth Bureau of Statistics (2006).

Then there is the problem created by the dramatic increase in the numbers of people on disability benefits, as Table 12.3 suggests.

Table 12.3 Unemployment and people on disability benefits in Australia, 1994–2004

	1994	**1996**	**1998**	**2000**	**2002**	**2004**
Unemployed (no.)	888500	736500	737800	626300	663300	586000
Disability benefits (no.)	436200	499200	555300	602400	623900	696700

Source: ABS (2005c); Commonwealth Bureau Statistics (2006).

There is good evidence that this increase reflects more than just an increase in the level of disability. Rather, it reflects decisions by Centrelink to move people who had been receiving unemployment and other income benefits (like supporting parent benefits) on to disability payments. In 2004, nearly 700 000 people were on disability benefits.

There are other ways in which the ILO/ABS definitions of 'labour force' and 'unemployment' help to disguise the extent of joblessness. The definition of the 'labour force' does not include those who continue their full-time education. Those who stay at school, or who have gone back to school or university because they cannot find work, are not counted as unemployed. ABS figures on youth unemployment are often represented as simply reporting on the numbers of young unemployed people without work. This, however, is not the case.

We need to remember that, to be 'counted' in the labour force, a respondent to the ABS questionnaire needs to be able to say they have worked for at least one hour in the survey period for income, and/or they have actively sought work in that period if they did not work for at least one hour for income. This is a fraught exercise in relation to measuring youth unemployment and/or education participation rates for young people, especially when it is done in relation to labour force participation rates. Many young people stay in the education system because they cannot get full-time employment. But, although they are full- or part-time students, many work part-time to help support themselves. The question is whether they are in the labour market or not.

The relatively low levels of youth unemployment sit alongside the near-complete disintegration of the full-time youth labour market (see Chapter 7). This shift was accompanied by an immense increase in school retention rates. The ABS decision to count as employed those young people who are without work but are undertaking some form of job training is also problematic in terms of understanding the magnitude of youth unemployment.

Another problem with the definition of unemployment is that it excludes people who are under-employed—that is, those wanting full-time waged work who are unable to find it. They include people who have worked over one hour in the previous week, and therefore do not officially count as being unemployed.

In summary, people may not be officially counted as unemployed because:

- they have worked in the survey period;
- they are under or over the appropriate age;
- they have not 'actively' sought work; or
- they are in some form of training or education.

The failure to pay attention to these quite tricky issues of defining and measuring unemployment is one reason why numerous myths about the problem of unemployment continue to flourish (see box).

Popular myths about unemployment

Three myths regularly surface when people talk about unemployment.

Myth 1: The unemployed don't want to work

The media are always happy to run stories about young unemployed people who will not take jobs when they are offered. There are also stories about a local employer who has repeatedly advertised for a worker to fill a vacancy but cannot get anyone to apply.

The problem with this is that, since the 1970s, there have been many more unemployed people than there are jobs available. In the 1990s (using the ANZ surveys of job advertisements), there were between 33 and 27 unemployed people for every job vacancy. Even in 2005–06 this continued to be the case. However, some economists are predicting that if the current economic growth pattern continues, it may lead to a point where there are more jobs than job-seekers.

Myth 2: Women are taking men's jobs

As we have seen, there has been a significant increase in the female labour force participation rate as large numbers of married women have moved into employment, while there has been a decline in the male labour force participation rate. This fact is sometimes used to argue that women have 'taken men's jobs'.

This is not the case. First, most jobs that women now do are either new jobs or jobs that have traditionally been women's occupations. Second, the high unemployment of the 1980s and 1990s has affected traditional men's jobs in labour-intensive and unskilled manufacturing industries. The sexual division of labour therefore explains why women do not in any simple sense compete for or take 'men's' jobs. It is clear that new jobs are emerging in the service sector, which tends to employ more women than men.

Myth 3: Young people cannot get jobs because they are illiterate, innumerate and lack a work ethic

This myth says that schools have failed to give students the requisite skills, knowledge and attitudes to work, which in turn has made them unemployable. This is a version of the 'blame the victim' approach—young people are unemployed because they have certain deficiencies.

The reality is much more complex. There has been a dramatic shrinkage in the full-time youth labour market since the early 1980s. At the same time, increasing numbers of young people from sixteen years of age are both in the labour market and studying. The dominant pattern is for full-time students to do part-time paid work. This reflects a dramatic shift in the school retention and education participation rates over the last twenty years.

At the same time, the ABS persists in running the line that some young people are at risk of failing to make the transition between school and employment. There appear to be a small but substantial number of young people who are neither studying nor employed. In 2004 the ABS suggested that about 14 per cent of young people aged fifteen to nineteen (or 193 800 people) were not 'fully engaged'. (ABS 2005c).

In interpreting this data, it is important to note that the ABS has defined this idea of being 'fully engaged' in ways that exclude young people who are working part-time. The need to be vigilant about reading and interpreting data like this is suggested by the fact that the ABS established that young women were much more likely not to be 'fully engaged' than young men. The reason for this was that 77 per cent of young women who were not 'fully engaged' were actually doing either unpaid housework and or were engaged in child care!

As for the idea that basic skills are in decline, there is little robust evidence to support this claim. The increased school retention rate—from 14 per cent in the early 1980s to 85 per cent in 2004—may suggest that literacy and numeracy rates have increased. Moreover, young people now have a number of new skills and different forms of literacy.

● THE PROBLEM WITH WORK

All the evidence points to processes of change that are disadvantaging some Australians while advantaging others. The distribution of employment and its benefits is connected to certain stubborn patterns of inequality.

There is no evidence that Australia's labour force is shrinking—yet. The number and proportion of people in paid employment has been growing over the last decade or so. The proportion of the total population in employment increased from 43.7 per cent in 1994 to 47.9 per cent in 2004–05. Likewise, there is no evidence of any dramatic decrease in the hours worked by full-time, part-time or casual employees. However, the fact that there has been a big increase in the numbers of people working part-time and casually points to the growth of under-employment as a persistent and serious problem, especially given that about a third of these workers say they want to work more hours.

We also need to be cautious about assuming that, following half a decade of reducing unemployment rates, Australia has solved the problems it was having with unemployment in the 1990s. As the ABS data show, after several decades of high average levels of unemployment (between 1982 and 1998), there has been a downward movement in the unemployment rate that has held until 2005–06. While this appears to be good news, it may reflect the ways the ABS has been defining and measuring unemployment rather than any real decrease in joblessness.

Back in 1988, part-time work accounted for 19 per cent of workers. Since the 1990s, this trend has accelerated. In 1994 it accounted for 24 per cent of the workforce. Since then, that rate has climbed even higher. In 2004–05, 28.4 per cent of workers were working part-time. The increase in part-time work parallels a major shift to casual employment that began in the early 1990s and has stayed relatively high ever since. In 1993, 23 per cent of workers (or 1.3 million people) were employed as casuals. In 2003, 26 per cent of employees (or 1.9 million people) were employed on a casual basis. It is important to understand that these two categories are referring to different kinds of experiences and industrial entitlements.

Casual workers can be employed on either a full-time or part-time basis. It is probably the case, as employers sometime argue, that casual employment suits some workers. Yet the ABS data suggest that in 2003 a third of men employed casually wanted more hours of work, while nearly a third of women working casually said they would like more hours. This preference was especially strong among men aged 35–54, with 55 per cent of them saying they wanted more hours.

Casual employment suits many employers and companies because it generates lower costs and increased flexibility. Casual employees generally do not have access to paid holiday leave or a range of other entitlements, and their employment can be terminated with little notice. Casual employment frequently entails low levels of training, poor career prospects and an increased risk of workplace injury, with little or no employer protection or job security. Casual employees also often report that their employers can insist on highly flexible working hours which suit the needs of the employer ahead of those of the worker. In 2003, 27 per cent of casual workers reported that their hours of work were altered on a weekly basis.

In both cases, the shift to more part-time work and casual employment is also tied to the feminisation of the workforce and to the continuing effect of ideas about women's responsibility for child care. The inequalities that are central to the sexual division of labour are persistent. Women of all ages are far less likely to work on a full-time basis than men of all ages. In 2003, only 42 per cent of women aged 25–29 were in full-time ongoing employment; this dropped to 25 per cent for women aged 35–39—a time when more women are having children.

In short, unemployment continues to be a problem—albeit a 'disguised' one. Under-employment, signified by the increase in part-time and casual employment, is also clearly a problem. As we show in Chapter 14, unemployment and under-employment play a significant role in entrenching basic patterns of economic and social inequality.

● EXPLANATIONS

To understand why unemployment and under-employment are problems, we need to ask why there are fewer full-time jobs in many different kinds of industries; why there are more part-time and casual jobs; and why more workers are working longer working weeks.

The contemporary problems of work result from decisions by business and political elites not to replace full-time jobs, or to create either casual jobs or part-time jobs. Unemployment and under-employment are the result of three types of decisions that have been made by employers in the private and public sectors (Bell 1997):

> Most businesses will normally seek to contain costs. In times of severe economic recession this can be done by sacking full-time workers. This reaction was on display in the most recent recession of 1989–1992 in the wake of the stock market crash of October 1987 and the general collapse of banks and finance companies in the late 1980s. This reduces wage costs and the costs associated with leave and other award conditions.

Managers and employers have also moved to contain costs by converting full-time jobs into part-time or casual jobs. Further, many companies and government employers believe that it is cheaper to contract out jobs that were once done from inside the company.

Many Australian companies have decided not to invest in creating full-time jobs in Australia. Instead, they have invested in labour-saving machines and information technology, or taken new jobs 'offshore' to low-cost economies. This has led to some far-reaching changes in the way work gets done.

The McDonaldisation of work

All of these dispositions are on display in what American sociologist George Ritzer (1993) calls the 'McDonaldization of work'. Ritzer was interested in the innovations in the production and sale of fast foods associated with the rise of fast-food giant McDonald's. In a simple sense, this company pioneered the redesign and restructuring of the work process, which on first glance involves a reduction in the number of full-time jobs and the employment of large numbers of young, unskilled casual workers—something made possible by the standardisation and automation of work processes. Ritzer's real insight was that what McDonald's had done was being emulated in a lot of industries other than fast-food restaurants.

Ritzer shows how the McDonald's approach has affected other services and companies, including 24-hour medical clinics, H&R Block tax offices, and the new large specialist supermarkets like Officeworks. As Ritzer shows, McDonaldising a workplace does not just involve changing the way workers do their work; it also affects the way customers experience the service or product they have come to buy.

McDonaldising involves using four principles to redesign work processes and relationships between employees, customers and the organisation.

Predictability and the abolition of choice

The first innovation the Kroc brothers introduced when they opened their first McDonald's restaurant was to simplify the choice of menu and to standardise and simplify the production process. McDonald's offers basically a small number of different kinds of hamburgers plus fries and various drinks. What they promise is a ruthless sameness in everything.

Anywhere in the world, even before customers enter a McDonald's restaurant, they know with certainty what they will find. With very slight variations, the same menu of foods is prepared and served the same way across the world.

Control over workers and customers

In a McDonaldised workplace, workers are required to perform simple and repetitive tasks, most of which need little or no expertise. One result is that workers either are not skilled or are deskilled by being required to perform those tasks. Workers are not permitted to join unions, most workers are young, and most leave once they are eligible for adult rates of pay.

This approach is even applied to customers. The promise was that customers would not have to wait for more than a few minutes at most for their hamburger. Customers are moved through the restaurant quickly, and harsh lighting and hard seats discourage them from staying for too long after the meal is consumed.

Automation, efficiency and calculability

The second key innovation introduced by the Kroc brothers was to automate the production and delivery of the hamburgers. By the 1950s, they had introduced machines and simplified production. Workers employed in a McDonald's restaurant needed no skill past pushing buttons and assembling the various elements of a hamburger. This was further enhanced by outsourcing the preparation of the various elements.

Every aspect of production and customer service has been thoroughly planned. This ensures predictability of time, labour and material resources.

Franchising

The Kroc brothers' final innovative logic was to use the franchising approach taken by the Coca-Cola company. Coca-Cola realised even before 1914 that one simple way to make a lot of money while cutting their own costs was to sell to other businesses the right to produce Coke.

The expansion of the McDonald's business has worked on the same basis. In effect, the would-be owner of a McDonald's restaurant buys the brand name and the various supplies. In turn, the central company outsources the supply of the various food products while offering long-term marketing and advertising, training to all McDonald's managers, and the strategic purchase of restaurant sites.

These elements have now been applied successfully by companies and services as diverse as Midas Muffler shops, H&R Block tax offices and specialist 'supermarkets' like Officeworks and Toys 'R' Us. An adaptation of them is also used by the large call centres that now supply services to banks, airline companies and numerous other industries.

Rationalising work using McDonald's style techniques and new technology has many advantages. Many of the dangerous, dirty and tedious jobs are now done by machines. However, the downside of technology in the workplace is that it displaces and deskills workers. McDonaldising work and introducing automated technologies has affected certain groups, like young people and people with few skills. It has, for example, seen the almost complete disappearance of the full-time youth labour market.

In Australia, the McDonaldisation of the workplace has been complemented by two other factors.

● AUSTRALIA RESTRUCTURED?

Australia has long been dependent on what it grew and mined. In the nineteenth century, the Australian economy began as a 'farm', supplying primary produce to Britain. Since the 1970s, we have become a 'quarry' as well as a farm, supplying coal, iron ore, gold, alumina and oil primarily to countries like Japan. This makes the Australian economy both vulnerable and dependent on what happens internationally to commodity prices:

- Primary producers involved in growing food crops have to deal with the effects of unseasonal climate, like droughts, floods and wind damage.
- Australia has also had to deal with long-term declining demand for particular primary commodities (like wool), which historically earned Australia a lot of our national income.
- We are vulnerable to price-fixing and competition between those countries and companies who are the major purchasers of our farm and mining goods, and we are also vulnerable to downturns in international prices for such commodities as gold, coal and iron ore.
- Since the early 1990s and into the twenty-first century, Australian primary producers have been buffeted by the global trade wars waged especially between the United States and Europe. This is currently affecting farmers involved in producing fruit like grapes, oranges and apples, who are being confronted by global gluts.
- Rural Australia is being 'restructured', and many once-thriving farming areas are becoming ghost towns as farms close down and young people leave country areas and towns to come to the city.
- Then there is the informational revolution associated with the dramatic technological changes produced by digital information.
- Unemployment and under-employment are consequences of the shift from an industrial economy to an informational economy (Castells 1996). Informational economies mean that the productivity and competitiveness of people, industries and nations increasingly become dependent on their capacity to efficiently generate, process and apply knowledge-based information. Informational economies become increasingly interdependent, and are organised on a global scale (Castells 1996: 66–7). This has major effects on the types of workers and skills needed by industries increasingly reliant on information technologies. As we head into the twenty-first century, there is clear evidence that e-commerce is making inroads into traditional ways of buying and selling goods.
- There have been significant changes in public policy, leading to a rapid decline in public sector investment. Unemployment and under-employment are also produced by government decisions (Langmore & Quiggin 1994; Bell 1997). Australian governments have reduced their investment in public works and in social infrastructure.

- Governments have also stopped employing large numbers of public servants and social and community service workers. In the 1990s, all levels of government downsized their workforces, abolishing hundreds of thousands of public sector jobs. Governments also privatised many government services in the 1990s.

CONCLUSION

Between 1945 and 1975, Australians lived in what Donald Horne (1974) ironically called 'the Lucky Country'. They enjoyed a long economic boom and full employment. Investment was booming, there was significant general economic growth, and Australia appeared to be an affluent society. As we saw in Chapter 7, many Australians got on with setting up 'nuclear families'. Most of the baby boomers (people born between 1945 and 1960) grew up in a society where economic growth, optimism and jobs were taken for granted.

Over the last 30 years, this has changed completely. Economic growth has been uneven, people are less optimistic, and unemployment and under-employment have proved to be a persistent part of many Australians' experience. It is not surprising that there is now anxiety about the future of work—and many other aspects of our society. This is partly because people feel that the problem of unemployment is only part of a larger process of change.

In this chapter, we have considered what is meant by both unemployment and under-employment. We have discussed what is meant by terms like 'labour force', the 'labour market', 'part-time work' and 'casual employment'. Finally, we have discussed the future of work, given the move towards persistent under-employment.

Yet we need to push the analysis deeper, which we do in the next chapters. These changes in the distribution of work are part of a larger and persistent pattern of inequality, which begins to explain why some people continue to be disadvantaged while others prosper. One of the essential paradoxes of our society is that, while many things now seem to be changing quite dramatically, other things are not. Inequality in the distribution of personal productive property (or wealth) is one of the most important features of a capitalist system. The way wealth (or productive property) is distributed, owned and used provides vital insight into the class structures of capitalist societies.

Discussion questions

12.1 What was the Australian Settlement and should we try to return to it?

12.2 Does work have a future?

12.3 What is problematic about the ways governments currently count the unemployed and under-employed?

12.4 Are unemployment and under-employment the result of laziness on the part of job-seekers, a lack of skills or a lack of investment in jobs?

The history of culture indicates that stupidity
is the twin sister of reason, it grows most
luxuriantly not on the soil of virgin of ignorance
but on the soil cultivated by the sweat of
doctors and professors. Great absurdities are
not thought up by those whose reason hovers over
daily affairs. It is not strange therefore that
the most intense thinkers were the producers
of the greatest idiocies.

Witold Gombrowicz, Diaries, Vol One (1988: 184)

13. CONFRONTING CLASS AND INEQUALITY

• • SUMMARY

Throughout this book, we have shown how Australia has been a white racist society, how men and women are not equal, and how work is being distributed unequally. In this chapter, we look at the general idea that Australia is an unequal society. Social inequality and class are long-standing conceptual themes in sociology. We begin by considering the idea of inequality before discussing some of the ways in which the concept of class has been used to make sense of and explain certain patterns of inequality. We also introduce and critically analyse the idea of an underclass.

One of the greatest philosophers of the twentieth century was Hannah Arendt (1958), who said that the single hardest thing we can ever do 'is to think what we do'. She was pointing to the often huge gap between the ways in which we live and experience our daily lives, and the effort involved in thinking. Nothing illustrates this problem like the chasm that opens up between our daily experience and the way social scientists try to think about or research the social character of our lives using ideas like 'inequality' or 'class'.

One reason for this gap has to do with the fact that, on the one hand, we live in little worlds consisting of our families, friends, local neighbourhoods, schools or workplaces. Most of us have intimate dealings with only a relatively small number of people, most of whom are usually the same kinds of people as we are. These little worlds exist on the basis of repetition of daily routines and rituals. We get up at the same time, have breakfast, get dressed, go to school or work, and relax at night in front of the TV. Such lives lead us to think that everyone else lives the way we do.

On the other hand, we also spend time in large public places like train stations, shopping malls or office blocks, and we read books and newspapers, surf the net or watch TV. Entering these larger, more public real or virtual spaces may suddenly confront us with difference. We may encounter a homeless person in dirty clothes sitting on a blanket in a major city street. We may briefly wonder what it would be like to do this on a daily basis before we pass by. Or we hear the news that a multi-billionaire like Kerry Packer has died and we may briefly wonder what it would be like to have that much wealth. However, the chances are that we won't spend much time thinking about these matters before we head back to the security of our secure little worlds. On the other hand, there is the world of the social scientist. The kinds of thinking that sociologists do about such things as inequality are likely to be experienced as strange, even confronting, by many Australians.

Many of us do not have the kinds of experiences in our daily lives that make inequality immediately apparent. Unless or until we cross certain social boundaries, or encounter other people who are richer or poorer than us, we are unlikely to see and experience inequality. One of the authors illustrates this issue with part of his life story, and also shows why inequality, in spite of the best efforts of some sociologists to persuade us otherwise, is not just an abstract idea.

Rob's story

I grew up in the 1950s in a low-income working-class family in a house in Footscray, a major industrial suburb of Melbourne. My house faced an iron foundry and was downwind from numerous abattoirs, meatworks and a rope factory. My grandmother owned the house, which was a small and simple three-bedroom weatherboard. The household included my grandmother, my parents and my brother. My father was an unskilled worker, and until I became a teenager my mother and grandmother were 'housewives'.

My family never had much money, but we seemed to cope. My father earned what was called the 'basic wage'. We ate all our meals in the kitchen. I shared a bedroom with my brother until I was fourteen. My family ate cheap but nutritious meals, in the English style. All through my childhood I had a small pile of treasured toys, including a teddy bear that had been in the family since 1929. We all wore cheap but adequate clothes.

Though there was only a small library of books (made up of the Bible, a medical reference book, *Robinson Crusoe*, a home handyman's book, and a six-volume history of World War II), my Nanna taught me to read when I was three, starting a lifelong affair with books. Until TV arrived, we sat at nights around a large wireless in the living room listening to the news, radio soapies and quiz shows. In 1958 we got our first television set (two years after TV broadcasts began).

Football (AFL-style) was the local sporting passion, and from the age of eight I went to as many matches at the local Western Oval as I could. I attended a local government-run primary school. I remember being puzzled when, at twelve years of age, along with hundreds of kids from the western suburbs, I was taken to the Lord Somers Camp for Industrial Children to 'see the sea' at Hastings. We had always had a short holiday, usually by some beach, ever since I could remember.

Subsequently, I went to a large, new high school built on the edge of a vast quarry-cum-rubbish tip. At fifteen, I was advised by a teacher to leave school and 'get a job' like most of my schoolmates did, because that was the normal thing to do. Although I had hated high school until then, I didn't leave school partly because I liked reading and partly because I didn't like being told what to do. I won a scholarship that meant my parents could afford to allow me to stay on to Year 12. This was quite rare for children living in the western suburbs of Melbourne. In 1966 I got my 'Matriculation'. Out of the 200 students who started high school, only 36 completed it, and only five that I knew of went on to university. Although universities then required hefty fees, I won a teaching scholarship. I was the first person in my extended family to complete secondary school and the first to attend and complete university.

At university in my first year, I discovered that there were only two other people who came from the 'western suburbs'. Later, in third-year university, I read a book about people like me called *Breakthroughs*, about working-class people who had 'defeated the odds' and gone to university. I had never thought about myself as 'working class' or indeed any other class. Yet I also vaguely intuited that I was different to almost everyone I met. The academics and the other students talked and acted differently. I wondered whether I deserved to be there. I would feel like this for decades—even as a university teacher, I thought that one day I would be 'found out'.

These intuitions were radically confirmed late in 1968 when I met and fell in love with a woman from a family of upper middle-class and well-off parents. When I visited her family for the first time for dinner, I was shaken. I discovered that, unlike my family, my girlfriend's family ate in a dining room, next to a whole room given over to a piano. I drank wine with my meal from exquisite crystal glasses and, worst of all, I discovered that they used different kinds of knives and forks to eat with. I had never encountered this before, and had to quietly ask which ones to use.

That night I crossed an important social boundary. I had always imagined everyone lived the way my family did. I discovered this was not necessarily so.

The point of this story is simple. It is not always easy to have an experience of inequality.

● THINKING ABOUT INEQUALITY

This personal story raises questions about inequality. Why is it hard to acknowledge or think about inequality? Why would many Australians find the claim that Australia is an unequal society so difficult to understand, let alone agree with?

Sociologists do not always help us to come to terms with inequality. Some write about inequality using jargon like 'class', 'stratification', 'ideology', 'social reproduction' or 'functional role differentiation'. These terms are often far removed from our own experiences. Thinking about (or theorising) inequality indicates the problem of trying to connect life experiences to either abstracted theories or highly technical research. Another common tendency is to use the word 'inequality' as if what the term means was already self-evident or clear. Greig et al. (2003), who wrote a whole book about inequality, spend a lot of time constructing an elaborate and interesting theory of inequality. Yet nowhere do they address in a simple, clear way what they mean when they talk about inequality, and about the complex relations between material—or economic—inequality and all the other kinds of inequality that see people being treated disrespectfully, abused or exploited.

Many Australians also believe we live in an equal society or that Australians are deeply egalitarian (Stilwell 1993; McGregor 1997) (see box).

We're all equal: Australians' beliefs in egalitarianism

- Australia is a classless society with few significant inequalities.

- Many Australians do not like to think of themselves as belonging to a class. Moreover, we should not use the language of class because only old-fashioned people like Marxists, communists and socialists use such words. People who use words like 'class' want to create discontent, are envious or have become irrelevant 'Marxists' or socialist fuddy-duddies.

- Even if people concede that there are classes, most Australians belong to one large middle class with small groups at either end, and those small groups are 'the rich' and 'the poor'.

- Any serious inequalities result from either 'natural' differences in intelligence, talent and skill, or are the product of individual differences in moral energy, ambition levels or the preparedness to work effectively and hard.

- If there are social differences and inequalities, they are usually quickly ironed out by governments or what is sometimes called the 'welfare state'. The welfare state is funded through 'our' taxes—this means the government takes from the more affluent to ensure that generous welfare payments are given to 'the poor'. This ensures that we all are more or less equal.

In this chapter, we outline the kinds of thinking we will need to engage in if we are to think carefully about inequality. This chapter needs to be read in conjunction with Chapter 14, where we present and discuss the kinds of empirical evidence that point to one conclusion: Australia is a society with significant and persistent social and economic inequalities, and those inequalities are important for determining the kind of society we have and the life experiences of ordinary Australians. However, before we can develop that argument, we need to think about the words and frameworks we might use to get insight into this matter of inequality.

● IDENTITY, DIFFERENCE AND INEQUALITY

In the first part of this book, we spent a lot of time discussing identity and the fact that people who live in Australia bring to bear a whole lot of identity markers which announce who they are both to themselves and to others. That is, 'identity' deals with both the inner qualities of 'self'—like feeling, thinking or making decisions about how to live—and with the way we negotiate our social lives with others. In this way, identity is essentially about relationships both between the inner or psychological dimensions of self and the external relationships we have with others. Equally, it is about the variety of relations we have with each other, which include intimate face-to-face relations as well as more abstracted relationships with people we never meet but who affect us nonetheless.

Because it is about relationships, identity is very much about important differences that acquire social significance. As we will stress, not all differences lead to unequal treatment or rewards, but all inequalities rely on differences. The differences that make up our identity cover a very wide array of dimensions, or identity markers, that include aspects of our bodies, our sexuality, gender, ethnicity and so forth:

- Our identity is always embodied. This goes to questions of body size and shape: whether we are tall, short, thin or fat. Some of us have all our limbs and senses, while others are blind or amputees or live with conditions like cerebral palsy or intellectual disability. It can involve skin colour or the colour of our hair—redheads and blondes have to put up with a lot of stereotyping. Or it can rest on the physical signs we use to determine age.
- It also involves our sexuality, as well as a truly basic identity distinction based on gender.
- Identity can be announced by our clothes and accessories as Goths and punks, businessmen in 'suits', street beggars and Muslims daily remind us. Our jobs also shape and announce our identity.
- Skin colour, language use and religion, as well as the kinds of foods we eat, can also announce our ethnicity.

Any one of us is a collage of these identity markers. For that reason, we can experience our identity as hopelessly muddled, deeply conflicted or well integrated—and this can vary from time to time or from one social setting to another. Equally, in terms of our relations with others and depending on the 'other's' view of us, we can be treated well, respectfully or even with awe in one social setting, yet be abused, spat at or even physically assaulted in another. This is because, around these identity markers and differences, all sorts of stereotypes and stories are constructed and used to shape our social relations with each other. Sometimes we know about this because the ways in which we are treated by other people are clearcut and easy. On other occasions, because of the common widespread and abiding capacity for hypocrisy, it is more subtle: many women, Muslims and gays know that, while discriminatory treatment is illegal, they nonetheless continue to feel that they are being subjected to subtle or silent discrimination.

This is where the boundaries between being merely different and being dealt with unequally can be hard to detect or define. As will become clear, not all differences are the basis for unequal treatment or reward. However, all the kinds of inequality that matter rely on some social understanding or practice that converts a difference into a basis for unequal treatment. Because inequality is about relationships between people, both individually and collectively, it necessarily involves matters both of difference and identity.

So what do we mean by inequality? We offer a formal overview of how we want to think about inequality.

● DEFINING INEQUALITY

Inequality is very much about different kinds of access to basic social and economic resources. The kinds of inequality we are interested in acknowledge that not all Australians enjoy the same or equal access to power, prestige, income and/or wealth. As we have shown in earlier chapters:

- White Europeans used their power and their ideas about 'race' and 'civilisation' after 1788 to position 'blacks' as inferior and sometimes even as sub-human.
- Men as a group have used their power over resources and their access to cultural institutions like schools, universities and the media to position women as inferior or subordinate.
- Adults have used their power over children and young people to position them as dependants and as vulnerable.

Inequality is first and foremost about different kinds of power. Inequality of power means that some people make decisions that others have to obey. As writers like Foucault point out, all of us have power. Power simply means the ability to shape our own life and the lives of others. However, it is social circumstances that make it possible for some people to affect the lives of others.

In this way, power seems somehow to be connected to positionality. Positionality points to the way some people enjoy strategic advantages over others because they have more of the things that we all value. For example, 'positionality' in the real estate industry addresses the idea that there are only a few house sites at the top of the hill, which makes them more valuable and more desirable. Likewise, wealth is positional because only a few people or groups have a lot of it. Power depends on some people having more of whatever their power rests on (e.g. more guns, troops, lawful authority or votes, or more people who they can order to do as they are told) than others.

Second, inequality is about differences in economic resources. Some people have considerable wealth or lots of property, while others do not.

Third, there are important differences in the value people give to other people, or what we can call 'status'. Again, status or prestige is positional. Status refers to the ways people value each other unequally. We still give people with a lot of formal education more esteem, while people who make large amounts of money may also enjoy high status—as long as they don't make money in ways others disapprove of.

Together, these inequalities of power, economic resources and status translate into an unequal capacity to participate in a range of social, economic and cultural activities. That is, positional differences in access to power, status, income and wealth translate into other kinds of social and economic inequalities—though the relationships between each of these are very complex. Having access to certain kinds of economic resources, like land, slaves or wealth, will affect the kinds of housing, health and opportunities for leisure and education people can access.

In a society like Australia, inequality arises out of the interplay between economic and social factors. Economic inequality is deeply implicated in social inequality. Having an inadequate income affects people's ability to enjoy a long and healthy life, to get a good education or job, to own their own house, and to enjoy certain kinds of leisure activities, like holidays or eating at restaurants.

Finally, social inequality tends to be persistent. While it is true that we can sometimes alter these arrangements, they are usually both systematic and persistent. We might guess that differences in these things will tend to be reproduced over time. Some families who already have a lot of wealth will be well placed to increase their wealth, while people living in poverty will face a major struggle to improve their position.

● EXPLAINING INEQUALITY

This schematic account of inequality raises many important questions, including:

- Do people live the way they do because they have choice or because they have no choice?
- Is social inequality of some kind inevitable?
- What factors best explain patterns of inequality?
- What can or should individuals, groups or governments do to alter patterns of inequality?
- When do explanations of inequality become justifications for it?

Many answers to these questions can be found within a variety of theoretical perspectives about inequality. Take the last question. Social differences and inequalities exist in all societies in relation to economic resources, status and power, and around these inequalities we find a lot of explanations, justifications and myths. As Crompton (1993: 1) observes, 'no persisting structure of economic and social inequality has existed in the absence of some kind of meaning system(s) which seek both to explain and to justify the unequal distribution of societal resources'. In any society, there are various justifications for why some people have more and others have less. And, to varying degrees, these reasons have been quite successful in encouraging people to accept as good or natural their 'station in life'.

Below, we look at the approaches to the issue of inequality offered by different social sciences:

- economists—who tell a story of individuals competing with each other;
- functionalist sociologists—who talk about how inequality is good for society;
- Marxists—who talk about the role of class; and
- feminists—who say relations between men and women are the original and primary source of inequality for women.

The stories told by economists and functionalist sociologists tend to favour or excuse inequality as inevitable or desirable. The stories told by both Marxists and feminists tend to be more critical, and we take more time to examine their claims.

● THE ECONOMISTS' STORY

Most economists, especially those belonging to the neo-classical tradition, talk about inequality as the consequence of individuals entering a marketplace to buy or sell goods or services. These economists start with the core idea that we are all individuals who rationally and selfishly pursue our own self-interest. They then say that individuals come together to buy or sell various things, including labour, and this creates a market process. Economists insist that the marketplace rationally harmonises the supply and demand for skills, labour, goods and services, needs and prices among a complex of individuals.

Individuals are said to be born with certain innate talents and attributes (e.g. intelligence and good looks), and we develop those attributes through schooling and training to give us skills. We take those talents and skills into the marketplace, either by offering ourselves to employers as wage-earners or by establishing a business and finding customers willing to exchange money for the commodities we offer. Economists say that if we work hard, make rational economic decisions, invest or save our money *and* enjoy a little luck we will do well. If we do not work hard and do not save, we become poor.

Most economists give little attention to things like inheriting significant amounts of money or property. To recognise such facts would undermine the central assumption (referred to as 'methodological individualism') that we all are born as individuals and make our own way in the world.

Economists claim the pattern of economic inequality is a consequence of millions of individual decisions taking place in free-market interactions. Provided markets are not 'interfered with' by governments or unions, they are said to be intrinsically rational mechanisms, like individuals, and together they allegedly produce the best outcomes—such as economic growth, wealth for all and universal happiness.

Thus people's standard of living is the result of their own choices and capabilities—plus a little good or bad luck. In other words, the wealthy are where they are today because they worked hard and used their skills and intelligence to the best advantage. Conversely, the poor are living in poverty because they are ignorant, stupid, lazy and do not try hard enough. The rest of us are said to be somewhere in between.

● SOCIOLOGICAL STORIES

It is not surprising that many conventional sociologists—especially those who talk about 'society' as a 'system' with its own needs and interests (i.e. structural functionalists)—reject the individualism of the economists' story. Most sociologists prefer to stress the ways that a society is patterned in terms of:

- the ownership of property;
- the sexual division of labour between men and women; and
- how much skin colour, ethnicity or religious affiliation is used as the basis for treating people as equals or as superiors or inferiors.

These things clearly play a role in shaping people's life-chances—how well people live, how long they live and what schools they attend.

Beyond that initial consensus, we find disagreements among sociologists, however. Some sociologists (especially those who identify themselves as functionalists) say social or economic inequality is good. Functionalist sociologists (e.g. Moore 1963) believe that any 'modern' or 'advanced' society has to ensure that individual skills and talents are matched with the right jobs. Inequality ensures that this is done, and is thus 'functional'.

The argument goes this way. To be functional and to survive, any society needs to ensure that the 'right' people are available and prepared to do the important jobs. Some people are said to be born with particular talents. Given the fact that it takes years of education, hard work and the forfeiting of pleasure to produce a brain surgeon or judge, it is necessary to give those people with talent encouragement and reward (i.e. financial status) when they finally make it. This not only attracts but compensates them for all those years of disciplined work and sacrifice. In the same way, you do not want to attract the most intelligent people to jobs like bus-driving or collecting the garbage, so you pay little for these jobs. In short, inequality is 'functional', or good for social order, because it ensures that the people with the right talents and skills go into the right jobs.

Other sociologists have rejected this approach. Some—in our view, rightly—have seen this less as an explanation and more as a justification.

Stratification theory

Other sociologists have spent a lot of time developing and refining what is called stratification theory. This is ideally suited to empirical research, relying on data collection and measurement. It purports to provide a portrait of inequality. One of its merits is its simplicity, and the way it uses the appealing domestic image of a layer cake to offer a metaphor for the way we think about inequality. According to this theory, there is a top layer, middle layers and a bottom stratum in society. This approach works well for people who do not want to think too hard and who believe that nothing really exists unless you can measure it. On this occasion, of course, the very act of measuring creates what is apparently real—namely, the layers or strata, and a whole raft of serious problems.

Stratification theorists are seeking to show that society is unequal because it is divided into so many layers, or strata. You can use status, income, occupation, level of education, amount of wealth or some other measure of inequality. You can have as many layers or strata as you like, because it all depends where the researcher draws the line. They can also engage in very sophisticated statistical analysis to show up 'patterns of co-variance' between, say, income strata and schooling or occupational outcomes.

Stratification theory is a good, if unhelpful, example of a style of research and theory that claims to be empirical but actually involves people sitting in their studies producing conceptual schemes without being too disciplined by reality. At least stratification theorists showed that the functionalist account ignores the fact that we do not know whether the 'right people' are in the right jobs. This is especially so if people are denied the opportunity of the schooling or skills necessary for those jobs. If they had been given access to a 'good' education they may have done better than their parents. Second, in an unequal society, it is not possible to find out who has what kind of talent. As a large amount of wealth is inherited, people from well-off families get a head start.

A third, more critical, approach to inequality has been developed by a tradition of Marxist and socialist theory, and more recently by various kinds of feminists. While there are many important debates between and among them, they say that the way things already are helps to keep things that way. In short, inequality produces more inequality.

● THE IDEA OF CLASS

Within the discipline of sociology, one of the traditional ways of explaining social stratification, poverty, wealth and inequality has been to talk about class. This tradition was active until the 1980s, when major studies using class were being produced in Australia by sociologists like A.F. Davies (1967), R.W. Connell (1977), Chris Chamberlain (1983) and J.S. Western (1983). Since then, class has faded somewhat from view. Apart from Pusey (2003), most of the recent books like Peel (1996, 2004) or McGregor (1997) that focus on class have not come from sociologists: these writers are respectively an historian and a journalist.

In Britain, Crompton (1993) has kept the faith and argues that 'the discourse of class has become one of the key concepts through which we can begin to understand inequality', and that 'class . . . is a major organising concept in the exploration of contemporary systems' (1993: 4–5). Class can be a baffling idea. As Raymond Williams (1976: 52) observed a long time ago: 'Class is a difficult word both in its range of meanings and in its complexity in that particular meaning where it describes a social division.' Because we agree with Crompton, and with these warnings in mind, let us try to be as clear as possible about a concept that is used in many different and complicating ways.

● MARX ON CLASS

In the 1840s, Karl Marx began to develop a broad theory of historical and social change that provided a large-scale and complex account of inequality. It was a theory that stressed the role of collective forms and relations of social and economic activity that relied on the concept of 'class'. (It is an infamous fact that he never once defined what he meant by this concept.)

After Marx's death, Marxism became a comprehensive and increasingly diverse body of theory about the ways in which power relationships and economic, social and cultural arrangements reflect and produce patterns of dominance and subordination. Later Marxists emphasise different points; there is no single Marxist position.

Karl Marx (1818–83)

In the 1840s, the young Marx became interested in finding out how the kind of radical social change he wanted to promote might happen. He concluded that all human societies had to worry about establishing the material basis for human existence, like ensuring that food, water and shelter were available. This took place by establishing certain relations of production. These relations of production were distinct from the ideas people had—which he called the 'ideal'. He did not discount ideas, since he saw them as implicated in the material processes. These processes included how they organised the production of food, clothing and housing, as well as the temples they built or art they made. Marx argued that all 'economic' activity involved:

- the use of tools;
- techniques;
- ideas; and
- social relationships.

He insisted that tools, techniques and ideas are used and created by people who live in particular social relationships.

Marx also argued that all complex societies operate on the basis of inequality, in which some people are the oppressed (i.e. 'slaves', 'serfs', 'working class'), who are tyrannised, coerced or cajoled by more powerful people to produce the basic food, clothing, housing, luxury items and wealth that make up any society's basic economic activity.

In part, the power of powerful groups rests on the fact that they already possess more weapons, land or wealth that other people. Ultimately, the powerful can shoot, hang or gaol the lower orders to ensure obedience. However, it is better if they are able to persuade the oppressed that there is nothing much they can do to alter the basic social arrangements. Many kinds of ideas have been used to justify inequality, including religion, law and science.

All of these ideas were used by Marx to reach his conclusion that all human history is about the rise and decline of 'classes', who struggle to define or change the ways in which economic production can take place and who will get the benefits of economic wealth.

While Marx saw all human history as a series of class struggles between the oppressed and the oppressors, he devoted most of his life to making sense of the rise of modern industrial capitalist economies. Marx maintained that understanding capitalist economies depended on understanding the conflict between two dominant class groupings—the new industrial and financial bourgeois class and the new propertyless industrial working class. The conflict was more complex than just a battle between two groups with opposing social interests. It was central to the way work was organised and how prices and markets operated. It also involved a complex tension between the means of production and the social relations of production:

- The means of production refer to the tools, techniques and ideas needed to produce things (i.e. land, factories, machinery and books, as well as processes like the division of labour and scientific ideas and technologies).
- The social relations of production refer to the relations between class groups, like the working class (or the proletariat), who laboured in the factories, mills, mines and potteries, and the great owners of financial and industrial capital.

Marx concluded that there was an inevitable conflict between the social organisation of production and the increasingly privatised ownership of the wealth generated. He may well have been right about this. However, he concluded that there was only one way for this conflict to be resolved: the working class had to become the dominant class. Marx remained curiously ambivalent about how this would happen: sometimes he thought workers would use peaceful parliamentary means, at other times he believed it would be by violent revolution.

According to Marx, there was a limit to how much oppression the working class could take. The realisation of the injustice and persecution they endured—or what he called 'class-consciousness'—was to play a special role. This, Marx argued, would result in the working class uniting in revolutionary or parliamentary action, which would produce a change in economic, political and social arrangements, bring an end to all class struggle, and lead to the dawn of a new classless era of complete human freedom and equality—the era of communism.

Later Marxists have continued to maintain that the pattern of economic inequality has little to do with individual talents or desires, and a lot to do with larger patterns and alliances of economic power. In the 1970s, Marxists like Connell (1977) and Wheelright & Buckley (1987) argued that class reflects how particular groups are positioned to control (or be controlled by) the ownership of the basic productive forms of wealth (e.g. land, capital or technology). They argued that economic inequality reproduces itself from generation to generation, and that individual efforts could work only in a pre-existing pattern (or structure) of class inequality.

The Marxist idea is true or useful in two important ways. First, it accurately 'predicts' or 'explains' the fact that, for much of the nineteenth and twentieth centuries, there was serious ongoing conflict between organised working-class movements (unions and socialist parties) and employers over things like democratic rights and over the level of wages and job security. These conflicts are found in all advanced Western societies, and in some developing ones like Russia and China.

Second, Marx got it right in the general sense when he insisted that there were major differences in the life-chances of the various classes. Capitalist economies rely on a fundamentally unequal distribution of wealth and income, and the distribution of these resources has proved remarkably impervious to change. Marx went too far in expecting that the working class would be driven into increasing poverty, but economic inequality has continued to characterise any capitalist economy.

However, the Marxist account is also untrue in one important respect. Because it relies on a reductionist and simplifying logic, Marxism treats the actual mess of social existence with cavalier disregard. It comprehensively fails to explain how and why different groups within the working class support all sorts of religious, racist, gendered or political views and values. It cannot deal with the detail of actual working-class people's lives and the effect that different kinds of education, exposure to ideas, gender differences, cultural taste, geography or ethnicity will have. Nor does it explain the prevalence of status consciousness within the working class itself. Class theory thus becomes another crude exercise in stereotyping: in the former Soviet Union in the 1930s, China in the 1960s and in Cambodia in the 1970s, Marxist ideologues made class identity the basis for horrifying exercises in political terror and mass murder that claimed the lives of many millions of victims.

Nor can the class reductionism of Marxism explain the fact that there were lots of other kinds of political and moral conflict over things like the abolition of slavery, the rights of women or the contest between religion and science that became a major part of the nineteenth century experience.

It was the problems with Marxism that led another German theorist, Max Weber, to refine the theory of class.

● WEBER ON CLASS

Max Weber's views on inequality and class are often put up as an alternative to those of Marx. In a number of important ways, Weber differed from Marx; however, they shared more than is usually recognised.

Unlike the Marxists and socialists of late nineteenth century Germany, Weber (1978) maintained it was not only economic factors that determined all aspects of our personal, social, political and cultural life. To this extent, Weber rejected the idea that class was able to explain all societies at all times. For Weber, ideas and institutions were at least as important. He had in mind ideas like 'rationality' and institutions like religious and bureaucratic organisations.

Weber gave more weight to people's capacity to choose to act. For Weber, people were active agents who had the ability to make decisions and choices about how they dealt with the constraints of their social existence. Weber also differed from the Marxist account in that he gave much more weight to the complexities inherent in the way status, honour and prestige are used to demarcate certain individuals and groups from others. Status, Weber argued, is important for understanding why some people rather than others enjoy certain privileges. Some people who enjoy privileged access to material goods belong to high-status groups rather than to an upper class.

In particular, Weber very shrewdly saw that the unified 'working class' that Marx hoped would adopt a revolutionary strategy and overthrow capitalism was much more likely to be diverted by status distinctions between, for example, blue-collar (or manual) workers and white-collar (or brain) workers, making working-class unity or political action next to impossible.

Where Weber did agree with Marx was that, in the economic system of capitalism, economic values and ideas were dominant and 'class' became the single most powerful shaper of people's lives and experiences. For Weber, class was important in capitalist societies. His account of class described a hierarchy of occupation and ownership (Crompton 1993) which included:

- the working class;
- the petty bourgeoisie;
- technicians and low-level management; and
- the upper classes, privileged by virtue of their possession of property and educaton.

Finally, Weber did agree with Marx that class was important because it helped to define the quality of a person's life. Class, according to Weber, involves a group of people sharing access to economic resources (including property, income and wealth), which in turn influence and shape their life-chances. These 'life-chances' include:

- the nature of people's education and level of skill;
- the kind of housing they live in;

- people's health and length of life; and
- their cultural tastes and pursuits.

In the 1960s, another blow was struck against the Marxist idea that class was the key to understanding social inequality. 'Second-wave feminism', associated with Friedan (1963), Greer (1967) and Millett (1971), argued that a preoccupation with class ignored an even more basic pattern of inequality to do with male–female relationships.

● FEMINISM AND GENDER INEQUALITY

There can be little doubt, as we showed in Chapter 9, that sex and gender provide the basis for another pattern of social inequality. We have already made the point that systematic misogyny and gender-blindness have long obscured the basic forms that the subordination of women has taken. Feminists argue that most social scientists, including those responsible for the economic stories and Marxist perspectives, ignore the effects of our gendered identity because they do not consider the significance of gender and sex.

Many feminists maintain that our society is patriarchal. In patriarchal societies, men as a group are said to enjoy dominant status, to have most of the wealth and income, and to take pleasure from various forms of power over women. This takes place in daily and intimate aspects of life. It happens in the family, the bedroom, the school, the wider public world of politics, government and paid work.

Feminists argue that men have most of the wealth and earn more income, and that this pattern of economic inequality helps to maintain gender inequality. Many feminists maintain that these patterns of economic inequality reflect and reinforce the fact that men and women already operate as socially and culturally unequal gender groups. Feminists argue that there is no innate reason why women cannot do the same kinds of socially valued activities as men. They argue that men as a group have an interest in leaving things alone because they will continue to be better off under existing arrangements.

● IS THE CONCEPT OF CLASS STILL USEFUL?

These days, it is hard to find intelligent people willing to identify as Marxists. Many have retired or else become post-modernists. Some neo-conservatives are too ready to put down talk of class, saying it is an outmoded concept, while some progressives seem too eager to use the concept of class as if it pointed clearly to social realities which no longer exist, or which are now fading. Yet there is a case to be made that, provided it is not used in a reductionist, over-simplifying or stereotypical way, class can still be a useful idea. The problem is how to use an abstract analytic idea to make sense of real people's lives and experiences.

So we are inclined to agree when Marxists say the social and economic aspects of a pattern of class inequality reinforce and reproduce each other. There is value, too, in the work of scholars like Manuel Castells (1996) when he shows how some of Marx's insights can be applied to contemporary Australia. In Australia today, scientific and industrial technology, combined with finance and industrial capital, is mostly owned by wealthy individuals and a variety of corporate businesses that dominate the Australian economy. Neo-Marxists like Castells argue that we have a capital-intensive economy controlled by individual and corporate owners of capital evolving into a new kind of information-capital intensive mode of production.

Yet there are many issues and basic questions that still swirl about the idea of 'class'.

- Is class an 'objective' structural aspect of all societies? What does it mean to say that class is an objective aspect of any society?
- Is class an analytical category of use only to theorists, which cannot refer to anything that is real about ordinary people's lives and experiences?
- Does class refer to the ways humans identify themselves as people belonging to a particular kind of group, with certain habits, feelings, beliefs and behaviours?
- If class is an objective feature of a society, how does this objective quality translate into real people's feelings, activities and beliefs? For example, if a sociologist asserts that there is a real (i.e. objective) working class, but we find that very few people either define themselves in this way or do not exhibit the feelings, activities and beliefs they are supposed to, what is the value of class categories?

These are all important questions—especially given many of the changes we have seen in the second half of the twentieth century and into the early part of the twenty-first.

Waged work has been critical in defining class. Industrial styles of work have also been critical in defining certain features of working-class life. Given the moves we are making towards non-industrial styles of work—and, indeed, the more general shift towards a post-employment society—we need to ask whether the notion of class is still helpful. In particular, we have seen globalising processes entail the relocation of manufacturing industries to newly developing countries in places like Asia and South America, where labour remains cheap and national governments are agreeable to investment. Traditionally, such industries provided the employment for the working class in countries like Australia, the United States and the United Kingdom. In a globalising world, is class a useful identity marker? What is the meaning, for example, of identifying someone as a member of the working class? Is identifying a person's class position the best way of recognising their lifestyle, patterns of consumption or the standard of education achieved?

Further, given that 'class' is supposed to describe the pattern of ownership of various productive resources, can we move from the fact of structure to the fact of real people doing, feeling or thinking anything? How do we move from an obvious structural feature of Australian society, like the fact that perhaps 10 per cent of the adult population own 90 per cent of the productive wealth of our society, to issues of agency and personal lifestyle?

We agree with writers who make the point that individual and collective identities which rely on work are increasingly losing their significance (Gorz 1984). Traditional markers which have been used to distinguish social classes (such as duration of education, type of employment or income) are losing their value as education retention rates rise along with unemployment rates. Similarly, the income of some 'working-class tradespeople' often exceeds the income of some professionals. Many 'struggling' families send their children to private schools, while some affluent parents send their children to state schools. In practical terms, the categories may be problematic because not everyone who receives a set income or has a particular type of work can be seen as 'working class' in many other aspects of their lives.

People who want to use the language of class often end up having to make essentialist assumptions. Essentialist thinking assumes that, by virtue of belonging to a group like the 'working class', all members are bound together by certain common features, and these are more important in terms of creating a collective unity than are any points of difference. However, as we have suggested, there are few people who belong to only one group. People who are in the 'working class' may also belong to groups defined by identity markers like gender, ethnicity, religion, age or body size, shape and health.

This does not mean we can simply throw out class as a concept. At the least, 'class' remains a useful analytic concept because it reminds us that not all of our activities are open or free choices. Class usefully refers to the idea that patterns of income and wealth distribution constrain action and choice. Class is also useful in referring to the way these patterns of resources point—though not always clearly—to the way people identify their interests and attempt to either reinforce whatever advantages they already have or rectify certain weaknesses.

We conclude with an exploration of the idea of an 'underclass' to make the point that what is needed is careful research.

● THE DISCOVERY OF AN 'UNDERCLASS'?

The discovery of an underclass of unemployed poor and disaffected criminals in Britain, the United States and Australia has been a prominent feature of media discussion and academic research since the 1980s (Wilson 1987). It is certainly the case that those Australians who cannot sell their labour power depend on government welfare to survive. Around 24 per cent of the adult population relies on social security payments; when you add dependants, this accounts for 34 per cent of the population. It suits government to portray this part of the population as dependent, while various academics have used this fact to suggest that this population may represent a threat to social order. In each of these countries, the discovery of an underclass coincided with discussion about 'crime waves' and unemployment (White

1994: 22–8). We believe there are serious problems with this argument.

The major restructuring of Australia's economy has produced, among other things, higher long-term unemployment and considerable social dislocation. In this context, debates about the most appropriate direction for national economic and social policies have incorporated the rediscovery of a 'new underclass'. From the left, for example, we hear concerns about the failure of 'economic rationalist' policies and cutbacks in state services, accompanying warnings that in the immediate future we are likely to hear more about the presence of a large and growing 'underclass' of people (White 1994). From the right come equally grim warnings. Conservatives see the new underclass as proof of the need for more cuts to welfare and a return to traditional values, like thrift and self-reliance, and a strengthening of the 'law and order' agenda.

Talk of an underclass relies on a range of social science models, as well as many images that emphasise threats to order and civility.

Thinking critically about the idea of underclass

Emphasising how the underclass debate reflects the politics of governance by experts does not deny the real consequences of global economic and social restructuring. The emergence of debates about an 'underclass' in the 1980s and 1990s reflects one of many social strains developing in a context of unprecedented social and cultural restructuring and the contradictory dynamics of late modernity (Beck 1992).

Classifying parts of the population is not unique to these past two decades. Once again, we see 'the poor' become the repository of collective fears generated by the respectable, the responsible and the expert. Policing or providing welfare to 'the poor' or 'the underclass' is reliant on particular perceptions of 'the destitute'. Whatever the perspective of policy prescription (whether it be in support of more *laissez-faire* or increased state intervention and guardianship by the state and/or the professional), regulation will continue to be the fate of those who fit the description of 'the underclass'.

● CONCLUSION

We have not been able to explore all of the stories, arguments and research on inequality or class. We can, however, say that economists are right when they say that markets make a significant difference. Markets rely on and reinforce the already existing unequal distribution of wealth and income. Feminists are also right to argue that the gendered division of labour and the inequalities between men and women are another key structuring principle in a country like Australia.

The claims of some sociologists that inequality is bad both for the society that allows it to continue and for its victims are also credible. One problem with social inequality is that the community as a whole is denied the opportunity to use and benefit from talents and skills that may never be discovered and used. Further, patterns of inequality can mean that the victims of inequality experience hardship, ill-health and distress, reducing their quality of life and preventing them from being happy and fulfilled citizens.

There is also some value in what Marxists say when they use the concept of class to talk about wealth and power. In some ways, they are right to talk about the structuring of inequality by class, and how it is integral to capitalist economies. Marxists have, however, been a bit shaky when they try to specify the ways class actually shape human action, thought and feeling, though it is still apparent (e.g. in the way unions continue to exist) that class works to some extent as a principle for organising collective action and thought.

From a moral point of view, inequality is an offence against most people's idea of a just society or social justice. When people are trapped in poverty, lifestyles and activities over which they have little control, it is clearly socially unjust. In Chapter 14 we turn to the question of economic inequality in Australia.

Discussion questions

13.1   What does the word 'class' describe or name?

13.2   Is 'class' a term only sociologists need to use, or does it describe real aspects of people's lives?

13.3   Is there an 'underclass' in Australia, or is this an example of middle-class prejudice about the poor?

13.4   What is the middle class?

13.5   Is social inequality inherited or made?

Chief Executive Officers (CEOs) are now earning more in a week than most workers make in a year ... CEOs' pay has blown out by more than 560 per cent since 1990 from $514,000 to $3.4 million ... In 1990 bosses took home 18 times as much as their average employee. In 2005 the ratio was 63 to 1.

The Melbourne Herald Sun, 28 January 2006

INEQUALITY IN AUSTRALIA 14.

- Summary

- The distribution of income

- Defining income inequality

- Information about economic inequality

- The distribution of income in Australia

- The distribution of wealth

- The idea of poverty

- The (Henderson) poverty line

- Absolute and relative poverty

- The poverty wars

- Conclusion

- Discussion questions

• • SUMMARY

While the advocates of globalisation have argued that increased free trade and economic restructuring are good for people, there is mounting evidence that Australia is becoming a more unequal society. In this chapter, we review this evidence. We begin by analysing some of the ways people talk about inequality, especially in terms of the distribution of income and wealth. We then focus on the problem of defining and measuring income inequality. We examine some research on economic inequality and ask whether income inequality in Australia has become worse in recent years. There is also concern about an increase in poverty, with some research suggesting that the incidence has doubled since 1975.

As Craig McGregor (1997) observes, Australians have long believed that they are part of a society where values like 'mateship' matter and where everyone is as good as everyone else. We take pride in employers having to pay their workers a decent 'basic' or minimum wage—unlike the United States. We even take pride in the 'tall poppy syndrome': anyone who gets a 'swelled head' is quickly cut back to size.

On this basis, many Australians feel reasonably confident that Australia is a classless society with few significant inequalities. Even if people concede that there are classes, they tend to add that most Australians belong to one large middle class with small groups at either end. Most Australians seem to live in their own home, get paid for the jobs they do, enjoy plenty of food, wear decent clothing and enjoy a wide range of leisure pursuits. So what possible basis could there be for thinking that Australia is a society with significant and persistent social and economic inequalities? There are several indications suggesting that this idea needs to be taken seriously.

The first is that, since the mid-1990s, the main source of income for between 26 and 28 per cent of Australian households has come from social security pensions and allowances. This means that one in three Australians (or between 34 and 37 per cent of the population) are reliant on government benefits and pensions (ABS 2005c).

Second—though this is a more ambiguous matter—poverty keeps on being 'rediscovered' in Australia. Ever since R.F. Henderson's first big 'discovery' back in the 1960s that upwards of 10 per cent of families lived below his 'poverty line', poverty has kept on being 'discovered'. Recent major studies of poverty in Australia (like Fincher & Nieuwenhuysen 1998; Harding et al. 2002; and Saunders 2005) have claimed that, since 1975, the number of Australians in poverty has virtually doubled, putting just over one in three Australians in poverty. Since 2001, however, a substantial controversy has erupted about the claim that poverty is getting worse. On one side is the economist Peter Saunders at the Social Policy Research Centre, advocating for the poverty-is-getting-worse view (Saunders 2005) and on the other a sociologist also called Peter Saunders, who works for the neo-conservative think-tank the Centre for Independent Studies, who rejects this view (Saunders 2004).

Finally, coinciding with the start of the twenty-first century, a number of researchers like Ann Harding (Harding et al. 2002) and Michael Pusey (2003) have presented research findings suggesting that 'middle Australians' feel 'worse off because they are sandwiched between affluent two-income professional couples . . . and unemployed and working poor families who receive more help from the government than they do' (Harding, in Gunn 2000: 3).

As we argued in Chapter 13, inequality is a complex idea. Debates like this remind us of the difficulties involved in using concepts like 'poverty' and 'inequality' as well as the difficulties that arise in dealing with the evidence available to support various views and value positions. For example, the idea that 'middle Australia'—or what Paul Kelly (2000a: 1) calls the 'battler middle class'—are being squeezed by 'the high fliers' and the 'rising poor' relies on surveys of what members of this oddly defined group feel is happening to them. Whether we can trust such feelings is dubious, given that Saunders (2005) points to evidence that remarkably few Australians have an accurate grasp of where they fit in the distribution of income.

Inequality is a controversial issue. Our ideas about it, and the variety of views people adopt towards it, are intimately connected to the way social relationships are shaped by the way power and resources are actually distributed, as well as by the real experiences people have. In order to get some clarity about these issues, we ask three basic questions:

- What do we know about the distribution of income—and wealth—in Australia?
- What kinds of evidence are there, and how good is it?
- How useful is the concept of poverty, and what problems are inherent in contemporary research into poverty?

Our answers to these questions indicate why we think that Australia is a society with significant and persistent social and economic inequalities, even though we only focus on economic inequality. Let's start with the distribution of income. How do we go about defining and measuring income inequality?

● THE DISTRIBUTION OF INCOME

We need to be very clear about what we mean by income. In a simple sense, income refers to the daily, weekly or monthly flow of money into people's hands. It comes from:

- selling their labour to employers;
- selling their skills or services;
- using their assets (or their wealth) to generate income; and
- government welfare and income support schemes.

Income is not the same thing as wealth—though the two are connected. If you have enough income, you can convert part of it into wealth by investing in property, buying shares or saving your income. Equally, if you own the right kind of wealth you can convert it into income. It is therefore likely that the underlying distribution of a community's wealth is a powerful factor shaping the distribution of income. Second, income needs to be defined as either before-tax or after-tax income. A further complication is that we also pay taxes other than income tax, like the GST—though we may not always be aware of this. Finally, there are both individual incomes and household or family incomes made up of the contributions of the various income-earners in the family. This raises difficult questions about whether to try to measure individual or household incomes.

Leaving aside these various complexities, using ABS data we can establish the various sources of income. Table 14.1 suggests something of the pattern over the last decade.

Table 14.1 Main sources of income, 1995–2004 (%)

Main source	1995	1998	2000	2004
Wages and salaries	57.5	56.8	56.7	58.0
Own business or partnership	6.1	6.0	6.4	6.2
Government pensions and benefits	28.4	28.4	28.7	26.6
Other	6.7	7.7	7.3	8.1

Source: ABS (2005c).

Table 14.1 points to the main sources of household incomes and accepts that real households may have a mix of these sources. It cannot tell us about this in any detail. A slightly different picture is presented in another ABS publication (ABS 2005c), using taxation and income support data. Using different assumptions and definitions that focus on individual sources of income these data suggest that, in 2000–01, 71.7 per cent of personal income came from wages and salaries, 11.2 per cent from government welfare payments, 7.5 per cent from investments, 7.0 per cent from unincorporated business income and 2.1 per cent from superannuation funds.

Even the simple snapshot in Table 14.1 suggests a degree of economic inequality in Australia. In a capitalist economy, it can be assumed that most people earning a wage will not be as well off as those whose income is derived from the ownership of property or from being self-employed. Equally, we can infer that those relying on government pensions and benefits will have smaller incomes than wage-earners.

It is interesting to note that, comparatively, Australia has one of the highest shares of income going to self-employed persons. The general picture is similar to that in Canada and the United

States, but it is different from places like Britain and very different from, say, Sweden, where there is a much smaller proportion of people defined as 'self-employed'.

● DEFINING INCOME INEQUALITY

While there are many complex issues involved in thinking about inequality, we do need some basic way of defining income inequality. One way is to start with the underpinning idea of income equality, which would occur if every person (or households, or other specified groups of people) had the same share of total income.

Using this idea, economists have constructed a picture of what income equality would look like by assuming that they can break up the population into groups. The conventional groups are either 'deciles' (i.e. 10 per cent of the population) or quintiles (20 per cent). At the same time, they can measure the total amount of income available to the population (found in gross domestic product or from Australian Taxation Office data) and establish what share of the total income each 'decile' or 'quintile' gets. This involves adding up the total share of income using the income measures before breaking it up into 10 or 20 per cent lots.

If we go back to the original idea of income equality, then a perfectly equal distribution of income can be represented as a 'straight line curve' (see Figure 14.1), showing what a perfectly equal distribution of income would look like. That is, in a situation of perfect income equality, each decile of the population would have the same share of total income as every other decile.

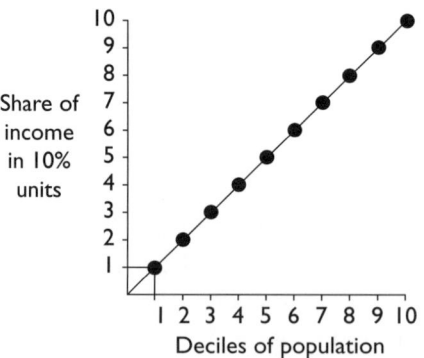

Note: A straight line curve results when each decile (or 10% of population) has access to each 10% lot of income. The analysis can also be done in quintiles (or 20%).

Figure 14.1 The straight line curve: Perfect income equality

Since no society we know about has ever had income equality, it is easy enough to work out how to describe income inequality. Income inequality can be mapped out using the graph of equality to show the actual curve of inequality (called the Lorenz curve after the economist who came up with this way of mapping income inequality). Economists measure inequality by breaking the total population of income-earners up into deciles or quintiles, and then asking what share of the total income each of these groups has. For example, it is easy enough to establish that the lowest decile may only have 1–2 per cent of the total amount of income while the top decile may have 25 per cent of total income. Plotting this on a graph can give us a curve of inequality. The deeper the curve, the more income inequality that society has.

Using this method, economists can report on the share of income in the hands of each decile—or each quintile—of the population. The method can be used to describe the share of income going to individuals and/or to households, and the researcher can also take account of any differences between before-tax and after-tax income.

One of the central problems with researching the distribution of income—and even more so of wealth—is that accurate information is often hard to find.

● INFORMATION ABOUT INCOME INEQUALITY

First, it is difficult to obtain accurate information about the amount of income people earn or their wealth holdings. There is one official source of information about income—the Australian Taxation Office (ATO); however, there are no equivalent good sources of data on wealth. Second, there may be doubts about the accuracy of information gained from people telling researchers or the government how much income or wealth they have. People often become secretive and some tell lies when they have large incomes and a lot of wealth to protect. It is thus likely that, at the top end of the income and wealth scales, people are not telling the whole story.

In trying to establish whether Australia has an equal distribution of income, we need to ask where we obtain evidence for describing the distribution of income. There are three main sources of public information about the distribution of income (see box), all of them federal government agencies.

Sources of income information
Income tax information

This is based on the annual income tax returns each income-earner is obliged to send into the ATO. In the case of the overwhelming number of income-earners who are wage- and salary-earning employees, the taxation they owe to the government is automatically collected by their employer each pay day and quite good data exist on this income. For people who are not employees, the data are less accurate and complete.

ABS Censuses

These are carried out by the Australian Bureau of Statistics in every household across Australia on one night every five years. Since 1976, the Census has included a question about the incomes of those in the household.

ABS Household Income and Expenditure surveys

The ABS Household Income and Expenditure surveys have been collecting data about income since 1976—roughly every six years or so. These surveys are taken from a representative sample of several thousand households. This survey tries to get as accurate an account as possible of their actual economic resources and expenditures. The information is collected using a mix of diaries and questionnaires to establish individual household incomes and expenditures, which are then manipulated statistically to give us an estimate of the distribution of income for all Australians. This means we are not looking at an actual count of the incomes of all households or individuals in Australia, but rather at a sophisticated guess about the income distribution for the total population based on what householders who fill out the various questionnaires are prepared to disclose.

Each source has its problems:

- No one source gives us a long-term and reliable historical picture of income distribution. The oldest data comes from the ATO, which has been collecting income tax from Australians since 1942–43. The ABS has been asking questions about income in the Census or Household Income and Expenditure surveys only since the 1970s. This means it is hard to establish what, if any, changes have taken place in the share of economic resources like income.
- It is fair to assume that there is some incentive for everyone dealing with the ATO to understate the extent of their income if they can. High income-earners have more income and therefore have more incentive to not tell the whole story: they have more to hide, and can afford better advice to help them achieve this goal.
- More generally, it seems that people do not feel easy about disclosing their incomes, even to ABS researchers. For example, up to a million householders fail to answer questions about income in the Census.

This means that any claims about the distribution of income have to be treated either sceptically or with caution.

If we consider the most common kind of evidence that is used—most of which is gathered and analysed by economists—what do we see?

● THE DISTRIBUTION OF INCOME IN AUSTRALIA

To start with total income, the data collected by the ABS suggests that there has been a substantial increase in real GDP income per head of population. This is actually a measure of the growth in the total worth of the Australian economy, and simply divides the total GDP income by total population. It shows that each man, woman and child in Australia started out in 1994 with $28 700 a year, which by 2004 had increased to $39 300 a year (see Table 14.2).

Table 14.2 Income growth per capita, 1994–2004

1994	1996	2000	2004
$28 700	$32 100	$36 400	$39 300

Source: ABS (2005c).

Table 14.3 suggests, in a slightly more realistic fashion, what the average weekly earnings were for all employees. This does not take into account the differences between full-time and part-time wage-earners or gender differences. For a point of comparison, we have added in the weekly benefit that a single aged pensioner received.

Table 14.3 Average weekly earnings for employees and single aged pensioner benefits, 1994–2004

	1994	1996	2000	2004
Employees				
Weekly	$533	$574	$653	$757
Annual	$26 650	$28 700	$32 650	$37 850
Single aged pensioner				
Weekly	$197	$197	$203	$232
Annual	$9 830	$9 830	$10 150	$11 600

Source: ABS (2005c).

While this begins to suggest the disparities between what average full-time workers might be getting and what a welfare beneficiary gets, it is only when we start to look at the overall pattern of income inequality that its extent becomes apparent.

We will start with a recent overview of income distribution for the half-century from the early 1940s to the early 1990s. Table 14.4 suggests both a high level of inequality and a degree of persistence in the pattern of income distribution. In this period the top quintile (20 per cent) of top income-earners has three times the share of total income available to the bottom two quintiles. Those in the top quintile of income-earners retained their share of total income across half a century. (We should also note when reading this table that, strictly speaking, the data inside this table are not comparable, since the data for 1989–90 refer to the share of income going to households.)

Table 14.4 Share of total income, 1942–43 to 1989–90 (%)

Year	Bottom two quintiles	Top quintile
1942–43	15	45
1968	20	38.8
1985–86	14.64	43.64
1989–90*	15	43.99

*Household distribution

Source: revised from Greig et al. (2003: 97).

It might be objected that this material is now dated and that Australia's economic performance, especially through the 1990s and into the twenty-first century, will have done a lot to improve the distribution of income. The issue of whether the distribution of income has become more or less equal over time involves some basic puzzles to do with the kinds of evidence available. As we have shown, there are problems with all the evidence used to describe distribution of income. These puzzles begin when we think about how well people understand their place in the distribution of income.

Recent discussion and debate about the 'disappearing middle' by Pusey (2003) remind us of the dangers of relying on how people understand their own circumstances. Michael Pusey (2003) claims that inequality is on the increase, and that one sign of this is that 'middle Australia' is being hollowed out. Pusey builds on his (1991) earlier work to claim that this is a result of decades of 'economic rationalist' policy-making. Pusey's book prompts two questions: what does he mean by the 'middling classes' or 'middle Australia'; and has it been—or is it being—'hollowed out'?

Pusey is unclear about who is in his 'middling groups', or why he has chosen to include the occupational or income-based cohorts he does. Second, while he relies heavily on the idea that those he interviewed feel that they are being squeezed, the data do not always 'add up' for Pusey in a way to which Saunders (2005) has pointed. Peter Saunders (2005) draws on research that compares how people locate themselves within the distribution of income with where they actually are in that distribution. He reports that most Australians are both poorly informed and terribly confused about this matter. Most people cannot accurately identify themselves in terms of where they fit into the pattern of income inequality. Saunders' research suggests that people who have lots of income consistently understate their income, and do not grasp how privileged they are. Equally, those with very little money consistently overstate the extent of their income. Saunders says that most of us cling to the belief that we belong to some amorphous 'middle class' or to 'middling Australia'. This is palpably not true, but it frames the confusions at work in Pusey's work.

Pusey wants to argue that there has been a contraction of 'middle incomes'. Whether this matters as much as the slicing away of the share of income that once went to the bottom four deciles of income-earners is another—though entirely salient—question. There is little doubt that there has been a deepening of income inequality in Australia. Yet—and here the evidence from the ABS (2006b: see Table 14.6 below) and Harding is clear—the middle are either holding their share of position or probably doing better. The net effect of two decades of government tax reform and social security reform has been to embellish the share of income going to two-income families, while single-parent and single-income families have been losers. Every time a government announces it is handing a tax reform over to the 'battlers' or to 'low-income' families, the net effect is to hand over more dollars the higher up the tiered income tax scale the benefit goes. When this is put in a context of the dramatic increase in part-time work and the generalised assault on 'real-wage' incomes over the past two decades, the picture is clear.

This discussion suggests why, if it is difficult to get a good picture of income distribution, it is even harder to establish whether income inequality is getting better or worse. This partly depends on what time period is being looked at. For example, we might pick a time frame like 1980–95 and use ATO income data to get a picture of shifts in the share of income. Table 14.5 paints a harsh picture for these years. The picture shows that the total distribution of before-tax income became more unequal. Translating Table 14.5—which measures gross income—we see that, again, most of the low- to middle-income groups lost their initial share of total income between 1982 and 1995 while the top quintile did much better.

Table 14.5 Changes in distribution of gross income by households (% of total income)

	1982	1986	1995
Lowest quintile	4.4	4.7	3.6
Second quintile	9.8	9.4	–
Third quintile	16.6	15.9	–
Fourth quintile	24.8	24.7	–
Highest quintile	44.1	45.6	47.9

Source: Saunders (1994: 214); ABS (1997d: 114).

Table 14.5 points to an increase in inequality signified by a loss of income for the bottom 60 per cent of income-earners and a rise in the share of the top 20 per cent. In particular, it seems that the lowest 20 per cent of income-earners lost a part of what small share of income they enjoyed. The highest income-earners, however, enjoyed a major rise in their income share during these years. Indeed, the highest income-earning decile got an increase equivalent to the *total* share going to the bottom 20 per cent! However, unless you take into account the effects of two major recessions accompanied by historically high rates of unemployment, this conclusion could be misleading: in 1982, Australia was in the grip of the worst post-1945 recession, with record levels of unemployment; by 1995, on the other hand, Australia had emerged from the even worse 1989–92 recession.

One other consideration is worth drawing attention to in regard to this time frame. The kind of research we have been using tends be gender-neutral or even gender-blind. It would be good if we could explore the question of how male and female incomes were faring through this period, but the data are not available. We certainly should recall the fact that women's income from wages tends on average to be lower than that of men. In 1994, women's pay averaged 85 per cent of men's average wages (ABS 1996b: 112). This means women tend to be more flexible in how they enter and leave the labour market. Most women cannot say they have been in a full-time waged job for more than ten years. In 1995, only 591 000 women, compared with 1.2 million men, had been in their jobs for more than ten years (ABS 1995: 111).

As Gregory and Hunter's (1995) research suggests, although women's participation rate has risen, not all women enjoy equal access to paid employment. As with men, so a woman's ability to get employment is affected by her socioeconomic status. Hunter and Gregory used Census data to examine the social and economic characteristics of each Census district (each one consisting of roughly 700 households across Australia), and ranked these districts by socioeconomic status. Between 1976 and 1991, the employment-to-population ratio fell generally. High-income, high-status neighbourhoods did much better than low-status, low-income neighbourhoods. This also has a gender aspect (cited in Probert 1997: 7):

- For men in the top 5 per cent of high-income, high-socioeconomic status (SES) areas, the employment-to-population ratio fell by 9 per cent.
- For men in the lowest 5 per cent of SES areas, the employment-to-population ratio fell by 37 per cent.
- For women in the top 50 per cent of SES areas, the employment-to-population ratio rose by 16 per cent; however, the ratio for women in the bottom 10 per cent of SES areas fell by 17.5 per cent.

These findings highlight the fact that not all women experience work in the same way. Being poor or working class, or living in particular neighbourhoods, affects the way people cope with changes in employment.

Moving into our own period, the available evidence suggests that there was no significant movement one way or the other in a distribution of income that is clearly unequal (see Table 14.6).

Table 14.6 Share of income by low-, middle- and high-income quintiles 1996–97 to 2003–04 (%)

	1996–97	**2000–01**	**2003–04**
Low-income	11.0	10.5	10.9
Middle-income	17.8	17.6	17.9
High-income	37.1	38.5	37.4

Source: ABS (2006c).

Again, we need to be careful how we understand this evidence. Between 2002 and 2004, the federal government made a one-off payment of $2.2 billion (announced in the May 2004 Budget) to families and carers, which increased gross household weekly incomes by $4.00. Second, these data come from the ABS Household Income and Expenditure surveys, not from the ATO tax data. Finally, the data are not comparable with other data: as the ABS acknowledges, it introduced certain changes to the methods used in calculating the distribution of income and expenditures in 2003–04. The only safe thing to do is to conclude that the pattern of income distribution remains unequal.

Given the relatively rich supply of data on income distribution, the problems involved in researching the distribution of wealth are even more daunting.

• THE DISTRIBUTION OF WEALTH

All societies have had small numbers of very wealthy people and many more people with little wealth. Australia is no exception. In many ways, the distribution of wealth is a very important matter. Yet it is hard to find any reference to wealth research in Saunders (1994), EPAC (1995) or most of the hundreds of references in Encel (1987, 1990). In 1986, the Hawke Labor government came under pressure to carry out a wealth inquiry, just as the Whitlam Labor government had established the Poverty Inquiry of 1973–75. The Hawke government successfully resisted this pressure, and the idea quietly disappeared.

This almost certainly reflects the fact that those who are wealthy are important politically. The decisions of small numbers of very wealthy and powerful people can shape the nature of our cities, our national culture or the extent of ecological damage in a particular region.

So what, if anything, do we know about the distribution of wealth in Australia? The answer is 'very little'. There are no regular surveys of wealth, the Census does not ask questions about wealth holdings, and there are currently few taxes that tap into wealth. The ABS does do research into what it calls the distribution of net worth by households. While there are major problems with how far this research goes, it does paint a picture of the distribution of net worth that is even more unequal than the distribution of income as shown in Table 14.7.

Table 14.7 Distribution of household net worth by quintile, 2003–04

	Lowest	Second quintile	Third	Fourth quintile	Top
Mean Household Net worth	$24 000	$142 000	$300 000	$502 000	$1.3 m
Share of total Net worth (%)	1	6	13	21	59

Source: ABS (2006c).

There is little other research evidence. Phil Raskall (1994) has done some interesting and well-informed guesswork on the issue. Back in 1979, Raskall did some pioneering research into what the data from death duties (since abolished) showed about the distribution of wealth. The higher the value of the dead person's estate, the higher the duty. So those who knew they would soon die gave much of their property away first. The Commonwealth government usually applied a gift tax to catch this movement of property. There was also a strong incentive to undervalue the estate and thus pay less in estate duty. The estate duty applied only to personal property, and did not touch the collective property owned by companies, trusts and the like. Finally, not every estate paid a death duty, especially if the initial value of the estate was too low to attract the tax.

With these qualifications in mind, and remembering how long ago his research was undertaken, it is perhaps surprising that Raskall found that the bottom four quintiles (or 80 per cent) of the population owned less than 10 per cent of the total wealth, while the top quintile owned 90 per cent. More recently, NATSEM, a Canberra-based research centre using a variety of computer-based simulations, estimated the total wealth in Australia in 1997 at $1.3 trillion, and calculated that the top 10 per cent of wealth-owners had 75 per cent of the wealth while the bottom 5 per cent had only 5 per cent of the total assets.

While there remain basic frustrations in terms of the data available, the distribution of wealth is clearly quite unequal. Data from the Australian Tax Office, which always needs to be treated with scepticism given the ease with which the really wealthy can manipulate their taxation returns to reduce their apparent incomes, suggest that the number of people with annual taxable incomes of over $1 million had continued to increase over the decade to 2005.

● THE IDEA OF POVERTY

Poverty attracts a far higher degree of attention from both the media and academics than wealth. Much of the social science research into poverty in Australia over the last 40 years has been done by economists, most of whom have at least acknowledged that Australians live in an unequal society. However, 'the experts' have long disagreed among themselves on some points, as the so-called 'poverty wars' (Saunders 2005) remind us.

We want to challenge the conventional idea that 'poverty' and 'the poor' are useful ways of thinking about aspects of inequality. This is because there are fundamental difficulties in using the idea of poverty—especially when trying to establish what an inadequate income might look like—and measuring poverty. Let us start with one common approach used in Australia, called the 'poverty line' approach.

● THE (HENDERSON) POVERTY LINE

In Australia since the mid-1960s, people have often thought about poverty using the Henderson 'poverty line'. Henderson's 'poverty line' measure was originally based on the premise that a family—a man at work and a wife at home with two dependent children—with a weekly income below the then basic wage (for 1966) of $33.00 per week would be poor. The basic wage was originally established at a level said by the Arbitration Court to enable a man, his 'dependent' wife and two children to have a 'frugal standard of subsistence'.

Henderson's poverty line became a politically acceptable way of framing certain debates—for example, about the adequacy of Australia's social security system. The poverty line has since been updated every year (using changes in household disposable income). It is still often used by critics of the government's level of social welfare spending to show how certain government benefits fall below 'the poverty line'. Table 14.8 represents an estimate of the various 'poverty lines' in dollar terms per week for various kinds of people and household units. If we use this table to calculate the numbers of people living in poverty, as defined by the use of the poverty line in 1990, we get Table 14.9.

Table 14.8 Poverty lines between 1981–82 and 1989–90 ($/week)

	1981–82	1985–86	1989–90
Single person aged under 25	69.50	101.10	139.80
Single aged person	64.80	94.00	132.60
Couple, plus two children	184.80	263.90	378.80
Sole parent, two children	133.40	192.20	275.00

Source: adapted from Saunders (1994: 268).

Table 14.9 shows that single parents constitute a significant and disproportionate number of poor Australians. Other groups likely to experience poverty are single young people and single older people. Indeed, if you are a single person and not involved in a larger household unit, you are at risk of being in poverty.

Table 14.9 Incidence of poverty in Australia, 1989–90

	Numbers	**% of this group in poverty**
All single people under 25	143 500	19.5
All single people over 60	225 000	27.9
Other single people	194 600	18.8
Childless couples	98 000	6.4
Couples with children	140 900	10.5
Single-parent families	190 500	58.0

Source: Saunders (1994: 270).

One recent exercise in measuring the incidence of poverty using the poverty line was undertaken by King (1998), who used a sophisticated computer simulation model (NATSEM) at the University of Canberra. King argues that, in the twenty years from 1975 to 1996, the incidence of households living in poverty has risen from 20.6 to 30.7 per cent. While in the earlier studies groups of both young and elderly singles seemed to be disproportionately at risk of being poor, there has been a swing towards young single people being most at risk. Again, single mothers are especially vulnerable (Shaver 1998). Critics have pointed to the arbitrariness involved in using a poverty line approach. However, as Saunders (1994) indicates, any alternatives will still be 'arbitrary'.

The other problem has been figuring out what the poverty line would be for groups of people or individuals who do not belong to the original poverty unit (i.e. a man, 'his' dependent wife and two children). This is the problem of establishing equivalence scales to show what the 'poverty line' is for a single nineteen-year-old man, or for a married couple in their thirties, or for a middle-aged woman with six children, because each of these households has different needs and costs. The core problem is that the word 'poverty' does not have a clearcut referent.

● ABSOLUTE AND RELATIVE POVERTY

Modern social scientists have conventionally distinguished between two kinds of poverty: 'absolute' and 'relative' poverty. It is said that absolute poverty refers to a circumstance where people are at risk of dying, or becoming seriously ill, because they do not have enough of the basics to stay alive. Death from starvation, illness and reduced life expectancy are the starkest possible evidence of absolute poverty. This idea then leads people to say that countries like Australia do not appear to have this kind of poverty. Relative poverty is a far more amorphous concept. It refers to the idea that, within a particular society, some people do not have enough income to share in what is seen to be an 'average standard of living'.

Having made this distinction, it still not easy to produce a simple or objective definition for either an absolute or a relative measure of poverty (see Atkinson 1987). For example, we could probably get nutritionists to say what the bare minimum of food and water is that would keep people alive. We could get them to look at the food and water intake of those Jews who survived Hitler's death camps in the 1940s, or at people who have just survived one of the recent African famines, to construct an objective absolute poverty index. One such index is the so-called Belsen Index, which says the average human needs a minimum of 600 calories of food a day to stay alive. As Davis (1997) shows, the British in India orchestrated the killing of between seven and thirteen million Indians in a series of policy-made famines in the 1870s by keeping daily food intakes below the Belsen Index level.

The idea of relative poverty raises many more questions. Can we—or should we—seek to construct an objective measure of relative poverty? Are the poor different from the rest of us? What counts as a 'socially acceptable minimum' below which we can say that someone is 'relatively poor'? In terms of developing good policy, is poverty in fact the problem, or is it actually inequality?

Some writers have argued that we need to look at what 'real' people in a 'real' community spend their money on, and examine their patterns of consumption. From this they say we can derive an index of consumption from which a minimum standard of living could be established.

In Britain, Peter Townsend (1979) developed an index of deprivation. He claimed that it was possible to define relative deprivation as affecting those people who 'lack the resources to obtain the types of diet, participate in the activities and have the living conditions and amenities which are customary, or at least widely encouraged, or approved in the society to which they belong' (1979: 30). However, critics have observed that what Townsend demonstrated is just a diversity in styles of consumption.

Other writers argue that we should look to the members of a community and ask them systematically what they think would constitute a minimal basis for 'living decently', or a minimal income level 'below which they could not make ends meet'. Again, there are difficulties involved in asking people with different actual living standards to establish a level below which they could not make ends meet or 'live decently'.

So what does the repeated 'discovery' of poverty over the last 40 years signify? At the height of an earlier 'rediscovery' of poverty in Australia, Sharp (1974) suggested:

it has sometimes been noted that such rediscoveries [of poverty] recur periodically. The clear implication is that the object of discovery has no neutrally independent existence, but has a good deal to do with ethical and social imperatives that find expression through the eye of the observer . . . At least initially the emphasis [here] is on why it is being observed and how it comes about that what was previously hidden can be discovered or rediscovered now.

Sharp then posed the question we need to revisit:

[W]hy should we assume that 'the truth' of the existence of poverty is any less ambiguous than the earlier assumption that it 'was no longer with us'? (Sharp 1974: 194)

The question Sharp posed then is as acute and relevant now as it was then. If it is legitimate to inquire into the distribution of income and the processes that produce 'poverty', along with the methods for doing this, it is equally legitimate to inquire into the social processes involved in this research and 'discovery' process, and their consequent impact on policy development.

● THE POVERTY WARS

The 'poverty wars' got underway late in 2001, following the release of a major report on the extent of poverty in Australia by the Smith Family. It was authored by Professor Ann Harding, the director of NATSEM—an economic modelling unit at the University of Canberra. Professor Peter Saunders of the Centre for Independent Studies (CIS), a Sydney-based neo-conservative think-tank, subsequently launched a blistering attack on this report. The subsequent 'poverty wars' have set the CIS, its journal *Policy*, and Peter Saunders (a former Professor of Sociology in the United Kingdom and the social policy spokesperson for the CIS) against some of the academic researchers.

The dispute was apparently about the extent of poverty in Australia, which Harding had used a computer model to estimate. Saunders at CIS claimed that this had produced an excessive estimate of the numbers of people living in poverty. Since then, there have been exchanges of fire as Saunders at CIS criticised various reports about 'poverty' by welfare organisations like St Vincent de Paul or the 2004 Senate report on poverty.

It would be fair to say that the CIS and spokespeople like Saunders (and Andrew Norton, the CIS spokesperson on education) promote an array of pro-'enterprise' and pro-'liberty' ideas common to the worldwide network of neo-conservative think-tanks whose history has been so well charted by Richard Cockett (1995). The neo-conservatives have a huge vested interest in promoting poverty research and talking up the idea of 'the poor'. As Saunders indicates in his *Kicking the Welfare Habit* (2004), he wants nothing less than the dismantling of the 'welfare state'.

In this strategy, 'the poor' and 'poverty' take on a key role. To neo-cons, 'the poor' are welfare dependants. This is because the welfare state gives people money for doing nothing. They are a burden to the taxpayer and a persistent source of moral and criminal depravity and economic inefficiency. In this respect, not much has changed since the late eighteenth century, when early liberal economists and self-avowed 'reformers' like Jeremy Bentham, James Mill and Edwin Chadwick condemned the effects on the poor of public income support.

Naturally Saunders will not concede that the pro-market directions taken by national economic policy since the early 1980s have promoted any increase in the extent of poverty. Hence his animus against the welfare lobby's view that poverty has become worse over the last few decades.

The protagonists on the other side in the 'poverty wars' are no less committed to talking about 'poverty' and 'the poor'. They include key welfare organisations like the Smith Family, the Brotherhood of St Lawrence and St Vincent de Paul, along with a number of academics employed in university research centres like the Social Policy Research Centre (SPRC) and NATSEM. The SPRC is headed up—confusingly—by another Professor Peter Saunders. (This Saunders is a widely published welfare economist who has assiduously promoted the value of doing research on poverty since the mid-1980s.) NATSEM, as already mentioned, is headed up by Professor Ann Harding, another leading welfare economist and specialist in economic modelling.

These players too have a clear interest in promoting 'poverty research' as part of their advocacy for more research (and research funding), and an increase in the scale of social policy expenditure. Both have an interest in promoting the discovery of 'poverty' and in documenting any alleged increase in its extent. After all, the welfare organisations are in the business of charity. As university research centres, groups like SPRC and NATSEM have long earned their keep by doing research for governments and welfare organisations on issues like poverty.

Among welfarists, there is no single agreed account of 'the poor'. They are most typically positioned as 'victims' of various 'structures', as people about whom negative moral judgments ought not be made, and as people on whom community resources ought properly to be expended. As William Ryan (1975) pointed out some decades ago, the general tendency among welfarists is also to identify a wide array of personal and social deficits (like inadequate education, lack of power, 'dysfunctional family life' or drug and alcohol use) as an explanation for why 'the poor' are poor. This is done as a prelude to defining professional solutions and programs that will fix the deficit. This is what Ryan calls 'blaming the victim'.

As Mitchell Dean (1991: 203) points out, we can only begin thinking well about poverty if we start by rejecting the empiricist assumption that: 'discursive entities such as "poverty", "pauperism", "the poor" and the laboring poor can only be analyzed by their degree of adequacy to the . . . reality of poverty'. Yet this is precisely what poverty researchers like Saunders of the SPRC and Saunders of the CIS are trying to do. The protagonists on both sides believe the debate can both be engaged and resolved only by empirical research involving some kind of counting or measuring exercise. The 'poverty wars' are being fought by people who each assume that it is possible by some means to establish the accuracy of their preferred 'measures' of poverty.

The issue of what an adequate or inadequate income is or should be involves both empirical and ethical dimensions. Adequacy is an evaluative idea. Establishing who is living an adequate or good life requires more clarity about what this ought to mean in both our own immediate society and in a global context. As we discuss in Chapter 20, global warming is a fact—2005 was the hottest year on record. The kind of discussion the Australian community should be having will need to address the intersection of economic, ecological and ethical values, and will need both political leadership and an informed community.

Assuming that poverty is real or measurable is not a useful starting point. Endless numbers of poverty researchers have insisted, as Peter Saunders (of the SPRC) does, that: 'The idea of poverty as a situation where people cannot meet their basic needs is enduring' (Saunders 2005: 6). Yet this idea leads only to fundamental confusion for two reasons.

First, for social science and government research on things like poverty, unemployment or the crime rate to take place, someone has first to define and measure them. Only by doing this can we 'discover' the evidence or benchmarks that enable us then to go on and say who is 'poor', how many 'unemployed' there are, or whether the 'crime rate' has gone up. It is no good saying that 'reality' will help us to determine what evidence or criteria we can use to discover poverty; if this was so, there would never be any need to discover anything. Rather, we need to take our intuition that there is something called 'poverty' and constitute it by defining it. So the fact that we rely on categories and on social scientific techniques to know about, 'invent' and 'discover' things like poverty needs to be accompanied by a lot of careful thinking.

The second basic problem is that there is currently no agreement about what 'basic needs' are, or how many people are unable to satisfy them. Saunders the welfarist is actually unable to say anything simple or clear about the 'basic needs' that are not being met. He is therefore unable to say who 'the poor' are, what 'poverty' looks like or how its extent might be measured.

● CONCLUSION

There are many ways in which inequality is experienced and constructed. In this chapter, we have focused on some of the economic dimensions of inequality to do with patterns of wealth and poverty. We have stressed the value of being thoughtful and careful, both about how we define economic inequality and how we go about getting credible evidence. The variety of approaches and the conclusions arrived at reflect some basic problems. Finding or 'discovering' good evidence when researching inequality or wealth is often difficult. In making the claim that the distribution of income and wealth is not equal, we need to observe that there are numerous difficulties involved for anyone wanting to do research on the patterns of economic inequality, leading to a need to insist on important qualifications about the evidence that is available.

There is also one very important bias at work in much of the empirical research on inequality. For too long, there has been a major preoccupation with researching poverty but almost no interest in researching wealth. We believe that this narrow preoccupation with poverty is unhelpful. Without ignoring the issue of poverty, there are broader issues about inequality which suggest that we should also be finding out more about how much wealth there is, who owns it, and how the unequal distribution of power and resources shapes people's lives.

It is perhaps not surprising that people who have the least access to valued resources like income, cultural capital and property should also suffer from being defined as deviant and as threats to society. How this happens has at least something to do with the way ideas about social order are developed and reproduced by institutions like the state and the mass media. In the next two chapters, we turn to the role of government and the media in generating images and ideas about certain groups of people and social problems.

Discussion questions

14.1 Is there an equal distribution of income and/or wealth in Australia?

14.2 How good is the evidence needed to answer these questions?

14.3 Is poverty real?

14.4 Why is there so much controversy about using the word 'poverty' or measuring it?

14.5 Why isn't the same amount of attention given to researching wealth as to researching poverty?

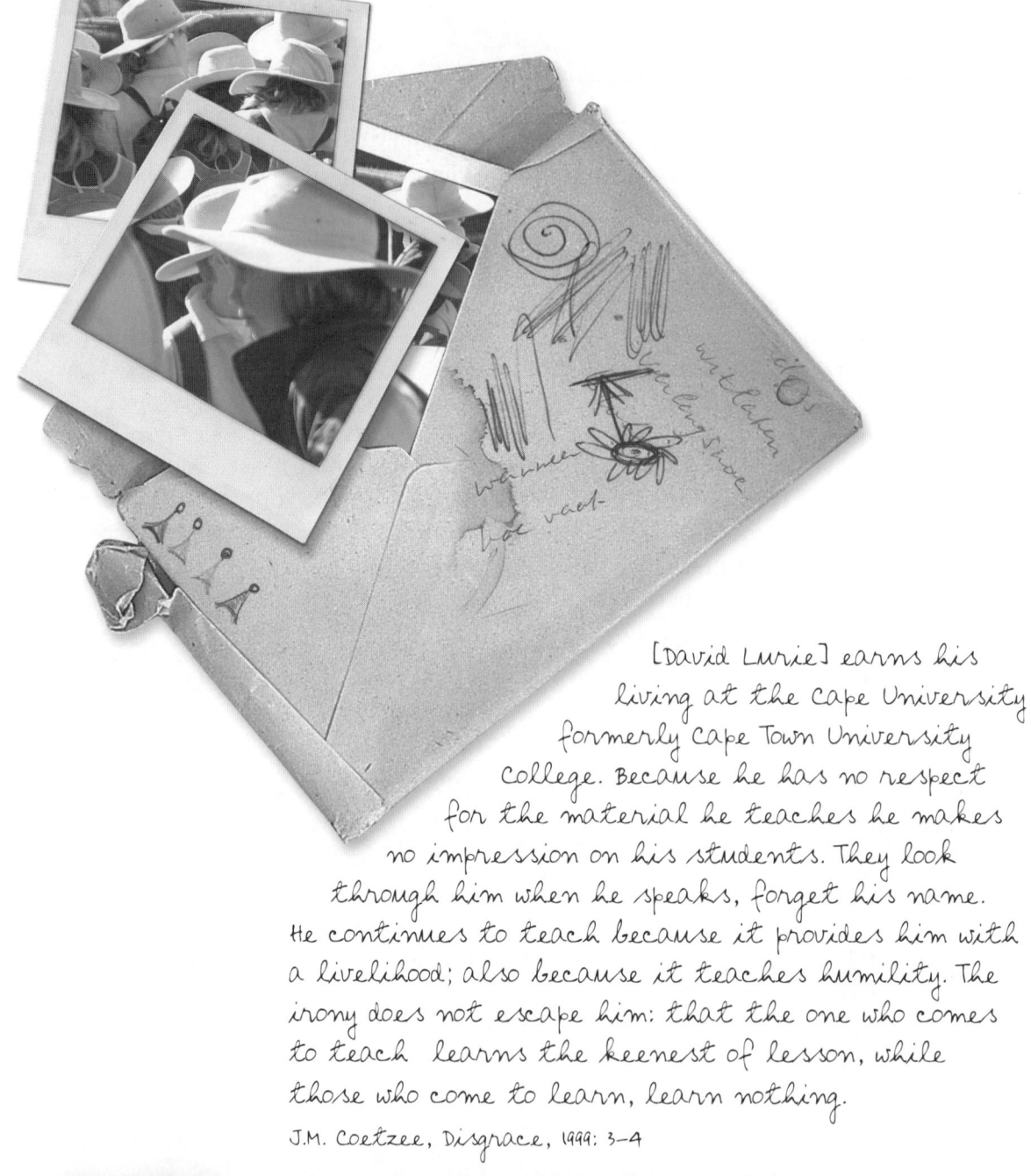

[David Lurie] earns his living at the Cape University formerly Cape Town University College. Because he has no respect for the material he teaches he makes no impression on his students. They look through him when he speaks, forget his name. He continues to teach because it provides him with a livelihood; also because it teaches humility. The irony does not escape him: that the one who comes to teach learns the keenest of lesson, while those who come to learn, learn nothing.

J.M. Coetzee, Disgrace, 1999: 3-4

15. EDUCATION IN A PERIOD OF CRISIS

• • SUMMARY

Education in a broad sense refers to all the things we learn to do inside families, households and society. In this chapter, we explore how people in countries like Australia have taken a universal social practice like education and redefined it as 'schooling'. We begin by establishing why Australians made schooling a near-universal part of the experience of children in the late nineteenth century. We then ask how sociologists have understood the evolution of modern schooling. Turning to the past few decades, we focus on the way a pervasive sense of social and economic crisis played a role in the decision to make schooling something in which the great majority of five- to 21-year-olds engage. We then consider the university sector and establish why small institutions catering to an elite have become a mass system. Finally, we reflect on the university experience of increasing numbers of students.

On weekdays in Australia's cities, suburbs or country towns, there are two moments of intense activity as masses of people clog our roads and fill buses, trains and trams. These are the times in the mornings and afternoons when around two-thirds of the entire population of Australia are on the move. There are two kinds of Australians who populate these 'peak hour' movements. One group comprises the nine million paid workers who go off to work or head home. The other group consists of the five million or so school, university and TAFE students travelling to or from their place of study.

These mass movements of people each day help to define what it means to live in a modern society. These two defining institutional arrangements give meaning and shape to our lives individually and collectively. Work and schooling are also intimately connected: schooling is understood to prepare us for work. And in terms of the themes of this part of the book, it is widely understood that work and schooling are somehow implicated in the far-reaching changes associated with globalisation. Like work, our experience of schooling has changed in often-dramatic ways over the last 30 years.

Education involves the acquisition of all kinds of knowledge, values and skills. It is a process that occurs naturally in any society or community. Education is a lifelong process occurring inside all the social relationships and activities to which we are exposed from the moment of our birth. Inside families and households, we learn to smile, eat, walk, control our bladders and bowels, throw a ball or play with a toy, put on clothes and talk. In this broad sense, education refers to all the things we learn to do inside families, households, on streets and in offices, where we have encounters with other people. Emile Durkheim, one of the key figures in early sociology, suggested that education is another way of talking about what later sociologists called socialisation.

The fact that people in countries like Australia have taken a universal social process like education and redefined it as 'schooling' may seem normal, but when we think about it, it starts to seem a little odd. The governments of modern societies decided over a century ago that education would best be provided universally through institutions called schools.

In this chapter, we ask some simple questions:

- Why did Australians make schooling a near-universal part of the experience of children in the late 1800s?
- How have sociologists understood the evolution of modern schooling?
- Why was schooling extended in the last decades of the twentieth century to include the majority of five- to 21-year-olds?
- Why have universities—once small, elite institutions—become a 'mass system'?
- Has the system of mass schooling changed the experience of being young and, if so, how?

● WHY COMPULSORY SCHOOLING?

In Australia, school attendance is now compulsory for all children aged between six and fifteen. The fact of legal compulsion, as well as the widespread cultural acceptance of schooling, are the reasons why some 3 343 900 children and young people were in primary or secondary schools in 2004–05 (ABS 2006c).

The fact that mass compulsory schooling is now such a normal part of our lives has led us to take it for granted. One advantage of thinking sociologically is that it helps to sustain and inform a sense of 'legitimate strangeness' about many of our everyday activities—like schooling. Why did this practice come about? Why do societies like ours believe it is good to place people in schools and formal educational institutions for their whole childhood and most of their life as a young person?

No less interesting is the modern belief that enrolment in some form of education or training should be as long as it is—to at least Year 12 and into post-secondary institutions. Although arguments to extend the time spent by young people in school are not new, the idea that they stay until age eighteen only started being taken seriously in the 1980s. More recently, we have heard calls to keep as many young people in universities and TAFE colleges as we can for as long as possible.

We have now entered the age of mass post-compulsory education. Around 900 000 people were enrolled in universities in 2006, while another 1.2 million students were enrolled in Technical and Further Education (TAFE) or Vocational and Educational and training (VET) colleges. This means that over five million people—or more than in one in four of all Australians—are enrolled in schools, universities and TAFE colleges. (A significant number of older Australians are also involved in Council of Adult Education courses and/or the University of the Third Age programs.) In short, Australians seem to have enthusiastically embraced the proposition that mass education for all children and young people, at least to age 21, is a good idea.

We know that mass compulsory schooling is a quite recent policy innovation dating back to the 1870s. So why was mass compulsory schooling introduced?

• WHY WAS MASS COMPULSORY SCHOOLING INTRODUCED?

Beginning with New South Wales and Victoria in the early 1870s, most of Australia's colonial governments introduced the principle of 'free, compulsory and secular' education. By passing Education Acts, these governments made it compulsory for children between five and twelve to attend a school.

There are two aspects of this policy innovation, one signifying acceptance of the idea that schooling was a good in itself, the other that the state should provide public schooling to all those who were not in some form of 'private' (i.e. religious) school. By the 1870s, there was widespread acceptance of the idea that schooling was good and that the defining characteristic of any modern society was widespread literacy and numeracy. This had not always been the case, however.

Until the seventeenth century, English schooling was only undertaken by the land-owning and commercial elites. There were only a few schools attended by a small proportion of the young people who were of school age. Most school students were members of upper- and middle-class families. (In the United Kingdom, there was one key exception: in 1697, Scotland made it legally obligatory that all children attend some kind of church-run school.) As Miller (1998) shows, this differed markedly from the commitment of northern European societies like the German states and Sweden to schooling: in Sweden, universal literacy had been achieved by the end of the eighteenth century (Miller 1998: 48).

Schooling then was generally understood as being less about giving people skills or knowledge and more about 'moulding character'. Governments did not build or staff schools. Most grammar schools were church-run schools providing an education in Greek and Latin as well as basic reading, writing and counting. Elite families also employed private tutors for their children. For those interested in trades like textiles, printing, carpentry, jewellery-making or surgery, a variety of craft skills were available to young people using a master–apprentice model.

Until the nineteenth century, the three universities in the United Kingdom (Oxford, Cambridge and Edinburgh) were religious institutions open to very small numbers of students, including children as young as eleven or twelve. From their inception in the twelfth century, universities taught languages, philosophy and mathematics in preparation either for life as a gentleman or for careers in the church, the law or medicine. From the sixteenth century, universities added the higher sciences like physics, astronomy and mathematics.

One of the consequences of the eighteenth century Age of Enlightenment was a belief cultivated among the increasingly numerous professions and commercial elites that schooling was a good thing. Inevitably, as ideas like the democratic notion that all citizens had a role to play in government won adherents, pressure mounted to include more and more children in the schooling process. In his *The Wealth of Nations* (1991), Adam Smith simply assumed that schooling in reading, writing and arithmetic was a fundamental characteristic of any 'civil society'. In 1839, even conservatives like the cultural commentator Thomas Carlyle declared that the fundamental task of schooling was to humanise: a man not educated was a man mutilated, as he put it.

The big issue in the nineteenth century was not whether schooling was a valuable activity, but who should pay for it, and how much of a role governments should play in requiring that all citizens receive a minimum level of education. Underneath the debate about the respective role of 'church' and 'state' was another about the extent to which the principle of democratic access by all was to be squared with the privileges of the elites. However, the determination of the various social and economic elites to ensure that their privileges were not compromised by any democratisation of schooling was never in doubt, as the history of schooling into our time has proved.

By the nineteenth century, Britain had a voluntary hybrid system consisting of private secular schools funded by pupils' fees that taught the '3Rs', religiously endowed 'public' (i.e. private) schools like Eton and Harrow to educate the elites, and a smattering of government-provided schools for everyone else. Efforts to introduce a principle of compulsion in Britain were rejected until the 1870s. Across the English Channel, things had been different for a long time: by the 1840s, governments in the German states (beginning with Prussia in 1763), Spain, France, Denmark, Holland and Switzerland had assumed responsibility for ensuring that all children received at least a primary education.

Through the nineteenth century, the Australian colonies emulated Britain, establishing their own hybrid systems with governments trying to regulate schooling through various kinds of government-run educational bureaucracies. The various colonial governments provided capital to build schools as well as subsidies to private secular and religious schools to pay teachers, encouraging the various churches to establish their own schools and establishing a state-run service to meet the needs of the lower orders.

In Victoria, when the government established its Board of Education in 1862, there were around 460 church-run schools and 187 state-run schools with enrolments of about 33 000 children—with an average enrolment of 55 children per school. By 1871 there were 107 000 children in Victorian schools, which was considerably less than half of the school-age population in that colony (Blake 1973: 168–78). Endless criticism shadowed the work of this board as costs rose dramatically through the 1860s.

The Higginbotham (1867) Royal Commission of 1867 showed that, of the 170 000 school-age children in Victoria, only 76 000 were getting any kind of regular schooling. Commissioner Higginbotham concluded that the system was 'scandalously ineffective, inefficient, and a waste of money' (Higginbotham 1867: 8). He also drew attention to the endless religious squabbling between the various churches, which was hindering a unified approach to the problem. It was due to religious opposition to the principle of universal education that liberal sponsorship of legislation for free, compulsory, secular education in Victoria was unsuccessful in 1867.

A variety of arguments were mounted in favour of the principle that all children should be required to spend a minimum number of years getting an education. One was the liberal appeal to the idea that education was such a powerful good that the state must ensure it was available to all. By the 1860s and 1870s, it had become an article of faith among the increasingly confident professional and liberal middle classes, as well as among working-class Australians, that everyone had a right to attend schools provided by the public purse. In 1850, John Ruskin summed up the arguments of many liberals:

> I hold it for indisputable that the first duty of the State is to see that every child shall be well housed, clothed, fed and educated till it attain years of discretion. But in order to do this, the Government must have an authority over the people of which we do not so much as dream. (Ruskin 1850: 117)

Other liberals, like J.S. Mill, had no trouble arguing for state intervention to secure the principle of compulsion: 'education is such a great human good that no one should choose not to be educated'. Indeed, by appealing to the old liberal idea that the churches should stay out of political processes—based on the doctrine of the separation of church and state—liberals could claim that the state could and must take control of education. In such a schooling system children would receive an education that was secular—that is, not religiously based. It was also increasingly becoming accepted that such attendance ought to be compulsory.

Closely linked to the liberal faith in schooling was the argument for modernity. By the 1870s there was a popular fear that too many young Australians were missing out on a basic education because of what was believed to be a haphazard and unsystematic system of schooling. The implication of this argument was that Australians needed to keep up with the latest modern trends, especially given what was perceived to be an increasingly competitive international context.

The idea that schooling provided a guarantee of social order was another key argument. Fear of disorder was closely linked to the fear of middle-class spokesmen that social order was threatened by a wave of crime bubbling up from an 'underclass' of poor and working-class people.

Central to the push for compulsory schooling was the trend to make childhood into a period of enforced economic and social dependency (Aries 1973). On the one hand, this meant the passage of laws outlawing certain kinds of child labour. Successive waves of reform legislation were implemented for the purpose of excluding children from the factories and mines, and to keep them off the streets. This movement of pro-childhood industrial reform would eventually capture most Australian children by increasingly restricting their access to the formal labour market. On the other hand, the reforming child-savers understood that it would not do to simply allow large numbers of children to lead unsupervised, unregulated and disorderly lives. Schooling would bring children into spaces where they would be regulated by adults.

Popular assumptions about the inherently troubled and troublesome character of young people confirmed in the minds of many that they could never be 'left to their own devices'. By the 1860s and early 1870s, there was also special concern about the growth in the numbers of poor and/or delinquent children. One central argument of educational reformers and liberal politicians leading up to the introduction of the compulsory education legislation in the 1870s was that education promised to prevent or at least arrest the otherwise unfettered growth of an 'urban criminal class' by instilling into students the virtues of being a law-abiding, hard-working citizen (Bessant 1987).

After an unsuccessful attempt in 1867 to introduce the principle of 'free compulsory and secular' education, the Victorian government successfully introduced legislation embracing this principle in 1872—again despite vehement opposition from the churches. (Successful passage of similar legislation in New South Wales in 1871 may have helped the Victorian advocates of the legislation.) The act established a Ministry of Education to provide for a system of legally compulsory attendance by all children at schools either run by the churches, or in the new state schools whose teachers were to be paid by the government and subject to regular inspection. The act applied to all children aged between five and fifteen, who were required to attend for a minimum of 60 days each six months. Parents who failed to send their children were liable to fines. The state schools were to provide only secular education.

Compulsory state schooling started in the heady days of the 1870s when the colonies enjoyed economic boom conditions. It was a time of prosperity and optimism, and it was not unusual to see schools popping up all over the countryside to cater for city and bush children alike. Teachers were trained in a rudimentary fashion and sent off to rural and metropolitan Australia. On the face of it, the legislation saw an immediate and dramatic increase in school attendance: by 1876, attendance in Victoria had risen from 144 049 (in 1872) to 231 560. Yet, as historians of education have pointed out, the introduction of this legislation was the start of a long struggle by the education system—including governments, the education bureaucracy and the burgeoning army of related experts including teachers and social scientists—to convert the idea of compulsory education into a reality by normalising schooling and the regulation of children's lives it entailed (Miller 1986).

In the cities and in rural Australia, many working-class families initially resisted the compulsory aspect of education. Many saw little practical value in having their children learn to read, write or do arithmetic. Many parents opposed the practice of sending their children to school because their children's labour contributed to the household income, and in many cases was crucial for the survival of the family. Conditions in country Australia from the late 1870s into the 1940s were hard and, for all family members, working just to survive was a necessity.

Children's labour was often depended on for maintaining the family economy. Carrying buckets of water for bathing, making beds, washing the floors, laundry and cooking were all part of their duties, and hard work must have affected school performance. Child labour was highly valued during sheep shearing, or fruit and vegetable picking seasons.

Paradoxically, legislation intended to ensure all young people 'had a childhood' had the effect of adding to an already heavy workload. Farm life for children meant many chores. Despite the attractive stories about Australia as a rural paradise, a good many of the young people living on the land experienced unremitting toil. Many children on the land continued to work as well as attending school. On the farm, this involved collecting the eggs and the morning's wood, milking cows, shovelling manure-laden yards and cleaning separator sheds. Daniel Herbert, who grew up in Victoria during the 1920s, recalled his typical day as a boy, which usually began at 5.45 a.m., summer and winter alike. It was only after he'd completed a list of jobs that he was sent off to school, 7 miles (11 kilometres) away, on his bike. On return from school, another list of chores awaited him. Older girls were valuable domestic workers in large families with few labour-saving devices. Girls also performed an important child-care role, looking after younger siblings on market and washing days or relieving their mother when she was pregnant with another baby. For girls, domestic work was expected at an early age when they were 'old enough to start pulling their own weight'. Girls often took responsibility for the younger children in the family at a very early age.

This was also true for children employed in the many factories in the inner cities, whose earnings often made the difference between being evicted and the family having a house over their heads. For many children, the new education legislation simply meant a double shift.

Yet the long-term effects of the introduction of compulsory schooling have been crucial to reshaping the contours of social experience, especially for succeeding generations of children and young people. So how have sociologists understood the evolution of modern schooling?

• SOCIOLOGISTS AND MODERN SCHOOLING

Social sciences like sociology have always been a central part of the processes they have tried either to understand or to explain. The development of sociology, for example, was part of the process in which the spread of reason and institutions like schooling were seen to define the modernisation of society.

As Pierre Bourdieu (1999) reminds us, the social sciences were part of the processes used by governments to investigate and then regulate people in modern nation-states. The poor, 'delinquent' children, criminals, schoolchildren, reformers, sexual and other deviants, the unemployed, factory workers, women and rural workers have all been thoroughly researched. Institutions like governments, schools, armies and advertising agencies came to see the social sciences as useful to their interest in discovering who and what was 'normal', and what could be done for those who were not. The development by psychologists like Francis Galton and Karl Pearson of powerful statistical tools like regression and correlation analysis, and their use by empirical sociologists in large social surveys, confirmed the practical value of the social sciences in the twentieth century.

One foundational figure in the development of modern sociology, Emile Durkheim, was deeply committed to the sociology of education and to promoting the role of the modern professions. In the twentieth century, sociologists from Talcott Parsons (1951) and Robert K. Merton (1967) to Jeffrey Alexander (1988) and James Coleman (1961) confirmed Durkheim's view that schooling was one of the central social institutions in any modern social order.

The functionalist and neo-functionalist traditions in sociology saw the introduction of mass compulsory schooling in entirely favourable terms. It was seen as a sign of the evolutionary and progressive transformation of pre-modern societies into modern rational societies marked out by the progressive consolidation of scientific and technological knowledge and training.

In the tradition of structural functionalist sociology, schooling was identified as one of the central institutions charged with reproducing both the ideas and practices that define any culture and the socially functional norms so vital to social order. This was its 'social control' function. Schooling was seen as a key site of secondary socialisation that would ensure the moral values or social norms that were indispensable for social order would be inculcated into the members of that society (Bessant & Spaul 1976).

Schooling was also treated as an institutional answer to the problem of how to ensure that the natural aptitudes and talents of individuals were synchronised with the functional needs of society. Schooling filled a vital role in ensuring that society's need for the right kinds of vocational skills were identified and met, thereby ensuring that the increasingly complex administrative, scientific and technological skills needed by modern economies and governments were available.

As many sociologists have argued, schooling played a role in ensuring that socially functional inequalities were normalised. Modern societies needed highly trained and educated professionals who had to forgo many years of the kinds of paid employment open to lower order occupations who needed fewer years of training.

In the 1970s, social inequality and poverty were 'rediscovered' in many societies, including Australia. In Australia, empirical research by Henderson et al. (1970) and Roper (1970) provided evidence of substantial economic inequality and the need for more public investment in schooling to advance what was called 'equality of opportunity'. Education became a highly politicised issue. Governments and many educationists argued that more access to schools and universities would create a more equitable and democratic society.

Equal opportunity strategies included increased public investment in schools and the opening up of universities as part of a larger project aimed at promoting social justice. Giving all children the chance to finish high school and go to university, rather than such a choice only being the preserve of those who could afford it, was one reason why in 1973–74 the Whitlam Labor government abolished university fees, introduced a system of income support for tertiary students and began pumping money into both public and private schools.

Ironically, feminists and Marxists of various kinds initiated a critique of the role of schools in reproducing basic kinds of inequalities. And, just as ironically, the commitment to public investment in schools and universities was suddenly reversed after 1975 in Australia courtesy of arguments that big government was ruining the economy (Bessant 1988a: 19–32, 1988b).

The radical critique of schools as institutions devoted to the reproduction of social inequality gathered pace through the 1970s. Far from being politically and culturally functional institutions, schools were held responsible for condemning large numbers of working-class people and/or women to low-income jobs. For writers like Bowles and Gintis (1976), the division of knowledge and learning into discrete subjects and disciplines pointed to some of the invisible ways schools became sites for legitimating and reproducing a class- and gender-based division of labour that characterised the capitalist political economy.

Training students to assume adult worker identities, far from enhancing equality of opportunity by offering people the opportunity for meritocratic advancement, actually reproduced the kinds of attitudes and skills functional to the reproduction of capitalist and patriarchal social relations (Miller & Davey 1990). This critical scholarship focused on both the formal and 'hidden' curriculum. In effect, the 'working class' were duped into believing that schools were about democracy and meritocracy when the system was actually designed to reproduce economic and social inequality and to further disadvantage those already being disadvantaged. Early feminist research (Mercer 1975) suggested that schools were primary sites of 'sex role socialisation', working to confirm the subordinate role of women by constraining girls through explicit curriculum practices as well as less visible kinds of educational processes to a narrow range of women's roles and occupations.

In the 1970s and 1980s, other writers expanded on this line of argument, pointing to the many complex ways that class and gender 'structures' reproduced persistent kinds of social inequality. The English neo-Marxist Paul Willis (1981) built on earlier Marxist insights while rejecting what he argued were overly simplified and deterministic accounts of the role played by schools.

According to Willis, the schooling system disadvantaged working-class students not only because their 'working-class culture' meant an absence of 'cultural capital' and thus opportunities for academic success, but because they could not decode the language and other cultural symbols. Rather than complying by going along with what were seen as pseudo-meritocratic competitions in school, they refused. That resistance took the form of youth cultures and counter-school cultures. Thus students' or young people's collective actions, music, politics and styles came to be seen as evidence of a resistance to class hegemony.

Willis's research paralleled the work of writers like Bernstein (1971), Bourdieu and Passeron (1977), Spender (1980) and Giroux (1981), who likewise focused on the role of language and the reproduction of what they 'cultural capital'—practices like reading books, playing musical instruments, going to art galleries and overseas travel. According to these writers, children from more affluent homes were likely to acquire this 'cultural capital' courtesy of their home and school lives, while children from lower socioeconomic backgrounds were not. As Dale Spender (1980, 1982) showed, young women were caught in a more invidious linguistic trap in which invisible patriarchal language games and categories reproduced masculine power.

In Australia, educationists like R.W. Connell drew on this tradition and focused on the idea of education as a form of 'symbolic violence'. This meant, as Connell et al. (1982) argued, that children in Australia's middle-class families came to the experience of schooling already equipped with certain expectations, values, attitudes and ways of talking, which assisted them to meet the challenges of exposure to academic cultures in school and university, and so helped to guarantee their success (Connell 1987). While he saw value in the idea of cultural capital, Connell was careful not to identify students simply as the passive recipients of cultural capital, emphasising the student's capacity to negotiate and renegotiate their relationships with families and between their families and schools (Connell et al. 1982). Connell's work encouraged an opening up of these arguments about education and class to include consideration of other identity markers like sexuality, gender, masculinity and ethnicity (Connell 1989: 291–303; Connell 2000; see also Kenway et al. 1998).

While neo-Marxist critiques of the schooling system continued to be produced in the 1980s and 1990s (e.g. Walker 1986; Poynting 1996), this critical tradition largely ceased to play any major role in shaping public discussion or policy-making after 1980. Issues of gender and ethnicity have had a more visible effect on Australian schools. This is evident in curriculum design and education policy-making, as teachers and bureaucrats acknowledged the need to promote gender equity, prevent sexual harassment and bullying, or ensure greater sensitivity to issues of ethnicity in a multicultural framework. However, these policy initiatives were forced to take a back seat as policy-makers rethought education policy.

In the 1960s and 1970s, education was popularly seen as an institution that had the capacity to create a more inclusive and equal society. By the late 1970s, however, policy-makers stopped worrying about using schools as an instrument to create a more equal society and started to worry about linking school and work. The most significant feature of education policy over the past 25 years has been a move to sweep up more and more young people aged fifteen to 21 into formal educational processes. The result has been a real change in the way schooling works.

• MASS POST-COMPULSORY EDUCATION IN A PERIOD OF CRISIS

The last 30 years have persistently been portrayed as a time of crisis (Mishra 1984; Hobsbawn 1994). It was a time characterised by a number of national and international economic recessions, which generated significant unemployment and under-employment. One common way of talking about this shift was to talk about the move from a Fordist capitalist system based on mass production industrial manufacturing and mass advertising to a post-Fordist capitalism shaped by the rise of knowledge, service and information industries. It was a time when the assumption that persistent economic growth was both practicable and desirable came under critical scrutiny. It was also a time when the Keynesian welfare state was given a major overhaul as part of a much larger process of restructuring. The development of Australian education during this period has been driven by a concern that schooling must address the basic national interest and economic needs.

In this context, the idea that schooling had an instrumental and vocational value became even more popular. Governments, employers and 'public opinion' increasingly treated schools and universities as places that prepared people for work and helped define the national economy. New kinds of education were said to be needed to provide for the 'new economy' and to help people fit into the new world of work. This was also a time when Australian politicians and policy-makers rediscovered the virtues of 'economic liberalism', while neo-conservative lobby groups argued for a 'back-to-basics' educational framework.

This changing context had major implications for the education system and for students and their families. From the mid-1970s, policy-makers began to rethink what they thought young people needed as they struggled to connect schooling and wage work (Mizen 2004: 23).

In 1974–75, Australians confronted their first major experience of economic recession and unemployment since 1939. The increasing youth unemployment rate was one of the first signs of trouble (Baird et al. 1981). Growing youth unemployment compounded anxiety about young people posing a threat to the social order. In this debate, schools were held responsible for all kinds of social, economic and moral problems.

Politicians were particularly concerned about the visibility of jobless youth, and what that might mean at election time. The undesirability of having too many young people excluded from the full-time workforce was reiterated by a chorus of experts and community organisations. Added to this was the reaction from school leavers and their families disillusioned by the impact of deteriorating employment opportunities on school leavers and their families.

Worse, large-scale and prolonged unemployment came to be seen as negating the lessons of schooling, producing a 'counter-work culture'—even an 'underclass' (Freeman 1980). According to experts and commentators alike, large-scale youth unemployment threatened a critical 'rite of passage' which all young people needed to face: the shift into the workforce.

This 'transitional opportunity' was no longer available to increasing numbers of school leavers. Instead, as one observer noted, the new circumstances meant that: 'these young people [were] running the streets, staying at home, taking drugs and getting into all sorts of mischief . . . we need a form of control' (Freeman 1980: 40).

Drawing on a mix of developmental psychology and functionalist sociology, 'good' discipline and a moral education were seen to equal effective socialisation—as a necessary, but allegedly largely absent, pre-condition for social cohesion. Gone was general support for the idea that a well-funded state education system was worthwhile because it would deliver opportunities to working-class children. There were many critics prepared to declare that the 'excessive freedom' allegedly rife in Australian schools was leading to a cohort of self-indulgent children prone to acts of anti-social behaviour (e.g. Kramer 1975: 5 & 12).

In the eyes of some critics, we were in the midst of a widespread trend towards 'soft option' subjects and a consequent decline in academic rigour. The lack of discipline allegedly contributed to the growth of 'permissiveness' and 'individual indulgence' (*ACES Review* 1976: 7). More specifically, a lack of respect for authority and the absence of self-discipline were held up as key reasons for social disorder and crisis (*Australian*, 6–7 February 1982). One group of conservative critics, who called themselves the Australian Council for Educational Standards, were quite vocal about 'declining values and principles', arguing that: 'Students are blatantly poaching on the most doubtful of adult preserves—tobacco, alcohol, drugs, sex—and committing all manner of offences . . . Who is to blame for this state of affairs? I believe it is the responsibility of those who have charge . . . [teachers]' (*ACES Review* 1976: 7). However, the concern with moral decline was to give way to a concern that schools were simply failing to be sufficiently practical and vocational.

● POLICY RESPONSES

By the 1980s, governments were alarmed as high youth unemployment rates showed no signs of abating. Through the 1980s and early 1990s, anxious governments commissioned reports like the Kirby Report (1985), the Blackburn Report (1985), the Finn Report (1991), the Carmichael Report (1992) and the Mayer Report (1992). These reports, together with numerous policy and academic debates in the 1980s and 1990s, played a major role in reframing educational policy—and the experience of many young people.

Schools were simultaneously treated as responsible for a full range of social and economic problems, and also as having a powerful and almost magical capacity to lift the nation out of the economic doldrums and produce a robust, internationally competitive economy. In such a context, talk about making Australia into the 'clever country', building a 'knowledge economy' and investing in 'human capital' provided a set of enduring and useful metaphors for policy-makers.

Both state and federal governments came increasingly to accept the value of human capital theory. By treating education as the 'engine room for economic recovery' and an institution that solved a variety of social problems—from unemployment to 'students at risk'—the virtues of investing in education became apparent. 'Human capital' is a popular idea that invites us to see people—or more specifically students—as commodities or objects, and education as an investment. Value is added to the commodity (the person) once certain knowledge or skills are added. 'Human capital' is a way of thinking and talking about education that became common in the late part of the twentieth century and that remains popular into the twenty-first (Marginson 1993: 31).

According to proponents of human capital theory, education adds value to both the individual and the community, and a relationship also exists between investment in education and the strength of the national economy. Human capital has been a very persuasive and effective metaphor because it refers to relationships between expenditure on higher education and increased national income or economic growth. These arguments have been deployed in a range of official reports to persuade government to fund particular kinds of education and training.

Correlations were drawn between the GDP and levels of education retention rates in countries such as Japan, Germany and the United States, which made Australia's performance look dismal in comparison. Such cross-national comparisons, combined with a perceived causal relationship between education levels and growth in GDP or employment, were motivating forces behind the move to extend and improve the quality of schools and universities.

Arguments about how education was critical for securing social order, and the dangers associated with students leaving school 'early', also played their part in these policy discussions. Young people who did not complete their schooling put themselves and society 'at risk'. Implicit in policies designed to keep students in education longer was the simple premise that they lacked certain employment-related skills and attributes (like a strong work ethic or high-quality literacy). Little was ever said about the possibility that the increases in joblessness may have been related to the absence of employment opportunities.

The way in which the 'problem' was described had a big influence on what was seen to be the 'solution'. If the problem was that too many people left school too early, then the solution must be to increase retention rates. By the 1980s, a plethora of policies—all directed towards increasing school participation rates—were being developed across Australia. Typical of those policies was the Victorian government's 1985 Blackburn Report, which argued for a ten-year plan designed to lift Year 12 'participation' rates to 70 per cent by 1995. It also argued that total enrolments in tertiary and TAFE education could be doubled (Blackburn 1985).

The consequences of such policy-making are now easy to see. All Australian children and young people between the ages of five and fifteen attend school. However, as Teese and Poleset (2003: 188–210) observe, this does not mean that significant inequalities have now been eradicated. Schools teaching young people from low socioeconomic status families continue to struggle against low levels of public funding to develop high-quality, motivating curricula. Many of those students continue to fail to complete their schooling or slide into low-paid, low-skill jobs. Equally, students from advantaged backgrounds go to well-resourced, highly motivating private and public schools and tend to go on to university and high-skill, high-income occupations.

In 2006, around two million Australians are also engaged in post-secondary education in universities or TAFE colleges. Abilities like reading, writing and numeracy are now considered vital for all adults/citizens. Moreover, governments and taxpayers spend a staggering amount of money to provide what is now defined as a vital aspect of public policy.

● EXPANDING POST-SECONDARY EDUCATION

Until the early 1970s, Australian universities were small, elite institutions catering to white, primarily male, affluent students. In 1946, Australia had a small university system with just eight universities and a total of just over 17 000 university students—or 2.3 per cent of the population aged seventeen to 22. By the 1960s, the Menzies Coalition government had sponsored a substantial increase in university enrolments. The student population had increased by 500 per cent to 91 000 by 1966, representing 7.8 per cent of the seventeen to 22 age cohort (Little 1970: 3).

It has only been over the last two to three decades that Australians have embraced a mass tertiary education system. As we mentioned above, there was much talk in the early 1970s about policies designed to promote 'equality of opportunity', which was then an important part of the ALP's identity and political commitments. Most policy-makers saw higher education as an investment in building a more egalitarian society. In 1974, the Whitlam government abolished university fees and expanded the provision of tertiary education, beginning what was to become a mass higher education system. In effect, the Whitlam government began to turn the system into what it is today.

Another Labor government (1983–92), led by Bob Hawke, sponsored further dramatic increases in the scale of university education. Between 1975 and 1996, the number of Australians in higher education rose from 273 137 to 631 025. By 2000, there were around 679 000 tertiary students and by 2004 this number had grown to 900 000. In terms of the participation rate in higher education, Australia—which in 1975 was in the lowest quarter of OECD states—had moved into the top quarter of OECD states by the twenty-first century.

One important change in thinking accompanied this big increase in student numbers, however. While the Whitlam government used taxpayer dollars to fund its expansion of tertiary education, the Hawke government reintroduced a partial system of student fees to fund the expansion of university places. In 1989, the then Minister for Education, John Dawkins

(1987–91), reintroduced a system of fees and paved the way for an incremental increase in student 'contributions'. The Hawke government's policy statements made it clear that the reintroduction of fees was aimed at opening up universities to even more students by helping to fund an expansion in student numbers. This expansion also involved merging the many Colleges of Advanced Education (set up in the 1960s to provide vocational education) with universities.

Since 1996–97, the Howard government has continued to reduce the level of public funding of universities while driving a further increase in student numbers.

On the one hand, growth in university enrolments has depended on students paying more for their tertiary education. Today, the majority of Australian university students pay a part of the cost of their education. This is a legacy of the Hawke government's promotion of the 'user pays' principle. This is done via what the Hawke government in 1988–89 called the Higher Education Contribution Scheme (HECS). It involves charging a student for part of the tuition costs of their degree, and then requires payment of those fees when the student has completed their degree. (The payment is collected via the income tax system.)

Public funding of universities has declined. By 1999, public funding of our universities consumed just 0.8 per cent of Australia's GDP. Only three countries in the OECD spent less of the public dollar on education than Australia: Japan, Korea and Luxembourg. By 2004, this has declined even further to just 0.6 per cent of GDP.

This has exacerbated the already considerable problems universities face in terms of maintaining the quality of teaching. The Howard government justified this policy move by talking up the capacity of universities to provide quality education, research and community outreach work while developing alternative revenue bases like full-fee-paying students. This has accompanied a major redefinition in policy terms of the university, in which the official talk is now of an 'enterprise university' (B. Bessant 1986, 1995; Considine & Marginson 2000). The Howard government has systematically ridiculed talk of crisis within universities—a concern that was given considerable public airing in a major Senate Report (Senate Employment Workplace Relations Small Business and Education Committee 2002).

• A UNIVERSITY SYSTEM IN CRISIS?

Australia now has the elements of a genuinely mass university system. As with any complex process of change, there are as many ways of narrating the change as there are interests and discursive traditions. One has been to talk about the 'globalisation of education' (Currie & Newson 1998). Another has been to talk about the birth of the modern 'enterprise university' (B. Bessant 1986, 1995; Considine & Marginson 2000) and the importance of universities in achieving national goals like building a 'knowledge economy'.

Talking about universities in these ways has tempted some academic commentators to talk about the recent shift to mass tertiary education in terms of 'decline', 'collapse', and the 'ruin' of the 'traditional' or liberal arts university. Alan Barcan (1994) provides a typical story of the death of the 'liberal university'. He blames egalitarianism, the subversion of the liberal idea of a community of scholars by Marxists, feminists and 'progressives', and the conversion of the former Colleges of Advanced Education into universities. Others, like Tony Coady (2000), bemoan the effect on universities of the language of 'markets and customers, quality assurance and a plethora of accountability mechanisms', leading to the idea that the task of tertiary training is to grind out 'graduates' at a certain rate for consumption by society. Raimond Gaita (1999) has likewise condemned the treatment of universities as a 'public service':

> More vocationally oriented courses determine the ways in which people speak of what's valuable in universities. And whether in one country it takes the form of business speak or whether in another country it takes the form of managerial newspeak, the fact is that in both places universities are turned into institutions which are meant to service something or other.

'Real universities', according to conservative critics like Coady or Gaita, should not have large numbers of students in them—nor should they offer degrees in practical or vocational areas such as nursing, teaching/education, architecture or social work. 'Real universities' are places where small numbers of intellectually gifted students are taught by scholars.

Part of the difficulty with these conservative accounts lies in their reliance on overly narrow ideas of 'the practical' on the one hand and the values of the liberal arts tradition on the other. Universities in Europe, from their origins in the eleventh century, had always engaged in vocational education and training—initially of doctors, priests and lawyers.

Although we might be critical of the modern conservative stories of the 'death of the university', there are many serious problems in Australian higher education that are not receiving the kind of practical attention they deserve. Some concern the need to work with far larger numbers of students that have enrolled in the universities over the last decade. This leads too many academics—most of whom have never been equipped with professional teacher training—to privilege the lecture model. The economically driven need to fall back on large lecture classes exposes the inadequacy of a traditional and crass pedagogy of knowledge transmission. Large classes have also meant increasing reliance on untrained and unqualified sessional teachers, who work alongside full-time academic teachers.

Another problem is the way modern university students are introduced to core intellectual abilities like reading, thinking and writing (Ramsden 1992). Many university teachers fail to engage in a solid and persistent exercise in showing new students what these activities look like, and how students can engage in them.

Bourdieu (1996: 6, 11) also described the normal, if lamentable, long-standing absence of reflexivity by too many university teachers:

The whole system of education as a particular historical structure finds expression in the communication which takes place between teachers and students. Misunderstanding and the fiction that there is no misunderstanding, are inseparable phenomena.

● THE CHANGING STUDENT EXPERIENCE

Increased education retention in the post-compulsory years and reduced access to the full-time labour market have had a major impact on young people's lives, including their incomes and their capacity to live independently. Over 30 years ago, in a study of the university experience, Graham Little (1970) made no reference to the need of university students to work for an income. Today, most students work part-time while they study full-time. Although any assessment of student/youth incomes has always been a difficult task, the effect of junior award rates has traditionally been to place young employees well below the 'poverty line'. The youth wage, which makes it lawful to discriminate against certain young people by paying them less than others for the same work, is one reason why many students have low incomes. Another is the precarious nature of the casual work that is now available.

Income from paid work—or from social security benefits—provides a measure of economic security and makes it possible for some students to have relative independence and a standard of living that sustains them through their studies. However, many young people who cannot get enough work, who are not able to draw on parental support and who are ineligible for the youth allowance live in relative poverty.

For many university students, the combination of paid work and the demands of university courses also creates new kinds of tensions and pressures. An increasing number of students need to earn an income by working longer and longer hours (Bessant 2003; McInnis et al. 2000b; Long & Hayden 2001). According to McInnis et al. (2000a), 26 per cent of first-year students reported part-time or casual employment as their main source of income in 1994. By 1999, that figure had increased to 37 per cent. The proportion of students working for eleven hours or more in paid employment rose from 40 per cent in 1994 to just over half of the study's respondents in 1999. McInnis et al. (2000a) observed a pattern of less attachments and commitment to university life and study on the part of students working long hours in paid employment. Long and Hayden reported similar findings that students work fifteen hours a week on average, with 70 per cent of full-time undergraduates employed during semester, and 87 per cent of part-time undergraduates working during semester (Long & Hayden 2001).

The increase in the number of 'working students' confirms what most academics already know. The phenomenon of part-time study combined with part-time or full-time work raises a range of issues for universities. It means less time for both formal study and extra-curricula activities, while the problem of student poverty has a direct impact not only on students' health, well-being and education, but also affects the fiscal viability of some campus services and facilities.

The nature of students' employment has a variable impact on their capacity to study. For students with regular secure work, planning class attendance and regular study arrangements was not a problem, but for those reliant on insecure work, the capacity to plan and attend regular tutorials, lectures or simply to be on campus at set times was extremely difficult.

The financial and work pressures mentioned above are also exacerbated by the increasing costs associated with being a university student. Increased fees and the push to encourage more and more students to pay full fees is having a big impact on the experience of university students.

● CONCLUSION

The introduction of mass compulsory schooling does not mean that other, more 'natural', kinds of education have been displaced. If anything, children and young people today are exposed to more educational complexity than any previous generations:

- Children and young people continue to be educated in household settings and their various communities.
- Increasingly, children and young people experience time in child-care centres, kindergartens, schools, TAFE colleges and universities.
- They are exposed to ideas, images and sounds provided by modern mass media: many children and young people will have seen more hours of television by the time they are twelve than they will spend in classrooms across their lifetime. In 2005, the ABS estimated that the 'average' child or young person was watching 22 hours of TV per fortnight.

The past few decades have been widely understood in terms of a pervasive crisis affecting the economy, the political process and society. The mid-1970s have typically been seen as a watershed marking a point when a number of key institutions changed. Full-time secure employment for all became a thing of the past, youth unemployment levels increased, and we witnessed a series of global economic recessions. This is to say nothing of the impact of accelerating technological changes on our social lives.

From the 1980s, we saw the steady extension of educational institutions, making formal education a near-universal part of the experience of all young people between five and 21, and increasingly affecting the lives of older Australians as well.

Discussion questions

15.1 How can we best understand the introduction of compulsory schooling for all?

15.2 How have changes to the economy, the labour market and family relations influenced education policy and the experience of being a student?

15.3 What happened in the mid-1970s, and how did it help shape the future of education in Australia?

15.4 What do social scientists and educationists mean when they talk about the 'corporatisation of education' or 'the enterprise university'?

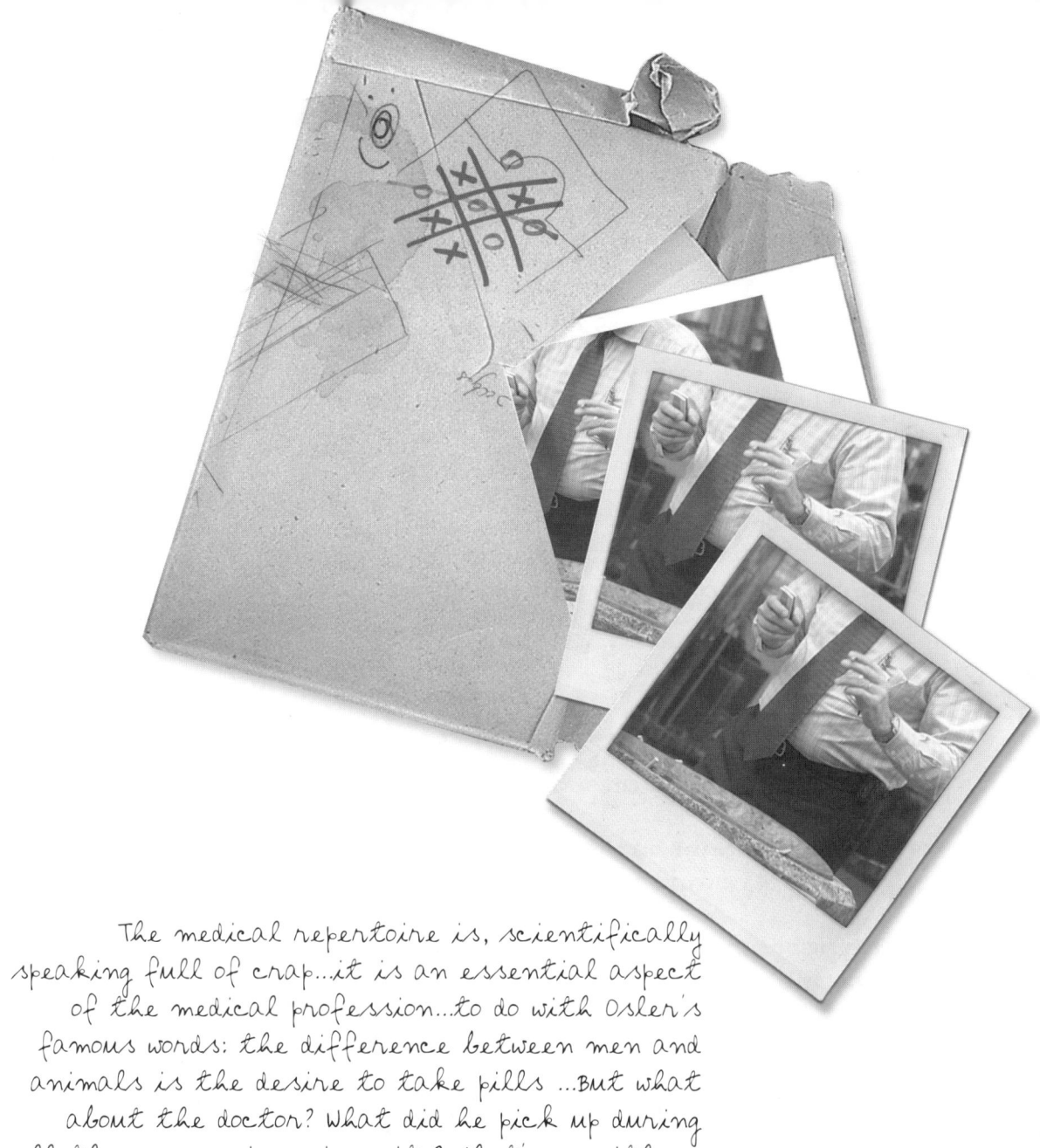

The medical repertoire is, scientifically speaking full of crap...it is an essential aspect of the medical profession...to do with Osler's famous words: the difference between men and animals is the desire to take pills ...But what about the doctor? What did he pick up during all those years in university? What's up with us doctors to prescribe all this useless shit?

Bert Keizer, Dancing with Doctor Death (1996: 67–8)

HEALTH AND ILLNESS IN AN UNEQUAL SOCIETY 16.

• • SUMMARY

By and large—especially when we make comparisons with other societies or explore the history of illness and diseases—we can readily agree that Australia is a 'healthy' society. Yet what does 'health' mean? Is it simply defined as the absence of illness? How much of what happens to a person's body is the result of purely biological factors like exposure to viruses and germs, and how much is a consequence of social relationships and cultural practices like diet and exercise? As we show here, the health of a person or an entire community involves an intricate overlapping of both biological and social processes.

In the early seventeenth century, the great philosopher and mathematician Blaise Pascal said our 'life in common' was lived out as if we were all prisoners in a chain-gang working as punishment in a salt mine. We are all manacled together and each day we see at least one of our fellows killed in front of us! If there is one aspect of our life that should remind us of the point of Blaise Pascal's famously bleak metaphor about the human condition, it is that we all live in and with a body that will one day give out on us.

Most of us treat this experience as an intensely individual and 'subjective' one. However, as sociologists from Brian Turner (1984) to Kevin White (2000) have insisted, while we may well experience sickness and illness as individuals and blame bad genes, germs, or a wicked lifestyle, there are powerful social processes that work *on* and *in* our bodies. This goes to both the ways we live in and use our bodies and to the social consequences of living in an unequal society.

This reference to our world reminds us that, in one sense, those of us who live in Australia enjoy comparatively good health:

- The average life expectancy for Australian men born in 2005 is now 78 years and for women 83 years—amongst the highest in the world (ABS 2005c: 6).
- Australia's infant mortality rate (at just under five infant deaths per 1000 live births) was among the lowest in the world in 2005.
- When asked to report on their health status, 85 per cent of Australians over the age of fifteen reported that they were in 'excellent health' (AIHW 2005a).

Australia is one of the 30 or so advanced societies collectively enjoying excellent health. We have no experience of the terrifying effects of scourge epidemics like HIV or tuberculosis, which have infected tens of millions of poor black Africans in countries like Kenya, South Africa or Tanzania. We have no experience of what is now routine in sub-Saharan Africa, where a minimum of 10 000 infants and children die each day from lack of food or simple gastro-enteritic diseases. In India, some ten million female foetuses were aborted in the decade up to 2005, reflecting a combination of widespread poverty and the cultural value put on males in that society. The social determinants of health and illness are no less obvious when we shrink the focus back to Australia (see box).

Facts about health and illness in Australia

- In 2005, Australia spent over $62 billion on its health services. There are approximately 2.5 physicians for every 1000 Australians, compared with 2.1 physicians per 1000 Canadians and 2.7 per 1000 Americans.

- The very affluence, level of public health expenditure and availability of new life-enhancing medical technologies now extend our average life expectancy; however, they also expose us to the risk of dying of diseases of the aged.

- This is why many Australians live under the shadow of the knowledge that they are likely to get a cancer. (It seems that one in three Australians will contract a form of cancer, and of those one in three will die from it.) Australians continue to experience and die from heart disease. Together, cancer, heart disease and stroke are the leading causes of death: the death rate per 1000 of population in 2004 was 183 for cancer, 130 for heart disease and 62 for stroke. Lung cancer continues to be the major cause of death from cancer (ABS 2005c).

- These statistics are closely connected to the Australian age profile of our society. Both cancer and heart disease are in some sense largely the diseases of an ageing population. It is now widely accepted that heart disease and vascular disease reflect patterns of diet, and of alcohol and tobacco consumption. Apropos the stereotypical image of 'the Australian' as a bronzed life-saver, the reality is that by the age of twenty, most young Australian men have stopped playing sport or exercising; the largest and fittest cohort of Australians are young women aged between twenty and 35, who are playing netball or attending aerobics classes.

- There is emerging evidence that those Muslim women who go into public spaces wearing a veil are at risk of developing osteoporosis, a condition which can partly be accounted for in terms of vitamin D deficiency. Vitamin D is largely derived from exposure to sunlight.

In effect, while biological factors such as genetic inheritance or bacterial and viral infections are at work in any experience of illness or health, there are also basic social and cultural factors involved as communities construct particular cultures of consumption, tell stories about our bodies and what is valuable about them, define some things as important health issues, and shape certain kinds of public health policies accordingly. The French feminist Simone de Beauvoir (1953: 69) put this point well when she argued that, as a social theorist, her interest was not in 'the body object as described by biologists that actually exists, but the body as lived in by the subject'.

Social patterns of inequality also impact on our experience of health and illness. We know that not all Australians enjoy the same kind of health:

- Aboriginal Australians still die earlier and in larger numbers than the rest of the population; the average life expectancy for Aboriginal people in 2005 was twenty years lower than for the white population, while infant mortality is five times higher for Aboriginal babies born in remote and regional areas in Australia.
- Even in the big coastal cities like Melbourne and Sydney, living in low-income areas is strongly connected to the fact that 'working-class' people seem to have a life expectancy up to ten years lower than people living in high-income areas (*Age*, 18 January 2001).

In the context of our discussion of contemporary forms of social inequality, data like these serve to remind us, as Greig et al. (2003: 39) put it, that: 'While an individual's health is played out as a "subjective" experience of their own body, the experience itself is a product of social inequalities that inscribe disease on the body.'

In the remainder of this chapter, we want to explore some of the social dimensions of health and sickness via some simple questions:

- To what extent are 'the body' and our experience of illness social matters?
- How do we know about health and illness?
- What do we know about the patterns of health and illness in Australia?
- Do patterns of social inequality affect our experience of health and illness and, if so, how?

THE BODY AS SOCIAL

It is important to remember that to be human is to be 'embodied'. This acknowledges first that there is an undoubted biological, or 'natural', aspect to living in a certain kind of body. Being tall or short, thin or fat, or male or female is determined to a considerable extent by genetic factors. Likewise, it acknowledges that our experience of illness owes a lot to biological factors like bacteria and viruses.

Equally, there is a highly significant social dimension to our embodied nature. We do things to and with our bodies that reflect the relationships we have with other people: we learn to swim or dance, to line up in queues, to apply tattoos or to circumcise male and female genitals, where and when we can have sex with each other, and the kinds of foods it is 'good' to eat.

It has taken sociologists quite some time to acknowledge our embodied nature. Indeed, it is fair to suggest that it has only been in the last 25 years or so that mainstream sociologists have acknowledged that being human entails being embodied. Work by Brian Turner (1984, 1996) is conventionally used to mark the onset of the modern interest in the body by sociologists. Turner's work was made possible in part because important work had been done prior to this time, much of it by people other than sociologists.

In the 1920s, French anthropologist Marcel Mauss (1985) theorised the way societies everywhere 'socialised' the body. By this he meant such practices as using tattoos, costumes and ritual to adorn the body, the ways communities seek to regulate the body through activities like marching, and how we learn to do new kinds of things with our bodies, such as learning to swim. Mauss seems to anticipate Foucault's work on governing the body when he identifies the varieties of regulation of our bodies as 'techniques of the body'. Likewise anticipating the work of Bourdieu, Mauss writes of the way the development of specific ways of using one's body is part of the development of a socialised 'second nature' he calls *habitus*—a process he believes is vital to the maintenance of social order.

In the 1930s, the great historian Norbert Elias (1978, 1984) wrote a large-scale psycho-social history of the 'civilising process' in Europe across the last one thousand years. Elias began with the slightly bizarre idea that 'pre-civilised' Europeans lived as pre-social creatures giving free rein to their emotions, and behaving in egotistical, greedy and violent ways. Elias set about showing how a culture of 'politeness' found in various dynastic courts provided a framework for regulating everyday life by setting up new social norms. His point was that the ways we now do these things with our bodies, and which we take so much for granted, was once a product of social learning. Written in German and published in Switzerland in 1940, Elias's work was largely unknown in the Anglo-American world until the 1970s.

In the 1940s, the feminist philosopher Simone de Beauvoir (1953) explored the way the social power and interests of men played a central role in shaping the sexual and bodily experiences of women whom she called the 'second sex'. Accepting the subordinate status of women as a social fact, de Beauvoir maintained that women's unequal social status had little to do with the alleged biological 'facts' traditionally employed to show that women were naturally inferior to men in terms of their intellectual, artistic or economic capacity. Rather, she argued, men pursued their interest in having women meet men's needs by living out certain roles (e.g. as wives and mothers) by suggesting women's subordinate capacity was legitimate because it was simply fulfilling women's 'biological destiny'. Her argument that female sexuality had little to do with hormones or genes, and much more to do with men positioning women as passive objects of desire, was just one of several shocking aspects of de Beauvoir's book. No less shocking was her claim that women played up to these expectations by accepting as 'natural' their role as passive objects of active male sexual desire. Years after her book appeared in France, her work became widely known in the English-speaking world as it was adopted by the feminist movement.

Into the 1970s and 1980s, people like the anthropologist Mary Douglas (1973) continued to explore the core idea that our bodies were as much social phenomena as they were biological matters. Douglas argues that the 'biological body' is shaped by the 'social body' so as to reflect, in mirror-like fashion, the dominant concerns of our culture. As Douglas (1973: 93) puts it:

> The social body constrains the way the physical body is perceived. The physical experience of the body, always modified by the social categories through which it is known, sustains a particular view of society. There is a continual interchange between the two kinds of bodily experience so that each reinforces the category of the other.

Douglas shows how all societies have constructed a clearcut distinction between what is 'pure'—and acceptable—and what is 'dirty'—and unacceptable or immoral.

In our own time and place—one dominated by powerful and prestigious medical professions—the metaphors of bacteria and infection supply a rich code of moral meanings to our understanding of politics and illness. Under the Nazis, Jews were represented as 'bacteria' infecting the German people, something 'Doctor' Hitler would fix by appropriate medicalised processes such as 'involuntary euthanasia' (Burleigh 1994). As Susan Sontag (1989), an American cultural theorist, points out, we now experience and describe illnesses like cancer, tuberculosis and HIV-AIDS in moral terms as much as we do in 'neutral' scientific terms.

Likewise, Foucault (1977) developed the Maussian tradition in the 1970s and 1980s to reveal a whole set of 'technologies of the body', illustrating how this worked inside such modern institutions as medical clinics and schools. Via his studies of classical Greek sexuality, Foucault showed how even sexual relations between older men and their young male lovers are codified and stringently regulated.

By the 1980s, sociologists began to develop these themes in a serious way. Some, like Armstrong (1983) and Reiger (1986), explored the impact of medical and expert knowledge on common experiences of illness or motherhood. Connell (1987) and Butler (1993) explored the social construction of sexualities. Brian Turner (1984, 1996) and Featherstone et al. (1991) showed how the body is produced socially by the organisation of society. There is now a vast sociological literature focused on the interplay of the body and a variety of social processes.

Traditional ways of thinking sociologically continue to exert an influence. The structural-functional imagination that has long helped to define mainstream sociology has developed Turner's work. Greig et al. (2003: 35) offer a typical expression of this when they argue that:

> At the broadest level societies *need their bodies* to be reproduced in a stable way, restrained in space, regulated over time and physically represented to conform to social dictates of normality. These are not individual initiatives, though it is on individual bodies that these processes are worked out, and it is by individuals that they are carried out. (emphasis added)

Our own view is a little different. As we have been at same pains to spell out in this book, we do not think sociologists assist clarity of thinking by insisting on the idea of 'society' at the level of abstraction summed up in the idea that 'societies *need their bodies* to be reproduced in a stable way'. Sociologists are better advised to pay attention to real people and the actual social relations through which we live out our lives. Real people are both constrained to act in certain ways by other people, and are able to exercise choice within the limits others allow. To acknowledge that we are embodied is also to acknowledge that our bodies are things that both constrain us and give us options.

Like the other elements of identity, living in a particular kind of body, or being well or sick or disabled, is a powerful way of being a particular kind of person. It enters into the way we conceive of ourselves and into the ways other people will relate to us (Duncan et al. 1985). Even more important is the impact our bodies and our health have on our identity. Our identity is in part shaped by embodied factors like whether we:

- are obese or too thin;
- are able-bodied or confined to a wheelchair;
- enjoy a robust workout in the gym or are dying of a terminal disease; or
- are living with a chronic illness or disability like asthma, arthritis or diabetes.

Our identity as an embodied being is not just about the unique and personal experiences of giving birth or enduring pain and dying, however. It also relates to the ways other people react to us and define us. These social factors affect things like the kinds of food we eat, the drugs and alcohol we use, the clothes we wear to particular social events, or the kinds of care or abuse to which we expose our bodies. And in a time when we increasingly rely on experts and professionals for our health care, this means others treat us with medicines, injections, massages, acupuncture or surgical interventions. In our time, even dying itself can now be a long, drawn-out affair as doctors and life-extending technologies are put to work to stave off the inevitable.

All these embodied factors have stories and social values attached to them. In our society, 'being fat' is bad, being pregnant is generally good (depending on who you are) and dying is sad. Some people with disabilities—like cerebral palsy—have historically been treated as hopelessly stupid and confined to some 'back ward' of a hospital, while blindness attracted some curious social responses. Even now, there is debate about whether babies identified in the womb as having Down Syndrome ought to be aborted.

Our bodies and the experiences we have of them are lived out in particular kinds of social relationships, largely with our families and friends. When things go wrong with our bodies, we enter into relationships with people and organisations trained to deal with our conditions—doctors, nurses, para-medical therapists, clinics and hospitals. They intervene in our lives, so it is no longer possible to separate what is personal from what is political and social.

One other reason why we do not like talking about 'society' as the source of our embodied self has to do with the fact that any society, as we have argued in the most recent chapters, is made up of groups of people who are both different *and* unequal in relation to each other. We use words like 'class', 'gender', 'age' and 'ethnicity' to describe some of these differences. As we have shown, these profoundly affect our identity but they are not just sources of identity. They are also involved in shaping the distribution of economic resources (including income, housing, schooling, clothing and leisure), the kinds of ideas and information available to people, and consequentially such basic life processes as the kinds of work we do, the kinds of food we eat, the kinds of suburbs we live in and the kinds of people we live with and relate to. All these matters are directly connected to our experience of health and illness. As we will see, these things all help to shape such basic facts as the length of people's lives, the kinds of illnesses people contract and how well they cope with them.

● THINKING ABOUT HEALTH AND ILLNESS

As we have stressed repeatedly throughout this book, we ought not begin with the assumption that many of the issues people in our community talk about so readily—like 'crime', 'unemployment', 'mental illness' or 'poverty'—are either simple matters to define or readily susceptible to objective knowledge. Too often it is simply taken for granted that when people— especially medical experts—talk about 'health' or problems like cancer, obesity or 'mental illness', they are referring to natural, objective and scientifically demonstrated matters. How objective are the data on 'mortality', 'morbidity' and 'health'?

To work out what we can know with some confidence about health and illness, we first need to do some hard thinking. Let us start with the simple idea of health.

● WHAT IS HEALTH?

Defining health or well-being is an unusually complex and difficult task. Most people will say they value health highly, along being part of a happy family and being loved. Yet what people say and what they do can be very different. For example, in Australia women go to doctors much more frequently than men. This is especially so when they go as mothers. This may explain why 'macho' men die earlier from undiagnosed and untreated conditions than women. Then there is the lack of connection between what people say and do. For example, Armstrong et al. (2000) report that 88 per cent of Australians aged eighteen to 75 years say they believe that they could be healthier if they increased their physical activity, and 92 per cent believe their state of health could improve by doing 30 minutes of moderate physical activity every day. Despite this, the average amount of time spent engaged in moderate exercise has fallen in recent years. There has been a marked decrease in vigorous activity from an average of 91 minutes per person each week in 1997 to 65 minutes per person in 1999. These falls were accompanied by a 44 per cent increase in the number of overweight and obese people (Armstrong et al. 2000).

Second, it is clear that different groups of people understand quite different things by the idea of 'health'. In defining health, mothers stress the absence of illness while fathers and young people emphasise fitness and healthy lifestyles. In identifying health risks, fathers and mothers identify lifestyle and environmental factors, while young people identify the risk of contracting AIDS or a cancer far more than their parents. In general, parents were more optimistic about their children's health than were young people. Seventy-five per cent of mothers and 80 per cent of fathers said their children enjoyed 'good health', while only 30 per cent of girls and 40 per cent of boys claimed to be healthy. Fathers, for example, thought their sons were healthy in spite of serious sporting injuries or chronic allergies (Brannen et al. 1994: 74–7).

Third, people may well believe that they are healthy when this is not actually the case. In one recent health survey, 83 per cent of Australians reported being in 'excellent health'. Yet this belief is not supported by the evidence. For example, large numbers of Australians live with crippling chronic diseases like asthma and arthritis. Asthma has become a major health problem. As many as two million Australians are thought to have the condition, and 19 per cent of them are young people aged between five and fourteen. Many Australians suffer from chronic back pain and headaches. Doctors prescribe a vast number (in excess of seven million) prescriptions for anti-depressants—among the highest rate in the world in 2004—while Australians continue to consume mountains of the ordinary painkillers and headache pills available in supermarkets.

● THE EXPERT VIEW

Expert knowledge plays a major role in our culture. For the better part of half a century, experts and officials have emphasised a 'positive' or normative view of health. The World Health Organisation (WHO), for example, defines health as a state of complete physical, mental and social well-being, and not just as the absence of disease or injury.

One consequence of expert dominance in the task of defining and measuring health or illness has been a privileging of individualistic and biologically determinist views of what causes illness (Brannen et al. 1994: 67). This approach involves holding individuals or communities responsible for changing their attitudes and practices. It also means that the ways people see health or various social practices that impact on health are generally ignored in favour of expert views about what issues are important and relevant. Dominant representations of particular health problems (e.g. AIDS and sexually transmitted diseases) has meant that other health issues important to certain groups become invisible (Emslie 1997). For example, it is clear that young gay and lesbian people suffer from a high level of physical bullying and emotional harassment, yet this issue is rarely acknowledged as a major health issue.

This does not mean that all the experts insist 'being well' can only be defined by the physical well-being of the individual. There are plenty of other experts who insist that well-being refers to the emotional, social and psychological well-being of not only the particular person, but the whole community. For instance, the idea of 'health promotion' targets community-based health involving strategies that emphasise what are seen as 'links' between social status and health (VicHealth 1999–2002).

Modern professionals like Richardson and Prior (2005) argue that the term 'healthy children' means children and their families are 'functioning normally'; that they are well looked after, protected from abuse, injury, premature death and illness; that they have access to appropriate health services; and that they enjoy the opportunity to develop to their full potential. It also requires that there are supportive social, psychological, economic and structural factors in the community which promote good health.

While we may well think this list of elements is eminently defensible, there are problems with this approach. For instance, Boss et al. (1995: 97) suggest that 'healthiness' is all about ensuring the 'normal functioning' of children and families. What does 'normal functioning' mean here? Why do experts like Richardson and Prior (2005) and Boss et al. include in their approach to young people's 'health' notions like 'emotional disturbance', 'risky behaviour', 'lack of emotional stability' or 'persistent immature behaviour' as issues of concern? Discussion about the 'new morbidities of youth' may also be another excuse to draw attention to adult fixations about young people as 'youth at risk'.

How realistic is it to assume that, to be healthy, children must have access to supportive social, psychological, economic and structural factors in the community which promote good health? For the better part of two decades, local and national governments in Australia have systematically reduced the level of public investment on child care, public education, public hospitals and community and psychiatric health services. There is widespread recognition that many of these services are now in crisis.

When experts argue for a wider, more inclusive view of what well-being looks like, they use an array of technical measures and 'scientific' data to make their claims appear authoritative. Yet many of the claims made by experts about what defines 'health' are not so much 'objective' or 'scientific' statements about what defines a person's well-being so much as morally charged assertions and assumptions.

This does not mean we should reject all the expert discussion and research about health, well-being or illness. In the following discussions, we take the view that research evidence on mortality (death) and morbidity (sickness and disability) offers some useful clues about the general health of Australians. But we need to ask who is doing the defining and counting.

● WHAT IS ILLNESS?

The World Health Organisation (WHO) distinguishes between a variety of circumstances, including:

- disease (acute or chronic);
- a disorder, injury or trauma; and
- other health-related conditions like pregnancy, ageing, stress, congenital abnormality or genetic disabilities or illnesses (WHO 1999).

Yet how do ordinary people and/or the experts know that these circumstances actually exist?

'Illness', 'sickness' and 'disability' may be thought to be a fairly 'obvious' circumstance. Being pregnant and giving birth to a baby, experiencing the symptoms of a bad head cold, or living with and perhaps dying from a terminal illness might all be thought to be a very real, natural, even objective kind of experience. Yet we know that this isn't so. Most people recognise sickness in themselves and those close to them. In most cases, being sick or having a disease is obvious because such conditions are typically accompanied by physical and emotional distress, discomfort, abnormal temperatures and high pulse rates. Sometimes, however—as in the case of diabetes, many cancers, high blood pressure or even glandular fever—it is not easy to recognise or respond to the symptoms of sickness. When the Human Immune Deficiency Virus (HIV) first made its presence felt in the early 1980s, doctors lacked a clear diagnostic set of tests and did not know how to define, let alone treat, the symptoms they were seeing.

The case of mental illness is no less tricky. We may be in the grip of some kind of emotional distress like depression or bipolar disorder and deny that the things we are experiencing add up to a diagnosis of these conditions.

We also know that many men fail to act on the basis of pains and other symptoms, preferring to suffer on in heroic silence—which is almost certainly one reason why men do not have the same life expectancy as women. Finally, there are many grey areas. One recent case has been the condition known as Chronic Fatigue Syndrome, which has only recently seen the development of a reliable clinical diagnostic test; until then, sufferers were frequently treated as neurotics.

How do governments and experts establish patterns of illness in a given community? When health experts release a report saying that 19 per cent of people aged twelve to nineteen suffer from asthma, how is this knowledge established? When a government health department announces that a group of people is at risk of contracting skin cancer or AIDS, how do they know this? They are most likely to be relying on specific kinds of either clinical or epidemiological research.

- Clinical research refers to the work done by doctors and other medical diagnosticians who examine patients or samples of their tissues or fluids, and make clinical assessments about the presence of various illnesses or conditions.
- Epidemiology is the collection, study and use of statistical research devoted to establishing what patterns of social activities and identity markers are implicated in the patterns of health and illness. Epidemiological research may draw on this clinical evidence, or it may draw on large-scale social surveys using questionnaires. In either case, it involves establishing large-scale patterns in the distribution or 'causes' of various illnesses. Epidemiologists also try to establish what aspects of a person's behaviour, lifestyles, an environmental exposure, or an inborn or inherited characteristic cause particular conditions (Last 1988).

It took decades of research to demonstrate clinically what epidemiologists had long shown statistically: that smoking cigarettes was closely linked to increased rates of lung cancer and heart disease. The revolution in genetics that has been gathering pace since the 1970s has further complicated the matter; research associated with the Human Genome Project has shown that many disabilities and illnesses have a genetic component as well as a social or environmental component.

As we have said, epidemiological research is based on one of several methods of collecting certain kinds of evidence or health data. First, there is the data routinely collected by doctors, clinics and hospitals when people present themselves for diagnosis and treatment. (Medicare, Australia's national health insurance scheme, offers a large national source of data on patterns of illness and injury.) This kind of evidence is used a lot by epidemiologists because it gives us some data about a lot of people; however, it assumes that people will take themselves off to a doctor or a hospital when they are sick. (For a useful discussion of how a range of social factors affect the collection and interpretation of all official statistics, see Miles & Irvine 1979.)

It is usually harder to define and count the rate of occurrence and the degree of mental diseases—despite the fact that the experience of depression is common for many of us. It is often difficult to say precisely when mental and emotional 'problems' are occurring.

Death is more obvious, especially as an outcome of illness or disease, though we normally require official and scientific procedures and reports from doctors, police and coroners—all of whom document and record data about who dies, why and when. Other outcomes relating to obvious bodily conditions such as giving birth are similarly easy to recognise: they produce results that are hard to ignore.

Then there are health surveys, where researchers select a sample of people and ask them to fill out a questionnaire where the person can report on a range of symptoms or experiences of illness (ABS 1991; Bowes et al. 1996). This may pick up trends or experiences not otherwise noticed, but again it depends on people reporting accurately.

• AN OVERVIEW OF HEALTH IN AUSTRALIA

In the eyes of many, being healthy is synonymous with being 'an Aussie', but what is the reality? One way of establishing how healthy/unwell we are is to consider how much money is spent on health services and how rapidly that investment has grown.

Table 16.1 Total health expenditure and rate of growth

| | Expenditure | | Rate of growth | |
| | Current prices(a) | Chain volume measures(b) | Current prices | Chain volume measures(b) |
	$m	$m	%	%
1992–93	35 098	44 764	n.a.	n.a.
1993–94	36 990	46 080	5.4	2.9
1994–95	39 216	47 733	6.0	3.6
1995–96	42 082	49 688	7.3	4.1
1996–97	45 296	52 182	7.6	5.0
1997–98	48 274	54 131	6.6	3.7
1998–99	51 726	56 785	7.2	4.9
1999–2000	55 427	59 435	7.2	4.7
2000–01	61 660	63 812	11.2	7.4
2001–02	66 541	66 541	7.9	4.3
2002–03(c)	72 183	69 306	8.5	4.2

(a) Comprises allocated recurrent expenditure, unallocated recurrent expenditure, capital expenditure/outlays and capital consumption. (b) Reference year is 2001–02. (c) Preliminary estimates.

Source: AIHW 2004.

Does this tell us how healthy we are? As Table 16.2 suggests, in terms of the usual indicators of health like life expectancy and mortality rates Australia is a modern healthy society.

• LIFE EXPECTANCY

Most Australians now enjoy a high average standard of health. This is using two standard measures, one of which is life expectancy. This is the estimate of how long a person born in a given year will live. The other measure is the infant mortality rate. Both measures have kept improving over the past century.

The average life expectancy for Australian men born in 2005 is now 78 years, and for women it is 84 years. These rates are amongst the highest in the world (ABS 2005c: 6). To put

Table 16.2 Key indicators of Australian health, 1988–98

Health status	Unit	1988	1989	1990	1991	1992	1993	1994	1995	1996	1997	1998
Life expectancy												
Male life expectancy at birth	Years	73.1	73.3	73.9	74.4	74.5	75.0	75.0	75.0	75.2	75.6	75.9
Female life expectancy at birth	Years	79.5	79.6	80.1	80.4	80.4	80.9	80.9	80.8	81.1	81.3	81.5
Male life expectancy at 65	Years	14.8	14.7	15.2	14.4	15.4	15.7	15.7	15.7	15.8	16.1	16.3
Female life expectancy at 65	Years	18.7	18.7	19.0	19.1	19.2	19.5	19.7	19.5	19.6	19.8	20.0
Male disability-free life expectancy at birth	Years	58.4	n.a.	n.a.	n.a.	n.a.	58.4	n.a.	n.a.	n.a.	n.a.	57.5
Female disability-free life expectancy at birth	Years	63.4	n.a.	n.a.	n.a.	n.a.	64.2	n.a.	n.a.	n.a.	n.a.	63.3
Mortality												
Total number of deaths	'000	19.9	124.2	120.1	119.1	123.7	121.6	126.7	125.1	128.7	129.4	127.2
Crude death rate (per 1000)	Rate	7.2	7.4	7.0	6.9	7.1	6.9	7.1	6.9	7.0	7.0	6.8
Standardised death rate (per 1000 population)	Rate	7.5	7.6	7.2	6.9	6.9	6.6	6.7	6.5	6.4	6.2	6.0
Infant mortality rate (per 1000 live birth)	Rate	8.7	8.0	8.2	7.1	7.0	6.1	5.9	5.7	5.8	5.3	5.0
Perinatal mortality rate (per 1000 live births and foetal deaths combined)	Rate	11.6	11.0	11.3	10.6	10.7	9.2	9.1	9.4	10.0	9.2	8.3
Disability												
Disability with specific restriction (per 1000 popn)	Per cent	13.6	n.a.	n.a.	n.a.	n.a.	13.6	n.a.	n.a.	n.a.	n.a.	16.1

Source: ABS (2000a: 58).

this in historical perspective, the life expectancy of white Australian men in 1886 was only around 48 years, and for women it was around 52 years. Achieving the Biblical 'three score and ten' (70 year) norm was something we had to wait for until the 1960s.

The rate at which babies die after birth is the other key indicator of the health status of a population. We should remember that, for most of human history, babies and small children comprised the group most vulnerable to a wide range of ordinary infectious diseases, including measles, diphtheria, typhoid, influenza and cholera. The Roman Empire had an infant mortality rate of one in two children before the age of one year.

Australia, like most other modern societies, has solved the problems of premature death and very high rates of infant mortality (see box).

Infant mortality rates in Australia

- In 1908, children under four years of age accounted for a quarter of all Australian deaths.

- In 2005, children under four accounted for only 1 per cent of all deaths (AIHW 2000a).

- Australia in 1950 had an infant (i.e. under twelve months) mortality rate of 24 deaths per 1000 live births.

Premature death and chronic illnesses occur chiefly because of exposure to chronic diseases like cholera and typhoid, which are spread by contaminated water supplies and poor sanitation— often in combination with malnutrition.

Contrary to popular belief, the great achievement of the nineteenth century was not scientific medicine—which developed new surgical procedures relying on new anaesthetic and antiseptic techniques. Infinitely more important were the efforts of governments to introduce public health measures designed to provide clean water to households and to get rid of the mountains of faeces produced daily in big cities. Most Australians live in large cities with assured high-quality supplies of water and modern systems for disposing of sewage. All this involves considerable government infrastructure and spending, and obviously high-density city and metropolitan communities tend to do better than those living in rural and regional Australia.

Apart from easily prevented deaths due to unclean water and inadequate sanitation, other diseases like AIDS, tuberculosis, leprosy and malaria remain major killers in the developing countries of Africa and Asia because of factors including inadequate mass vaccination programs, or a refusal to take appropriate prevention programs—like the use of condoms.

Besides the infrastructure costs of quality water and sewerage systems, how much do Australians spend on health? This indicates why, in general, Australia is a healthy society. Health service expenditure in Australia was estimated to be $50.3 billion in 1998–99. The rate of growth in 1998–99 was 5.3 per cent, the highest annual growth rate in health spending in the last decade (AIHW 2000b). The majority of this growth related to the areas of pharmaceuticals and medical services. The introduction of the Private Health Insurance Incentive Scheme and the Private Health Insurance Rebate Scheme also helped to boost Commonwealth government funding quite dramatically.

Expenditure on health services per capita (or person) in 1998–99 was $2671—an increase of $148 from 1997–98 (AIHW 2000b).

● WHAT KILLS US TODAY?

It is fairly clear that, as societies modernise, they are able to control preventable diseases, and thereby both reduce infant mortality and increase life expectancy. Ensuring that everyone has clean water and effective sanitation, and that people can buy and store nutritional food in healthy ways, are simple yet effective ways of overcoming preventable diseases that thrive when these conditions are absent. By and large, any modern society with a market capitalist economy is able to meet these conditions.

One result is that we now live longer. Precisely because of this accomplishment, we also now die from diseases and illnesses that are directly related to the increased longevity and to the way people who live in societies organise their work and life opportunities.

Today, Australians no longer die from epidemic infectious diseases. Instead, degenerative heart and vascular disease (leading to hypertension, diabetes, heart attacks and strokes) and various kinds of cancer are the major causes of death. Almost half of all deaths in 2005 were the result of cancer or heart and vascular disease. And these diseases are effectively—though not exclusively—diseases of the elderly. Of all the deaths reported in 2005:

- 27 per cent were due to cancer;
- 22 per cent were attributed to heart disease;
- 9 per cent were caused by stroke;
- 5 per cent were due to chronic lung disease; and
- 4 per cent were caused by pneumonia and influenza (AIHW 2005a).

Likewise, young people in the early twenty-first century no longer die from epidemic gastrointestinal or respiratory diseases like typhus, diptheria, whooping cough or tuberculosis— diseases from which vast numbers of young people continue to die in many so-called developing countries in Africa and Asia. Young Australians die in far smaller numbers, and do so largely as a result of external causes like car accidents, the use of illicit drugs and, to a lesser extent, suicide.

Table 16.3 provides us with a snapshot of the mortality rates to be found in Australia. It shows that a variety of cancers and heart disease are the two leading and most common causes of death.

Table 16.3 Causes of death in Australia, 1988–98 (per 100 000 population)

Causes of death	1988	1989	1990	1991	1992	1993	1994	1995	1996	1997	1998
Leading causes											
Cancer	184	183	181	181	181	180	181	177	177	171	168
Ischaemic heart disease	199	200	186	176	177	162	161	151	145	138	128
Stroke	99	78	72	69	67	65	67	63	61	56	53
Selected cancers											
Male lung cancer	65	64	60	60	59	57	59	56	55	52	53
Female lung cancer	17	18	18	17	18	19	19	19	20	19	19
Female breast cancer	27	27	27	27	25	27	27	26	25	24	23
Prostate cancer	31	32	31	37	34	35	35	33	33	29	29
Skin cancer	6	6	6	7	7	7	7	7	7	6	6
Heart disease and diabetes											
Male ischaemic heart disease	271	271	237	250	235	219	216	204	196	183	171
Female ischaemic heart disease	143	145	127	136	130	117	118	109	105	101	93
Diabetes mellitus	13	13	13	13	14	14	15	14	15	14	13
Motor vehicle traffic accidents											
Male 15–24 years	55	49	42	38	31	33	30	32	32	29	27
Female 15–24 years	19	17	15	13	12	11	11	11	11	10	9
Suicide											
Male 12–24	28	24	27	27	27	25	27	25	25	31	27
Female 12–24	4	3	4	6	6	4	4	6	4	1	6
AIDS-related	1	2	4	3	4	4	4	4	3	2	1

Source: ABS (2000b: 28–9).

• LIFESTYLE DISEASES OR SOCIAL INEQUALITY?

In the last few decades, it has become conventional to argue that the kinds of diseases which kill us today reflect lifestyle choices or risks. The favoured culprits include smoking tobacco, drinking alcohol, avoiding exercise, eating too much and/or eating foods with unhealthy fat sugar and salt levels, and too much exposure to the sun. Considerable time and effort have been put into epidemiological research to validate this claim. Governments have also put a lot of money and effort into health promotion campaigns designed to get us up and off the couch and out there jogging, 'slip, slop, slapping', dieting and eating healthy foods, giving up smoking and alcohol use, and so on. This might be viewed as an exercise in constructing health as a moral choice, which unfortunately some of us choose not to make.

The Australian Institute of Health and Welfare (AIHW) (2000b: 39) exemplifies this tendency when it argues that a welcome decline in heart disease in the late 1990s was a consequence of people quitting smoking and eating fewer fatty foods. (It also pointed to the development of new and improved drugs and surgical interventions.) Evidence cited suggested that five major risk factors stood out:

- smoking—the AIHW said this was responsible for 10 per cent of all disease in Australia (20 per cent of adults smoke regularly);
- physical inactivity—responsible for 7 per cent of all disease (one-third of Australians aged over fifteen do no regular exercise);
- high blood pressure—responsible for 5 per cent of all disease;
- obesity—the culprit in 4 per cent of all disease; and
- insufficient fruit and vegetables in diet—the cause of 3 per cent of all disease (AIHW 2000b, see also AIHW 2003).

Table 16.4 Exercise levels from selected risk status

	Age group (years)							
	18–24	25–34	35–44	45–54	55–64	65–74	75 and over	Total
Risk status	'000	'000	'000	'000	'000	'000	'000	'000
Exercise level								
Sedentary								
Did not exercise	377.7	721.7	911.6	800.8	586.0	430.3	486.6	4314.6
Other	26.3	19.3	41.0	27.4	*8.9	19.0	*11.7	153.6
Low	679.0	1125.5	1144.9	1026.8	662.6	442.9	289.4	5371.1
Moderate	440.3	657.6	665.5	637.9	483.2	371.9	184.4	3440.8
High	261.1	279.8	157.5	122.8	59.2	20.0	*4.1	904.6
Total	1784.3	2803.9	2920.6	2615.6	1800.0	1284.1	976.2	14 184.7

* estimate has a relative standard error of between 25 per cent and 50 per cent and should be used with caution
Source: ABS (2001).

There is enough epidemiological research to suggest that we should not reject outright such well-established links as those between tobacco use, lung cancer (and other lung disease) and heart disease. However, we think explanations offered only in terms of 'lifestyle choice' are simplistic, unless they also incorporate the role played by social inequality.

There is simply too much evidence pointing to the way social inequality intersects with so-called lifestyle risk factors to ignore the fundamental ways in which illness and health are closely linked to the unequal distribution of social and economic resources. Or, to put this more bluntly, if you are working class and/or live on less than an adequate income, you stand a far higher chance of having more illness, encountering life-threatening conditions like heart disease or cancers and/or dying earlier than people higher up the social hierarchy. (For reviews of this literature, see Fein 1995; Turrell et al. 1999; and Greig et al. 2003.)

This evidence suggests that there are major relationships between living in certain kinds of spaces (which have industrial activity and resultant pollution), doing certain kinds of work which expose workers to high risks or simply not having enough money or the kinds of information other people have. This is not to say that being fat, eating poorly, doing little if any exercise or smoking heavily do not have bad consequences. It is simply that there are more complex social relations at work in distributing the risk of illness or premature death.

There is striking evidence found in the classic studies done in Britain by Marmot (1998) and by Marmot and his colleagues (1978, 1991) which suggests that lifestyle risk factors explain key disease patterns—like heart attack and stroke—far less well than class factors. These studies also clearly scotch the myth that high-paid, high-status people work in jobs or in ways that 'cause' heart attacks and that working-class people in labouring jobs are better off in this regard: the reverse is actually the case.

Marmot's studies were carried out within England's highly stratified public service, which is characterised by major inequalities of job type, income and status. The occupational range studied embraced people in high-paid, high-status professional or managerial roles (Class 1) through to people working as unskilled labourers (Class 5). This research showed that lifestyle risk factors (exercise, smoking, blood pressure and excess weight) accounted for less than one-third of the difference in disease rates found across the five occupational classes.

The studies led Marmot to propose what he called a 'social gradient of disease' model. That is, the class or status differentials explain patterns of disease more robustly than the so-called lifestyle risk factors. For example, research on the incidence of coronary heart disease showed that lifestyle did not account for the 400 per cent difference in the rate of heart attack between those in Class 1 and those in Class 5. The so-called individual risk factors only accounted for 40 per cent of his difference.

Epidemiological research on diseases like lung cancer and other respiratory diseases clearly indicates that, while smoking is a factor, so too is class. One study of the industrial areas in the Hunter and Illawarra regions of New South Wales revealed the impact of industrial pollutants on the respiratory health of people living in Australia's old 'steel cities' (Lewis et al. 1998: 459–63). More generally, a British study by Knox and Gilman (1997) of childhood cancers and leukemias that killed some 22 000 children between 1953 and the 1980s pointed to the powerful effect of environmental factors in these deaths. The research was able to distinguish between normal rates of these cancers and the abnormally high incidence of these illnesses in heavy industrial areas. Working-class families lived in close proximity to oil and petroleum refineries, steelworks, plastics manufacturers or car manufacturers.

The poorest Australians undoubtedly experience more ill-health than do people who enjoy elite incomes, work in elite occupations or live in elite suburbs. Australians can be found living along a 'social gradient of disease' that matches the unequal distribution of economic and social resources—a distribution that has actually become worse (King 1998) over the past two decades. Turrell et al. (1999: 32) sum up this situation as follows:

> the evidence of SES and health in Australia is unequivocal: those who occupy positions at the lower end of the socio-economic hierarchy fare significantly worse in terms of their health. Specifically persons variously classified as low SES have higher mortality rates for most major causes of death, their mortality profile indicates they experience more ill-health, and their use of health care services suggests they are less likely to act to prevent disease or detect it at a symptomatic stage.

The evidence in support of this conclusion is quite clear. Much of this research relies on National Health Surveys carried out in 1992 and 1995:

- Walker and Abello's (2001) study of self-reported disease shows that people in the bottom decile of income report worse health than those in every other decile.
- For young people (aged fifteen to 24) in the bottom (quintile) of income, circulatory disease is 110 per cent higher for males compared with those in the top quintile, as is the incidence of respiratory disease (White 2002a).
- Older people (65 and over) in the lowest quintile have more diabetes (15 per cent) than those in the top quintile, more lung cancer (28 per cent for men) than those in the top quintile, and more coronary heart disease (10 per cent for men and 15 per cent for women) than do those in the top quintile. They also experience more strokes (16 per cent for men and 65 per cent for women), than do those in the top quintile (Mathers 1994).
- Blue-collar workers have far higher death rates from various diseases than do professional workers; the death rate from diabetes is 110 per cent higher; that from lung cancer is 99 per cent higher; from cardiovascular disease it is 62 per cent higher; and from pneumonia and influenza it is 206 per cent higher (Mathers 1994).

Typically, combinations of low income, unemployment and working-class occupations, and the associated geographic clustering of people in these circumstances who experience a range of environmental hazards, provide a stronger explanation of why people in these circumstances have more illness and die prematurely than trying to explain patterns of morbidity and mortality only by reference to lifestyle risk factors.

In short, health and illness are not experienced equally or randomly. This in turn is closely connected to the ways we live in unequal relationships with each other. The distribution of illness and premature death is a social process, and cannot simply be explained by people making foolish lifestyle choices. This point is borne out strikingly by the case of Australia's Aboriginal and Torres Strait Islander population.

● THE EXCEPTIONAL HEALTH STATUS OF ABORIGINAL COMMUNITIES

In a society that is unequal in terms of its distribution of income and wealth, people who live in poor economic circumstances are especially prone to different patterns of disease and illness, and in some cases do not get the kind of medical treatment they need. This is especially true of Australia's Indigenous peoples, whose health profile is reminiscent of that encountered in Third World countries.

Here the data indicate that Australia has nothing to be proud of. Our Aboriginal and Torres Strait Islander communities have an appalling record with regard to the rate of infant mortality. In 2005, despite impressive reductions, the infant mortality rate was still running at around fifteen infant deaths per 1000 live births. The average number of years an Aboriginal baby can expect to live continues to be significantly lower than for comparable white Australians.

In 2005, life expectancy for all Australians was 78.4 years for males and 83.1 years for women. In contrast, life expectancy was only 56.9 years for Aboriginal men and 61.7 years for Aboriginal women. Among Indigenous Australians, heart disease is still the dominant killer, responsible for 27 per cent of male deaths and 33 per cent of female deaths. A large social survey carried out in 2002 suggested that Indigenous people were twice as likely to rate their health as poor in comparison with non-Indigenous Australians, and were one and a half times more likely to have a long-term illness or disability than white Australians (ABS 2004).

This discussion about the intersection of a society characterised by significant social inequalities and the unequal distribution of illness points us towards the role played by modern experts and their knowledge in defining and treating medical and health problems. As we will see, the modern health professions are part of this problem.

• THE HEALTH PROFESSIONS IN AN UNEQUAL SOCIETY

Medical practitioners and associated health-care professionals now occupy a key role in defining both what counts as a legitimate health problem and who is entitled to intervene medically. As a group, medical practitioners—including general practitioners, surgeons and specialists, as well as allied professions like dentists, pharmacists and psychologists—enjoy high social status, high average incomes, have more tertiary education than most other occupations, and enjoy the legal protection of governments to maintain a monopoly control over the services they provide.

Through the twentieth century, governments have moved to provide a legal basis for determining who can operate as a doctor, nurse, pharmacist or psychologist by establishing the conditions to be met for registration and practice as a professional. This has the effect of establishing a legal monopoly over the supply of health services, and is testimony to the legal and social authority of these professions.

To practise as a health professional, several very high hurdles need to be jumped. In the case of doctors this includes entry into a recognised medical program, six or more years of study and supervised practice prior to registration. Professional associations such as the Australian Medical Association (AMA) or the Australian Psychological Association (APS) have strict rules governing things like teaching programs and admission to their professions. They are also extremely powerful lobby groups which safeguard the wages and working conditions of their members.

In 2005, Australia had some 49 500 medical practitioners, including general practitioners and specialists (AIHW 2005a: 1). This is 248 medical clinicians per 100 000 of population. This compares with countries like Canada (209.5 doctors per 100 000) and New Zealand (218.7 per 100 000). Most OECD countries are showing a continuing growth in the number of doctors.

We have said that the medical and related health professions are part of the larger problem of social inequality. This is so in a number of different ways. First, the distribution of Australia's medical and health services is far from being equal. In particular, regional and rural Australians have very poor access to medical services. This is a problem Australian governments have attempted to deal with for some time by introducing schemes and incentives intended to encourage health workers to practise in rural Australia. In 2005, fewer than 8000 medical practitioners (or only 15.6 per cent) worked in rural or remote Australia in contrast to the overall population distribution of 28.7 per cent living in rural and remote areas (AIHW 2005b: 3). It is no surprise to find that other kinds of health practitioners, like chemists, psychologists, physiotherapists, podiatrists, nurses, dentists and orthodontists, also work primarily in the large cities and their suburbs. However, it is the unequal power of the heath professions that deserves more attention.

● THE POWER OF THE HEALTH PROFESSIONS

It is fair to suggest that Australians are heavily reliant on the medical and health professions. In part, this reflects the real capacity of doctors and hospitals to ameliorate pain and suffering, hold death at bay and to produce 'cures' for many of our health problems.

Advances in medical knowledge and technologies have meant that many once life-threatening or debilitating diseases and conditions like hypertension, advanced heart disease, kidney and liver failure are now manageable, while diseases like HIV, which once posed significant threats to life, are now treatable. Health professionals make valuable contributions to our lives, and many women are now able to enjoy relatively pain-free childbirths thanks to medical intervention. There are now procedures like IVF available to overcome infertility and cochlear inplants can restore hearing to the profoundly deaf. The impact of relatively simply discoveries such as the polio vaccines and subsequent immunisation of children made a major difference to the quality of life of millions of people. Similarly, antibiotics and surgical interventions have saved the lives of numerous people who would otherwise have died from relatively simple infectious diseases and improved the quality of life for most of us. And, with the completion of the Human Genome Project and its mapping of the human genome, many more possibilities exist for the early detection and treatment of some cancers and other genetic conditions.

Yet the history of medicine is not a simple story of endless progress. In 1977, McKinlay and McKinlay estimated that the medical profession was responsible for only a 3.5 per cent reduction in the death toll from heart disease, stroke and cancer. In 1994, Bunker estimated that medical interventions had added about five years to the average lifespan of people in Western societies. This says nothing of the damage done by medical interventions (see box).

The downside of medical interventions

- Doctors throughout the modern world, from Scandinavia to the United States, compulsorily sterilised millions of men and women deemed to be 'sub-normal' or 'disabled' between 1912 and the late 1960s. This was a policy pursued by eugenicists who believed this would fix a number of 'genetic' problems in a scientifically valid way.

- The over-prescription of antibiotics—especially for use in livestock production—has seriously weakened the capacity of many older antibiotics to treat new and more resistant strains of bacteria. As a result, some hospitals now have worrying levels of highly resistant infections. There is mounting concern from toxicologists about the entry of these antibiotics into our rivers and soils.

- There is concern that some medical procedures are being used excessively. For some decades after 1950, circumcision was routinely practised on young male babies as a 'hygienic' measure. In the 1920s and 1930s, doctors in Melbourne and Sydney routinely excised the clitoris of young girls suspected of infantile masturbation. There is mounting concern about the fact that Australia now leads the world in terms of the number of caesarean births carried out.

- There are areas of medicine, like psychiatry, where the capacity to explain or understand quite basic conditions has hardly progressed in a century or more, and where, as recently as the 1940s and 1950s, psychiatrists treated certain psychoses by inserting instruments through the nose into the patient's brain to cut out a section of the frontal lobe.

It was against the backdrop of the history of medicine that, in 1974, Ivan Illich caused a furore when he claimed that the major medical problem of our time was what he called an epidemic of 'iatrogenic illness'—that is, doctor-caused illness. In this way, Illich (1975) developed an interesting critique of medical power.

Illich on medical power

Illich (1975) pointed to the statistics on procedures that went wrong, leading to disability or even death. He showed how even routine medical interventions (like a powerful antibiotic) could cause other problems (like vaginal yeast infections), requiring further medical interventions.

Illich's contribution to the debate was loud and sometimes misguided. He depended too much on ideas derived from his Catholic belief system that suffering and pain were good and were part of God's plan for us. He also misrepresented the history of childbirth, grotesquely arguing that modern medical interventions had overwhelmed the older communal practice of midwifery.

Illich nonetheless raised some serious questions about what he also called medically induced dependence—that is, the incapacity of ordinary people to manage their own health without expensive and sometimes unnecessary medical interventions. He drew attention to the paradoxes associated with, and the prices we pay for, living in what Weber called the 'iron cage of rationality', and what Giddens (1990) has suggested is the hallmark of any modern society dominated by 'symbolic tokens' and 'expert knowledge'.

Sociologists before and after Illich have had a lot to say about professionals and expert knowledge.

● SOCIOLOGISTS ON PROFESSIONALISM

The development of different professions was closely related to the growth in mainstream structural functionalist sociology, and in particular the accounts of professionalism produced by classical sociologists like Durkheim (1957), Parsons (1964) and Merton (1967), whose work constituted the conventional sociology of the professions between the 1940s and the 1970s.

Like Giddens (1990), Durkheim and Parsons saw the role of the modern professions and their knowledge as central to the emergence of 'modern societies'. Professions provided the intellectual foundations—found in their theoretical and technological knowledge base—and the ethical practices that made any 'modern society' possible. Parsons emphasised the professionals' intellectual authority, said to provide the foundations for the Enlightenment Project, therefore making science and rationality the primary source of the modern professions' authority and legitimacy.

Parsons' (1964) model of professionalism established an authoritative and dominant model for studying and defining professions. It set out to establish the criteria—or traits—that defined 'real' professions from non-professionals and para-professionals. Parsons took it for granted that there were 'authentic professions'—like medicine or the law—and that the traits which characterised these professions could then be used to establish whether other occupational groups passed the test or were simply lesser 'vocational occupations' or 'semi-professionals'—like social work, teaching or nursing.

Parsons' model relied on identifying the foundational traits and values said to define authentic professions. These included:

- a high level of altruism—putting others first;
- ethical practice, governed by a code of practice;
- the consolidation of a unique body of scientific or theoretical knowledge which defined the profession and informed practice;
- professional autonomy secured by the existence of a professional association which certified that people were eligible to be part of the profession; and
- monopoly access to a body of knowledge.

In Parsons' eyes, professionals were both intellectually and ethically superior to other occupations, and their competence, skills, knowledge and expertise were based in scientific knowledge and gained through specialist education. They were agents of rationality, logic and reason, and had a legal entitlement to practise to the exclusion of others—a right maintained through new professional associations rather than unions or guilds. Needless to say, many occupational groups have basked in the esteem which Parsons' model seemed to accord them. Using this 'trait model', doctors and dentists could claim that they were professionals, while nurses and 'ancillary staff' were merely 'para-professionals'.

In Australia, the popularity of the 'trait model' has meant that many 'para-professionals' struggled for decades to achieve state-sanctioned definitions of certified knowledge and monopoly control over access to employment or private practice. This was a battle that peaked for groups like nurses and teachers in the 1970s and 1980s. By the end of this period, professional associations won state support for regulation of training standards, registration and codes of practice.

The critique

The 1960s and 1970s saw various challenges to the older functionalist sociology of the professions. Neo-Marxists like Donzelot (1970) and Habermas (1973) argued that science was not value-free, as Parsons had argued, but represented certain dominant social interests and values and functioned as an instrument of domination. According to this critical sociology, professions were implicated in the reproduction of capitalism (Pemberton & Boreham 1976: 29; see also Johnson 1972).

Since the 1980s, interest in the professions as a subject of sociological research and/or theoretical reflection has declined. This can partly be explained in terms of the fate of particular intellectual traditions like the decline of structural functionalist and Marxist sociologies and the rise of anti-foundationalism, evident in post-modernism, post-structuralism and cultural studies.

The once-strong interest in the professions has now been supplanted by a less specific interest in 'governmentality'—an interest informed by the work of Foucault. This burgeoning area is represented, for example, in the work of Rose (1990), Hunter (1996) and Dean and Hindess (1998). It means that the once sharply focused attention given to the professions has become obscured as those using a 'governmentality' approach explore a diverse array of historically evolving techniques for governing the self, implicating families, the media, the state and the professions.

Irrespective of these particular critical traditions, it is possible to critically examine the trait model to ascertain how much it is a description of occupational activities and how much of it is self-serving fantasy.

● CONCLUSION

Australians like to think of themselves as a healthy people. Being healthy is an important part of our national identity, closely tied to the special status our beaches and sporting prowess enjoy. It is also an important part of our personal identity. Our experience of our bodies as fat or thin, sick or disabled is an important aspect of our social identity, shaping the ways we live and the ways other people relate to us. In this chapter, we have shown that there is some support for the general idea that we enjoy a generally high average level of health. Yet we cannot avoid the fact that the state of our bodies and minds in health and sickness is caught up in important social processes.

As embodied creatures, we experience ourselves and each other through and with our bodies. Being well or disabled, healthy or dying does have an irreducible biological component, but it is also overlaid with social judgments and relationships. Knowing whether we are well or sick is rarely a uniquely personal experience.

Worse, the actual patterns of health and sickness are closely connected to the basic fact that we live in an unequal society. As the evidence mounts that certain basic patterns of inequality are being consolidated or extended, this has to be a source of some concern about the health of all Australians.

Discussion questions

16.1 What do you think defines 'health'?

16.2 Identify some of the social ideas and practices that contribute to ill-health.

16.3 How much are people responsible for their experience of heart disease or cancer?

According to his obituary, the actor
Robert Mitchum, when released from jail
after serving time for marijuana possession,
was asked what it was like inside the
slams. He replied 'Not bad. Kind of like Palm
Springs without the riffraff'.
James Lee Burke, 2000, Purple Cane Road: 113)
(Note: replace 'Palm Springs' with Byron Bay or
Portsea and you get the point)

CRIME, DEVIANCE AND POWER 17.

● ● SUMMARY

There is widespread concern about a crisis in Western cultural and moral values. This is said to be producing an unprecedented epidemic of depression, hopelessness, drug abuse, suicide, crime and 'anti-social behaviour'. How credible are these ideas about social order and groups of people who threaten that order? To answer this, we outline and discuss four traditions that have been influential in shaping the ways people have thought about deviance and crime. We start with Durkheim's account of deviance, and examine the value of the conventional sociologists' conception of deviance. We then explore other more critical theories, which involve the work of symbolic interactionist and radical approaches to the conventional idea that some people are either naturally different, bad or criminal, or are made this way by society. We explore the work of Foucault, who rejects the conventional approach to madness, deviance and criminality. We argue against any biological or narrow sociological account of deviance, highlighting instead the role played by power in defining who or what is deviant or criminal.

Australia, like other societies, has long been characterised by persistent forms of social and economic inequality. As we have shown, Australians do not have equal access to well-paid, satisfying, full-time jobs, nor do we all enjoy equally long and healthy lives. There is clear evidence pointing to the unequal distribution of income and wealth. The clear distinctions between elite private schools and public schools point to one of the mechanisms that reproduces the unequal distribution of wealth and income.

By and large, public discussion of these matters is muted or absent—especially in the media. It is much more common to find energetic discussion in our media about the decline of moral standards and the shocking increase in crime, violence and disrespect for law.

In a context characterised by dramatic social and economic change, which has exacerbated the patterns of inequality, it is perhaps not surprising that there should be widespread concern about social order, a disintegration of community values and alleged increases in the rate of 'anti-social' and criminal activity.

Back at the end of the nineteenth century, after a period of no less dramatic social and economic change, there was both popular anxiety about social order and significant pioneering exercises by sociologists like Durkheim to define social order and the threats posed by 'deviants, delinquents and criminals'. In our time, public spokespeople bemoan the loss of respect for traditional values and the rise of 'anti-social' behaviour. Right-wing columnists like Andrew Bolt complain about the loss of patriotic values (*Herald Sun*, 3 February 2006). Archbishop Jensen in Sydney tells us that homosexuality is a sin against God and His authority. Pundits like Richard Eckersley (1993) and John Carroll (2005) have long argued that we confront a 'crisis in Western values' which is evident in the erosion of cultural and moral authority, producing an unprecedented epidemic of depression, hopelessness, drug abuse, suicide, crime and anti-social behaviour committed especially, but by no means exclusively, by young people. Academic research in Australia and overseas (Rutter et al. 1998; National Crime Prevention 1999) endlessly 'discovers' a complex mix of social, psychological, social and biological factors operating (even in the womb) which place some people 'at risk' of becoming criminals. The major daily newspapers routinely carry headlines like 'Violent Crimes by Young Soar' or 'Graffitti Costs Millions' (*Herald Sun*, 24 January 2006).

The fascination with crime and social disorder has many sources. It certainly has nothing to do with any real increase in crime or ordinary violence, even though there is a widespread view that we are subjected to ever-increasing rates of crime. In the United Kingdom since 1998, the Blair Labour government has regularly polled citizens on this matter, confirming that this is indeed a widespread belief. As Simmons and Dodd (2003: 6) report, over 38 per cent of people surveyed believed that crime had risen 'a lot' and another 35 per cent believed it had risen 'a little' over the previous two years, even though available data showed that it had actually fallen by 17 per cent since 1999. This perception seems to be closely related to the kinds of newspaper people read. Some 48 per cent of readers of the populist tabloid newspapers believed crime had risen 'a lot' compared with only 26 per cent of readers of broadsheets or quality newspapers (Simmons & Dodd 2003: 6). The perception that crime is always on the rise tempts many politicians to declare 'war on crime' or to 'get tough on crime'—especially just before or during an election. The release of any criminological research on the murder rate or the incidence of car thefts is likewise an excuse for a frenzy of media analysis and much canvassing of public opinion.

Even though there are very substantial problems in treating crime rate statistics, all the available evidence—as the Australian Institute of Criminology (1992) has been arguing since its inception—makes one big point: societies like Australia have become progressively more law-abiding and less violent.

The preoccupation with crime and social disorder has other sources. It may reflect our curiosity about the 'dark side' of ourselves, where anxieties about death, emotions like anger and a fascination with violence at times conflict with the normal day-to-day requirements of living peaceably with each other. It undoubtedly connects to the voyeurism that brings out crowds of people to crime scenes involving theft or murder or a road accident. It also seems to feed off our capacity to feel anxious. Numerous surveys show that there is a widespread contemporary fear of being raped, mugged, robbed, murdered or of having one's children assaulted. Whether these concerns have any basis in reality is quite a separate matter—as we discuss later. These anxieties in turn lie behind the politicisation of law and order policy: media reports of murder or rape cases invariably trigger calls for tougher penalties or even the restoration of capital punishment leading populist politicians to promise they will be 'tough on crime'.

Popular concern about issues of law and order mirror a long-standing interest by sociologists in crime and social order. Most of the great names in the sociological pantheon (including

Durkheim, Parsons, Wirth, Merton, Becker, Douglas and Erikson) made their names with studies of what sociologists have long called 'deviance' or 'social pathology', to say nothing of crime and 'the criminal'. This preoccupation has produced a vast body of theoretical speculation and a rich research literature about street gangs, criminals, homosexuals, drug-users, prostitutes and similar 'deviant' groups.

Whether this is a socially useful interest is debatable. That it is extraordinarily one-sided is undeniable when this vast literature addressing normal crime is contrasted with the almost complete lack of attention paid by sociologists (and by criminologists and psychologists) to the hugely more violent, damaging and destructive crimes committed by governments. The daily global homicide rate produced by governments murdering their own citizens (using famine, death camps and ethnic cleansing) ran at about 14 000 deaths a day across the twentieth century, and this excludes the death toll caused by wars. State-sponsored genocide carried out in the Soviet Union after 1932 saw between fifteen and twenty million civilians murdered by Stalin's government. The German Holocaust after 1941 killed millions of Jews, Poles and Russians, homosexuals and people with disabilities. In the early 1960s, the Chinese government killed at least 20 million peasants. Yet Smelser's (1994) authoritative overview of twentieth century sociology or Giddens' best-selling sociology textbook (1997) are entirely silent on the issue of state crime. The authoritative *Oxford Handbook of Criminology* (Maguire et al. 2002) likewise devotes just one paragraph of its 1400 pages to state crime. One recent significant exception to this silence is Michael Mann's (2005) work on ethnic cleansing.

These considerations indicate why we need to think about how sociologists have approached the issue of criminality, social order and what many continue to call 'deviance'. Conventional sociologists have long assumed that they know who the deviants and the criminals are. We are not so sure this confidence is well placed.

Discussions about crime and deviance, and the research done by sociologists and criminologists, raise major questions about how knowledge of our society is produced. As we have insisted at numerous points throughout this book, we are not entitled to complacently treat 'facts' about things like the crime rate as if they reflect some natural and objective state of affairs. As we have shown, there are always real people involved in a variety of practices that produce the knowledge we claim to have about our world.

In the spirit of thoughtfulness which Pierre Bourdieu (2004: 85–114) calls 'reflexivity', we need to ask some difficult questions:

- In the sociological treatment of deviance, is being different or bad an objective fact that distinguishes some people from the rest?
- Is being bad or mad a consequence of social definitions that can change from time to time or place to place?
- Can we ever know who is really bad or different?

- How do we know about things like the crime rate?
- Can we ever explain deviance or crime in terms of scientific laws and causal explanations?
- How do patterns of social inequality affect the disposition to crime?

We begin by identifying some of the ways conventional sociologists have thought about social order, crime and deviance.

• SOCIOLOGISTS ON DEVIANCE, DELINQUENCY AND CRIME

In the context of those dramatic social and economic changes now referred to as the Great Transformation, Anglo-American and European intellectuals and many of these societies's elites throughout the nineteenth century were endlessly concerned about the threat to social order that the 'dangerous classes' were believed to pose to society. What today some people call an 'underclass' then included:

- all or part of the working classes;
- most of the 'the poor'; and
- a criminal class.

In the nineteenth century, governments, journalists, church leaders and the emergent social scientists of the day understood these groups to be far more numerous themselves—and very different. Sometimes referred to as the 'black people' or the 'perishing classes', they were objects of both fear and pity, given that 'they' were chronically likely to erupt in an orgy of revolutionary violence in pursuit of something called democracy, or else indulge in some good old-fashioned rioting and crime. On the basis of these well-documented social prejudices (see Garland 1985, 1991; Pickens 1995), sociology—and its sub-discipline, criminology—went on to construct a long-standing disciplinary and 'scientific' preoccupation with 'deviance', 'delinquency' and 'criminality'.

It is not irrelevant that most sociologists in the nineteenth and twentieth centuries (at least up to the 1950s) have generally come from the middle or upper classes. They have found it easy to treat the working classes and 'the poor' as lazy, anti-social, uneducated, unskilled and given to seeking immediate gratification—all of which adds up to the idea that they were just plain 'different'. They then converted these social prejudices into theoretical questions and scientific research programs. This has helped to render these prejudices more or less invisible while appealing to the authority to which anyone using 'scientific method' can lay claim.

Much of this sociological—and criminological—enterprise has rested on one sublimely simple proposition: there is a social and moral consensus which makes 'society' possible—a consensus about which significant numbers of the 'lower orders' were either ignorant or even antagonistic.

After all, the core idea of deviance requires that there be something from which some people can deviate. From this simple proposition came an early and still influential endeavour to address deviance and crime: the structural functionalist tradition. As Ryan (1975) argues, the preoccupation with developing a 'scientific method' for studying society has invariably begun with the premise that there is a single social-cum-moral order. Using that idea as a benchmark, it has been possible to show how the lives of the 'poor', the 'criminal' and the 'unemployed' are different to that order, then to use that difference as the source of and explanation for their deviant experience. Ideas about the causal value of a concept like 'the culture of poverty' have been especially useful in 'explaining' why the poor are poor or the unemployed are unemployed. (See our discussion of the 'underclass' idea in Chapter 13.)

The sociologists who have contributed to this mainstream tradition developed views about deviance, delinquency and crime that were popular in the nineteenth century and which continue to be so even today. In some respects, those ways of seeing social order and deviance continue to be part of today's 'common sense'.

● THE STRUCTURAL FUNCTIONALIST APPROACH TO DEVIANCE

Emile Durkheim, one of the 'fathers' of sociology, pioneered a structural functionalist theory of deviance. As we have shown in Chapter 3, Durkheim's account of deviance is based on a larger theory which treats society as a system akin to the human body. For functionalists, social health means the same thing as social order. Social order is guaranteed when everyone accepts the moral values of 'society' and all members of the community accept their roles.

Durkheim's premise was that social order depends on the existence of a moral consensus, and that society establishes standards of behaviour and thinking which are functional for that society. This means that rules which determine what is normal and right behaviour in a society not only help to maintain 'social order' but actually constitute society itself. Social order is gained through extended and complex processes of education, punishment and rewards. Social order is the task of social control agencies like schools, families, the church—all of which ensure that most people integrate the rules for right behaviour (or the norms) into their own personality. And if the moral order collapses, then so does society.

Durkheim claimed that in any society, especially those manifesting a robust moral order, there would always be some individuals who did not fit:

- Some people would always be different from what was described and prescribed by the dominant social and moral rules of their society—these were the deviant.
- Some people acted in ways that society regarded as bad or reprehensible but not criminal especially if they were young—these were the delinquent.
- Finally, some people breeched not only the moral order but the formal legal codes of society—these are the criminals.

Durkheim argued that deviance, delinquency and crime were best understood as steps along a continuum of difference. Further, these differences were a natural and inevitable aspect of any society.

Durkheim insisted on treating forms of deviance as a 'social fact'. Social facts are numerical statements that record the frequency of certain kinds of behaviour. Those Durkheim was interested in included statistics like the 'crime rate' or the 'suicide rate'. Durkheim did not treat social facts as a consequence of individual choice. The behaviours he called 'deviance', 'crime' or 'delinquency' were not an individual's activity or the consequence of some individual choice or decision. Rather, society caused aggregate trends to operate. Social facts capture the operation of society on individuals. Crime or suicide rates rise or fall, and Durkheim believed these rates were the 'social facts' which a properly scientific sociology could best explain. He also felt that it was possible to identify other social facts at work, like an increase in aggregate wealth or a rise in the unemployment rate. These, Durkheim said, were the explanatory 'structural' or aggregate facts that determined other social facts. A properly scientific sociology could therefore explain one social fact—like the crime rate—by reference to other structural social facts. These ideas have proved remarkably persuasive and long-lasting.

To add to this framework, Durkheim also—in common with later functionalists—distinguished between two types of deviance: normal deviance and anomic deviance (see box).

Types of deviance

Normal deviance

Normal deviance is the kind of deviance said to be positive and 'good' for society. Normal deviance occurs in any society with a strong moral constitution, and is beneficial because it helps to maintain boundaries that mark out very clearly to observers what is acceptable behaviour and what is not. Normal deviance performs a preventative or educative role. When people are re-educated or even punished for transgressing the boundaries of acceptable behaviour, then all the 'normal', conforming people see what might happen to them if they misbehave and are reminded of the need to stay on the straight and narrow.

Anomic deviance

The second type of deviance according to Durkheim—and his successors like Robert K. Merton—is less desirable. Anomic deviance is what happens when social order itself has weakened, social bonds are breaking down and people are becoming more and more individualised. In this condition of anomie (Durkheim's term), large numbers of people break the rules and so the suicide rate or the crime rate increases.

Merton's theory of anomic deviance

In the late 1930s, Robert Merton (1957) developed a variation on Durkheim's account of deviance which became one of the most cited sociological theories of deviance. Merton, like Durkheim, wanted to know whether there were structural conditions which caused deviance. Merton argued that 'society' tried to create a good quality of life for its citizens; further, social structures were designed to achieve those aspirations/goals. He went on to claim that all societies link their aspirations to particular sets of moral beliefs, and thereby create institutions which try to realise those social goals.

According to Merton, 'social order' is the result of people being satisfied because they have conformed to social expectations. He argues that there is an inclination for some groups and individuals to become anomic when they focus on achieving socially accepted goals, but are not concerned about the means by which they realise those desires. Anomie can develop in some groups if they want the material goods at any cost—even if it means cheating, stealing or murdering to obtain the outcome.

After Merton, functionalists tended to argue that deviant behaviour implied problems with the socialisation process. A lot of sociological research was done between the 1930s and the 1970s demonstrating that such structural factors as rising divorce rates, falling school retention rates, declining church attendance rates and unemployment cause crime rates to rise or fall. Underpinning much of this research were assumptions about how 'deviant' or 'criminal' people have either escaped normal socialisation or have been socialised into a deviant culture.

In the 1990s, there was a dramatic revival of this tradition in America, where extremely long-lived and socially conservative sociologists like Amitai Etzioni and James Coleman argued that behaviours like membership of political parties or belonging to bowling teams could be used as evidence of the strength of 'civil society'—which is the antithesis of an 'anomic' society.

● PROBLEMS WITH THE STRUCTURAL FUNCTIONALIST ACCOUNT

There are many problems with these assumptions for our time. First, there is a problem with the concepts of 'social order' and 'moral consensus'. Take the work of a modern Australian criminologist like John Braithwaite (1989), who claims that there is a clear distinction between conventional society and the 'delinquents' and 'criminals' who exhibit unconventional and/or criminal attitudes, values and behaviours. Braithwaite (1989: 3, 9) writes that 'most criminal laws in most societies are the subject of overwhelming consensus . . . because criminal behaviour is mostly harmful by any moral yardstick and agreed to be so by most citizens'. But is this so? Much of the 'evidence' Braithwaite relies on comes from opinion surveys, which tell us that most people do not approve of rape, murder or theft. But is this reliable evidence of a binding moral consensus?

First, the people who answer questionnaires about values often give answers that they think the researcher wants to hear, but which do not necessarily reflect their own actual views or behaviour. Second, Braithwaite (1989: 13) weakens his argument when he claims that there is a social consensus about crime held by most people and that multiple moral codes and beliefs are a reality in modern society. These contradictory claims are not addressed by Braithwaite.

As to the reliability of opinion polls, we should ask whether we are best guided by what people *say* or by what they actually *do*. Stanley Milgram's famous studies on obedience to authority (1973) indicate one answer. Milgram found using surveys that most people said they did not approve of causing pain to helpless people. He then constructed an experiment in which participants believed they were administering increasingly severe electric shocks to others. Most people obediently administered what they thought were real and painful shocks to the subject in the name of science, although they believed the subject was in considerable pain or even about to have a heart attack. The key question this raises is whether we can rely on what people say they value in response to social surveys as an indicator of the strength of a given moral consensus—or whether we are better guided by people's actual behaviours.

There is another no less fundamental problem which renders deeply problematic the whole history of sociology's pretensions to be regarded as an objective science of society. The problem has to do with the belief that social facts are objective statements of real things. The tendency to treat the 'crime rate' or the 'suicide rate' as if they are entirely natural and obvious facts is unwarranted. Unlike Durkheim or Merton, we should not assume that 'crime' or 'deviance' are objective facts. Words like 'crime', 'murder', suicide' or 'violence' are frequently used as if their meanings were self-evident and able to be applied easily to some simple 'fact' or activity. Abe Fatteh (1997: 37) takes a much more robust approach to this matter when he says 'there is no universal or agreed upon definition [of crime] . . . It means different things to different people . . . all attempts to define it are doomed'. Fatteh's point is that criminal acts or deviant people are not things, nor are the criteria that make something 'criminal' or 'deviant', 'natural' or 'objective' facts because these things are the product of many often complex social practices and beliefs.

Let us look at the way a 'social fact' like the crime rate is produced.

● MEASURING THE CRIME RATE

Many people believe that defining and counting criminal activities is a relatively straightforward exercise. They would say that crime is whatever the law says it is. However, the issue of how we 'know' about crime becomes more complex when we attempt to 'measure' the crime rate. The dimensions and frequency of activities like 'crime' or 'unemployment' depend on how we define what we set out to measure. Added to this is the very real problem involved in finding the people who are doing the things we want to measure. The category 'crime' requires us to establish how transgressions of law are both defined and detected. The problem with measuring crime is that the outcome depends on:

- who is doing the counting;
- why they do the counting;
- what criteria they use to count activities as criminal; and
- the willingness of people who may be doing criminal things to be 'discovered' and 'counted'.

It is certainly the case that the laws of a country like Australia may define the 'criminal' act. Even this is problematic when we remember that, in Australia, there are seven state and federal systems of law, each with its own legal statutes. It is also the job of others (i.e. victims, police, lawyers, judges and juries) to decide whether a crime has actually been committed.

Many people and possibly even law enforcement officials may believe that a crime is a 'fact'. It is important to make the point that any event which is called a 'crime' and possibly counted as one is not 'real' until someone decides that the event or activity happened and meets the criteria for being treated as a crime. Far from being an 'objective' fact, the process of converting human conduct into a crime statistic involves a complex process of social negotiation and definition. Let us say that someone discovers a dead person. The body bears all the signs of deadly wounds. Yet is it 'obvious' that a crime like murder has been committed?

In Australia, one famous case makes this point in striking fashion. In 1998, the Australian press reported extensively on a matter, first brought to the attention of police in the mid-1980s, which began with the discovery of a woman's body in a farmhouse. The woman, who had two bullet wounds to her head, was initially counted as a 'suicide'. This was so in spite of the fact that the victim had apparently shot herself in the head not once, but twice, and with a bolt action rifle! In the first official inquiry—and acting on police advice and reports—the coroner reluctantly treated this as a 'suicide'. A decade later, the case was reopened and a second coroner's inquiry determined that the woman had been killed and by a serving police officer. (In spite of that official finding, the police officer in question has never been tried for the offence.)

The central point here is that those human actions that become a crime can only become so after someone else has defined them that way. Against the commonsense assumption that the 'facts speak for themselves', human conduct that becomes a crime statistic has been through an elaborate process of selection, negotiation and decision-making. The construction of a 'crime rate' reflects decisions on the part of those who define, classify and record certain behaviour as 'crime'. The extent to which this occurs was first revealed in a classic piece of research by Aaron Cicourel (1968).

Cicourel examined two police departments in two American cities with relatively identical social, economic and demographic characteristics. Yet one of these cities had a high youth crime rate while the other's was low. Cicourel followed police on to the streets of these two cities to discover that the different crime rates reflected nothing other than quite different policing practices. In one city, an ambitious police force liked to generate high arrest and juvenile process rates. In the other city, police preferred to administer justice on the streets. This involved the full range of corporal punishment including the issuing of back-lane discipline to black and Chicano juveniles and serious talks with the young person's parents if they were seen to have come from 'a respectable family'. Justice looked different in these two cities.

Likewise, Black (1970: 738) showed in his study of policing practices in three American blue-collar working-class areas that police prefer to deal with and record serious crimes (felonies) rather than misdemeanours. In his study, 72 per cent of felonies were recorded and reported as crimes, but only 53 per cent of misdemeanours were treated as crime. Later, Sherman and Glick (1984) pointed to many failures by police to file official crime reports, or to make regular and serious errors in reporting crime. Most recently, Charles Katz (2003) followed a special police unit on to the streets as it gathered intelligence about gangs. He concluded that the police disregarded official guidelines in gathering and recording data, and collected it in such ad hoc ways that the police administration decided the data should not be used: 'Violations of "counting rules" were so flagrantly disregarded that users of police gang data would be unsure as to the nature and reliability of the data' (2003: 510–11). Worse, he found evidence that police were making the data available in the community, so that employers and teachers were often using it to the disadvantage of the young people being labelled—often wrongly—as gang members.

Only once there is agreement that a crime has been committed is it possible to 'count' criminal activities. This means there is nothing natural or objective about crime because the way the idea or category is defined varies according to the specific time and place. Usually, when we try to establish the amount of crime being committed, we ask whether the measurement of crimes includes:

- all reports to police of such offences;
- all the arrests of people who allegedly committed those offences; and
- all the convictions of persons for these offences.

What about the many events that are not reported to police? It is likely that large numbers of petty offences and minor crimes go unreported, and there is no way of monitoring such activity.

It is very difficult to compare crime rates across long stretches of time, even within the one country or the one state. Laws reflect social attitudes and values that change over time. It has been established, for example, that only a third of rape events were being reported until the 1980s. New crimes, like rape in marriage, credit card fraud or computer hacking, are still being added. Old crimes, like abortion, 'homosexuality' or certain kinds of drug-use, are 'decriminalised'. Moreover, many minor and major crimes go undetected. This makes it difficult to conclude that 'the crime rate has increased or decreased between 1850 and 2005'.

This fundamental problem led a group of sociologists known as the symbolic interactionists to reject the idea that 'deviance' or 'criminality' is obvious, easily measured and discovered. This led to some interesting developments in rethinking deviance and crime.

● SYMBOLIC INTERACTIONISTS ON CRIME AND DEVIANCE

The symbolic interactionist approach to rethinking deviance and crime, and by implication the core idea of 'social order', really took off in the 1960s and 1970s. (It is often referred to as 'labelling theory', or sometimes as 'ethnomethodology'.) This tradition is associated with the work of American writers like Harold Garfinkel, Alfred Schutz and Peter Berger. It produced specific studies on deviance by Ervin Goffman (1961), Howard Becker (1963), Jack Douglas (1970), Aaron Cicourel (1968) and Stanley Cohen (1972), among others. Their accounts were quite different from the functionalist stories.

Symbolic interactionists did not accept the functionalist claim that there was a clear distinction between conventional and non-conventional groups in any society. They questioned the claim that criminality was easily identifiable and that certain clear markers, certain behaviours, pointed objectively to deviance or to criminality.

Symbolic interactionists reject ideas about how 'society' coerces people into either conformity or deviance. They argue that deviance is actually a process in which some people define an activity as deviant, and then force other people doing those 'deviant' things into accepting the consequences of this process. Implicitly, symbolic interactionists were introducing the idea of power into their account of the processes of 'discovering' and detecting deviance—though they did not always handle this very clearly.

One consequence of this approach is that, if being 'deviant' involves being 'different' from what someone else or a powerful group says is normal, most people at some point in their lives will be treated as deviant. Being different is in fact more the norm than any idea of an over-arching 'normality' from which only a few deviate. This led symbolic interactionists to argue that the 'outsider' is someone who is labelled as such. This makes the idea of deviance proposed by Durkheim or Merton begin to look a little strange.

The symbolic interactionists' approach to crime and deviance includes several claims.

- Social reality is what people define as being real.
- Social reality depends on how we understand the meaning of each other's activities. Human action, according to symbolic interactionists like Geertz, is symbolic action which is full of ideas, rules, words and values.
- Social reality is not external to people in the way that structural functionalists say it is. Social reality is the consequence of people's interactions, agreements and interpretive rules involving the use of symbolic techniques of communication that are grounded in language.
- Language is identified as being an important part of interaction between people, and language is symbolic action. Symbolic interactionists also give attention to non-linguistic communication, such as gestures and body posture. Language is symbolic in that it names an object, feeling or behaviour, or can be used to interpret an action as meaningful; it also helps to fix reality and make it seem stable or orderly. We use language to describe things that are not actually available to us—something that happened yesterday, or things we want to happen next year. We use language to tell stories about what is good (or what is evil), and we use it to tell the truth (or lies).
- All social encounters involve and require constant interpretation, which helps people to establish what is happening around them. What is 'actually' happening is not the critical issue, because in one sense there is no special position from which a person can say with any final authority what is 'actually' happening. The critical thing is to realise that we are engaging in interpretive processes, and it is those processes that shape what and how we see. Equally, some actions are more or less clearcut: planning to and actually cutting someone's throat is clearly murder.
- All social action involves interaction, where individual participants simultaneously experience and interpret each other. Being labelled a 'deviant' results from an interpretation—often by someone who has more power than another person.

Symbolic interactionists say that, rather than seeing deviant status as inherent in the individual or the deviant act, it needs to be seen as the result of other people defining someone as deviant. W.I. Thomas's and D. Thomas's (1929) observation that once people define situations as real they become real in their consequences suggests the potency of interpretations. In other words, if someone defines you as deviant, and they have the power to make that definition apply, then you are likely to be treated as deviant. Parents, teachers, psychiatrists, police and welfare workers all have this kind of power.

So how do symbolic interactionists research 'deviance'? Symbolic interactionists focus on specific social encounters and what they call 'insiders' accounts'. (An insider is anyone directly involved in a given social interaction.) Any social action is an encounter founded on reciprocal action. It involves constant interpretation and reciprocal actions in which each person is influenced by, as well as influencing, the other. Symbolic interactionists also speak of an audience who may participate in the encounter.

Goffman's study of encounters indicates how each of us monitors ourselves and others constantly, even as we adjust our presentation of self in the light of:

- what we imagine they want us to be;
- what we want them to be;
- what they are doing to make us be what they want us to be; and
- what we are doing to make them be what we would like them to be.

Interactionists are interested in small-scale interactions between people. Symbolic inter-actionists prefer to produce small-scale descriptive accounts of people's life-worlds, focusing on the meanings they attribute to certain things. They like looking, for example, at interactions between police and young people, at how the police interpret the behaviours of the young people, at how straight the young people stand when being talked to by the police or how much 'respect' the young person shows the police officer, and at what consequences follow from the interpretations made by the police.

Participant observation is the symbolic interactionist's preferred way of getting information about how people act in and interpret the world. Making observations from within the group means the researcher gains an understanding of the values, knowledge and belief systems in other people's lives. Observation and interaction with those being studied is usually preferred to controlled experiments and large-scale sample surveys based on questionnaires.

Symbolic interactionists often reject, or at least have little time for, structural causal explanations of deviance. Generally, they do not try to develop causal or explanatory theories that attempt to copy 'scientific' models of research.

● LIMITATIONS OF SYMBOLIC INTERACTIONISM

After decades of functionalist theories of deviance, the interactionist or labelling approach arrived like a cool breeze at the end of a long, hot day. But as time went by, people began making some serious and critical observations:

- Their approach to deviance and crime often became a relativist exercise, where neither truth nor secure moral judgments seemed possible, including anything said by the interactionists.

- Some critics claimed that interactionists offered a voyeuristic sociology, where sociologists reported on how they spent time with rapists or murderers, or watched violent or vicious events and got a buzz out of doing this.
- Finally, given the interactionists' stress on the power of the rule-makers, they did not offer any account of where the power came from, or even what form it took. Worse, because of the focus on small-scale and face-to-face interactions, they could never explain how some people came to be rule-makers in the first place.

Labelling theorists and symbolic interactionists made the critical point that conventional sociologists who stressed the 'objectivity' of being deviant or criminal in certain ways did not recognise how politics and power are essential to defining some activities as 'deviant' or people as 'criminal—and how the same activities, when done by other people, can be rendered normal or even desirable. This point has been made in the most telling fashion by feminist criminologists.

● FEMINIST CRIMINOLOGY

Most feminists take a critical approach to 'mainstream'—or what some call 'malestream'— knowledge or research. Most feminists would say that their job as researchers is to provide critical analysis as well as to try to engage in emancipatory practices which support women. This is very much an 'engaged' or 'committed' view of research or knowledge. We should also remember that there is no single feminist view about knowledge or the basis of valid theory:

- Some feminists argue that all forms of rational knowledge reliant on 'scientific method' are positivist and reflect male-centred values and practices designed to reinforce male power, and must be rejected.
- Others argue that it does not matter what methods are used, so long as their application to research reflects the experiences of those women being studied.

For most feminists, the social sciences have been part of an apparatus that supported the continued oppression of women. Modern feminists also mostly agree that sexism is codified both in disciplines like sociology and in the justice system.

First, criminologists informed by feminist thinking argue that 'criminality' is primarily a masculine construct. Representations of the 'criminal' or 'delinquent' have traditionally been based on the figure of the male. Feminists like Oakley (1979) and Carrington (1993) point to a preoccupation with the male in deviancy theory. Official statistics have also been identified in highlighting the fact that two features characterise the 'criminal': being male and being young. For feminists like Cain (1989), this is because male social scientists could not see gender and could not speak about men and women.

Second, feminists argue that women are either invisible or are significantly misrepresented within criminological theory and research (Smart 1976; Heidensohn 1992; Cain 1989; Carrington 1993). In other words, the part played by women and girls as victims and perpetrators in stories of delinquency and criminality are rarely considered (Gelsthorpe and Morris 1988). Although it was acknowledged that girls and women were capable of criminal and delinquent acts, female criminality was usually benchmarked against male experiences of criminality, rather than the other way around.

Third, feminists argued that the primary concern of the criminal justice system was safeguarding the sexual virtue or chastity of women—especially young women—and ensuring that they went on to fulfil their sex role—that is, to become a satisfactory wife and mother. For feminist criminologists like Kerry Carrington (1993) and Adrian Howe (1998), what gets women and girls into real trouble is their refusal to accept their 'legitimate' sexuality—their refusal to be integrated into a culture of femininity.

Since the 1970s another tradition, often referred to as 'post-structuralism', has produced a distinctive perspective on deviance.

• POST-STRUCTURALISTS RETHINK CRIME AND DEVIANCE

We refer here to the work of Michel Foucault. Though Foucault rejected the application of the 'post-structuralist' label to his work, his attempt to move beyond explanations couched in structuralist terms like gender warrants some attention. His work has sponsored an interesting body of research and theory. See Dean and Hindess (1998) for a collection of work by Australian 'Foucauldians', while innovative work by writers like Garland (1985, 1991) testifies to the value of Foucault's work.

In a way, Foucault's approach to deviance and crime parallels certain features of the symbolic interactionist approach to social reality, which focuses on the processes operating in specific institutions that lead to some people being defined as mad, bad or criminal. Foucault made the same kind of point about the role of psychiatric clinics and institutions like prisons. Like the symbolic interactionists, Foucault explored what he called the micro-practices of power and control in places like police cars, schools, courts or psychiatric clinics. However, Foucault was not interested in the details of human interactions—a hallmark of the symbolic interactionist approach. His characteristic and much more abstracted approach stressed the role of theoretical schemes developed by the social and medical sciences—or what he called 'discourses'.

At the same time, his work looks a bit like the feminist interest in the way power works to define certain people and behaviours in highly gendered ways. Foucault, however, rejected what he called the determinism found in mainstream feminism's insistence that power flows in a single and uniform (i.e. patriarchal) way across society. Foucault rejected all structuralist or totalising explanations of power and social order, preferring to emphasise the complex and multiple forms power can take.

In effect, Foucault takes the radical's interest in power and the symbolic interactionist's interest in the way particular practices inside specific institutions like gaols, hospitals and schools are used to control people to develop his own kind of analysis. He does this by emphasising the role of what he calls 'government' (see Foucault 2000).

● GOVERNMENT AND POWER

Foucault argues that we should use the idea of government to refer to two kinds of social practice. The first is what the state does by way of discovering social problems and making policy. Foucault reminds us that modern states and their politics are actively involved in regulating and policing their citizens. Most governments also try to monopolise power over important resources and processes. Modern governments maintain standing military forces and police forces, which provide a potentially violent basis for securing state power. They:

- ensure there are no other serious competitors who could claim a superior right to govern;
- possess a capacity to make laws, and have superior access to weapons of destruction and coercion; and
- routinise and make predictable certain choices and judgments (this involves 'the rule of law').

When possible, modern governments try not to rely on guns and physical force, and prefer the rule of law. Governments like to monopolise legitimacy, the ability to make rules and laws, and the use of force. To achieve this, governments generate and control the making of laws, which are simply rules that determine the right procedures and actions. Modern governments prefer the use of non-violent means to regulate, control, know and manage people. This involves:

- economic rules and policies (regulating investment, property rights, employment or production quality);
- studying and managing complex environmental issues (air pollution, global warming or energy use);
- knowing about and regulating personal and family issues (births, deaths, marriages, domestic violence);
- trying to shape community relations (violence, property, associations like football clubs, racial tolerance issues); and
- managing complex health, education and welfare activities and institutions.

As Foucault (1979) argues, the growth of certain kinds of knowledge, especially the social sciences (or what Foucault calls the 'human sciences'), enhances the capacity of modern states to govern their citizens.

The second way in which Foucault uses the term 'government' points to the way all sorts of other institutions, like schools, clinics, hospitals and prisons, and the experts and professionals who staff these institutions try to regulate people's lives. Foucault uses the term 'government' to refer to a far more dispersed mode of regulation.

● THE SOCIAL SCIENCES, KNOWLEDGE AND POWER

Foucault's emphasis on the way knowledge about people is used to construct truths about certain types of people and then to regulate them is likely to prove one of his most important contributions to sociology. Power, according to Foucault, relies on claims to know certain things and to be able to access truth. Foucault rejects the proposition that there is a basis for anyone ever being able to say they have the 'absolute truth'; rather, people who claim to have the truth are just using a variety of social or political techniques to force other people to accept that claim. He calls these 'truth practices'.

The power of social scientists and professionals rests partly on their ability to impose their ideas on others. This depends not so much on superior intellectual capacity as on political techniques like ridiculing people with alternative views and excluding them from committees or jobs. From Foucault's perspective, the main purpose of the human sciences is to define, categorise and regulate people by using criteria like 'rational' to define and then identify the irrational, and 'normal' to define and identify the 'abnormal'.

Foucault points to the ways language is organised into what he calls 'discourses', which are used to create these 'truth practices' and to produce their 'power effects'. His idea of discourse is close to T.S. Kuhn's (1969) idea of 'paradigm', which talks about the social ways in which particular knowledge systems about the world are developed and depend on complex patterns of questions and assumptions, the definition of which counts as evidence for a particular perspective.

A discourse is a pattern of language used by a group of people who assert a certain reality. It relies on key concepts, their definitions and a range of techniques claiming the world exists in a particular way. Foucault makes two major points about discourse. First, there is no way of escaping the power of any one discourse, except by moving into another. That is, there is no single master discourse which gives us absolute access to reality—nor can we appeal easily to 'reality' to resolve disputes between different discourses. All knowledge of reality is mediated by discourses (particularly language and techniques), so we can never claim to know reality as it 'really' is.

Second, Foucault says the use of language in certain discourses works in particular ways to know and categorise people (e.g. certain diagnoses of mental illness or certain categories of delinquents). This activity has seen the arrangement of people into various classifications of 'normal/abnormal', 'sane/mad', 'healthy/unhealthy', 'criminal/law-abiding', 'adjusted/maladjusted' and so on. The idea of 'normal' is very important and necessary to the process of identifying who is different. Foucault argues that, since the eighteenth century, Western governments have increasingly measured and regulated their populations using statistics to build up a picture of the population.

Foucault spent much of his time reading historical documents to understand why we understand madness, deviance or criminality in the ways we now do. Nikolaus Rose (1990) argues that, from the nineteenth century, the social sciences have been used to identify people as abnormal or mad or criminal so that they can be incarcerated, excluded, confined or hospitalised.

Normalising judgments work at getting people who are defined as abnormal to become more 'normal'. Teachers, for instance, talk about 'lazy' or 'slow' students, who after appropriate counselling and 'special education' become 'high-performance students'. Many Year 12 students still do a public examination which incorporates processes of normalisation in the judgment of the quality of their work. The result is a written and recorded system upon which people are distributed according to how they are assessed and classified. Such enterprises have been important for informing government about how best to educate the population so they will become useful and well-adjusted citizens. They also lead to state interventions such as mass compulsory schooling, public health and dentistry, family planning, kindergartens, physical education, urban planning and sex education. And they lead to campaigns aimed at first identifying, then eradicating, slums, poverty, prostitution, alcohol and drug-use, illiteracy, delinquency and criminality.

This discussion is a useful introduction to the way crime has been understood in a time of dramatic social change, when there is evidence that social inequalities are proving stubbornly persistent.

● CRIME IN AN UNEQUAL SOCIETY

The last three decades have seen sweeping social, economic and political changes in most Western societies. Whole industries and occupations have disappeared as new digital technologies have transformed the workplace and the home. In countries like Britain, America, Canada, Australia and much of Europe, these changes have been accompanied by entrenched long-term unemployment and under-employment, wage cuts and mounting evidence of socioeconomic inequality.

It is perhaps not surprising that some criminologists and sociologists have pointed to these kinds of changes and used them to explain the contemporary experience of crime. In the 1980s, writers like John Julius Wilson (1987) began to talk about an 'underclass' of permanently unemployed, poor, largely black and immigrant communities. The emergence of an 'underclass', said Wilson, explained the persistence of property crimes and crimes of violence. Since the 1990s, Australian policy-makers have taken their cue from British discussion and begun to talk about persistent 'social exclusion' characterised by long-term unemployment, poverty and crime. These ideas are part of a longer history of what Ian Taylor (1997) has called a 'political economy of crime'. For well over two centuries, social scientists and criminologists have argued that poverty and unemployment breed crime. Yet the fact that an idea has been around for a long time does not automatically make it a good or useful one.

Increasing rates of unemployment in the leading economies of the West during the 1970s spurred criminologists to carry out research on the unemployment–crime link. Many of Australia's leading criminologists have argued for just such a direct causal link. In the late 1980s, Rob White (1989: 146) claimed that: 'At the economic level, it can be suggested that more and more young men will turn to crime to make ends meet.' Similarly, Polk and Tait (1990: 21) argued for a deterministic relationship between youth unemployment and criminality, maintaining that: 'One potential consequence of the resultant large pool of new marginal youth has been a turn to illegal forms of activity.'

An extensive international literature on this proposed link (Chiricos 1987; Weatherburn 1992a: 4; Bagguley & Mann 1992) appeared to lend support to the idea that crime rates rose during periods of unemployment. Chiricos (1987) concluded from his analysis of some 65 research studies that unemployment rates were positively linked to crime rates. The argument that there is a positive link between crime and unemployment was extended into an argument that many 'Western' countries were witnessing the emergence of an 'underclass' (cf. Bessant 1995).

Yet some criminologists were sceptical about such simple causal explanations. In the early 1980s, North American research by Tithe et al. (1982) gently undermined the claim that unemployed young people were especially at risk of becoming criminal. In the United States, Duster (1987: 302) argued that 'unemployment surely does not cause crime in any simple linear fashion, and certainly not in any direct one-to-one relationship. In [North America] the easy demonstration is the Great Depression.' Heidensohn (with Hahn-Rafter 1995: 184) argued 'that not everyone accepts that there is a positive and causal link' between crime and unemployment. In Australia, Don Weatherburn (1992a) argued that much of the research did not show a consistent disposition on the part of crime rates to closely shadow changes in unemployment rates.

On both sides of this debate, it seems that too many sociologists had forgotten some of the striking arguments made by one of the greatest criminologists, Edwin Sutherland (1994), who argues strongly against the thesis that criminal behaviour was 'caused' by unemployment—or by the poverty associated with unemployment. First, as Sutherland (1994: 24–5) notes, there is the problem of white-collar crime:

First, the [unemployment/poverty crime link] presents a generally skewed picture of crime given that it omits almost entirely the behavior of white collar criminals . . . criminologists have tended to restrict their attentions largely to cases processed through the criminal courts. Given the vast majority of defendants passing through the system come from the lower socio-economic classes this would suggest a narrow view of the 'crime problem'.

The problem of white-collar crime is important for people who want to draw some link between being unemployed and/or poor and crime. This is precisely because white-collar crime involves people who are employed, frequently in senior positions inside companies and governments, and/or who have an upper-class background or enjoy high incomes. As Sutherland (1994: 25) puts it:

Secondly, the generalization that criminality is closely associated with poverty obviously does not apply to white-collar criminals. With a small number of exceptions, they are not in poverty, were not reared in slums or badly deteriorated families. Even if poverty is extended to include the economic stresses which afflict business in a period of depression, it is not correlated with white collar criminality. Despite the relative wealth of those in the corporate world crimes in the field of investment and management have escalated rapidly over the past few decades. This neatly inverts the traditional correlations made by criminologists between poverty, unemployment and crime.

Sutherland also points out that many of those who commit white-collar crimes are never convicted and their crimes are never recorded. ('Out-of-court' settlements result in further 'non-convictions'.) Unlike the 'crimes' of people from working-class backgrounds, the unlawful acts of white-collar criminals are 'often less visible' and relatively 'immune because of the class bias of the courts and the power of their class to influence the administration of the law' (Sutherland 1994: 23).

Finally, there is a larger problem which Sutherland pointed to when he notes (1994: 25) that: 'Criminological theory has not adequately explained lower class criminality. Thus, the emphasis on socio-pathic and psycho-pathic factors have not been related to cases involving white collar or corporate crime.' Whether criminologists have explained lower-class crime adequately is arguable. Sutherland is surely right, however, to suggest that, by failing to include white-collar crime in the normal or mainstream criminological framework, there is no capacity to test the adequacy of any of the usual theories advanced to explain 'normal'—that is, working-class—crime.

The value of Foucault's work on the role of the social sciences in identifying and regulating certain population groups and Sutherland's concern with the social or class biases at work in sociology are suggested when we look at the currently fashionable attempts to identify working-class families said to be 'at risk' of producing anti-social behaviour and criminals.

• CLASS BIAS AND THE SOCIAL SCIENCES

Sociologists and criminologists have, in the modern period, used a number of code words like 'large families', 'broken families' or 'dysfunctional families' when they research the links between crime and working-class, poor families. In each case, there is a mountain of research which apparently confirms how 'broken', 'large' or 'dysfunctional' families are criminogenic—that is, they produce 'anti-social' behaviour and criminals.

The 'broken family'—where one of the parents is absent due to divorce, separation or bereavement—has attracted persistent attention among empirical researchers concerned with families and crime. Into the twenty-first century, sociologists continue to discover that 'broken families' produce significant numbers of delinquent and criminal young people (Dembo & Schmeidler 2000; Chung et al. 2002; Dembo & Schmeidler 2003a: 204–5; Dembo & Schmeidler 2003b).

Other criminologists have looked to the problems of family size, almost always understood as the problem of 'large families' (Regoli & Hewitt 1991: 181–206). Family size, usually measured in terms of the number of children in a household, features repeatedly in empirical investigations of the link between families and crime. Typical of such claims is Leflore (1988: 640), who argues that the pressures posed by very large families have a marked impact on the ability of parents to care adequately for their children. An American study by Tygart (1991: 535) argues that 'large families' mean parents find it more difficult to supervise their children adequately. In the best known of contemporary longitudinal British studies (Farrington 1996: 71–83), the researchers argue that 'large families' correlate with delinquency.

Finally, research has been done on 'dysfunctional families' that produce criminals. Criminologists' efforts to identify the role of the domestic rumblings of family life in the creation of crime and delinquency have never been less than exhaustive. 'Parental failure' is said to be evident in poor emotional relationships between parents and their children, and in the inability of parents to exercise effective child-rearing or parenting skills.

David Farrington is arguably the best known British advocate for inserting a concern with 'dysfunctional families' into a 'human development' approach to the study of 'criminal careers'. Farrington (1996, 1997) began work with D.J. West on a 'prospective longitudinal survey' of over 400 'traditional' working-class British boys in 1961. Researchers interviewed the boys at regular intervals between the ages of eight and 32 years. They also surveyed the boys' parents with respect to factors such as income, family size, employment, child-rearing practices and 'degree of supervision', as well as interviewing their teachers to establish general patterns of school behaviour among the children. The boys' peers were invited to 'rate' factors such as 'daring', 'dishonesty', 'popularity' and 'troublesomeness'. Farrington's team 'tested' the boys at various chronological stages for intelligence, 'impulsivity', development and attainment, as well as 'assessing' the impact of living conditions, employment, relationships with parents, leisure activities and other pursuits, such as 'drinking, fighting and offending behaviour' (Farrington 1997: 15–44).

Farrington argues that 'inconsistent' and 'poor' parenting has a direct bearing on the emergence of delinquency. He and his colleagues argue that parental attitudes and the quality of supervision and discipline are vital to preventing the onset of 'anti-social behaviour'. Farrington (1996: 12–15) suggests that 'cool, rejecting parents tend to have delinquent children . . . [as do] parents who let their children roam the streets unsupervised from an early age [while] . . . warm, loving parents tend not to have delinquent children'. 'Erratic and inconsistent discipline' is also considered a major cause of delinquency (Farrington 1996: 10). This all matters because the 'anti-social' tendencies that mark out 'the delinquent' can be the start of a 'criminal career'. West and Farrington (1977) define 'anti-social' to include such things as an 'unstable job record, heavy gambling, heavy smoking, drug use, drunk driving, sexual promiscuity, spending time hanging around the street, anti-social group activity, violence and anti-establishment attitudes' (Farrington 1997: 364).

Subsequent studies in America, New Zealand and Australia have replicated Farrington's longitudinal and multivariate analysis (see Utting et al. 1993 for an overview of these studies).

That these arguments coincide with a good deal of populist and simplistic media commentary does not necessarily mean they should not be taken seriously. That this kind of research mimics the views of fundamentalist Christian propaganda and neo-conservative think-tanks which promote traditional or socially conservative views about the proper role of 'strong fathers' and nurturant mothers, permissive approaches to child-rearing, sexuality and divorce, or the sinfulness of gays and lesbians may equally just be a coincidence. However, some careful and critical thought may indicate why there are some very real problems with drawing too quick and easy a link between certain kinds of working-class and/or poor families and crime.

One of the key problems in the literature claiming to find a causal link between broken families and crime is a failure to specify what particular factors characterising families— broken or otherwise—are supposed to lead to crime. As Wells and Rankin (1986: 8) note:

> Despite the sizeable body of empirical research extending back to the turn of the century, the broken home question remains unsettled and ambiguous. A major shortcoming in the literature is the virtual absence of any systematic conceptual specification and corresponding empirical measurement of the broken home as a sociological variable. Although it seems straightforward on its face, more careful

analysis reveals it to be a summary gloss for a multiplex combination of family structural and interactional conditions.

It is simply not clear what it is about the 'broken family'—in comparison with the so-called 'intact family'—that predicts 'delinquency' or 'criminality'. As Utting (1994: 20) points out: 'Family structure—in this instance being raised in a one-parent family—may be of less direct significance than the quality of care and supervision that individual parents are able to provide.'

These observations also relate to the claim that large families are criminogenic. As with the 'broken family' model, the link between the number of children in a household and delinquency is at best weak. For example, though Farrington (1996: 14–15) argues for a correlation between family size and delinquency, he also allows that this is secondary to the nature and quality of family relations—particularly between children and parents. Similarly, Leflore (1988), in an American study, found only a tenuous relationship between family size and delinquency, concluding that 'the home environment may be more important than family structure variables for some youths'. As Rutter and Giller (1983: 109) argue, the claim that there is a close connection between family size and offending is largely unfounded.

That working-class, coloured and immigrant families and low-status families in Britain, America and Australia have tended throughout the twentieth century to have more children than white, middle-class or elite couples may well have something to do with the fixation on family size in the sociological literature. This raises the question of how certain social prejudices may have entered into the 'constructive schemes' of modern criminologists looking for a causal link between certain kinds of families and crime.

There are some very powerful elements in the constructive schemes at work in modern social science. There is the very simple idea, common among sociologists and criminologists, that 'anti-social behaviour' or 'crime' are readily identifiable—even measurable and objective— phenomena. Then there is the idea of a quasi-organic process of human development in which everything done to a child before it is five shapes its future. Finally, there is the simple idea that human conduct can be readily explained by 'causal factors' like the quality and quantity of maternal love, and that lifelong causality is at work. This gives rise to very confident claims, exemplified by David Farrington (1997: 361):

> criminal behavior does not generally appear without warning: it is commonly preceded by childhood anti-social behavior (such as bullying, lying, truanting and cruelty to animals) and followed by adult anti-social behavior (such as spouse assault, child abuse, and neglect, excessive drinking and sexual promiscuity). The word 'anti-social' of course involves a value judgement, but it seems likely that there would be a general agreement among most members of western democracies that these kinds of acts interfered with the smooth running of Western society.

There are several early warning signs about this claim. First, it is simply quite unclear what meaning the idea of 'anti-social behaviour' has, except to designate forms of conduct the researcher dislikes—and which, on this occasion, Farrington acknowledges 'involves a value judgement'. Farrington (1994) understands 'anti-social' behaviours to include being 'troublesome and dishonest' in primary school, being 'aggressive and frequent liars' at twelve to fourteen, being a 'bully' at fourteen and engaging in 'heavy drinking', 'heavy smoking', 'using prohibited drugs', 'heavy gambling' and frequent, early, unprotected and promiscuous sex by eighteen. It is salutary to remember that West and Farrington (1977) had earlier included having an 'anti-establishment attitude' in their definition of 'anti-social'.

In Australia, as numerous health and social surveys suggest, many if not most young people at eighteen have engaged in 'heavy drinking', have 'used prohibited drugs' and have engaged in frequent, often unprotected sexual activities. A substantial minority of young people are also engaged in 'heavy gambling' and 'heavy smoking'. The proposition that these activities signify 'anti-social behaviour' in a society where these attributes and activities are also widely practised and used as hallmarks of sophisticated behaviour by many adults is, frankly, quaint.

Does Farrington really want us to believe that the behaviours he refers to as 'anti-social'—either singly or in aggregate—are actually capable of 'interfering with the smooth running of Western society'? The proposition that heavy drinking, smoking and gambling are anti-social activities might come as something of a surprise to the liquor, tobacco and gambling industries. These industries constitute a substantial proportion of any modern country's economy as measured, for example, by gross domestic product providing employment for millions of workers and supplying major sponsorships for sporting and cultural events.

The very ubiquity of behaviours such as bullying, cheating and lying, which some may say are the very qualities needed for success in politics or the business world, might suggest that they have hardly impacted on 'the smooth running of Western society'. Indeed, among certain elites, sexual promiscuity and/or lying on the scale associated with various well-known but nameless presidents, prime ministers, cabinet ministers or corporate bosses suggests that, far from being 'anti-social', these behaviours are widely practised and even highly praised behaviours. The idea that there is some kind of 'causal' connection in place between 'anti-social' forms of human conduct, the selection of which plainly reflects only Farrington's value set, and criminal conduct is so questionable as to be laughable.

The fact that Farrington and those replicating his work in Australia have chosen to focus on low-status, working-class and poor families is an invisible yet major problem. Should any of the observable differences between the poor, minority and working-class families and elite families be properly understood as deficiencies or as differences—and whose judgment is to prevail? The research focus on low-status, working-class, coloured and immigrant families is a traditional preoccupation of academic research. Why aren't upper-class alcoholism, sexual promiscuity, emotional abuse or drug-taking researched to the same extent?

We can say that the quality of both the emotional life and parenting styles found among contemporary Australian families is very diverse. Australian social scientists need to take into account the fact that theirs is a society with both Indigenous peoples and immigrant groups that include significant populations of Catholic Irish, Catholic Italians, European Jews, Catholic Mexicans, Buddhist Vietnamese and Muslim Arabic peoples.

This might suggest, in an area notoriously subject to fads, fashions and advice-mongering by well-meaning experts, that it might be unwise to reduce parenting or ideas about 'effective parenting skills' to a single set of expert-derived criteria. It is undeniable that a small number of parents engage in unacceptable behaviour. It is a sad fact that the most likely killer of a child under twelve in Britain and Australia is the child's mother. Equally, there is evidence to suggest that some families across a wide spectrum of ethnicities and class backgrounds engage in brutal emotional, sexual or physical abuse of their children. The core question remains: what is to count as a parenting deficiency, and what should be understood simply as differences in child-rearing practice or as differences in managing family relationships?

As Stan Cohen (1972, 1992) has pointed out in relation to British criminology, the very selection of 'factors' for study in a lot of criminological research mitigates against any simple notion of 'objectivity'. Finally, it is especially striking that the empirical research on working-class families has the actual effect of silencing or muffling the voices of the subjects. Hil & MacMahon (2004: 4), in a recent commentary on juvenile justice research, note that the resulting literature is:

> remarkable for its lack of attention to the views and experiences of those actually caught up in the criminal justice system. We continue to know little about the lived experience of those involved in processes of criminal justice or about the ways in which these experiences relate to everyday life in communities and neighborhoods.

● CONCLUSION

Too many sociologists continue to cling to the idea that there really is a 'reality' about deviance or 'crime' which justifies an objectivist approach. The idea of 'deviance' and 'crime' as natural, obstinate and ever-threatening facts of life perpetrated by an objectively discoverable body of people ('the criminal') has continued to be recycled by the popular media and conventional sociology, and has proved remarkably resistant to critical thought.

When contemporary sociologists and criminologists do research on crime, as Braithwaite (1989) points out, they continue to do it as an 'empirical' and 'scientific' enterprise. This continuing commitment to the defining elements of 'naturalism' is found in:

- the practice and refinement of empirical measures of things like crime rates, arrest rates and recidivism rates; as well as
- the use of multivariate analysis and the search for correlations between 'variables' like class, education, ethnicity, gender, age and geography—and, more recently, unemployment and the crime rate.

Certain deep or 'meta-theoretical' assumptions continue to underpin contemporary research, including the beliefs that:

- there is a single objective and coherent social and moral reality called 'society' against which 'deviance' and crime' can be defined; this is part of the postulate of phenomenalism central to empiricism;
- deviant and criminal conduct is sufficiently stable, objective or observable to make these phenomena either amenable to study or to conceptualising within the canons of sociology or criminology established as properly 'scientific';
- the qualities defining certain patterns of conduct as 'deviant' or 'criminal' are inherent in those forms of conduct or behaviour itself and not in the relation between the behaviour and observers. That is, 'crime' and 'deviance' are 'objective' behaviours giving rise to 'observables' like 'the crime rate'; and
- the search for a 'general theory of deviance' or a 'general theory of crime' remains a deeply sensible and credible exercise, justified by the unity of these behaviours and the censures they attract across the otherwise variable range of cultures, situations and contexts (see Wilson & Herrnstein 1985). Pursuing causal and 'multivariate' explanations and developing and refining criminological 'theory', understood in Merton's terms as a deductive form, is still a central objective and task for the modern sociology of crime.

Discussion questions

17.1 Are some human behaviours always inherently bad or wrong?

17.2 Is it possible for us to know accurately about the level of crime in a society like Australia?

17.3 In what sense is crime caused by things like unemployment or poverty?

17.4 Are popular concerns about the crime rate justified?

I'm with you on the free press. It's the newspapers I can't stand.

Tom Stoppard,
Night and Day (Act I)
(1978)

KNOWING THE WORLD: 18.
THE AUSTRALIAN MEDIA

● ● SUMMARY

In the light of claims that Australia has become an 'information society' in a globalising world, we address some questions about the role of the mass media in Australia. We begin by asking what the media are. We focus first on the way the media define our relation with the world by adding to our face-to-face social relationships and interactions, and then on their role as a major part of a modern corporate economy. Second, we ask about the kinds of effects the media have and consider some arguments about the positive and negative effects. We then present a short case study on the relation of press reporting to political processes, addressing the serious issue of heroin use.

Our electronic world

A striking feature of modern life is the way we all seem to swim in an ocean of electronic media:

- Many of us wake to the sound of the radio; we switch on the TV to eat breakfast, while others read the daily newspaper on the internet or attach the earplugs of the MP3 player as we head off to school or work.

- At school, home or work, more of us are using the internet to access information for an essay, buy shares or do our banking, chat on a bulletin board, run an e-conference or send email.

- At night, many of us sit by the TV as we have dinner, or perhaps hire a DVD to watch the latest movie on our new plasma or LCD TV.

- At any time of the day, we can access 24-hour global news reports from CNN, or watch TV shows like the *Dave Letterman Show* live from New York either on TV or on the internet.

- We rely on the media for our knowledge of what is happening in the world and who matters in it. Big events like the death of a pop star, the terrorist attacks on New York on 11 September 2001, the US-led invasion of Iraq, or the Boxing Day tsunami get saturation exposure on TV.

- Groups and organisations of all sorts, from major corporations to terrorist networks like Al-Qaeda, use their access to TV or the internet to get leverage on public opinion; the true genius—some might say evil genius—of Osama bin Laden lies in his grasp of the power of media publicity.

- We sometimes construct a sense of community using the media. After the 9/11 terrorist attacks in New York or the tsunami, many Australians with no direct connection to the event were deeply shaken by the endless cycling of media reports. Many people across Australia formed a virtual community—upset and shocked by the scale of the violence or disaster.

The above box suggests why social theorists talk about 'globalisation' and point to the rise of information-based and media industries like Microsoft or Google as a key aspect of globalisation. Other writers refer to the emergence of an 'information society', or even a 'post-modern society', arguing that the modern media are redefining how we know everything and anything. As one leading post-modernist, Jean Francois Baudrillard, insists, only the media representations of the world are real.

Before we rush to agree, we need to recall that there is a long history of hyper-gloomy and/ or hyper-optimistic assessments of the impact of innovations in mass media (see box).

The impact of media innovations

- In the mid-nineteenth century, as newspapers began to achieve mass circulation and cheap books started to circulate more widely, critics like Mathew Arnold (1867) claimed that this would debauch public morality and lead to the death of good taste and the moral values that make a civilisation great.

- In the 1930s, Walter Benjamin (1968) claimed that the spread of film and radio created a fascist aesthetic. Other writers worried about the vulgarising of good taste when artists produced kitsch, pointing to Walt Disney's 1941 film *Fantasia* which used the music of J.S. Bach and Stravinsky in conjunction with Disney cartoon figures.

- In the 1950s, Frederick Wertheim (1951) was convinced that mass-produced comics would produce a tidal wave of juvenile delinquency, while John McDonald (1951) was no less convinced that rock'n'roll would produce the same evil effects.

- The introduction of television in the mid-1950s was accompanied by claims that it would both unleash a revolution in education and kill off any desire to read books.

- Images of violence or sexuality on film and TV screens remain a perennial source of dire warnings about the evil effects of such images—especially on children.

This list of meaningless claims or unsubstantiated anxieties reminds us of both the ease with which large generalisations can be advanced with no evidence, and the ways social scientists arrive at painfully silly conclusions. The list also reminds us that what people want to believe is usually more important than careful thinking or thoughtful analysis of relevant evidence.

In this chapter, we ask some basic questions that might lead to a more cautious estimation of the effects of the media on how we live and think:

- What are the media and how do they work?
- Does the evolution of the mass media change the quality of our social lives and relationships?
- Has our world become smaller because we are now familiar with larger parts of the world beyond the intimate life-world of our family, friends, school or place of work?
- Who benefits from the globalisation of the media?

● THE MODERN MASS MEDIA

The mass media can be divided into several forms (see box).

The mass media

The print media

- Major daily newspapers like *The Australian*, *The Age* and the *Herald-Sun* (in Melbourne), the *Sydney Morning Herald*, the Brisbane *Courier Mail*, the *West Australian*

- Weekly, monthly and specialist newspapers, and an array of big-circulation magazines like the *Australian Women's Weekly*; also other smaller magazines like *Men's Health*, *Playboy*, *Dolly* and *Girlfriend*, which cater for special interests

- An enormous variety of books. Australia is a society with high levels of literacy, book purchase and library borrowing

The electronic media

- A diversity of radio stations, run mostly by private business companies, a government network (the ABC and SBS) and community groups (over 95 per cent of homes have more than three radios)

- Privately owned free-to-air city and regional TV network companies (like the Seven, Nine and Ten networks), as well as the government-run ABC and SBS TV networks, and subscription TV channels provided by Foxtel (more than 94 per cent of Australian homes in 2005 had at least one TV set)

- A growth industry in home- and institution-based computers that are multimedia and linked via the internet; also a diversity of interactive visual computer games and electronic game systems, like the xBox (approximately 71 per cent of Australian homes now have a computer and 67 per cent of Australians surveyed had sent or received an email in the survey week in 2004)

The audio-visual media

- Films shown commercially in cinemas and/or available for sale or hire in DVD format at the local video shop

- Photography, such as the new digital cameras that are linked to computers

- Pre-recorded audio media, such as compact discs, DVDs and audio-cassettes, most of which are based on digital technology

Information technology

- Computers, modems, the internet and email

- New telecommunications technologies, like 3G mobile phones which link into email do digital photography and download data

- Optical fibre networks carrying a large amount of digital information, including freely downloadable music from a computer into an MP3 player

THINKING ABOUT MEDIA TECHNOLOGIES AND SOCIAL LIFE

In a literal sense, any form of media works by 'mediating' between ourselves and the larger world. We draw on the work of social theorists like David Harvey (1990) and Anthony Giddens (1990) to make a very important point about the way print and electronic media extend or expand both the content and the possibilities of the 'social'.

For a very long time, in what we can loosely define as 'pre-modern societies', people constructed their most important social relationships and activities on a face-to-face basis—and most of us continue to do so even now. In a simple sense, all those people who lived in pre-modern societies filled up the social with face-to-face relations and activities. For most of human history, people have lived in this way—usually in small-scale families and communities. The world they knew was the world as they experienced it directly through their senses. This world was bounded by two things: who people could talk to and how far they could travel. Mostly this was done on foot, or occasionally by horse-power.

It was a world people made together on the basis of talking with each other; this world was often an intensely oral culture. The development of culture, and of moral and religious beliefs, was an oral achievement. People spoke with and listened to each other, telling long stories in epic poems like Homer's *The Odyssey* and *The Iliad*, which were passed on from generation to generation. They invented all sorts of belief systems, and told stories about gods and spirits to make sense of the world. They worked in the presence of others in that world to produce food, clothing and shelter. They developed richly expressive activities like dance, music and art to celebrate the things that mattered (like sex, birth, the cycle of producing crops or flocks of animals and death) and to try to comprehend the things they did not always fully understand, like the origins of the world. The limits of the world were set by how far people could travel. It was very much the kind of society which existed among the numerous 'Aboriginal' communities in Australia before the white invasion of 1788.

In pre-modern settings, the 'social' referred to whatever took place in a specific time and place, or what we call the 'here and now', and involved face-to-face interactions. However, at some point—and we do not know precisely when—human communities invented forms of writing which involved developing a script, the technology to produce it (like pens, clay tablets or paper) and the ability to read it. Writing was the first medium of extended communications, and it was the first medium that began to affect the nature of the social.

As long ago as 10 000 years, drawings and a simple system for counting things were invented. The Egyptians invented hieroglyphs about 3100 BCE, and by 2900 BCE traders and clerks in Ur were using cuneiform to record and count the holdings in warehouses and were also using cuneiform script. By 1600 BCE, early Greek scripts (Linear B) were in use, and by 750 BCE the Greeks had evolved a fully developed alphabetical script: see Olson (1994).

Writing on clay tablets—and later on skins and paper—had one immediate effect: it meant that people could now communicate with each other outside of the face-to-face relationship. Writing made the exchange of complex ideas and information possible, and in ways that abolished the time and space of the 'here and now'. This innovation also meant that written words could now stand in for what people could no longer see or touch immediately. The evolution of writing systems both required and produced groups of people (writers, priests and later intellectuals and even various kinds of scientists) who were skilled in reading and writing. The power of writing is such that people would sometimes believe that the words they were reading or writing were more real than the things to which they referred.

Writing was, and remains, the most powerful of the techniques of mediated communication. Even now, in schools and universities, we use a combination of face-to-face modes of teaching and learning (based on speech and practical tasks in the 'here and now' of the classroom) and the medium of writing (found in books and journals, or increasingly via online technologies).

The invention of writing was succeeded by other media like the development of printing in the fifteenth century, which made possible the mass production of texts and images, culminating in the mass-circulation newspapers of the nineteenth century, which used photography to supply images to go with the text.

An amazing burst of technological innovation inevitably changes the social quality of the space across which people can speak or listen to each other. This is what the invention of the telegraph, the telephone and recording of voices and music did in the nineteenth century. The subsequent development of film, radio and TV had the same effect, making it possible to throw voices, sounds and images across ever larger spaces, and thereby expanding the domain of the 'here and now'.

The next radical shift in technology involved the dramatic speeding up of calculation and information storage and retrieval. This was made possible by digitalising information and embedding techniques of calculation and information analysis and retrieval inside electronic computers. The first working computers were operating by the late 1940s. The clever idea (introduced in the 1980s) to link computers to each other via the global telephone system made the awesome power of digital information analysis, storage and retrieval available on a global scale in the 1990s. In principle, every living human being is now linked immediately to every other human being via the internet.

For David Harvey (1990), 'modernity' is all about the development of these kinds of new technologies. He points to the way the spread of communications technologies—most dramatically the invention of the telegraph in the 1840s and then the spread of the telephone in the 1880s—further compressed time and space; information which had taken weeks or months to travel suddenly became available almost instantaneously. By the 1930s, cricket fans could listen to 'live' broadcasts of Australia–England Test cricket at Lords.

Harvey says that taking into account the speed at which people can now fly from Sydney to London or New York, or the speed with which electronic business activities (like the sale of shares or currency) can be transacted, has produced a compression of both time and space. Harvey illustrates this point by suggesting that the globe is now only one-fiftieth of the size it was in the 1560s: this is because a jet airliner is roughly 50 times faster than a sixteenth century sailing ship. For Harvey, the most recent technologies—like global TV news services or the internet—are at the heart of the 'globalisation' experience, and also ensure we are moving into a 'post-modern' period.

For a sociologist like Anthony Giddens (1990), what he calls 'modernity' is characterised not by the compression of time and space so much as by the extension of the social world, which becomes increasingly 'virtual'. This, Giddens says, leads to the 'emptying out' of those practices found in the social space and time that distinguished 'pre-modern societies'—that is, the time and space of the 'here and now'.

For Giddens (1990: 18), 'modernity', or what we have called the 'modernising process', 'increasingly tears space away from place by fostering relations between absent others, locationally distant from any face-to-face situations . . . and locales are thoroughly penetrated by and shaped in terms of social influences quite distant from them'. It is clear that modern media technologies in all their forms are key elements in this process.

For Giddens, there are two mechanisms that produce what he calls a 'stretching of time and space', which work to remove us from the immediacy of the face-to-face world. These mechanisms are 'symbolic tokens' and the growth of 'expert systems' of knowledge.

The key symbolic tokens of our time include:

- money, which we use to buy goods and services or simply to evaluate the value of things;
- the units of time (minutes, hours and days), which we use to organise all sorts of relationships and activities; and
- various kinds of official knowledge, such as unemployment data, gross domestic product, poverty or fertility rates, which we use to inform ourselves about our communities. Modern governments, experts and the news media rely a lot on these statistics to tell stories about things like social problems, progress or our place in the world.

Our society is also increasingly reliant on the work of 'experts' and their 'expert systems'. As Max Weber indicated, the expansion of technical rationality—which he argued characterised, even defines, 'modern societies'—depends on the availability of very complex technologies and systems. We depend on these working properly, and this means we have to trust the experts and officials who run the array of complex systems.

Giddens (1990: 16) suggests that 'modernity' is all about living in and depending on ever larger, more complex and extended and abstracted 'expert systems' and 'symbolic tokens'. This does not mean that most of the important social experiences in our life are not still based on face-to-face relationships with family, friends, lovers and work colleagues. Rather, in the kind of modern society in which we live, we also come to depend on people we never meet or know in any sense intimately to do things that make our life-world possible. Giddens calls this the 'disembedding of social systems'. In such a setting, we also come to rely on 'continual inputs of knowledge affecting the actions of individuals and groups' (Giddens 1990: 17). In this respect, we can think of things like:

- the endless release of research-based warnings about the latest SARS outbreak;
- official social and economic statistics to tell us how unemployment rates are falling, putting pressure on housing interest rates; or
- media reports and commentaries on social and political events and problems, which helps us to work out what to think and who we will vote for at the next election, or whether we are being too permissive in raising our children.

Theorists like Giddens and Harvey tell us in a somewhat abstracted way how the modern media play a part in shrinking time and place. Though the rich intimate relations we have with friends and family remain a crucial part of our experience of the social world, our experience now also includes extended or abstracted social relations. This means we continuously rely on people like journalists and TV cameramen for basic knowledge about our world.

This theoretical account might lead us to the idea that we are all experiencing these media technologies in the same way. Nothing, of course, could be further from the truth. Technological determinism has been a recurrent bad habit of thought in the social sciences; however, people come to media technologies like newspapers, TV and the internet with different intentions and interests in using those technologies.

So how should we think about the spread of the mass media over the last century? One way is to look at how social scientists have, in George Lakoff's (2005) terms, framed discussions about the effects of the mass media.

● CONSERVATIVE REACTIONS

The oldest tradition of media studies was associated with literary critics—people like Mathew Arnold (1976). Arnold claimed that the new mass newspapers and the production of cheap books were responsible for the 'debasement' of culture and the spread of ugliness, coarseness and bad taste. This response belongs to a frankly elitist and conservative tradition that drew a straight-line connection between the 'rise of the masses', democratic political change and the spread of 'low' (i.e. 'popular') culture, courtesy of the mass media. In the twentieth century, writers like Ortega Y Gasset (1968) and George Steiner (1986), watching the spread of radio, cinema, TV and 'popular music', have agreed. The implications of this tradition are on full display in Steiner's *In Bluebeard's Castle*, his famous diatribe in favour of what he calls high culture.

Those who work in the conservative tradition make a lot out of the 'mass' nature of the modern media. Until around the fourteenth century, in places like China, Japan, India, the Middle East, Europe and England, the 'media' consisted of expensive, hand-copied books and manuscripts that were usually in the hands of a tiny proportion of the population. Few people could afford to buy the manuscripts, and a very small number were literate enough to read these texts. The invention and expansion of the printing press in the fifteenth century changed this, although it was a slow process.

Production of books gradually increased. Then came the invention of the telegraph and the telephone, which made the world smaller in quite dramatic ways after the 1860s. The late nineteenth century saw the rise of mass-circulation newspapers. Since that time, we have experienced a continuous avalanche of inventions in the twentieth century, with the development and spread of:

- popular photography;
- audio recordings (from cylinders to CDs and tapes);
- cinema;
- radio (from crystal wireless to transistor);
- television (including videotape and VCRs); and
- computers.

For conservatives, the rise of the mass media represents a struggle between 'high' culture and 'low' or 'mass' culture—a struggle which mass culture has won.

Conservatives in Europe and England, like Alexis de Tocqueville, Mathew Arnold, F.R. Leavis and George Steiner, have written mournfully about the 'decline of civilisation'. In Australia, this position is taken by people like John Carroll (2005). There is also a left-wing version (see Adorno 1980) which says the achievements of Western civilisation have been debased by capitalist mass media. This story reflects a bleak view of the values of 'ordinary people' and the achievements of modern culture.

According to conservatives like George Steiner (1986) and Orlega Y Gasset (1968), in 'the good old days' before democracy, industry and modernity took over wealthy aristocrats dominated society. These aristocrats were few in number, but had 'good taste'. They set the standards of beauty and creativity. Further, they had the money and taste to employ great artists like Giotto, da Vinci and Rembrandt. They commissioned great writers like Chaucer, Shakespeare or Dante, architects and sculptors like Cellini and Michelangelo, and musicians like Monterverdi, Mozart or Bach to create 'great works of art'.

In the eighteenth century, however, came the 'revolt of the masses', evidenced in democracy and the Industrial Revolution. The rise of the masses was linked to new technology which supported the growth of the mass media. Instead of art meeting the needs of the few, it became 'popular'. The result, according to this story, is a culture of rubbish and kitsch, disposable throw-aways and mass entertainment, where no one knows the value of anything unless it is a dollar value. Instead of excellence, we get mediocrity. We use mass-produced plastic cups instead of high-quality, finely hand-crafted silver goblets. We look at posters rather than great paintings like the Mona Lisa. We watch poorly acted and scripted TV soaps instead of Shakespearian plays.

These conservatives also claim that the machinery of mass culture has debased the great works of art. This is because mass culture has 'popularised' art. They point to Walt Disney's rendition of Bach in the cartoon *Fantasia*, or to the use of da Vinci's *Mona Lisa* to promote a toothpaste.

● SOCIOLOGICAL FUNCTIONALISTS

Many sociologists have argued that the conservative account is wrong and that the modern media industries are both useful and functional to modern society. Mainstream sociologists—especially those who like structural and functional interpretations—have tended to a more benign view, treating the mass media as a system that produces negative, sometimes neutral or beneficial effects. This tradition of media researchers has used empiricist (i.e. survey) research methods to establish 'the effects of the media' on the audience (Singer 1980; Dusseyer 1979; McQuail 1986). Conventional sociologists, drawing on the work of American writers like Talcott Parsons and Robert Merton, say that every society needs a flow of communications to survive and prosper, and that modern society needs this more than others.

The modern mass media are simply the latest version of something each society has always had to have. According to this conventional sociological account (e.g. White 1964: 13–21), the mass media are at best functional, and at worst benign. Modern commercial films, radio, TV and newspapers simply provide communication channels for messages, information or entertainment that people value, use and need. They also argue that if the media were a real problem, people would stop using them or buying their services. Even advertising, it is argued, meets people's needs for information.

Writers in this tradition say the conservatives' account of the destruction of 'high culture' by 'mass culture' is either meaningless and/or untrue. They claim there never was a time when any society dominated by an aristocracy (with its elite privileges and values and whose members commissioned high art) was also a decent, well-behaved and humane society. In sixteenth century England, when Shakespeare was writing his plays, Londoners—including the nobility—would routinely leave the playhouse to visit the bear-pits to watch dogs and bears tear each other to pieces. After that, they would head off to Tyburn to watch a public burning of heretics or the execution of traitors. In the twentieth century, Ilse Koch, the female commandant of a Nazi German death camp, regularly sat listening at night to Bach's music as she tanned the skins of Jews killed that day in the camp.

This more benign account argues that the modern mass media enhance people's access to great works of art. Television brings Shakespeare to the masses while Puccini's operas can be seen by millions. Cinema, as a distinctively modern art form for the masses, brings new styles of writing, acting and imagination to more people: great film-makers like Bergman, Spielberg, Kurosawa or the Coen brothers illuminate the human condition.

Here, issues of good or bad taste are irrelevant when what is at issue is the smooth, economically and culturally functional circulation of ideas and information and the supply of entertainment. The modern media are functional to society because of the prosperity and employment they generate. This account recognises that the modern media industries are big money-makers and employers. They are also at the forefront of the apparent transformation of a nation like Australia from an industrial to a post-industrial society.

● CRITICAL RESPONSES

Marxist and feminist theorists contributed to a critical tradition, which argued that the mass media have long been a key part of a capitalist or patriarchal society, working to justify and reproduce class and/or gender inequality (Bennett 1977; Hall 1978; Chomsky 2002). Marxist and many feminist writers have stressed the way the mass media work to make inequality and exploitation seem either reasonable or invisible. Some radicals argue that newspapers and TV are inherently 'pro-capitalist' or 'anti-woman'. This is because the media are run or owned by capitalist businessmen and/or dominated by men. Marxists claim that the modern media are not neutral, but are at the centre of modern capitalist economies. The media play a key role in big business.

Not only are the media part of the business and corporate world, sharing anti-union and anti-strike attitudes with other businesses, they also legitimise inequalities by portraying them as normal, natural or inevitable, or they censor evidence of oppression and inequality. In other words, the media function as a primary agent of 'false consciousness'.

A sophisticated version of this story was developed by writers like Stuart Hall, who was associated with the Birmingham School of Critical Cultural Studies. Rather than a picture of simple class or gender oppression, they claim the media carry the contradictions of such a society while supporting an often-precarious status quo. Hall (1978) claims the working classes have three options in respect to social inequality and oppression: they can resist; they can attempt to negotiate with the elites; or they can be co-opted.

These writers see the media as part of a range of leisure activities which drain the working classes of their energy for radical social change. They argue that the media give young working-class people language, clothing, hairstyles and music which become 'a means of expression through which groups in subordinate structural positions attempted to negotiate or oppose the dominant meaning system'. Brake (1987), for example, argues that working-class youth cultures:

> arise as attempts to resolve collectively experienced problems resulting from contradictions in the social structure . . . they generate a form of collective identity from which an individual constructs an identity outside that ascribed by class, identity and occupation. This is nearly always a temporary solution and in no sense a real material solution but one which is solved at the cultural level. (1987: ix)

This translates into the claim that 'youth cultures' provide young people with a way of expressing symbolic forms of protest and opposition. However, these forms of expression do not pose serious challenges to the social order of capitalism because any genuinely critical sting has been softened.

It seems clear that the modern media are part of the big-business sector. A long time ago, Henry Mayer (1964) argued that any modern media company was indistinguishable from any other capitalist business enterprise in terms of four core features (see box).

The modern media organisation

- Modern media organisations exist as companies whose shares are available for sale on the stock market. Their market value and assets make them very valuable.

- Media organisations are run by boards of directors. Their members are typically wealthy and powerful men, and are usually also found on the boards of other companies.

- A TV or newspaper company operates to make a profit; if it fails to do so, it will go out of business.

- A normal pattern of unequal power relations operates within these companies between the owners and managers and the workers, who are paid to produce what the company requires.

At the start of the twenty-first century, a small number of companies own most of our commercial media. These media companies, like Rupert Murdoch's News Limited or James Packer's media conglomerate, are huge in terms of turnover and profit. The mass media have to succeed as any other business must do in a market economy. As consumers, we purchase access to the media by paying for a newspaper, magazine, CD or film, or renting a video or a film. In each of these cases, there is a market of consumers and a business system (or market) of suppliers and producers. Yet in some cases, like radio or television, we do not seem to pay for what we get. How does a TV station earn its way?

In fact, most of the commercial media are heavily dependent on advertising. This leads to a surprising feature of the political economy of some parts of the commercial media, such as 'free-to-air' radio or commercial TV. If you ask what they sell, the answer is that they sell audiences to advertisers. Unlike most other industries, the electronic media sell their audiences. TV and radio stations need to sell air-time to advertisers. Their ability to do so depends on the companies' ability to demonstrate the size and nature of their audience. This includes knowing how many men, women and children watch particular shows, as well as the levels of these groups' incomes and their purchasing habits. Such factors determine the level of advertising fees the companies can charge advertisers.

In Australia, for a long time now, Nine has been the top-rating TV network in terms of the total size of its audience. This means the Nine Network can charge the highest advertising rates, especially at peak viewing times (between 6.00 p.m. and 9.30 p.m.). This is also true of the mass print media like newspapers. Customers certainly buy their newspapers. Yet the price covers only a small part of the cost of producing the paper or magazine—let alone making a profit. Newspapers and magazines rely heavily on selling advertising space to earn their income—and make a profit.

What of the larger claim that the modern media help to prop up the existing social and economic order? One response to this claim has been made by the post-structuralists.

● POST-STRUCTURALIST AND POST-MODERN THEORIES

Over the past few decades, the field of media studies has been redefined as a form of cultural studies, informed by post-structuralist and post-modernist frameworks. Post-structuralist and post-modern theorists argue that that media images carry a near-infinite variety of meanings and messages. As Garnham (1990: 1–55) points out, the post-modernist insistence on the actual incoherence of the meanings of media images and text seems to affect the way those like Baudrillard or Kroker, who work within this tradition, write. We recall that post-modernists like Lyotard (1984) make the following points:

- There is no ultimate 'truth' if truth is understood as some correspondence between the way things actually are and the various systems of knowledge or the technologies like writing or images we have to catch reality.

- Post-modernists reject the 'commonsense' belief that words correspond with things/objects in the world. Words do not correspond with things but shape the way we see things: words correspond only with other words.
- Any society and any process of historical change is so complex that no single theory or scientific claim can describe it. Instead, a multiplicity of social relations exists.

When these propositions are applied to the modern media, post-modernists deny that the media report on reality in ways which we can judge as 'true' or 'untrue'. Instead, they maintain the media become a system of meanings and images which refer only to other meanings and images. For example, post-modernists may say that Princess Diana became famous not because she was good or worthy, but because she was famous and constantly photographed—equally, there was no essential truth about Diana: her image could be filled with many different kinds of meanings depending on who was looking at her. Generally, post-modernists argue that the media are simply an enormous factory for manufacturing illusions. When some fans see a TV character shot, die or marry, they can fall into deep grief or ecstasy; this is a classic post-modern experience because people can no longer distinguish what is 'true' from what is not.

These arguments are part of the fervour of debate about the negative and beneficial effects of the media. We have see variants of these views ever since the invention of printing, newspapers and more modern forms of media like comics, TV, radio and film. Every year, 'new' debates erupt about the effects of too much violence or sex on TV (or more recently in video games).

● EFFECTS OF THE MEDIA

As we have said already, these kinds of arguments are part of an ongoing history of concern expressed by 'responsible' people about the 'bad' effects of the mass media. 'Responsible' people nowadays get upset about perceived links between crime and the modern media. These people have a field day when it is 'discovered', as it was with the two boys who killed a two-year-old boy in Britain in 1994, that the older boys had seen a video of the film *Chucky*. (The movie's main character was a homicidal infant doll that killed people.) This was said to 'prove' that violent films corrupt young, innocent children and breed violence.

Is there anything problematic about such explanations and the claim that there are strong causal links between a certain kind of media 'input' and a certain negative behavioural 'output'? The way we frame the question is crucial to the answers we get. No research can ever be free from assumptions. If, for example, you ask, 'What effect does X (violence, sex or bad news) have on an audience?', this is different from asking, 'How do audiences use images of X (violence, sex or bad news)?' The first question already presupposes that it is both possible and desirable to look for causal links based on the assumption that much of our behaviour is determined by external factors. Conversely, to frame the question in terms of how a given audience uses the media assumes that people have a lot of choice about how they read a newspaper or watch and understand a TV news item.

Since it is useful to develop some basic critical skills, let us keep the role of assumptions in mind as we examine three typical claims made about the media.

Claim 1: Television is a visual medium

If we assume that seeing is the basis for believing or knowing anything, we may want to approach TV as a visual medium. This points us towards the idea that TV is predominantly a visual medium. However, there is a simple test of this claim which you can easily carry out.

Before the nightly TV news starts, turn off the sound, watch the next half-hour and try to grasp or understand what is being reported using only the visual images. What sense can you make of these soundless images? The answer is almost nothing. TV may look like it is a visual medium, but it is strikingly reliant on the spoken word to make any sense.

Claim 2: TV is more objective than newspapers, because words can lie but visual images cannot

Survey after survey in Australia suggest that a large majority of people do not trust print media to be accurate or 'objective'. They say they prefer TV news because you can believe what you see. The claim that TV is more objective than newspapers is difficult to test directly. It certainly relies on the simple assumption that seeing is believing, and therefore that cameras capture the truth better than journalists who use words. We have already tested this simple idea in the claim that TV is a visual medium and suggested that, without words, TV news makes no sense.

One further test involves establishing how much detail a TV news item offers in comparison with a newspaper item on the same news item. Try using a watch to time the longest item on the TV news and compare that with the longest newspaper report the next morning, then judge which of the two forms of media is the most credible.

You may also want to think about the credibility of the images. Do the images being presented actually refer to the news item? TV networks have been criticised for using certain footage that has no relationship to the news item. Others have been outed by TV shows like the ABC's *Media Watch* for screening what are in effect propaganda documentaries prepared by PR companies on behalf of corporate clients. Or, to test the basic assumption that cameras or images can never lie, you might want to think about how different techniques—the way the person with the camera angles the images, the way light is used and the editing of shots—actually transmit different messages.

Claim 3: Images of violence on TV or video/film make people want to go out and kill or commit violent acts

One of the most persistent anxieties many people—especially parents—have about TV and film is the effect on children of viewing violence. Many a psychologist has achieved their fifteen minutes of fame by producing research findings or laboratory data to confirm such a link.

In debates about the media, most of the negative arguments about bad media effects rely on certain assumptions about people being conditioned and shaped by their social environment via the socialisation process. If you ask, 'What effect does X (violence, sex or bad news) have on an audience?', this question assumes that media audiences and consumers are passive and ready to be shaped by what they see or hear. This kind of research, and the larger debate about 'effects', are shaped by an underlying assumption that the modern audience is passive and easily influenced. Much of this debate is based on socialisation theory, which sees people as actors whose roles and norms of behaviour are shaped and determined by primary and secondary socialisation.

What if we ask, 'How do young people use TV?' There is growing evidence from modern research which indicates that people are not shaped by what they watch; rather, when confronted by some form of media, people actively select from what the media is putting out and relate it to their own symbolic meaning systems, creative intentions and practices. Livingstone's (2002: 166–210) work indicated that, even if the TV is constantly on in a living room, people are not passive, apathetic, uncritical viewers at all. Far from being the passive viewers of popular mythology, audiences actively collaborate with the screen to create and recreate a web of meanings that are relevant to them and are anchored in their own lives. Willis's research (1990) indicates that young people are highly literate watchers who actively select and interpret what TV offers. This approach to the study of media suggests that people have familiarity with and understanding of different TV genres (comedy, drama, soaps). Most people do not mistake fiction for reality.

What we are saying is that, although the mass media like TV offers a one-way form of communication, this does not mean that communication is actually one-way. For communication to exist, there needs to be interaction between the sender of the messages and the receiver who interprets the message. In other words, the message can be given many different meanings.

Older forms of communication (newspapers, TV and radio) typically involve a one-way process (from sender to receiver), while more recent information technology, such as the internet, allows for a more genuinely interactive process. With the internet, users become both senders and receivers; they get to shape the information as they are simultaneously shaped by it. People not only interpret the messages they receive in a variety of ways, they also have the opportunity to 'invent' themselves. This is done through the dialogues in which they engage. They can take on a different gender, age, ethnicity—these identity markers can be altered on the net. People do this regularly and in different ways as they converse electronically through the media and across cyberspace (Porter 1997: 201–11).

Ultimately, our capacity to think carefully about issues like the effects of the media on our community will require very fine-grained research. In the case study which follows, we demonstrate the complex interplay between political processes and media reporting by addressing the issue of heroin use.

A case study: The press and heroin policy

From the 1980s through into the twenty-first century, the sale and use of heroin in Australia has been at the centre of an ongoing policy crisis. While heroin use is widely understood to be central to a range of criminal justice, public health and social policy problems, the inability—or refusal—by governments to move beyond the criminalisation of heroin use has stymied any ability to address the actual as distinct from the fantasised problems with heroin use.

For example, in July 1997, following a bevy of committee inquiries and task forces, Commonwealth, state and territory health ministers agreed to adopt a version of 'harm minimisation' by initiating a 'safe injection room' trial to begin in the Australian Capital Territory. However, on 17 August 1997, Prime Minister Howard announced that the Commonwealth would not support such a trial. There is strong evidence (see McArthur 1999; Lawrence et al. 2000) that a month-long media-led intervention killed off an initiative which had resulted from four years of policy research and development. A campaign by leading commercial radio personalities like Alan Jones, John Laws and Stan Zemanek, as well as the Sydney *Daily Telegraph*, persuaded John Howard that he lacked public support for this policy innovation. Howard subsequently reinstated a 'zero tolerance' strategy.

Central to many policy-making practices are both media representations of problems and media-based narratives about how governments and public opinion are connected inside the electoral cycle. The press, using a variety of linguistic devices such as 'constitutive metaphors' (Schon 1998), often help to constitute a policy problem. The press not only play a significant role in 'reality constitution', but their interventions in the political process of making—or breaking—consensus can also be quite important. They can, for example, stand in for 'the public' or for public opinion, or they can set about mobilising or focusing public opinion through the use of forums like telephone polls or Letters to the Editor. Alternately, they can put a brake on change or reform proposals by reaffirming long-standing or 'traditional' ideas or representations of problem populations or practices, and send these endlessly back into a policy-making network. On rare occasions, they can generate and then 'run' a political or policy crisis which can lead to radical policy change, the resignation of a minister or even an entire government.

It has long been conventional for journalists to represent what they do as an empiricist enterprise based either on eyewitness accounts or interviews by journalists, with photographs used to add veracity. Far more useful is the idea that the media, and the press in particular, produce not 'news' but 'olds', and do so within a relatively closed framework in which not too much reality is actually allowed to intrude because this would force a major recasting of the routinised approach to 'reporting the news'.

In effect, the press create and use modern myths in their reporting of heroin use. It produces narratives about experienced professional heroes/helpers fighting the villains or helping the victims, who are in fact the same group: perpetrators when they are 'drug traffickers', or victims when portrayed as 'junkies' or 'addicts'.

● CONCLUSION

Against the conservatives and the radicals, Willis (1990) and others argue that shows such as TV soaps are a popular genre because they offer images, ideas and activities which ordinary people may either identify with or reject. The media also offer escapism and fantasy.

Contrary to the claims of highbrow critics, who worry about the effects of mass culture, people constantly interpret, judge and rework the material they see, read and hear, finding points of identification in their own lives. And, although certain forms of mass media do communicate via a one-way process, communication involves interaction between the sender of the message and the receiver, who interprets the message.

Discussion questions

18.1 Are people 'cultural dopes' when it comes to watching TV or listening to the radio, or do we have an ability to think critically about what we watch and hear?

18.2 Has Western civilisation gone into a steep decline by losing sight of the values that matter because of the effects of the modern mass media?

18.3 Do talkback radio hosts have too much power?

18.4 Would we know more or less about our world if all the TV news shows were stopped?

We do not inherit
from our parents,
we borrow from our
children.

Anon

19. SUSTAINABILITY

- Summary

- What is sustainability?

- Why has sustainability come to be seen as an important issue?

- New social movements

- Sustainability and the environmental movement

- Economic liberalism

- Privatisation

- Deregulation

- Conclusion: Sustainability in an era of economic liberal policy?

- Discussion questions

● ● SUMMARY

Over the past two decades, 'sustainability' has become an idea central to social practices on the part of governments, policy-makers, organisations in the public, community and private sectors and citizens. We begin with a discussion of sustainability. We then ask why it has become such an important contemporary idea. We discuss one recent explanation for the preoccupation with 'sustainability' offered by Ulrich Beck in terms of his theory of 'risk society'. We then turn to the role played by new social movements like the environmental movement. Finally, we explore the paradox that the successes of the environmental movement have occurred at the very time that a major 'sea change' has been taking place in the political and policy-making cultures of most Western societies, understood as a shift away from a mixed economy (informed by a Keynesian tradition of social liberalism) involving intensive state involvement in economic management, and towards an 'economic liberal' policy model which emphasises market-based activities.

Each day, Australians are confronted by such things as the need to separate their rubbish and put recyclable material into one bin and ordinary rubbish in another, and choosing between asking for plastic supermarket bags or purchasing a reusable 'green' bag. Or they may see some of the following on the nightly TV news:

- Enthusiasts for wind power generators clash with local residents who complain about the 'unsightly' or 'noisy' giant propellers and claim they will reduce their enjoyment of the coastal views or cut the value of their properties.
- Governments announce a further extension of water restrictions for an indefinite period in major cities.
- Protestors picket supermarkets that refuse to sell anything but eggs laid by battery hens and laboratories engaged in producing genetically modified food products.
- Greenpeace boats crewed by environmental activists monitor larger Japanese whaling boats in the international waters off the coasts of Australia, trying to prevent the whaling vessels from killing whales—while also trying to avoid being sunk by those whalers.
- Environmental peak bodies like the Australian Conservation Foundation (ACF) complain that the Howard government is failing to give anything like the proper level of support to the Kyoto Protocols for reducing the emission of greenhouse gases like carbon dioxide.
- 2005 was declared to be the hottest year on record in Australia and the Weather Bureau suggests this is evidence of global warming.
- Debates about the virtues and social and environmental costs of nuclear power in the context of growing concern about fossil fuels heating the earth.

These things point to some basic shifts that are taking place in the way people in societies like Australia understand themselves in relation to the world. While it may be hard to measure these shifts, there is little doubt that many Australians now think and live differently to the ways they would have understood their place in the world in, say, 1950 or even 1970. What we are seeing are changes in the ways we think about and use energy sources like oil or electricity, consume water, drive cars, and worry about pollution and the purity of what we eat. Increasing numbers of people are also experimenting with new ways of living, either voluntarily or because they have no choice. The preoccupation with sustainability is another way of thinking about the development of new kinds of sensibilities, which includes thinking about issues in global ways.

Over the past two decades, 'sustainability' has become a core idea and a source of new kinds of behaviour for governments, policy-makers, organisations and ordinary citizens. The language of 'sustainability' is now applied to many different things: we hear talk of sustainable environment, sustainable land care, sustainable water systems, sustainable policy, sustainable economy, sustainable consumption, sustainable growth, sustainable relations and so on. Sustainability is also being invoked even when people don't actually use the word. This is evident, for example, in conversations about what to do with nuclear waste, pesticides, the soaring demands of energy and the option of nuclear power and renewable energy, problems of transport and biodiversity—they are all discussions about sustainability.

Further evidence of the popularity of sustainability is the number of times the language of sustainability appears in the titles of state, federal and local government departments and in the names of research centres. In the late 1990s, Australian governments committed themselves to what has come to be called the 'triple bottom line'. This means that governments say they will scrutinise their activities and policies to ensure they supply three kinds of sustainability: fiscal, environmental and social.

'Sustainability talk' is also scattered throughout much of advertising material to which we are subjected and it can be seen in many of our bookshops, which now have shelves full of books on sustainability and the environment.

Finally, sustainability is an idea which has caused a lot of public controversy and even conflict. The idea of sustainability can act as a point of division, separating people along major political, economic, social and cultural fault lines. Considering the impact of an idea like sustainability leads us to ask several questions:

- What does 'sustainability' mean?
- Why are more people recognising sustainability as a significant social issue, and why has the concept of 'sustainability' caught on in the way it has?
- Does the work of Ulrich Beck (1992) on 'risk society' illuminate or obscure our understanding?

- What does the fact that 'sustainability' has become a concept central to both significant social conflict and political debate in our time tell us about our society?

We begin with a discussion of sustainability before asking why it has become an important issue in recent years. We consider two kinds of explanations. One is provided by Beck (1992) in his account of the rise of 'risk society'. Another looks to the role played by new social movements (Touraine 1985, 1988), like the environmental movement and what is sometimes called the 'new class' (Gouldner 1979).

• WHAT IS SUSTAINABILITY?

Although there is plenty of evidence to point to the contested nature of sustainability, there is enough consensus for a broad account of what it refers to. Sustaining something means maintaining it. In this sense, sustainability derives semantically from the conservation movement. McDaniel (2002: 1457) for example argues that, despite the ambiguities surrounding the concept of sustainability, it 'has become the keystone of the global dialogue about the human future. But what exactly do we intend to sustain and what will that require of us?' As McDaniel goes on to explain: 'The dialogue about sustainability is about a change in the human trajectory that will require us to rethink old assumptions and engage the large questions of the human condition.'

However, as many ecologists and environmentalists argue, if this kind of conservation is to occur, many other things will need to be changed. Writers like Goldie et al. (2005: 1), for example, talk about sustainability in terms of the globe's land, atmosphere, sea and all who inhabit those places:

> Sustainability refers to the capacity of our planet—or what biologists call the biosphere—to provide for the full range of human concerns in the long term. In Australia we are faring well economically but both our social and environmental systems are showing evidence of serious damage. At a global level, inequity and inequality of opportunity lie at the heart of global sustainability, terror and wars. If we are to survive as a species, there will need to be a drastic change in conventional values, economic structures and social arrangements.

Sustainability generally refers to ideas and actions that are critical to the quality of our individual and collective lives, health and indeed very survival of all human and non-human life on the planet. The prospect of a sustainable future involves issues like population growth and whether each of us can live a full life within the context of the planet's means. This is an important question, given that there are more people alive today than ever before, and given that more people live longer lives and enjoy standards of living that were simply unthinkable a few decades ago.

Sustainability can be used to refer to things such as a sustainable community, sustainable farming practices, or a sustainable economy or business. Much of the discussion of sustainability depends on an often highly technical discussion of data and measurements of everything from energy use or economic growth and consumption to numbers of people, plants or animals. Paul Ginsborg (2005) uses measures of growth to explain what is not sustainable and to advocate the need for action. He argues that in a hundred years, between 1890 and the 1990s, the global economy expanded by 1400 per cent. World industrial output increased 40 times, while our use of energy increased thirteen times. Pollution of the atmosphere has quadrupled in the last 50 years (Ginsborg 2005: 37).

Ginsborg points out that the richest 20 per cent of the world's population are responsible for 86 per cent of all private consumer spending. The poorest 20 per cent, on the other hand, account for only 1.3 per cent of private spending. Meanwhile, there are 1.4 billion people who do not have regular access to drinking water. In short, 'those who are the richest and consume the most, pollute the most' (2005: 38–9).

Yet much of the talk about sustainability encompasses more than natural resources and the environment, or issues of air pollution, clean soil and the supply of clean water. Contemporary ideas of sustainability include areas like the economy, politics, social and community life. The term 'sustainable communities', for example, usually refers to things like building and maintaining social infrastructure like public transport, health and education systems. It means ensuring citizens of a given community have employment opportunities with adequate incomes, as well as a political or social system that is free from intimidation and the arbitrary exercise of oppressive power.

• WHY HAS SUSTAINABILITY COME TO BE SEEN AS AN IMPORTANT ISSUE?

What we offer here is an outline of Beck's (1992) concern with the environmental crisis and how that relates to the evolution of a 'risk society'. This discussion is used to show why we need to be careful when offering large-scale or abstracted theoretical explanations. Talk about risk has become central to many of the key social and natural science disciplines. What is this talk about, and why did it begin to surface in the 1980s and 1990s?

For centuries, the idea of risk was the preserve of gamblers. From the eighteenth to the twentieth centuries, first actuaries associated with the insurance industry, and more recently emergency services, have made the concept of 'risk' central to their professional calculations or interventions. It has even entered into the upper echelons of social theory.

More recently, 'risk' has become a central metaphor used by contemporary social theorists to discuss the regulation of human affairs in 'late modernity' in terms of what is called 'risk society' (Beck 1992; Kelly 1998; Lupton 1999). Some of the leading social theorists of our time are now preoccupied with the category of risk, meant to define the leading quality of an entire social order. Given the extraordinary importance attached to 'social theory'—not least by its practitioners—it is not surprising that the idea of risk has moved on to a broader intellectual and cultural stage. For this, Ulrich Beck has something to answer.

Beck's work (1992, 1998) contributes to one of the central themes of contemporary social theory, and builds on a persistent interest among sociologists and theorists about how best to characterise societal development. Since August Comte, social theorists have been curious about how to define and describe the evolution of 'modern society'. Beck coined the idea of the 'risk society' and thereby made his mark on this tradition.

When he spoke of 'risk', Beck (1992) referred to the kinds of anxiety or uncertainty posed by environmental catastrophe, the threat of nuclear war or epidemic diseases like AIDS. The notion of 'risk society' also contributed to long-standing debates about how to identify the shift from 'modernity' (or 'industrial society' or 'capitalism') to a 'post-modern' (or 'post-industrial') condition or 'informationalist society'.

Beck (1992, 1998; Beck et al. 1993) and others, like Giddens (1990), explain what is now happening by claiming it is part of a transition from one type of society ('classical', 'modern' or 'industrial' society) to another ('risk society', 'post-industrial' or 'post-modern' society). According to Beck, modern societies are in transition from being a 'class society' to a 'risk society'. This, he says, means that modern societies are now passing from being 'class-based' and concerned to distribute 'socially produced wealth and related conflicts' (1992: 20) to becoming 'risk-producing societies', where people have to address the consequences of excessive production like environmental hazards.

Beck (1998: 9) says transition also involves the claim that society 'has become a laboratory where there is nobody in charge'. According to Beck, a defining feature of our phase of modernity (what he calls 'radicalised modernity') is that our society now produces a range of hazards and risks for which no one is actually responsible, and for which there are frequently no apparent explanations.

Within industrial society, risks were produced locally and there were appropriate respondents (e.g. the welfare state) which accepted responsibility for locally produced risks and dangers, and which took collective responsibility through statutory protection and compensation for accidents, illness or unemployment. Although Beck (1998: 17) focuses on the manufacture of ecological hazards, he indicates that the same mechanisms which produce ecological hazards are also producing 'the disintegration of nuclear families, stable labour markets, segregated gender roles, [and] social classes'. These he identifies as the spread of new technologies, globalisation and the marketisation of what were once public services. As he emphasises, these factors mean that nobody is in control, and nobody is responsible (Beck 1998: 12). What is left is recognition of the reality and the emotions involved in dealing with the new forms of 'organised irresponsibility' through the use of the old schemes. According to Beck (1998: 16):

> the modes of determining and perceiving risk, attributing causality and allocating compensation have irreversibly broken down, throwing the function of bureaucracies, states, economies and science into question. Risks that were calculable under industrial society become incalculable and unpredictable in risk society.

As Beck argues, we face a basic problem in our time. This problem is that most people operate with the belief that they can interpret and explain what is happening by using traditional or 'industrial' modes of understanding and categories which assume some institutional or social responsibility, when these categories and expectations have actually been rendered irrelevant.

The transition out of a modern industrial society involves the rise of an increasingly individualised society which can be seen in the demise of old institutions and the loss of the traditional institutions socialising power. As Beck explains:

> Risk society begins where tradition ends, when, in all spheres of life, we can no longer take traditional certainties for granted. The less we can rely on traditional securities, the more risk we have to negotiate.
>
> There is an important line of argument which connects the theory of risk society, in this context to the processes of individualisation in spheres of work, family life and self-identity. (Beck 1998: 10)

According to Beck, the transition occurs in phases. In the first phase of the 'risk society', he argues that society continues making 'decisions and acts on the pattern of simple modernity' (Beck 1998: 17). For Beck, 'risk society' is characterised by an increasing dependency on the individual along with a new social commitment to lifestyles and market mechanisms. Market competitive mechanisms, rather than traditional ties, are said to create greater risk as well as new modes of social integration. This shift in conditions of integration, in conjunction with other changes like the collapse of the youth labour market and general unemployment, are of major significance to 'youth'. Amongst other things, this involves changing modes of integration where the competitive mechanisms of the market are increasingly determining the patterns and the rules of social life rather than the traditional ties (like class, clan and family) (Beck 1992).

Generally, Beck's work might be linked to the widespread loss of optimism and hope 'diagnosed' by many academic social theorists—many of whom seem to have little to do with the social movements that have erupted in the last few decades. Habermas is typical of the academic pessimists who pointed to the 'exhaustion of utopian possibilities' in the 1980s following the collapse of Marxism as a theoretical project and the subsequent disintegration of European communist states. Psychologists like Tversky (1990: 75) concur, suggesting that the experience of risk is coloured by pessimism: when people now take a risky decision in business or in other life-shaping decisions: 'There are a few things that would make you feel better, but the number of things that would make you feel worse is unbounded.'

Risk is now said to embody an anxiety that social order and personal well-being alike are under threat. Van Swaaningen (1997: 174), for example, argues that the rise of a 'risk society' discourse indicates that 'society [is] no longer oriented towards positive ideals but towards the negative ideal of limiting risk. Solidarity is no longer based on a positive feeling of connectedness but is expressed in a negative communality of fear'. We could ask when 'society' was ever oriented to 'positive ideals'. Van Swaaningen's is a fantasy which may belong more to certain sociological discourses that identify 'society' with a unitary 'moral order' than to any actually existing historical society. Holloway and Jefferson (1997: 265; see also Holloway and Jefferson 2000) may be closer to the mark when they observe: 'In an age of uncertainty, discourses that appear to promise a resolution to ambivalence by providing identifiable victims and blameable villains, are likely to figure prominently in the state's concerted attempts to impose social order.'

What, then, of the large claims that we can understand the rise of sustainability as a consequence of what Beck et al. (1993) suggest is part of a transition from one type of society to another? We are not persuaded that abstracted theorising about such a transition is all that useful, or even all that empirically verifiable. We do not think that gesturing at the idea that we have become a 'risk society' or that this has happened as a consequence of the 'fact' that nobody is in control or that nobody is responsible (Beck 1998: 12) is all that helpful.

Rather, we see the current interest in sustainability as a consequence of collective movements of people concerned about how we live on the planet. Through collective action involving protest activity and publicity campaigns, they have attempted to get governments and the larger community to acknowledge that there are major environmental issues and that there is a pressing case to change the ways in which we live.

• NEW SOCIAL MOVEMENTS

The last three decades have been marked by considerable agitation for fundamental social, economic and political change. New social movements have played a conspicuous part in this agitation for change (see box).

Significant social movements

- Anti-war movements which have protested everything from illegal military invasions by rogue states like the Soviet Union, China and the United States to the indiscriminate use of land mines

- The civil rights movement in the United States, the anti-apartheid movement in South Africa and black rights movements in countries like Australia

- The women's movement

- The gay liberation movement

- Green and environmental movements

- Pro-democracy movements in Eastern Europe and the former Soviet Union, as well as in places like the Philippines and Indonesia

- Islamist movements in a variety of countries like Iran, Pakistan, Indonesia, Saudi Arabia and Iraq

- Anti-poverty and anti-globalisation movements from Live Aid rock concerts to anti free-trade campaigns

- Human rights movements from support for the rights of asylum seekers to anti-torture campaigns

Not all of these movements have been successful, or been as conspicuously active in processes of social transformation. There have been world-changing successes like the collapse of the former Soviet bloc or the overthrow of apartheid in South Africa, and significant gains in terms of civil rights for women, gays and indigenous peoples in many countries. Other movements, like the anti-poverty movements, have hardly made a dent in the problem of poverty in places like Africa.

It is not surprising that social theorists have tried to make sense of these movements in various ways—not always successfully. As social theorists like Habermas were bemoaning the loss of utopian hopes and the collapse of the radical politics, various pro-democracy movements were busily undermining the rule of every communist one-party state in eastern Europe—a process completed by December 1991.

Other theorists (e.g. Inglehart 1977; Jennett & Stewart 1989; Pakulski 1999) over-generalise by claiming to see in the rise of these social movements the end of an entire era and style of 'materialistic' politics, and the emergence of entirely novel kinds of 'post-materialist' politics. The argument from Inglehart (1977) is that post-1945 politics were dominated by people who grew up in the era of mass unemployment in the 1930s, and devoted themselves to securing affluence, economic growth and welfare state-type policies. By the 1970s, the long boom (1945–75) had delivered the goods. This enabled a new politics based on a younger, more affluent electorate and their 'post-materialist' concerns like peace, sexual rights (for women or gays), or with human rights or green issues to transform the political landscape.

There are parallel arguments that highlight the novelty of the new social movements, claiming that they are agents of what are called 'identity politics'—which is said to distinguish them from older political groupings associated with working-class and materialist politics. Calhoun (1994: 9–36) exposes the anti-historical tendencies inherent in these arguments.

While there is some truth in this characterisation, it overstates the case for a major and recent transformation in the political cultures of Western societies in two ways. First, it understates the historical role of social movements driven by explicit moral values. Hochschild (2005), for example, documents the success of one of the modern social movements that began in Britain with a view to abolishing slavery in the British Empire. We could equally recall the role of the movement for civic rights for women (1880–1920) or the peace movement's role in creating intra-national governance bodies like the League of Nations (after 1919) or the United Nations (after 1945).

Second, it overstates the extent to which the everyday political preoccupations with mundane issues of economic security and effective economic management continue. Government concern with managing employment, the rates of economic growth, taxation, levels of expenditure on health welfare and education, and national security have not been displaced by the new 'post-materialist' politics in the past 30 years.

A careful examination (e.g. Papadakis 1991) of the Australian experience since 1980 indicates that at no point in the years since then has any major party or government given more than the politically necessary amount of acknowledgment or accommodation to 'post-materialist' values or politics. Far from seeing any general transformation of the political environment as a result of these kinds of social movements, a better case can be made that both kinds of politics have long coexisted.

This point is implicit in the work of Alain Touraine (1985, 1988), who offers insight into the character of social movements. Touraine provides a salutary response to the grand social theory promoted by the likes of Beck and Giddens. He (1988) offers an effective critique of abstracted social theory couched in terms of societal models and the privileging of structural-functional explanations that talk either about 'society's needs', or about 'modernity' or 'post-modernity'. This partly reflects Touraine's preference for doing empirical and practical research on social movements. At a time when social theorists like Habermas were bemoaning the loss of utopian hope or political optimism and the collapse of transformative politics, Touraine was working with and researching a variety of social movements.

Touraine (1979) spent much of the 1970s working with his team of sociologists in a kind of action research project advising Solidarity, the Polish trade union and Catholic movement, in its successful campaign in helping to bring down the one-party communist state in Poland.

Touraine understood the strengths and weaknesses of social movements struggling to engage in social or political change.

Touraine's account of social movements is informed by a dissatisfaction with the structuralist tendency to ignore the details of how social change takes place. Touraine reminds us that both social order and social change take place as the result of the work of real people. Given the variety of social movements, Touraine seems to have been less interested in constructing a general theory of social movements than in suggesting some of the features they share.

His point is that social movements, characterised by utopian impulses and intent on radical change from early Christianity on, have long been major agents of social transformation. There are interesting questions about how the historical imagination operates to inform various social movements. Some social movements seem to have a model society based on a real or imagined past that they wish to reinvent, while others seem intent on an imagined future state of affairs. There are also interesting questions about the extent to which social movements consist of people who share a single unifying vision or else function as collectives with divergent views about the ends and the means to be adopted. However, if we are to gain any insight into what makes some social movements successful and others less so, it is necessary to acknowledge their uniqueness as much as it is to identify their commonalities.

This is a useful point at which to turn to the rise of the environmental movement and its attempt to put the state of the environment and the idea of 'sustainability' at the forefront of contemporary political consciousness.

● SUSTAINABILITY AND THE ENVIRONMENTAL MOVEMENT

The environmental movement has long been a mass movement with a range of members of widely varying ages and social backgrounds, with often quite diverse views about the goals and the means to be adopted. The environmental movement is a loose coalition of groups that includes traditional conservationists, ecologists, Green parties, anti-nuclear campaigners, Friends of the Earth, Green-peace activists, social ecologists, 'deep ecologists' (the 'fundamentalists' of the movement), animal liberationists, eco-feminists, perma-culturalists, alternative energy and alternative technologists, organic and bio-dynamic farmers, eco-tourism promoters and environmental entrepreneurs.

While its origins lie in the environmentalist or Green movements of the 1970s, the intellectual basis of the current preoccupations with sustainability was laid in the 1950s. Though it somewhat over-simplifies matters, the origins of the concern with sustainability can be traced back to the work of Rachel Carson (1971) and a book she wrote in 1962 called *Silent Spring*, which documented the widespread use of pesticides in almost every area of the American landscape. Carson's revelations so alarmed governments and citizens in many modern societies that they were galvanised into action.

In *Silent Spring*, Carson demonstrated that chemical insecticides then in use (chlorinated hydrocarbons and organic phosphates) were easily manufactured, but that their effects on the health of humans, non-human organisms and ecosystems were long-lasting and serious. She discovered that, from 1947 to 1960, the annual production of chemical-based pesticides had increased fivefold, to about 650 million pounds; sprayed over wide areas, many more organisms than intended fell pray to the destructive power of chemical insecticides than had originally been intended. Carson drew on her studies of ecology to show the way DDT worked on this web of life.

Particularly alarming was the discovery that concentrations of these pesticides built up in the fatty tissues such as the testes and the egg follicles of ovaries, and in the milk of mammals such as cows and human beings. DDT severely affected their longer-term viability by the increased preponderance of cancer and reduced fertility rates. Worse, she showed that the insects which were the original targets of these chemicals had shown a remarkable capacity to develop resistance to the very insecticides meant to eradicate them—but when this transpired their natural predators were usually dead from the very same chemicals and so greater and more diverse forms of poisoning were often engendered—an ecologically vicious cycle.

Carson also showed how the dangers to humans of chemicals in foodstuffs were not being taken seriously by public regulatory boards such as the US Food and Drug Administration, which determined the minimum allowable levels of pesticide residues in foodstuffs when any residue at all is dangerous.

In the light of these findings, Carson made a number of suggestions that she thought would help redress, or at least ameliorate, this lethal situation, including that people should have the right to live unendangered by such indiscriminate use of highly toxic chemicals; that there should be a zero tolerance of all known poisons in foodstuffs imposed by the relevant regulatory bodies; and that biological means of pest control be researched and adopted instead of the chemical means then currently in use.

The early responses to *Silent Spring* were exemplary. Powerful political and economic interests within government departments and in the chemical industry worked to expand and promote the use of dangerous substances even when dangers were known. Elements in the industry and government criticised and tried to discredit the work. The detractors were predominantly spokespeople and apologists for the chemicals industry, some of whom also threatened to sue the publishers of *Silent Spring* for libel. But Rachel had done her homework, checking and re-checking all her sources, and there were no libel claims made against her.

The fact that the book itself became a best-seller however meant that it had a major impact on public opinion. Carson died from cancer not long after its publication, but not before she had given evidence to government inquiries. *Silent Spring* has been credited with being instrumental in the establishment of the Environmental Protection Agency (EPA) in the United States and many other countries, including Australia. It has not been out of print since it was published 40 years ago, and it has been translated into many languages. It also helped to galvanise the modern environmental movement.

The development of modern industrial societies was always accompanied by concern about the environmental effects of industrialisation. Nineteenth century concerns about sustainability saw governments legislate to bring in the first pollution laws, move to establish systems to regulate and safeguard public health, and to establish public parklands (Howes 2005). In countries like the United States and Australia in the late nineteenth century, people identified as progressives or social liberals became environmental enthusiasts, campaigning to get public support to set aside large areas of public land for environmental use and value. As early as the first decade of the twentieth century, US President Teddy Roosevelt mobilised public opinion in favour of passing laws setting aside large areas for national parks.

If Carson's *Silent Spring* (1971 [1962]) provided a very important impetus to public discussion about the state of the environment, it was only because there were already intellectuals, scientists and policy-makers interested in and/or alarmed about the effects of decades of economic growth and industrial development. In 1960, member states of the European Club of Rome issued a report warning about the possible consequences of unrestrained growth. A small number of economists were sensitive to the arguments of the nineteenth century pessimist Thomas Malthus, who claimed to have discovered there was an inverse ratio between food supply and population growth. In 1971, the biologist Paul Erlich published *The Population Bomb*, claiming the world was heading into an era of disastrous population growth and global famine. (These predictions helped to sponsor major campaigns to introduce population control policies in countries like India, Japan and China, involving the use of abortion, condoms and coercive sterilisation.) In short, even in the 1960s there were people receptive to Carson's revelations of the dangers posed by indiscriminate use of pesticides.

As scientists did more work on other environmental risks, the groundwork for the emergence of large-scale environmental movements was being laid. McDaniel (2002) argues that the concept of sustainability first came to public notice courtesy of a series of books released in the 1970s by Wes Jackson, Lester Brown's *Building a Sustainable Society* (1981) and *How to Save the World: The World Conservation Strategy*, published in the 1980s by Robert Allen. Green and conservation movements picked up the theme of sustainability as one way of persuading governments, policy-makers and the community that sensible action could be taken to prevent an environmental catastrophe.

According to Howes (2005: xxi-xxii), sustainability had become a key idea by the 1980s:

> the 1980s we saw the emergence of a mass movement that expanded and incorporated researchers who produced knowledge that helped 'the cause'. They eventually shifted from the status of political fringe-dwelling outsider groups to attending

major policy making forums on sustainable development. Some had even owned their own political parties and successfully ran for office.

Howes (2005: xxii) goes on to point out that, despite their title, these 'anti-globalisation movements' were not essentially against globalisation because their key concerns were about 'realising a more sustainable, fair and just interlinking of societies'.

The combination of political pressure brought to bear by the environmental movement and the steady increase in electoral support for Green parties in Australia and in other countries has produced significant policy achievements. Governments, however reluctantly, have been pressured into passing environmental legislation and into establishing environment ministries and environmental protection agencies. Industries now face stricter controls. There is more collaboration between national governments, who are obliged to attend international summits and issue a plethora of international declarations and protocols like the Kyoto (1999) Greenhouse Gas Emission Control Protocols. Governments have been required to pay attention to new renewable energy sources like solar power and wind generation. A question mark has again been raised over the long-term future of oil as a basis for a society so heavily reliant on the automobile, especially since the major price increases in petrol in 2005–06 following the US invasion of Iraq in 2003.

What is striking about these successes of the environmental movement is that they have occurred at the very time a major 'sea change' was taking place in the political and policy-making cultures of most Western societies, including Australia. This 'sea change' is best understood as a shift away from a 'mixed economy' model—informed by a Keynesian tradition of social liberalism giving rise to intensive state involvement in economic management—and towards an 'economic liberal' model which emphasises market-based activities. On the face of it, the new policy paradigm should have been intensely hostile and resistant to the kinds of arguments mounted by the environmental movement for more government intervention.

This paradoxical conjunction is a reminder of how normal policy-making and political processes involve contestation and conflict. If anything, the years since 1983 have been a period of intense political transformation and political contestation, possibly without parallel since the 1930s.

● ECONOMIC LIBERALISM

It has almost become a cliché to say that the boundaries between the state, economy and civil society have been extensively redrawn in most Western societies since the 1970s (Cerny 1989; Arato & Cohen 1992). The relations between the state and civil society, knitted to a liberal-Keynesian pattern from the 1940s to the 1970s, have indeed both unravelled and been reworked (Arato & Cohen 1992).

This has been seen by some as a core feature of the process called 'globalisation', while others have seen it as a part of a 'new bourgeois counter-revolution' (Przeworski 1989). A less dramatic way of describing what has happened is to note how most major political parties have adopted some version of 'economic liberalism'. In Australia, Michael Pusey (1991) has used the term 'economic rationalism' to describe this policy model.

While it has been conventional to treat 'economic liberalism' as an ideology adopted only by conservative parties, this significantly downplays the active role of ostensibly social democratic parties like the Australian Labor Party in adopting an economic liberal policy framework. In Australia, successive federal Labor governments under Hawke and Keating (1983–96) and the Howard Coalition government (1996–) have driven a major policy process of radical change in most portfolio areas. They have also put pressure on state and local governments to fall in line with what can be described as an 'economic liberal' policy model.

The triumph of economic liberalism involved governments changing the ways in which language and practices were used so that words like 'market', 'customers', 'user-pays' and 'deregulation' became part of everyday talk. Economic liberalism is best understood as the political mobilisation of traditional, even mainstream, 'neo-classical' and 'marginal utility' schools of economics designed to:

- supplant any value system used in determining what is good or useful with the criteria of economic efficiency and profitability; and
- justify two central political objectives.

The first requirement is to reduce the scale and impact of the public sector in terms of its revenue-raising, expenditure activities and capital borrowings, and to see a greater share of the economy given to the private sector. The second imperative is to reduce the share of national income going to wage-earners and to redistribute that share of national income to capital owners and investors—either as corporate or as private individuals.

As Cockett (1995) has pointed out, the triumph of economic liberalism attests to a durable effort involving intellectual analysis, detailed policy research and propaganda over decades on the part of pro-market groups. In Australia, we have seen two chief strategies for giving effect to the economic liberal model: privatisation and deregulation. However, to grasp the radical nature of the policy changes introduced since the early 1980s, we need to remember how Australian governments engaged in a range of social and economic activities across the first 80 years of the twentieth century. In the 1980s, public sector and community services and amenities were mostly only supplied by governments because these goods and services were defined as public or 'social goods'. Many of these services did not always return profits, and in many cases they were unable to do so because they were in the form of a 'social good'. The pattern of services and amenities offered in the public sector until the 1980s reflected a long-standing agreement between interest groups, political parties and citizens about the kinds of goods and services which it was felt were either too important or not appropriate to be left to the vagaries of the market. In a few instances, these goods and services were owned and operated by government or by a statutory authority, and in some cases by a government business enterprise (GBE). Until the 1990s, there were state-owned banks, airline companies, gas and electricity services, and telecommunications companies. In some cases—like health and education—there were private systems operating alongside the public system.

Public sector and community services and amenities were traditionally financed by government revenues from taxes and charges, or by government borrowings. The repayment of the borrowings came from the government's monopoly of revenue from taxes, charges and rates.

Governments at all levels borrowed heavily from the world capital markets to finance the extensive provision of capital goods (including everything from schools and hospitals to roads, port facilities and even power stations, dams or freeways). This was possible because these services required considerable investment and large expenditures. Governments normally borrowed money at lower interest rates because they were seen as low credit risks.

From the 1960s, all of these 'traditional' approaches to policy-making came under sustained attack from academic economists, journalists and from 'New Right' think-tanks like the Institute of Public Affairs (IPA). The arguments involved an all-out attack on government intervention and regulation. At least four main arguments were deployed (see Kelsey 1995 for a critical account of these arguments in detail).

The main claim advanced was that governments—and especially Labor governments—were irresponsible and hopeless managers of the national economy or the community's finances. It was argued that 'big government' provided the best explanation for a succession of recessions (in 1974–60, 1981–83 and 1989–92). According to the stories of economic liberals, anything governments tried to do to manage the economy was economically irrational. The claim was that only markets can do these things rationally. It was argued that governments had accumulated such astonishingly high and 'crippling' levels of debt during the 1980s and early 1990s that they could not be allowed to drag the community further into debt. To allow governments to borrow money—no matter how laudable the projects or how necessary they might be—would be 'criminal folly'.

This argument also depended on what was called the 'crowding-out' hypothesis. The argument was that, at times of poor economic performance or recession, it was silly to allow governments to squeeze out the private sector from the capital market and squander scarce capital by reckless expenditures, budget deficits, mounting public debt or extravagant borrowings. Third, advocates for a new economic liberal model argued that:

- the business sector needed new 'incentives' and opportunities for investment;
- until the level of business activity improved there would be no economic recovery; and

- governments would continue to see a shrinking in their revenue base as the tax pool dried up and their welfare expenditures grew as more poor and unemployed people applied for social security payments.

Finally, the role of governments in providing a base level of income support for people on low incomes (because of unemployment, sickness, disability or other reasons) came under sustained attack. According to economic liberals, the 'welfare state' promoted laziness, immorality and criminality. The assumption was that providing social security income would somehow undermine the work ethic.

● PRIVATISATION

As John Ernst (1993) observes, these arguments were used to promote the wholesale makeover of 'traditional' government policies and programs. One result was a drive to 'reform' community services and the supply of public goods (like roads, energy, welfare services, schools and health care) by way of a 'contracting out of the state'. As Ernst (1993: 31) explains, the resulting 'contract culture':

> mandates a set of relationships which essentially mirror market transactions. The world, including the political domain, is made up of buyers and sellers (or purchasers and providers). As in the market, individual transactions and individual claims are recognized to the exclusion of collective action and group claims. This potentially atomizes the process of democratic decision making . . . the Kennett government has abandoned many of the formal and informal structures for community consultation for the more passive techniques of obtaining feedback (and 'voice') through consumer surveys and opinion polls.

Since the 1980s, the evolution of the new economic liberal policy model has meant that privatisation has become one central way of capturing what the new policy model is about. Fran Collyer (1996: 24–6) notes that privatisation encompasses 'a range of financial management and political strategies, such as franchising, contracting out, lease back arrangements, the imposition of user charges, and reductions in government services'. That is, privatisation has been a broad strategy (see box), involving everything from the selling off of assets to market liberalisation, enhancing competitiveness, increasing the role of market forces and improving public sector performance (Domberger & Piggot 1986: 145).

Privatisation strategies

Asset sales

Since the late 1980s, federal and state governments have embarked on a sell-off of all or part of virtually all major public utilities and institutions, like the Commonwealth Bank and the various state banks, Telstra and public transport systems, to the private sector. This is an important and high-profile part of the policy of 'privatisation'. In large measure, it is a form of asset stripping of valuable properties, systems or assets in which public funds, and often a good deal of intellectual capital, have been invested over decades.

Contracting out services

The largest—but not always most visible—aspect of privatisation has been the move to sub-contract out public and community services. This has been evident at both the state and local government levels, and has affected areas like transport or cleaning services; prisons; the supply of information systems to government-sponsored fire and ambulance services; and a wide range of community services dealing with children, women and families. These services have been contracted out to the non-government charity sector, often with the intention of shedding government employees.

Corporatising public sector activities via the new managerialism

Governments have introduced new styles of 'private sector' management practice and culture into statutory authorities. This is called 'corporatisation' and it is argued this will make the public sector more efficient, leaner and better able to meet the needs of the community.

Privatising infrastructure

This aspect of privatisation is in some ways the most radical expression of the new paradigm, since it envisages a whole new approach on the part of governments to ensuring that basic infrastructure is supplied to the community. Labor and Coalition governments alike since the late 1980s have been encouraging private investment in public utilities like bridge-building, police stations, freeway construction or transport links between airports and the capital cities. This is called 'private investment in infrastructure'.

• DEREGULATION

Over the past three decades, deregulation has provided a complementary policy theme to privatisation. Several key sectors—the banking and financial sector, secondary industry and Australia's unique system of industrial relations—have borne the brunt of the commitment to deregulation. Beginning in 1983, the new ALP government under Bob Hawke deregulated the

Australian dollar, letting currency markets set the level of the Australian currency. Beginning in 1984–85, the entire banking and finance sector—previously strongly controlled to regulate things like home loans and to prevent foreign banks' entry into Australia—was undone. One result was a boom in lending and speculative activity that led directly to the crash of 1989 and the complete collapse of the state-owned banks.

A second target of deregulation was the regime of tariff protection established in the early 1900s to encourage Australian industry to employ local workers. Through the 1980s and 1990s, advocates for free trade systematically promoted the virtues of abolishing tariffs, ignoring the fact that key trading partners like Japan and the United States had no intention of cutting protection to their own industries. Successive 'industry plans' adopted tariff reduction goals for the car industry, textiles and footwear, effectively closing down whole industries and leading to a long-term unemployment effect for older male blue-collar workers. The denouement to this free trade reform agenda came in 2004 with the Australia–United States Free Trade Agreement which, as Weiss et al. (2004) demonstrate, opened up Australia to US imports with no equivalent rights of access by the US market.

Finally, the full weight of the deregulatory reform agenda was brought to bear on Australia's system of industrial relations. Advocates for industrial deregulation argued that the system gave too much power to unions, added a cost burden to industry through unnecessary bureaucratic red tape and denied workers 'freedom of choice'. These arguments won adherents even among the Labor governments of the 1990s. This entailed the dismantling of the old industrial relations systems—moves designed to weaken the union movement and to introduce individual workplace agreements. This involved the removal of regulations and laws that protected workers, along with the new laws and arrangements designed to erode the capacity of trade unions to safeguard workers. Thus, rather than collective bargaining, we now have individual contracts. Rather than regulations like those requiring employers to provide a set number of hours' work for shift workers, we have greater 'flexibility' (to employers), which mean an employee can be told to go home soon after arriving at work because there are too few customers.

Beginning under the Labor government in 1991 and completed under the Howard government in 2005–06, successive waves of industrial deregulation reform have been designed to remove moribund 'rigidities' to 'free up options' and provide 'choice' and flexibility for individual workers. Deregulation and the erosion of collective solidarities is intended to expose the individual worker to the open market. In the workplace, this means more short-term contracts, a major expansion in part-time jobs, much more low-paid work, and increased exploitation of vulnerable people such as migrant workers, those living in poverty and young people.

All this had serious implications for securing sustainable communities, workplaces and economies, to say nothing of the environmental issues involved. Deregulation exposed many people to the excesses of 'the marketplace', causing personal hardship and enormous stress on family and community relations. We saw steep increases in poverty levels and a widening gap between 'the rich' and 'the poor'—all of which raise serious questions about the future viability of our liberal democracy as well as the quality of people's lives.

Economists like Fred Argy (2003) argue that we are also seeing a steady erosion of egalitarian values, a trend that can be explained in terms of changing political dynamics—particularly the loss of a sense of community caused, amongst other things, by a strong commitment in Canberra to economic liberalism. As Argy explains, the 'pillars' of an egalitarian society have been eroded:

- Australia's welfare safety net has more holes in it. While pensions have been treated well, other welfare recipients have 'fallen markedly behind and are subject to ever tougher severe breaching penalties'.
- The unskilled and those with minimal credentials, as well as people living in disadvantaged regions and suburbs, have not shared proportionally in the benefits of improved efficiency and have become an emerging class of 'working poor'.
- Other key determinants of equality of opportunity, such as housing, education and health, also indicate that we are moving toward a two-tier society.
- Moreover, the balance of power has swung markedly against low-paid and unskilled workers (Argy 2003).

Policies that promote equity, protect the environment or simply counter the worst effects of economic liberalism usually cost money—something which is not appreciated in the current context. It is also a milieu in which the longer term benefits of such policies are either overlooked or interpreted as 'rigidities' and inefficiencies which are detrimental to economic growth.

The compatibility of sustainable communities and a sustainable environment with economic liberalism is a contentious issue. While some people believe a liberal economy provides a necessary resource base for an equitable and sustainable society and environment, others disagree. According to the critics, a *laissez-faire* economy promotes vicious forms of social Darwinism and individualism, and intensifies competition at the expense of cooperative relations. In this context, the natural environment becomes a resource to be exploited for economic growth while more people are encouraged to spend money and consume more material goods.

● CONCLUSION: SUSTAINABILITY IN AN ERA OF ECONOMIC LIBERAL POLICY?

By the end of the twentieth century, for the first time in the ecological history of the planet an acute awareness of the finite and fragile nature of global resources had come to be seen by experts as a serious problem. The optimistic nineteenth century view of the infinite availability of nature to humankind had been replaced by a more pessimistic—or more realistic—understanding of how we can live on the planet with a sense of future (Ginsborg 2005: 36). The idea of sustainability plays a central role in signifying this new awareness.

The brief overview of the new policy framework offered here might imply that the kinds of values and concerns promoted by the environmental movement were not completely successful. How, then, should we explain the conjunction of the sustainability in a period dominated by economic liberalism? We think that finding the answer is not too difficult. In both cases, the success of the economic liberal reform agenda and the more partial successes of the environmental movement both point to the normal practices of politics. Both kinds of political ideas and values have enjoyed the successes they have because the advocates of economic liberalism *and* environmental values have engaged in political mobilisation using well-tested techniques for enlisting support, doing research, promoting their ideas and winning the hearts and minds of voters and policy-makers.

This conclusion is not something people who engage in abstract social theory and offer large and simplifying generalisations are likely to accept. Using words like 'modernity' and 'post-modernity' in searching for essentialist descriptions to proclaim 'the death of politics' or the demise of the nation-state is a symptom of an unwillingness to pay attention to the details of what is happening.

It is easy to gesture at the proposition that, over the past 200 years, the practices and institutions of governance have been implicated in the epochal transformations in lived experience that we too casually refer to as 'modernity' (Giddens 1993). The recent 'discovery' of the problem of theorising the relations between 'state' and 'civil society' (Keane 1988: 1)—especially when many theorists identify the 'economic market' with 'civil society'—is problematic, although exactly why this should be so is not so easy to explain. The 'state and civil society' problem has been with us for a long time, but so has basic and persistent controversy about the nature of that relationship.

In the early part of the twenty-first century, there ought be neither premature pessimism nor applause at the 'death of the state' brought about by the revival of economic liberalism. So, when a sociologist like Michael Pusey (1991) says the rise of 'economic rationalism' among Canberra's public servants points to the question of the social meaning of modernisation, culture and public morality in a supposedly 'post-modern' world, this is not helpful.

For all the economic liberal talk about 'shrinking the state' or 'demolishing the welfare state', both remain stubbornly real. There *have* been major changes in the way Australian governments function and make policy, involving new kinds of partnerships between government and business and with the non-government community sector. As Cerny (1989: 196) noted a decade and a half ago in terms that continue to be salient, we now have:

> an infinitely more complex state than before, one not simply intervening more or getting weightier, but one also drawn into the structures of everyday life by the

changes and gaps and tensions within everyday life itself—whilst the private and personal have expanded and contracted too in complex ways. To 'get the government off our backs' as President Reagan wished to do, often paradoxically requires more intervention, not less.

Far from shrivelling up or 'dying', the Australian 'welfare state' now spends a larger proportion of national income than at any point in its history. Whether the current mixture of policies and income support systems actually benefits people, or functions on a basis of respect, or meets core ideas like justice is another question—one addressed recently by Mark Peel (2004) in his account of the trials of low-income people trying to lead decent lives as they battle the Centrelink system.

The mediations and the antagonisms between 'state' and 'civil society' are the daily work of the intellectually trained who have important positions in both sites of social action. To put it simply, people continue to engage in political and ethical debate, to organise themselves in movements, unions, lobby groups and political parties, and to work as journalists, public servants, teachers, academics and human service professions, where they intervene in the public sphere. This is how we can understand the continuing role of movements like the environmental movement, and what is sometimes called the 'culture wars'.

The fact that the Howard government was determined to push the Australia–United States Free Trade Agreement (AUSFTA) through to sign-off, and did so with the support of the opposition, did not prevent the Australian Conservation Foundation (ACF) from making vigorous criticisms. The ACF pointed out that AUSFTA had the potential to impact seriously on Australia's environment (see box).

The Australia–United States Free Trade Agreement

- The Australia–United States Free Trade Agreement obliges the Australian government to pay damages to American investors if Australian laws on the environment, human rights or labour standards 'significantly interfere' with their investments.

- The agreement commits Australia to ensuring that its environmental laws are not a barrier to trade in services. If they are, Australia can be taken by the US government to a specially convened dispute settlement panel, which will be able to rule that the law must be repealed or compensation paid. This component of the agreement could increase pressure for the privatisation of our national parks or park services, and make it harder for Australian governments to regulate water use and distribution.

- The Australian Conservation Foundation also raised important questions about our quarantine laws, referring to the prospect of those laws being weakened in the future (www.tradewatchoz.org/AUSFTA/Index.html#Environment).

The idea of sustainability and the role of the environmental movement continue to be central to many basic political debates and conflicts. Older-style unions—especially those involved in the timber industry—have been at the forefront of heated conflict between Green activists, the state and loggers. Closer to our own time, the various elements of what are sometimes called the 'culture wars' point to the continuing vitality of political and intellectual controversy. Neo-conservative intellectuals and commentators attack what they see as the politically correct posturing of those who advocate multiculturalism (Blainey 1984), the 'black-armband' view of Aboriginal history (Windschuttle 2002), the virtues of the welfare state (Saunders 2005) or the 'excesses' of the environmental movement (Bolt 2006). Progressive and social liberals respond just as vigorously. This is as it should be.

Discussion questions

19.1 What do you think sustainability is?

19.2 Do Green activists overstate the case about issues like global warming?

19.3 How much should we trade off the benefits of economic growth and affluence for securing the long-term sustainability of the globe, its people and the life which depends on it?

20. CONCLUSION: AUSTRALIA AND GLOBALISATION

The idea of 'globalisation' has been used in all sorts of ways by all sorts of people to explain changes taking place over the last 30 years or so. Our question here is simple: does its widespread use point to the value of sociology or of talking and thinking sociologically? Lloyd (1995: 13) thinks not, commenting sharply that the widespread use of the concept is not a victory for clear thinking. We are inclined to agree.

Since Robertson's pioneering use of the word 'globalisation' (1985, 1992: 8), the term has become part of our daily language. (It is now even in the *New Oxford Dictionary*). The term 'globalisation' was first used in books by American management writers, like Porter (1990). Asking what it is that is being 'globalised', Lloyd notes that typical answers include (1995: 14):

- standardising products and consumer preferences on a global basis;
- globalising styles of work;
- globalising modes of communication;
- globalising knowledge and culture;
- globalising decision-making and power;
- globalising innovation and the rapid spread of new technologies; and
- globalising competition.

Some writers claim that globalisation essentially refers to the spread of the power and influence of multinational (or transnational) companies. Companies like Sony, General Motors, Philips or News Limited may or may not have national headquarters in one country, and their operations span the world. Such companies pursue global strategies and 'their international activities are linked and coordinated on a worldwide basis' (Bureau of Industry Economics 1989: 2). Powerful multinational or transnational corporations are increasingly central to the 'new world order' (Giddens 1991). Porter's claim that 'Firms, not nations, compete in international markets' (1990: 330) makes this point. Some say that the power of these companies is so great that nation-states or societies do not matter any longer—or at least, not in the ways they used to. One result, according to Giddens, is that nation-states are no longer the main players in the modernising process. Although phrases like 'world order' overlook the abundant evidence of disorder and disorganisation in the world, Giddens (1991) claims that we now live in a 'new world order'.

For Giddens, globalisation has four key features:

- The global order is still based on nation-states, but their role is weakening.
- In the global order, nation-states operate in a world capitalist economy dominated by multinational and transnational companies.
- Globalisation depends on an international division of labour, where nation-states play a variety of roles supporting that arrangement. Some countries (e.g. Australia)

supply raw materials. Other countries (e.g. Japan) provide expensive and finished industrial or electronic goods, while others (e.g. India or China) supply cheap, plentiful consumer goods. New industries are developing that supply information management or intellectual and research services. These industries carry out what Reich (1994) calls 'symbolic work'. Castells (1998) claims that this indicates the emergence of a new form of capitalism, which he calls 'informationalism'. This refers to the leading role played by information technology like personal computers and the internet.

• The global order is also a world military order, in which global security is provided by certain 'superpowers', like the USA or the European Union.

Many writers agree, arguing that:

• The globalising process is shaped by multinational (or transnational) corporations. More people are working for transnational corporations which may have their head offices located on the other side of the globe from where the workers are, or may even be located in 'virtual space'.

• Bankers can invest in 'global markets' through electronic technology, moving billions of dollars in a fraction of a second.

• People across the world recognise as universal symbols such as McDonald's golden arches and the Coke bottle.

• In a globalised world, we rely increasingly on extended and abstracted relationships with people which are made possible by global television news offered by CNN or through email and the internet.

Sociologists add to the globalising of economic activities, globalisation in culture, communications systems and the impact of mass migrations of people (Waters 1997). For many writers, 'globalisation' is seen as a new phase (or period) in history that is either 'post-industrial' or 'post-modern'. Others, like Giddens, argue that 'globalisation' is more about the unfolding or extension of the process of modernity.

We cannot explore the intricacies of all the definitions of 'globalisation' (see Waters 1997: 38–93), or the problems with different models (see Hirst & Thompson 1999). We can, however, think about the ways in which people use an idea like 'globalisation'.

● A CRITICAL NOTE ON GLOBALISATION

So how useful is the idea of gloablisation? What should we make of a standard definition like Waters' (1997: 3) when he says globalisation is: 'a social process in which the constraints of geography on social and cultural arrangements recede and in which people become increasingly aware that they are receding'? We have no problem if people want to use a word like 'globalisation' to describe a complex pattern of change in the ways Waters points to. Broadly speaking, 'globalisation' can be used meaningfully to refer to a process in which various social, economic, political and cultural relationships and activities get stretched out and may in some cases become increasingly global in their dimensions. However, this is not how the word is being used.

The first problem is that people are using the word 'globalisation' in completely idiosyncratic and diverse ways: there is simply no agreement about what it means. Harris (1993: 17) has noticed the absence of an agreed-upon definition of 'globalisation'. As a consequence, far too much discussion of 'globalisation' borders on the vacuous. McGrew (1992: 13–14) claims that globalisation involves:

> the multiplicity of linkages and interconnections that transcend the nation-state (and by implication the societies) which make up the modern world system. It defines a process through which events, decisions, and activities in one part of the world can come to have significant consequences for individuals and communities in quite distant parts of the globe.

The second problem is that people use it to *explain* why things are happening; abstract concepts are useful as shorthand names, but they explain nothing and encourage us to forget the active role played by men, women and institutions in producing change. Too much 'globalisation' talk involves treating it as a 'thing' or a 'force' that is outside human control and beyond political debate.

The great Russian writer Mikhail Bakhtin (1992) raged against what he called 'theoreticism'. 'Theoretism' is the kind of thinking practised by large numbers of modern social scientists and theorists. It is bound up with the implicit status hierarchy in the social sciences which puts 'theorists' above those people (empiricists) who merely describe or count things in the world. It works by abstracting from real human activity anything that is generalisable, and treating the resulting idea or category as if it were something real (see Bakhtin 1992; Morson & Emerson 1989: 5–15).

We can see this tendency at work in one recent confused discussion of 'globalisation' by Makinda (1989: 4; see also Clark 1997), who asks about the ways in which 'globalisation' constrains or facilitates the choices of foreign policy-makers. Makinda (1989: 5) suggests first that: 'globalisation could be seen as a "symptom of wider political and economic policies" and "the product of specific state policy choices"'. He then contradicts himself by adding that 'globalisation is a modernisation and restructuring process which cannot be ignored by governments'.

A further consequence of the ways people use the idea of globalisation is the impression that, whatever is meant by globalisation, it is irresistible or inevitable. This idea is what Catley (1996: 222–3) is getting at when he suggests that:

> the globalising of Australian capitalism . . . has become unavoidable, necessary and desirable. It is unavoidable because the extension of the world market and the rapid technological change has made the survival of small, rich, idiosyncratic semi-capitalist societies untenable. This restructuring then has become necessary if Australia is to arrest the long-term decline in its living standards . . .

Far from being irresistible or inevitable, the policies that Australian governments adopted in the 1980s and 1990s were a consequence of deliberate policy-making processes and political decisions. In each case, we can identify real politicians and bureaucrats who adopted a certain approach to solving what they thought were real problems. It is not helpful to suggest that 'globalisation' made the Hawke government deregulate the Australian dollar in 1983. We can trace out the very complex and highly political story of how the Hawke government made up its mind in ways that show the government always had clear options and choices about this decision.

Then again, it is not clear whether the alleged novelty of 'globalisation' is all that new. In 1917, the Russian revolutionary leader Lenin wrote a book titled *Imperialism*, in which he described a world economy that looked very similar to the one people today describe using the word 'globalisation'.

There is a problem about whether the idea of 'globalisation' imposes an appearance of order and stability in ways that overlook the conflicts, tensions and contests entailed by the term. Some sociologists and social theorists argue that globalisation can be described as a shift from an industrial to a post-industrial society, or a shift from modernity to post-modernity. For a criticism of claims that our society is becoming post-modern, see Frankel (1993).

It is not easy to see how or why 'globalisation' represents a distinctively new period in history. Giddens (1999) argues that globalisation is an extension of trends already present in the modernisation process, rather than a distinctively new mode of social experience or existence. This would suggest that globalisation is not a new phenomenon, but that the effects of modernising are continuing to affect the lives of more and more people.

One final point. As Mestrovic (1997) points out, Giddens (1993) and Castells (1998) over-emphasise the rational and progressive aspects of modernity and globalisation. Both have systematically refused to address the terrible examples of local ethnic hatreds which have produced 'ethnic cleansing' and genocide in Europe, or resurgent anti-foreigner and anti-Semitic campaigns in places like Germany and Austria. In short, there are major problems with the way people—including sociologists—use the 'globalisation' concept. We need to remember that processes like McDonaldising and restructuring the workforce are historical, and are the consequences of human choice and judgment. Globalisation is part of an historical process involving people who make choices and exercise judgments in circumstances that are not always of their own making.

Globalisation is not an enormous natural event, like a bushfire or an earthquake. It is not something done to people or to governments. Globalisation is a shorthand way of describing the ways people act in certain ways. It has many features, and develops differently within the constraints of the history, culture and social relationships of any particular country. The experience of globalisation is a consequence of policies and practices designed to 'integrate' Australia into the global economy. These policies reflect the views of governments and business leaders inside Australia and outside that Australia needs to be exposed to the global economy.

To think well about the kinds of experiences of change, we need to reinstate a role for human action and choice. The rise of 'economic rationalist' policies has been crucial to the way the Australian Settlement (1901–70) has been dismantled (Quiggin 1997). This has been a key source of the processes of change in Australia. As Peter Beilharz (1996) argues, the federal Labor government's (1983–96) 'modernisation' project in the 1980s and 1990s was based on a vision of a revitalised Australian industrial sector exporting to global markets. That modernisation project required certain 'reforms':

- A structural redesign of Australian institutions occurred which would lead to economic reconstruction. Those rearrangements included new arguments and practices aimed at subordinating the schooling and education systems to the needs of the economy. School and university 'students' became 'customers', education become more 'vocational' and universities were required to be more 'entrepreneurial'.
- The public sector was urged to 'corporatise' and adopt an 'enterprise culture'. This involved strengthening managerialist procedures, abolishing lifetime tenure for public servants and teachers, and copying private sector behaviours through greater reliance on the user-pays principle and a strengthening of management prerogatives (Considine 1988; Considine and Painter 1997).
- The community sector was to be more accountable and competitive. In 1994, the Keating government outlined its National Competition Policy. Contracting out of government services, the establishment of private gaols and universities, and the adoption by universities, welfare groups and hospitals of 'corporate missions' and 'corporate identities' resulted as these agencies tried to improve their place in a competitive market.

Many of these developments (both real and alleged) are often contradictory, and are not unique to Australia. They are also matters in which politicians, policy-makers and ordinary citizens have a role to play in determining how we should live into the future.

GLOSSARY

aboriginal Generally a word used by Europeans to describe any indigenous community in a society shaped by invasions by other peoples. Used in Australia to describe the first people. For a long time the word was coloured with racist assumptions like the idea that 'aboriginals' were 'primitives' or 'savages'.

absolute poverty A definition of poverty which assumes that we have an absolute minimum need for food, water and shelter without which life cannot be sustained. The term is used in comparison with the idea of **relative poverty**.

action Any kind of human conduct. Sociologists understand action as social interaction. Max Weber thought all action and interaction was rationally comprehensible because of the role played by intentions as motivations for action. Alfred Schutz thought otherwise, saying there was no rational connection between peoples' intentions, actions or their explanations offered after the event.

action research A form of ongoing social research typically used in a situation involving a group of people pursuing some kind of change. The action researcher feeds research findings back to the people engaged in change thereby helping to evaluate progress being made.

adolescence A stage in the life of people situated between childhood and adulthood. The socially constructed discourse of adolescence enables adults to treat young people as 'troublemakers' or 'vulnerable' and 'at risk' even as many economic and social factors appear to be prolonging the period.

age A person's age is a central source of identity, social value and potentially of discrimination.

ageism A form of discrimination that relies on negative assessments of a person's age, and is particularly directed against children, young people and the elderly.

agency The word used by many modern sociologists to communicate the idea that society or other 'forces' do not manipulate us like puppets. The idea of human agency refers to our capacity to be self-aware, to know what we are doing, to give good accounts of why we have done what we have done and a will to act. Some social scientists argue that we are self-interpreting symbolic and expressive creatures, who are rational because we seek to direct, interpret, monitor and change our activities and that we do so mostly in the context of relationships with other similarly equipped creatures. It is often used in opposition to the idea of **structure**.

anomie Durkheim used this word to describe a situation where people lived in a society which lacked a basic moral consensus.

anthropology The study of traditional or pre-modern societies. Anthropology shares much with sociology in terms of the range of social experience and relationships studied. It has traditionally relied on participant observation research techniques.

authority Is a form of legal, intellectual, political or moral power. A person in a position of authority can require other people to think or act in a particular way.

belief Humans seem able to entertain a very wide range of ideas about themselves and the world. Some beliefs rely on tradition, others on faith, some on science and others on common sense. Most sociologists imagine they can distinguish clearly between these kinds of beliefs, though on what basis (tradition? faith? etc.) they do so is not clear.

bureaucracy A hierarchical form of organisation. Bureacracies rely on written rules for defining and managing the work of officials, and work is characterised by a high degree of uniformity and predictability. Weber said that modern societies were dominated by bureaucratic forms of organisation and authority.

capital In a narrow sense any kind of economic resource which possession of enables people to use for productive purposes. It can come in any form, for example, land, racehorses, gold bullion, office buildings or shares. Its origins lie in processes of military invasion or in institutions like slavery. Its perpetuation relies on the use of power or force to preserve the unequal distribution of these resources. People who should know better now refer to other kinds of capital like 'social capital'—or trust—or intellectual capital—education and skill—as if these metaphors have transmuted into nouns.

capitalism Though the word was first used in the 1890s in Germany it refers to a durable economic and social order based on the private ownership of productive wealth. Such an order relies on the fact that large numbers of people have to sell their labour in order to live. Historically, capitalism involves making more and more things/activities into commodities that can be bought and sold; including labour itself, services (e.g. education, child care) and tangible goods (e.g. food, clothing). Capitalist economies are characterised by extreme inequality in regard to income and wealth and by dynamic change and growth. Long-believed to be doomed to explode, capitalism has proved more durable than most Marxists supposed likely.

church Both a building and an organisation in which people in the west practise their religion.

citizen A member of a modern political community (i.e. the nation-state) who possesses formally defined rights and responsibilities by virtue of membership of that nation, typically including the right to vote.

class A classic sociological concept with its origins in Marxist and socialist traditions. In general the idea tries to represent the ways economic and social resources are unequally distributed in all societies. Marxists believed that competition between different classes explained large scale social change. Both its meaning and the research done to try and describe or explain how class works have been troubled by lack of clarity or consensus about what it is, how it worked or how it might be researched.

colonialism Refers to the extension of European economic, cultural and political controls over the world. It began with the discovery of America in 1492 and included establishing colonies in India, Asia, the Pacific (including Australia) and Africa over the next four centuries. Australia retains some of its colonial ties such as our head of state who is the monarch of Great Britain.

community A word long used by sociologists to describe the kind of social relations imagined to exist before the rise of modern industrial societies where most people live in big cities. Tinged with nostalgia, and like other cognate words (e.g. **globalisation**), the word means less and less the more it is used.

conflict theory A group of theories, including Marxism and feminism, which argue that all social orders are characterised by social conflict, typically between classes or gender groups, over which group should control valued resources like wealth, power and property. The forms conflict takes includes everything from peaceful competition to criminal violence.

culture Another big idea social scientists use to refer to all of the varieties of beliefs, knowledges, language practices, expressive behaviours, religious practices and social rituals. It seems to include everything people use a word like 'society' to name. Social scientists use binaries like 'society' and 'individual' to set loose permanent confusion and a lack of clarity.

democracy A set of ideas and institutions that give effect to ideas about the rights of individuals ('citizens') to form governments and have their freedoms and rights respected. Set loose in the late seventeenth century, democratic movements have, by the late twentieth century, ensured that most modern nation-states are democratic in some way.

demystification One of Max Weber's key concepts used to define the way modern societies come to be emptied of the symbolic and ethical values that religion and magic once conferred. This 'death of God' is a consequence of the rise of science, technology and bureaucracy and, while the world is made rational by these activities, Weber says they do not provide any satisfying meaning.

determinism Refers to attempts made by scientific sociology to discover or establish causal or probabilistic explanations. For example, the idea that unemployment causes suicide is a determinist account. Determinism is much-favoured by those working within a **positivist** framework. It is closely aligned with attempts to construct biological and psychological theories of human behaviour which inevitably encounter the problem of **indeterminacy**.

deviance A classic sociological idea, grounded in **functionalist** assumptions, that assumed it was possible and desirable to categorically identify and explain the existence of people who differed from some imagined social norm. Like certain other ideas (e.g. **community** and **globalisation**) it is best treated as an empty signifier open to so many meanings as to be meaningless, and, since its assumption is patently false, as a useless idea (i.e. all societies have a clear-cut and compelling moral consensus about everything).

dialectics An idea about how human knowledge changes historically. Philosophers like Hegel used this to point to the social and historical construction of particular systems of ideas and beliefs and to show how apparently new ideas actually retain rejected bits of older ideas. For example, sociologists like Comte disliked the idea of 'God' yet their use of the idea of 'society' appears to be another version of the God concept.

discourse Refers to the ways in which power is legitimated through frameworks of knowledge production. In particular, discourse involves the use of language to name reality. Discourse is a body of knowledge that can become powerful because it shapes the way we come to know the world. The naming of reality or of a truth is a highly political act which results in government or regulation. There are continuous contests over whose voice is given effect (e.g. there are constant struggles over who gets to say what is and what is not 'violence' or what is or what is not 'feminist' action).

discursive practices Describe post-modernists ideas on power, knowledge and refer to particular methods of promoting certain discourses.

division of labour A given production process, such as making a car, which can be broken down into a number of smaller components and given to separate workers. Modern industrial processes began to use this technique in the eighteenth century. The sexual division of labour refers to the way some jobs are only or largely done by men and others only by women.

double hermeneutic A phrase used by Giddens to name an interactive process that starts with social scientists collecting data from the social world as part of their research. The material is then analysed and theorised before the research results are fed back into the same community. This feedback process has the capacity to change the social world of the community, possibly in major ways.

education A generic word to describe any of the ways people acquire moral, social or technical abilities and ideas. Because of the rise of compulsory mass **schools** most people now equate it with schooling.

embodied Refers to sociologists' recent 'discovery' that people have bodies that change shape and appearance from birth, are constantly eating and drinking, experience the intense pleasures of sex, feel sorrow and sadness, are not always well—and which ultimately must die. Being embodied confers identity—our age, skin colour and physical shape influences the way other people react to us or define us.

emotions Embracing a wide array of feelings and moral responses, sociologists since Weber have treated them with suspicion, contempt or neglect believing them to be sources of **irrationality** which **modernity** would somehow bypass. Sociology has led an impoverished existence since this bad judgement.

emotivism The idea that all ethical principles or values are only the expression of feelings and, as such, can have no validity or authority, unlike solid 'facts'. It is argued that values cannot be rationally assessed or compared; instead that 'facts' provide the bedrock of scientific descriptions, generalisations, theories and laws.

empirical research Research based on asking questions and using certain systematic and thoughtful techniques of inquiry into some aspect of 'reality'. Empirical research can use participant observation, surveys, questionnaires, historical documents, photographs and anything else that helps investigate 'reality'. For some narrow-minded sociologists, empirical research refers only to certain styles and techniques of statistical analysis.

empiricism A philosophy that argues that the only credible kind of knowledge is that based on facts or things found in the world which we can see, touch, measure or feel.

environment A generic word to describe the natural and social context in which humans construct their webs of social life. Against the idea that humans can do anything they like, those who understand the dynamics and constraints of any natural habitat understand there are limits to food production, energy use or consumption of air and water.

epidemiology One kind of research used by health and medical researchers. It involves the collection, study and use of statistical data devoted to establishing what patterns of social activities and identity markers are implicated in the patterns of health and illness.

epistemology Refers to any attempt to claim that there is a secure foundation for the things we say we know to be true. Philosophers have argued that those foundations might include experience (empiricism) or ideas put there by God (idealism) or as part of the human brain (rationalism). Modern pragmatists like Richard Rorty do not see any point in looking for a foundation for knowledge.

essentialism Is the idea that social categories (and practices) are known and recognised in terms of an assumed essence or a basic nature said to be shared by all those belonging to the group in question. Essentialism is based on the idea that a person by virtue of membership to a certain group share, with all other members of that group, certain interests and experiences.

ethics Refers to the branch of philosophy that asks what reasons we rely on to ascertain what is the good or right thing to do. More generally, it refers to all of the practical problems we have and all the processes we go through when working out, in a social setting, what we ought to do. Many social scientists think they do not matter and should be kept well away from 'objective' social science research. This may explain why social sciences like economics and psychology regularly produce atrocities like neo-liberal economic policies or eugenics respectively.

ethics clearance Now a normal procedure in universities and research organisations. Most authorities who monitor and regulate social research only require an ethics clearance if the researcher comes in contact with people or animals that are capable of feeling and this involves describing the proposed research and evaluating any risk to people.

extended family Any family where more than two generations of family members live together or where there may be numerous relatives and even domestic servants living together.

facts Since the nineteenth century, positivists and empiricists have encouraged a belief in the existence of objective facts which are said to be truthful statements about the world, free of ethical or theoretical significance. Most modern philosophers doubt that such facts have ever existed or are likely to be 'discovered'.

family Long said to be a core, if not the fundamental, institution upon which the survival or health of any society or community depends. In most modern societies the status and wellbeing of families is a source of basic social and political controversy. They are said to come in different forms (e.g. nuclear or extended) and to come as single parent families, same sex families and so on.

female The qualities associated with being a woman. Much debate has raged between advocates of biological and sociological **determinism**, a debate relying on heavy doses of gender **essentialism**.

feminism A number of critical political and social theories designed to promote the liberation of women from oppressive male-centred values and the privileging of men's status, wealth and power. Feminists insist that for too long women have been ignored by orthodox social science and theory and that women have the same right to respect and fairness as men.

Fordism The name given to the recent history of industrialism. It is characterised by high wages, mass production of consumer goods and mass advertising relying on an ever expanding mass media. Fordism delivered a rise in the standards of living for many working people in countries like Australia, the USA and Britain after the 1920s and especially after 1945.

function A concept often used by orthodox sociologists—following Durkheim and Parsons—to explain why social roles and social institutions exist in any given society. For example, 'the family' exists because society needs it to socialise new members of society.

fundamentalism Since the 1980s it has become common to refer to certain extremist adherents of Christian, Hindu, Jewish and Islamic faiths as fundamentalists. This meant to point to the way some adherents of these faiths dislike many if not all the features of modern democratic scientific, tolerant and secular societies, and are prepared to use violence and coercion to restore 'traditional' moral or political beliefs. Fundamentalists of all kinds tend to hate homosexuals, dislike modern women and want to see their belief system govern their community.

gender Refers to the ways social practices and relations between males and females (as marked by biological sex differences) are ordered, defined, regulated, valued, institutionalised and reproduced. It also refers to the experiences and identities of both women and men.

gender essentialism The idea that a single fundamental or essential woman's or man's experience/s or encounter/s can be separated from all other parts of the woman's or man's identity (e.g. her/his sexuality, ethnicity, parental status and so on). In other words, gender essentialism is when one assumes that the woman's/man's essential reality can be identified and represented as being separate from all other aspects of the woman's or man's life.

globalisation An idea that emerged in the 1980s to refer to and/or to explain the impact of new patterns of economic, political and cultural activity, especially those relying on communications technology and the rapid flow of finance capital. The world is said to be shrinking, creating a single, expanded, globalising free market and removing the need for nation-states. Globalisation is arguably a largely meaningless idea with numerous contradictory definitions. Its value seems limited given that it refers to longstanding economic patterns of activity. Claims made by globalisation theorists, for example about the death of nation-states, are grossly overstated.

government Any organisation possessing legal authority and responsibility for the good order of a territory and able to use violence to protect the peoples living in that territory from disorder, crime or invasion. Australians enjoy three levels of government which may explain a high level of distrust on their part about politicians.

governmentality Refers to the ability to manage or guide the conduct of others. It is an activity that is not exclusive to the business of the state, but occurs in various contexts such as public organisations like education institutions and in family relations. Governmentality relies on an ability to access information on those being governed that is then used to anticipate social problems.

health Defined by the World Health Organization (WHO) as a state of complete physical, mental and social wellbeing and not just as the absence of disease or injury.

HECS The Higher Education Contribution Scheme refers to a tertiary fee payment arrangment that was introduced under the Hawke Labor government in 1988–89 and was the brainchild of Professor Bruce Chapman. It involves charging a student for a part of the tuition costs of their degree and then requires payment of those fees when the student has completed their degree (the payment is collected via the income tax system). Fees of this kind are for Commonwealth supported places. Some students who are not eligible for government support places pay full fees which are considerably higher.

hetero-sexism The assumption that everyone is, or ought to be, heterosexual. It is an assumption that also privileges heterosexuality and discriminates against non-heterosexuals.

homosexuality People who are sexually attracted to people of the same gender are referred to as homosexual while some make a distinction 'gay' men and 'lesbian' women. The assumption that sexual attraction can be pigeonholed in this way may be a suspect premise.

idea A fundamental concept. Debate has raged since the Greeks first used this word whether our ideas come from our senses (like sight or smell) and therefore work as images of 'real' things in the world or whether we construct ideas (like numbers or ideas like 'time' and justice) in our heads to make sense of things out in the world, or whether there is some complex interplay between both activities. Debate rages still while most people use the word in a muddled and unclear way.

identity Refers to the ways we experience ourselves as well as the ways other people interpret and interact with us. It always has at least two dimensions—an 'inside' and an 'outside' dimension. We use all sorts of identity markers like age, ethnicity, gender, clothing, music tastes, religion etc. to mark an identity.

ideology An older idea advanced, mostly by Marxists, that human knowledge promotes the values and the interests of powerful elites. It has been argued for example, that economics is the ideology of businessmen and companies who claim that it is simply a scientific way of thinking about the economy. Critics say ideologies offer at best a partially true account of what is going on and often cover up the bad consequences of the way a given social elite dominates a society.

indeterminacy The disordered, imprecise, ambiguous and contradictory aspects of our social relationships, experiences, beliefs, aspirations and interactions. Good sociology and social theory is comfortable with indeterminacy.

inequality Refers to the various ways in which all societies and social relationships exhibit patterned differences in power over resources and decision-making. These differences relate to economic resources like land or money, access to weapons or organisational power, or cultural resources like knowledge. These inequalities can be explained in terms of class, gender, physical ability, ethnicity, religion or age, and many inequalities are passed on from generation to generation.

interpretative sociology One of the primary approaches to doing sociology and social research. It involves researching the ways in which people use symbolic techniques such as speaking, listening, reading and writing. It also means describing and intrepreting the intentions, values, rules and symbolic meanings social actors use to live and work inside institutions. Versions of this approach include symbolic interactionism, ethnomethodology, social constructionism and phenomenological sociology.

irrational/irrationality As a progeny of Enlightenment thinking about **rationality**, **sociology** has long treated key aspects of the human condition like **religion**, **emotion** and **ethical values** as irrational. This judgement is arguably irrational: it certainly relies on many untested and unargued assumptions about the nature of **facts** and **theories**, and the **objective** basis of **science**.

knowledge Refers to all the socially constructed and sanctioned patterns of beliefs and theories about the world which one or more groups of people believe to be true. There are many kinds of knowledge including common sense knowledge, scientific knowledge and professional knowledge, and there are many practices that produce knowledge. In modern societies, expert and scientific knowledge have great credibility and authority.

liberalism Arguably the tradition of ideas that provides the dominant ideas we have about the nature of people, economies and societies as well as of states and policy making. There has been a discernibly liberal tradition since the work of John Locke. Liberals think about the person as an individual, and about liberty. The trouble starts in the debate between those who emphasise the right to be free from coercion versus the right to be free to pursue one's own idea of welfare. This is one way of identifying the difference between economic liberals who emphasise freedom from coercion and social liberals who emphasise an idea of freedom as the right to flourish.

life expectancy A statistical estimate of how long a person born in a given year will live.

lifestyle diseases Diseases such as cardiovascular disease and cancer which appear to be linked to overeating, cigarette smoking, drinking alcohol and under-exercising. Lifestyle diseases are at epidemic levels in Australia.

market liberalisation This is based on a view about 'the big expansionist government'. The idea is that governments are big spending and have a Keynsian approach to economic policy largely responsible for the prevailing fiscal and social problems. It is a perception that fuelled talk about a need for greater government accountability and for a leaner bureaucracy including the imposition of a managerialist style of public administration.

Marxism Marxists say all societies have their own history arising from the ways people clustered together in various classes organise their economic activities. All societies experience considerable change and much of this is expressed as class conflict. In all societies the primary kind of power is economic power. In modern societies capitalists own the various forms of wealth (e.g. land, finance, industrial capital), while the working class owns little or nothing of the productive wealth except their capacity to sell labour; both classes operate in a capital-intensive economy. Most Marxists say you cannot understand human action unless you relate it to people's position in the class structure.

masculine The concepts masculine and feminine both go beyond physical sex difference.

meta narratives refers to inclusive stories or theories about social relations and historical progresses. Meta narratives are also on occasions referred to as grand narratives.

metaphor A figure of speech that can be defined as a trope of resemblances which constitute a displacement and an extension of the meaning of the word. A metaphor works to turn something literal into something figurative. In short, metaphors involves a process of transferring and carrying over meaning. Metaphors invite us to see an association between two apparently unrelated areas or objects that the metaphor connects.

mode of production A Marxist idea referring to the distinctive and dominant form of production (e.g. slave, feudal or capitalist) and the various class groups associated with this that make up the history of societies.

morality The word used to refer to the codes and rules people draw on when working out what the right thing to do might be.

morbidity Used by health researchers to refer to patterns of illness or disease.

mortality Used by health researchers to refer to the number of deaths and to the death rate of a given social group.

nationalism Ideas about the special qualities of a community allegedly found in its history, religion, geography or in some racial or ethnic qualities of its people. Many modern nation-states depend on ideas about an ideal racial or ethnic community to provide the foundation for government and a nation's boundaries. Nationalism provides one primary source of collective identity.

nation-state An idea about the relationship between certain communities defined by language, religion or ethnicity and their governments who exercise authority over a defined geographic area.

normalise refers to social and institutional practices that are based on a belief system like sexism or racism that uses differences—like physical appearance or behaviours—to mark off those who do not fit within the average range.

nuclear family The form of family where two biologically linked generations live together. The adults are a man and woman who are married to each other and who have biologically or legally related children whom they look after until the children are adults. Once touted as the universal form of family life, we now understand that family forms are very diverse and fluid both within a given society and across history.

ontology Any more or less coherent set of claims about the ultimate nature of reality. Religious people believe god/gods created the universe while secular humanists think of the universe as a consequence of scientific laws or happenstance. Most Australians don't give a rats and prefer to put another prawn on the barbie.

participant observation A technique central to interpretative sociology or ethnographic research. It involves the researcher living with or closely observing a social group and becoming sufficiently exposed to all or even part of a complex social reality so that the group's elaborate rules, invisible meanings, complex motives, ambiguous actions and feelings can be reported to other people.

patriarchy The name of any pattern of social arrangements in which men as a group have superior status, greater wealth and far more power than women as a group. Historical evidence points to the existence only of patriarchal societies.

positivism Refers to the ambitious idea that social scientists should copy the methods of the natural sciences so that they, too, can discover 'facts' and measure 'variables' so as to produce good explanations that are predictive or possibly even law-like statements—or 'theory'. Positivism is difficult to define and there are many different versions, though most believe in a unitary scientific method based partly on induction and empiricism, and partly on deduction and the use of mathematics or statistics.

post-modernism An influential, expansive, sometimes incomprehensible mass of ideas and themes spread among all sorts of intellectuals in modern societies that rejects the rationalism and scientism of the Enlightenment. Post-modernists tend to reject big sweeping generalisations about the directionality of history favoured for example, by Marxists; the applicability of large generalisations about class, gender or power to social problems or the applicability of realist and natural scientific methods of knowing things to the social world.

power A characteristic of human relationships that operates between people. Power is everywhere. Power refers to the capacity of one person or a group to compel another to do something they would otherwise not do. Power is not always oppressive, it can also be positive and does not have to be exercised in a personal way. Power often rests in knowledge claims and in the ways space is used and designed.

profession Orthodox sociologists claim that professions are defined by altruism—that is, putting others ahead of oneself—by reliance on a code of practice, by the consolidation of a unique body of scientific or theoretical knowledge that defines the profession and informs practice, and by autonomy secured by membership of a professional association. Most of these claims are questionable.

qualitative research Any kind of research associated with interpretative sociology that attempts an indepth account of the meanings and rules for making sense of a particular social setting, event or relationship.

quantitative research Any kind of research that involves the collection and measurement of large amounts of relatively simple and unambiguous, even 'objective', data with a view to producing generalisations about the actions or beliefs of large numbers of people, typically collected via surveys of a sample population.

racism The belief that it is possible to generalise about a group of people using superficial differences like skin colour. These generalisations are then used to claim that members of a particular 'race' are superior or inferior to other races. Racism relies on profound ignorance, lots of hatred and the absence of any sense of humour.

random sample A type of sample whereby the researcher selects 'by chance' a number of people to represent an entire population. It is assumed that the larger a random sample, the more confidence the researcher can have that statements made about the sample will also be true of the whole population.

rationalisation Used by Weber to describe the redesign of social relationships and practices through precise rules and abstract and/or technical styles of calculation. Bureaucracies are said to represent the most rational organisation.

rationality A longstanding idea about humans who are said to have the capacity to be rational or to be reasonable. Beginning with classical Athens the quality of rationality has been defined in terms of our capacity to develop mathematical systems, to think logically or to develop a variety of empirical and scientific ways of describing or measuring the world. It may well be that all these forms of rationality depend on non-rational beliefs.

relative poverty Refers to the idea that a good way of measuring or defining poverty in a society should begin by establishing how most people live and what expectations they have about the consumption of food, clothing, housing and other goods and services, so that those who fall beneath this standard are said to live in poverty.

religion For the longest part of human history, humans have believed they lived in a world or cosmos both made for them and ruled over by the gods or a single god. These divine powers were central to basic sense-making stories about the nature of reality, the condition of human existence, the need for basic ethical rules for living and the possibilities of life after death. As a product of the Enlightenment sociologists have long treated religion as irrational and/or doomed to die out before the onrush of science and secular reason. The sociological obituary for religion has proved somewhat premature.

representative sample One way of doing survey research. A group of people who mirror the larger population in terms of the characteristics (such as age, sex, intelligence or political beliefs) are looked for by the researcher.

research Any process of discovery or inquiry into any aspect of the natural and social world. There are only a relatively small number of ways of doing research, but each has zealous advocates which encourages a lot of arcane debate and controversy. No matter how rigorous the methods used, bad questions, dubious assumptions or ethically dubious intentions can all produce bad research that fails to address pressing human needs or adds pain and misery to the human experience.

role Mainstream sociology holds that members of a society, via the process of socialisation, acquire a set of scripted values, behaviours and aspirations appropriate to a variety of functional identities (e.g. 'man', 'woman', 'husband', 'wife', 'worker', 'boss') because without these roles society would collapse.

schools Compelling all children of a certain age to attend school (i.e. compulsory mass schooling) is a central defining feature of all modern societies. The wisdom of this is now a taken-for-granted fact; its role in reproducing social disadvantage is an uncomfortable but little researched aspect of all such societies.

science In the Anglo-American world the word conjures up test tubes and men in white coats. The Germans more sensibly have one word (*wissenschaft*) to denote any methodical study and then talk of the art sciences (*kunstwissenschaft*), the human sciences (*geistes wissenschaft*) or the physical sciences (*naturwissenshaft*) on the basis that different things need different kinds of methods of study.

sex Can refer to the identities we assume as masculine men or feminine women, as well as to the organs traditionally assumed to distinguish men from women, as well as to the act of intercourse.

sexism The belief that members of one sex both individually and collectively are inherently superior to the other. Most feminists are concerned about male sexism which relies mostly on biological or religious beliefs which ignore the findings of modern genetics and on an abililty to generalise.

sexual division of labour Occurs when men and women do different kinds of work according to their gender (i.e. women care for the children and cook the dinner while men mow the lawns, fix the cars and put the rubbish out). Although the sexual division of labour has meant that women have been more heavily involved in child care and domestic work than men, anthropological studies indicate a wide variation in the tasks of men and women across different societies.

social facts These are special kinds of facts that say something significant about a society as a whole. Thus the 'crime rate' or the 'suicide rate', because they are said to reflect the degree of social order and moral consensus, are social facts.

social movement Any collective organisation of people promoting some kind of social change. Recent examples include trade unions, the Nazi movement, the women's movement, environmentalists, peace and anti-nuclear movements and a variety of democracy and peoples' movements.

social order The idea promoted, especially by structural functionalists, that all societies tend naturally to equilibrium. Society requires that every member of society works for the order and stability of society. Social order is the normal condition of any social system and is achieved through extended and complex processes of socialisation, education and sanctions (i.e. punishments and rewards). It is reinforced by social control agencies like schools, families, social workers or churches, which ensure that most people make the rules for 'right' behaviour (or the norms) part of their own personality.

social sciences The term embraces a wide array of disciplines including anthropology, sociology, social theory, criminology, psychology, history, political science and economics. The fruit of the Enlightenment, they have hosted many basic and yet to be resolved debates about both what is meant by the idea of 'social' and what is meant by 'science'.

socialisation The idea that society creates and shapes its members through a lifelong process of learning and regulation of beliefs, ideas, knowledges, aspirations and activities. It is usually divided into two parts: primary socialisation (said to be what happens in the early part of life, occurring mainly inside families) and secondary socialisation (which occurs later).

society Understood by many sociologists as an ordered social system, a structured totality with a life and interests of its own. In society people are said to understand themselves as free and rational individuals who (although free) are coordinated and regulated to perform the roles given to them through the process of socialisation. Individuals interact in predictable ways that are said to be largely predetermined by the system's value consensus. According to this view, people as social actors are either cultural puppets or victims constrained by social forces or **structures** that compel them to behave in certain ways.

sociological imagination A way of thinking about ourselves and our social and historical context made possible when we lift ourselves out of our immediate surroundings and the common sense we rely on. The sociological imagination means thinking about the various social connections and the histories that shape our worlds.

sociology One of the essential products of Enlightenment social thought, sociology has long been a core social science. The central tradition has sought to mimic the natural sciences (by discovering facts, developing theories and advancing law like statements) but alternative and critical traditions like Marxism, symbolic interactionism and post modernism have resisted the appeal of positivism.

structural functionalism A traditional style of sociology which focuses on the whole of society, its structures and mechanisms for securing order and consensus.

structure This is one of the most used words in sociology and, like some important key words (e.g. 'society', 'system' or 'culture'), it is a rarely defined metaphor that encourages us to see and think in particular ways that are not always helpful. It is used to point to things or processes which constrain people to do certain things (e.g. 'gender is a structure that forces women to be submissive to men'). It may also point to the ways certain rules and systems, like those found in a language, enable people to speak, write and understand each other. It is a very unclear term that lies at the heart of the 'structure-agency' debate, which may suggest to some people that sociologists live in a perpetual state of confusion.

survey A technique of research that asks a number of people (who make up a sample) to answer questions or to respond to statements so that the researcher can make certain claims about the whole population.

sustainability A key idea that emerged at the end of the twentieth century. It is used to point both to issues of resource depletion (as the world uses up clean air, water and non-renewable energy supplies), to problems like global warming and greenhouse gas emissions and to the value of embarking on policies to use these resources more wisely, and for the long term benefit of the whole global community.

symbolic interactionism A style of sociology associated with Herbert Blumer (1900–87), who emphasised the symbolic nature of social interaction and the idea that social reality is constructed by human beings. Symbolic interactionists stress the use of interpretation as a technique of social research.

terrorism Involves the use of extreme, often random, violence aimed at ordinary men, women and children and is designed to spread fear and coerce whole communities into supporting the political values and ambitions of the terrorist organisation. Both governments and social movements use terror. Over the past century governments have been the most systematic and violent agents of terrorism, though the media and governments have been able to persuade many of us that terrorism is the weapon of small, weak social movements.

The Great Transformation Refers to the process of modernising that started around the eighteenth century and continues today.

The youth wage This is a law that makes it legal to discriminate against certain young people by paying them less than others for work that is of the same value.

theory A word with a number of different meanings, including the belief that it is possible to develop scientific explanatory–predictive generalisations, as well as high-order generalisations or simply big sense-making stories.

utilitarianism The dominant ethical system in modern western societies developed in the eighteenth century. Its advocates, from Bentham through to Mill to Singer, say that whatever causes us happiness is good and that humans are equipped to identify whatever causes them happiness. Bentham added that it was the task of government to promote the greatest happiness of the greatest number of people.

utility The technical and philosophical term for happiness or pleasure that is central to the ethical doctrine of utilitarianism.

Weberian sociology Weberians argue that social action cannot be reduced to economic practices or ideas. They say we need to recognise the vital role of ideas and related symbolic and cultural forms of social expression. They also stress the symbolic (or meaningful) nature of social action and focus on the role of key institutions like bureaucracy and the role of scientific rationality under the conditions of modernity.

work Any action undertaken by humans to transform some aspect of the world to meet expressive, artistic, religious or biological survival needs or wants. More narrowly its use has been confined to the employment and income generating activities of people in modern capitalist economies with a distinction drawn between those who work for others (i.e. wage earners) and those who work for themselves (i.e. professionals, property owners, tradespeople and shop keepers).

REFERENCES

Aapola, S., Gonick, M. & Harris, A. (eds) 2005, *Young Femininity: Girlhood, Power and Social Change*, Palgrave Macmillan, New York.

ABA (Australian Broadcasting Authority) 1996, *What Are They Listening To?* AGPS, Canberra.

Abraham, J.H. 1973, *Origins and Growth of Sociology*, Penguin, Harmondsworth.

ABS (Australian Bureau of Statistics) 1991, *1989–1990 National Health Survey: Summary of Results*, ABS, Canberra.

—— 1993, *Suicides Australia 1982–1992*, Cat. No. 3309.0, ABS, Canberra.

—— 1994a, *Permanent Arrivals*, Cat. No. 3412.0, ABS, Canberra.

—— 1994b, *Trends in Mortality by Cause of Death in Australia*, Cat. No. 3313.0, ABS, Canberra.

—— 1995, *Australian Women's Year Book*, ABS, Canberra.

—— 1996a, *Household Use of Information Technology, Music, New Music and All That*, Australian Broadcasting Authority, Canberra.

—— 1996b, *Social Trends 1996*, Cat. No. 4101.0, ABS, Canberra.

—— 1997a, *Labour Force 1990–1997*, Cat. No. 6203.0, ABS, Canberra.

—— 1997b, *Models and Youth Unemployment: A Discussion Paper*, ABS, Canberra.

—— 1997c, *Census of Population and Housing*, Cat. No. 2015.0, ABS, Canberra.

—— 1997d, *Social Trends 1997*, Cat. No. 4101.0, ABS, Canberra.

—— 1998, *Labour Force 1998*, Cat. No. 6203.0, ABS, Canberra.

—— 1999, *Marriages and Divorces*, Cat. No. 3370.00, ABS, Canberra.

—— 2000a, *Australian Social Indicators 2000*, Cat. No. 4101.0, ABS, Canberra.

—— 2000b, *Social Trends 2000*, Cat. No. 4101.0, ABS, Canberra.

—— 2001, *National Health Survey*, ABS, Canberra.

—— 2004, *National Aboriginal and Torres Strait Islander Survey 2004–05*, ABS Cat. No. 2034.0, ABS, Canberra.

—— 2005a, *Aboriginal and Torres Strait Islander Peoples*, Cat. No. 2034.0, ABS, Canberra.

—— 2005b, *Australian Migration, 2004–05*, Cat No. 3412.0, ABS, Canberra.

—— 2005c, *Australian Social Indicators 2005*, Cat. No. 4101.0, ABS, Canberra.

—— 2005d, *Divorces in Australia 2004*, Cat. No. 307.0, ABS, Canberra.

—— 2006a *Labour Force*, Cat. No. 6203.0, ABS, Canberra.

—— 2006b, *Australian Social Trends 2006*, Cat. No. 4102.0, ABS, Canberra.

—— 2006c, *Australian Year Book 2006*, ABS, Canberra.

ACES, 1976, *ACES Review*, vol. 3, no. 4, June–July.

Adams, R. 1960, 'An Inquiry into the Nature of the Family', in G. Dole & R. Carneiro (eds), *Essays in the Science of Culture*, Crowell, New York.

Adorno, T.W. 1980, *Minima Moralia*, NLB, London.

Adorno, T.W. & Horkheimer, M. 1972, *Dialectic and Enlightenment*, NLB, London.

Agamben, G. 1997, 'The Camp as the Nomos of the Modern', in H. de Vries & S. Weber (eds), *Violence, Identity and Self Determination*, Stanford University Press, Stanford, pp.106–18.

Agnew, R. 2001, 'Building on the Foundation of General Strain Theory: Specifying the Types of Strain Most Likely to Lead to Crime and Delinquency', *Journal of Research in Crime and Delinquency*, vol. 38, pp. 319–61.

AGPS 1994, *Style Manual for Authors, Editors and Printers*, 5th edn, AGPS, Canberra.

Ainley, J., Batten L. & Miller, H. 1984, *Patterns of Retention in Australian Government Schools*, ACER, Hawthorn.

Aitken, S. 2001, *Geographies of Young People: The Morally Contested Spaces of Identity*, Routledge, New York.

Alaheto, T. 2003, 'Economic Crime: Does Personality Matter?', *International Journal of Offender Therapy and Comparative Criminology*, vol. 47, no. 3, pp. 335–55.

Albright, M. 2003, *Madam Secretary: A Memoir*, Macmillan, London.

Alexander, J. 1988, *Theoretical Logic in Sociology*, (4 vols), UCLA Press, Berkeley.

—— 1990, *Structure and Action*, Columbia University Press, New York.

Allen, R. 1980, *How to Save the World: The World Conservation Strategy*, Rowman & Littlefield, Boston.

Allen, S. 1973, 'Class, Culture and Generation', *Sociological Review*, vol. 21, pp. 437–46.

Anderson, B. 1989, *Imagined Communities*, Verso, London.

Anderson, T.L. & Leal, D.R. 2001, *Free Market Environmentalism*, rev. edn, Palgrave, New York.

Andruss, Van, Plant, C., Plant, J. and Wright, S. 1990, *Home! A Bio-regional Reader*, New Society Publishers, Philadelphia.

Angus, G., Wilkinson, K. & Zabar, P. 1994, *Child Abuse and Neglect Australia 1991–92*, Child Welfare Series no. 5, AIHW, Canberra.

Arato, A. & Cohen, J. 1992, 'Civil Society and Social Theory', in P. Beilharz, G. Robinson & J. Rundell (eds), *Between Totalitarianism and Postmodernity*, MIT, Cambridge.

Arblaster, A. 1988, *The Rise and Fall of Western Liberalism*, Oxford University Press, Oxford.

Archer, D. & Gartner, R. 1978, 'Legal Homicide and its Consequences', in Kutash, I., Kutash, S. & Auchinloss, L. (eds), *Violence: Perspectives*, Jossey-Bass, San Francisco.

Arendt, H. 1954, *The Origins of Totalitarianism*, HBJ, New York.

—— 1958, *The Human Condition*, University of Chicago Press, Chicago.

—— 1963, *Eichmann in Jerusalem*, Penguin, Harmondsworth.

—— 1968, *Men in Dark Times*, Penguin, Harmondsworth.

Argy, F. 2003, 'In Search of Sustainability; The Future of Australian Egalitarianism', paper presented to the In Search of Australian Sustainability Conference, Canberra, December, <www.isosconference.org.au/entry.htm>.

Aries, P. 1973, *Centuries of Childhood*, Penguin, Harmondsworth.

Aristotle 1976, *Ethics*, trans. J. Thompson, and Introduction by J. Barnes, Penguin, Harmondsworth.

Armstrong, D. 1983, *The Political Anatomy of the Body*, Cambridge University Press, Cambridge.

Armstrong, T., Davies, J. & Bauman, A. 2000, *Physical Activity Patterns of Australian Adults*, Australian Institute of Health and Welfare, Canberra.

Arnold, M. 1976 [1865], *Culture and Anarchy*, Hutchinson, London.

Aronowitz, S. & Di Fazio, W. 1994, *The Jobless Future*, University of Minnesota Press, Minneapolis.

Aspin, L. 1987, *The Family: An Australian Focus*, Longman Cheshire, Melbourne.

Atkinson, A.B. 1987, 'On the Measurement of Poverty', *Econometrica*, vol. 55, no. 4, pp. 49–64.

Attwood, B. 1989, *The Making of the Aborigines*, Allen & Unwin, Sydney.

—— 2005, *Telling the Truth About Aboriginal History*, Allen & Unwin, Sydney.

Australian Institute of Criminology 1992, *Australian Criminal Statistics 1788–1988*, AIC, Canberra.

Australian Institute of Health and Welfare (AIHW) 1992, *Australia's Health 1992*, AIHW, Canberra.

—— 1998, *Medical Labour Force 1998*, no. 16, AIHW, Canberra.

—— 1999, *Australia's Young People: Their Health and Wellbeing 1999*, AIHW, Canberra.

—— 2000a, *Australia's Health 2000*, AIHW, Canberra.

—— 2000b, *Health Expenditure Bulletin, No. 16: Australia's Health Services Expenditure to 1998–99*, June, AIHW, Canberra.

—— 2003, *Australia's Young People: Their Health and Wellbeing*, AIHW, Cat. No. PHE 50, Canberra.

—— 2004, *Australia's Health 2004*, AIHW, Canberra.

—— 2005a, *Australia's Health 2005*, AIHW, Canberra.

—— 2005b, *Health Expenditure Bulletin, No. 20: Australia's Health Services Expenditure to 2004–2005*, June, AIHW, Canberra.

Australian Law Reform Commission and Human Rights and Equal Opportunity Commission 1997, *Seen and Heard: Priority for Children in Legal Process, LRC and HREOC*, Report No. 84, AGPS, Canberra.

Australian Treasury 2001, 'Public Good Conservation and the Impact of Environmental Measures Imposed on Landholders', *Economic Roundup*, pp. 93–103.

Avineri, S. 1970, *The Social and Political Theory of Karl Marx*, Cambridge University Press, Cambridge.

Avril, K. 1992, 'Little Depraved Felons', *Australian Historical Studies*, no. 99, October, pp. 319–24.

Bacon, F. 1978 [1597], *Meditationes Sacrae*, English trans., Oxford University Press, Oxford.

Bagguley, P. & Mann, K. 1992, 'Idle Thieving Bastards: Scholarly Representations of the Underclass', *Work Employment & Society*, vol. 6, no. 1, pp. 112–26.

Bahktin, M. 1992, 'Philosophy of the Act', in *Art and Answerability: Early Philosophical Essays*, University of Texas, Austin.

Baird, G., Gregory, R. & Gruen, F. 1981, *Youth Unemployment, Education, and Training*, ANU, Canberra.

Bannister, R. 1987, *Sociology and Scientism: The American Quest for Objectivity, 1880–1949*, University of North Carolina Press, Chapel Hill.

Barbalet, J.M. 1998, *Emotion and Social Structure*, Cambridge University Press, Melbourne.

Barcan, A. 1994, 'The Liberal University: Death and Transfiguration', *Education Research Perspectives*, vol. 24, no. 2, pp. 1–17.

Barratt, M. 1980, *Women's Oppression Today: Problems in Marxist Feminist Analysis*, Verso, London.

Barratt, M. & Phillips, A. (eds) 1992, *Destabilizing Theory: Contemporary Feminist Debates*, Polity Press, Cambridge.

Batten, M. & Russell, J. 1995, *Students at Risk: A Review of Australian Literature, 1980–1994*, ACER, Melbourne.

Baudrillard, J. 1987, *The Evil Demon of Images*, Power Institute, Sydney.

Bauman, Z. 1991, *Modernity and the Holocaust*, Polity Press, Cambridge.

—— 1998, *Globalisation*, Cambridge University Press, Cambridge.

Bavin-Mizzi, J. 1995, *Ravished: Sexual Violence in Victorian Australia*, UNSW Press, Sydney.

Baxter, J., Gibson, D. & Lynch-Blosse, M. 1990, *Double Take*, AGPS, Canberra.

Beauvoir, S. de 1953, *The Second Sex*, Cape, London.

—— 1953, *The Second Sex*, (trans H. Paisley) Alfred Knopf, New York.

Beck, U. 1992, *Risk Society: Towards a New Modernity*, Sage, London.

—— 1998, 'Politics of Risk Society', in J. Franklin (ed.), *The Politics of Risk Society*, Polity Press, Cambridge.

—— 1999, *World Risk Society*, Polity Press, Cambridge.

—— 2000, *What is Globalisation?*, Polity Press, Cambridge.

Beck, U., Giddens, A. & Lash, S. (eds) 1993, *Risk Society and Late Modernity*, Polity Press, Cambridge.

Becker, H. 1963, *Outsiders: Studies in the Sociology of Deviance*, Free Press, London.

Beder, S. 1997, *Global Spin: The Corporate Assault on Environmentalism*, Green Books, Devon.

Beilharz, P. 1996, *Transforming Labour*, Cambridge University Press, Melbourne.

Belkap, J. 1989, 'The Economic Crime Link', *Criminal Justice Abstracts*, March, pp. 140–57.

Bell, S. 1997, *Ungoverning the Economy*, Oxford University Press, Melbourne.

Benjamin, W. 1968, *Illuminations: Essays and Reflections*, (trans and intro H. Arendt), HBJ, New York.

Bennett, T. 1977, *The Mass Media as Definers of Reality*, Open University, Milton Keynes.

Benton, T. 1984, *The Rise and Fall of Structural Marxism*, Macmillan, London.

Berger, B. 1963, 'On the Youthfulness of Youth Cultures', *Social Research*, vol. 30, no. 4, pp. 329–54.

Berger, P. 1966, *Invitation to Sociology*, Penguin, Harmondsworth.

—— 1967, *The Sacred Canopy*, Doubleday, New York.

—— 1970, *A Rumour of Angels*, Doubleday, New York.

Berger, P. & Berger, B. 1983, *The War Over the Family*, Hutchinson, London.

Berger, P. & Kellner, H.F. 1974, *The Homeless Mind*, Penguin, Harmondsworth.

Berger, P. & Luckman, T. 1971, *The Social Construction of Reality*, Penguin, Harmondsworth.

Berlin, I. 1969, *Four Essays on Liberty*, Oxford University Press, Oxford.

—— 1981, *Against the Current: Essays in the History of Ideas*, ed. H. Hardy, Oxford University Press, Oxford.

Berman, M. 1982, *All That is Solid Melts into Air*, Simon & Schuster, New York.

Bernstein, B., 1971, *Class Codes and Schooling* (2 vols), Routledge & Kegan Paul, London.

Bessant, B. 1986, 'Privatisation and Academic Freedom', *Australian Universities' Review*, vol. 29, no. 2, pp. 11–15.

—— (ed.) 1987, *Mother State and Her Little Ones, Children and Youth in Australia 1860–1930*, Centre for Youth and Community Services, Melbourne.

—— 1995, 'Corporate Management and its Penetration of University Administration and Government', *Australian Universities Review*, vol. 38, no. 1, pp. 59–62.

Bessant, B. & Spaul, A. 1976, *Politics of Schooling*, Pitman, Melbourne.

Bessant, J. 1986, 'Schools Under Scrutiny During a Period of Depression 1890–1910', *Melbourne Studies in Education*, vol. 27, no. 1, pp. 32–61.

—— 1988a, 'Meeting the Demands of the Corporate Sector', *Journal of Australian Studies*, no. 22, pp. 19–32.

—— 1988b, Public Criticisms of Schooling During Periods of Economic Crisis, PhD thesis, La Trobe University, Bundoora.

—— 1990, 'An Historical Perspective on The Standards Debate of the 1970s and 1980s', *Melbourne Studies in Education*, vol. 30, no. 2, pp. 63–71.

—— 2000, 'Social Action and the Internet: New Forms of Political Space', *Just Policy: A Journal of Australian Social Policy*, nos 19/20, pp. 108–18.

—— 2001, Student Poverty in the Enterprise University, unpublished paper.

—— 2003, 'The Problem of Poverty Amongst Tertiary Students: Why It's Missing from the Poverty Agenda', *Melbourne Studies in Education*, vol. 44, pp. 69–88.

—— 2004, 'Interview with "Penny"', Youth Work Project RMIT University, Melbourne.

—— 2004, 'Mixed Messages: Youth Participation and Democratic Practice', *Australian Journal of Political Science*, vol. 39, no. 2, pp. 387–404.

Bessant, J. & Hil, R. 1997, *Youth and the Media*, National Clearing House for Youth Studies, Tasmania.

Bessant, J., Hil, R. & Watts, R. 2003, *Discovering Risk: Social Research and Policy Making*, Peter Lang, New York.

Bessant, J., Sercombe, H. & Watts, R. 1998, *Youth Studies: An Australian Perspective*, Addison Wesley Longman, Melbourne.

Bessant, J. & Watts, R. 1995, 'Violence in Schools: A Preliminary Report', *Discourse*, vol. 15, no. 2, pp. 49–60.

Bessant, J., Watts, R., Dalton, T. & Smyth, P. 2006, *Talking Policy: How Policy is Made*, Allen & Unwin, Sydney.

Best, S. & Kellner, D. 1991, *Postmodern Theory: Critical Interrogations*, Macmillan, London.

Biddulph, S. 2004, *Manhood*, Collins–Dare, Melbourne.

Bilton, A., Bonnett, K., Jones, P., Sheard, K., Stanworth, M. & Webster, A. 1996, *Introductory Sociology*, 3rd edn, Macmillan, London.

Bittman, M. 1991, *Juggling Time*, Office of the Status of Women, AGPS, Canberra.

Bittman, M. & Pixley, J. 1997, *The Double Life of the Family*, Allen & Unwin, Sydney.

Black, D. 1970, 'The Production of Crime Rates', *American Sociological Review*, no. 35, pp. 733–48.

Blackburn, S. 1985, *Ministerial Review of Post-compulsory Schooling*, vols 1 and 2, VGPS, Melbourne.

Blainey, G. 1966, *The Tyranny of Distance*, Sun Books, Adelaide.

—— 1975, *Triumph of the Nomads*, Macmillan, Melbourne.

—— 1984, *All for Australia*, Methuen, Sydney.

Blake, L. 1973, 'Free, Compulsory and Secular', in L. Blake (ed.), *Vision and Realisation*, Education Department of Victoria, Melbourne.

Bloch, E. 1995, *The Principle of Hope*, vol. 3, trans. N. Plaice, S. Plaice & P. Knight, MIT Press, Cambridge, MA.

Bloom, H. 1994, *The Western Canon*, Harcourt, Brace Jovanovich, New York.

Blumer, J. 1969, *Symbolic Interactionism*, Prentice-Hall, Englewood Cliffs.

Bohmann, J. 1991, *New Philosophy of Social Science*, MIT Press, Cambridge, MA.

Bohme, G. 1977, 'Cognitive Norms, Knowledge Interests and the Constitution of the Scientific Subject', in E. Mendelsohn (ed.), *The Social Production of Scientific Knowledge*, Reidel, Dardrent, pp. 129–41.

Bolt, A. 2006, *Still Not Sorry: The Best of Andrew Bolt*, Angus & Robertson, Sydney.

Boss, P., Edwards, S. & Pitman, S. 1995, *Profile of Young Australians*, Churchill Livingstone, Melbourne.

Boswell, J. 1988, *The Kindness of Strangers*, Random House, New York.

—— 1990, *The Kindness of Strangers*, Vintage, New York.

—— 1993, *In the Care of Strangers*, Basic Books, New York.

—— 1994, *Same Sex Unions in Early Christianity*, Vintage Books, New York.

Bouma, G. 1992, *Religion: Meaning, Transcendence and Community in Australia*, Longman Cheshire, Melbourne.

—— 2001, 'Globalisation and Localization: Pentecostals and Anglicans in Australia and the United States', in C. Cusack & P. Oldmeadow (eds), *The End of Religions? Religion in the Age of Globalisation*, University of Sydney Press, Sydney.

—— 2003, 'Religion and Spirituality', in I. Macallister, S. Dowrick & R. Hassan (eds), *The Cambridge Handbook of Social Sciences in Australia*, Cambridge University Press, Melbourne.

Bouma, G. & Hughes, P. 2000, 'Religious Residential Concentrations in Australia', *People and Place*, vol. 8, pp. 18–27.

Bourdieu, P. 1994, *Homo Academicus*, Polity Press, Cambridge.

—— 1996, *Academic Discourse: Linguistic Misunderstanding and Professorial Power*, Polity Press, Cambridge.

—— 1999, *Practical Reason*, Polity Press, Cambridge.

—— 2004, *Science of Science and Reflexivity*, Polity Press, Cambridge.

Bourdieu, P., Accourdo, A., Balazs, G., Beaud, S., Bonvin, F., Bourdieu, E., Bourgois, P., Broccolichi, S., Champagne, P., Christin, R., Faguer, J., Garcia, S., Lenoir, R., Œuvrard, M., Pinto, L., Podalydès, D., Sayad, A., Soulie, C. & Wacquant, L. 1999, *The Weight of the World: Social Suffering in Contemporary Society*, Polity Press, Cambridge.

Bourdieu, P. & Passeron, J. 1977 *Reproduction in Education, Society & Culture*, Sage, New York.

Bowes, G., Hibbert, M., Caust, J., Patton, G. & Rosier, M. 1996, *The Health of Young People in Victoria: Adolescent Health Survey*, Centre for Adolescent Health, University of Melbourne, Melbourne.

Bowles, S. & Gintis, H. 1976, *Schooling in Capitalist America*, Routledge & Kegan Paul, London.

Bradbury, B. & Jantti, M. 2001, 'Child Poverty Across 25 Countries', in B. Bradbury, S. Jenkins & J. Mickelwright (eds), *The Dynamics of Child Poverty in Industrialised Countries*, Cambridge University Press, Cambridge.

Bradley, G. & Stock, J. 1993, *Students at Risk, Identification and Intervention: A Case Study*, Sage, New Pines.

Braithwaite, J. 1989, 'The State of Criminology: Theoretical Decay or Renaissance?', *Australian New Zealand Journal of Criminology*, vol. 22, no. 3, pp. 12–27.

Braithwaite, J. & Barker, M. 1977, 'Bodgies and Widgies as Folk Devils of the Fifties', in P. Wilson & J. Braithwaite (eds), *Juvenile Delinquency in Australia*, University of Queensland Press, Brisbane.

Brake, M. 1979, *The Sociology of Youth Culture and Youth Sub Cultures*, Routledge & Kegan Paul, London.

—— 1985, *Comparative Youth Culture: The Sociology of Youth Cultures and Youth Sub Cultures in America, Britain and Canada*, Routledge & Kegan Paul, London.

—— 1987, *Comparative Youth Cultures*, Routledge & Kegan Paul, London.

Bramwell, A. 1989, *Ecology in the Twentieth Century: A History*, Yale University Press, New Haven.

Brannen, J., Dodd, K., Oakley, A. & Storey, P. 1994, *Young People, Health and Family Life*, Open University, Buckingham.

Braudel, F. 1984, *The Wheels of Commerce*, Collins, London.

Braverman, H. 1974, *Labour and Monopoly Capital: The Degradation of Work in the Twentieth Century*, Monthly Review Press, New York.

Brooks, A. 1997, *Academic Women*, Open University Press, Buckingham.

Brooks, P. 1980, *Speaking for Nature: How Literary Naturalists from Henry Thoreau to Rachel Carson have Shaped America*, Houghton Mifflin, Boston.

Brooks-Gunn, J. 1984, 'The Psychological Significance of Different Pubertal Events to Young Girls', *Journal of Early Adolescence*, vol. 4, no. 4, pp. 315–27.

Broome, R. 1984, *The Victorians: Arriving*, Fairfax, Syme & Weldon, Sydney.

Brotherhood of St Laurence 1981, Submission to the Department of Employment and Youth Affairs Review of the Community Youth Support Scheme, December.

Brown, L. 1981, *Building A Sustainable Society*, Norton, New York.

Brown, P. & Jordanova, L. 1982, 'Oppressive Dichotomies: The Nature/Culture Debate', in E. Whitelegg et al. (eds), *The Changing Experience of Men and Women*, Martin Robertson, Oxford.

Browning, C. 1990, *Ordinary Men*, Cambridge University Press, Cambridge.

Brownlee, H. & McDonald, P. 1992, 'A Safe Place for Children', *Family Matters*, no. 33, December, pp. 12–17.

Bryson, L. 1992, *Welfare and the State*, Macmillan, London.

—— 2001, 'New Differences Between Men and Women', in H. Irving (ed.), *Unity and Diversity: A National Conversation*, ABC Books, Sydney.

Bryson L. & Thompson, F. 1977, *An Australian Newtown*, Kibble Press, Malmsbury.

Bryson L. & Winter, I. 1998, *Social Change, Suburban Life*, Allen & Unwin, Sydney.

Bryson, L., Winter, I. & Lazzarini, V. 1997, 'Australian Newtown Revisited: Global Restructuring and Local Difference', *Labour and Industry*, vol. 7, no. 2, pp. 35–54.

Bunker, J. 1994, 'Improving Health: Measuring Effects of Medical Care', *Millbank Quarterly*, vol. 72, no. 2, pp. 222–58.

Burdekin, B., 1989 (report), *Our Homeless Children, Inquiry into Youth Homelessness*, Human Rights and Equal Opportunity Commission, AGPS, Canberra.

Bureau of Industry Economics 1989, *Globalisation: Implications for Australian Information Technology Industry*, AGPS, Canberra.

Burke, J.L. 2000, *Purple Cane Road*, Orion Books, London.

Burke, K., 1944, *The Grammar of Rhetoric*, University of Chicago Press, Chicago.

Burkert, W. 1987, *Homo Necans: The Anthropology of Ancient Greek Sacrificial Ritual and Myth*, University of Chicago Press, Chicago.

Burleigh, M. 1994, *Death and Deliverance: Euthanasia in Germany*, OUP, Oxford.

Burnley, I., Murphy, P. & Fagan, R. 1997, *Immigration and Australian Cities*, The Federation Press, Sydney.

Burt, C. 1938, *The Young Delinquent*, 3rd edn, University of London, London.

Butler, J. 1993, *Bodies that Matter: On the Discursive Limits of 'Sex'*, Routledge, New York.

Butlin N.G. 1983, *Our Original Aggression*, Allen & Unwin, Sydney.

Cain, J. & Hewitt, J. 2004, *Off Course: From Public Place to Marketplace at Melbourne University*, Scribe, Melbourne.

Cain, M. 1989, *Growing Up Good*, Sage, Newbery Park.

Caldwell, J. & Ruzicka, L. 1978, 'The Australian Fertility Transition: An Analysis', *Population & Development*, no. 41, pp. 81–103.

Calhoun, C. 1994, 'Social Theory and Identity Politics', in C. Calhoun (ed.), *Social Theory and the Politics of Identity*, Blackwell, Oxford.

Callan, V. & Noller, P. 1991, *Marriage and the Family*, Methuen, Sydney.

Canadian Council on Social Development 2002, *The Progress of Canada's Children 2002*, Canadian Council on Social Development, Ottawa.

Canguilhem, G. 1990, *The Normal and the Pathological*, Zone Books, New York.

Carcach, C., Grant A. & Conroy, R. 1999, *Australian Corrections: The Imprisonment of Indigenous People*, Trends and Issues Paper no. 137, Australian Institute of Criminology, Canberra.

Carrington, K. 1993, *Offending Girls: Sex, Youth and Justice*, Allen & Unwin, Sydney.

Carroll, J. 1998, *Western Humanism*, Text, Richmond.

—— 2005, *Western Humanism*, 2nd edn, Text, Richmond.

Carson, E., Fitzgerald, P. & Roche, S. 2000, *A New Social Contract: Changing Social and Legal Frameworks for Young Australians*, Report to the National Youth Affairs Research Scheme, National Clearinghouse for Youth Studies, Hobart.

Carson, R. 1971 [1962], *Silent Spring*, Penguin, Harmondsworth.

Caspi, A., Henry, B., McGee, R., Moffitt, T. & Silver, P. 1995, 'Temperamental Origins of Child and Adolescent Behaviour', *Child Development*, vol. 57, no. 2, pp. 357–406.

Cass, B., Cappo, D., Edgar, D., George, J., Knox, B. & Setches, K. 1994, *The Heart of the*

Matter: Families at the Center of Public Policy, Discussion Paper prepared by the National Committee for the International Year of the Family, AGPS, Canberra.

Castells, M. 1996, *The Rise of the Network Society, The Information Age: Economy, Society and Culture*, vol. I, Blackwell, Oxford.

—— 1998, *End of Millennium: The Information Age: Economy, Society and Culture*, vol. III, Blackwell, Oxford.

Castles, S. 1992, 'Australian Multiculturalism', in G. Freeman & J. Jupp (eds), *Nations of Immigrants*, Oxford University Press, Melbourne.

Castles, S. & Miller, J. 1993, *The Age of Migration*, Macmillan, London.

Catley, B. 1996, *Globalising Australian Capitalism*, Cambridge University Press, Melbourne.

Cerny, P.G. 1989, *The Changing Architecture of the State*, Sage, London.

Chalk, G. & Jonasson, S. 1990, *Genocide: A Historical and Sociological Perspective*, CUNY Press, New York.

Chamberlain, C. 1983, *Class Consciousness in Australia*, Allen & Unwin, Sydney.

Chapman, B. & Pope, D. 1992, 'Government, Human Capital Formation and Higher Education', *Australian Quarterly*, Spring, pp. 275–92.

Chiricos, T. 1987, 'Rates of Crime and Unemployment: An Analysis of Aggregate Research Evidence', *Social Problems*, vol. 34, pp. 187–212.

Chomsky, N. 2002, *Media Control: The Spectacular Achievement of Propaganda*, Seven Stories Press, New York.

Christian Research Association 2005, *Australian Community Survey, 2001*, <www.cra.org.au>.

Chung, L., Hill, K. & Haukens, J. 2002, 'Childhood Predictors of Offence Trajectories', *Journal of Research in Crime and Delinquency*, vol. 39, no. 3, pp. 60–90.

Cicourel, A. 1976, *The Social Organisation of Juvenile Justice*, Heinemann, London.

Clark, C.M.H. 1962, *A History of Australia: From the Earliest Times to the Age of Macquarie*, Melbourne University Press, Melbourne.

Clark, I. 1997, *Globalisation and Fragmentation*, Oxford University Press, Oxford.

Clarke, G. 1982, *Defending Ski Jumpers: A Critique of Theories of Youth Subcultures*, CCCS Occasional Papers, University of Birmingham, Birmingham.

Clarke, J., Hall, S., Jefferson, T. & Roberts, R. 1976, 'Sub-Cultures, Cultures and Class', in S. Hall & T. Jefferson (eds), *Resistance through Rituals*, Hutchinson, London.

Coady, A. 2000, 'Universities and the Ideals of Inquiry', in A. Coady (ed.), *Why Universities Matter*, Allen & Unwin, Sydney.

Cockett, R. 1995, *Thinking the Unthinkable*, HarperCollins, London.

Coetzee, J.M., 1998, *Boyhood: Scenes from a Provincial Childhood*, Vintage, London.

—— 1999, *Disgrace*, Vintage, London.

Cohen, S. 1972, *Folk Devils and Moral Panics*, Martin Robertson, Oxford.

—— 1992, *Against Criminology*, Transaction Books, New Brunswick.

—— 1997, 'Intellectual Skepticism and Political Commitment: The Case of Radical Criminology', in P. Walton & J. Young (eds), *The New Criminology Revisited*, Macmillan, London.

Colebrook, J. 1988, *A House of Trees*, Corgi, London.

Coleman, J. 1974, *Relationships in Adolescence*, Routledge, London.

Coleman, C. & Moynihan, J. 1996, *Understanding Crime Data: Haunted by the Dark Figure*, Open University Press, Buckingham.

Coleman, J. 1961, *The Adolescent Society*, Free Press, Glencoe.

Collini, S. 1979, *Liberalism and Sociology*, Cambridge University Press, Cambridge.

Collins, R. 1975, 'Violence in the Sociological Tradition', in *Theory and Society*, vol. 7, no. 2, pp. 16–37.

Collyer, F. 1996, 'Measuring the Impact of Privatisation: A Review of Current Methodological Issues', *Just Policy*, no. 7, pp. 16–27.

Committee of Inquiry into Labour Market Programs 1985, *Report of the Committee of Inquiry into Labour Market Programs*, AGPS, Canberra,

Commonwealth Bureau of Census and Statistics 1972, *Australian Year Book 1972*, AGPS, Canberra.

—— 1973, *Australian Year Book 1973*, AGPS, Canberra.

Comte, A. 1877, *System of Positive Philosophy*, Longman Green, London.

Connell, R.W. 1975, *How to Do Small Surveys: A Guide for Students in Sociology, Kindred Industries and Allied Trades*, 2nd edn, School of Social Sciences, Flinders University.

—— 1977, *Ruling Class, Ruling Culture*, Cambridge University Press, Cambridge.

—— 1985, *Teachers' Work*, George Allen & Unwin, Sydney.

—— 1987 *Gender and Power: Society, the Person and Sexual Politics*, Polity Press, Cambridge.

—— 1989, 'Cool Guys, Swots and Wimps: The Interplay of Masculinity and Education', *Oxford Review of Education*, vol. 15, no. 3, special issue: Gender and Education: Current Issues, pp. 291–303.

—— 1995, *Masculinities*, Allen & Unwin, Sydney.

—— 2000, *Men and Boys*, Allen & Unwin, Sydney.

Connell, R.W., Ashenden, D., Kessler, S. & Dowlett, G. 1982, *Making the Difference: Schools, Families and Social Division*, Allen & Unwin, Sydney.

Considine, M. 1988, 'The Corporate Management Framework as Administrative Science: A Critique', *Australian Journal of Public Administration*, vol. 47, no. 1, pp. 11–29.

Considine, M. & Marginson, S. 2000, *The Enterprise University*, Cambridge University Press, Melbourne.

Considine, M. & Painter, M. (eds) 1997, *Managerialism: The Great Debate*, Melbourne University Press, Melbourne.

Criminal Justice Commission 1999, *Prisoner Numbers in Queensland*, Criminal Justice Commission, Brisbane.

Crompton, R. 1993, *Class and Stratification: An Introduction to Current Debates*, Polity Press, Cambridge.

Cunningham, S. & Turner, G. *The Media in Australia*, 2nd edn, Allen & Unwin, Sydney.

Currie, J. & Newson, J. (eds) 1998, *Universities and Globalization*, Sage, Thousand Oaks.

Dalton, V. 1999, *Aboriginal Deaths in Prison, 1980 to 1998: National Overview 1997–98*, AIC Trends and Issues Paper no.131, AIC, Canberra.

Danziger, K. 1993, *Constructing the Subject: Historical Origins of Psychological Research*, Cambridge University Press, Cambridge.

Davies, A.F. 1967, *Images of Class: An Australian Study*, Allen & Unwin, Sydney.

Davis, M. 1997, *Late Victorian Holocausts*, Verso, London.

Day, D. 1996, *Claiming a Continent: A History of Australia*, HarperCollins, Sydney.

Dean, M. & Hindess, B. (eds) 1998, *Governing Australia*, Cambridge University Press, Melbourne.

Dean, M. 1991, *The Constitution of Poverty*, Routledge, London.

Dembo, R. & Schmeidler, J. 2000, 'A Structural Model of the Impact of Family Factors on Serious Delinquency', *Journal of Child and Adolescent Substance Use*, vol. 10, no. 2, pp. 17–31.

—— 2003a, 'A Classification of High-Risk Youths', *Crime & Delinquency*, vol. 49, no. 2, pp. 201–30.

—— 2003b, *Family Empowerment Intervention: An Innovative Service for High-Risk Youths and their Families*, Haworth, Binghampton.

Department of Employment, Education and Training (DEET) 1995, *Trends in Education 1990–1995*, AGPS, Canberra.

Department of Employment, Education, Training and Youth Affairs (DEETYA) 1997, *DEETYA Job Futures 6*, Analysis and Evaluation Division, DEETYA, Canberra.

Department of Justice (Vic.) 1993, *Children's Court Statistics 1992*, Department of Justice, Melbourne.

de Vaus, D. 1995, *Surveys in Social Research*, 4th edn, Allen & Unwin, Sydney.

—— 2005, *Diversity and Change in Australian Families: A Statistical Profile*, Australian Institute of Family Studies, Melbourne.

Diggins J.P. 1996, *Max Weber: Politics and the Spirit of Tragedy*, Basic Books, New York.

Domberger S. & Piggott, J. 1986, 'Privatisation Policies and Public Enterprise', *Economic Record*, vol. 62, pp. 145–62.

Donzelot, J. 1970, *Policing Families*, Pantheon, New York.

Douglas, J. 1970, *Deviance and Respectability: The Social Construction of Moral Meaning*, Basic Book, New York.

Douglas, M. 1973, *Natural Symbols: Explorations in Cosmology*, Penguin, Harmondsworth.

Doyle, T. 2000, *Green Power: The Environment Movement in Australia*, UNSW Press, Sydney.

Dryfoos, J. 1990, *Adolescence at Risk: Prevalence and Prevention*, Oxford University Press, New York.

Dubet, F. 1993, 'On the Logics of Social Action', *Thesis Eleven*, vol. 17, no. 1, pp. 17–34.

Duncan, P., Ritter, P., Dornbusch, S., Gross, R. & Carlsmith, J. 1985, 'The Effects of Pubertal Timing on Body Image, School Behaviour and Deviance', *Journal of Youth and Adolescence*, vol. 14, pp. 227–36.

Durkheim, E. 1938, *The Rules of Sociological Method*, University of Chicago Press, Chicago.

—— 1957, *Professional Ethics and Civic Morals*, Routledge & Kegan Paul, London.

—— 1965 [1912], *The Elementary Forms of the Religious Life*, Free Press, New York.

—— 1973, 'Homo Duplex: the Dualism of Human Nature and its Social Conditions', in R. Bellah (ed.), *On Morality and Social Order*, University of Chicago Press, Chicago.

—— 1974 [1933], *The Division of Labour*, Free Press, New York.

—— 1982 [1897], *The Rules of Sociological Method*, Free Press, New York.

—— 1987 [1951], *Suicide: Study in Sociology*, Free Press, New York.

Dusseldorp Skills Forum 1998, *Australia's Youth: Reality and Risk*, Dusseldorp Skills Forum, Sydney.

Dusseyer, I. 1979, *Crime News: A Study of 40 Ontario Newspapers*, University of Toronto, Toronto.

Duster, T. 1987, 'Crime, Youth and Unemployment and the Black Underclass', *Journal of Research in Crime and Delinquency*, vol. 33, pp. 300–16.

Dwyer, P. 1997, *Opting Out Early: School Leavers and the Degeneration of Youth Policy*, National Clearing House for Youth Studies, Hobart.

Eagleton, T. 1988, *Literary Theory*, Oxford University Press, Oxford.

Eckersley, R. 1988, *Casualties of change: The Predicament of Youth in Australia*, Australian Commission for the Future, Melbourne.

—— 1992, *Apocalypse Now? Youth and the Challenge to Change*, Commission for the Future, Melbourne.

—— 1993, 'The West's Deepening Cultural Crisis', *The Futurist*, Nov–Dec, pp. 8–12.

Eckersley, R. 2002, *Environmentalism and Political Theory*, UCL Press, London.

Eckersley, R. 2004, *Well and Good: Meaning and Happiness*, Text, Melbourne.

Edgar, D. 1998, 'Relationships in the 90s', *The Weekend Australian*, 7–8 March, p. 17.

Edwards, M. 1998, *Social Policy, Public Policy*, Allen & Unwin, Sydney.

Egan, G. 1986, *The Skilled Helper*, Dunlop, Chicago.

Eichler, M. 1983, 'Beyond the Monolithic Bias in Family Literature', in M. Eichler (ed.), *Families in Canada Today*, Gage, Toronto.

Eisenstein, H. 1984, *Contemporary Feminist Theory*, Allen & Unwin, Sydney.

Eisenstein, Z. 1988, *The Female Body and the Law*, UCLA Press, Berkeley.

Elias, N. 1970, *Introduction to Sociology*, Blackwell, Oxford.

—— 1978, *The History of Manners: The Civilizing Process* (vol. 1), Blackwell, Oxford.

—— 1984, *The Civilising Process*, (2 vols), Blackwell, Oxford.

—— 1998, *The Norbert Elias Reader*, eds J. Goudsblom & S. Mennell, Blackwell, Oxford.

—— 1999, *The Germans*, Blackwell, Oxford.

Elkin, A.P. 1954, *The Australian Aboriginal*, Angus & Robertson, Sydney.

Emslie, M. 1997, A Chance to Avoid Illness: Responding to the Health Needs of Young Gay Men and Lesbians, unpublished paper, RMIT, Melbourne.

Encel, D. 1987, *Poverty and Aspects of Inequality in Australia: An Annotated Bibliography*, Social Welfare Research Centre, University of New South Wales, Sydney.

—— 1990, *Aspects of the Distribution of Income and Wealth in Australia: An Annotated Bibliography*, Social Welfare Research Centre, University of New South Wales, Sydney.

EPAC 1995, *Income Distribution in Australia*, AGPS, Canberra.

Erlich, P. 1971, *The Population Bomb*, Ballantine Books, New York.

Ernst, J. 1993, 'The Bower Bird Government and the Boat of State: The Theory of Governance in Victoria', *The Australian Rationalist*, no. 35.

Ernst, J. & Webber, M. 1996, 'Ideology and Interests: Privatisation in Theory and Practice', in M. Webber (ed.) with Mary Crooks, *Putting the People Last: Government Services and Rights in Victoria*, Hyland House, Melbourne.

Eze, E. (ed.) 1997, *Race and the Enlightenment: A Reader*, Blackwell Oxford.

Fagot, B.I., Gramant, L. & Johanssen, B. 1985, 'Differential Reactions to Assertive and Communicative Acts by Toddler Boys and Girls', *Child Development*, vol. 56, no. 4, pp. 30–49.

Farrington, D. 1978, 'The Family Backgrounds of Aggressive Youths', in L. Hersov, M. Berger & S. Schaffer (eds), *Aggression and Anti-Social Behaviour in Childhood and Adolescence*, Pergamon, Oxford.

—— 1994, *The Influence of the Family on Delinquent Development*, in C. Henderson (ed.), *Crime and the Family*, Family Policy Studies Centre, London.

—— 1996, *Understanding and Preventing Youth Crime*, Rowntree, London.

—— 1997, 'Human Development and Criminal Careers', in M. Maguire, R. Morgan & R. Reiner (eds), *The Oxford Handbook of Criminology*, Oxford University Press, Oxford.

Farrington, D., Gallagher, B., Morley, L., St Ledger, R. & West, D. 1986, 'Unemployment, School Leaving and Crime', *British Journal of Criminology*, vol. 26, no. 4, pp. 89–101.

Fatteh, E. 1997, *Criminology, Past Present and Future: A Critical Overview*, Macmillan, London.

Featherstone, M., Hepworth, M. & Turner, B.S. (eds) 1991, *The Body: Social Process, and Cultural Theory*, Sage, London.

Fein, O. 1995, 'The Influence of Social Class on Health Status: American and British Research on Health Inequalities', *Journal of Internal Medicine*, vol. 10, pp. 577–86.

Fernandez-Armestos, P. 1997, *Truth: A History and a Guide for the Perplexed*, Black Swan, London.

Fielding, N. 1993, 'Qualitative Interviewing', in G. Gilbert (ed.), *Researching Social Life*, Sage, London.

Finch, C. n.d. (c. late 1990s), *Australia Sports Injury Data Dictionary*, <www.ausport.gov. au/partic/datadict.html>.

Fincher, R. & Niewenhuysen, J. (eds) 1998, *Poverty Then and Now*, Melbourne University Press, Melbourne.

Fiske, J. 1990, *Understanding Popular Culture*, Unwin Hyman, London.

Flannery, T. 1998, *Throwim Way Leg: An Adventure*, Text Publishers, Richmond.

Foucault, M. 1977, *Discipline and Punish*, Penguin, Harmondsworth.

—— 1979, 'Omnes et Singulatim: Towards a Criticism of Political Reason', in S. McMurrin (ed.), *The Tanner Lectures on Human Values* (vol. 2), Cambridge University Press, Cambridge.

—— 1980, *Power/Knowledge: Selected Interviews and Other Writings, 1972–1977*, Pantheon, New York.

—— 1981, 'Questions of Method: An Interview with Michel Foucault', *Ideology and Consciousness*, vol. 8, pp. 7–26.

—— 1986, *The History of Sexuality* (vol. 3), Pantheon, New York.

—— 2000, *The Essential Foucault: Power* (vol. 3), The New Press, New York.

Fox, R. 1967, *Kinship and Marriage*, Penguin, Harmondsworth.

Frame, J. 1990, *State of Siege*, Angus & Robertson, Auckland.

Frankel, B. 1993, *From the Prophets Deserts Come*, Kibble Press, Melbourne.

Freeman, G. 1980, 'Comments for Discussion', in 'School to Work Transition', Victorian Consultative Committee on Social Development, papers presented at workshop, July and VCCSD Forum, 27 August.

Freeman, G. & Jupp, J. 1992, *Nations of Immigrants*, Oxford University Press, Melbourne.

Friedan, B. 1963, *The Feminine Mystique*, Norton, New York.

Friedenberg, E. 1959, *The Vanishing Adolescent*, Basic Books, New York.

Friedrichs, D.O. (ed.) 1998, *State Crime*, 2 vols, Dartmouth, Aldershot.

Fuchs, S. 2005, *Anti-Theory*, Zone Books, Cambridge.

Fuller, S. 2005, *The Intellectual*, Icon Books, London.

Furlong, A. & Cartmel, F. 1997, *Young People and Social Change: Individualisation and Risk in Late Modernity*, Open University, Buckingham.

Gadamer, H.G. 1989, *Truth and Method*, 2nd edn, Continuum, New York.

Gaddis, A. & Brooks-Gunn, J. 1985, 'The Male Experience of Pubertal Change', *Journal of Youth and Adolescence*, vol. 14, pp. 61–9.

Gagnon, J. & Simon, W. 1973, *Sexual Conduct*, Aldine, Chicago.

—— 1987, 'The Scripting of Oral–Genital Conduct', *Archives of Sexual Behaviour*, vol. 16, no. 1, pp. 1–25.

Gaita, R. 1999, *A Common Humanity*, Text, Richmond.

—— 2000, 'Truth and the University', in A. Coady (ed.), *Why Universities Matter*, Allen & Unwin, Sydney.

Garber, M. 1993, *Vested Interests: Cross Dressing and Cultural Anxiety*, Harmondsworth, Penguin.

Garfinkel, H. 1967, *Studies in Ethnomethodology*, Prentice Hall, Englewood Cliffs.

—— 1967, *Studies in Ethnomethodology*, Prentice-Hall, Englewood Cliffs.

Garland, D. 1985, 'The Criminal and His Science: A Critical Account of the Formation of Criminology at the End of the Nineteenth Century', *The British Journal of Criminology*, vol. 25, pp. 109–37.

—— 1991, *Punishment and Modern Society*, Oxford University Press, Oxford.

Garnham, N. 1990, *Capitalism and Communications*, Sage, London.

Gasset, Ortega Y. 1968, *The Revolt of the Masses*, Allen & Unwin, London.

Gelsthorpe, L. & Morris, A. 1988, 'Feminism and Criminology in Britain', *Journal of British Criminology*, vol. 28, pp. 93–110.

Gibb, D. 1973, *The Making of 'White' Australia*, Victorian Historical Association, Melbourne.

Giddens, A. 1974, *Capitalism and Modern Social Theory*, Cambridge University Press, Cambridge.

—— 1979, *Central Problems in Social Theory*, Macmillan, London.

—— 1982, *Profiles and Critiques in Social Theory*, Macmillan, London.

—— 1984, *The Constitution of Society*, Polity Press, Cambridge.

—— 1987a, *Social Theory and Modern Sociology*, Polity Press, Cambridge.

—— 1987b, *The Nation State and Violence*, Polity Press, Cambridge.

—— 1990, *The Consequences of Modernity*, Polity Press, Cambridge.

—— 1991a, *Modernity and Self-Identity: Self and Society in the Late Modern Age*, Polity Press, Cambridge.

—— 1991b, *Sociology: An Introduction*, Polity Press, Cambridge.

—— 1993, *New Rules of Sociological Method*, Polity Press, Cambridge.

—— 1997, *Sociology*, 3rd edn, Polity Press, Cambridge.

—— 1999, *Runaway World: How Globalisation is Reshaping our Lives*, Profile Books, London.

Gilding, M. 1997, *Australian Families: A Comparative Perspective*, Longman, Melbourne.

Ginsborg, P. 2005, *The Politics of Everyday Life: Making Choices, Changing Lives*, Yale University Press, London.

Giroux, H. 1981, *Ideology, Culture & the Process of Schooling*, Falmer Press, London.

—— 1997, *Channel Surfing: Race Talk and the Destruction of Today's Youth*, Macmillan, London.

Glezer, H. 1991, 'Juggling Work and Family Commitments', *Family Matters*, no. 28, pp. 6–10.

Glover, J. & Woollacott, T. 1992, *Social Health Atlas of Australia*, vol. 2, Cat. No. 4385.0 South Australian Health Commission and ABS, Canberra.

Glyn, A. 1992, 'The Costs of Stability: The Advanced Capitalist Countries in the 1980s', *New Left Review*, November, pp. 71–95.

Goffman, E. 1961, *Asylums: Essays on the Social Situation of Mental Patients and Other Inmates*, Doubleday, New York.

—— 1969, *The Presentation of Self in Everyday Life*, Penguin, Harmondsworth.

—— 1974, *Frame Analysis*, Houghton-Mifflin, San Francisco.

Goldberg, D. 1993, *Racist Culture*, Blackwell, Oxford.

Goldhagen J. 1996, *Hitler's Willing Executioners*, Knopf, New York.

Goldie, J.G., Douglas, B. & Furnass, B. 2005, 'An Urgent Need to Change Direction', in J. Goldie, B. Douglas & B. Furnass (eds), *In Search of Sustainability*, Sustainable Population Australia, Sydney, pp. 1–17.

Gombrowicz, W. 1988, (trans L. Vallee), *Diary Volume 1*, Northwestern University Press, Brampton.

Goodstein, E.S. 2002, *Economics and the Environment*, 3rd edn, John Wiley, New York.

Gorz, A. 1984, *End of the Working Class*, NLB Books, London.

Gottfredson, M. and Hirschi, T. 1990, *A General Theory of Crime*, Stanford University Press, Stanford.

Gough, K. 1967, 'Is the Family Universal: The Case of the Nayar', in N. Bell & E. Vogel (eds), *A Modern Introduction to the Family*, Free Press, New York.

Gouldnet, A.J. 1979, *The Future of Intellectuals and the Rise of the New Class*, Seabury Press, New York.

Graff, G., 2003, *Clueless in Academe*, New Haven, Yale University Press.

Graham, C. & Burvill, P. 1992, 'A Study of Coroners' Records of Suicide in Young People, 1986–88 in Western Australia', *Australian and New Zealand Journal of Psychiatry*, vol. 26, pp. 30–9.

Greer, G. 1967, *The Female Eunuch*, Angus & Robertson, Sydney.

—— 1970, *The Female Eunuch*, Paladin Books, London.

Gregory, R. & Hunter, B. 1995, *The Macro Economy and the Growth of Urban Ghettos and Urban Poverty in Australia*, discussion paper no. 325, Centre for Economic Policy Research, ANU, Canberra.

Greig, A., Lewins, F. & White, K. 2003, *Inequality in Australia*, Cambridge University Press, Melbourne.

Grieve, N. & Burns, A. (eds) 1994, *Australian Women's Contemporary Feminist Thought*, Oxford University Press, Melbourne.

Grint, K. 1991, *The Sociology of Work: An Introduction*, Polity Press, Cambridge.

Gruen, F. & Grattan, M. 1993, *Managing Government: Labor's Achievements and Failures*, Longman Cheshire, Melbourne.

Gunn, M. 2000, 'Class Divide Reaches the Playground', *The Australian*, 22 June.

Habermas, J. 1971, *Knowledge and Human Interests*, Beacon Press, Boston.

—— 1973, *Legitimation Crisis*, Beacon Press, Boston.

—— 1984–86, *A Theory of Communicative Action*, 2 vols, Polity Press, Cambridge.

—— 1990, *Moral Consciousness and Communicative Action*, trans. C. Lenhardt & S. Nicholsen, MIT Press, Cambridge.

—— 1992, *The Structural Transformation of the Public Sphere*, MIT Press, Cambridge.

—— 1993, *Justification and Application: Remarks on Discourse Ethics*, trans C. Cronin, MIT Press, Cambridge.

—— 1998, *Facts and Norms*, MIT Press, Cambridge.

—— 1999, 'The Uncoupling of System and Life-world', in A. Elliott (ed.), *The Blackwell Reader in Contemporary Social Theory*, Blackwell, Oxford.

Hacking, I. 1999, *The Social Construction of What?*, Harvard University Press, Cambridge.

—— 2002, *Historical Ontology*, Harvard University Press, Cambridge.

Hall, S. 1978, *Policing the Crisis: Mugging, the State and Law and Order*, Macmillan, London.

Hall, S. & Jefferson T. (eds) 1976, *Resistance Through Rituals*, Hutchinson, London.

Hammersley, M. & Atkins, P. 1983, *Ethnography: Principles in Practice*, Tavistock, London.

Hanley, N., Shogren, J.F. & White, B. 2001, *Introduction to Environmental Economics*, Oxford University Press, Oxford.

Hansen, S., Jesperson, P. & Rasmussen, I. 2000, *Towards a Sustainable Economy: The Application of Ecological Premises to Long-Term Planning in Norway*, Macmillan, London.

Haralambos, M., van Krieken, R., Smith, P. & Holborn, M. 1997, *Sociology: Themes and Perspectives*, Longmans, Melbourne.

Harden, I. 1992, *The Contracting State*, Open University Press, Buckingham.

Harding, A., Lloyd, R. & Greenwell, H. 2002, *Financial Disadvantage in Australia 1999 to 2000: The Persistence of Poverty in a Decade of Growth*, Smith Family, Sydney.

Harre, R. 1986, 'The Steps to Social Constructionism', in R. Martin & P. Light (eds), *Children of Social Worlds: Development in a Social Context*, Polity Press, Cambridge, pp. 287–95.

Harris, A. 2001, 'Dodging and Weaving; Young Women Countering the Stories of Youth Citizenship', *International Journal of Critical Psychology*, vol. 4, no. 4, pp. 183–99.

Harris, A. & Fine, A. (eds), *All About the Girl: Culture, Power and Identity*, Routledge, New York.

Harris, R. 1993, 'Globalization, Trade and Income', *Canadian Journal of Economics*, vol. 26, no. 2, pp. 753–76.

Hartley, R. 1989, *What Price Independence?* Australian Institute of Family Studies, and Youth Affairs Council of Victoria, Melbourne.

Hartley, R. & McDonald, P. 1994, 'The Many Faces of Families', *Family Matters*, no. 37, pp. 6–19.

Hartmann, H. 1970, 'Capitalism, Patriarchy and Job Segregation by Sex', in Z. Eisenstein (ed.), *Capitalist Patriarchy and the Case for Socialism*, MR Press, New York.

Harvey, D. 1989, *The Condition of Post Modernity*, Blackwell, Oxford.

—— 1996, *Justice, Nature and the Geography of Difference*, Blackwell, Oxford.

Hawken, P., Lovins, A.B. & Lovins, L.H. 2000, *Natural Capitalism: The Next Industrial Revolution*, Earthscan, London.

HCSV 1993, *School Students and Drug Use 1993*, Health and Community Services Victoria, HCSV, Melbourne.

Heidensohn, F. 1992, *Women in Control? The Role of Women in Law Enforcement*, OUP, Oxford.

Heidensohn, F. with Hahn-Rafter, N. 1995, *International Perspectives in Feminist Criminology*, Open University Press, Milton Keynes.

Held, D. 1980, *Introduction to Critical Theory: Horkheimer to Habermas*, University of California Press, Berkeley.

Hempel, C.G. 1970, *Philosophy of Natural Science*, Prentice Hall, Englewood Cliffs, New Jersey.

Henderson, H. 1996, 'What's New in the Great Debate about Measuring Wealth and Progress?', *Challenge*, vol. 39, no. 6, pp. 50–6, <www.homeoffice.gov.uk/docs/ptp.pdf>.

Henderson, R.F., Harcourt, A. & Harper, R. 1970, *People in Poverty: A Melbourne Survey*, Cheshire, Melbourne.

Hessler, R. 1992, *Social Research Methods*, West Publishing, St Pauls.

Higginbotham, G. 1867, *Report of the Royal Commission on Education in Victoria*, Victorian Parliamentary Papers, p. 1867.

Hil, R. & McMahon, T. 2004, *Families and Juvenile Crime*, Peter Lang, New York.

Hill, D.M., White, V., Williams, M. & Gardner, G. 1993, 'Tobacco and Alcohol Use Among Australian Secondary School Students in 1990', *Medical Journal of Australia*, vol. 158, pp. 228–34.

Hinkson, J. 1987, 'Post-Lyotard: A Critique of the Information Society', *Arena*, no. 80, pp. 34–57.

Hirst, P. & Thompson, J. 1999, *Globalization in Question* (2nd edn), Polity Press, Cambridge.

Hite, S. 1977, *The Hite Report*, Dell Publishing, New York.

Hobsbawm, R.J. 1994, *Age of Extremes: The Short Twentieth Century, 1914–1991*, Verso, London.

Hochschild, A. 2005, *Bury the Chains*, Macmillan, London.

Hocking, J. 2004, *Terror Laws: ASIO, Counter-Terrorism and the Threat to Democracy*, UNSW Press, Sydney.

Hollway, W. & Jefferson, T. 1997, 'The Risk Society in an Age of Anxiety: Situating Fear of Crime', *British Journal of Sociology*, 48(2), pp. 255–66.

—— 2000, 'The role of anxiety in fear of crime', in R. Sparks & T. Hope (eds), *Crime Risk and Insecurity: Law and Order in Everyday Life and Political Discourse*, Routledge, London.

Holton, G. 1988, *Thematic Origins of Scientific Thought: Kepler to Einstein*, 2nd edn, Harvard University Press, Cambridge.

Hopkin, S. 1996, 'Synthetic Ecstasy: The Youth Culture of Techno Music', *Youth Studies Australia*, no. 15, pp. 12–17.

—— 2002, *Girl Heroes: The New Force in Popular Culture*, Pluto Press, Sydney.

Horne, D. 1964, *The Lucky Country: Australia in the Sixties*, Penguin, Ringwood.

Howe, A. 1998, (ed.) *Sexed Crime in the News*, The Federation Press, Sydney.

Howes, M. 2005, *Can Government Save the Planet? Responses to Environmental Risk in the USA, UK and Australia*, Allen & Unwin, Sydney.

Hoyle, R., Harris, J. & Judd, C. 2002, *Research Methods in Social Relations*, (7th ed), Wadsworth/Thompson, Belmont.

Hughes, K. 1997, *Contemporary Feminism 2*, Longman, Melbourne.

Hughes, R. 1986, *The Fatal Shore*, Random House, Sydney.

Hume, D. 1882, *Essays: Moral, Political and Literary*, Longman Green, London.

Humphries, S., 1981, *Hooligans or Rebels: An Oral History of Working Class Childhood and Youth 1889–1939*, Blackwell, New York.

Hunter, I. 1993, *Government and Culture*, Macmillan, London.

—— 1996, *Rethinking the School*, Allen & Unwin, Sydney.

Huntington, S. 1996, *The Clash of Civilizations*, Norton, New York.

Hynes, H.P. 1989, *The Recurring Silent Spring*, Pergamon, New York.

Illich, I. 1975, *Medical Nemesis*, Calder Boyer, London.

Inglehart, R. 1977, *The Silent Revolution: Changing Values and Political Styles Among Western Politics*, Princeton University Press, New Jersey.

Irigaray, L. 1987, 'Sexual Difference', in T. Moi (ed.), *French Feminist Thought*, Blackwell, Oxford.

Ironmonger, J. (ed.) 1989, *Households Work*, Allen & Unwin, Sydney.

Jakubowicz, A. 1981, 'State and Ethnicity', *Australian and New Zealand Journal of Sociology*, vol. 17, no. 3, pp. 4–13.

James, W. 1906, *Pragmatism*, Dover Books, New York.

—— 1964, *The Varieties of Religious Experience*, University of Chicago Press, Chicago.

Jay, M. 1972, *The Dialectical Imagination*, Heinemann, London.

Jennett, C. & Stewart, R. (eds) 1989, *Politics of the Future: The Role of Social Movements*, Macmillan, Melbourne.

Johnson, L. 1993, *The Modern Girl: Girlhood and Growing Up*, Allen & Unwin, Sydney.

Johnson, T. 1972, *Professions and Power*, Macmillan, London.

Jones, B. 1982, *Sleepers Awake! Technology and the Future of Work*, Oxford University Press, Melbourne.

Jones, S. 1993, 'We Are All Cousins Under the Skin', *The Independent*, 12 December.

Joyce, P. (ed.) 1995, *Class*, Oxford University Press, Oxford.

Juredeini, R., Kenny, S. & Poole, M. (eds) 1997, *Sociology: Australian Connections*, Allen & Unwin, Sydney.

Kamin, L. 1976, *The Politics of IQ*, Penguin, Harmondsworth.

Kant, I. 1997 [1764], *Observations on the Feeling of the Beautiful and Sublime*, Cambridge University Press, Cambridge.

Katz, C. 2003, 'Issues in the Production and Dissemination of Crime Statistics', *Crime & Delinquency*, vol. 49, no. 3, pp. 485–516.

Katz, J. 1988, *Seductions of Crime*, Basic Books, New York.

—— 2002, *How Emotions Work*, University of Chicago Press, Chicago.

Keane, J. (ed.) 1988, *Civil Society and the State*, Verso, London.

—— 2001, *Reflections on Violence*, Verso, London.

Keizer, B. 1997, *Dancing with Mister D: Notes on Life and Death*, Nan Talese, New York.

Kellehear, A. (ed.) 1996, *Social Self, Global Culture: An Introduction to Sociological Ideas*, Oxford University Press, Melbourne.

Kellner, D. 1992, 'Popular Culture and the Construction of Postmodern Identities', in S. Lash & J. Friedman (eds), *Modernity and Identity*, Blackwell, Oxford.

Kelly P. 1992, *The End of Certainty*, Allen & Unwin, Sydney.

—— 1993, *The End of Certainty*, Allen & Unwin, Sydney.

—— 1998, Risk and the Regulation of Youth(ful) identities in an Age of Manufactured Uncertainty, unpublished PhD thesis, Deakin University, Melbourne.

—— 1999, 'Wild and Tame Zones: Regulating the Transition of Youth at Risk', *Journal of Youth Studies*, vol. 2, no. 2, pp. 193–211.

—— 2000a, 'Our Split Personality Society', *The Australian*, 17 June.

—— 2000b, 'The Dangerousness of Youth at Risk: The Possibilities of Surveillance and Intervention in Uncertain Times', *Journal of Adolescence*, vol. 23, no. 4, pp. 463–76.

Kelsey, J. 1995, *Economic Fundamentalism*, Pluto Press, London.

Kemmis, S. 1981, *Research Approaches and Methods: Action Research*, Deakin University, Geelong.

Kenway, J., Blackmore, J., Rennie, L. & Willis, S. 1998, *Answering Back: Girls, Boys, Teachers & Feminism in Schools*, Routledge, New York.

Kenway, J. & Willis, S. 1991, *Hearts and Minds: Girls, Schooling and Self-Esteem*, Falmer Press, London.

King, A. 1998, 'Income Poverty Since the 1970s', in R. Fincher & J. Nieuwenhuysen (eds), *Poverty Then and Now*, Melbourne University Press, Melbourne, pp. 71–102.

Kinnear, P. (ed.) 2001, *The Idea of a University: Enterprise or Academy?* Discussion Paper No. 39, The Australia Institute, September.

Kinsey, A. 1948, *The Sexual Behaviour of the Human Male*, Saunders & Co., Boston.

Klamer, A. & Leonard, T. 1994, 'What's An Economic Metaphor?', in Mirowski, P. (ed.), *Natural Images in Economic Thought*, Cambridge University Press, Cambridge.

Knox, E. & Gilman, E. 1997, 'Hazard Proximities of Childhood Cancers in Great Britain from 1953 to 1980', *Journal of Epidemiology and Community Health*, vol. 51, pp. 151–9.

Kohn, M. 1999, *The Race Gallery*, Pimlico, London.

Kolakowski, S. 1982, *Marxism: Main Themes and Currents*, 3 vols, Blackwell, Oxford.

Kramer, L. 1975, *Australian Council for Education Standards*, Review, ACES, vol. 2, no. 4.

—— 1989, 'Principles of Education Reform for Australia', *Newsweekly*, 15 February.

Krivanek, J. 1988, *Heroin Myths and Reality*, Allen & Unwin, Sydney.

Kuhn, T.S. 1969, *The Structure of Scientific Revolutions*, University of Chicago Press, Chicago.

Kumar, K. 1978, *Prophecy and Progress: The Sociology of Industrial and Post Industrial Life*, Penguin, Harmondsworth.

Lacquer, W. 1980, *Making Sex*, Harvard University Press, Cambridge.

Lakoff, G. 1999, *Moral Politics: How Neo-Conservatives and Liberals Think*, University of Chicago Press, Chicago.

—— 2005, *Don't Think of an Elephant: Know Your Values and Frame the Debate*, Scribe Publications, Melbourne.

Lakoff, G. & Johnson, M. 1980, *Metaphors We Live By*, University of Chicago Press, Chicago.

—— 2003, *Metaphors We Live By* (2nd edn), University of Chicago Press, Chicago.

Lakoff, G. & Nunez, R., 2000, *Where Mathematics Comes From*, Basic Books, New York.

Langmore, J. & Quiggin, J. 1994, *Work for All*, Melbourne University Press, Melbourne.

Lansdown, G. 2001, *Promoting Children's Participation in Democratic Decision Making*, UNICEF, Innocenti Research Centre, Florence.

Larsen M. 1976, *The Rise of Professionalism*, UCLA Press, Berkeley.

Laslett, P. 1979, *The World We Have Lost*, Methuen, London.

Last, J. 1988, *A Dictionary of Epidemiology*, Oxford University Press, New York.

Laub, J. & Sampson, R. 1988, 'Unraveling Families and Delinquency: A Re-analysis of the Gluecks' Data', *Criminology*, vol. 26, no. 3, pp. 355–79.

Lawrence, G., Bammer, G. & Chapman, S. 2000, 'Sending the Wrong Signal: Analysis of Print Media Reportage of the ACT Heroin Prescription Trial Proposal, August 1997', *Australian and New Zealand Journal of Public Health*, vol. 24, no. 3, pp. 254–64.

Layder, D. 1994, *Understanding Social Theory*, Sage, London.

—— 1997, *Modern Social Theory: Key Debates and New Directions*, Routledge, London.

Leflore, L. 1988, 'Delinquent Youths and Family', *Adolescence*, vol. xxiii, no. 91, pp. 47–59.

Leser, D. 1996, 'Pauline Hanson's Bitter Harvest', *The Age Good Weekend*, 30 November.

Lewis, B. 1994, *Islam and the Rest*, Oxford University Press, New York.

Lewis, P., Hensley, M., Wlodarczyk, J., Toneguzzi, R., Westley-Wise, V., Dunn, T. & Calvert, D. 1998, 'Outdoor Air Pollution and Children's Respiratory Symptoms in the Steel Cities of New South Wales', *The Medical Journal of Australia*, vol. 169, pp. 459–63.

Leys, S. 1999, *The Angel & The Octopus*, Duffy & Snellgrove, Sydney.

Levinas, E. 1996, *Emmanuel Levinas: Basic Writings*, Indianna University Press, Bloomington.

Little, G. 1970, *The University Experience: An Australian Study*, MUP, Melbourne.

Livingstone, S. 2002, *Young People and the New Media*, Sage, London.

Lloyd, P. 1995, 'The Nature of Globalization', in EPAC, *Globalisation: Issues for Australia*, EPAC Commission Paper No. 5, AGPS, Canberra, pp. 11–23.

Lomborg, B. 2001, *The Skeptical Environmentalist: Measuring the Real State of the World*, Cambridge University Press, Cambridge.

Long, M. & Hayden, M. 2001, *Paying Their Way: A Survey of Australian Undergraduate University Student Finances 2000* (Executive Summary), Australian Vice-Chancellors' Committee, September.

Lopez, R. 2000, *The Origins of Australian Multiculturalism*, Melbourne University Press, Melbourne.

Luckin, D. 2000, 'Environmental Taxation and Red–Green Politics', *Capital and Class*, no. 72, Autumn, pp. 161–89.

Lukes, S. 1979, *Emile Durkheim: His Life and Work*, Allen Lane, London.

Lupton, D. (ed.) 1999, *Risk and Subcultural Theory: New Directions and Perspectives*, Cambridge University Press, Melbourne.

Lyotard, J.F. 1984, *The Postmodern Condition*, University of Minnesota Press, Minneapolis.

MacDonald, G. & Baldwin, G. 1991, *Long Time Gone*, Pinevale Publications, San Francisco.

MacDonald, J. 1951, 'The Bodgie', Unpublished BA Honors Thesis, University of Sydney.

MacIntyre, A. 1981, *After Virtue*, University of Notre Dame Press, Philadelphia.

Macintyre, A. 1988, *Whose Justice? Which Rationality?*, University of Notre Dame Press, Notre Dame, IN.

—— 1990, *Three Rival Versions of Moral Enquiry*, University of Notre Dame Press, Notre Dame, IN.

Maguire, M. 1997, 'Crime Statistics, Patterns and Trends', in M. Maguire, R. Morgan & R. Reiner (eds), *The Oxford Handbook of Criminology*, 2nd edn, Oxford University Press, Oxford, pp. 135–88.

Maguire, M., Morgan, R. & Reiner, R. (eds), 2002, *Oxford Handbook of Criminology*, 3rd edn, Oxford University Press, Oxford.

Makinda, S. 1989, 'Globalisation as a Policy Outcome', *Current Affairs Bulletin*, CAE, Sydney.

Makkai, T. & McAllister, I. 1993, 'Immigrants in Australian Society', in J. Najman & J.S. Western (eds), *A Sociology of Australian Society*, Macmillan, Melbourne.

Manent, P. 1998, *The City of Man*, trans. M. LePain, Princeton University Press, Princeton.

Mann, M. 1989, *War and States*, Polity Press, Cambridge.

—— 2005, *The Dark Side of Democracy: Explaining Ethnic Cleansing*, Cambridge University Press, Cambridge.

Mannes, M. 1959, *Subverse: Rhymes for our Times*, Faber & Faber, London.

Marco, G.J., Hollingworth, R. & Durham, W. (eds) 1987, *Silent Spring Revisited*, American Chemical Society, Washington, DC.

Marcuse, H. 1972, *One Dimensional Man*, Sphere, London.

Marginson, S. 1992, 'The Politics of Post-Compulsory Curricula', in T. Seddon & C.E. Deer (eds), *A Curriculum for the Senior Secondary Years*, Australian Council for Educational Research, Melbourne.

—— 1993, *Education Credentials in Australia: Average Positional Value in Decline*, CSHE Working Paper 93, University of Melbourne, Melbourne.

—— 1997, *Markets in Education*, Allen & Unwin, Sydney.

Marmot, M. 1998, 'Contribution of Psychosocial Factors to Socio-economic Differences in Health', *Milbank Quarterly*, vol. 76, pp. 403–33.

Marmot, M., Rose, G. & Shipley, M. 1991, 'Health Inequalities Among British Civil Servants', *Lancet*, vol. 337, pp. 1387–9.

Marmot, M., Rose, G., Shipley, M. & Hamilton, P. 1978, 'Employment Grade and Coronary Heart Disease in British Civil Servants', *Journal of Epidemiology and Community Health*, vol. 3, pp. 244–9.

Marr, D. & Wilkinson, M. 2004, *Dark Victory*, 2nd edn, Allen & Unwin, Sydney.

Marshall, T.H. 1950, *Citizenship and Social Class*, Cambridge University Press, Cambridge.

Martin, J. 1978, *The Migrant Presence*, Allen & Unwin, Sydney.

Martin, J.J. 1993, *The History and Power of Reading*, Princeton University Press, Princeton.

Marx, K. & Engels, F. 1971, *The Communist Manifesto*, Penguin, Harmondsworth.

Mathers, C. 1994, *Health Differentials Among Adult Australians Aged 25–64*, AIHW, Canberra.

Matthews, H., Limb, M. & Taylor, M. 2000, 'Young People's Participation and Representation in Society', *Geoforum*, vol. 30, pp. 135–44.

Mauss, M. 1985, 'A Category of the Human Mind: The Notion of Person, the Notion of Self', in M. Carruthers, S. Collins, & S. Lukes (eds), *The Categories of the Person*, Cambridge University Press, Cambridge.

Mayer, H. 1964, *The Press in Australia*, Lansdowne Press, Melbourne.

McAllister, I. & Kelly, J. 1984, 'Immigrants' Status, Earnings and Politics', in J. Jupp (ed.), *Ethnic Politics in Australia*, Allen & Unwin, Sydney.

McArthur, M. 1999, 'Pushing the Drug Debate: The Media's Role in Policy Reform', *Australian Journal of Social Issues*, vol. 34, no. 2, pp. 149–62.

McBryde, I. 1987, 'Goods from Another Country', in J. Mulvaney & J. White (eds), *Australians to 1788*, Fairfax, Syme & Weldon, Sydney.

McCloskey, D. 1999, *Crossings: A Memoir*, Vintage, New York.

McDaniel, J. 2002, 'Spirituality and Sustainability', *Conservation Biology*, no. 16, pp. 1461–4.

McDonald, K. 1995, 'Morals is All You've Got', *Arena Magazine*, December, pp. 18–23.

McDonald, P. 1988, 'Family Formation in Victoria, 1881–1891', in C. McConville & G. Davidson (eds), *The Colonial Family*, Allen & Unwin, Sydney.

—— 1993, 'Family Trends and Structure in Australia', *Australian Family Briefings No. 3*, AIFS, Melbourne.

—— 1994, 'What are the Issues?', *Family Matters*, no. 37, pp. 4–5.

McGregor, C. 1997, *Class in Australia*, Penguin, Ringwood.

McGrew, T. 1992, 'A Global Society', in S. Hall, D. Held & T. McGrew (eds), *Modernity and its Futures*, Polity Press, Cambridge.

McInnis, C., Hartley, R., Polesel, J. & Teese, R. 2000a, *Non-Completion in Vocational Education and Training in Higher Education: A Literature Review Commissioned by the Department of Education, Training and Youth Affairs*, Centre for the Study of Higher Education, University of Melbourne, Melbourne.

McInnis, C., James, R. & Hartley, R. 2000b, *Trends in the First Year Experience in Australian Universities*, Centre for the Study of Higher Education, University of Melbourne, Melbourne.

McKay, J. 1989, *Phoenician Farewell*, Ashwood House, Melbourne.

McKeown, T. 1979, *The Role of Medicine*, Princeton University Press, Princeton, New Jersey.

McKinlay, J. & McKinlay, S. 1977, 'The Questionable Effect of Medical Measures on the Decline of Mortality in the United States', *Millbank Quarterly*, vol. 55, pp. 405–28.

McLelland, D. 1978, *Karl Marx: A Biography*, Macmillan, London.

McMahon, A. 1997, 'Sex and Social Life', in R. Jureidini, S. Kenny & M. Poole (eds), *Sociology: Australian Connections*, Allen & Unwin, Sydney.

McMullan, B. 1996, 'A Fair Distribution of Work: An Equity Issue for the 21st Century', Speech to John Curtin Memorial Breakfast, 24 November.

McPherson, C.B. 1968, *Origins of Possessive Individualism*, Oxford University Press, Oxford.

McQuail, D. 1986, 'Diversity in Political Communications: Its Sources, Forms and Future', in P. Golding et al. (eds), *Communicating Politics*, Leicester University Press, Leicester.

McRobbie, A. 1980, 'Settling Accounts with Subcultures: A Feminist Critique', *Screen Education*, Spring.

Mead, G.H. 1934, *Mind, Self and Society*, University of Chicago Press, Chicago.

Mead, M. 1963 [1935], *Sex and Temperament in Three Primitive Societies*, William Morrow, New York.

Meekosha, H. 2002, 'Virtual Activists? Women and the Making of Identities of Disability', *Hypatia*, vol. 17, no. 3, pp. 67–88.

Melucci, A. 1996, *Challenging Codes: Collective Action in the Information Age*, Cambridge University Press, Cambridge.

Mendes, P. 2003, *Australia's Welfare Wars: The Players, the Politics and the Ideologies*, UNSW Press, Sydney.

Mercer, J. (ed.) 1975, *The Other Half*, Penguin, Ringwood.

Merton, R. 1967, *Social Theory and Social Structure*, rev. edn, Free Press, Glencoe.

—— 1967, 'Insiders and Outsiders: A Chapter in the Sociology of Ideas', *American Journal of Sociology*, vol. 78, no. 1, pp. 9–47.

Mestrovic, S. 1997, *Anthony Giddens: The Last Modernist*, Routledge, London.

Miles, I. & Irvine, J. 1979, 'The Critique of Official Statistics', in J. Irvine, I. Miles & J. Evans (eds), *Demystifying Official Statistics*, Pluto, London.

Miles, S. 2000, *Youth Lifestyles in a Changing World*, Open University Press, Buckingham.

Milgram, S. 1973, *Obedience to Authority: An Experimental View*, Harper & Row, New York.

Miller, J. 1997, *God has Ninety Nine Names: A Journalist's Journey Through a Militant Middle East*, Simon & Schuster, New York.

Miller, P. 1986, *Long Division: State Schooling in South Australian Society*, Wakefield Press, Adelaide.

—— 1998, *Transformations of Patriarchy in the West, 1500–1900*, Indiana University Press, Bloomington.

Miller, P. & Davey, I. 1990, 'Family, Schooling and the Patriarchal State', in M. Theobald & R. Selleck (eds), *Family, School and State in Australian History*, Allen & Unwin, Sydney.

Millett, K. 1970, *Sexual Politics*, Doubleday, New York.

—— 1971, *Sexual Politics*, Sphere, London.

Mills, C. Wright 1970, *The Sociological Imagination*, Penguin, Harmondsworth.

Mishra, R. 1984, *The Crisis of the Welfare State*, Wheatsheaf, Harvester.

Mitchell, W. & Sherington, G. 1987, *Growing Up in Illawarra: A Social History 1834–1984*, Allen & Unwin, Sydney.

Mizen, P. 2004, *The Changing State of Youth*, Palgrave Macmillan, New York.

Mol, H. 1971, *Religion in Australia*, Nelson, Melbourne.

Montaigne, M. de, 1994, *Essays 1580–88*, University of Chicago Press, Chicago.

Moore, S. & Rosenthal, D. 1993, *Sexuality in Adolescence*, Routledge, London.

Moore, W. 1963, 'But Some are More Equal than Others', *American Sociological Review*, vol. xxviii, no. 1, February, pp. 13–18.

Morgan, D. 1975, *Social Theory and the Family*, Routledge & Kegan Paul, London.

Morson, G. & Emerson, C. (eds) 1989, *Rethinking Bahktin: Extensions and Challenges*, North Western University, Evanston.

Mostert, N. 1992, *Frontiers*, Pimlico, London.

Muecke, S. 1992, *Textual Space: Aboriginality and Cultural Studies*, UNSW Press, Sydney.

Mukherjee, S. 1994, 'What is So Good About the Low Crime Rate in Japan?', *Australian Rationalist*, no. 37, pp. 7–19.

—— 1997, 'The Dimensions of Juvenile Crime', in A. Borowski & I. O'Connor (eds), *Juvenile Crime, Justice and Correction*, Longman, Melbourne, pp. 4–24.

Mukherjee, S. & Dagger, D. 1990, *The Size of the Crime Problem in Australia*, 2nd edn, Australian Institute of Criminology, Canberra.

Mulvaney, J. 2002, 'Difficult to Found an Opinion: 1788 Aboriginal Population Estimates', in G. Briscoe & I. Smith (eds), 'The Aboriginal Population Revisited: 70,000 Years to the Present', *Aboriginal History Monograph*, vol. 10, pp. 1–8.

Murdock, G.P. 1949, *Social Structure*, Macmillan, New York.

Murphy, J. 2000, *Imagining the Fifties: Private Sentiment and Political Culture in Menzies' Australia*, Pluto Press, Sydney.

Murray, J. 1974, *Larrikins*, Cheshire Press, Melbourne.

Nagel, T. 1986, *The View from Nowhere*, Oxford University Press, New York.

National Committee on Violence Against Women 1993, *The National Strategy on Violence Against Women*, Office of the Status of Women, Department of the Prime Minister and Cabinet, Canberra.

National Crime Prevention 1999, *Pathways to Prevention: Developmental and Early Intervention Approaches to Crime in Australia*, Commonwealth Attorney-General's Department, Canberra.

NCADA 1992, *Statistics on Drug Use in Australia 1992*, H&HCS, Canberra.

Neiman, S. 2002, *Evil in Modern Thought*, Princeton University Press, Princeton.

Nelson, J., Megill, R. & McCloskey, D. 1987, *The Rhetoric of the Human Sciences*, University of Wisconsin Press, Madison.

Neruda, P. 1977, 'Too Many Names', *Estravagario*, trans. T. Gunn, New Publishing, London.

Neville, A. 2002, *State of the Family*, Anglicare Australia, Melbourne.

Newman, Cardinal J.H. 1960 [1873], *The Idea of a University*, Rinehart Press, San Francisco.

Newton, I. 1996 [1687], *Philosophia Naturalis Principia Mathematica*, Cambridge University Press, Cambridge.

Nicholson, L. 1997, 'The Myth of the Traditional Family', in H.L. Marsh (ed.), *Feminism and Families*, Routledge, New York.

Nisbet, R. 1974, *The Sociological Tradition*, Open University, Milton Keynes.

Oakley, A. 1979, *Becoming a Mother*, Martin Robertson, Oxford.

Ochiltree, G. 1990, *Children in Australian Families*, Longman Cheshire, Melbourne.

Offe, C. 1983, *The Contradictions of the Welfare State*, Blackwell, Oxford.

—— 1996, *Modernity and the State*, Blackwell, Oxford.

Offer, D. 1969, *The Psychological World of the Teenager: A Study of Normal Adolescent Boys*, Basic Books, New York.

Offer, D. & Baittie, B. 1970, 'On the Nature of Adolescent Rebellion', in S. Feinstein, P. Giovacchini & A. Miller (eds), *Annals of Adolescent Psychiatry*, Basic Books, New York.

Offer, D. & Offer, J. 1968, 'Profiles of Normal Adolescent Girls', in *Archive of General Psychiatry*, vol. 19, pp. 513–22.

—— 1972, 'Developmental Psychology of Youth', in S. Shamsie (ed.), *Youth: Problems and Approaches*, Lea & Febiger, Philadelphia, pp. 43–68.

—— 1988, *The Teenage World: Adolescents' Self-Image in Ten Countries*, Plenum Medical, New York.

O'Grady, C. 1992, 'A Rising Star in the Prosecution of Juveniles in Victoria', *Youth Studies Australia*, vol. II, no. 4, pp. 10–17.

Ollman, B. 1975, *Alienation: Marx's Theory of Man under Capitalism*, Cambridge University Press, New York.

Olson, D. 1994, *The World on Paper*, Cambridge University Press, Cambridge.

Paglia, C. 1990, *Sexual Personae*, Penguin, Harmondsworth.

Pakulski, J. 1999, *Social Movements*, Longman Cheshire, Melbourne.

—— 2004, *Globalising Inequalities*, Allen & Unwin, Sydney.

Palmer, A. 2000, *Colonial Genocide*, Crawford House Publishing, Adelaide.

Palmer, P. 1998, *The Courage to Teach*, Jossey-Bass, San Francisco.

Papadakis, E. 1991, 'Does the New Politics have a Future?', in F.G. Castles (ed.), *Australia Compared: People Policies and Politics*, Allen & Unwin, Sydney.

Parsons, T. 1951, *The Social System*, The Free Press, New York.

—— 1963 [1942], 'Age and Sex in the Social Structure of the United States', in R. Grinder (ed.), *Studies in Adolescence*, Macmillan, London, pp. 28–49.

—— 1964, 'The Professions and the Social Structure', in T. Parsons, *Essays in Sociological Theory*, The Free Press, New York.

—— 1971, *The System of Modern Societies*, Prentice Hall, Englewood Cliffs.

Pearson, G. 1983, *Hooligan: A History of Respectable Fears*, Macmillan, London.

Peel, M. 1996, *Good Times, Hard Times: The Past and the Future in Elizabeth*, Melbourne University Press, Melbourne.

—— 2004, *The Lowest Rung*, Cambridge University Press, Melbourne.

Pemberton, A. & Boreham, P. 1976, 'Towards a Reorientation of Sociological Studies of the Professions', in A. Pemberton, P. Boreham & P. Wilson (eds), *The Professions in Australia: A Critical Appraisal*, University of Queensland Press, Brisbane.

Perelman, S.J. & Olbrechts-Tyteca, L. 1969, *The New Rhetoric*, Reidel and Co., Amsterdam.

Peterson, C. 1997, *Looking Forward Through the Life Cycle*, 3rd edn, Prentice-Hall, Englewood Cliffs.

Pickens, D. 1995, *The Faces of Degeneracy*, Cambridge University Press, Cambridge.

Piggott, J. 1987, 'Privatisation and Public Economics: Some Neglected Issues', in P. Abelson (ed.), *Privatisation: An Australian Perspective*, APA, Sydney.

Pinker, T. 2000, *Hegel*, Oxford University Press, Oxford.

Platt, J. 1988, 'What Can Case Studies Do?', in R. Burgess (ed.), *Studies in Qualitative Methodology*, JAI Press, London.

Polanyi, K. 1973, *The Great Transformation*, Octagon Books, New York.

Polk, K. 1994, *When Men Kill: Scenarios of Masculine Violence*, Cambridge University Press, Melbourne.

Polk, K. & Tait, D. 1990, 'Changing Youth Labour Markets and Youth Life Styles', *Youth Studies*, vol. 9, no. 1, pp. 21–33.

Porter, D. 1997, 'Cyberdemocracy, Internet and the Public Sphere', in D. Porter (ed.), *Internet Culture*, Routledge, New York.

Porter, M. 1990, *The Competitive Advantage of Nations*, Macmillan, London.

Porter, R. 2000, *The Enlightenment*, Penguin, Harmondsworth.

Poynting, S. 1996, *Cultures of Schooling*, Allen & Unwin, Sydney.

Poynting, S. & Noble, G. 1996, 'Rekindling the Spark: Teacher's Experience of Accelerative Learning', *Australian Journal of Education*, vol. 42, pp. 37–48.

Presdee, M. 1987, 'Made in Australia: Youth Policies and the Creation of Crime', Occasional Paper No. 3, University of South Australia, Adelaide.

Probert, B. 1997, 'Women in the Labour Market', in K.P. Hughes (ed.), *Contemporary Australian Feminism 2*, 2nd edn, Addison Wesley Longman, Melbourne, pp. 305–31.

Probert, B. & McDonald, F. 1996, *The Work Generation: The Future of Work*, Brotherhood of St Laurence, Melbourne.

Proctor, Robert N. 1995, *The Cancer Wars: How Politics Shapes What We Know and Don't Know About Cancer*, Basic Books, New York.

Przeworski, A. 1989, *Capitalism and Social Democracy: Studies in Marxism and Social Democracy*, Cambridge University Press, Cambridge.

Pusey, M. 1991, *Economic Rationalism in Canberra: How a Nation-building State Changed Its Mind*, Cambridge University Press, Melbourne.

—— 2003, *The Experience of Middle Australia: The Dark Side of Economic Reform*, Cambridge University Press, Melbourne.

Putnam, H. 2005, *The Is/Ought Distinction and Other Essays*, Yale University Press, New Haven.

Putnam Tong, R. 1998, *Feminist Thought: A Comprehensive Introduction*, 2nd edn, Allen & Unwin, Sydney.

Quiggin, J. 1997, *Great Expectations*, Allen & Unwin, Sydney.

Ramsden, P. 1992, *Learning to Teach in Higher Education*, Routledge, London.

Raskall, P. 1994, 'Inequality in Australia: What We Know and What We Don't', in P. Raskall & P. Saunders (eds), *Economic Inequality in Australia: Some Factors Causing Inequality*, vol. 2, SSEI Monograph No. 2, Social Policy Research Centre, UNSW, Sydney.

Rawls, J. 1999, *Justice as Fairness: Theory of Justice Reconsidered*, Harvard University Press, Cambridge.

Regoli, R. & Hewitt, J. 1991, *Deliquency and Society: A Child Centered Approach*, McGraw Hill, New York.

Reich, R. 1994, *The Work of Nations*, Basic Books, New York.

Reiger, K. 1986, *Rationalising the Home*, Oxford University Press, Melbourne.

Reynolds, H. 1987, *Frontier*, Penguin, Ringwood.

Rich, A. 1984, 'Compulsory Heterosexuality and Lesbian Existence', in A. Snitow et al. (eds), *Desire: The Politics of Sexuality*, Virago, London.

Richardson, S. & Prior, M. (eds) 2005, *No Time to Lose: The Wellbeing of Australia's Children*, Melbourne University Press, Melbourne.

Rieff, P. 1996, *Triumph of the Therapeutic*, Penguin, Harmondsworth.

Rifkin, J. 1996, *The End of Work*, G.P. Putman, New York.

Ritzer, G. 1993, *The McDonaldization of Society*, Forge Press, Thousand Oaks.

Roach Anleu, S.L. 1995, *Deviance, Conformity and Control*, Longman, Melbourne.

—— 2001, *Deviance, Conformity and Control*, 2nd edn, Longman, Melbourne.

Roberts, K. 1983, *Youth and Leisure*, Allen & Unwin, London.

Robertson, R. 1985, 'The Relativisation of Societies: Modern Religion and Globalization', in T. Robbins, H. Shepherd & J. McBride (eds), *Cults, Culture and the Law*, Scholars Press, Chicago.

—— 1992, *Globalization*, Sage, London.

Robinson, M. & Watson, D. 1995, 'Domestic Violence—Gendered Abuse', *Social Alternatives*, vol. 14, no. 1, pp. 5–7.

Rogers, R. 1992, 'HIV and Harm Reduction', *Youth Studies Australia*, Summer, pp. 23–7.

Roper, T. 1970, *The Myth of Equality*, National Union of Australian Universities, Melbourne.

Rorty, R. 1999, *Philosophy and Social Hope*, Penguin, Harmondsworth.

Rose, N. 1990, *Governing the Soul: The Shaping of the Private Self*, London, Routledge.

—— 1996, 'The Death of the Social? Refiguring the Territory of Government', *Economy and Society*, vol. 25, no. 3, pp. 327–56.

Rowse, T. 2005, 'Notes on the History of the Aboriginal Population', in D. Moses (ed.), *Genocide and Settler Society*, Berghahn Books, New York.

Ruskin, J. 1850, *The Stones of Venice*, Chapman & Hall, London.

Russell, C.S. 2001, *Applying Economics to the Environment*, Oxford University Press, New York.

Russell, G. 1989, *The Changing Role of Fathers*, University of Queensland Press, Brisbane.

—— 1994, 'Sharing the Pains and Pleasures of Family Life, *Family Matters*, vol. 37, pp. 13–19.

Rutter, M. & Giller, H. 1983, *Juvenile Delinquency: Trends and Perspectives*, Penguin, Harmondsworth.

Rutter, M., Giller, H. & Hagell, A. 1998, *Antisocial Behaviour by Young People*, Cambridge University Press, Cambridge.

Ryan, W.S. 1975, *Blaming the Victim*, Vintage, New York.

Sacks, O. 1994, *The Man Who Mistook His Wife for a Hat*, Paladin, London.

Said, E. 1997, *Covering Islam*, Vintage, New York.

Saul, J.R. 1997, *The Unconscious Civilisation*, Penguin, Ringwood.

Saunders, P. 2004, *Kicking the Welfare Habit*, Duffy & Snellgrove, Sydney.

Saunders, P.G. 1994, *Welfare and Inequality*, Cambridge University Press, Melbourne.

—— 2005, *The Poverty Wars*, UNSW Press, Sydney.

Savage, H. 1992, *England's Dreaming: Sex Pistols and Punk Rock*, Faber & Faber, London.

Sawyer, M., Sarris, A., Baghurst, P., Cornish, C. & Kalucy, R. 1990, 'The Prevalence of Emotional and Behaviour Disorders and Patterns of Service Utilisation in Children and Adolescents', *ANZ Journal of Psychiatry*, vol. 254, pp. 323–30.

Scarry, E. 1986, *The Body in Pain*, Oxford University Press, New York.

Schmitt, C. 1996, *The Concept of the Political*, University of Chicago Press, Chicago.

Schon, D. 1998, 'Generative Metaphor: Perspective on Problem Setting in Social Policy', in A. Ortony (ed.), *Metaphor and Thought*, Cambridge University Press, Cambridge.

Schutz, A. 1986, *The Correspondence of Alfred Schutz and Aaron Gurwitch*, University of Indiana Press, Bloomington.

Scruton, R. 2004, *The West and the Rest*, ISL Books, London.

Seigel, J. 2005, *The Idea of the Self: Thought and Experience in Western Europe Since the Seventeenth Century*, Cambridge University Press, Cambridge.

Self, W. 1993, *Cock & Bull*, Collins, London.

Sen, A. 1992, *Re-examining Inequality*, Oxford University Press, Oxford.

Senate Employment Workplace Relations Small Business and Education Committee 2002, *Universities in Crisis: Report into the Capacity of Public Universities to Meet Australia's Higher Education Needs*, Commonwealth of Australia, Canberra.

Senate Standing Committee 1992, *Physical and Sports Education*, Commonwealth of Australia, Canberra.

Sennett, R. 1988, *Authority*, Faber & Faber, London.

Sennett, R. & Cobb, R. 1989, *The Hidden Injuries of Class*, Vintage, New York.

Sercombe, H. 1992, 'Youth Theory, Marx or Foucault', *Youth Studies Australia*, vol. 11, no. 3, pp. 51–4.

—— 1995, 'The Face of the Criminal is Aboriginal', in J. Bessant, K. Carrington & S. Cook (eds), *Cultures of Crime and Violence: The Australian Experience*, La Trobe University Press & Victoria Law Institute, Bundoora.

—— 1997, Naming Youth: The Construction of the Youth Category, unpublished PhD thesis, Murdoch University, Perth.

Shapin, S. 1997, *The Scientific Revolution*, University of Chicago Press, Chicago.

Sharp, G. 1974, 'Interpretations of Poverty', *Australia and New Zealand Journal of Sociology*, vol. 12, no. 2, pp. 17–29.

Shaver, S. 1998, 'Poverty, Gender and Sole Parenthood', in R. Fincher & J. Nieuwenhuysen (eds), *Australian Poverty: Then and Now*, Melbourne University Press, Melbourne, pp. 276–92.

Shaw, G.B. 1907, 'Major Barbara (Preface)', in G.B. Shaw, *Prefaces*, Collins, London.

Shergold, P. 1985, 'Discrimination Against Australian Migrants', in I. Burnley, S. Encel & G. McCall (eds), *Immigration and Ethnicity in the 1980s*, Longman Cheshire, Melbourne.

Sherman, L. & Glick, B. 1984, *The Quality of Police Arrest Statistics*, Police Foundation Report 2, Washington DC.

Shorter, E. 1983, *A History of Women*, Penguin, Harmondsworth.

—— 1988, *Women's Bodies*, Penguin, Harmondsworth.

Siahpus, M. & Borland, R. 2001, 'Socio-demographic Variations in Smoking Status Among Australians Aged 18: Multivariate Results from the 1995 National Health Survey', *Australian and New Zealand Journal of Public Health*, vol. 25, no. 5, pp. 438–42.

Sica, A. 1988, *Weber, Irrationality and Social Order*, Cambridge University Press, Cambridge.

Sidoti, C. 1997, 'Young People and Racism', paper presented to Youth and Racism Conference, Australian Catholic University, Ascot Vale.

Silverblatt, I. 2004, *Modern Inquisitions: Peru and the Cultural Origins of the Civilized World*, Duke University Press, Durham.

Simmel, G. 1949, 'The Sociology of Sociability', *American Journal of Sociology*, vol. 55, no. 3, pp. 254–61.

—— 1950, *The Sociology of Georg Simmel*, Free Press, New York.

Simmons, J. & Dodd, T. (eds) 2003, *Crime in England and Wales 2002–2003*, National Statistics, London.

Singer, B. 1980, *Feedback and Society*, D.C. Heath, Lexington.

Sklair, L. 1991, *The Sociology of the Global System*, Harvester Press, Brighton.

Slee, R. 1995, *Changing Theories and Practices of Discipline*, Falmer Press, London.

Smart, C. 1976, *Women, Crime and Criminology*, Routledge Kegan, London.

Smelser, N. 1994, *Sociology*, UNESCO, Sage, London.

Smith, A. 1991 [1776], *The Wealth of Nations*, 2 vols, Liberty Press, Baltimore.

Snooks, G.D. 1994, *Portrait of the Family Within the Total Economy*, Cambridge University Press, Melbourne.

Sofsky, W. 1997, *The Order of Terror: The Concentration Camp*, trans W. Templer, Princeton University Press, Princeton.

—— 2003, *Violence: Terrorism, Genocide, War*, Granta Books, London.

Sontag, S. 1989, *AIDS as Metaphor*, Penguin, Harmondsworth.

Spencer, H. 1965, *The Study of Sociology*, Free Press, New York.

Spender, D. 1980, *Man Made Language*, RKP, London.

—— 1982, *Invisible Women: The Schooling Scandal*, London, Writers and Readers.

Stanley, S. 1990, 'Doing Ethnography, Writing Ethnography', *Sociology*, vol. 24, no. 4, pp. 617–27.

Stanley-Hall, G. 1904, *Adolescence: Its Physiological, Biological, Psychological, Historical and Cultural Aspects*, 2 vols, Bono & Liverwright, New York.

Steiner, G. 1986, *In Bluebeard's Castle*, Faber & Faber, London.

Stilwell, F. 1993, *Economic Inequality: Who Gets What in Australia?*, Pluto Press, Sydney.

Stoppard, T. 1978, *Night and Day*, Faber & Faber, London.

Stratton, J. 1992, *The Wild Ones*, Black Swan Press, Perth.

Stricker, P. & Sheehan, P. 1982, *Hidden Unemployment: The Australian Experience*, Institute of Applied and Economic Social Research, University of Melbourne, Melbourne.

Stringer, E. 1996, *Action Research*, Sage, London.

Sumner, C. 1992, *The Sociology of Deviance: An Obituary*, Open University, Milton Keynes.

Sutherland, E. 1994 [1940], 'White Collar Criminality', in J. Jacoby (ed.), *Classics of Criminology*, Waveland, Illinois.

Suzuki, D. & Dressel, H. 2002, *Good News for a Change: Hope for a Troubled Planet*, Allen & Unwin, Sydney.

Sykes, R. 1989, 'Blacks, Whites and Racism', in *Black Majority*, Hudson, Melbourne.

Tait, G. 1992, 'Reassessing Street Kids: A Critique of Sub-cultural Theory', *Youth Studies Australia*, vol. 11, no. 2, pp. 12–16.

—— 1995, 'Shaping "At Risk Youth": Risk, Governmentality and the Finn Report', *Discourse*, vol. 16, no. 1, pp. 123–34.

—— 2000, *Youth, Sex and Government*, Peter Lang, New York.

Taylor, C. 1985, *Language and Human Action: Collected Papers, Vol. 1*, Cambridge University Press, Cambridge.

Taylor, C.A. 1977, 'Interpretation and the Sciences of Man', in F. Dallmayr & T. McCarthy (eds), *Understanding and Social Inquiry*, University of Notre Dame Press, Notre Dame, IN.

Taylor, I. 1997, 'The Political Economy of Crime', in M. Maguire, R. Morgan & R. Reiner (eds), *The Oxford Handbook of Criminology*, 2nd edn, Oxford University Press, Oxford.

Taylor, I., Walton, P. & Young, J. 1973, *The New Criminology: For a Social Theory of Deviance*, Routledge & Kegan Paul, London.

Teese, R. & Poleset, J. 2003, *Undemocratic Schooling: Equity and Quality in Mass Secondary Education in Australia*, Melbourne University Press, Melbourne.

The Age, 2006, Letters to the Editor, 9 January.

The *Herald-Sun*, 2006, 24 January.

—— 2006, 28 January.

—— 2006, Andrew Bolt column, 3 February.

Thomas, W. & Thomas, D. 1929, *The Child in America*, Alfred Knopf, New York.

Thompson, E.P. 1967, 'Time, Work, Discipline and Industrial Capitalism', *Past and Present*, vol. 38, pp. 56–97.

—— 1968, *The Making of the English Working Class*, Penguin, Harmondsworth.

Thornton, B. 1997, *Eros: The Myth of Ancient Greek Sexuality*, Westview Press, Boulder.

Tithe, C., Villemez, W. & Smith, D. 1982, 'The Relationship of Unemployment to Crime and Delinquency', *Journal of Social Issues*, vol. 24, pp. 105–14.

Toennies, F. 1963, *Community and Association*, Harper & Row, New York.

Toffler, A. 1974, *Future Shock*, Pan Books, London.

Toohey, B. 1995, *Tumbling Dice*, Heinemann, Sydney.

Toulmin, S. 1957, *The Philosophy of Science: An Introduction*, Hutchinson University Library, London.

Touraine, A. 1971, *The Post Industrial Society*, Wildwood House, London.

—— 1979, *Solidarity*, Cambridge University Press, Cambridge.

—— 1985, 'An Introduction to the Study of Social Movements', *Social Research*, vol. 52, pp. 749–88.

—— 1988, *The Return of the Actor*, University of Minnesota Press, Minneapolis.

Townsend, P. 1979, *Poverty in the United Kingdom: A Study of Household Resources and Standards of Living*, Penguin, Harmondsworth.

Tran Nam, B. & Neville, J. 1988, 'The Effects of Birthplace on Male Earnings in Australia', *Australian Economic Papers*, vol. 27, no. 5, pp. 83–101.

Travers, P. & Richardson, S. 1994, *Living Decently*, Oxford University Press, Melbourne.

Tsolidis, T. 1993, 'Difference and Identity: A Feminist Debate Indicating Directions for the Development of Transformative Curriculum', *Melbourne Studies in Education*, vol. 21, pp. 51–62.

Tucker, S. 2004, 'Youth Working: Professional Identities Given, Received or Contested?', in J. Roche, S. Tucker, R. Thomson & R. Flynn (eds), *Youth in Society*, 2nd edn, Sage, Thousand Oaks, pp. 81–9.

Turgenev, I. 1974 [1877], *Virgin Soil*, Penguin, Harmondsworth.

Turner, B.S. 1984, *The Body and Society*, Blackwell, London.

—— 1996, *The Body and Society*, 2nd edn, Sage, London.

Turrell, G., Oldenberg, B., McGoffog, I. & Dent, R. 1999, *Socioeconomic Determinants of Health: Towards a National Research Program and Policy*, QUT Press, AusInfo, Canberra.

Tversky, A. 1990, 'The Psychology of Risk', in W. Sharpe (ed.), *Quantifying the Market Risk Phenomenon for Investment Decision-making*, Institute for Chartered Financial Analysts, Charlottesville.

Tygart, C. 1991, 'Juvenile Delinquency and Number of Children in Family', *Youth and Society*, vol. 22, no. 2, pp. 525–36.

UNICEF 1994, *Progress of Nations*, UNICEF, New York.

United Nations, 2005, *World Youth Report 2005: Young People Today and in 2015*, Department of Economic and Social Affairs, New York.

United Nations Department of Economic and Social Affairs 1998, *Demographic Yearbook 1996*, United Nations, New York.

Utting, D. 1994, 'Family Factors and the Rise in Crime', in A. Coote (ed.), *Families, Children and Crime, Institute of Public Policy Research*, IPPR, London.

—— 1995, 'When the Talking has to Stop', *The Guardian*, 22 February.

Utting, D., Bright, J. & Henricson, C. 1993, *Crime and the Family: Improving Child-rearing and Preventing Delinquency*, Family Policy Studies Centre, London.

Vamplew, W. (ed.) 1988, *Australians: Historical Statistics*, Fairfax, Syme & Weldon, Sydney.

van Swaaningen, A. 1997, *Critical Criminology*, Sage, London.

VicHealth, 1999–2002, *Strategic Directions*, Victorian Health Promotion Foundation, Melbourne.

Victorian Government 1985, *Ministerial Review of Post-compulsory Schooling, Vols 1 and 2*, VGPS, Melbourne,

Wadsworth, G. 1992, *Rachel Carson: Voice for the Earth*, Lerner Publications, Minneapolis.

Wadsworth, Y. 1997, *Do It Yourself Social Research*, 2nd edn, Allen & Unwin, Sydney.

Walby, S. 1992, 'Post Post Modernism: Theorising Social Complexity', in M. Barratt & A. Phillips (eds), *Destabilizing Theory: Contemporary Feminist Debates*, Polity Press, Cambridge.

Walker, A. & Abello, A. 2001, *Changes in the Health Status of Low Income Groups in Australia 1977–78 to 1995*, NATSEM Discussion Paper No. 2, NATSEM, Canberra.

Walker, J.C. 1986, 'Romanticising Resistance, Romanticising Culture: A Critique of Willis' Theory of Cultural Production', *British Journal of Sociology*, vol. 7, no. 1, pp. 59–80.

—— 1988, *Louts and Legends: Male Youth Culture in an Inner City School*, Allen & Unwin, Sydney.

Wall, W.D. 1947, *The Adolescent Child*, Methuen, London.

Wallerstein, I. 1974, *The Modern World System*, Academic Press, New York.

Waring, M. 1987, *Counting for Nothing*, Allen & Unwin, Hutt River.

Waters, M. 1997, *Globalisation*, Routledge, London.

Watson, D. 2003, *Death Sentence: The Decline of Public Language*, Allen & Unwin, Sydney.

Watts, R. 2002, 'The "Idea of the University": Australian Conservatives and the Public University', *Melbourne Studies in Education*, vol. 43, no. 3, pp. 13–24.

Weatherburn, D. 1992a, 'Economic Adversity and Crime', *Trends and Issues*, no. 40, Australian Institute of Criminology.

—— 1992b, 'On the Quest for a General Theory of Crime', *Australian New Zealand Journal of Criminology*, vol. 26, no. 2, pp. 78–91.

Webber, M. & Ernst, J. 1996, 'Privatisation in Review', in M. Webber (ed.) with M. Crooks, *Putting the People Last: Government Services and Rights in Victoria*, Hyland House, Melbourne.

Webber, R. 1994, *Living in a Step Family*, ACER, Melbourne.

Weber, M. 1947, *The Theory of Social and Economic Organisation*, trans. A. Henderson & T. Parsons, The Free Press, Glencoe.

—— 1949, 'Objectivity in Social Science', in E. Shils & H. Finch (eds), *The Methodology of the Social Sciences*, The Free Press, New York.

—— 1974, *The Protestant Ethic and the Spirit of Capitalism*, Allen & Unwin, London.

—— 1977, *From Max Weber: Essays in Sociology*, eds C. Wright Mills & H. Gerth, Routledge & Kegan Paul, Boston.

—— 1978, *Economy and Society*, 2 vols, trans. G. Roth & C. Wittich, University of California Press, Berkeley.

Weber, Marianne 1974, *Max Weber: A Life*, John Wiley & Sons, New York.

Weiss, L., Thurban, E. & Mathews, J. 2004, *How to Kill a Country: Australia's Devastating Trade Deal with the United States*, Allen & Unwin, Sydney.

Wells, L.E. & Rankin, J.H. 1986, 'The Broken Homes Model of Delinquency: Analytical Issues', *Journal of Researching Crime and Delinquency*, vol. 23, no. 1, pp. 13–29.

—— 1991, 'Families and Delinquency: A Meta Analysis of the Impact of Broken Homes', *Social Problems*, vol. 38, no. 1, pp. 33–49.

Wertham, F. 1954, *The Seduction of the Innocent*, Knopf, New York.

West, D. & Farrington, D. 1977, *The Delinquent Way of Life*, Heinemann, London.

Western, J.S. 1983, *Social Inequality in Australia*, Macmillan, Melbourne.

Western, J. & Najman, J. 1999, *Australian Sociology*, 2nd edn, Macmillan, South Melbourne.

Wheelwright, E. & Buckley, K. (eds) 1987, *Essays in the Political Economy of Australian Capitalism*, ANZ Book Co., Sydney.

White, D. 1964, 'Mass Culture: Another View', in B. Rosenberg & D. White (eds), *Mass Culture*, The Free Press, New York.

White, K. 2000, 'Health and Illness', in R. Juredenei & M. Poole (eds) with S. Kenny, *Sociology: Australian Connections*, 2nd edn, Allen & Unwin, Sydney.

—— 2002a, *An Introduction to the Sociology of Health and Illness*, Sage, London.

—— 2002b, 'The Sociology of Health and Illness', in R. Juredenei & M. Poole with S. Kenny, *Sociology: Australian Connections*, 3rd edn, Allen & Unwin, Sydney, pp. 328–48.

White, R. 1989, *No Space of Their Own: Young People and Social Control in Australia*, Cambridge University Press, Melbourne.

—— 1990, 'Making Ends Meet: Young People, Work and the Criminal Economy', *Australian*

New Zealand Journal of Criminology, vol. 22, pp. 136–50.

—— (ed.) 1993, *Youth Sub Cultures: Theory History and the Australian Experience*, National Clearing House for Youth Studies, Hobart.

—— 1994, 'The Making of the Youth Underclass', *Policy Issues Forum*, Autumn, pp. 22–8.

White, R. & Alder, C. (eds) 1994, *The Police and Young People in Australia*, Cambridge University Press, Sydney.

White, R., McDonnell, L. & Harris, A. 1996, 'Researching Youth: A Practical Guide', *Youth Studies Australia*, vol. 15, no. 3, pp. 18–25.

Whyte, W. 1955, *Street Corner Society*, 2nd edn, University of Chicago Press, Chicago.

Wickham, G. & Hunt, A. 1994, *Foucault and the Law: Towards a Sociology of Law as Governance*, Pluto, London.

Wild, R. 1974, *Bradstow*, Angus & Robertson, Sydney.

—— 1978, *Social Stratification in Australia*, Allen & Unwin, Sydney.

Wilde, O. 1891, 'The Decay of Lying', in O. Wilde, *Intentions*, Macmillan, London.

Williams, R. 1976, *Keywords*, Fontana, London.

Willis, P. 1981, *Learning to Labour: How Working Class Kids Get Working Class Jobs*, Columbia University Press, New York.

—— 1990, *Common Culture*, Open University, Milton Keynes.

Wilson, J. 1987, *The Truly Disadvantaged*, University of Chicago Press, Chicago.

Wilson, J.Q. & Herrnstein, R.J. 1985, *Crime and Human Nature*, Basic Books, New York.

Wilson, P. 1988, 'Beyond the Rhetoric on "Law and Order"', *Legal Services Bulletin*, vol. 13, no. 2, April.

Wilson, W.J. 1987, *The Truly Disadvantaged: The Inner City, the Underclass and Public Policy*, University of Chicago Press, Chicago.

—— 1996, *When Work Disappears: The World of the New Urban Poor*, Knopf, New York.

Windschuttle, K. 1982, *Unemployment*, rev. edn, Penguin, Ringwood.

—— 1984, *The Media*, Penguin, Ringwood.

—— 2002, *The Fabrication of Aboriginal History Vol. 1: Van Diemen's Land, 1803–1847*, Macleay Press, Paddington.

Withers, G. & Pope, D. 1985, 'Immigration and Unemployment', *Economic Record*, vol. 61, pp. 554–63.

Wittgenstein, L. 1953, *Philosophical Investigations*, Blackwell, Oxford.

Wooden, M. 1998, 'The Labour Market for Young Australians', Dusseldorp Skills Foundation (ed.), *Australia's Youth: Reality and Risk*, Dusseldorp Skills Foundation, Sydney.

World Health Organisation (WHO) 1999, *ICIDH-2: International Classification of Functioning of Disability, BETA-2 Draft*, Full Version, Geneva.

Wotherspoon, G. 1986, 'The Loner', in G. Wotherspoon (ed.), *Being Different*, Hale & Iremonger, Sydney.

Wurm, S. 1972, *Languages of Australia and Tasmania*, Mouton, The Hague.

Wyn, J. & White, R. 1997, *Rethinking Youth*, Allen & Unwin, Sydney.

Yates, L. 1983, 'The Theory and Practice of Counter Sexist Education in Schools', *Discourse*, vol. 3, no. 2, pp. 232–70.

—— 1993, *The Education of Girls: Policy, Research and the Question of Gender*, ACER, Melbourne.

—— 1997, 'Gender Equity and the Boys Debate: What Sort of Challenge is It?', *British Journal of Sociology of Education*, vol. 18, no. 3, pp. 337–47.

Yeatman, A. 1990, *Bureaucrats, Technocrats, Femocrats: Essays on the Contemporary Australian State*, Allen & Unwin, Sydney.

Yinger, J.M. 1981, 'Towards a Theory of Assimilation and Dissimilation', *Ethnic & Racial Studies*, vol. 4, no. 3, pp. 249–64.

Young, J. 1992, 'Ten Points of Realism', in J. Young & R. Mathews (eds), *Rethinking Criminology: The Realist Debate*, Sage, London.

INDEX